W9-BBQ-011

SPECIAL ADVERTISING SECTION

Appreciation·
Achievement·Being·
Belonging·Becoming·
Development·Diversity·
Enhancement·Enjoyment·
Positive Experiences·
People·Friends·Family·
Flexibility·Freedom·Fulfillment·
Happiness·Health·Hopes·Identity·
Improvement·Integrity·
Knowledge·Nurture·
Opportunities·Opinions·
Satisfaction·Security·
Truth·Dreams

Quality of Life

What is your definition of QUALITY of life? At The Gallup Organization, you'll work in a culture that SUPPORTS you not just professionally, but personally. Whether your PASSION is building new business, managing consulting projects, or assisting executives, you'll have the OPPORTUNITY to do what you do BEST every day. We'll help you discover your TALENTS and build STRENGTHS.

How do we know that life is BETTER at Gallup? **A recent survey by Vault.com of 2,500 consultants ranks Gallup #1 in corporate culture.** At Gallup, we offer more than just a job — we offer you a FUTURE.

 GALLUP

www.gallup.com/careers

BUILD
YOUR
FUTURE

"With Toyota, I am most likely to succeed."

The Toyota Way of doing business centers on respect for others and the continued growth of everyone. In order to maintain this high-performing environment, we need the best people. People just like you.

At Toyota Motor Sales, USA, Inc., we take pride in what the Toyota name represents – innovation, quality, and reliability. TMS is the U.S. sales, marketing, and distribution arm that oversees operations in 49 states for Toyota, Scion and Lexus products.

We invite you to explore our Undergraduate Program opportunities and discover how you can achieve greater success as part of a team of which you too can be proud of.

These training programs will give you invaluable exposure to the automotive industry:

+ Customer Relations   + Logistics
+ Technical Service   + Sales, Marketing & Service

You have the education, now get the experience you need with a summer internship in fields ranging from advertising to eBusiness and technical support to vehicle service:

+ Corporate Summer Intern Program
+ Technical Service Summer Intern Program

We offer an excellent salary and benefits package including medical, dental and vision plans and a vehicle lease program.

For more information on employment opportunities, please visit us at: www.toyota.com/talentlink

 TOYOTA | toyota.com/talentlink

The media's watching Vault!
Here's a sampling of our coverage.

"For those hoping to climb the ladder of success, [Vault's] insights are priceless."
– *Money magazine*

"The best place on the web to prepare for a job search."
– *Fortune*

"[Vault guides] make for excellent starting points for job hunters and should be purchased by academic libraries for their career sections [and] university career centers."
– *Library Journal*

"The granddaddy of worker sites."
– *US News and World Report*

"A killer app."
– *The New York Times*

One of Forbes' 33 "Favorite Sites"
– *Forbes*

"To get the unvarnished scoop, check out Vault."
– *Smart Money Magazine*

"Vault has a wealth of information about major employers and job-searching strategies as well as comments from workers about their experiences at specific companies."
– *The Washington Post*

"Vault has become the go-to source for career preparation."
– *Crain's New York Business*

"Vault [provides] the skinny on working conditions at all kinds of companies from current and former employees."
– *USA Today*

ManhattanGMAT
the new standard

the world's largest GMAT-exclusive test preparation provider

Our Curriculum

ManhattanGMAT's exclusive curriculum was designed in accordance with our philosophy of test preparation, which centers on a balance between two competing emphases: test-taking strategies on the one hand, with in-depth content understanding on the other. The heart of the curriculum is the acclaimed ManhattanGMAT Strategy Guide Set, seven content-based books (five math and two verbal), and they are available through the ManhattanGMAT online store; they are also sold at Barnes & Noble and Amazon.com. The set, along with three other books and various online resources, is provided to all ManhattanGMAT program students.

Nine-Session Preparation Courses

Meet once per week in our popular group course, either in-person or live and online from your home or office.

Private Instruction

Work with one of our expert tutors (all of whom have scored 750+ on their official GMAT tests), who will design a customized program to suit your needs.

The Quest for 750 Workshop Series

Complete your preparation with emphasis on the most advanced content: data sufficiency, quantitative skills, and sentence correction.

Free GMAT Preview Classes

New to the GMAT? Learn GMAT test basics, principles of adaptive testing, and how to prepare at an online or in-person free GMAT workshop.

Questions?

Call Student Services at 800-576-4628 or send an email to studentservices@manhattangmat.com.

Get schedules and sign up at www.manhattangmat.com or 800-576-4628.

Boston:
140 Clarendon Street
Ground Floor
Boston, MA 02116
617-585-5665

Chicago:
222 West Ontario Street
Fourth Floor
Chicago, IL 60610
312-274-1591

New York:
138 West 25th Street
Ninth Floor
New York, NY 10001
212-721-7400

San Francisco:
870 Market Street
Sixth Floor
San Francisco, CA 94102
415-402-0218

Southern California:
at Pepperdine University in
Encino, Irvine, Long Beach,
Pasadena, West LA and
Westlake Village

Global:
Live instruction online in
our virtual classroom with
students from around the
world.

ManhattanGMAT corporate: 138 West 25th St, 7th floor New York, NY 10001 212-721-7400

THE VAULT
COLLEGE CAREER BIBLE

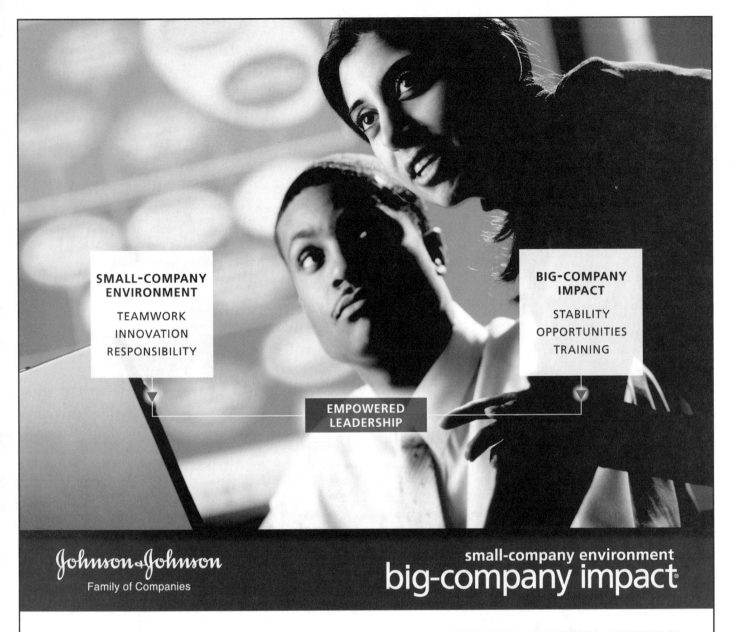

SMALL-COMPANY ENVIRONMENT

TEAMWORK
INNOVATION
RESPONSIBILITY

BIG-COMPANY IMPACT

STABILITY
OPPORTUNITIES
TRAINING

EMPOWERED LEADERSHIP

Johnson & Johnson
Family of Companies

small-company environment
big-company impact

You're looking forward to a career where your education and talents can make a difference. You'd like to find a small-company environment where you can build your professional skills in a supportive atmosphere of teamwork and innovation. At the same time, you're attracted to the stability, world-class leadership development, and career opportunities that can be found with a global business leader.

MEDICAL DEVICES & DIAGNOSTICS   CONSUMER   PHARMACEUTICAL

Who says you have to choose?

Johnson & Johnson companies celebrate and promote small-company environments that respond to the needs of individuals and teams. Through more than 230 operating companies, we are the world's most comprehensive and broadly based manufacturer of health care products for the consumer, pharmaceutical, and medical devices and diagnostics markets.

Discover the many small-company environments behind the big-company impact of the Johnson & Johnson companies.

find more
www.jnj.com/careers

ASIA-PACIFIC
EUROPE/MIDDLE EAST/AFRICA
LATIN AMERICA
NORTH AMERICA

THE VAULT
COLLEGE
CAREER BIBLE

VAULT EDITORS

Copyright © 2006 by Vault Inc. All rights reserved.

All information in this book is subject to change without notice. Vault makes no claims as to the accuracy and reliability of the information contained within and disclaims all warranties. No part of this book may be reproduced or transmitted in any form or by any means, electronic or mechanical, for any purpose, without the express written permission of Vault Inc.

Vault, the Vault logo, and "the most trusted name in career information™" are trademarks of Vault Inc.

For information about permission to reproduce selections from this book, contact Vault Inc.150 W. 22nd St. New York, New York 10011-1772, (212) 366-4212.

Library of Congress CIP Data is available.

ISBN: 1-58131-419-1

ISBN 13: 978-1-58131-419-9

Printed in the United States of America

Acknowledgments

We are extremely grateful to Vault's entire staff for all their help in the editorial, production and marketing processes. Vault also would like to acknowledge the support of our investors, clients, employees, family, and friends. Thank you!

Visit Vault at **www.vault.com** for insider company profiles, expert advice,
career message boards, expert resume reviews, the Vault Job Board and more.

VAULT CAREER LIBRARY

vii

Table of Contents

Shelton State Libraries
Shelton State Community College

Visit Vault at **www.vault.com** for insider company profiles, expert advice,
career message boards, expert resume reviews, the Vault Job Board and more.

VAULT CAREER LIBRARY

ix

Visit Vault at **www.vault.com** for insider company profiles, expert advice,
career message boards, expert resume reviews, the Vault Job Board and more.

VAULT CAREER LIBRARY

xi

Visit Vault at **www.vault.com** for insider company profiles, expert advice,
career message boards, expert resume reviews, the Vault Job Board and more.

VAULT CAREER LIBRARY   xiii

Visit Vault at **www.vault.com** for insider company profiles, expert advice,
career message boards, expert resume reviews, the Vault Job Board and more.

VAULT CAREER LIBRARY   **xv**

Introduction

Maybe you're facing the end of your college career; maybe you've already graduated. Either way, you're facing the question you've been asked all your life: what are you going to do when you grow up? Only now, this question is no longer hypothetical. So what are you going to do?

First: relax. Whether you're a college junior, senior or recent graduate, the world will not end if you don't have a job lined up just yet. Almost everyone has difficulty figuring out what he or she wants to do with the rest of his or her life, and absolutely everyone goes through the painful process of finding that first "real" job. You're in good company. According to studies by the National Association of Colleges and Employers (NACE), only 45 percent of college graduates have jobs waiting for them when they graduate, but about three-quarters find work within six or seven months after graduation.

Moreover, after several years of layoffs and hiring freezes, the U.S. job market began picking up in 2004 and continued to add jobs in 2005. The market for more recent grads is even better. According to a September 2006 survey conducted by NACE, 2006 graduates are entering the most promising job market in four years. Respondents to the NACE's Salary Survey reported that employers expected their college hiring in 2006-2007 to be 17.4 percent higher than in 2005-2006. In addition, 52 percent of employers expect to hire more new college graduates this year than before; as factors they cite company growth and a wish to develop leadership. And there are other good signs—according to the survey, some grads are getting multiple job offers and with earlier start dates and, in the case of business, engineering and IT degree holders, higher starting salaries than in previous years.

Still, for most first-time job seekers, finding that first gig is never easy. This Vault guide will help you get a leg up on the competitive job search, and will assist you in narrowing your search by giving you an overview of popular industries, careers and resources.

Start with your career center

Whether you're currently enrolled or a recent graduate, your college career center is a good place to start your job search. Counselors at the career center can often provide help with resumes and interviewing, and the center also usually has job and internship listings, as well as contact information for alumni in your field of interest who are willing to provide advice to wide-eyed newbies. (Remember, you can still use your college career center even after you've graduated.)

Attend career fairs

Career fairs—veritable smorgasbords of employers and job options—are another place to test out the job market waters. According to the NACE's Job Outlook 2007 Fall Preview, published in the fall of 2006, employers like to visit career fairs to get a sense of their applicant pool. An overwhelming majority of the survey's 257 respondents—94.9 percent—said that they liked the fact that career fairs allowed them to both spread their brand to students and meet those students informally. With employers visiting an average of 27 campus and six commercial fairs per year, these events present terrific opportunities to make face-to-face impressions before floods of resumes pile up in HR inboxes.

Narrow your career options

Figuring out what you'd like to do is half the battle; once you've done that, your job search will automatically become more focused. After you've decided on an industry or position, look for information about the day-to-day responsibilities such a job will entail. It's tough to really understand what it's like to work at a place or position without these tips, which is why Vault provides "Days in the Life" notes and Q&As for many different occupations. Some of these are included in this book; others can be found in Vault's guides on specific industries or on www.vault.com.

Visit Vault at **www.vault.com** for insider company profiles, expert advice, career message boards, expert resume reviews, the Vault Job Board and more.

VAULT CAREER LIBRARY   1

Don't stress

All that said, don't stress out too much over choosing your first job. Gone are the days of working 40 years at one company and leaving with a gold watch; today's job market is much more fluid—most professionals starting their careers today will work in at least five different industries or functions before they retire. For a generation of young, curious and versatile graduates, that is an exciting prospect.

Good luck!

The Team at Vault

THE COLLEGE
STUDENT
JOB SEARCH

Use the Internet's
MOST TARGETED
job search tools.

Vault Job Board

Target your search by industry, function, and experience level, and find the job openings that you want.

VaultMatch Resume Database

Vault takes match-making to the next level: post your resume and customize your search by industry, function, experience and more. We'll match job listings with your interests and criteria and e-mail them directly to your in-box.

On-Campus Recruiting and Internships

On-Campus Recruiting and Career Fairs

If you want to start your career at a large company, being a college student puts you in a good position to do so. Many major employers recruit college students at targeted campuses. Employers in professional services fields such as accounting, consulting, and investment banking hire large classes of graduating students each year as analysts, while major employers in other industries often recruit new grads into management development programs. (These same employers normally hire many juniors as interns. Many students who intern at a company are extended full-time offers after graduation.)

The best place to find out which companies recruit at your school is your career services office. Companies generally visit the campus in the fall to give presentations to interested students; some colleges also hold career fairs, at which HR representatives from these companies collect resumes and speak with students. If you think you might be interested in a company, don't fail to go to these presentations!

If you're interested in a company, make sure you attend all presentations made by that company and speak to at least one company representative. Sometimes this rep will be an HR professional, sometimes a manager in the department that is recruiting, and still other times the rep will be a new hire at the company, often an alumnus of your university. Be sure that you get the business card of the representative with whom you connect the most strongly. Then follow up with an e-mail expressing your interest and perhaps making an on-target inquiry or two. This will show your motivation and initiative—and remember, companies want to hire students who are interested in them and motivated to work for them. Don't overdo it, however; writing your new contact every week is overkill.

Later in the fall, these companies hold a first round of interviews with students on campus or very near campus, often at the career center. Students who pass the first round then visit the company's offices for a second day of interviews that takes a half-day or full day. The same process is followed for internships, though recruiting for summer internships generally happens at the beginning of the spring semester.

The Importance of Interning

If you're reading this book as an underclassman or early in your senior year, you're in good shape—many college students don't begin thinking about careers until late in their senior year or (gasp) after graduation. If you're one of the early birds, make sure you take advantage of your time by getting experience through a summer and/or school-year internship.

What is an internship?

An internship is a sort of trial run at a company—and one of the best ways to test out a potential career field or employer. Internships can last two weeks or a full year, though most of them are for a three-month period or so. Most internships take place over the summer, though others may be available over the fall or spring semester or of a duration of your choosing. Similarly, the majority of internships are full time, though some are part time.

Why do an internship?

You might be tempted just to take a job to earn money. There's nothing wrong with that—but there's so much more right with doing an internship. For example, if you want to break into a field that's tough to crack, like entertainment or advertising or politics, the very best way to get a job in the field is to have interned in it. Not only will you have great experience on your resume, you'll meet plenty of contacts and potential mentors. Similarly, interning at a top company puts you on the fast

Visit Vault at www.vault.com for insider company profiles, expert advice, career message boards, expert resume reviews, the Vault Job Board and more.

VAULT CAREER LIBRARY

5

track to getting a full-time offer from that firm—or one of its competitors! Most large companies are much more likely to hire a former intern than someone "right off the street." Even if you don't end up working for your employer, you'll have some invaluable and difficult-to-obtain experience on your resume.

But I need to get paid!

Don't think that doing an internship means giving up on pay altogether. It's true that many internships are unpaid or only offer college credit—at the same time, these are often small, interesting organizations or companies in glamorous industries. But many others offer some kind of payment, from a stipend or travel allowance to a very generous salary. Others offer interesting perks, including travel and the chance to attend exclusive industry events.

Tips for applying to internships

Let's say you've found an internship that interests you. That's great! The first thing you should do is to follow all the instructions. Here's a short checklist of things you need to do when applying for internships.

Apply by the deadline. A few months before the deadline is even better—a small organization might just take the first qualified intern who applies.

Follow the instructions! If you're asked to provide a writing sample, don't send your photo portfolio. If you're asked to provide a reference, start canvassing your teachers and professors.

Make sure your resume is up to date and thoroughly spellchecked. If you've never written a resume, go to your school career guidance center and ask for help. And ask an experienced professional or two that you trust to review your resume. If you are applying for internships in different fields, you may need to have more than one version of your resume highlighting different experience. Make sure that your most current contact information is on the resume.

Don't ignore the cover letter. Make a persuasive case in your cover letter, which should be tailored to each internship, that you really want to intern at the company. Do your research and be specific—and honest—about why the opportunity is right for you. Again, make sure you carefully proofread the cover letter. Let a trusted friend or teacher read it as well.

Follow up. If you're really interested in an internship, there's nothing wrong with a quick call or e-mail a few weeks after the application to let the organization know how interested you are. But don't pepper them with phone calls every day.

Carpe diem. If you're really interested in an internship, but your qualifications aren't quite right, apply anyway and stress your real interest. Many organizations would rather have a truly excited and motivated intern than one that just meets the qualifications on paper.

Take experience over money. You can always earn money. The window of opportunity for internships isn't eternally open. If you're really broke, consider taking a part-time job in order to work at the internship you really want.

Intern anytime

Most companies with internships have formal programs during the summer, when they hire a number of college or high school students. However, many companies also hire during the school year, so if you're starting your senior year, it's not too late to get that all-important professional work experience.

And, even if you've graduated from college, you can still intern to gain experience if you haven't landed a full-time job. We can't stress this enough: if you can manage it financially, interning in a profession in which you have long-term interest is almost always more preferable than taking a paying job that has nothing to do with your interests. If you're a college graduate, this may mean moving home or working a night job for fewer hours and less pay. Years down the road, we're sure you'll agree that it was worth it.

For information on internship programs, refer to the *Vault Guide to Top Internships*, which has information on more than 750 top programs, and check out the Internship Board at www.vault.com for up-to-date listings.

Make Sure You Don't Blow Your Internship

Remember that scene in *Grease* when the Rydell High kids are singing about the summer? Danny "had me a blast," while for Sandy it "happened so fast." It seems a strange comparison, but many summer interns at America's leading companies describe their summers the same way. Not all experiences are quite so rosy, but in any case, young employees get both a feel for their corporate culture and a taste of the workforce during the course of these often finely crafted programs. Whether their time is spent doing substantive work that affects the company, or just making Starbucks runs all summer, there is a goal in mind. Summer interns need to spend those precious weeks making a favorable impression in order to get that all-important full-time offer.

Granted, the reason that many summer programs are so carefully organized and lavish is so that interns will want to come back. In many programs, "you have to seriously mess up not to get [an offer]." Much more commonly though, interns are not afforded such leeway, and need to be aware of what it takes to secure a full-time position. First and foremost, while the fate of the company may not hinge on the work interns produce, optimum effort must still be made on assignments. Simply put, no matter if it seems insignificant, "whatever work you do, make sure to do a good job," advises one recruiter. Satisfying this requirement may mean punching the clock after the summer sun has disappeared for the night. Most businesses do not take kindly to employees who leave a vapor trail out the door when the five o'clock whistle blows.

Also extremely important are the connections, however informal, made with established employees. This is especially true with mid-level and senior employees who have a say in who gets hired. Those who assume that a stellar academic record and a shiny pair of Ferragamo wing tips are a substitute for engaging conversation may be in for a rude awakening come Labor Day. Successful networking can be accomplished by working for a variety of people or through socialization inside the office. Attendance at company social events, when offered, is an "important way to build personal relationships within the company" as well. Whether cruising the halls or knocking a few back at the local pub, a gregarious persona cannot be discounted— "office wallflowers just will not cut the mustard," says one corporate insider. On the other hand, there are limits; for instance, insiders at Goldman Sachs tell a cautionary tale wherein one investment banking associate who failed to get an offer was snubbed "as a result of excessive brown nosing."

At the same time, summer interns need to be careful about exposing, or more to the point imposing, their personality on their fellow employees. At some companies, for example, "you're not allowed to be rude to anyone—secretaries, the lady in the cafeteria, or whoever it is." Even fast-paced offices with a reputation for "screamers" may be averse to bringing in new people who will perpetuate a harsh culture. "Some summer interns behave completely inappropriately," says a source at a Wall Street firm. "One recent summer associate had a big mouth and she screamed a lot. She made enemies in only eight weeks, including some managing directors."

Of course, even when interns generally play their cards right, one wrong move may stand between them and a job offer. For instance, an insider tells Vault that one would-be full-timer was not asked back to his company after "arguing with a partner at a softball game about what position to play." Another inexplicably turned over an entire assignment to an unqualified subordinate. Perhaps the most extreme example involved an overly enthusiastic intern at one firm who, while on a company retreat, stripped off his clothes and hopped into the hot tub. That's a little too much information!

Visit Vault at **www.vault.com** for insider company profiles, expert advice, career message boards, expert resume reviews, the Vault Job Board and more.

VAULT CAREER LIBRARY

7

How to Take Advantage of Your Internship

The internship craze is reaching new heights. Nearly three-quarters of all college students do internships today as compared to 1 in 36 in 1980. These numbers have made many employers a bit uneasy. After all, these employers are, for the most part, getting all this labor for free, or at most a small stipend. Isn't there something a little bit wrong with that? Many employers think so. That won't stop them from taking the sweet deal, but they won't feel good about. That's where you —the intern— come into the picture. The intern has an extremely receptive and grateful audience at his internship, an audience that aims to please. Consequently, if the intern plays his cards well, he or she can do extraordinary things during his two- or three-month stint.

1. Be there first

At most internships, especially those that take place in the summer, the company or organization will have several interns for a particular time period. If possible, arrive a week or so before the other interns. First, you will get more individual attention in the beginning and consequently can establish yourself as the "favorite" intern.

Second, you may be able to get the first pick of the assignments. Third, you may get the first pick of the desks, or wherever they will seat you. Employing this rule to its extremes, interns have been known to use this seemingly simple technique to get the later-arriving interns to become their "pseudo-interns"—farming out menial tasks to them so they can concentrate on more substantive work.

2. Look around

Once you get inside a company, you should not feel restrained by the department that you're working in—or even to your assigned supervisor. Figure out what you most want to do in the organization and schmooze the person who does it. A good way to do this is to ask them to lunch. A good line is: "I'm trying to absorb as much information as I can in this internship, and what you do seems particular interesting. I wonder if you are available for lunch anytime this week." They will almost always say "Yes." When they describe what they do at lunch, try to relate the skills that they employ to skills that you have. For example, if they tell you about the press release they are writing for company X, slip in how that's similar to your college newspaper writing experience. Hopefully, they will then offer you a chance to draft a press release.

If not, try to give them another nudge, but make it gently. "Oh, writing press releases seems like so much fun!" you can add, or something to that effect.

3. Never complain

When you are given menial errands to do, take it in good cheer. No one likes a whiner. If you feel like you must say something, couch it in humor. One State Department intern remembers telling his boss: "Although being a Deputy Assistant Secretary of Photocopying has its moments, I was wondering if I could do more substantive work here." It got his message across—and worked. Remember: As long as you do a few things that look impressive, you won't have to put on your resume that for 99 percent of the time you ran errands and photocopied stuff. So instead of complaining about your menial tasks— or even non-verbally complaining by acting dour—express an interest in doing substantive work, and be as specific as possible. Specificity shows interest.

Resumes

What can you do?

Rule number one: employers don't really, truly care what you did at your last job. They care about what you can do for them. They wonder about your potential for future success working for them. Your resume must answer these questions.

As Shannon Heidkamp, recruiting manager for a division of Allstate Insurance says, "People need to ask themselves 'What value can I offer this prospective employer?'" These before-and-after samples tell potential employers what skills each employee used, what tasks they accomplished and what honors they garnered—skills, tasks and honors that can be applied to future jobs. Specific job openings, whether advertised through newspaper ads, Internet sites or inter-office memos, come with specific job descriptions. If you find out about the job through a friend, ask for a copy of the job description. Your job is to meet those requirements by listing your qualifications that most closely meet these prerequisites.

Ten seconds

Studies show that regardless of how long you labor over your resume, most employers will spend 10 seconds looking at it. That's it.

Because of the masses of job searchers, most managers and human resource employees receive an enormous number of resumes. Faced with a pile of paper to wade through every morning, employers look for any deficiency possible to reduce the applicant pool to a manageable number. Thus, your resume must present your information quickly, clearly and in a way that makes your experience relevant to the position in question. That means condensing your information down to its most powerful form.

So distill, distill, distill. Long, dense paragraphs make information hard to find and require too much effort from the overworked reader. If that reader can't figure out how your experience applies to the available position, your resume is not doing its job.

Solve this problem by creating bulleted, indented, focused statements. Short, powerful lines show the reader, in a glance, exactly why they should keep reading.

Think about how to write up your experience in targeted, clear, bulleted, detail-rich prose.

Visit Vault at **www.vault.com** for insider company profiles, expert advice, career message boards, expert resume reviews, the Vault Job Board and more.

VAULT CAREER LIBRARY

9

Sample Resumes

Sandra Pearson

Sandypear@ivillage.com
11 Hillhouse Aavenue
New Haven, Connecticut 06511
(203) 555-8103

Education:

Yale University, New Haven, CT
Bachelor of Arts, May 2005; Double Major
Psychology and History
2001 National Merit Scholar Award
2000 Micehouse National Laboratory Internship

Skills:

Microsoft Word, Excel
Editing and proofreading
Proficient Spanish
Graphic design

Work Experience:

Project Hand in Hand 2005
Consultant to teach adults an accredited course on creating curriculum based on the Multiple Intelligence theory

Toddling On Up 2002-2004
Teacher, day care provider; creator of art curriculum and designer of weekly programs

Yale Greenpeace Office 2004
Distributed information on recycling, made presentations; visited, advised and reorganized locations in the Yale and New Haven Communities

Learning Disabilities Center at Yale 2002
Performed various clerical duties; read onto tapes and copied materials for special needs members of the Yale community

XYZ Vacuums
Sales representative for high-quality vacuum cleaners

Activities:

Kappa Beta Sorority 2003-2005; Social Chair 2004-2005
Community Relations Council 2003-2004
Black Alliance at Yale; Publicity Manager, 2003-2004
Yale Gospel Choir 2002-2005
Black Caucus at Yale; co-founder 2002-2005
Roots Theatre Ensemble; costume designer 2002-2003, actress 2002-2004
Yale Antigravity Society 2004

Farley Suber

345 Fenwick Street   Elton Park, CO 79403   (750) 555-4212

Objective:

Seeking an entry-level position in sales or marketing

FARLEY CRAFTILY DISGUISES HIS GAPS IN WORK EXPERIENCE

Education:

Bachelor of Arts in Communication (Public Relations) May 2004
Minor: Business/Liberal Arts
University of Chicago, Chicago, IL
Cumulative GPA: 3.1 out of 4.0

Experience:

LONS Computing Systems
Sales and Marketing Representative
- Applied marketing skills to increase sales of Macintosh computers
- Cultivated client relationships, increasing customer satisfaction and repeat sales
- Placed advertising in magazines including *Men's Health*, *GQ* and *Wired*
- Wrote press releases on new computer products

Broadway Master Theatre
Marketing Assistant
- Assisted with the planning, creation and distribution of theatrical press releases
- Wrote radio advertisements
- Tracked attendance based on information from reservationists and box office attendants
- Handled photo releases mailings to be distributed to the media sources

Honors and Interests:

- **Senior Honors:** Senior cumulative average of 4.0 out of 4.0
- **Terrence S. Duboff Award:** Award for academic achievement excellence in communications
- **NCAA Division 1 Golfer:** Winner of the Greenview Collegiate Classic 2004, 2nd Place finalist 2004 NCAA MidWest Cup
- **Chi Phi Sigma Fraternity:** Rush Chairman, Scholarship Chairman, Standards Board, Senior Steering Committee

Visit Vault at **www.vault.com** for insider company profiles, expert advice, career message boards, expert resume reviews, the Vault Job Board and more.

VAULT CAREER LIBRARY   11

It's what you did, not what your name tag said

Resumes should scream ability, not claim responsibility. Employers should be visualizing you in the new position, not remembering you as "that account assistant from Chase." While some former employers can bolster your resume by their mere presence, you don't want to be thought of as a cog from another machine. Instead, your resume should present you as an essential component of a company's success.

Think broadly

Applicants applying for specific job openings must customize their resume for each position. Many job hunters, particularly those beginning their careers, apply to many different jobs.

A person interested in a career in publishing, for example, might apply for jobs as a writer, proofreader, editor, copywriter, grant proposal writer, fact-checker or research assistant. The applicant may or may not have the experience necessary to apply for any of these jobs. But you may have more skills than you think.

When considering the skills that make you a valuable prospect, think broadly. Anybody who's worked a single day can point to several different skills, because even the most isolated, repetitive jobs offer a range of experience. Highway toll collection, for instance, is a repetitive job with limited variation, but even that career requires multiple job skills. Helping lost highway drivers read a map means "Offering customer service in a prompt, detail-oriented environment." Making change for riders translates as "Cashiering in a high-pressure, fast-paced setting." But unless these toll-booth workers emphasize these skills to prospective employers, it'll be the highway life for them.

Selected history

A lot of things happen in everyone's day, but when someone asks "How was your day?" you don't start with your first cough and your lost slippers. You edit. Resumes require that same type of disciplined, succinct editing. The better you are at controlling the information you create, the stronger the resume will be.

When editing your history to fit the resume format, ask yourself, "How does this particular information contribute towards my overall attractiveness to this employer?" If something doesn't help, drop it. Make more space to elaborate on the experiences most relevant to the job you are applying.

Similarly, if information lurks in your past that would harm your chances of getting the job, omit it. In resume writing, omitting is not lying. If some jobs make you overqualified for a position, eliminate those positions from your resume. If you're overeducated, don't mention the degree that makes you so. If you're significantly undereducated, there's no need to mention education at all. If the 10 jobs you've had in the last five years make you look like a real life Walter Mitty, reduce your resume's references to the most relevant positions while making sure there are no gaps in the years of your employment.

Cover Letters

The Cover Letter Template

Your Name
Your Street Address, Apartment #
Your City, State and Zip
Your E-mail Address
Your PHONE NUMBER
Your FAX NUMBER

WONDERING WHAT GOES ON A COVER LETTER? HERE'S A STEP-BY-STEP GUIDE

Contact's Name
Contact's Title
Contact's Department
Contact's Company Name
Contact's Street Address, Suite #
Company City, State Zip
Company PHONE NUMBER
Company FAX NUMBER

Date

Dear Ms./Mr. CONTACT,

The first paragraph tells why you're contacting the person, then either mentions your connection with that person or tells where you read about the job. It also quickly states who you are. Next it wows them with your sincere, researched knowledge of their company. The goal: demonstrating that you are a worthy applicant, and enticing them to read further.

The second and optional third paragraph tell more about yourself, particularly why you're an ideal match for the job by summarizing why you're what they're looking for. You may also clarify anything unclear on your resume.

The last paragraph is your goodbye: you thank the reader for his or her time. Include that you look forward to their reply or give them a time when you'll be getting in contact by phone.

Sincerely,

Sign Here

Visit Vault at **www.vault.com** for insider company profiles, expert advice, career message boards, expert resume reviews, the Vault Job Board and more.

VAULT CAREER LIBRARY

13

Date

Placement of the date, whether left justified, centered or aligned to the right, is up to your discretion, but take the time to write out the entry. If you choose to list the day, list it first, followed by the month, date and year, as follows: Tuesday, December 13, 2005. (Europeans commonly list the day before month, so writing a date only in numbers can be confusing. Does a letter written on 4/7/04 date from April 7, or July 4?)

Name and address

Your name and address on the cover letter should be the same as the one on your resume. Uniformity in this case applies not only to the address given, but the way the information is written. If you listed your street as Ave. instead of Avenue on your resume, do so on your cover letter too.

Your header can be displayed centrally, just like the resume header—including your name in a larger and/or bolded font. But in most cases, the heading is either left justified or left justified and indented to the far right hand side of the page.

If you choose to list your phone number, make sure that you don't list it somewhere else on the page.

Next comes the address of the person you are writing. In many circumstances, you'll have the complete information on the person you're trying to contact, in which case you should list it in this order:

• Name of contact

• Title of contact

• Company name

• Company address

• Phone number

• Fax number

However, in other cases, you have less than complete information to go on. This is particularly true when responding to an advertisement. If you have an address or phone or fax number but no company name, try a reverse directory, such as Superpages (www.superpages.com), which lets you trace a business by either its address or phone number.

When you're trying to get the name of a contact person, calling the company and asking the receptionist for the name of the recipient (normally, though not always, head of HR) may work. But usually, companies don't list this information because they don't want you calling at all. So if you call, be polite, be persistent, ask for a contact name, say thank you and hang up. Don't identify yourself. If you have questions, wait until the interview.

If you don't get all of the info, don't worry. There are several salutations to use to finesse the fact that you've got no idea who you're addressing. Some solutions are:

To whom it may concern: A bit frosty, but effective.

Dear Sir or Madam: Formal and fusty, but it works.

Sirs: Since the workforce is full of women, avoid this outdated greeting.

Omitting the salutation altogether: Effective, but may look too informal.

Good morning: A sensible approach that is gaining popularity.

Format

Unlike the resume, the cover letter offers the writer significant room for flexibility. Successful cover letters have come in various different forms, and sometimes those that break rules achieve success by attracting attention. But most don't. Here are some basic guidelines on what information the body of a cover letter should deliver.

First paragraph

To be successful, this first paragraph should contain:

• A first line that tells the reader why you're contacting him or her, and how you came to know about the position. This statement should be quick, simple and catchy. Ultimately, what you're trying to create is a descriptive line by which people can categorize you. This means no transcendental speeches about "the real you" or long-winded treatises on your career and philosophy of life.

• Text indicating your respect for the firm's accomplishments, history, status, products or leaders.

• A last line that gives a very brief synopsis of who you are and why you want the position. The best way to do this, if you don't already have a more personal connection with the person you're contacting, is to lay it out:

I am a (your identifying characteristic)

+

I am a (your profession)

+

I have (your years of experience or education)

+

I have worked in (your area of expertise)

+

I am interested in (what position you're looking for)

And thus a killer first paragraph is born.

Middle paragraph(s)

The middle paragraph allows you to move beyond your initial declarative sentences, and into more expansive and revealing statements about who you are and what skills you bring to the job. This is another opportunity to explicitly summarize key facts of your job history. The middle paragraph also offers you the opportunity to mention any connection or prior experience that you may have with the company.

Tell the employer in this paragraph how, based on concrete references to your previous performances, you will perform in your desired position. This does not mean making general, unqualified statements about your greatness such as "I'm going to be the best you've ever had" or my "My energetic multitasking will be the ultimate asset to your company."

Comments should be backed up by specific references. Try something along the lines of "My post-graduate degree in marketing, combined with my four years of retail bicycle sales would make me a strong addition to Gwinn Cycles' marketing team."

Or: "Meeting the demands of a full-time undergraduate education, a position as student government accountant and a 20-hour-a-week internship with Davidson Management provided me with the multitasking experience needed to excel as a financial analyst at Whittier Finance."

Visit Vault at **www.vault.com** for insider company profiles, expert advice,
career message boards, expert resume reviews, the Vault Job Board and more.

VAULT CAREER LIBRARY   **15**

Many advertisements ask you to name your salary requirements. Some avoid the problem altogether by ignoring this requirement, and this may be the safest route—any number you give might price you out of a job (before you have the chance to negotiate face-to-face at an interview). Alternatively, you might be pegged at a lower salary than you might otherwise have been offered. If you must give a salary requirement, be as general as possible. The safest bet is to offer a general range ("in the $40,000s"). Put the salary requirement at the end of the paragraph, not in your first sentence.

Some cover letter writers use another paragraph to describe their accomplishments. This makes sense if, for example, your experience lies in two distinct areas, or you need to explain something that is not evident on your resume, such as "I decided to leave law school to pursue an exciting venture capital opportunity" or "I plan to relocate to Wisconsin shortly." Do not get overly personal—"I dropped out of business school to care for my sick mother" is touching, but will not necessarily impress employers.

Final paragraph

The final paragraph is your fond farewell, your summation, a testament to your elegance and social grace. This should be the shortest paragraph of the letter. Here, tell your readers you're pleased they got so far down the page. Tell them you look forward to hearing from them. Tell them how you can be reached. Here's some sample sentences for your conclusion.

Thank you sentences:
Thank you for your time.
Thank you for reviewing my qualifications.
Thank you for your consideration.
Thank you for your review of my qualifications.

Way too much:
It would be more than an honor to meet with you.

A note of confidence in a callback:
I look forward to your reply.
I look forward to hearing from you.
I look forward to your response.
I look forward to your call.

Over the top:
Call me tomorrow, please.

Interviews

Getting Ready

Would a seasoned attorney stride into a courtroom on the day of an important case without having considered every angle of the case? Would a professional climber arrive in Kathmandu without provisions and maps of Mount Everest? Nope. If you want to sway the jury or reach the summit, you've got to go into the big event prepared. The same is true of going into an interview. Preparation is an essential part of the interview process and one that is easy to overlook or shortchange.

According to polls, most job candidates spend less than an hour preparing for their interviews. No one is going to make you prepare for an interview, least of all the people who will be asking the questions, so it's up to you to get ready on your own.

Unprepared interview subjects often give poor interviews, says Clift Jones, an account director at Bozell Worldwide Advertising. "One of the biggest mistakes people make is to come in with no agenda. They don't know why they want the job, anything about the unique strengths of the company or why they'd be a good match. They're eager and little else. It's much more impressive if they've put a lot of thought into what they want from a situation and what they have to offer before they come in."

By preparing for the interview you'll be doing yourself a favor. Remember: more time spent in preparation means less anxiety on the day of the interview. It's a relief to have something relevant to say, a cogent question on your tongue, a collection of stories underscoring specific elements of your prodigious competence, when the interviewer's anticipatory eyes fall on you and it's your turn to speak.

In addition to alleviating pre-interview stress, being prepared has several other benefits:

- It shows the interviewer that you care enough about the position, the company and the industry to research its current status and future.
- It suggests that once you're hired, your preparation for meetings and assignments will be equally as sound.
- It shows respect for the interviewer and the company he or she works for.
- It provides more opportunities for you and the interviewer to have a meaningful conversation in which you can find common ground.

Research

Research is a vital preparation tool. Over time, companies, like countries, develop distinct cultures and inner languages. In some cases the language of a corporation or industry can become so specialized that an outsider will have trouble understanding it. The job candidate who learns an organization's lingo well enough to speak it during the interview just might, like a long-lost relative, be embraced with a cry of, "He's one of us!" and welcomed into the fold.

Where can someone find this kind of insider knowledge? Vault produces a series of profiles and surveys on organizations that can help the information-hungry interviewee. Other user-friendly, if more company-friendly, sources of information include the packets prepared for a company's stockholders. Any stockbroker will send you these, provided you assure them of your interest in someday purchasing stocks through them. A company's human resources, treasury or public relations office will be happy to send you an annual report (which will include a company's financial, marketing and product report), a prospectus (which includes the name of the CEO and a list of major players), or a 10K report (which contains a company's historical and financial information).

Trade magazines, (or "the trades") industry insider magazines, can apprise you of current events, hirings and firings, trends and other relevant issues. Libraries, career centers, and web sites can also be valuable information-gathering places. Spending a day at the library is an especially good way to get the job search going if you're just starting out.

Visit Vault at **www.vault.com** for insider company profiles, expert advice, career message boards, expert resume reviews, the Vault Job Board and more.

VAULT CAREER LIBRARY

17

Perhaps the most direct way of getting the real skinny on a company is to talk to someone who works there. Speaking to someone in a position similar to the one in which you're interested, can give you vital insights into the company's modus operandi and expose some of the rats in its cellar—or executive suites. If you don't know anyone who's had experience at the company, you might ask around to see if you have any less obvious connections to the industry or a parallel field.

As in other areas of the job search, it's a good idea to treat your preparation for the interview as a job. You might, for example, want to keep a notebook for observations on the companies with which you've interviewed. Or, you might collect the information you gather in an interview folder. Not only will this give you some practice—a warm-up in the organizational skills important in any job—but it will also help you focus and take the preparation process a little more seriously. Some especially important things to remember are the names, numbers and extensions of any contacts with whom you've spoken, the dates and times when those contacts occurred, lists of reasons why you're interested in a particular organization, and potential obstacles or drawbacks associated with a company.

Review your resume

Before the interview, your resume is probably going to be the only thing the interviewer knows about you. In most cases, whoever is going to interview you will have that resume close at hand and might even have memorized key elements of it, so it's important you to be totally familiar with what you've written. Take some time to review what you've done and to observe how it's represented. If you haven't updated your resume in a while, you might discover serious omissions. Maybe you've left off an important experience, or maybe you've forgotten about an experience that could take center stage during the interview. If you can't remember something on your resume, your interviewer may think you are lying.

Check the dates of past jobs for any gaps you might be asked to explain. If you were out searching for the last living grizzly bear in Arizona for those few months when you weren't working, spend some time thinking about how you can turn this to your advantage in the interview. Those tracking skills might prove your passion, bravery and tenacity, for example. Just as importantly, this offbeat experience might help you establish a connection with your interviewer and give him or her an insight into your character.

Consider doing some role playing as you review your resume. Try stepping outside yourself and look at your resume hypercritically, as an employer looking to hire you would. Based on your resume, try imagining questions you'd ask yourself and reasons for not hiring yourself. Once you've imagined the on-paper preconceptions this person likely has of you before you meet him, you can come up with an effective plan for exceeding these expectations face to face.

Because computers play such a vital role in the workplace, it's a good idea to review before the interview exactly which programs you know. If you have experience with any of the programs the company uses, you can make an immediate positive impact on the organization. If you're particularly ambitious, you can give yourself this computer advantage by finding out which programs the company uses and familiarizing yourself with them before the interview.

Emotional preparation

Even if you've made yourself into a walking tome of facts and figures, computer programs and trade lingo, you might not make a good impression unless you're emotionally prepared for the interview. In a mad rush to do whatever you have to do to land a job, you may not take the time to ask yourself how you really feel about this job.

The interview is as much a forum for you to find out if the company and the job fit your needs as it is for the company to discover whether or not you're right for them. You may have to give up some aspects of your dream job, but the goal is to sacrifice as little as possible. What do you want from a job? What are you good at doing? What do people compliment you on?

In the ideal situation, the interviewer and the interviewee are equally interested in finding a perfect fit. Look out for yourself. Ask hard questions about work conditions, drawbacks and low points. If asked tactfully and backed up with research, well-directed questions of this sort won't offend a responsible interviewer. After all, a happy employee is going to be more productive than someone who hates his job.

But if you choose unwisely the first time, don't worry—jobs are no longer forever. People change careers nowadays about as often as their hairstyles. Chances are, even the person who interviews you, if he or she hasn't been living in a cave with blind fish, will understand that you probably won't be with the company for life. Gone are the days of the 1950s "company man" who signed up after college and stayed on until he retired. Nevertheless, choosing a job and career right the first time saves a lot of time and angst.

At the Interview

The meeting and small talk

If you're old enough to be vying for a job that requires a serious interview, you've probably met a lot of people in your life. Extend those social skills to the people in the office. Maintain solid eye contact and a firm handshake. This proven greeting combination implies strength, confidence, competence and honesty. Consider the alternative: shifty eyes and a limp handshake.

After the initial meeting and a stroll back to the interview room, the next phase begins—small talk. The interview hasn't officially begun, but make no mistake: your ability to talk about the weather is being measured up. The topic of conversation might in fact be the weather, a brief discussion of the latest media frenzy, the game last night, a round or two of the name and geography game. Small talk is meant to relax you, so allow yourself to be relaxed. Remember though, that you're still in an interview and anything you say can be used against you in the decision process. Answer small talk questions briefly, honestly, diplomatically and tactfully. Be witty, but not obscene or clownish.

The main event

At some point, the interviewer will shift to the heart of the matter and begin to ask questions pertaining to the job and your fitness for it. Often these questions will follow a description of the available job and an explanation of the company and what it does.

Often the segue from the small talk session into the more serious portion of the interview will be marked by a description of what the company does. Your interviewer might ask you what you know about the company, and after you give your answer (astute and detailed, due to your extensive research) the interviewer will talk about the company, the job, the industry, their plans for the future. This is a good time to demonstrate your listening skills. Let them see that you're listening and interested, and pay attention to what they're saying. Take notes on the notepad you remembered to bring.

Focus

Before anything else is said it might be helpful, here, to dispense an all-purpose interviewing bromide: remember to focus. Once the middle, substance portion of the interview begins, the interviewer is primarily interested in your past job performances and possibly your life performances in as much as they relate to the open job. He or she wants to know how your experience and personality will translate into the available job. For example, when the interviewer says, "Tell me about yourself," they're interested in your work experiences, not the fact that you were born in deepest February when the moon was on the wane, and frost obscured the windowpane. Your interviewer will be thinking of little else except whether or not

Visit Vault at **www.vault.com** for insider company profiles, expert advice, career message boards, expert resume reviews, the Vault Job Board and more.

VAULT CAREER LIBRARY

19

you will be able to do the job. (This does not mean that you should purge yourself of all personality—it's fine to mention that you like ice fishing—but you should keep your eye on conveying your fitness for the job.)

During the interview you should act like a boxer in the ring. You want to land as many substantive punches as possible, and you want every one of your answers to count. If you use up a lot of your time and energy on false punches—statements that fail to focus on the job and why you're a good person to fill it—the interviewer is going to decide you're wasting time. If you feel yourself getting off topic and talking about something that's not really relevant, it's all right to mention this. Your interviewer will appreciate the fact that you reined yourself in—this demonstrates control, maturity, an understanding of the bottom line and well-developed communication skills.

Honesty

Any lies you tell about your background and accomplishments will come back to haunt you. Similarly, unless you're an experienced actor, any affectations in attitude or manner will be detected by an experienced interviewer. Interview situations are stressful enough; you don't need to add method acting to the mix. Be honest without dwelling on your weaknesses. Be the best version of yourself. Practiced interviewers will appreciate your candor. They'll know they're dealing with an honest person.

Who's doing what for whom? It is better to give than to receive

Often, an applicant will blithely run through a litany of reasons why the position fits his career paths without mentioning what skills, insights or vision he can bring to the position. It's a good idea to steer clear of this trap. Often when thinking of a position, especially one that is perfect for our career aspirations, we tend to think about it in terms of what it has to offer us. Your love for the position, however, should not be the focus of the interview. The spotlight, from beginning to end, should shine on the myriad reasons why you'll be indispensable to the company once you're in the position.

Finding common ground and bonding

Employers, being human, will often hire someone they like—someone who reminds them of themselves at the same age, or someone to whom they are connected in whatever way—instead of the person who will perform best in the job. It's far more difficult to turn a friend down for a job than it is to nix someone about whom you have no particular feeling. So try subtly and deftly (it's easy to go overboard and become an Eddy Haskell) to form a connection with the employer.

If you can discover what kind of person you're dealing with, what his or her passion is, it will be easier for you to become a bit of a chameleon for bonding purposes. Any connection you can discover with the person can help. Find a topic such as a shared alma mater or an outside interest upon which you can build a connection. Do what you can to size the person up. If they mention a hobby or a recent vacation, express real interest. If you can get them to like you as a person, in addition to making them feel you're the best candidate for the job, you'll have done yourself a tremendous favor.

Making an end run

Trying to use humor or other methods of endearment in an interview is risky, but so are most business ventures. Similarly, being completely straightforward in the interview holds risks, but telling the emperor he has no clothes might impress some interviewers.

We all know at least one person who has a knack for making immediate connections, one of those people who never meets a stranger. But the ability to establish an instant rapport with someone can be learned. Think about those people in your life who have a knack for meeting people. What are their secrets? How do they do it? Are they able to project a genuine enthusiasm, a guilelessness that disarms people? While it can be dangerous to try to take on someone else's personality for an interview, try to discover ways you can better connect with someone. The following is a list of things you might want to keep in mind when trying to forge a bond with your interviewer.

- Listening. Remember your grade-school teachers. "Don't just listen. Show me you're listening." Let the interviewer see your interest and enthusiasm. Concentrate on what they're saying.

- Read 'em and weep. Or make 'em laugh. Try to discover what motivates your interviewers. What kind of person do they look like? How are their offices decorated? Do some research on your interviewer. Find out who they are and what they do outside of work. What are their hobbies and passions? It's amazing how much even the most reserved person will open up if you find the right subject.

- If they're trying to be funny, don't be too nervous to laugh.

Asking for the job

If you know you want the job, don't be afraid to let the interviewer know this, point blank. If an interviewer senses wishy-washiness, they'll offer the job to someone else. They want to hire someone who wants the job, not someone who will grudgingly accept it. Express interest in the position and the company.

Questions to Expect: The Quality Search

Interviewers, inevitably, seek the ideal candidate. To become this perfect hire, put yourself in the mind of the interviewer. Take a good look at yourself. What does this person look like? How does this person dress, and carry him or herself? Which qualities does this interviewee demonstrate in his or her answers?

Increasingly, interviewers will ask behavioral questions—questions that seek to understand you through the prism of your past behavior and accomplishments.

One cool customer

If you're the person who can step into the bloody heart of the fray with ice water in your veins when the office resembles Custer's camp on the Little Bighorn, then you'll be a valuable asset to the company. If, on the other hand, you get frazzled when someone asks for the company's address, you might be a dangerous liability when the bullets start to fly and scalps are being taken. So your interviewer is going to be watching you to see how you handle the stress of the interview and your ability to remain composed. The following are some questions you should know how to answer by the time you're sitting in the hot seat:

- You're in customer relations and an unsatisfied customer is complaining bitterly about the product or service. How do you handle the situation?
- You've been given multiple tasks. There is no way you can complete all of them on time. What do you do?
- Describe some situations that really bother you.
- You're right. You know you're right. And, yet, everyone is taking issue with what you say. How do you react?
- How well do you handle pressure in the workplace?

Visit Vault at **www.vault.com** for insider company profiles, expert advice, career message boards, expert resume reviews, the Vault Job Board and more.

V\ULT CAREER LIBRARY

21

How bad do you want it and what will you do to get it?

During the interview, one quality for which your interviewer will undoubtedly be searching—in your answers, handshake, appearance and voice—is enthusiasm about the industry, the company and the particular job opening. They're counting on you to bring in a jolt of fresh-faced exuberance. You can express your energy and aggressiveness in the interview, but true excitement is difficult to fake. Here are some questions designed to measure the true level of your enthusiasm.

- What do you feel are your best and worst qualities, and how will these relate to the position?
- What interests you about this position, industry, organization?
- What are your long-term career goals?
- What motivates you?
- How important is winning to you?
- What is the most difficult thing you've ever had to do. Why?
- Has anyone ever really pushed you? How did you respond?

Where you've been and what you've done

What you've done in the past serves as the clearest indication of what you'll be able to do in the future. If you can portray yourself in your interview as someone with a string of past successes by telling honest anecdotes in which you emerge as the hero, you're on your way to winning the job at hand.

Remember, however, that an experienced interviewer will be on to you like your first grade teacher if you try to snow him or her. Here are some questions you should know how to answer in the category of past performance:

- Describe your duties at [this particular position].
- Of which of your past accomplishments are you most proud?
- What, based on your experience, have you found to be your optimal work conditions?
- What are the most valuable lessons you've learned from past work experiences?
- Which of the skills you've picked up at the positions listed on your resume do you feel will best translate into this position and why?
- What are your long-term goals in this industry and at this company?
- Describe a problem you encountered at one of your jobs and how you handled it.

Writing and rapping

These two arts form the bedrock of civilization and important skills for any job. Any experienced interviewer will be searching for soundness, if not outright eloquence, in written and oral communication. Your oral communication abilities will be on display, from the moment you meet the interviewer until the time you bid them adieu.

Your writing skills will be evaluated in the resume and cover letter, and sometimes in a formal writing sample. Those mistakes on your resume—the misspelling of your own name, the missing dot in your e-mail address—will imply a dangerous lack of attention to detail and may be viewed by a potential employer as the tip of the iceberg. If this person can't manage these small details, he or she may think, then how will they be able to handle the larger requirements of this job?

It's a good idea to remember that communication extends beyond just words. Facial expressions, gestures, style and cleanliness of dress, tone of voice, posture, scent and hairstyle send a message of one kind or another to your interviewer from the moment you stride confidently through the office door. So think about these questions.

- Compare and contrast your oral and written communication skills.

• What experience have you had with public speaking? In your view, what are the key attributes of a successful public speaker?

• Let's say someone refuses or is hesitant to embrace your ideas. How do you persuade that person you're right?

• What problems have you had with past employers and co-workers and how did you deal with these situations?

Visit Vault at **www.vault.com** for insider company profiles, expert advice, career message boards, expert resume reviews, the Vault Job Board and more.

V∧ULT CAREER LIBRARY   **23**

Schmoozing/Networking

Schmoozing to Find a Job Through People

"I tell my clients that 15 percent of jobs are filled through the newspaper, five percent are filled through companies like mine, and 80 percent are filled through word-of-mouth," says Beth Anrig, the owner of Beth Anrig and Associates, a job placement service in Connecticut. Anrig places individuals in positions in a wide variety of industries, ranging from banking to publishing. "Do you know how most jobs are filled?" Anrig asks. "A manager asks a couple of people if they know anyone good."

We've moved past the point where we expect that jobs will be mainly filled through company recruiting and advertising. According to widely cited statistics, 75 to 80 percent of all job seekers find their new position through referrals; most openings never see the light of day (or newsprint). By schmoozing, you make word-of-mouth work in your favor. You can learn about a variety of industries and make friends and contacts upon whom you can call for career advice or assistance. Now how to do it?

Schmoozing to Find a Job When in School

If you're still in school, you have golden schmoozing opportunities all around you. Many students forget that there are numerous people at their university who already know them and are predisposed to want them to succeed—their professors. If you think your history professor only knows about the French Revolution, think again. He's probably pretty savvy about life in this century as well.

Make sure you are on a first-name basis with each and every one of your professors. Even if you're enrolled in huge lecture classes and can barely see the prof, figure out when his or her office hours are (hint: they'll be printed on the syllabus or posted on the office door) and go. Most professors only see students when they're begging for extensions on papers or explaining how they slept through the midterm. Your schmoozing should come as a welcome change.

Introduce yourself to your professor at the beginning of the semester. Tell them you're looking forward to taking the class, and if you're majoring (or thinking about it) in the subject, let them know that too. If you have any questions about something in lecture or are curious about something you've read, ask. But make sure to ask non-class-related questions as well. How did they get interested in sociology? What research are they doing now? Can they recommend any other good classes?

Because, after all, you ultimately want to get a job after you graduate, ask your professor for advice about that too. What have other students in his/her subject done after graduation? What does the professor recommend you do? You'd be surprised how many professors consult with companies part time. If you're at a larger university, you might want to consider taking a class at your school's business or law school, as professors at professional schools often have an even wider variety of career contacts.

Tap alumni resources

Other woefully underused routes to schmoozing for a job in school are career counselors and alumni.

Career counselors want to help you get a job. That's their job. At the same time, they also have to find jobs for the other couple of thousand students at your university. But you, smart schmoozer that you are, have an advantage—not all those students are going to bother to schmooze their career counselors. As early as possible in your school career, go to your school career center, introduce yourself and discuss your career goals. Thank your counselor for any particularly good advice or leads he gives you. Most students neglect career counselors until the spring of their senior year. Don't make the same mistake.

Visit Vault at **www.vault.com** for insider company profiles, expert advice, career message boards, expert resume reviews, the Vault Job Board and more.

VAULT CAREER LIBRARY 25

Alumni already have a point of similarity with you. Ron Nelson points out, "Just having that little thing like a school connection takes you from 'Who the hell are you and why are you calling me?' to 'Oh, okay, you went to Vanderbilt too, what can I do for you?' It's not a big thing, but it's enough."

Tamara Totah, the former headhunter for The Oxbridge Group, also recommends using alumni contacts from your school, although she cautions that you should never directly ask them for a job. "The minute they hear that they get worried," she says. "Talk to them about what different opportunities may be available in the industry. People will spend 30 minutes with you. They know how tough it is."

Schmoozing for a Job Out of School

Once you're out of school, you'll have lost (sniff!) some of the support structure for which all your tuition dollars paid. What happens when you've found a job, and then realized that you're not too happy with it? Don't be afraid—most people in this age of downsizing, corporate restructuring and increasing specialization change careers at least six times during their lives. With all the job hopping, people increasingly accept that job changing is a part of life. Your schmoozing talents will help you ease these transitions.

The informational interview

It's not a job interview—exactly. But it does get you face-to-face with someone in an industry that interests you. Informational interviews are an invaluable opportunity to learn about the inside scoop into the career field that interests you. Many people are prepared to spend 10 minutes to an hour of their time talking to those looking for a job, assessing their skills and background, and giving them some pointers in breaking into their chosen field.

Says Beth Anrig, "I tell all my clients that the best thing to do is to set up informational interviews." One caveat—"never call them that," she says. Informational interviews sound too much like interviews, and that sounds like asking for a job. Everyone is over-networked, in the official sense. No one has the time anymore to do something that is just like a job.

So don't frame the "informational interview" as any kind of interview. Instead, say that you want to talk with them, or get coffee or chat. Your goal is to have a conversation, not an interview. Ask semipersonal questions: What got you started in this industry? What other careers did you consider? Are you happy in your choice? At the same time, talk honestly and openly about your own career aspirations, and why the industry in question appeals to you. If you click, keep the person abreast of your career progress and decisions.

But never, says Totah, our erstwhile New York headhunter, ask for a job outright. "If they don't have one and you ask that, they're going to want to boot you out five minutes later," Totah says. "Believe me, if you're talking about careers, they know you want a job. If they like you and they can help you in some way they will." Schmoozing means you don't spell it out.

When calling someone for an informational interview, make it clear you are not asking for a job. The point is, if they like you, they will help you find a job. Appeal to your contact's expertise. "Everyone likes to give advice," says Anrig. "If you tell them that you are calling because a mutual acquaintance has suggested they are a real authority in their field or an inspiring example, they will be hard-pressed to turn you down."

Though the informational interview isn't a job interview (exactly), it's still important to do your research on the company and the industry. It's rude to waste someone's time during the workday, and it doesn't reflect well on you. "Most people are very generous about helping people make connections," says Wicke Chambers, our communications consultant from Atlanta. "I have a lot of business contacts and am willing to call up and set up informational interviews for people coming out of college and recent grads. I myself am approached for interviews constantly."

However, Chambers says, "What I do mind is people asking to talk to me about my job and then having absolutely no idea what they want. I've interviewed with people who don't know whether they want to be a florist, an airline pilot or a public relations executive. I don't care a hill of beans if someone hasn't at least got an idea about what they want to do and how I can help."

Visit Vault at **www.vault.com** for insider company profiles, expert advice,
career message boards, expert resume reviews, the Vault Job Board and more.

VAULT CAREER LIBRARY   27

TO BUILD BEAUTY, WE NEED TALENT.

"At L'Oréal, success starts with people. Our people are our most precious asset. Respect for people, their ideas and differences, is the only path to our sustainable long-term growth."

Laurent Attal, President and CEO, L'Oréal USA

John P.
Packaging development engineer

Vincent T.
Marketing manager

Alice F.
Formula development engineer

L'ORÉAL
WORLD LEADER IN BEAUTY PRODUCTS

Join us. Staying on top of a dynamic industry means we need ambitious, flexible and high-performing people. L'Oréal USA: It's fast-paced. It's stimulating. It's rewarding. And most of all, it's what you make it.

L'Oréal USA Management Development Program
Marketing ▪ Sales ▪ Finance ▪ Information Systems ▪ Logistics ▪ Manufacturing ▪ Research & Development

If you are an imaginative and results-focused graduating senior with an entrepreneurial spirit and commitment to excellence, then L'Oréal USA may have the opportunity for you. Upon entering our rotational training program, you will become an integral part of our team, with concrete responsibility from day one. You will work alongside top professionals who shape the industry, contributing to the creation of ideas and the processes that turn those ideas into realities. In addition to professional development training held at our Management Development Center, we offer competitive compensation and benefits. Learn more about this exciting full-time opportunity and apply at **WWW.LOREALUSA.COM.** Equal Opportunity Employer.

WORKPLACE DIVERSITY

Overview

Every year, many new college and professional school grads get their first jobs as entry-level employees in Corporate America. The client service industries in particular—management consulting, investment banking, law and accounting— employ a new army of young worker bees every fall season. Lured by the opportunity to make a great deal of money and gain a broad education in the business world, recent grads often enter the corporate environment with no understanding of the written and unwritten rules of Corporate America to guide their behavior. They simply expect their new employers to train them completely.

This section of *The College Career Bible* is for the benefit of those with little practical experience with the inner workings of the corporate world. Women and minorities need to be particularly savvy in navigating the maze of office protocol and politics. The corporate world has historically been a heterosexual, white male playground. Women usually lack the prior experience, role models and mentors to guide their climb up the corporate ladder. Minorities face those and additional obstacles. Often, new female and minority hires start their jobs ready to conquer the world, only to find their enthusiasm and confidence eroded as they face each additional pitfall. And no wonder. They see few successful survivors of their kind at the top of the ladder. In 2002, only 11 Fortune 1000 companies were led by women. Among *Fortune*'s list of the "Best 50 Companies for Minorities," only 24 percent of officials and managers that the employers honored were actually minorities.

Visit Vault at **www.vault.com** for insider company profiles, expert advice, career message boards, expert resume reviews, the Vault Job Board and more.

VAULT CAREER LIBRARY   31

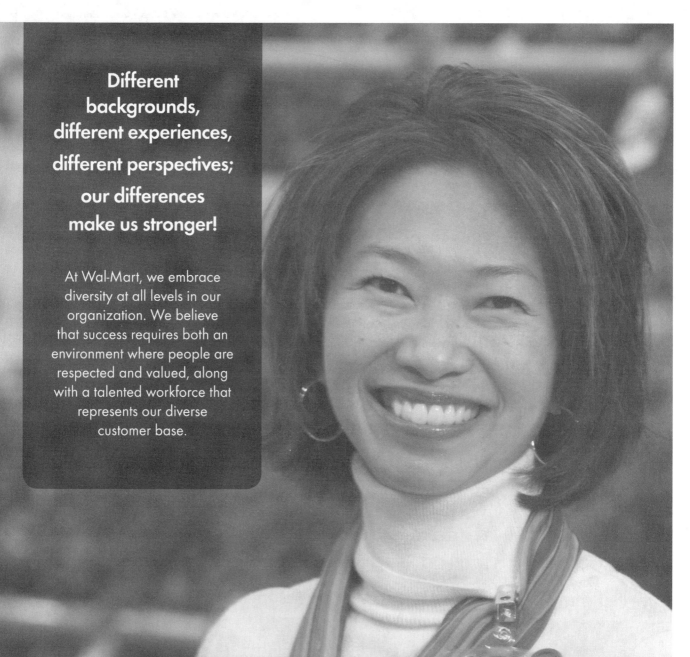

Mentors

A Crucial Advantage

What makes the difference between a career that thrives and one that stalls? For many women and minorities, the narrow gap between failure and success is bridged by mentorships. Mentors are people who share their general business knowledge, as well as their knowledge of a specific company, with lucky mentees (someone who mentors take under their wings). Here is some advice on how to make these valuable relationships work for you.

The importance of mentors for women and minorities

Decision-makers often consciously or unconsciously bond with and champion those who remind them of themselves. Minorities in particular need in-house mentors who champion them because they usually don't have natural role models and networks at their company. Mentors will educate you about your company's office politics and cultural norms, teach you valuable job skills and pass on industry knowledge.

You mentor does not need to share your minority status. In fact, a straight white male mentor can be a major asset in your rise up the corporate ladder. It takes time, patience and investment to develop a meaningful relationship with someone who seems to be very different from yourself—but it is worth it.

Mentors can keep you with an employer

After several years at the prestigious consulting firm Booz Allen Hamilton, Cathy Mhatre had her first child. Mhatre credits her mentors at Booz Allen with keeping her at the firm. "I've now been at Booz Allen for six years, which is unusual for any consultant. One of the main reasons I am still here is because there were people who wanted to keep me here." Mhatre estimates that she has "four to six" mentors at the firm, and advises, "Because women mentors are scarce in general, find enlightened men."

Identifying Potential Mentors

Find out if your employer assigns you a mentor—then keep looking

Increasingly, employers assign mentors to incoming employees—a practice that has been common at law firms for some time and is spreading rapidly to other industries as well. Some consulting firms have entire mentor family trees—with a "founder" mentor, his or her mentees, their mentees, and so on. Make sure to take advantage of these mentors, who have specifically volunteered to serve as resources.

At the same time, the most valuable mentors are normally the ones that evolve from everyday working relationships. If someone appears willing to share their experience and skills with you and takes an interest in your career, it is likely that they would like to mentor you in some way.

Mentors can be found inside or outside your company. Look around your department, your company and the professional business organizations to which you belong. Identify people you really admire with whom you cross paths. Don't limit yourself to obvious choices (e.g., the most popular/powerful executive, the person who had your job before you, the person of the same race or gender as you). Any impressive, intelligent and insightful person you meet can evolve into a future mentor.

Visit Vault at **www.vault.com** for insider company profiles, expert advice, career message boards, expert resume reviews, the Vault Job Board and more.

VAULT CAREER LIBRARY

33

Mentors within the company can help champion or cultivate you. In your company, mentors know all the players, politics and pitfalls. Ideally, they are well respected and secure in their positions. They may be a few rungs up the corporate ladder and can help you understand different managers' personalities and preferred working styles, office politics and the lessons they have learned.

Mentors outside of work provide objectivity. Choose mentors outside of your office who know your personality and have wisdom from a wide range of experiences. Develop relationships with at least one or two people who have no impact on your career to whom you can openly vent, turn to for perspective and ask for candid feedback. You will appreciate their distance when a work issue is too controversial to discuss with a fellow colleague, even in confidence.

In many cases, you may not even need a personal relationship with these people in order to learn from them. Observe their traits from a distance, and emulate them when you get in a position of power. For example, one director at Oracle recalls that he admired a manager who recognized hard work by comping subordinates on expensive dinners and hotel rooms. This director is now implementing this practice, which breeds loyalty.

Approaching potential mentors

Be patient and build connections through regular interactions, evolving conversations in the office, over lunch or outside of the office. Don't wait for a potential mentor to invite you to lunch or coffee—you make the offer. Tell them you would love to hear about their background (people love to talk about themselves). Be direct in seeking their counsel in dealing with your own professional situations. Try to get on projects with them so you can demonstrate your personality and performance. If you do a good job with them, hopefully they will be impressed (and even see themselves in you). Bond over nonprofessional common interests. An African-American woman discovered a shared love of cooking with a senior white male executive, who often sought her out to exchange recipes.

You can try approaching speakers at seminars or classes; they may be receptive because they like working with younger, ambitious people who remind them of their younger selves and who are receptive to their wisdom.

Establish a broad group of mentors

Cultivate different mentors for different areas of your professional life. You should not expect one person to provide all of the counsel and guidance you need to get ahead. Pick and choose different people you admire for different reasons and use them as a resource in areas where they shine. Quality matters too—one or two superstar mentors may do you more good in the end than a dozen slackers. Company and independent organizations for women and minorities are a great way to expand your network of mentors.

Getting the most from a mentor

Once you have mentors, be open to their advice. Do not be defensive—they have nothing to gain in giving you this advice. Mentors will only value and continue your relationship if you're communicative and sincerely value their counsel. Make sure you report back to them on your successes and setbacks.

How to Get a Mentor

Mary Cranston, chair of law firm Pillsbury Winthrop LLP

Mary is the chairperson of one of the largest law firms in America. She has been practicing law since 1975, and has litigated over 300 class-action cases in state and federal court, focusing on antitrust counseling and litigation, and securities litigation. She has been named to the *National Law Journal*'s list of the 100 Most Influential Lawyers in America, and *California Daily Journal*'s list of the 100 Most Influential Lawyers in California.

Her advice on how to get a mentor:

Be a good mentee. Approach individuals who have skills you want to acquire. If you just say, "Help me," they will be less likely to help. But if you say, "I had a great idea; can we work on it together?" your chances are much higher. Think about how you can contribute to the relationship, then you're more likely to get help from a mentor.

Tips for Building a Relationship with a Potential Mentor

Kristi Anderson, executive recruiter, TMP Worldwide

Show overwhelming interest in their kids! Pretend you like their kids, remember their names and ask about them often. Remembering to ask who won that high school football game will go a million miles in endearing yourself to a potential mentor.

Ask your mentor for advice often, even when you don't need it. People, especially successful people, like to hear themselves talk and to demonstrate their wisdom. Don't ask dumb or simple questions with a definitive answer, but ask your mentor open-ended questions regarding his style and experience in handling a particular business situation. Then just sit back and feign interest in the long-winded response. Even when I don't need the advice, I will pose such a question to a mentor. It makes a mentor feel like he is bringing you along in your professional development.

Tips for Mentees

It's not enough to find a good mentor—it's just as important to use them correctly. Here are a few tips to make the most of your mentor relationship.

- Find mentors at all levels of the company. The classic mentor is someone a few levels above you in an organization—close enough to your experience to guide you upwards in the ranks, experienced enough to have some pull. But you can also gain experience from mentors at your level and at other companies as well. Your business school professors are another invaluable set of potential mentors.

- Don't approach someone and formally ask them to be your mentor. This kind of act is akin to handing your business card to someone and asking them to be your contact—it's too artificial to take root. If someone wants to be your mentor, they will indicate that fact through the interest they take in you.

- Keep in touch with your mentors. Mentorship is a relationship, and relationships are built from frequent, informal contact. This is important even when your mentor is assigned to you by your company. If you move on from a company, stay in touch with your mentor there.

- Establish trust. Everything you discuss with your mentor is between the two of you.

- Have realistic expectations. Your mentor is an advisor and advocate—not someone to do your career networking for you, or someone to cover your errors.

Visit Vault at **www.vault.com** for insider company profiles, expert advice, career message boards, expert resume reviews, the Vault Job Board and more.

V∧ULT CAREER LIBRARY

35

Tips for Mentees (continued)

• Don't pass up the opportunity to have a mentor. Having a mentor can make a major difference in your career path and your self-confidence.

Finding a Mentor During a Meltdown

Ashley Fieglein, director, General Atlantic Partners

During my investment banking career, I learned the importance of choosing a mentor even though I was the only woman in an all-male office. Four years into investment banking, with hundreds of hours of lost sleep under my belt, I reached a moment where I really needed to let go. A client had yelled at me. I had a stack of work on my desk guaranteeing another lost weekend. And I had gotten a call saying that two of the projects were "urgent" and needed yesterday. I felt panicked. I noticed the teardrops on my desk, even though I wasn't aware I was crying. I got up and closed the door to my office. And the hysteria set in. I sobbed. And then I suddenly realized that I really wasn't going to be OK.

I picked up the phone and called one of the senior bankers with whom I had worked very closely over the previous four years. He showed up in my office in a matter of minutes. In spite of my embarrassment, I let him rub my back while I sobbed. He closed the door, gave me a glass of water and waited until I caught my breath.

He offered to help manage the situation, to get me more support and to get me more time. And then he sent me home. No arguments allowed, though I protested that things had to get done, but he insisted that they would be OK I think he probably stayed extra hours that night to oversee the analysts working on my projects. I was sound asleep in my bed, catching up on some long overdue rest.

When I came back in the next morning, everything seemed manageable. The client who had reamed me the night before had called back to apologize. The work was no longer insurmountable. And the urgency had subsided.

My newly-found mentor never said a word to me about the incident afterwards. I ended up calling him crying at least once or twice more, and he always supported me kindly. He always took my tears seriously. He understood that this was my way of expressing anger. And I completely trusted his support of me.

Appearance

Take extra care in your appearance. It is the first impression you make in terms of your professional credibility, and it will be easy for others to be judgmental of your looks. As a new hire at the bottom of the food chain, you should not be making any personal statements with your clothes. Nothing should distract from the quality of your work. Strive to look well-groomed and polished, a look you can achieve on any budget.

Presentation Counts

Siobhan Green, project manager

At my performance evaluation for my first job, I was shocked to be rated poorly on my professional appearance. When I asked what that meant (I had a good wardrobe and thought I was more or less fitting in with the other staff), I was told that I should "dress more like Judy." So I watched her and noticed the difference. I didn't wear makeup and she did. Her hair, face and nails were always impeccable—and mine weren't.

The president of our company, whom I often accompanied to client meetings as a note taker, was the one who gave me the low review. He didn't really know what made Judy look more professional than me, but it bothered him enough to mention it to my supervisor and note it on my evaluation. I realized that if I wanted to continue working in that company, wearing nice suits would not be enough. I would have to make sure my nails were always clean and polished, get my hair trimmed regularly, and wear some eyeliner and lipstick, at least for meetings with clients and senior managers.

- **Dress appropriately for your industry and for your position.** Dressing outside your company norm suggests a lack of judgment and cultural fit.

- **Dress well to appear older.** Often, women and minorities can look much younger than their age. Remember that you will interact with senior executives and clients who are two to three times your age. One easy way to appear older, and more professionally credible, is to dress in a more subdued, conservative style. If you are wearing a suit, you are less likely to be mistaken for the summer intern or bike messenger.

- **Women should avoid inappropriately sexy clothes.** There is no quicker way to hurt your professional credibility. If you want to be taken seriously, observe limits: don't bare your midriff, wear low-cut necklines, see-through blouses or Ally McBeal-length miniskirts. Save it for the weekend (unless you are coming into the office). Use the 50 percent rule for judgment calls: if at least half the women go without pantyhose, wear open-toed shoes or moderately short skirts, then you can.

- **Minorities can display ethnic style—in moderation.** Wearing a kente-cloth pocket square with your suit is fine, but coming to work in a full-on dashiki is not. If you wear a piece of clothing for religious reasons (a yarmulke or a headscarf, for example), select pieces in subdued colors and make sure the rest of your clothing fits company standards.

- **Geeky isn't chic in the workplace.** Does your wardrobe consist of square glasses and faded T-shirts with funny slogans? Then you'll need to invest a little bit of time and money in upgrading your look. Overhauling your image will boost your self-esteem and the respect you command from others. Unfortunately, the bottom line is that co-workers in corporate America can be even more superficial than bullies in the schoolyard.

    – No clue what to wear? Buy some fashion magazines, ask your stylish colleagues some questions about where they shop, or talk to a sales clerk in the men's department in a classy department store or chain like Brooks Brothers.

Visit Vault at **www.vault.com** for insider company profiles, expert advice, career message boards, expert resume reviews, the Vault Job Board and more.

VAULT CAREER LIBRARY   37

– Replace your glasses with simple wire frames.

– If you work in a formal dress environment, aim to have three or four tailored suits, twice as many shirts and ties, two pairs of dress shoes (one brown and one black) and four casual outfits for Fridays. If you work in a business casual environment, aim to have at least four or five nice slacks (e.g., black, gray, khaki, navy blue, olive), twice as many shirts to mix and match and two pairs of casual shoes (one brown and one black). Women should buy simple suits in neutral colors (black, brown, gray). Your mint green pantsuit may look smashing on you, but it's so memorable that you won't be able to wear it more than once a month. A simple black skirt suit, on the other hand, can be worn at least once a week. In addition, you can split up the skirt and the jacket and wear them with other items to create more work-ready looks.

– Remember that sock color needs to match shoe or pant color. And never wear athletic socks with a suit! Women, if you're wearing a skirt, wear non-shiny nude or black hose only.

Dressing Right Brings Respect
Former management consultant

When I started working, I brought with me all my clothes and shoes from college and summer jobs. I learned very quickly that while chunky heels and open-toed shoes, fitted tops and above-the-knee skirts weren't necessarily prohibited, I felt much better about myself and the respect I got from senior management by dressing more conservatively. And so my career wardrobe began with new French blue button-down shirts and conservative black pants.

- **Get your hair cut once a month** by someone other than your mother. Men, part your hair on the side instead of the middle.

- **In America, follow American standards.** Overseas, it can be quite common for corporate employees to wear the same outfit several times a week and not shower every day. Be forewarned that Americans who work in a corporate environment are typically extremely superficial about wardrobes and downright fanatical about personal hygiene. If you want to fit in as much as possible, shower and use deodorant every day, and try to have at least five fresh outfits in your wardrobe, one for each day of the week.

Dealing with Stereotyping

People stereotype others out of ignorance and convenience, not malice. As a minority in the corporate world, you may find yourself subtly or blatantly treated differently than your peers because of your assumed strengths, weaknesses and traits. This special treatment may not necessarily be unpleasant or negative. But you need to identify who is making what assumptions, and how these erroneous assumptions impact your work life. If there is any negative impact on your image at the company, and hence your long-term professional development, it is important to address the situation gracefully and request the same treatment your peers receive.

Stereotyping is often unconscious on the part of your colleagues. For example, there's an old stereotype that all Asians are good at math. And maybe you are Asian and really are quite good at math. So on, say, your first management consulting project, it seems to make sense for you to do the back office analysis while someone else interviews the client executives. But the more you do the back office number-crunching, the better you become at it, and the more it makes sense for you to do it again next time. Eventually, if you keep holing up with your calculator, you will fall behind in developing communication skills, professional presence and client relationships. Break the cycle and make sure you are learning an appropriately broad set of skills before you become pigeonholed as the "expert" of one task.

In the next section, we will outline common stereotypes for women, minorities and gay men. Specific ethnicities, age groups and sexual orientation will trigger specific stereotypes. These examples are meant to give you some idea of direct and indirect discrimination you may face based on commonly-held stereotypes. Generally, stereotypes stunt your professional development by skewing the mix of work you get, while your peers receive a more balanced training.

If you decide you are fine with the situation because it is an anomaly, is short-term or has upsides, that's fine. If you want to change the situation, you have to speak up early before the precedent is repeated too often. Whether or not you want to address the stereotype directly, at least you can inform your manager that you would like to broaden your skill set and get a good mix of challenging and diverse work. Don't approach your boss complaining. Tell him your reasoning and your proposed solutions, so that you steer the conversation toward getting his support for one option and the transition itself is assumed. The sooner you demonstrate consistent, undeniable interest and accomplishment in the areas outside of the stereotype, the sooner people will see you as a unique individual. It is not fair that it takes extra work, but the investment is worth it.

Visit Vault at **www.vault.com** for insider company profiles, expert advice, career message boards, expert resume reviews, the Vault Job Board and more.

VAULT CAREER LIBRARY   39

Common Stereotypes: Women

Assumption	Situation	Solution
You are bad at math but good at writing.	Whenever project tasks are distributed amongst the team, you always get the qualitative, not quantitative, tasks. You don't become better at math. If you are put on a quantitative task and have trouble with it, you are removed from the task instead of trained to do it better.	Make it a priority to learn new things, especially when you first start your job. Do not let yourself be removed from quantitative projects.
You are suited to detailed administrative work.	You are assigned administrative duties no one else wants: taking notes at the meetings, booking travel for the team, making copies, ordering lunch, getting coffee for clients, setting up or cleaning up a meeting.	Volunteer someone else for the task and try to get your manager's backing.
You are eye candy and probably not that bright, because you're attractive.	You are excluded from important meetings, but trotted out on fun business development outings so older male clients can flirt with you. People gossip about you.	Make sure your work stands on its own. Do not dress in a revealing or sexy manner.
You are too sensitive and emotional.	You don't get direct feedback about your performance so you don't advance. People are afraid you will cry, so they treat you gently. When you do cry, people assume you cannot handle stressful work.	Seek out truthful feedback. Remove yourself from stressful situations and control your temper and emotions.
You are timid.	People forget to ask you for your opinion because they assume you won't have one. You stop forming opinions because you are never asked about them, stunting your critical thinking and communication skills.	Practice expressing yourself. Build alliances. Emulate strong speakers.
You are a pushover.	You are asked to do work that no one else wants to do, like staying late in the office for a last-minute assignment, cleaning up other's unfinished work and delivering bad news for other people.	Learn your boundaries. Embrace the word "No," especially if these requests do not come from a manager or senior executive.
You are a token hire.	Especially in a macho environment like investment banking or sales, your peers don't believe you made it here on merit, and do not give your work and opinions equal respect.	Work twice as hard to prove yourself. Try not to be too sensitive about routine male-bonding behaviors.
Work is not as important to you as it is to your male co-workers. Your family comes first.	Co-workers will not ask you for help on tough assignments. Your manager may be reluctant to invite you on business trips or to late-night client dinners.	Meet every deadline. Do not discuss family visits or shopping excursions, especially if you take time off for these activities. Clearly state you interest in attending a client event.

The de facto secretary

Women are often unconsciously slotted into an administrative role and given routine, detail-oriented work. While these projects may be important, and it's vital to be able to pitch in during a time crunch, it's difficult to shine by doing these routine tasks. The requests may seem benign at first. Can you take the notes during the meeting? Can you prepare FedEx packages? Can you coordinate the next meeting or the next business trip? If you are the most junior person on the team, assume that status is the reason for getting these chores. In the corporate world, the guy at the bottom of the food chain takes care of all the scrub work. The more machismo-laced an environment you work in, the more pronounced the hierarchy will probably be. Check with the second-most junior person to see if he had all the same "chores" before you arrived. Make sure you pass those duties on right away when a more junior person joins the team.

If you are not the most junior teammate, you may have been designated as a secretary for the team because of your gender. How should you handle the request? If the need is legitimate and you are the most appropriate person to perform the task (e.g., because you have the time or because your piece of the work is not as time-sensitive), go ahead and do it, and don't take it personally. If the need is not legitimate, or you are not the most appropriate person for the job, do not accept the role! Ask your manager to pass the chore to a secretary or another member of your department. Or tell your manager you would like to rotate the responsibility around the team because you took the duty last time. You could simply say, "I'm sorry. I don't have time to do that and meet my other deadlines. Can someone else pitch in?"

If a client asks you to do something administrative, go ahead and do it … once. Make sure you raise the issue with your manager and get his backing before you tell the client you cannot the second time. If you are asked to do something really demeaning, like making coffee, smile sweetly or make a little joke and say you don't know how to.

If you are the only woman on the team and you are constantly performing the admin duties, you will diminish your professional credibility and stunt your professional development compared to your male peers. Address the situation politely but directly with your manager and/or other perpetrators. Here are two common scenarios women in the corporate world face and how to address them.

The note-taker

You are always asked to take notes "because you have the best handwriting." This statement could be absolutely true—some guys really have atrocious handwriting!

But when you take notes, you are busy looking down at the paper and writing down what everyone else says. As a result, you don't get to participate in the discussion as much. At review time, your manager won't recall hearing you speak in meetings, forgetting that he asked you to take notes. He'll have the impression that you are timid (playing right into another common stereotype of women). Furthermore, if you are writing madly in a future meeting that includes a client or a senior executive, you lose the opportunity to interact with and impress an important person. You may even be mistaken for a secretary yourself.

If you are the most junior person on the team, you may have to take notes until someone new is hired. If you are not the most junior person, get a reality check from a trusted peer or manager in the office who is removed from the situation at hand. "I want to ask your opinion because I'm not sure if I am being too sensitive. Who takes notes in your meetings?"

The cyclical nature of stereotyping comes from the fact that the more you do something, the better you become at it than everyone else, so then everyone wants you to continue doing it. After several meetings of being the note-taker, you learn to outline exactly how your boss likes it, type everything up with graphs and charts inserted, and distribute to the group quickly. Of course everyone will want you to keep doing it because no one else does it as well. But continuing the role compromises your professional development, self-respect and the respect of your peers, even if it is gradual and unintentional.

Visit Vault at **www.vault.com** for insider company profiles, expert advice, career message boards, expert resume reviews, the Vault Job Board and more.

VAULT CAREER LIBRARY   41

Talk to your manager directly, but avoid any suggestion that the offense was intentional (even if you suspect it was). Address the professional rationale behind your request and your proposed solutions. "I don't want to always be the note taker because it prevents me from participating in the discussion in a meaningful way. The issues are so interesting I'd like to share my thoughts next time. Let's rotate the responsibility, or bring a secretary into the meeting to take the notes."

Be prepared to be brushed off as being hypersensitive. "Uh oh, you're not a militant feminist are you? You are way too sensitive!" Don't back down when faced with such resistance. Stand your ground, and calmly respond. "I know it's easy for you to jump to that conclusion, but humor me, and let's rotate the responsibility. I really would like to join in the conversation next time, and I think I have proposed fair solutions." Just make sure you don't clam up in the next meeting!

The teacher

Maybe you're repeatedly asked to train new hires. Why are you singled out every time? Is it because you are friendly, patient and verbal compared to your other colleagues? Is the responsibility of training only assigned to top performers who uphold the highest standards of work quality? Is training a total pain in the neck, and your boss knows you'll be a pushover? Ask your boss or the person who trained you how the responsibility is assigned. Then you can evaluate how you want to deal with the situation.

Perhaps you don't mind this assignment because you enjoy getting to know the new hires right away, you get a break from your normal workload and you get to expense more meals on the company. Or the training assignments reflect the fact that you're a star at the company. Maybe you actually hate sitting alone in your office all day crunching numbers and you really want to be a teacher at heart, so the opportunity to train new employees is a dream niche for you.

Now for the downsides. Because training is administrative, you may be expected to carry your full load of "real" work on top, meaning that you are working much later nights than everyone else to get everything done. Is training worth compromising your personal time? On the other hand, if your manager does reduce your workload to accommodate your training assignments, over time you might fall behind your colleagues in terms of advancement because you spend your days teaching and mentoring new hires instead of getting more challenging projects and interacting with senior colleagues and clients. Is training worth compromising your professional development?

Want to get out of doing training? Tell your boss you have already conducted the training twice as many times as the last person who did it. Or point out that you have missed client meetings because of training, which is detrimental to both your development and your relationship with your client. Suggest setting up a random system to rotate the responsibility amongst your peers by drawing numbers or assigning it alphabetically by last name. Or suggest that people pair up in teams to conduct training, so it's not as time-consuming for each person.

Address and Retrain Your Manager Immediately If You Feel Singled Out

Sonja Beals Iribarren, former director at Disney

As the most junior member of the team, I accepted the fact that I drew the duty of making copies during meetings, should the need arise. That I was often the only woman in the room seemed only a coincidence until a new, younger—and male—analyst joined the team. I think we were both shocked when my boss again asked me to step out and make a few copies at the next meeting. I did so without complaint, in the name of team spirit, but did speak to my boss privately immediately afterward and told him that I wanted that duty to fall to the new junior member of the team. I tried to keep the focus on the seniority issue and away from any discussion about gender, which I felt might be interpreted as militant feminism and would not ultimately serve my purpose. I was concerned that people's perception of me would be negatively affected if I continued to accept this duty without comment. It's not about making the copies—it's that people expect you to stand up for yourself. Honestly, I wouldn't be surprised if scenarios like these aren't a test to see how you handle yourself in these situations.

Common Stereotypes: Minorities

Assumption	Situation	Solution
You are good at math but bad at communicating.	You are always given back office analyses, but never put in front of senior executives or clients to present your findings.	Don't just hand over analyses to your manager with no explanation or interpretation. If you do a good job articulating your work to your boss, you can make the next step of presenting to others.
You have a chip on your shoulder.	People assume you are difficult to work with, keep their distance and minimize interaction. You leave the job without any significant relationships, mentors or networks to help you later on.	Be careful how you express your views. Show your casual, humorous side often.
You share the same traits as everyone else of your demographic.	You are compared to the other minority of the same race as you in the department. You are called the wrong name, as if people can't tell you apart. You compete with each other for the token slot.	Establish your identity and distinguish yourself.
You do not speak English well.	You are not given time to speak in meetings or written assignments.	Work to perfect your writing and speaking skills. Ask for and excel at, writing and speaking assignments.

People naturally categorize things into convenient buckets and make assumptions about those categories. Establish your own identity, and avoid "competing" with the one other person in the office of your race. For example, let's say that you are one of two Asian-American analysts in your starting class of twelve new hires. People you don't work closely with may mix you up and call you the wrong name. As a more serious pitfall, you may be compared to each other all the time, and there may also be an assumption that only one of you will be promoted.

Don't take it personally if the other person of your ethnicity is not quick to establish a close friendship with you. She may want to establish her own identity. It is an immature reaction on her part, but an explainable one. If a friendship is meant to be, over time it will develop as you both settle in to your new jobs.

Ways of establishing your personal identity include:

• Socialize with a variety of your peers.

• Befriend the perpetrators. People will not mistake you for someone else if they get to know you. Talk about things you have in common. Let them get to know you as a person with distinct interests, rather than a token minority.

• Correct people if they call you by another name. You can do this nicely, but don't let them persist in thinking you are someone else. Correct the person on the spot, introduce yourself and laugh it off to help the perpetrator save face. "It's a big office, so I often forget names of people I've only met once or twice, too."

• Establish natural friendships with peers of your ethnicity. There is no advantage to discriminating against people who look like you, and you come off like a jerk. And you might be sacrificing a friendship with someone with whom you would otherwise really connect because of shared experiences and insights.

Visit Vault at **www.vault.com** for insider company profiles, expert advice, career message boards, expert resume reviews, the Vault Job Board and more.

VAULT CAREER LIBRARY 43

Don't Assume You Will Bond Over Race

Former strategic planning analyst

During my interviews for a competitive position at a Fortune 100 company, I continually asked about the obvious lack of African-American employees in the department. To dispel my concerns, the recruiting manager arranged for me to meet a very senior African-American officer in the company, even though I would not actually be working with him in my prospective job.

Without thinking twice, I openly asked him about the dearth of African-Americans at the company. He replied, "If you are one of those black people who needs to be around other black people, you won't find them here!"

Shocked and disappointed, I quickly learned that not all people of color view themselves as leaders or mentors of junior employees of their same race. On the contrary, many prefer to ignore ethnicity and maintain distance from other colleagues of color in order to avoid labeling.

Geography Matters

Victor Hwang, former corporate lawyer, current COO LARTA (a nonprofit think tank)

If you're a minority, geography matters. I love Austin, Texas. I spent my formative years there. I love country music, barbecue, Longhorn football and big hair. I never encountered any overt prejudice in my professional life in Austin, but one does start to feel worn down after the third time someone has confused you with your minority co-worker, every lunch at a sushi restaurant starts a talk about "other Chinese food," and people think that your parents are Thai because they're from Taiwan. It may or may not be prejudice, really it's just ignorance, but it does take a toll on your self-esteem.

So I moved to Los Angeles and never looked back. There has been such a difference in my sense of professional opportunity since I've moved to Los Angeles. Climbing the professional ladder is hard enough already; one should eliminate as many controllable obstacles as possible.

College Career Bible • 2007 Edition
....

Workplace Diversity: Dealing with Stereotyping

Common Stereotypes: Gay Men

Assumption	Situation	Solution
You are creative.	People come to you with more questions and projects that involve visual aesthetic, creative design or marketing, whether or not that is part of your job function.	Make it a point to shine in other areas. Make sure those areas are visible to management.
You don't have traditional masculine interests.	You are not invited to sports or bar outings. You miss out on the opportunity to network and bond out of the office.	Bring up your participation in sports, your home teams or your favorite non-gay bars and clubs. Invite yourself along.
You are checking out all the straight men in the office at all times.	Guys keep their distance. You are made to feel self-conscious.	Don't make any sexual references or jokes. Never flirt with or date co-workers.
You are flamboyant.	You are not put in front of the most conservative, stodgiest clients or senior executives.	Be mindful of corporate culture, behave conservatively and give people time to get to know you.
You are the token gay friend everyone wants.	Female colleagues want to be your best friend, talk to you about boys and fashion. Colleagues don't respect the same professional vs. personal boundaries with you. You're called "Will" from the popular show *Wiill and Grace*.	Be mindful of your interactions with others. Act professionally and conservatively, focus on work. Give people time to get to know the real you.

Visit Vault at **www.vault.com** for insider company profiles, expert advice, career message boards, expert resume reviews, the Vault Job Board and more.

V\ULT CAREER LIBRARY   **45**

VAULT'S
DIVERSITY CENTRAL

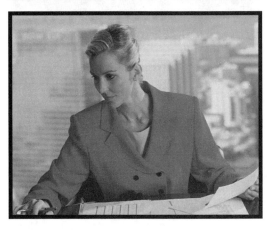

Diversity Employer Directory

Baker Hughes Incorporated

2929 Allen Parkway, Suite 2100
Houston, TX 77019-2118
Diversity Contact Phone: 713-439-8600
www.bakerhughes.com

To be a global company, Baker Hughes is building a diverse workforce that includes men and women from more than 90 countries where we operate. Such diversity will enable us to understand local cultures and provide service that creates value for customers around the world. Baker Hughes recruiting programs reach students from universities on five continents and our development programs provide opportunities for them to advance their careers. Our ongoing effort to develop and maintain a high performance culture starts with our Core Values of Integrity, Teamwork, Performance and Learning and with our Keys to Success. We employ succession planning efforts to develop leaders across all our businesses that embody these Core Values and represent the diversity of our customer base. We constantly hire and train employees from around the world to ensure that we have a well-trained workforce in place to support our business plans.

Below are some of the schools Baker Hughes Incorporated is currently recruiting from:

Colorado School of Mines; Florida Institute of Technology; Louisiana State University; McNeese University; Michigan Tech University; Mississippi State University;MIT; Montana Tech University; New Mexico Tech University; Oklahoma State University; Southern University; Stanford University; Texas A&M University; Texas A&M Kingsville; Texas Tech University; University of Houston; University of Louisiana - Lafayette; University of Maryland; University of Oklahoma; University of Texas-Austin; University of Texas - San Antonio; University of Tulsa; University of Wyoming;

Bristol-Myers Squibb

345 Park Avenue
New York, NY 10154-0037
Diversity Contact Phone: 212-546-4000
www.bms.com/career/data/workdive.html

Different perspectives make it possible.

At Bristol-Myers Squibb, we're a diverse team of talented and creative people -- each with a different perspective. We value each person's unique contributions and inspire each other to develop the innovative solutions that extend and enhance the lives of our patients around the world.

Flexibility makes it possible.

At Bristol-Myers Squibb, our people find fulfillment in their work, extending and enhancing the lives of patients around the world. And they have fulfilling lives at home too. Bristol-Myers Squibb offers a flexible range of work/life programs that help our employees at each stage of their lives. We're proud to be ranked in the top 100 of Working Mother Magazine's "Best Companies for Working Mothers.

Opportunities make your growth possible.

Ask yourself - how far do you want to go? At Bristol-Myers Squibb, we're determined to be the company where our employees can achieve their career goals. We offer a range of opportunities to help you get there. It's simple. Your growth helps us to better extend and enhance the lives of patients around the world.

Schools Bristol-Myers Squibb Recruits from

Undergraduate-level students may pursue internship, co-op and permanent job opportunities in many business divisions and functions across BMS and its family of health care companies.

Visit Vault at **www.vault.com** for insider company profiles, expert advice, career message boards, expert resume reviews, the Vault Job Board and more.

VAULT CAREER LIBRARY 47

Credit Suisse

11 Madison Avenue
10th Floor
New York, New York 10010

Diversity Contact:
Erica McMahon
Undergraduate Diversity Recruiting
Phone: 212-538-3785
E-mail: Diversity.recruiting@credit-suisse.com
www.credit-suisse.com/standout

CREDIT SUISSE

CREDIT SUISSE BA EXPLORER PROGRAM - COLLEGE FRESHMEN AND SOPHOMORES

The BA Explorer program is a pioneering three-day educational outreach program that encourages undergraduate students of African, Latino, and Native American descent and all majors to learn more about the world of business. Students learn about Wall Street and Credit Suisse. This unique program offers students the opportunity to learn first-hand about the exciting world of financial services and expose them to the many professional opportunities within the industry.

DOUGLAS L. PAUL SCHOLARSHIP FOR ACHIEVEMENT - COLLEGE SOPHOMORES

Credit Suisse will offer $5,000 scholarships to a number of college sophomores of African, Latino, and Native American descent. Recipients of the scholarships will be selected based on their academic excellence, leadership abilities, and interest in the financial services industry. In addition to monetary resources, Doug Paul Scholars will have the chance to participate in our 10-week rotational program in New York. This program provides students with an educational opportunity to learn about the various areas of an investment bank, with rotations in Equities, Fixed Income, and Investment Banking. Scholars will receive a stipend for the duration of the 10-week program. During the program, students are given mentors to provide valuable insight into Credit Suisse, Wall Street, and financial services.

Undergraduate Schools Credit Suisse Recruits from:

We recruit from top undergraduate programs. For more information, please visit our website: www.credit-suisse.com/standout

Fitch Ratings

One State St. Plaza, 33rd Floor
New York, NY 10004
www.fitchratings.com

FitchRatings

Genentech

1 DNA Way
South San Francisco, CA 94080-4990
www.gene.com/gene/about/diversity/index.jsp

Genentech

IN BUSINESS FOR LIFE

Diversity is core to Genentech's values and culture. We are committed to developing an inclusive work environment where diversity of thought, style, culture, skill sets and perspective is valued and celebrated in support of individual performance and potential, as well as our business goals and mission.

Diversity is integral to our culture and how we conduct our business. It is evident in who we are, the patients we serve, the physicians with whom we partner, the vendors we rely upon, and the communities in which we work. It strengthens our organization and contributes to our competitiveness. We are inclusive; we demonstrate respect and appreciation for diversity and encourage the richness of ideas, approaches and points of view that it enables.

Financial Management Professional Training Program (NAVY)

153 Ellyson Avenue, Suite A
Pensacola, FL 32508-5245
Phone: 850-452-3783
www.navyfmtp.com

The Financial Management Trainee Program (FMTP) recruits high quality, prospective civilian financial managers for Department of the Navy Activities. The FMIP is a 28-month program of professional development through academic and on-the-job training. Entry level positions as Analysts, Accountants, and Auditors are available. Applicants may have any academic major; but those applying for Accounting and Auditor positions require 24 semester hours of accounting (6 hours may be in business law). A minimum cumulative GPA of 2.95 in an undergraduate degree from a nationally accredited university/college is required.

Undergraduate Schools NAVY Recruits from

Nationally accredited colleges and universities

JC Penney

PO Box 10001
Dallas, TX 75301-8115
Phone: (972) 431-1000
www.JCPenney.com

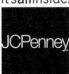

Communication Subcommittee Mission Statement

Improve communications by enhancing the sensitivity level surrounding diversity & work-life impacting customer service and associate satisfaction/productivity.

Personnel Relations Subcommittee Mission Statement

To foster the upward mobility of women and minorities into all levels of management, including senior management positions, by enhancing our current recruitment programs and implementing career development plans that allow the Company to retain, train and promote qualified women and minority associates.

Work-Life Issues Subcommittee Mission Statement

Identify Work-Life Issues that affect each associate's ability to perform to full potential. Encourage a supportive work environment that allows associates to maximize their contributions towards company objectives.

Schools JCPenney recruits from

Open to all accredited colleges and universities

Visit Vault at **www.vault.com** for insider company profiles, expert advice, career message boards, expert resume reviews, the Vault Job Board and more.

VAULT CAREER LIBRARY

49

Johnson & Johnson

501 George Street
New Brunswick, NJ 08901
www.jnj.com/careers

Johnson&Johnson
Family of Companies

Today's customer and employees come from all over the world and represent different ages, cultures, genders, races, sexual orientation, and physical capabilities. Through their life experiences, they provide a diversity of thought and perspective that must be reflected in our corporate culture. To ensure we continue to build a diverse workforce, we partner with the following organizations from a college recruiting perspective: National Society of Black Engineers, Society of Hispanic Professional Engineers, SWE, CGSM, GEM, National Society of Hispanic MBA, NBMBAA, Reaching Out, Disco, MBA Diversity Forum, and INROADS. We're part of the NSBE, SHPE, NBMBAA, and NSHMBA Board of Affiliates.

Undergraduate Schools Johnson & Johnson Recruits From:

Howard; FAMU; Morehouse; Hampton; U Puerto Rico, Mayaguez

M & T Bank Corporation

One M&T Plaza, 11th Floor
Buffalo, N.Y. 14203
Phone: (716) 842-5445
www.mandtbank.com/campus

At M&T, employees are our most important asset. In fact, our success is attributable to the talent and dedication of our employees. Therefore, M&T demonstrates its return commitment by supporting both diversity and the unique talents of our employees throughout the organization.

To foster an inclusive environment, M&T continually drives initiatives such as diversity awareness training, diversity recruitment, supplier diversity and community involvement. In addition the bank has a dedicated diversity council focused on important employee issues.

Through these efforts, M&T strives to deliver on our commitment to become one of the best companies to work for in the nation.

Undergraduate schools M&T Bank recruits from

Amherst; Bowdoin; Brown; Carnegie Mellon; Canisius; Colgate; Columbia; Cornell; Dartmouth; George Washington; Georgetown; Hampton; Harvard; Howard; Ithaca; Johns Hopkins; Lafayette; Morehouse; Mt. Holyoke; Niagara; Penn State; Princeton; RIT; Smith; Spelman; Swarthmore; SUNY Binghamton; SUNY Geneseo; Syracuse; University at Buffalo; University at Maryland; University of Notre Dame; University of Pennsylvania; University of Rochester; University of Virginia; Vassar; Wellesley; Williams; Yale

Osram Sylvania

100 Endicott St.
Danvers, MA 01923
www.sylvania.com/AboutUs/Careers/

Diversity Contact:

Leah Weinberg, Manager, Diversity Inclusion
Phone: (978) 750-2761
Recruiting Email: Diversity.recruiter@sylvania.com

OSRAM SYLVANIA is committed to developing an increasingly diverse workforce with fair and open access to career opportunities. We cultivate an inclusive, supportive climate, thereby enabling us to better meet the needs of our employees and customers. We believe that variety of opinion, approach, perspective, and talent are the cornerstones of a strong, flexible, and competitive company. Affinity groups, a mentoring program, and strategic relationships with professional organizations and colleges all support OSRAM SYLVANIA's commitment to an inclusive environment where every talented individual can be proud to work.

Undergraduate Schools Osram Sylvania Recruits from

Bucknell; WPI; Bentley; GA Tech; Notre Dame; Ohio; Alfred; RPI; Bryant; UWisc; Penn State; UKY; Olin

Pulte Homes, Inc.

100 Bloomfield Hills Parkway, Suite 300
Bloomfield Hills, Michigan 48304
Diversity Contact Phon: 248-647-2750
www.pulte.com

The way it should be®

At Pulte, we view diversity as a business priority, it is critical to our success. Innovation is one of our core business strategies, so leveraging diversity just makes sense! We believe in the value of each other's differences and in treating one another fairly and with respect and dignity. We are working hard to ensure that our future workforce reflects the diversity of our customers, partners, trade contractors, stockholders and the communities around the nation that have embraced our beautiful homes and neighborhoods. We need the insight, creativity and perspectives that a range of diverse employees can bring to the table in order tobecome a stronger, smarter and more innovative company.

As our workforce continues to evolve to reflect the growing diversity of our communities, our ability to understand, value and incorporate differences becomes increasingly important. Diversity, like any other part of our long-term business plan, requires focus and resolve. Our commitment starts at the top and filters through every geographic area. A few of the things that we're doing to maintain diversity in our culture: diversity training, outreach and scholarship programs and web-based communications.

Pulte is proud to sponsor our employee-run Diversity Council and Women's Leadership Council to ensure that everyone in our organization visibly encourages and values the contributions and differences of employees from various backgrounds. Key objectives of both councils include:
- Creating a more inclusive environment for all employees
- Heightening and increasing employee and management awareness
- Increasing representation of women and diverse employees at all levels of the organization through focused training, development, mentoring and retention plans
- Increasing our capabilities and results in recruiting diverse employees into our workforce

At Pulte, our employees may all look different, but they share one thing in common: an unbridled passion for what we do...we deliver the homes that people dream of!
If you are excited about opportunities at Pulte Homes, we want to talk to you! Please visit us at www.pulte.com.

Visit Vault at **www.vault.com** for insider company profiles, expert advice, career message boards, expert resume reviews, the Vault Job Board and more.

VAULT CAREER LIBRARY

51

Sodexho

200 Continental Drive, Suite 400
Newark, DE 19713
www.sodexhousa.com

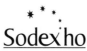

Our Committment

Diversity and inclusion is a strategic imperative at Sodexho. We measure our progress and report out our results on a quarterly basis along with our financial performance. Managers are held accountable for diversity results with a direct link to their incentive compensation. The use of an innovative scorecard provides managers with their progress.

Sodexho believes that workforce diversity is essential to the Company's growth and long-term success. By valuing and managing diversity at work, Sodexho can leverage the skills, knowledge, and abilities of all employees to increase employee, client, and customer satisfaction.

Managing diversity at work is a process of inclusion; it is a means of achieving superior individual and group performance by recognizing and celebrating each employee's unique contribution toward meeting the Company's business objectives.

Sodexho believes that management's ability to respect and manage employee differences is essential to attracting diverse employees, and building diverse, high-performing work teams, which will allow us to more effectively serve our clients and enhance the Company's competitive advantage in the marketplace.

Sodexho's commitment to workforce diversity is part of a dynamic, inclusive process for building organizational excellence, by ensuring that all employees are full partners in the Company's growth and financial success

Our Diversity Vision

Diversity and inclusion is an inherent part of our culture and business growth. The energy and talent at all levels of the organization is unleashed, resulting in innovative solutions that contribute to a spirit of team, service and progress. With diversity and inclusion as a competitive advantage, Sodexho is an employer of choice and the benchmark for customers, clients and communities domestically and globally.

Undergraduate Schools Sodexho Recruits From:

Brigham Young University, California State Polytechnic University; Culinary Institute of America; Howard University; Indiana University of Pennsylvania; Johnson & Wales - Charlotte; Johnson & Wales-Providence; Kansas State University; Kendall College; Lexington College; Massachusetts Maritime; Mercyhurst College; Michigan State University; Morgan State University; New Mexico State University; North Carolina Central University; Penn State University; Purdue University; San Diego State University - Imperial Valley Campus; San Francisco State University (Assc Member); Trident Technical College; Tuskegee University; University of Central Florida; University of Houston; University of Maryland - Eastern Shore; University of Massachusetts; University of Memphis; University of Wisconsin - Stout; Widener University

LEADERSHIP
DEVELOPMENT
PROGRAMS

The Scoop on Leadership Development Programs

If you're looking to get an early boost for your career after graduation, consider applying to a rotational training program.

These programs, which can be found in literally every industry and type of employer, are typically offered by large employers who aim to hire recent graduates and groom them as future company leaders.

Because the programs can be found at many different types of employers, they vary widely. For starters, they can go by any number of names and labels, though they usually have the words "management," "leadership," "training," or "development" in their titles. They also vary with respect to duration, number of rotations, number of employees hired into the program each year and other details.

There are common threads that tie these programs together, however. After joining them, trainees generally rotate through many different departments/areas in order to get an overview of the different parts of an organization. Employees are also offered formal training courses and mentorship relationships as part of the program. But most importantly, these programs are all designed to train the future leaders of an organization. Because of this, employees who go through these programs not only receive the best training their organizations have to offer, but are also "tagged" as potential leaders whose progress in the organization is followed even after they graduate from the training program.

Why rotate?

The central goal of a rotational training program is to provide trainees with an overview of an organization's operations.

"The more well-rounded employees are in understanding all of the operations in a hotel, the better they'll be as a general manager," explains Nancy Vu, Manager of Field Employment and Recruiting at Hilton Hotels Corporation. Hilton hires recent graduates into what it calls its Leader-in-Training (LIT) program. In Hilton's program, a trainee rotates through about a dozen different hotel departments in a six- to eight-month period.

"We want them to understand how each department links to one another," says Vu. "We want our trainees to get their feet wet in all these areas. Then they have a better understanding of what goes on in the rest of the hotel."

Michael Danubio, Manager of College Relations for Staples agrees that the breadth of experience is the key to the retailer's Merchandise Training Program, which rotates trainees through both store and headquarters rotations over an 18-month period.

"The most valuable thing they get out of this is seeing the full cycle of the business," says Danubio. "Once they're done, they've seen a big chunk of our merchandising operation."

Formal training and mentoring

Most rotational training programs incorporate formal training and mentorship that go above and beyond what most recent graduates encounter when they join their first employers. For example, for Staples' Merchandise Training Program, trainees take seminar-type courses on everything from "pricing to negotiation skills to supply chain logistics," says Erin Egnatchik, a recent graduate of the program. "That training has been opened up to other associates [in Staples' Framingham, Mass., headquarters], but it's required for Merchandise Training Associates," says Egnatchik.

Debbie Bertan, Director of College Relations for Citigroup says that the training and mentoring offered through the company's rotational programs (called the Management Associate Programs) is one of the program's main advantages. Citigroup hires recent graduates into a two-year rotation program in its Retail Distribution Group, and Citibanking Technology Solutions group (internal information technology positions) units.

Visit Vault at **www.vault.com** for insider company profiles, expert advice, career message boards, expert resume reviews, the Vault Job Board and more.

V∧ULT CAREER LIBRARY   55

"It's much more structured when you join a [Management Associate] program," says Bertan. "There's training at various intervals. Most of the associates start with some specific training that the whole group goes through, and then there's training specific to the Management Associate's specific needs. There's also softer skills training—for example, training in leadership and communication skills."

But it's not just seminar-type training that new employees receive. In many cases, trainees are matched up with managers who serve as formal mentors during their time in the program. And because of an employee's status as a "future leader," he or she is also likely to pick up more informal mentors, too.

"When you enter through one of these training programs, there's more emphasis on mentorship," explains Citigroup's Bertan. "There's also greater exposure to senior leaders—partially through events and/or through networking."

Starting on the ground floor

Just because rotational management training programs are intended to groom and train recent graduates as future leaders doesn't mean that new employees have it easy. In many programs, trainees are required to pay their dues as entry-level employees.

For example, in the retail industry, trainees often start with a store-level rotation. This is the case at both Staples and TJX. In Citigroup's Retail Distribution Group Management Associate Program, trainees may start behind the teller window.

"They probably think 'What am I doing here? I just paid 100 grand for my education and I'm wearing a red shirt in a store,'" says Staples' Michael Danubio. "But the reality is once they come into the home office, they realize how invaluable that experience is."

Danubio says that a recent hire into Staples' Merchandise Training Program made a point of telling him how valuable his in-store experience turned out to be. "[Once he got to Staples' headquarters office] he was working for a senior inventory analyst that handled the furniture," recounts Danubio. "He said that from Day 1, he knew what people were talking about. They were talking about specific SKUs that he learned about when he was in the store. It would have been a much longer ramp-up time if he hadn't had that experience."

At Hilton Hotels Corporation, trainees start with the unglamorous tasks related to normal hotel operations. "When they go through the housekeeping rotation," says Hilton's Vu, "They're required to make a certain number of beds, clean a certain number of rooms."

Because trainees in Hilton's program often go on to become managers at the hotel at which they train, the dues-paying is more than just a matter of learning the operations, says Vu.

Grooming leaders

From those humble entry-level rotations, however, future company leaders are created. Says Vu of Hilton's rotational program (which was established originally in 1988 as the Hilton Professional Development Program. "We have directors and VPs who came through that program and are still with us."

Because companies treat trainees as future leaders, a lot of attention is typically paid to their development. For this reason, some rotational training programs are small in size. Staples, for example, only currently hires two people a year into its Merchandise Training Program. "The organization internally can only sustain so many people at one time," says Danubio, "Because it takes a lot of internal coordination and training, and we want to make sure that we're giving them the resources they need here."

Once trainees "graduate" from rotational programs, companies usually track them through their career. Part of the reason for this is to make sure that the programs are working.

"We want to make sure that there's a reason to be supporting a program, so we track the career progression of the Management Associates we hire," says Citigroup's Bertan.

A consequence of tracking trainees this way, of course, is that graduates of training programs are always identified as such in the companies' human resource records, which is no small thing. "The real advantage is they are accelerated leadership programs," says Bertan. "This is our pipeline to train our future leaders."

Vault Q&A: Suzanne Rickard, Citigroup Management Associate Program

Suzanne Rickard is a 2003 graduate of New York University (the Stern school of business undergraduate program). After graduation she joined Citigroup's Management Associate Program in the company's retail banking division. She took time out to talk with Vault about her experience with Citi's rotational program.

Vault: Tell me a little bit about Citigroup's Management Associate Program

Rickard: The program is a two-year rotational program. The way it's set up is that you have the opportunity to rotate and train as well as perform in different functions within the retail bank. You start out with a financial associate rotation, being the person who takes deposits for clients at the teller window—handling money, etc. Then you have training as a customer service officer where you answer clients' questions and assist them with any banking related issue.

The next rotation was as an account representative, which they call Client Financial Analyst (CFA). During that rotation, I was able to open accounts for clients and also received my Series 6 and Series 63 licenses as well as my Life and Health License, so I was able to sell investment and insurance products. There's also an operations rotation, a corporate headquarters rotation, as well as a commercial, small business banking part.

Vault: How big is the program?

Rickard: In my class in the retail bank area there are 11 associates. In total [at Citigroup], I believe it's maybe 200 or 300. I think it's been in existence for many years but has taken on a variety of structures. For the retail bank section, it could range from as small as five or so people to as large as our class, which is 11 people. They do a hiring process three times a year, in the spring, summer and fall.

There's a program for each different section of the company. For the credit card department there's a different program, for human resources there's a different program, and so on.

Vault: Where are you now in the program?

Rickard: I've already done the consumer rotation. I've also dealt with operations—that's the back office, making sure that everything balances in terms of money at the end of the day and also dealing with audits. The rotation I'm in right now is the commercial, small business banking position.

Vault: So how long is each rotation?

Rickard: The financial associate rotation was about three months, the service officer rotation was two or three months, the CFA portion is about five or six months, the operations one where you deal with audits is about three or four months. The corporate project rotation, it's supposed to be a short one, but I stayed about five months.

Visit Vault at **www.vault.com** for insider company profiles, expert advice, career message boards, expert resume reviews, the Vault Job Board and more.

VAULT CAREER LIBRARY   **57**

Vault: What sort of corporate project did you work on?

Rickard: I did a rotation in [Citigroup's headquarters in] Long Island City with one of the main directors of a new product. So I dealt with the marketing of the product. I dealt with the legal group. I dealt with the finance group. I dealt with other cross-functional issues. Having a product with Citibank, you have to make sure it works with everyone else and that they can sell it too.

Vault: What kind of product was it?

Rickard: It's called CitiGold. It's a premier bank product for high net worth clients. It's a type of checking account that looks to consolidate the clients' account relationships. So for example, you can open a brokerage account with that product or handle your credit card accounts through that account. We want clients to feel like they can consolidate all their finances with us, where you can have banking, borrowing, brokerage and insurance, which are all interrelated.

Vault: You mentioned other cross-functional issues in working on this project? What types of other departments did you deal with?

Rickard: I worked with our customer service group, our online system group and others. Basically everything that goes into producing and processing a financial product. It was interesting— a lot of work starting from scratch, but it's been going well.

Vault: And where were your other rotations?

Rickard: For the operations rotation, I was at a very busy branch at 34th Street that was across from Macy's. The day-to-day traffic at that branch was nonstop. They had three floors in the bank at that branch, and we dealt in the millions [of dollars]. I was there around the holidays, dealing with hundreds of people coming in and out constantly.

Vault: So what do you do in an operations role?

Rickard: I'm basically making sure transactions are being done properly, approving transactions if they're large amounts, making sure all the cash "proves" [checks out against transactions].

Vault: So with that much cash moving in and out I'm curious as to how much slips through the cracks on a daily basis?

Rickard: That branch was really good. Everyone was pretty accurate, consistently. The operations manager had been with the bank for I think 20 or 30 years, and had done operations at the bank at a lot of different branches. He had a lot of experience and knew the type of people to hire and what systems to have.

So training with him, I knew what things to recognize what to look for, it ran like a well-oiled machine. But sometimes it would get a little hectic because there were maybe 15 people or so taking clients, asking you to help them. You're constantly being asked questions, and there's not a whole lot of time to have lunch, or do other things. You're there for a couple hours after the bank closes, making sure that everything "proves out." At the end of the day you may feel like you've just gone through a frenzy but you're also happy that everything worked out for the clients as well as the staff.

Vault Q&A: Lena Davie, Staples Merchandise Training Program

After graduating from Xavier University in Cincinnati with a degree in marketing, Lena Davie was recruited into Staples' customer service rotational program. The retailer's customer service program is one of a few rotational programs Staples offers; others include a merchandise training program and a logistics training program.

Davie, who is the first Staples employee to be recruited into the rotational program, took some time out from her schedule to discus her experience at Staples—and why she finds customer service such a good fit for her.

Vault: Tell me a little bit about the program and the different positions you've rotated through.

Davie: Customer service is divided into Staples Business Delivery, which is for businesses with fewer than 20 employees, and Contracts, which is for companies with more than 20 employees. Typically our call centers service one business unit. We have two facilities for each business unit in the U.S.—in Englewood, NJ and Rochester, NY for Contracts, and Framingham, MA and Florence, KY for SBD. We also have two locations in Canada, in Halifax and Saskatchewan.

Employees in the centers are divided between order resolution, handling inquiries, and then we have our frontline sales and customer service teams, that handle orders.

The program I joined is two years. I spent a year in Kentucky, where I worked in various business units in the Business Delivery organization, did QA and monitored calls. After that year, I moved to Rochester NY, with our Contracts division for six months. Now I'm in Framingham, MA at our headquarters, working on a specific organization-wide project—it's a process improvement rotation for the Business Delivery Unit.

So I got the field aspect being in Kentucky and Rochester, and since coming into Framingham, I've had the corporate experience.

Vault: And where will you be going after your current rotation?

Davie: I've actually been hired by the company, and I'll be transitioning to the Rochester Call Center where I'll be a team manager. I'll be managing front-line associates who are working with customers.

Vault: How do customers place their orders?

Davie: We have orders that come in a variety of ways. Some come in via Staples.com, some cover in over the phone. We do orders by chat, we can also do orders by e-mail, and that's just for Staples Business Delivery. In the Contracts division, 90 percent of orders come through the Internet, though we also take them over the phone and then by fax.

My first rotation in the program was learning how to take calls. It helped me understand what my team was doing on the front line. I actually did three rotations in the Kentucky center—the first team was a frontline customer service sales team, the second team was the order resolution team, the third team was the quality assurance team.

I was taught the basics, starting with how to take a call. I've had that fundamental training in every location I've gone to, and it helps you build your foundation. I had one-on-one training with the trainer in the specific location. They give you that individual attention, because you are going to be a future manager.

I also had management training in Kentucky. That really helped me understand what the core values are at Staples. For management training, the HR manager with the center would conduct it once a month, and every new supervisor would have to go through the course.

Vault: What sort of courses were they?

Visit Vault at **www.vault.com** for insider company profiles, expert advice, career message boards, expert resume reviews, the Vault Job Board and more.

V∧ULT CAREER LIBRARY   **59**

Davie: How to give poor performance feedback, how to get along with your peers, how to make sure you're easily approachable, those sorts of things. They're topics that are important to make sure that you're a good manager. It was very helpful. I did the management training the whole time I was there.

Vault: How did you end up with Kentucky as your first rotation?

Davie: The location was decided by the business, and it was additionally decided because I was coming from Cincinnati it would make most sense to start in Kentucky.

The second location I was able to choose—I was able to choose between Englewood and Rochester. I'm from Northeast Ohio, so Rochester wasn't that far from there, and also our director of the Contracts division was located in that center, so it was opportunity for me to have that one-on-one relationship with her.

Vault: Were you set up with a formal mentor for the program?

Davie: Definitely. I have a wonderful mentor; I was assigned a mentor from our service improvement team. She's located here in Framingham, and she's been my mentor the whole program. The customer service organization is a very small, close organization. Really all of the directors have put effort and time to help my development. I can go to any of the four directors and they can help lead me where I need to go.

With my mentor, we had one-on-one sessions every two weeks, as if I was actually on her team. And then I could talk to her if I ever needed to talk to her. Once she was on pregnancy leave and wasn't in the office. I sent her an e-mail and sure enough, she responded.

Vault: How did you decide to go into customer service? Was this something you thought about when you were in school?

Davie: Coming out of school, I was thinking about going into nonprofit, so this was the other end of things.

But it has definitely been a great fit. Because I wanted to help people succeed, a customer service organization fits me. I'm really a coach. I want to help people continue to provide excellent service. I need to be one-on-one with my people. I need to talk to them. I need to be real and not always numbers-driven for them. It was a great fit for me, and it still is.

I'm expecting to stay in customer service, I think there are a lot of opportunities at Staples as we continue to grow. Because I'm very people-driven, the operations part is very close to my heart.

The people at Staples are really unique, you find people who care about the business, and focus on quality. You don't think you're in a corporate environment. I don't know how many people can say that every time you go to a new building you have a new family, I have a family Rochester, in Kentucky and in Framingham.

Vault: Have you had any issues with coming in as a recent college graduate on a "fast track" managing employees with more tenure at the company?

Davie: One thing I was always told is "You should be known for your work ethic and your quality." Most people do not know how old I am. I can be out of college and be 26 or I can come out of college and be 21. If you do great work, it doesn't matter. Not only do you have to work hard, but you do have to show an interest in people. You have to make sure that people know you want to work with them, not over them.

Vault Q&A: Young Yuk, Intuit's Rotational Development Program

As he was graduating from the University of California at Berkeley in 2004 with a degree in electrical engineering and computer science, Young Yuk knew for sure he didn't want to be an engineer or programmer. Beyond that, though, he wasn't too sure. He found a good chance to explore possible career paths as part of the first class of Intuit's Rotational Development Program.

Vault: How did you find out about Intuit's rotational program and why did it appeal to you?

Yuk: Coming out of college, I knew I didn't want to do engineering and programming anymore, so I wanted a transition job. The Rotational Development Program, even the phrase, got me excited. I randomly learned about it just through the career center e-mail list, luckily. .

I didn't know such programs existed until senior year of college, but now I think there's more buzz around these types of programs. I'm heavily involved in college recruiting, so I go to most events and share my perspective on the program. People are very interested. I think people think of the program as a means to rise up the corporate ladder faster. I don't necessarily like that correlation, but it's there.

When you get out of college, most people still don't know what they want to do. This is a good way to accelerate your career development. You get hands-on experience rather than just hearing about it or doing informational interviews. You also learn to think like a person in that job and can ask the right questions.

And with the people I work with who are in their 30s and 40s, when I talk to them, they always say they wish they had done something like this.

Vault: So you explored other similar programs?

Yuk: Yes. I think the difference between our program and others is that other companies are focused on one function like marketing and you get to rotate within that function. With our program, you rotate across multiple functions that are core to the business and mostly focused on delivering for customers.

Vault: How is the program structured?

Yuk: It's a 27-month program, so two years and three months. Every six months, we rotate into a different core business function: marketing, product management, product development—which is optional, if you're qualified, process excellence—which is like operations, and strategy.

Everyone starts off in Tucson, AZ for three months at our call center. This is not necessarily one of our rotations, but we go there to learn about our products and learn about our customers by providing technical phone support. That period in Tucson serves as a springboard for our first rotation. Intuit has a very high attention to customer-driven innovation, it's one of our buzzwords, having that perspective is very important

Vault: So everyone does that rotation together?

Yuk: Yeah, it's almost like The Real World, everyone gets an apartment that they share with a person in the program, and you get a car. The apartment and car are provided by Intuit. You get to know each other for three months. That's one of the things I'll look back on most fondly, that I made 11 good friends in the Boot Camp, which is what we call it.

Vault: So then where do you rotate to?

Yuk: The rest of the rotations are primarily in Mountain View, our headquarters. There are occasional rotations elsewhere.

Generally there's a big list of opportunities available, and we get to talk to leaders and managers on what our top three or five rotations would be. Then the leaders and all of our advisors get into a room and make decisions, combining business need and personal desires. There's no interviewing or anything like that.

Everyone hits marketing and product management. If you have a background in it, you can do programming. There's a process excellence rotation, which is Six Sigma related, improving internal business processes. There's also a strategy rotation, but only a few of us have done that so far.

Vault: What rotations did you do?

Visit Vault at **www.vault.com** for insider company profiles, expert advice, career message boards, expert resume reviews, the Vault Job Board and more.

VAULT CAREER LIBRARY

61

Yuk: Product development, marketing, product management, and strategy.

I did programming, because I wanted to prove to myself that I can do that at Intuit, and learn how it's done at our company, even though I knew coming in that I didn't want to do that long term. Marketing, that was a stretch of my brain, because it's thinking in a totally different way than engineers do. At the highest level, marketers are selling the product, you can't just blast them with all the details up front. Engineers like to be specific with how things work. While I enjoyed my marketing rotation, I don't think I could be as successful at it.

Product management was an easier transition given my technical background.

I enjoy strategy because it's very being in the front end of things, looking for new businesses, and also I like the fact that we Intuit has a focus on not just the market but looking at the customer problems, which I enjoy.

All the rotations have given me a tremendous amount of self-awareness, we explicitly have discussions with managers and advisors and among each other about what we like to do, what we don't like to do, all the time.

Vault: What happens after you finish your last rotation?

Yuk: I'll be done in December. It's a new process, so what they're going to do is have us talk to hiring managers for about three weeks. Shouldn't be much a surprise as to what the offer should be. Some of us know they want to go into product management, some know they want to go into marketing. I would be content with a full-time strategy job.

I think there might be a job outside for me that might be better. One thing that's great is I can have honest discussions with our managers and leaders about what I want to be doing 5 to 10 years out. We think it's important that people are happy and doing work that they are passionate about. One of our leaders thinks that if Intuit helps someone recognize their passion and supports them in finding that dream job, he/she would leave as a promoter of the company as a great place to work, with a focus on individuals' goals.

Vault: Do you have events with the others in the program regularly?

Yuk: We meet up all the time. After every six months, we have two to three days for development and fun. We have a full day on something around leadership, or maybe something around effective written communication, and then we'll have a whole day of group bonding activities. During the rotation we have monthly meetings, and also there are a slew of courses that they offer to all employees that we tap into.

Vault: Anything else you'd like to talk about?

Yuk: There's one aspect of my job that I would like to mention. We get the opportunity to do white space projects where you get to drive a project with 10 percent of your time and run with it. The project that I've been driving, with a team of eight to 10 people, has as its goal trying to accelerate people's development.

So far, what we've done is interview leaders across the company for an hour—we go to all levels of the organization from managers to executives—we ask them questions about leadership, career and personal development. Then we document this all and share it across the company through a wiki. Each person has a profile and there's a diagram of their journey of their career inside and outside Intuit. So employees in the company are getting to know their leaders and where they're coming from, and are getting exposed to different career paths. It helps us understand what paths might be available for us looking forward.

At first we thought, we were going to learn tips on how to rise up the corporate ladder faster, but instead, our team has walked about with great life lessons that we're trying to apply today.

Intuit leaders invest heavily on teaching. I don't know that at other companies leaders would be willing to share their personal stories and be honest about mistakes they've made. It's our company culture that helps foster this.

Osram Sylvania

100 Endicott St.
Danvers, MA 01923

Diversity Recruitiment Contact:
Leah Weinberg
Manager, Diversity Inclusion
Phone: (978) 750-2761
E-mail: Diversity.recruiter@sylvania.com
www.sylvania.com/AboutUs/Careers/

OSRAM SYLVANIA is committed to developing an increasingly diverse workforce with fair and open access to career opportunities. We cultivate an inclusive, supportive climate, thereby enabling us to better meet the needs of our employees and customers. We believe that variety of opinion, approach, perspective, and talent are the cornerstones of a strong, flexible, and competitive company. Affinity groups, a mentoring program, and strategic relationships with professional organizations and colleges all support OSRAM SYLVANIA's commitment to an inclusive environment where every talented individual can be proud to work.

Schools Osram Sylvania Recruits from

Bucknell; WPI; Bentley; GA Tech; Notre Dame; Ohio; Alfred; RPI; Bryant; UWisc; Penn State; UKY; Olin

Visit Vault at **www.vault.com** for insider company profiles, expert advice, career message boards, expert resume reviews, the Vault Job Board and more.

V∧ULT CAREER LIBRARY 63

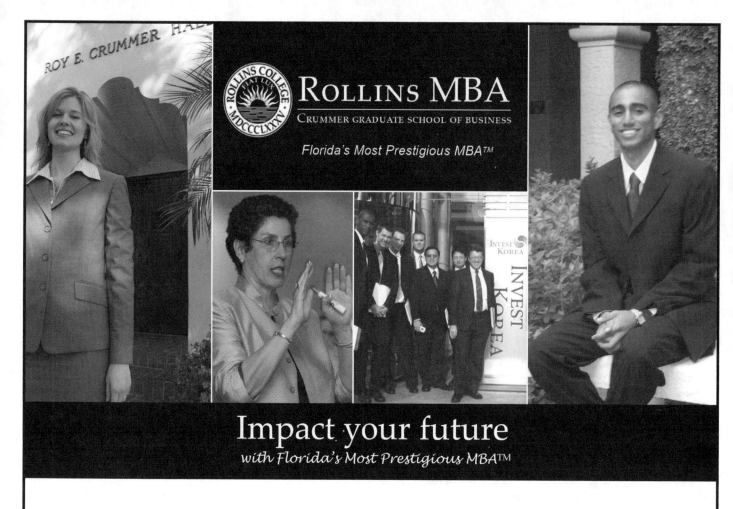

Impact your future
with Florida's Most Prestigious MBA™

ROLLINS EARLY ADVANTAGE MBA FAST FACTS:

- 21-month full-time program for recent college graduates
- Ranked in Top 50 for Full-time MBA by *Forbes*, August 2005
- Full and partial tuition scholarships available for full-time MBA students
- International study trip included in tuition
- Global and domestic consulting projects integrated into program
- Notebook computer included in tuition
- Curriculum designed to fit ALL undergraduate majors

- Mentor program
- Concentrations in Finance, International Business, Marketing and more
- MBA level internship opportunities
- Extensive career management services
- Designated Center for Leadership Development including leadership coaching
- Student-run Collegiate Entrepreneurs Organization which supports future entrepreneurs
- AACSB International accreditation

LEARN MORE ABOUT THE EARLY ADVANTAGE MBA

Jacqueline Brito, Director of Full-Time MBA Admissions

jbrito@rollins.edu, 800-866-2405, ext. 6320

www.crummer.rollins.edu

Ranked #1 MBA in Florida by *Forbes*, August 2005

Ranked #1 in the South, America's Best Colleges, *US News & World Report*, August 2006

Recognized by *Entrepreneur Magazine* for leading Entrepreneurship program, September 2006

GRADUATE
EDUCATION

Get the BUZZ on Top Schools

Considering Graduate School

Graduate School: To Go or Not To Go

When it comes to graduate school, there are two main schools of thought. The first, (led by anxious parents everywhere) says, "Go right away! Otherwise, you'll forget what it's like to be in school, and you won't be able to study! And you'll never get a decent job in the real world anyway!" If this voice is the one currently pounding in your brain, tell it to be quiet and go take a nap. Then, listen to the more rational side of the debate, often specified in small print on graduate school applications: most graduate students are in their late twenties, as schools like it if you have both life and professional experience before pursuing a higher degree.

Of course, not all graduate degrees are created equal. First there are professional degrees (law, teaching, medicine) versus academic degrees (literature, art history). Some programs take only a year, others seem to take the rest of your life. Also, certain professions essentially require you to have more than a B.A. before even considering them (particularly in academia). Other fields are more willing to take a chance on a brash young thing, such as yourself.

Ultimately, the best thing to do is to ask people who are experienced in your chosen field. Ask them if they think you would be best off going to grad school right away, or if they feel you should wait awhile. Ask them about the best schools, and the best degrees for what you want to do. Don't forget to ask them if their companies ever pay for employees to get more education. Frequently, a company will chip in and give an employee flexible hours, in return for a guarantee of work for a certain period of time after he or she has graduated.

One thing graduate school should not be is a last resort. It is too expensive and time consuming to do without really knowing that it's what you want to be doing—at least for the time being.

Graduate School Options: Certification vs. a Degree

There are a multitude of factors you need to take into consideration when deciding whether to pursue an advanced degree, attend local classes towards a certificate, or study for and take your certification exam. The following factors will aid in your decision-making:

- **Stage in life.** Don't let an arbitrary and subjective detail like your age get in the way of your education or professional advancement. If you really want to do it, it doesn't matter whether you're 25 or 125.

- **Stage in career.** Will the degree help you in your career progression? If you have already broken into a field and have amassed experience in it, probably not. If you're looking to change jobs to another company, you may want to consider it. If you're an independent consultant and want to ensure that new clients find you credible, you may want to go back to school.

- **Impact on income.** Can you afford to go to school full time? Can you find a good part-time program while you continue to work? Is it worthwhile to take out a loan? Will your employer help you out with a tuition assistance program?

- **Impact on relationships.** How will your time away from your friends and family impact your relationships? What's more important to you right now and in the future?

- **Volatility of field.** Is this field going to be around in the future—or are there tell-tale signs that it will be replaced by technological advancements or radically altered so that your specialty won't be needed? Check out trends and professional forecasts on web sites like Vault.com and SHRM.org for more insight.

- **Return on investment.** What are the benefits of each option?

Visit Vault at **www.vault.com** for insider company profiles, expert advice, career message boards, expert resume reviews, the Vault Job Board and more.

VAULT CAREER LIBRARY 67

- **Time and money.** Do you need this education by a certain deadline, for a certain reason and on a certain budget? If so, certification will be much quicker and cheaper to attain than a degree. If time and money are of no concern, do both.

- **True motive.** Are you looking to make more money? Then, depending on your current employer's compensation system, you may have to change jobs to a company that rewards its employees based on education rather than tenure. Also, if you are over 40, it probably won't make a difference if you have another degree if you already have over 15 years of career-relevant experience.

- **Theoretical education.** If you want this, school is often a better option.

- **Practical application.** Certification might make more sense here.

It's no secret that having an advanced degree will make you more marketable in the job market, should you need to change employers. If you're just starting out or trying to break into a field, you should definitely pursue a relevant degree; it will open up doors for you and get you more money from the get-go. If you're already established in the field and have a wide array of experience, you'll probably be OK without a degree for future internal advancement—although getting a degree certainly wouldn't hurt you for credibility and possible job changes. Furthermore, achieving a professional certification (e.g., PHR/SPHR) is a boon for degreed professionals and seasoned ones alike.

Attending local college-run certificate programs can give you some added, high-level insight into areas of interest, but won't substitute for a degree or certification. And as far as which school to attend, research all the possibilities and select the one that's right for you. The right program may not be at a "big name" university, but at a smaller institution that offers you the perfect education and training. Be sure to check out the alumni association and career placement office to find out where the school's graduates have landed jobs and which companies actively recruit from the school. The decision to pursue either an advanced degree or certification all comes down to what you feel more comfortable with and your personal career goals.

Considering Graduate School?

Applying to graduate school can sometimes be a daunting task. Even after completing thorough research, selecting the college or university and submitting the application, applicants are frequently left with unanswered questions and legitimate concerns about the evaluation process.

Some of the commonly-asked questions students have at this stage of the process are: "How much emphasis is placed on my undergraduate grades?" "Are my standardized test scores strong enough?" "How important are my written essay and work experience to my application?" and "Who makes the final admission decision?"

International students, required in almost all cases to submit a test score or documentation indicative of their ability to study in English, are faced with additional criteria by which their application will be judged, and may therefore find the evaluation process that much more intimidating. It should help to know that the application and evaluation process is relatively straightforward.

Regardless of the program, the evaluations are based on two main criteria:

- Academic background

- Personal background

In order to determine if one's academic background is admissible, the applicant is asked to submit official undergraduate and or graduate transcripts indicating one's coursework, showing credits and grades in these courses; a standardized test score (such as the GRE or GMAT) specifically requested by the program; and a TOEFL or TOESL test score report, if applicable.

To determine if one's personal or professional background is admissible, an applicant is asked to submit two or more letters of recommendation, preferably from academic or professional references; a written essay(s), which may pertain to a specific topic or reflect the applicant's objective in pursuing the degree program; and a resume or curriculum vitae summarizing the applicant's work experience to date.

In addition, some programs may request a portfolio or sample of one's work. Many schools will request a personal interview after evaluating the application. This may be done in person or over the telephone.

Academic background

The admission committee will begin by reviewing the main indicators of how well one will do in a graduate degree program: undergraduate grades, standardized test scores and TOEFL or TOESL score.

When reviewing the undergraduate or graduate grades, the committee will look closely at the overall grade point average, as well as grades in the major or concentration. The standardized test score is examined, and depending on the type of program, special consideration may be given to a particular section of the test.

Personal background

While the grades and test scores are the most objective measure of the applicant's ability, the personal and professional criteria can do much to enhance an applicant's profile. The written essay, which for some schools may take the place of a personal interview, provides evidence of an applicant's writing ability and his or her motivation to pursue the program.

Letters of recommendation describe an applicant's skills and abilities in the workplace or the classroom. The resume informs of areas outside the classroom where a student may demonstrate competence or knowledge. The combination will provide a clear picture of an applicant's admissibility and subsequent selection for the program.

Application tips

There are a few things you can do to ensure the smooth processing and evaluation of the application. The overall appearance of your application indicates your professionalism and organizational abilities, so be sure to write neatly or type your application, essay and resume (checking for any spelling or grammatical errors). International students should keep in mind any cultural differences such as the order of first and last names. Also, make sure to complete and send in your application in a timely manner—try not to leave it all for the last minute—especially if you're hoping for financial aid. Give ample notice to the people writing your recommendations, and leave yourself time to correct mistakes or find any additional information that might be required. You might even consider making a schedule for yourself so you don't cram all of your preparation into the week or two before the deadline.

Answer all questions on the application completely and, if necessary, attach any additional information on separate sheets of paper. Make every effort to have official transcripts and translations sent directly from your previous university. Lastly, try to have standardized test scores sent to the university in advance, so they arrive at about the same time as your application.

The most important piece of advice that a prospective graduate student could receive is this: do not hesitate to ask questions. There are many ways to obtain answers to specific questions about admissions policies: you can search the web, attend university information sessions, and e-mail, write, fax or telephone the admissions office. Knowing the answers to your questions will help you discover whether your academic and personal profiles match your school of choice and allow you to go through the admission process with greater confidence. Good luck.

Visit Vault at **www.vault.com** for insider company profiles, expert advice, career message boards, expert resume reviews, the Vault Job Board and more.

VAULT CAREER LIBRARY

69

Use the Internet's
MOST TARGETED
job search tools.

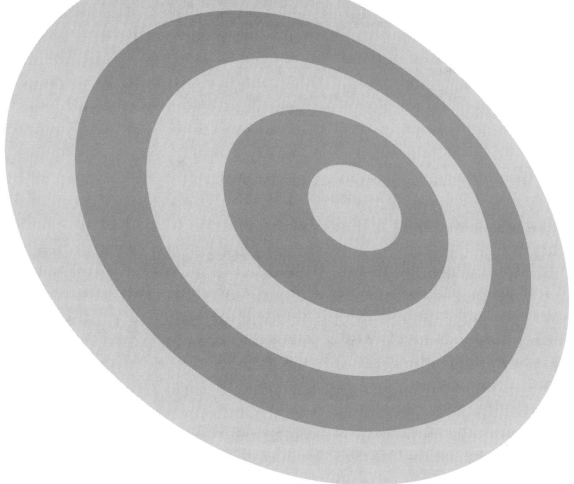

Vault Job Board

Target your search by industry, function, and experience level, and find the job openings that you want.

VaultMatch Resume Database

Vault takes match-making to the next level: post your resume and customize your search by industry, function, experience and more. We'll match job listings with your interests and criteria and e-mail them directly to your in-box.

V∆ULT

> the most trusted name in career information™

Law School

Choosing a Law School

Which law school should you attend? In some ways, this question seems simplistic: you want to go to the best law school that will admit you. But what defines a good law school? There are many books about law schools and surveys that rank them, notably the annual issue published by *U.S. News & World Report*, and it is a good idea to review these publications. Even to the uninitiated, some names pop up immediately: Harvard, Yale, Stanford, Columbia. By reputation and stringent academic requirements, schools like these claim to take only the cream of the crop. And a prestigious law school, with its higher profile, might lead to better employment opportunities after graduation than a less well-known school. But there are considerations other than reputation.

Admittedly, it's hard to wade through the volumes of press materials each law school will send you. Review the course catalogs, certainly, but also look for statistics about the percentage of graduates who go on to litigation, corporate law or other areas of the law, and the kinds of practices they join to get an idea of the kind of training the school focuses on. It's also a good idea to visit the school in person and, if possible, sit in on some classes. "I think it's important to meet with the students at the school," says one recent graduate, "because you get the real facts about what the school is like. Go to whatever mixers they set up for their applicants, if you can."

Another element you should consider is location. Not all of the best law schools are in big cities, but being in an urban setting has a number of advantages. You will have direct contact with many law firms, city agencies and government offices with the resources to hire interns and law students. "Going to a law school in a big city meant that I could have a variety of internships and summer jobs without worrying about housing or moving," says one junior corporate litigator. Many firms also prefer to hire summer associates from local schools. If you have your eye on practicing in New York, for example, it's often a good idea to go to a New York school. You'll be in closer proximity to interview at local firms and some classes (such as criminal law or professional responsibility) may focus on New York state law.

And then there are more practical considerations. Will the school provide housing? If you live off campus, what will your daily commute be like? Are you ready to pick up and move alone or to take your family to a new city or state? Can you afford the tuition? Do you share the school's philosophy and emphasis? Is there a particular professor with whom you want to work?

Ultimately, the decision of which law school to go to is as personal as it is practical. Even if it's important to know school statistics and rankings, your choice needs to be a school that will teach the skills you want to learn, in a location where you can live comfortably. This is especially true if you are embarking on a second career and hesitate to uproot your whole life.

Law School Reputation

Reputation is a subjective quality, usually based on other subjective qualities and usually measured in national rankings and local prestige.

Every year, *U.S. News & World Report* publishes an issue devoted to ranking the colleges and universities of the United States. This is the ranking that people talk about for law schools. The magazine looks at subjective factors like ratings by academics, lawyers and judges, as well as statistical data like LSAT (Law School Aptitude Test) scores, bar passage rates, and acceptance and rejection rates. It conducts opinion polls and gathers statistics on average LSAT scores and undergraduate grade point averages (GPAs). Employers often use the rankings to determine which schools merit an on-campus interviewing visit. And, in a chicken and egg way, the fact that the law firms are paying more attention to those law schools leads to better applicants at those schools, since that's where law students see good career prospects. If you've missed the latest print issue, you can review the rankings online at www.usnews.com.

Visit Vault at **www.vault.com** for insider company profiles, expert advice, career message boards, expert resume reviews, the Vault Job Board and more.

VAULT CAREER LIBRARY 71

National ranking systems like those published by *U.S. News* have been criticized for subjectivity and an overdependence on reputation without considering issues like who gets jobs, what graduates think of their law school, and so on. Some critics, including a coalition of law school deans, have come up with alternative rankings. For more information about alternative rankings and criticism of subjective national rankings, refer to *Judging the Law Schools*, an "unauthorized ranking" of law schools by Thomas E. Brennan, a former Chief Justice of the Michigan Supreme Court (www.ilrg.com/rankings), and *The Ranking Game*, from Indiana University School of Law-Bloomington (monoborg.law.indiana.edu/LawRank/index.html). However, most lawyers and clients still use the *U.S. News* rankings as a yardstick of prestige

A school that ranks in the top of the *U.S. News* list, a "national" law school, offers advantages in the form of portability of degree. Students who attend national schools typically have an easier time finding jobs in different geographical regions than do those coming from lower-ranked schools. A national school may also have highly regarded faculty. "I went to the best law school I got into and would encourage everyone to do the same," says a Harvard alum working in a large Boston firm. "Law school is about getting a credential and access to the career, not an experience unto itself. It's called a professional school for a reason."

Of course, many successful corporate lawyers haven't gone to Harvard or Yale. A local school can be an excellent strategic and financially sound decision, especially for someone who knows the geographic area in which he wants to practice. And all firms hire from the top of their local school class. "I have realized that if you don't get into a top-10 national school, it is sometimes better to go to a local school with many local connections to firms than to go to a second-tier national school in a state in which you won't practice," says a Boston associate. "For example, people in Boston who went to Boston College Law School have good luck landing jobs in firms even though there are a lot of second-tier national schools ranked above them."

If you're lucky enough to get into several schools with good programs in areas of law that interest you, then you just need to think about personal comfort. This is where money and location come into play.

Advice for the 1L

Work steadily

Even if you've been a last-minute, overnight crammer your whole life, that system will not serve you well in law school. There is just too much material for that to be humanly possible. "Don't ever expect to cram," says one graduate, "or leave things to the last minute. You'll drown." Not only will you be memorizing an enormous amount of information, but you will also need to be so familiar with legal principles and reasoning as to be able to use them in a new context on exam questions. You have to work steadily from the very beginning of your first year so that you don't get overwhelmed at the end.

Interact

Set up study groups with serious students and attend them regularly. Go to your professors during their office hours with issues you don't understand. And, as scary as it is, ask questions in class and be prepared to participate. You are not merely being social. Everyone has different strengths and discussing your questions with fellow students can help you understand often complex issues. Yes, it's tempting to see classmates as rivals—why do you want to help others when the tests are graded on a curve? "It's easy to get caught up in the competitiveness, so be careful," says one third-year lawyer. Warns another graduate, "If you're overly competitive, the other students will avoid you like a plague." In reality, a good litigator engages in discussion and a good law student will get used to this at an early stage. Furthermore, law school can be intense, lonely and isolating. A support system can help you keep your sanity in the worst moments.

Don't panic

Law school grades can be brought up in your second and third years. If you feel lost at sea in the beginning, rest assured—the odds are that most of your classmates don't know what they're doing either. And there's no way to tell who's going to get the best grade. The student who speaks confidently in class may not have the skills to analyze issues on paper, while the quiet, insecure student who takes copious notes and studies on weekends might get the only "A" in the course. So don't spend time worrying about other students' skills—concentrate on your own.

Make use of study guides

There are many study guides available to the first-year law student. You can listen to tapes, study from flash cards, buy professional outlines, attend lectures and even take additional courses. Find what works for you and most accurately emphasizes what your professor emphasizes (she's putting the test together, after all).

Be prepared in class

Do your reading and be prepared to answer questions. Some professors are ruthless inquisitors; others are more interested in fostering general class discussions. Either way, you'll lower your stress level if you are prepared to be called on and give intelligent answers. One litigator offers this tip: "I usually reviewed what I studied right before class, so it was fresh."

Review

You might have done the reading for class and taken good notes, but just because you read or wrote it down once doesn't mean you know it cold. Set aside time regularly to review your notes and previous materials to build up that store of accessible knowledge you'll need to call on for the final exam. Repetition is the key.

Don't get sucked in

Try to keep up with your friends outside law school and engage in some extracurricular activities, even if it's just going to the movies occasionally or playing a game of basketball. The advantage of interacting with your fellow law students is also its disadvantage: you're all in the same boat. Talking about law 24 hours a day can be exhausting and counterproductive; you can get immersed and caught up in your fellow students' panic attacks or intense competitiveness. "I made a lot of friends in law school," says one former law student, "but I lost some friends, too, because I didn't keep in touch with all my friends from before law school." You will likely have more time and feel less pressure in your second and third years and you will be glad not to have alienated your non-law school friends. Escaping from the law once in a while will actually make you a better student in the long run, and it is an important lesson to keep in mind when you actually become an attorney.

LSAT 101

For many students, few things are more dreaded than standardized testing, and the LSAT is among the most fearsome tests of all. The Law School Admissions Test is used to evaluate a candidate's verbal and math skills as well as her analytical thinking. The exam can be arduous and exhausting, but it is a necessary element of applying to law school. The LSAT is administered by the Law School Admissions Council four times a year and most schools require that you have taken the LSAT before you apply to law school. The test is roughly three and a half hours long and similar to the SAT—only harder. The test breaks down into the following sections:

Visit Vault at **www.vault.com** for insider company profiles, expert advice, career message boards, expert resume reviews, the Vault Job Board and more.

V\ULT CAREER LIBRARY   73

- **Logical reasoning** (Two sections, 35 minutes each, 48 to 52 questions total). This section tests your ability to dissect an argument. The questions each consist of an argumentative passage of three or four sentences. There is usually a flaw with the argument, and your job is to find out what it is. Occasionally the argument is valid, and your job is to determine the conclusion. This section is pretty dense, so be prepared to do some thorough reading.

- **Analytical reasoning/games** (One section, 35 minutes, approximately 24 questions). This is traditionally one of the hardest sections of the LSAT. The best description of these "games" is that they involve logical reasoning of a system of relationships. You'll usually have to draw a diagram to figure out the relationships based on the rules given to you. There are four games and there are five to eight questions for each game.

- **Reading comprehension** (One section, 35 minutes, approximately 24 questions) As a lawyer, you're going to read through hundreds of cases, statutes, documents and memoranda. Reading comprehension is extremely important. This section includes four passages, each roughly 400 to 500 words long and followed by five to eight questions. You must read each section and be able to answer each set of questions correctly.

- **Mystery section** (One of the above sections, possibly a little different in format).

- **Writing sample** (30 minutes). The writing sample will be on a topic chosen by the test committee. The essay is forwarded to all the schools to which you are applying, but, according to an admissions official at an accredited law school, their office relies more on the applicant's personal statement than the LSAT essay to evaluate a candidate's writing abilities. The essay is not factored into the total LSAT score. Rather than count on your work being ignored, however, you should be prepared to formulate an argument and present it clearly under pressure.

The LSAT is graded on a matrix that converts the raw score (0-100) to a 120-180 scale. There is no passing score, but it becomes increasingly harder to move up in the matrix. You don't need to get all the questions right in order to get a perfect score, but your score can drop based on the answer to a single question.

There are many courses designed help you to "beat" the LSAT, including Kaplan, the Princeton Review and the LSAT Center Course. These courses teach specific strategies for tackling each section. The LSAT doesn't change that much from year to year, so if you study older tests and practice a lot, you'll improve your chances of doing well on the real thing.

Business School

Why the MBA?

Is it a quant boot camp where students find themselves chained to their laptops and their spreadsheets? Is it a country club where students mix and mingle, discussing future business plans over cocktails? Or is it a mandatory two years that would-be CEOs must serve in order to get that bump in salary and that chance to rise into upper management?

The school part

Business school is definitely school. Particularly in the first year, when students in many programs take "core" classes in fields like accounting and corporate finance, the workload at business school is often described as "overwhelming." In class, students learn marketing strategies and management theories, negotiation tactics, the heavy quantitative lifting of valuing a company and other useful business concepts. Many business schools utilize "business cases" to illustrate concepts the students learn. Through these cases, students study the way these concepts have played out in real-world situations.

The business part

But business school is often as much about careers as it is than books and learning. While at school, future MBAs often have one foot in the classroom and the other in the working world. For starters, unlike their graduate, law or medical school counterparts, very few business school students enroll in the programs without having first gained experience in the working world. (Most programs require some work experience and will reject candidates who don't have it.) The program itself is also shorter—the traditional full-time MBA program is two years, which serves as less of a hiatus from working life than other graduate programs. In fact, some students in full-time MBA programs continue to consult or work part-time with their former employers throughout their time at business school.

For some students, business school is a necessary step in their career path. In the investment banking and consulting industries, many large employers will not promote employees past the analyst level until they have received their MBA. It is common practice for these budding bankers and consultants to attend business school after a two- to three-year stint as an analyst following college; some of them return to their firms as associates.

Many other students earn their MBA degrees through evening classes while working full-time. For many of these evening and executive MBA students, getting an MBA is especially attractive because their employers are footing the bill for their degrees.

Career-minded

More so than students at other graduate programs, students at business school enroll to accomplish specific objectives related to their careers. According to a survey published by the Graduate Management Admission Council (GMAC—the organization that administers the GMAT business schools admissions test), about half (51 percent) of business school students use the MBA degree to enhance opportunities in their current occupation or industry; the other half (49 percent) seek to switch careers. Often, career switchers are experienced professionals who have worked in the corporate world in a non-business function (engineering, for example), who wish to transition to a business-oriented management track.

And on the whole, MBAs are satisfied with their degrees. According to a survey of the MBA graduates of the class of 2003 conducted by GMAC, more than two-thirds of graduates from business school feel the value of their MBA is outstanding or excellent (22 percent indicated the value to be good, while 9 percent indicated it was fair and 3 percent described it as poor).

Visit Vault at **www.vault.com** for insider company profiles, expert advice, career message boards, expert resume reviews, the Vault Job Board and more.

VAULT CAREER LIBRARY 75

What you'll gain

Most business school students expect to make more money once they graduate. This opportunity certainly exists. Any business school student who lands at a top investment bank or consulting firm (the two largest industry employers of MBAs) will find themselves immediately making $100,000+ a year. And in general, having an MBA on your resume puts you in a better position to negotiate and command a higher salary (even if you return to the same industry or even same company that you worked at previous to business school).

However, landing a six-figure job is no guarantee. During tough economic times, MBA hiring takes a larger hit than undergraduate hiring or direct-from-industry hiring—in part because of the cost of hiring MBAs. Many graduates of the class of 2001 and 2002 found themselves jobless for up to a year or more after graduation.

But there are other reasons to get the degree other than a bump in salary. Many recruiters and managers find MBAs to be more polished professionals in certain respects. According to the *Corporate Recruiters Survey* published by GMAC, recruiters find the following skills both highly attractive and well developed in MBA graduates:

• Ability to think analytically

• Quantitative skills

• Ability to integrate information from a wide variety of sources

• Information-gathering skills

GMAT 101

The following article is provided by Vault's partner, Manhattan GMAT. Learn more about the GMAT exam and about ways to prepare at www.manhattangmat.com. Sign up for the official test by calling 1-800-GMAT-NOW, or by going to the official GMAT web site at www.mba.com.

The GMAT is the Graduate Management Admission Test, a standardized test used by business schools as a measure of an applicant's academic ability. Schools require applicants to take the GMAT and submit their scores in order to be considered for admission to MBA and other business-oriented degree programs. The GMAT is a computerized test; administered six days a week, 52 weeks a year (except holidays), and it can be taken virtually anytime. However, it can only be taken once per month and five times per year. The cost to take the exam is $225.

The computerized GMAT CAT

The GMAT is offered ONLY on computer, which means that you do not use a pencil and paper to answer test questions. Instead, you will sit in front of a computer screen at an official testing center and take the GMAT in its CAT (Computer Adaptive Test) form. The basic features of the CAT format are as follows:

• You will see only one question on the screen at a time. Therefore, you may not skip around in a section and answer questions in the order that you please. Once you answer a question, you are not allowed to return to it, but you must answer each question in order to move to the next.

• The test is designed to adapt to your personal ability by giving you questions that reflect how well you have answered previous questions. Test questions are not pre-set in advance. Instead, as you take the test, new questions are generated for you based on how well you are doing. The test begins with a question of average difficulty. If you answer it correctly, you will receive a slightly harder second question. If you do not, you will receive a slightly easier second question. Your third question, in turn, will be based on your response to the second question and its difficulty level. In this way, the computer zeros in on your ability level and assigns you a corresponding score.

- Due to the GMAT's computer adaptive format, scores are not determined solely by the number of correct answers. Correct responses to difficult questions are worth more than correct responses to easy questions. Therefore, in order to score well you must be able to answer the more difficult questions correctly.

- No matter your ability level, the CAT presents you with a fair mix of questions for the content areas within a given section. For example, in the math section, all test-takers receive roughly the same mix of arithmetic, algebra and geometry questions.

- Prior to the exam, there will be a computer tutorial designed to help you become familiar with computerized testing. You will be allowed as much time as you need to review the computerized format and practice entering in answers.

GMAT format

- *Section 1:* You will be asked to compose two 30-minute essays. The first essay will ask you to analyze a given argument. The second essay will ask you to analyze a given issue. This section is called the Analytical Writing Assessment (the AWA).

- *Section 2:* You will be given 75 minutes to answer 37 multiple-choice quantitative questions. These questions come in two forms: (a) Problem Solving questions, which ask you to solve a variety of arithmetic, algebraic and geometric math problems and (b) Data Sufficiency questions, which ask you to decide whether or not you are given sufficient information to solve a given math problem.

- *Section 3:* You will be given 75 minutes to answer 41 multiple-choice verbal questions. These questions come in three forms: (a) Sentence Correction questions, which ask you to choose the most grammatically accurate way of expressing a given sentence, (b) Critical Reasoning questions, which ask you to assess the logic of short arguments, and (c) Reading Comprehension questions, which ask you to read short passages (up to 350 words each) and answer content, inference and application questions based on the information presented.

The timed-portion of the GMAT lasts three and a half hours. You are allowed a five-minute break between each section. Note: the GMAT does not include any questions that test your business knowledge. It is designed solely to measure your writing, quantitative and verbal ability.

GMAT scoring

- After taking the GMAT, you will receive both quantitative (Section 2) and verbal (Section 3) subscores. Each subscore ranges from 0 to 60. These subscores are then combined into an overall score, which ranges from 200 to 800 and this is what is typically considered your GMAT score. You will also receive a separate score, ranging from 0 to 6, on the AWA essay portion of the exam (Section 1). Your scores are accompanied by a percentile ranking that tells you how you did in relation to everyone else who took the test. If you score in the 85th percentile, this means that 85 percent of all GMAT test-takers scored at or below your level.

- The median overall GMAT score is approximately 520. However, to be considered for top business schools, you will generally need a score of at least 600. In fact, according to the 2004 *U.S. News* business school rankings, 10 of the 15 business schools report that their average GMAT scores are in the 700+ range.

- Scores are reported to you immediately. After completing the GMAT, you are given the option of either viewing or canceling your scores. If you think that you did not do very well, you may cancel your scores (without seeing them!) and they will not be reported to any business schools, although the business schools will be notified of the cancellation on future score reports. Keep in mind, however, that once you cancel your scores, you will not be able to view them. Also, you will not be refunded your test registration fee. Your AWA essay-writing score is determined separately (graded by ETS writing professionals and a software program called Robo-reader) and mailed to you approximately two weeks after the test. The test fee covers reporting of these scores to five schools, and additional score reports can be purchased for $28.

Visit Vault at **www.vault.com** for insider company profiles, expert advice, career message boards, expert resume reviews, the Vault Job Board and more.

VAULT CAREER LIBRARY **77**

Medical School

The History of Medical Schools in the U.S.

The very first medical school in the original 13 colonies was founded in 1765 by John Morgan at the University of Pennsylvania, which at the time was known as the College of Philadelphia. The faculty had been trained at the University of Edinburgh and used British medical education as the model. Thus, the first medical school in the United States was built within an institution of higher learning. It promoted bedside learning that was to supplement medical lectures. The medical school was within a few blocks from the Pennsylvania Hospital that was founded by Benjamin Franklin.

Medical education in that era included formal lectures for a semester or two and several years of apprenticeship. There was no formal tuition, no prerequisite academic preparation and written exams were not mandatory. With the progress of science in the 19th Century started the new era of medical education calling for full-time investigators and teachers in biochemistry, bacteriology, pharmacology, etc. In the 1870s, the first teaching hospital, the Hospital of the University of Pennsylvania, was built. Teaching hospitals are those that teach future physicians the art of medicine, and thus have residents and medical students working alongside the main doctors (known as attendings).

Medical school in the 20th Century

The birth of modern medical education in the United States and Canada is often attributed to Abraham Flexner, a professional educator, who in 1910 published the Flexner Report for the Carnegie Foundation. The report was a commentary of the state of medical education at the time. It criticized the fact that there were too many medical schools, many of which were substandard. At the time the report was published there were 155 medical schools in the United States and Canada and only 16 of these required two or more years of college work as an admission requirement. (Many of the others came into being simply to make money from tuition as opposed to actually providing a quality education.) Flexner proposed a four-year medical school curriculum—two years of basic science education followed by two years of clinical training. He also proposed the requirements for admission to include the high school diploma and a minimum of two years of college science. The report resulted in the closure of many medical schools that were not incorporated within a university; this way, medical education would be associated with institutions known for academic excellence. In 1935 there were 66 MD granting institutions that survived the reform, 57 of which were part of a university.

These improvements in medical education were followed by the birth of standardized testing for medical school admissions. The Medical College Admission Test (MCAT) was developed in 1928. It was implemented to improve attrition rates that at the time ranged from 5 to 50 percent. By 1946 attrition rates at medical schools in the U.S. decreased to 7 percent.

The student body

As for the student body in these early medical schools, it will come as no surprise that the students were white and male. Medical schools were closed to African-Americans, except for a few older medical schools in the north. The first African-American to graduate from a northern medical school was Dr. David J. Peck, who graduated from Rush Medical School in Chicago in 1847. Between 1868 and 1904 seven medical schools for African-Americans were established. Unfortunately, by 1923 only Howard University Medical School in Washington and Meharry Medical School in Nashville remained open. Things were not much better for women. The first medical school for women, The Women's Medical College of Pennsylvania, was founded in 1850, and eventually came to be known as the Medical College of Pennsylvania. Drexel University eventually took over the school, and it is now known as Drexel College of Medicine. The first woman to graduate from a medical school in the U.S. was Dr. Elizabeth Blackwell. She graduated first in class from Geneva Medical College (now SUNY Upstate Medical University College of Medicine) in New York in 1849. The first African-American woman to

Visit Vault at **www.vault.com** for insider company profiles, expert advice, career message boards, expert resume reviews, the Vault Job Board and more.

VAULT CAREER LIBRARY 79

graduate from a medical school in the U.S. was Dr. Rebecca Lee Crumpler who graduated from the New England Female Medical College in Boston in 1846.

Med school today

Today there are 125 MD granting institutions, most of which still follow the curriculum that was proposed by Flexner and all of which require the MCAT. Thing have changed however, most notably the student and medical school faculty body. Each year, a little over 17,000 students start their first year of medical schools, close to 30 percent of whom are minorities. In 2004, 50 percent of the entering class of medical students and 45 percent of the graduating class were women.

A Brief Overview: Applying to Medical School

The application process begins long before you start filling out your med school applications. You've got to do your homework. Your academic requirements, grades, MCAT scores and interviews will determine where you apply and were you attend medical school.

Undergraduate academic requirements

One of the biggest myths surrounding the medical school application process is that the applicant must be a science major, particularly a biology or chemistry major. In actuality, a medical school applicant may major in any subject area he or she chooses. Regardless of the major one chooses, an applicant only needs to complete medical school admission prerequisites. Prerequisites differ from school to school, but the standard usually consists of eight semester-long classes broken down as follows:

- Two semesters of basic chemistry
- Two semesters of organic chemistry
- Two semesters of biology
- Two semesters of physics

Most medical schools also require one to two semesters of basic college English or writing courses. The good news is that most undergraduate institutions have similar requirements in order to graduate, and fulfilling these requirements will typically also take care of the medical school prerequisite. But be aware that some medical schools will not accept Advance Placement (AP) English credit to satisfy this requirement, and will expect at least another semester of English. Also, some schools require one to two semesters of mathematics, particularly calculus. You should research your schools of interest to find out what prerequisites to complete in order to be considered for admission. This information is usually readily available on the medical school's web site or through your pre-medical advisor.

With only eight to 10 semester classes devoted to the prerequisites required for admission, students can use the rest of their time to major in any subject area they choose. Many students end up choosing biology or chemistry anyway because the common medical school prerequisites coincide with the prerequisites for a biology or chemistry major. Also, many students feel that a strong background in biology or chemistry will help prepare them for the MCAT. But if one examines the data provided by the Association of American Medical Colleges (AAMC) showing the correlation between MCAT score and undergraduate major, there is no evidence indicating a background in biology or chemistry will provide a higher MCAT score (data available at http://www.aamc.org/students/mcat/examineedata/char99.pdf).

If a biology or chemistry major doesn't affect MCAT scores, which major should you choose and why? Well, who better to give advice on this question than successful medical school applicants? In the chapter dedicated to academics, students will give you general academic advice, as well as reasoning behind their choices in majors. While there is a vast array of reasons behind their choices, you will find one unifying theme: pick a major that you will enjoy. Not only do students usually do better in subject areas they enjoy, but college only lasts four years. If you don't enjoy your major for those four years, you'll probably be miserable and regret the decision in the long run.

The MCAT

The Medical College Admission Test (MCAT) was designed to assess knowledge of scientific principles and concepts through the use of problem solving, critical thinking and writing. In short, the MCAT tests both aptitude and knowledge. One could think of it as a synthesis of the SAT, which tests aptitude, and the ACT, which tests outside knowledge. First developed in 1928 as a way to decrease attrition rates in medical school, the MCAT has undergone several revisions, the most recent of which was to change the subject material to emphasize the skills and concepts identified by physicians and medical educators as prerequisite for the practice of medicine. The paper form of the test was also converted to a completely computerized format in 2007. The test is developed by the Association of American Medical Colleges (AAMC) in conjunction with its member U.S. medical schools. The MCAT is an unavoidable challenge that must be faced when applying to any medical school. It is one of the critical factors that medical schools use to evaluate an applicant, so it must be taken seriously.

In 2007, the MCAT will be offered on 22 separate testing dates, 20 of which are between April and September, with the other two test dates in January. The test is administered in Thomson Prometric Testing Centers, which are facilities set up throughout the country for the administration of various computer-based standardized exams. It is usually recommended that students take the MCAT about 18 months before they plan to enter medical school though they can take as far in advance as needed and up to three times total without needing special permission. For instance, if you plan on entering medical school in the fall of 2008, you should plan to take the test around April of 2007. The bottom line is that a medical school needs your MCAT scores to evaluate your application and it takes about 30 days for scores to be released after the test date, so plan accordingly.

The only way to register for the MCAT is online at www.aamc.org/mcat. You will be able to register at this web site six months prior to the test date. It is highly recommended that you submit your registration early to ensure that you will be able to take the test at your first choice test center and to avoid any late fees. This will help to alleviate the additional stress of having to travel to an unfamiliar location to take the test. It is important to note that there is absolutely no walk-in registration.

You can take the MCAT up to three times each year, although you must complete an exam before registering to take another. Please note that when your scores are reported to medical schools, all of your previous scores are sent. Therefore, it is best to feel fully prepared before attempting to take the test. Never take the official test for mere practice.

Taking the MCAT is expensive! In 2006, the regular examination fee was $210.00 with a late registration fee of $50.00. There is no indication that these prices will be reduced in the future, so be prepared to pay at least this much at the time you register for the test.

Content of the MCAT

The MCAT is composed of four sections: Physical Sciences, Biological Sciences, Verbal Reasoning and the Writing Sample. All of the sections consist of multiple choice questions except for the Writing Sample, which consists of two essays. The number of test questions for each section, the order of the exam sections and the time allotted are as follows:

Section	Number of Questions	Time (in Minutes)
Physical Sciences	52	70
Verbal Reasoning	40	60
Writing Sample	2	60
Biological Sciences	52	70

Visit Vault at www.vault.com for insider company profiles, expert advice, career message boards, expert resume reviews, the Vault Job Board and more.

VAULT CAREER LIBRARY   81

The Verbal Reasoning section consists of several passages, each about 500 to 600 words long, taken from the "humanities, social sciences, and areas of the natural sciences," which are loosely defined areas. These topics are often not tested elsewhere on the MCAT. Each passage is followed by five to 10 questions based on the information presented in the passage. All of the information needed to answer each question is provided in the accompanying passage so you should not need to apply any outside information you may have studied.

The Physical Sciences section is designed to assess your reasoning in general chemistry and physics. The Biological Sciences section is designed to assess your reasoning in biology and organic chemistry. For a complete list of specific topics covered in each section, check the official MCAT web site at www.aamc.org/mcat. Each section contains 10-11 problem sets, each about 250 words in length that describe a situation or problem. Each problem set is followed by four to eight questions. There are also approximately 10 questions found in each section not accompanied by a passage. Unlike the Verbal Reasoning section, the Physical and Biological Sciences sections do expect you to have a background in these areas and use information you have studied before the test to answer the questions.

The Writing Sample consists of two 30-minute essays. This section of the MCAT is designed to assess your ability to develop a central idea, synthesize concepts and ideas, write clearly, and use proper grammar, syntax and punctuation. Each Writing Sample item provides a specific topic that you must respond to by typing your response. The topics vary widely from your opinions on global warming to whether or not you agree with a common adage, but do not include religious or emotionally charged issues or issues related to the application process or your decision to pursue a career in medicine.

The MCAT is truly a grueling test, but luckily, the total exam length has decreased significantly with the implementation of the computerized format. The overall length of the test day is about five-and-a-half hours. There are three optional 10-minute breaks.

How the MCAT is scored

Your total score on the MCAT is a composite of the score for each of the four sections. For each multiple choice section, your raw score is calculated by adding the number of questions you answer correctly. It is important to note that there is no penalty for incorrect answers, unlike some of the other standardized tests. Since there are multiple versions of the MCAT given at any one time, it is necessary to convert the raw scores to a scale to take this difference into consideration. For the three multiple choice sections of the test, the scaled scores range from a low of 1 to a high of 15. For the writing sample, each of your essays is read by two different individuals. Each individual score ranges from 1 to 6 and the total raw score is then converted to an alphabetic scale ranging from J (lowest) to T (highest). The alphabetic score is obtained from the summation of the scores received on each of your essays.

MCAT resources

It is critical for you to be proactive when preparing for this ever-important test. You should talk to students who have taken the test before you and stay in touch with your pre-medical advisor, if available, to be aware of all upcoming deadlines. The best place to check out the nitty-gritty details of the MCAT is at the official MCAT web site, www.aamc.org/mcat. A practice online test is offered at www.e-mcat.com.

The AMCAS Application

For most applicants, the formal application process for medical school starts with filling out the AMCAS application, which can be accessed through the Association of American Medical Colleges web site at www.aamc.org. This electronic application is typically known as the "primary" application, and is a common application that goes out to all of the medical schools to which you are applying. Almost every medical school in the country requires you to send them this initial application so that they can screen applicants for their individual or "secondary" applications. The primary AMCAS application requires that you fill out personal information, record grades for your classes, describe extracurricular activities and write a personal statement. You must also send them an official copy of your transcript. Along with your primary application, AMCAS will also send your MCAT scores to medical schools. Secondary applications are sent by individual schools after they screen your primary application. These often require you to write several additional essays and fill out more personal information, but this is highly dependent on the school, so you should be prepared for the extra time commitment and pay close attention to the unique deadlines for these supplemental applications.

Please note that there are a few schools that do not require AMCAS, and you must apply to these schools directly. Most of these schools take part in the Texas Medical and Dental Schools Application Service, including the University of Texas Southwestern, Texas A&M University and Texas Tech University. Further information about this process can be found at www.utsystem.edu/tmdsas/HomepageMS&Pre-HlthAdv.htm.

There are several key points to consider when deciding what schools to apply to. No matter the credentials you possess, you should apply to at least one school where your chances for admittance are higher than at most other schools, often called a "safety." The chance of getting into your state school is often better than your chances for getting into a private school because your state schools are required to accept more applicants from your state. Typically, 80-90 percent of a state school's student body consists of in-state residents. It is always wise to apply to your state schools, even if you prefer not to go there now; you may change your mind if that is the only school you are accepted to. However, just because the odds are in your favor at state schools, do not think that admission is guaranteed at any medical school. The disclaimer here is that even so-called "perfect" applicants get rejected from medical schools, so be aware that the process is imperfect and thus can be unfair to even the most deserving candidates.

It is always a good idea to apply as early as possible. Some schools have a rolling admissions process in which they send out acceptances throughout the interview season, and as the number of acceptances goes up, it gets more competitive for the late interviewees. There is also an early decision program in which certain medical schools participate. This program requires that you apply to only one participating school, which requires filling out the AMCAS by August 1, and waiting to hear back.

If accepted, you will know by October 1, and you must attend this medical school. You can only apply to other medical schools once you have been rejected from you early decision school or received an official release from them allowing you to apply elsewhere. Check with individual schools to see if they participate in this program.

There is no magic number of schools to apply to, but the majority of students send their AMCAS application to between 10 and 30 different schools. If you get more interviews than you care to attend, you can always withdraw your application from individual programs, so it is better to apply to a lot of medical schools and get plenty of interviews, rather than apply to a few schools and get a small number of interviews. With that said, it is important to realize that AMCAS charges an application fee of $160 for one medical school designation, and then charges an additional $30 for each additional medical school. Individual schools often charge an additional fee for their secondary applications, most of them around $50, so be aware of this additional cost of applying.

Visit Vault at **www.vault.com** for insider company profiles, expert advice, career message boards, expert resume reviews, the Vault Job Board and more.

V/\ULT CAREER LIBRARY

83

INDUSTRY
OVERVIEWS

Accounting

Why Accounting?

What exactly is accounting, and why do we need it? Accounting is a system by which economic information is identified, recorded, summarized and reported to be used by decision makers.

So what does that mean?

Put simply, accounting is the language of business. An accounting system essentially tracks all of the activities of an organization, showing when and where money has been spent and commitments have been made. This aids decision making by allowing managers to evaluate organizational performance, by indicating the financial implications of choosing one strategy over another and by highlighting current weaknesses and opportunities. It allows managers to take a step back, look at the organization, and assess how it is doing and determine where it should be going.

Accounting, however, is not the exclusive domain of Big Business. In all likelihood, you have been managing your own personal accounting system for years—it's called your checking account. Every time you record an entry in your check ledger, you are acting like an accountant. Your check ledger is an accounting log of all of your deposit and withdrawal activities, helping you identify your cash inflows and outflows and letting you know how much money you have left in the bank. It lets you know where your money went and helps you make decisions on how to plan your future purchases and expenses. If this log is not regularly balanced for accuracy, you would have an inaccurate picture of your cash position and might spend more than you have (a common situation, given the popularity of overdraft protection features offered by banks).

You get the picture. Now, imagine these functions performed on more complicated items and on a much larger scale. While you might have 500 checkbook transactions in a year, many organizations might have that many transactions every minute. This is what an accountant does. And, just as you would eventually be lost without a relatively accurate checkbook, organizations would not be able to make useful decisions without an accurate accounting system. Anyone who has pulled out his or her hair trying to balance their checkbook should have an appreciation for both the importance and challenges of accounting.

Why accounting?

So why would anyone choose a career in accounting as opposed to another business profession, like investment banking or management consulting? Isn't accounting boring and tedious?

As we discussed earlier, accounting has always had an image problem, stuck in the public consciousness as a profession populated by math geeks who love crunching numbers but little else. While this stereotype may have been accurate at one point in history, it no longer presents an accurate picture of what the career is like. While the basic mechanics of accounting can certainly become tedious, such functions are increasingly becoming automated, with accountants focusing more on analysis, interpretation and business strategy.

In fact, accounting has been rated one of the most desirable professions available. According to *The 2002 Jobs Rated Almanac*, "accountant" was the fifth best job in terms of low stress, high compensation, lots of autonomy and tremendous hiring demand. Furthermore, the National Association of Colleges and Employers' Winter 2002 Salary Survey ranked the accounting services industry first among the top five employers with job offers for graduating college students.

Visit Vault at **www.vault.com** for insider company profiles, expert advice, career message boards, expert resume reviews, the Vault Job Board and more.

V/\ULT CAREER LIBRARY 87

Accounting Uppers and Downers

Uppers

- **Collegial work environment.** Public accounting firms, particularly the Big Four firms (Deloitte & Touche, Ernst & Young, KPMG and PricewaterhouseCoopers), tend to hire large classes of newly graduated accountants. Being surrounded by so many people with similar interests and concerns makes acclimation to the firm and the job much more agreeable. It also provides fertile ground for networking opportunities. According to one public accountant, "I started with a class of almost 100 other college graduates, and we bonded quickly through all of the training and client work. While most of these people have since left the firm, I still keep in touch with most of them, which is great since they've all fanned out to dozens of interesting companies. I've already turned some of them into clients and am working on many others. The networking opportunity is tremendous."

- **Applicability to many functions.** A strong knowledge of accounting is applicable across all management functions, including purchasing, manufacturing, wholesaling, retailing, marketing and finance. It provides a base from which to build broad knowledge about virtually all business functions and industries. As the collectors and interpreters of financial information, accountants develop comprehensive knowledge about what is occurring and close relationships with key decision makers, and are increasingly being called upon to offer strategic advice. Senior accountants or controllers are often selected as production or marketing executives because they have acquired in-depth general management skills.

- **Exposure to different companies.** Public accounting offers rapid exposure to a number of different clients and activities, accelerating the rate of attaining skills and experience. According to one Big Four audit senior who specializes in entertainment industry clients, "I've been with the firm for less than three years, but I've become intimately involved in work for large industry players like Sony, Viacom and Disney, as well as for a good number of smaller entertainment and media companies. Being able to learn about the business of entertainment from the industry's benchmark companies has really sped up my professional development. Few professions would have offered me such a great learning opportunity."

- **Better hours and less stress than investment banking and management consulting.** The hours and travel required by the accounting profession are much less stressful and more predictable than that found in investment banking and consulting. In public accounting, you generally know you'll be very busy for a few months out of the year and then settle in to a manageable 40- to 45-hour workweek, whereas I-bankers and consultants are notorious for regularly pulling 60-80 hour weeks (at least) and hopping on planes at a moment's notice. "As hard as I worked as an accountant, my life has truly been swallowed by my I-banking job," says one former auditor who, after attaining an MBA, is now an investment banker. "I pretty much work six days a week, with at least part of my Sunday spent on some work item or another. I actually had a life when I was an auditor—not anymore."

- **Great for women.** The profession has taken great strides to implement flexible work arrangements and other initiatives to provide lifestyle choices for women. According to the Bureau of Labor Statistics, women now account for approximately 60 percent of the accounting profession, with the outlook for women accountants looking bright. According to a CFO survey by Robert Half International, 58 percent of CFOs believe that the number of women accountants in management-level positions (such as vice president or chief financial officer) will increase in the next five years. According to one partner who has worked for several large firms, "At the risk of sounding politically incorrect, my 17 years of experience have shown me that women tend to make better accountants than men. In my observation, men often tend to be focused on the big picture, while women are more acutely aware of intricate detail. Well, accounting demands a detail-oriented approach more than any other skill, so you do the math."

Downers

- **Lower pay than investment banking and consulting.** The more manageable lifestyle has its tradeoff: lower pay. On average, starting base salaries in accounting are 15 to 20 percent lower than investment banking or consulting, not including the bonus incentives that can significantly increase a banker's or consultant's overall pay package. According to the same former auditor/current investment banker from above, "I do make a lot more money as an I-banker—I mean a LOT—which does make up somewhat for losing my personal life, but it doesn't feel that way all the time. Sometimes it seems that, if you divided my I-banking compensation by the number of hours I spend working, I would be making about minimum wage." Bonus incentives are much smaller in public accounting, if they exist at all. "You'll never become 'stinkin' rich' on an accountant's wage," adds one Big Four tax partner, "but I like to think that, since we are supposed to be conservative and intelligent in matters pertaining to money, we know best how to take care of our money and make it work for us. You will definitely lead a comfortable life."

- **Many bosses with different priorities.** Accountants, particularly public accountants, are usually assigned to multiple projects at any given time and must prioritize and, when needed, learn to say "no." This is particularly true in public accounting, where multiple, simultaneous projects for different clients are commonplace. According to one auditor, juggling projects "has honestly been the hardest part of my job. Forget the clients, they're relatively easy to deal with—it's the partners on those clients that get you. They all want you to focus on their projects first. On more than one occasion, a partner has screamed my head off, really got down and cursed, because of a perceived 'lack of focus' on my part. You just have to try to explain your situation, try to demonstrate that you have everything covered, and move on." However, this premium on time management is also present in investment banking and consulting.

- **Relatively conservative, conformist cultures.** Accountants are generally looking to see if reported numbers conform to one set of regulations or another (Generally Accepted Accounting Principles, the Internal Revenue Code, SEC regulations, etc.). This emphasis on regulations (in fact, one might say that the entire accounting industry exists because of regulations) translates into a generally risk-averse culture and ethos that emphasizes conformity.

- **Pressure to stay "chargeable."** This is one of the subtler, yet highly sensitive parts of being an accountant. Like attorneys, public accountants generally work under billable hour arrangements (they are paid by clients for each hour billed). This means that they must account for every single hour they work and accurately allocate them to each project they work on, whether client-related or otherwise. Being "chargeable" means billing a high percentage of your hours to work performed for paying clients as opposed to non-billable projects. This tracking of billable hours, while often tedious, is absolutely crucial to the profession—it is the basis for how public accounting firms determine revenue, expenses, profitability, efficiency, performance and a host of other metrics. With such vital items at stake, timesheets and chargeability often are the subject of much stress and consternation.

"Yeah, we can work 60 hours in a week," says one audit senior, "but not all of those hours are chargeable to a client. Some days, you can spend time on a proposal for new business, some time on developing a new product or service, and some time on performing general research on a specific issue. All of these activities are important to continued success, but they hurt you because none of them are chargeable to a specific client. In other words, the firm isn't getting paid for this work. While the firm values this non-chargeable work, it doesn't want you doing too much of it—it wants you out there making money for the firm. So when you find yourself doing this stuff, your chargeability goes down and your performance numbers suffer, which can hurt your reviews, your paycheck and ultimately your future at the firm. However, you can't err on the other side either—you bill too many hours to your clients and you run the risk of going over budget and having the client give you the third degree on why the job is taking you so long. It can be pretty stressful."

Visit Vault at **www.vault.com** for insider company profiles, expert advice, career message boards, expert resume reviews, the Vault Job Board and more.

VAULT CAREER LIBRARY **89**

Public vs. Private Accounting

While there are many ways to classify accountants, the most common division is between public and private accountants. Public accountants mainly deal with financial accounting (the preparation of financial statements for external parties such as investors). Private accountants deal with both financial and management accounting.

Public accountants

Public accountants are paid a fee for services provided to individuals, businesses and governments. Public accounting firms vary greatly in size and the type of services provided. Most public accounting firms provide some combination of auditing, tax and management consulting services. Small firms mainly provide tax or bookkeeping services for smaller companies and organizations that do not have internal accounting departments. Larger firms usually provide these services to firms that have internal accounting departments. Because all public companies are required to have yearly audits, the large public accounting firms are extremely important for fulfilling this requirement.

The four largest accounting firms are known as the "Big Four," and are among the most well-known organizations throughout the world. (Previously, it was the Big Eight, which became the Big Six and then the Big Five when PriceWaterhouse and Coopers & Lybrand merged to form PricewaterhouseCoopers. Because of the collapse of Arthur Andersen, we're now down to the Big Four.) The Big Four includes:

- Deloitte & Touche
- Ernst & Young
- KPMG
- PricewaterhouseCoopers

Many students pursuing accounting careers aim to start their careers at one of the Big Four firms. These firms have offices throughout the United States, as well as in many other countries, and recruit at a majority of the top schools throughout the world.

In addition to the Big Four, there are thousands of other accounting firms ranging from small proprietorships to large international partnerships. The difference between these firms and the Big Four is size, often measured in terms of billings. The Big Four have billings in excess of $1 billion a year. A large majority (97 percent) of companies listed on the New York Stock Exchange are clients of the Big Four.

Regional accounting firms represent clients that do most of their business within the U.S., although they may also have a few international clients. The largest regional firms can be thought of as somewhat smaller versions of the Big Four. And as the category name suggests, these practices tend to be stronger in certain regions. If you're considering working for a regional public accounting firm, be sure to research the quality of the firm's practice in your area. Vault publishes the *Vault Guide to the Top Accounting Firms*, which provides detailed insider information on the largest regional firms.

Local accounting firms operate in a small number of cities and tend to focus on small businesses and individuals. These organizations conduct more tax and tax planning engagements, and traditionally handle more of the bookkeeping responsibilities for their clients.

While most people start their careers at a public accounting firm, many gain valuable experience in public accounting and switch to the private sector after two years (or however long it takes them to get certified as a CPA). Accountants with public accounting experience are well positioned to take financial officer roles at corporations, government agencies or non-profits.

Private accountants

Private accountants work for businesses, the government or nonprofit agencies.

Corporations—Most corporations have an internal accounting group that prepares the financial information (both tax and audit) for the public accountants, tracks company performance for internal evaluation and works with management on issues related to acquisitions, international transactions and any other operational issues that arise in the running of the company. Within corporations, there are several roles that an accountant can take on:

- Internal auditors perform financial accounting tasks within an organization. Typically, these employees will perform audits of specific divisions or operational units of a company.

- Management accountants can work in several different areas of a corporation. On the finance side, accountants can work in the financial planning and analysis or treasurer's group, analyzing potential acquisitions and making funding decisions for the company. On the accounting side, there are opportunities within the accounting group to handle tax issues and to work with external auditors to prepare financial statements such as SEC filings. Additionally, on the accounting side, opportunities exist to work within specific divisions to track costs and analyze operational performance.

Government agencies—Government accountants can work at the federal, state or local level. Many government organizations have large accounting departments to analyze the performance and allocation of their funds. The Department of Defense (DOD), the General Accounting Office (GAO), the Internal Revenue Service (IRS) and the Securities and Exchange Commission (SEC) typically hire large numbers of accountants for services and evaluations within the organization. Accountants at the IRS typically review individual and corporate tax returns. The SEC hires experienced accountants to evaluate filings made by public companies. These accountants ensure that firms are complying with SEC regulations.

Nonprofit organizations—Accounting for nonprofits is very similar to for-profit accounting; they both follow Generally Accepted Accounting Principles (GAAP). In addition to understanding GAAP, nonprofit accountants must also understand the FASB standards written specifically for these organizations as well as the tax regulations also specific to those organizations. (For example, nonprofit organizations are typically exempt from federal taxation.)

The accounting groups in these organizations are typically smaller than those in for-profit companies, so an employee may be responsible for more than one area of accounting (e.g., both financial statements and tax issues).

Public or private?

According to many college professors and career services counselors, most college students interested in accounting should try to start their careers in public accounting. This route carries a number of benefits, including higher salaries, more interesting and diverse work, exposure to many different industries and the ability to fulfill a requirement for certification.

One senior manager at a Big Four firm captures the general opinion of the majority of people we spoke with: "For someone just out of college, public accounting is really the only way to go," he says. "You gain experience and get up the learning curve much more quickly. A public accountant will perform three or four audits of entire companies in a year, whereas a private accountant could be stuck monitoring cash ledgers—one account—for a year. Even in the long term, there are benefits. You have more control over your career progression. In private, you'll often see highly productive and talented individuals mired in their jobs or limited to lateral career moves because they have to wait for the people above them to retire or otherwise leave the company. Public accounting is much more of a meritocracy—you'll advance as fast and as high as you want to."

However, public accounting life is not for everyone. Private accountants generally don't travel nearly as much as public accountants, and their work schedules are much more stable—they rarely have to pack a briefcase and go to a client at a

Visit Vault at **www.vault.com** for insider company profiles, expert advice, career message boards, expert resume reviews, the Vault Job Board and more.

VAULT CAREER LIBRARY

91

moment's notice. Private accountants also do not have to deal with the chargeability issue (the pressure on public accountants to work on billable projects as much of the time as possible). Finally, they are not required to get their CPA and thus do not have to deal with the rigors of fulfilling the grueling certification requirements.

The CPA

Becoming a CPA is no easy task. It demands a higher education commitment than most other career paths. To qualify for certification, you must meet the requirements of the state or jurisdiction where you wish to practice. The state requirements are established by the state board of accountancy and vary from state to state. Because of these variations, first determine where you are planning to practice accounting and then review that state's certification requirements on the web site for the state's CPA society or board of accountancy.

Becoming a certified public accountant entails the successful completion of: (a) 150 credit hours of college-level education, which translates to five years of college and graduate level work; (b) getting passing grades on all four parts of the Uniform Certified Public Accountants Exam (the CPA exam); and (c) the requisite amount of accounting work experience as mandated by each state, often two years or so.

What you can do without becoming a CPA

You most certainly can perform accounting functions without being certified, and there are many successful people in the profession who have taken this route. Non-certified accountants are not required to fulfill the five-year requirement; they aren't even required to have a degree in accounting (although, obviously, it helps). A traditional four-year degree is all that is necessary to be a non-certified accountant. The actual functions of an accountant are not, as the saying goes, rocket science, and complicated mathematics is rarely needed; thus, advanced certification might not seem necessary. Internal auditors, management accountants and tax personnel may all practice their professions without the CPA or any other professional designation.

Furthermore, many accounting professionals (CPAs and otherwise) contend that the CPA exam is nothing more than a rite of passage, an intense exercise in memorization that adds little actual value to your technical development as an accountant. These people generally feel that all of the information you crammed into your brain disappears once the exam is over. Many of them even said that this "brain drain" should happen since much of this information will never be seen in your actual practice; if you ever do need it, you can quickly look it up.

What you can't do

However, not being certified has a few significant drawbacks. Foremost among these is that it can be career limiting—most public accounting firms will not promote an auditor above a certain level (senior associate; these levels are discussed later in this guide) without at least passing the exam.

There are a couple of important reasons for this. First, only a CPA may sign an audit opinion. This signature is crucial, as it signifies that the auditor believes that the financial statements reasonably represent the company's actual financial position, giving the users of these statements more confidence that they can rely on them to make their decisions. Thus, an auditor without a CPA can not perform one of the most important activities of the profession.

Furthermore, a failure to pursue certification is often interpreted by public accounting firms as a lack of commitment to the profession, and few firms are willing to invest resources in someone who might leave the profession altogether (especially when there are so many others out there who are willing to pursue certification).

Another downside of not having a CPA is that you would miss out on the credibility that the certification carries. As with other advanced professional certifications, the CPA tends to give the stamp of "expert" in the eyes of the public and thus more perceived confidence in the accountant's abilities. Such credibility could mean the difference to a recruiter who's deciding between two otherwise comparable job candidates.

One final, ever-so-important downside of not having a CPA: you'll make less money. According to the staffing agency Robert Half International, the CPA can, on average, increase a candidate's base salary by 10 percent, with specialized fields (such as forensic accounting) commanding even higher salaries.

Now, this is not meant to scare you into pursuing the CPA, nor is it meant to suggest that you are a slacker if you don't pursue the CPA. You can still have a successful career in accounting without it. For example, public tax accountants generally do not sign off on audit opinions, and tax returns generally do not require the signature of a CPA. However, pursuing the CPA opens you up to many more opportunities and can only help a career in accounting. Thus, plans for certification should be seriously considered by anyone looking to break into the accounting field.

Visit Vault at **www.vault.com** for insider company profiles, expert advice,
career message boards, expert resume reviews, the Vault Job Board and more.

V∆ULT CAREER LIBRARY   **93**

Accounting Employer Directory

BDO Seidman, LLP

130 E. Randolph
Suite 2800
Chicago, IL 60601

Recruiting Contact:
Phone: (312) 240-1236
Please see www.bdo.com/careers to submit a resume or to contact BDO Seidman.

BDO Seidman, LLP
Accountants and Consultants

Undergraduate schools BDO recruits from:
BDO Seidman actively recruits on campuses nationwide

Explore a path with an established and growing organization.

BDO Seidman provides assurance, tax, financial advisory and consulting services to a wide range of publicly traded and privately held companies. Guided by core values of integrity, trust, professionalism, independence and service for almost 100 years, BDO Seidman is a firm for energetic self-starters who want to make an impact early in their careers.

Serving clients through 34 offices and more than 300 independent alliance firm locations nationwide, BDO Seidman is also an independent member firm of BDO International, the 5th largest accounting and consulting organization in the world.

Amper Politziner & Mattia

2015 Lincoln Highway
P.O. Box 988
Edison, NJ 08818
Phone: (732) 287-1000
Fax: (732) 287-3200
www.amper.com

Anchin, Block & Anchin

1375 Broadway
New York, NY 10018
Phone: (212) 840-3456
Fax: (212) 840-7066
www.anchin.com

Berdon LLP

360 Madison Avenue
New York, NY 10017
Phone: (212) 832-0400
Fax: (212) 371-1159
www.berdonllp.com

bmc

2609 Keiser Blvd.
Wyomissing, PA 19610
Phone: (610) 927-4910
Fax: (610) 927-9809
www.bmcvision.com

BKD LLP

Hammons Tower
901 E. St. Louis Street, Suite 1800
P.O. Box 1900
Springfield, MO 65801-1900
Phone: (417) 831-7283
Fax: (417) 831-4763
www.bkd.com

Cherry, Bekaert & Holland LLP

1700 Bayberry Court
Suite 300
Richmond, VA 23226-3791
Phone: (804) 673-4224
Fax: (804) 673-5799
www.cbh.com

Citrin Cooperman & Company, LLP

529 Fifth Avenue, 2nd Fl.
New York, NY 10017
Phone: (212) 697-1000
Fax: (212) 697-1004
www.citrincooperman.com

Clifton Gunderson LLP

301 SW Adams Street
Suite 600
Peoria, Illinois 61602
Phone: (309) 671-4560
Fax: (309) 671-4576
www.cliftoncpa.com

Crowe Chizek and Co. LLC

330 East Jefferson Boulevard
South Bend, IN 46601
Phone: (574) 232-3992
Fax: (574) 236-8692
www.crowechizek.com

Deloitte & Touche USA LLP and its subsidiaries

1633 Broadway
New York, NY 10019
Phone: (212) 489-1600
Fax: (212) 489-1687
www.deloitte.com

Accounting Employer Directory, cont.

Dixon Hughes PLLC
1829 Eastchester Dr.
High Point, NC 27261-2612
Phone: (336) 889-6168
Fax: (336) 889-2812
www.dixon-hughes.com

Eide Bailly LLP
3203 32nd Avenue, SW
Fargo, ND 58103
Phone: (701) 239-8500
Fax: (701) 239-8611
www.eidebailly.com

Eisner LLP
750 Third Avenue
New York, NY 10017
Phone: (212) 949-8700
100 Campus Drive
Florham Park, NJ 07932
Phone: (973) 593-7000
www.eisnerllp.com

Elliott Davis, LLC
200 E. Broad Street
PO Box 6286
Greenville, SC 29606
Phone: (864) 242-3370
Fax: (864) 232-7161
www.elliottdavis.com

Ernst & Young LLP
5 Times Square
New York, NY 10036-6530
Phone: (212) 773-3000
Fax: (212) 773-6350
www.ey.com

Frank, Rimerman + Co. LLP
60 South Market Street, Suite 500
San Jose, California 95113
Phone: (408) 279-5566
Fax : (408) 279-8284
www.frankrimerman.com

Friedman LLP
1700 Broadway
New York, NY 10019
Phone: (212) 842-7000
Fax: (212) 842-7001
www.friedmanllp.com

Goodman & Co.
One Commercial Place
Norfolk, VA 23510-2119
Phone: (757) 624-5100
Fax: (757) 624-5233
www.goodmanco.com

Grant Thornton LLP
175 West Jackson Boulevard
20th Floor
Chicago, IL 60604
Phone: (312) 856-0200
Fax: (312) 602-8099
www.grantthornton.com

J.H. Cohn LLP
4 Becker Farm Road
Roseland, NJ 07068
Phone: (973) 228-3500
Fax: (973) 631-6221
www.jhcohn.com

Kennedy and Coe, LLC
3030 Cortland
P.O. Box 1100
Salina, KS 67402
Phone: (785) 825-1561
Fax: (785) 825-5371
www.kcoe.com

KPMG LLP
345 Park Ave.
New York, NY 10154-0102
Phone: (212) 758-0700
Fax: (212) 758-9819
www.us.kpmg.com

Larson, Allen, Weishar & Co., LLP
220 South Sixth Street
Suite 300
Minneapolis, MN 55402-1436
Phone: (612) 376-4500
Fax: (612) 376-4850
www.larsonallen.com

Mahoney Cohen & Company, CPA, P.C.
1065 Ave. of the Americas
New York, NY 10018
Phone: (212) 790-5700
Fax: (212) 398-0267
www.mahoneycohen.com

Marcum & Kliegman LLP
10 Melville Park Road
Melville, NY 11747
Phone: (631) 414-4000
Fax: (631) 414-4001
www.mkllp.com

McGladrey & Pullen LLP
3600 American Blvd. West
Third Floor
Bloomington, MN 55431-1082
Phone: (952) 835-9930
Fax: (952) 921-7702
www.mcgladrey.com

Moss Adams LLP
1001 Fourth Avenue
31st Floor
Seattle, WA 98154-1199
Phone: (206) 223-1820
Fax: (206) 652-2098
www.mossadams.com

Parente Randolph LLC
Two Penn Center Plaza
Suite 1800
Philadelphia, PA 19102-1725
Phone: (215) 972-0701
Fax: (215) 563-4925
www.parentenet.com

Visit Vault at **www.vault.com** for insider company profiles, expert advice,
career message boards, expert resume reviews, the Vault Job Board and more.

VAULT CAREER LIBRARY   **95**

Accounting Employer Directory, cont.

Plante & Moran PLLC
27400 Northwestern Highway
Southfield, MI 48034
Phone: (248) 352-2500
Fax: (248) 352-0018
www.plantemoran.com

PricewaterhouseCoopers LLP
300 Madison Avenue
New York, NY 10017
Phone: (646) 471-3000
Fax: (813) 286-6000
www.pwc.com/us

Rachlin Cohen & Holtz, LLP
Suntrust International Center
One SE Third Ave, Tenth Floor
Miami, FL 33131
Phone: (305) 377-4228
Fax: (305) 377-8331
www.rachlin.com

Rehmann Group, The
5800 Gratiot Rd. Suite 201
Saginaw, MI 48603
Phone: (989) 799-9580
Fax: (989) 799-0227
www.rehmann.com

Reznick Group
7700 Old Georgetown Road
Suite 400
Bethesda, MD 20814
Phone: (301) 652-9100
Fax: (301) 652-1848
www.reznickgroup.com

Rothstein Kass
4 Becker Farm Road
Roseland, NJ 07068
Phone: (973) 994-6666
Fax: (973) 994-0337
www.rkco.com

Virchow, Krause & Co.
10 Terrace Court
Madison, WI 53718
Phone: (608) 249-6622
www.virchowkrause.com

Vitale Caturano & Company
80 City Square
Boston, MA 02129
Phone: (617) 912-9000
Fax: (617) 912-9001
www.vitale.com

Weiser LLP
135 West 50th Street
New York, NY 10020
Phone: (212) 812-7000
Fax: (212) 375-6888
www.weiserllp.com

Wipfli LLP
11 Scott Street
Wausau, WI 54403
Phone: (715) 845-3111
Fax: (715) 842-7272
www.wipfli.com

WithumSmith+Brown
5 Vaughn Drive
Princeton, NJ 08540
Phone: (609) 520-1188
Fax: (609) 520-9882
www.withum.com

Advertising

An Introduction to Advertising

The concept of advertising existed long before we had a term for it. In 981A.D., the great Viking explorer Eric the Red left Norway to survey an island west of Iceland. Except for the southern coast this new land was little more than a gigantic iceberg. But Eric was a natural at advertising. To persuade immigrants to leave Norway and settle the island, he painted a picture of temperate climate, rolling meadows and lush farmland. To top it all off, he named it Greenland. Eric created a brand. Hundreds of land-starved Vikings boarded longships and headed west for this so-called "greenland."

Advertising is defined as the art of positioning and creating brands and persuading consumers to buy them through messages in mass media. The clothes you wear, the cars you drive, the food you eat and the soft drinks you consume are all brands.

Advertising is a creative and inclusive field unique in the business world. "Advertising agencies are idea stores, and just about everyone gets in on the act," says Chuck Bachrach, media director of the Los Angeles-based full-service advertising agency Rubin Postaer and Associates. "If you have a fire in your belly and want to work with smart, creative, fun people in a business that's virtually blind to race and gender, there's no business quite as satisfying."

Branding

David Ogilvy, founder of Ogilvy & Mather, knew something about brands, having created icons like The American Express Card and Rolls Royce. He defined a brand as: "The intangible sum of a product's attributes: its name, packaging and price, its history, its reputation and the way it's advertised." The best way to understand a brand is to think of it as a friend. We choose brands in exactly the same way we choose friends. Brands are friends; products are strangers. Branding is an emotional process of involvement.

At its most basic level advertising, like friendship, is a three-stage process—awareness, trial and repeat. In the first stage, awareness, you hear about a brand. In the second stage, trial, you're persuaded to buy it and try it. If you like it, you buy it again and again. You're a repeat customer. Along the way, you find that you and the brand share the same values. You wouldn't think about using anything else.

A brand is an image, a conception in consumers' minds. Implicit within the image is a unique promise of value and trust that distinguishes it from its competitors. The job of an advertising agency is to use every tool at its disposal to clothe the brand with substance and endow it with personality—to make it a trusted friend.

Media Options

Once an advertising campaign is constructed, it needs to be, well, advertised. Here are the primary conduits for advertising.

Television

Network television: A network is any group of local television stations electronically joined to broadcast the same program at the same time. Network TV is essential for advertising national brands and reaches an audience of 99 percent of U.S. TV households. It offers advertisers a large choice of programs, each with their own demographics, ranging from Saturday morning children's shows to news and sports, to soap operas and prime time shows.

Spot television: Spot television is the purchase of advertising time on a market-by-market basis. Perhaps a brand has only recently entered a new geographic market and needs an advertising branding push only in that location. Or maybe the brand is only available or distributed in a select number of markets (e.g., In-n-out Burgers, a fast-food chain, is only located in

Visit Vault at **www.vault.com** for insider company profiles, expert advice, career message boards, expert resume reviews, the Vault Job Board and more.

VAULT CAREER LIBRARY

97

California, Nevada and Arizona). In such cases, spot television makes sense. Additionally, buys can incorporate specific market characteristics. For example, viewing levels increase in cold weather markets during the winter, as Northerners cuddle in front of the cozy electronic hearth that is the television set.

Cable television: Introduced in 1960 to improve reception in remote areas, cable television now rivals the networks for audience. According to a lead researcher at Viacom, almost 84 percent of all television homes receive cable—that's 91 million homes! Cable TV provides advertisers with fairly precise demographic, psychographic and geographic targeting, and a more affluent audience than broadcast television because it only exists in households that can afford it. (Demographics are a basic, objective descriptive classification of consumers, such as their age, sex, income, education, size of household, ownership of home and so on.) Most cable TV channels are programmed for narrowcasting—attracting a specific demographic or interest. ESPN is all sports all the time. Animal Planet is designed for animal lovers. AMC aims for aficionados of old movies. If there's an interest with a sufficient audience, you can bet there is or will be a cable channel devoted to it, and advertisers wanting to reach that audience. Cable programs don't attract as many viewers, but wasted audience—those who fall outside of the demographic or interest group—is minimal.

Print advertising

There are three types of print advertising media—consumer magazines, trade magazines, and national and local newspapers.

Magazines have a great deal to offer advertisers, with ads that have a long shelf life. Unlike TV viewers, readers take their time with a magazine. They refer back to it from time to time, increasing ad exposure opportunities, and they can, and often do, pass magazines on to friends and relatives.

Consumer magazines: In these publications, the editorial content appeals to the general public or a specific segment of the public. Educated and affluent consumers tend to be heavy magazine readers and light TV viewers. Consumer magazines offer audience selectivity. They can deliver a defined segment with a minimum of "wasted" (nontargeted) delivery. There are entire magazines devoted to particular subjects (e.g., *Road & Track*, *Golf Digest*, and so on). Magazines also sometimes offer regular features devoted to particular subjects that interest advertisers. For example, *The New Yorker* may offer an issue with a special travel section. Airlines, car rental companies and hotel advertisers in the featured area use the issue to target consumers.

There is an adage in the advertising industry: "The more you tell, the more you sell." Magazines offer room for long, detailed copy and are the perfect environments for products, like drugs or electronic devices, that require extended explanations.

Trade magazines: Aimed at professionals in a particular industry, these magazines are typically not sold on mainstream newsstands, though there are exceptions, such as *Variety* (for media industry insiders).

Newspapers: People get involved with what affects them personally—in their neighborhoods, at their workplace—and newspapers give them that local information more than any other media vehicle. Smart media buyers leverage these opportunities. Sections like these are replete with ads. Typical newspaper readers are college-educated, in their mid-forties and a very attractive audience to automotive, electronics and travel advertisers. National newspapers like *The Wall Street Journal* and *USA Today*, and local papers like the *San Francisco Chronicle* or *The Washington Post*, offer a variety of advantages to advertisers. Newspapers are a perfect medium for limited time offers and new product announcements. They underscore the axiom that all advertising is local. Research shows that an ad in the *Charlotte Observer* that mentions Charlotte in the headline will attract more attention than an otherwise identical ad that omits the name of the city in the headline. And, just as in magazines, there is plenty of room for long, detailed copy required for technically oriented brands, like high performance automobiles.

Radio

Radio can be a useful part of a media plan. Like television, radio (AM & FM) is divided into network and spot (local). And like cable TV, it's narrowcasted—it offers stations that play music in virtually every flavor, talk shows, sports programs and news channels. But unlike its broadcast sibling, radio only offers sound, so you can't see the product. In addition, consumers often listen to the radio when they are driving or away from their homes, so they may not absorb the information as readily.

But radio also is much less expensive than TV. Its single dimension—sound—forces copywriters to stimulate the listener's imagination. The average radio station plays up to twenty radio commercials in an hour. In order to break through the "wallpaper" of background noise, intrusive delivery is everything. Music, pacing, humor, audio mnemonic devices—the Green Giant's "Ho, ho, ho," for example—are employed to capture the listener's attention. Some advertisers even use the weather to their advantage. Coca-Cola and other soft drink marketers have issued standing orders for commercials to be played when the temperature reaches 90 degrees. In a media plan, radio ads can target audiences at a relatively low cost. It's also a good way to "surround" consumers with a brand; not as effective by itself, but useful as a way to increase brand recognition and affection.

Out-of-Home

Out-of-home advertising ranges from billboards to bus signs to kiosks to spectacular signs in Times Square. It's used not to build but to reinforce an ad campaign. Only one copy point, or benefit, can be registered.

Major Career Paths in Advertising

Account services

Account services professionals manage the relationship between the agency and the client. They are the first line of contact with the client—and the first line of defense. Essentially, they are the project managers for advertising client accounts.

The account services hierarchy ranges from account coordinator at the entry level, to account directors (also called management supervisors) who oversee one or more client relationships in their entirety. Account services people are marketing and communications consultants; they must know as much about the brand as the client, and more about how to advertise it.

Successful account services pros must be all of the following.

- **Integrators.** Account people craft the communications marketing plan and insure that all of the agency's resources are working together to make the plan a reality.

- **Organized.** Account services professionals are detail-oriented, and masters of multitasking and following up. They are keepers of the overall timetable for ad production, placement and communication.

- **Generalists.** They must have a working knowledge of every agency discipline ranging from evaluating copy and art to media and production.

- **Advocates.** They are the client's advocate within the agency, and the agency's advocate to the client. Diplomacy and eloquence are key.

- **Students and lovers of advertising.** They must immerse themselves in advertising and marketing and learn the lessons of past and current successes and failures.

Visit Vault at www.vault.com for insider company profiles, expert advice, career message boards, expert resume reviews, the Vault Job Board and more.

V∧ULT CAREER LIBRARY   99

- **Cheerleaders.** As leaders of the team, account people must be superb "people" people, exhibiting grace under pressure. "When everyone's walking around moping because the client hates the new campaign, or there's been a screw up somewhere, it's my job to get everyone back on track. In account services, the glass is always half full," an account supervisor at a large agency notes (cheerfully).

Media services

Broadly, media services is responsible for the planning and buying of print, broadcast, out-of-home (billboards) and interactive media in the most effective and efficient way possible. Media planners are the strategists—they determine when and where it's most advantageous to buy advertising space for any given campaign. Buyers actually negotiate for, and purchase, the media space.

But that's hardly the whole story. These media specialists are also key members of the advertising branding team. They must find environments that extend and reinforce the brand image of their clients—and buy space for advertising those brands. Armed with consumer research, both proprietary and purchased, media professionals not only know the target audience's media habits—the programs they watch and listen to, the magazines and newspapers they read—they also know what influences consumers to make purchasing decisions. Purchase decision influencers are people who have a lot of influence over the purchase but aren't the "target market." For example, while men may purchase suits, women have significant influence over which suits their male partners and companions buy.

The result of the media specialists' research and work is the media plan for the advertising campaign. Major media outlets will then compete to get on the plan (that is, to secure a portion of the client's ad budget for their magazine or television network or newspaper). The plan itself contains recommendations on where the client should spend their media budget to achieve the campaign's goals in the most efficient way. The plan outlines how many people the media recommendation reaches, how many times the commercial or print ad will run, and the total audience impressions the plan will attract.

Once the plan is approved, media vehicles like television stations, newspapers and magazines that weren't included in the plan fight to get included. So, in the midst of a buy, buyers not only have to contend with the job of purchasing media, they also have to entertain presentations from disappointed media sales reps. Media buyers, especially, frequently socialize with sales representatives from media organizations on a regular basis.

Creative services

Many people outside of the industry view creative as the "romantic" part of the business. Romantic and exciting though it may seem, copywriting and art direction is hard work. Creative services jobs are indeed exciting, but failure is easy to come by.

Once the creative strategy is set (by the account services folks) and approved by the client, and once the consumer research has been transformed into a media plan, it's time for the Big Idea—a creative translation of the strategy into a compelling and persuasive ad. And there is nothing more difficult than facing a hard deadline and sitting at a desk, well into the night, staring at a blank sheet of paper, in an office littered with balled up sheets of paper, while thinking, "Lord, send me an idea!"

Copywriters, who write the copy (words, script, whatever) and art directors, who visually design the ads, work as a team. Together, they create ads, not only for the current campaigns but for "back up"—campaigns that are continually tested in the event that the current advertising loses its effectiveness, or "wears out"—campaigns as well.

The creative process, for new ads, is initiated by the client. Let's say the client calls the account executive and requests a four-color ad for *Modern Maturity* magazine. The account executive writes a creative strategy statement for the ad (obviously aimed at an older audience) and takes it to the creative supervisor. The creative supervisor assigns the ad to a copywriter and art director team with a due date. Once the ad is completed and approved internally, the copy and layout are presented to the client.

Account planning/research

Account planning, an import from British advertising agencies, is a relatively new discipline in the United States. Most of the larger agencies and many of the smaller ones have embraced it. Account planning uses qualitative research to determine why consumers behave the way they do. Planners function as the voice of the consumer within the agency, and their main goal is to gain a deeper understanding of the way consumers react to their clients' product or service. Planners burrow into the consumer's mind, plumbing for insights about the product, its position and competition, and research is their tool. They live with the brand and its consumers. The insights they gain are considered the target market's psychographics—their attitudes, opinions and values. These consumer psychographics help copywriters and art directors create more effective advertising.

Traffic

Traffic managers are the keepers of the creative process—schedules and approvals reside in their domain. If account services professionals are like the generals, setting and managing the overall strategy, traffickers are the foot soldiers and work with creative, media and the account group to insure that all deadlines are met. Print publications and broadcast stations have unchangeable closing dates. In addition, it's traffic's responsibility to see that the ads are approved at every stage of their development and forwarded to the media on time. Successful traffic managers are organized, detail-oriented and able to work under pressure. It is a difficult, highly stressful job.

Production

There are two types of production specialists at advertising agencies—print and broadcast. Print production specialists are schooled in every aspect of the print production process and are experts at making ads look great in magazines, newspapers and out-of-home venues. Most print production advertising professionals are hired from printing companies and other graphic design outlets.

Broadcast producers are in charge of the actual production of TV and radio commercials. They work closely with the creative

Visit Vault at **www.vault.com** for insider company profiles, expert advice, career message boards, expert resume reviews, the Vault Job Board and more.

VAULT CAREER LIBRARY   101

Advertising Employer Directory

24/7 Real Media, Inc.
132 West 31st Street, Floor 9
New York, NY 10001
Phone: (212) 231-7100
Fax: (212) 760-1774
www.247realmedia.com

BBDO Worldwide Inc.
1285 Avenue of the Americas
New York, NY 10019
Phone: (212) 459-5000
Fax: (212) 459-6645
www.bbdo.com

Burrell Communications Group
233 N. Michigan Avenue
Chicago, IL 60602
Phone: (312) 297-9600
Fax: (312) 297-9601
www.burrell.com

DDB Worldwide Communications Group Inc.
437 Madison Avenue
New York, NY 10022
Phone: (212) 415-2000
Fax: (212) 415-3414
www.ddb.com

Dentsu Inc.
1-8-1, Higashi-shimbashi, Minato-ku
Tokyo, 105-7001, Japan
Phone: +81-3-6216-5111
www.dentsu.com

DoubleClick Inc.
111 8th Avenue, 10th Floor
New York, NY 10011
Phone: (212) 683-0001
Fax: (212) 287-1203
www.doubleclick.com

Euro RSCG Worldwide Inc.
350 Hudson Street
New York, NY 10014
Phone: (212) 886-2000
Fax: (212) 886-2016
www.eurorscg.com

Fallon Worldwide
50 S. Sixth Street
Minneapolis, MN 55402
Phone: (612) 758-2345
Fax: (612) 758-2346
www.fallon.com

Foote Cone & Belding Worldwide
100 W. 33rd Steet
New York, NY 10001
Phone: (212) 885-3000
Fax: (212) 885-2803
www.fcb.com

Goodby, Silverstein & Partners
720 California Street
San Francisco, CA 94108
Phone: (415) 392-0669
Fax: (415) 788-4303
www.goodbysilverstein.com

Grey Global Group
777 Third Avenue
New York, NY 10017
Phone: (212) 546-2000
Fax: (212) 546-1495
www.greyglobalgroup.com

Harte-Hanks, Inc.
200 Concord Plaza Drive
San Antonio, TX 78216
Phone: (210) 829-9000
Fax: (210) 829-9403
www.harte-hanks.com

Interpublic Group of Companies, The
1114 Avenue of the Americas
New York, NY 10036
Phone: (212) 704-1200
Fax: (212) 704-1201
www.interpublic.com

JWT
466 Lexington Avenue
New York, NY 10017-3176
Phone: (212) 210-7000
Fax: (212) 210-7299
www.jwt.com

Leo Burnett Worldwide
35 W. Wacker Drive
Chicago, IL 60601
Phone: (312) 220-5959
Fax: (312) 220-3299
www.leoburnett.com

McCann Worldgroup
622 3rd Avenue
New York, NY 10017
Phone: (646) 865-2000
Fax: (646) 487-9610
www.mccann.com

Ogilvy & Mather Worldwide
309 West 49th Street
New York, NY 10019
Phone: (212) 237-4000
Fax: (212) 237-5123
www.ogilvy.com

Publicis & Hal Riney
2001 The Embarcadero
San Francisco, CA 94133
Phone: (415) 293-2001
Fax: (415) 293-2619
www.hrp.com

Saatchi & Saatchi Worldwide
375 Hudson Street
New York, NY 10014-3620
Phone: (212) 463-2000
Fax: (212) 463-9855
www.saatchi.com

TBWA Worldwide
488 Madison Avenue
New York, NY 10022
Phone: (212) 804-1300
Fax: (212) 804-1200
www.tbwa.com

Young & Rubicam Inc.
285 Madison Avenue
New York, NY 10017
Phone: (212) 210-3000
Fax: (212) 210-4680
www.yr.com

Aerospace & Defense

Aerospace and Defense Industry Overview

Smart segment

The aerospace industry consists of companies which produce aircraft, missiles, satellites and propulsion systems, as well as the firms which maintain and develop these products. Aerospace and defense are closely allied, with the same companies frequently serving both civilian and military markets. The majority of civil aerospace ventures are related to the manufacture of planes for the transport of goods or passengers, while defense uses planes for combat, transport and reconnaissance. Satellite construction and maintenance also forms a growing part of this industry because of their applications in the areas of communications, entertainment, research and global positioning systems (GPS). According to the Bureau of Labor Statistics (BLS) there were some 2,800 companies doing business in aerospace and defense in 2004 (the latest year for which data was available).

We have liftoff

The aerospace industry took off (pun intended) following the Wright brothers' first successful flight in 1905. As with many new technologies, airplanes were first used extensively in a war—namely, World War I, for reconnaissance, bombing and aerial combat. Following the war, when the U.S. found itself with a surplus of military aircraft and pilots with not much to do, the postal service opted in 1918 to use them to start a transcontinental air mail service, which ran from New York to San Francisco. To keep costs down, 12 spur routes were spun off to independent contractors—thus were the familiar friendly sky-flying companies of American Airlines, United Airlines, TWA and Northwest born.

Passenger flights did not become a reality until Ford introduced a 12-seat plane, which made carrying people potentially profitable. Pan American Airways, the first airline with international destinations, was founded in 1927, with other airlines adding international routes in the 1940s. Remarkably, airlines remained generally profitable during the Great Depression. Following this period, World War II brought many advances to the civilian air transport sector. Innovations initially intended for bombers made passenger planes larger, faster, able to carry heavier payloads and to fly at higher altitudes. The 1970s saw the introduction of supersonic air travel with the advent of the Concorde—which is now defunct.

Looking up

The civil aviation sector suffered a severe economic blow following the attacks of September 11, in the form of a forced grounding of planes immediately after the attacks, as well as the rapid institution of stringent airport security measures—all of which led to a sharp decline in orders for new planes after 2001. The following year, the top 10 commercial airlines, the biggest customers for these aircraft when business is good, lost more than $12 billion, with key players like United Airlines' parent company UAL and US Airways filing for bankruptcy. Employment in the industry hit a 50-year low in 2004. But by the end of that year, aerospace sales, orders, exports and employment had all experienced a significant uptick. The number of U.S. commercial jetliners delivered increased for the first time in two years, while civil aircraft sector revenue increased to $35 billion. According to the Aerospace Industries Association (AIA), this favorable trend continued in 2005 with increases across all sectors of the industry—sales, for one, were up 9.2 percent. The body's 2006 predictions are similarly rosy.

Visit Vault at **www.vault.com** for insider company profiles, expert advice, career message boards, expert resume reviews, the Vault Job Board and more.

VAULT CAREER LIBRARY   103

Plane dealing

The bulk of the aerospace industry is taken up by firms producing civil aircraft for commercial airlines and cargo transportation, as well as those for general aviation, like leisure planes, helicopters and corporate jets. But the lucrative nature of defense contracts shouldn't be underestimated: the U.S. government is planning to spend a whopping $439 billion on defense in 2007. Boeing, with its wealth of (sometimes controversial) defense contracts in addition to its commercial airplane business, dominates the aerospace and defense industry as a whole, closely followed, ranked according to sales, by EU firm EADS, which owns bitter Boeing rival Airbus; defense contract leader Lockheed Martin; and ship- and submarine-builder Northrop Grumman. Other major players are Raytheon, Textron, United Technologies and Embraer, while leading jet engine manufacturers include GE Aircraft Engines, Pratt & Whitney and Rolls-Royce.

De-FENSE!

In the area of companies that specialize in fulfilling defense contracts, Lockheed Martin and Northrop Grumman lead the pack, followed by Boeing, Raytheon, and BAE Systems. European companies are not far behind, though. With U.S. companies increasing spending and reeling in contracts, transatlantic rivals have no choice but to step up efforts to compete, and are slowly building up market share in America. EADS, for example, the EU's biggest defense and aerospace company, announced in 2006 that it will build UH-145 helicopters for use by the U.S. Army, Coast Guard and Department of Homeland Security. Back at home, Lockheed Martin maintains a healthy dominance in the sector thanks in part to its score of one of the richest defense deals in history, when in 2001 it beat out Boeing for a fighter jet contract worth $200 billion. Other major players on the international end include British Aerospace and Marconi Electric Systems (BAES), which picked up U.S.-based United Defense Industries for $4.1 billion in March 2005, and Italy's Finmeccanica. EADS has also established several partnerships recently with Northrop Grumman and Lockheed Martin.

The defense portion of the industry has been affected not only by the war on terror and mega mergers, but also by a shift in the way warfare is practiced. Since the Cold War, modi operandi among Pentagon types have shifted from "shock and awe"—never mind the start of the most recent war in Iraq—to a focus on equipment that's smarter, leaner and more mobile.

In order to keep on the bleeding edge of warfare technologies, the aerospace and defense industry spent about $38 billion on R&D in 2005. Developments in the industry include General Atomics' unmanned Predator drones, which saw success in Afghanistan. Unmanned jets and other computer-guided equipment are seen as preferable to traditional manned craft, as they are less costly to operate and pose less risk (obviously) to military personnel in combat. Other buzz on the industry's war front concerns "network-centric warfare," an area toward which the top defense contractors have shifted resources in recent years. In this approach, computers, satellites and sensors are all integrated so that soldiers and their planes, tanks and other equipment receive a constant stream of precise, real-time information about what's happening on the front lines.

Securing the homeland

Another major shift in the defense industry since 2001 is the growth of companies focusing on domestic (aka "homeland") security. This sector includes everything from audio and video surveillance equipment to disease and bioterrorism identification and secure communications equipment. In May 2006, the Bush administration announced an open-ended $2 billion contract for the design and implementation of devices for the Secure Border initiative, the latest version of a plan to patrol U.S. borders. Similar, previous attempts at high-tech surveillance have not been unqualified successes. Video cameras, ordered in the 1990s, were never installed or didn't work; ground sensor systems alerted agents to unauthorized intruders such as passing trains and desert animals; and a $6.8 million unmanned aircraft crashed in 2006.

Armies for hire

The Pentagon is increasingly—and controversially—relying on manpower from private military contractors (PMCs) to bolster its missions in Iraq, Afghanistan and elsewhere. These projects can include rebuilding power and sanitation systems and other logistical support, or (more notoriously) conducting interrogations and security operations. While the military outsourced just one percent of its work, mainly for airfield maintenance, during the first Gulf War in the 1990s, contractors are, according to Brookings Institute fellow P.W. Singer, handling as much as 30 percent of the military's services today, including reconstruction, during the ongoing activities in Iraq. These contractors include well-known giants like Halliburton subsidiary KBR (formerly Kellogg, Brown & Root), which has a nearly $4 billion contract for oil field reconstruction and maintenance in Iraq, as well as many smaller firms.

The latter are catching the eye of aerospace and defense giants like Northrop Grumman, which recently acquired the PMC Vinnell. But they are also drawing attention from Congress, the media and the public, who question oversight of these organizations and wonder if the military should be outsourcing so much of its operations to people who, in some cases, are seen as mercenaries.

Spatial relations

The first object launched into space was a German rocket in 1942—though exploration did not begin in earnest until 1957, when Russia's Sputnik become the first manmade object ever to orbit the planet. Yuri Gagarin became the first person in space in 1961, and Neil Armstrong and Buzz Aldrin walked on the moon in 1969. But since then, there has been less interest in the awesome fiscal outlays necessary for manned space missions. NASA's budget was reduced by over half between 1994 and 2006, and the *Columbia* and *Challenger* shuttle disasters did little to recommend the program to public or political favor. Most manned space flights today are for the purposes of launching and repairing satellites and performing experiments. Unmanned exploratory missions, however, have continued, with a robotic probe sent to Mars in 2004.

In the space sector, which is made up of satellite and rocket manufacturing and launch services, familiar names lead the pack, including Boeing, Northrop Grumman and Lockheed Martin, which picked up a hefty NASA contract in June 2005 (capped at $700 million) to develop a satellite designed to collect scientific data on Jupiter and from the solar system as a whole. Major aerospace and defense companies continue to build space activities into their long-term investment plans, even though shooting for the stars won't turn cash flow positive in any time frame outside of a science fiction novel.

Closer to Earth, space pursuits have resulted in the launch of satellites for such useful purposes as GPS devices, communications, weather prediction and research, television and radio. Specialized leaders in this field include Alcatel Space, Astrium, Orbital Sciences and Arianespace, a division of EADS. Government and military demand for satellite bandwidth is expected to quadruple in the next decade—and, as such, the two groups (which can't seem to launch satellites fast enough) have been attaching their tech to civilian birds.

Space cowboys

The star players are keeping an eye on a pack of upstarts in the space race, private companies that rely on individual investors rather than federal dollars. If successful, these private liftoff firms promise to radically alter the space exploration game by stripping it of the costs, bureaucracy and $400 hammers that often accrue around federally funded projects. One major impetus for commercial space ventures was the Ansari X Prize, a $10 million bounty for the first privately-funded, -manned and largely reusable spaceship to reach space twice in two weeks. The prize, modeled after the Orteig Prize, which Lindberg claimed in his transatlantic flight, was won by Scaled Composites' SpaceShipOne in June 2004. To capitalize on the success of these prizes, NASA announced several Centennial Challenges, cash prizes awarded for innovations necessary to make space flight less costly and more feasible.

Visit Vault at **www.vault.com** for insider company profiles, expert advice, career message boards, expert resume reviews, the Vault Job Board and more.

VAULT CAREER LIBRARY   **105**

Later in 2004, an unmanned rocket built by a small California company was set to carry an experimental satellite into orbit for the Defense Department in a project involving no federal dollars. The Bush Administration has come out in favor of increased involvement by such private companies in missions to send people to the moon and, one day, to Mars. In addition to these types of missions, many space visionaries—some of whom formerly headed the dot-com pack back in the Internet boom days—see all sorts of opportunities up beyond the clouds, ranging from tourism to mining for oxygen and precious metals. A few brave entrepreneurs, including Virgin chief Sir Richard Branson, who in 2004 announced a space tourism company called Virgin Galactic, have made inroads into space. Branson's aim is for people to experience short, suborbital trips for around $200,000 per ticket starting in 2008. Currently, space tourism is limited to individuals with exceedingly high net worth, who can afford the tens of millions of dollars necessary to send them beyond the mesosphere.

Fly right

Professionals who work in the aerospace product and parts manufacturing sector, the BLS reports, enjoy earnings that are substantially higher, on average, than those of their counterparts in other manufacturing sectors. Most jobs in the sector are in the areas of skilled production and management. The BLS reports that, in 2004, 62 percent of jobs in aerospace manufacturing were in large establishments employing 1,000 or more workers. In addition, aerospace employment stopped a five-year skid in 2004, as the industry added 18,900 new jobs. Employment numbers, according to the AIA, have been gently increasing since 2004. Women are still scarce in the industry, making up only 11.3 percent of U.S. aerospace engineers in 2004, despite the fact that women earning doctoral degrees in aerospace increased by 150 percent between 1994 and 2001.

Aerospace & Defense Employer Directory

Airbus
1, Rond point Maurice Bellonte
31707 Blagnac Cedex
France
Phone: +33-5-61-93-33-33
Fax: +33-5-61-93-49-55
www.airbus.com

BAE Systems
6 Carlton Gardens
London
SW1Y 5AD, United Kingdom
Phone: +44-1252-373-232
Fax: +44-1252-383-000
http://www.baesystems.com

Boeing Company, The
100 N. Riverside Plaza
Chicago, IL 60606-1596
Phone: (312) 544-2000
Fax: (312) 544-2082
www.boeing.com

General Dynamics Corporation
3190 Fairview Park Dr.
Falls Church, VA 22042-4523
Phone: (703) 876-3000
Fax: (703) 876-3125
www.gendyn.com

General Electric Company
3135 Easton Tpke.
Fairfield, CT 06828-0001
Phone: (203) 373-2211
Fax: (203) 373 3131
www.ge.com

Honeywell International Inc.
101 Columbia Rd.
Morristown, NJ 07962-1219
Phone: (973) 455-2000
Fax: (973) 455-4807
www.honeywell.com

L-3 Communications Holdings
600 3rd Ave.
New York, NY 10016
Phone: (212) 697-1111
Fax: (212) 867-5249
www.L-3Com.com

Lockheed Martin
6801 Rockledge Dr.
Bethesda, MD 20817-1877
Phone: (301) 897-6000
Fax: (301) 897-6704
www.lockheedmartin.com

Northrop Grumman Corporation
1840 Century Park East
Los Angeles, CA 90067-2199
Phone: (310) 553-6262
Fax: (310) 553-2076
www.northgrum.com

Parker Hannifin Corporation
6035 Parkland Blvd.
Cleveland, OH 44124-4141
Phone: (216) 896-3000
Fax: (216) 896-4000
www.parker.com

Raytheon Company
870 Winter St.
Waltham, MA 02451-1449
Phone: (781) 522-3000
Fax: (781) 522-3001
www.raytheon.com

Rockwell Collins
400 Collins Road N.E.
Cedar Rapids, IA 52498
Phone: (319) 295-1000
Fax: (319) 295-5429
www.rockwellcollins.com

Textron Inc.
40 Westminster St.
Providence, RI 02903-2596
Phone: (401) 421-2800
Fax: (401) 421-2878
www.textron.com

United Technologies Corporation
One Financial Plaza
Hartford, CT 06103
Phone: (860) 728-7000
Fax: (860) 728-7979
www.utc.com

Visit Vault at **www.vault.com** for insider company profiles, expert advice, career message boards, expert resume reviews, the Vault Job Board and more.

VAULT CAREER LIBRARY   107

Agriculture

Agriculture Industry Overview

Feed me

The agriculture industry's broad scope includes everyone from farmers and ranchers to scientists who devise new and better foods and the businesspeople who keep it all running. The various disciplines within the industry seek ways to more efficiently feed Earth's ever-growing population while improving profit margins for food-related businesses. Allied industries provide the infrastructure that makes this possible, including rail and road transportation, pesticides and fertilizers, and processors that transform raw products into comestibles.

Agriculture's not just food, though: rather it covers everything that is grown or raised for consumption. Cotton and wool are agricultural products, as are animal byproducts, ornamental plants, tobacco, lumber and the various fruits and grains used to produce alcohol. The industry, unsurprisingly, is massive, accounting for 1 percent of U.S. gross domestic product. Though that might not seem like a lot, 1 percent of $12,500,000,000,000 is a hefty chunk of change.

Bread and circuses

Despite its significant contribution to the GDP, agriculture is very risky and often unprofitable. Profit margins, especially for crops such as soybeans, wheat and corn, are very low, so these plants are frequently grown on large, industrial farms, as tiny returns per acre make small-scale farming economically unfeasible. Fruits and vegetables offer higher returns on lower acreage, but the investment in plants, soil preparation and the necessary labor-intensive harvesting makes the likelihood of farmers breaking even in the first few years unlikely.

Farmers are also at the mercy of pests, plant diseases and weather, the king of all X-factors. While insecticides and pest- and disease-resistant strains of plants can mitigate these risks, they of course cannot be entirely controlled. Heat, drought, flooding, storms and other "acts of God" work havoc on yields and, in extreme circumstances, can even lead to famine. The weather doesn't even have to be especially dramatic to drive up prices: the per-bushel cost of 2006 corn has gone up 28 percent, a two-year high, due to a hot, dry spell in the Midwest in July.

Further complicating matters is the fact that commodities such as corn, soybeans, and wheat are subject to market forces. To wit: a good harvest suppresses the price of a commodity and lowers profits, while a poor one raises prices but causes shortages. This relationship between productivity and profit has plagued agribusiness for decades. Government subsidies for corn, wheat, milk, cotton and a number of other farm products also affect the equation. Designed to hedge risks and lessen farmers' financial burden, these subsidies keep agricultural commodity prices artificially low in domestic markets and around the world.

All of the issues detailed above have forced the consolidation of farms and processing firms. Today, the real players in the industry are all big companies such as Cargill, Archer Daniels Midland, Tyson, Perdue, Bunge and Pilgrim's Pride. ConAgra, at one time a major farming firm, is currently divesting its agricultural business to focus on branded and value-added packaged foods. Meanwhile, Bayer, Dow and DuPont all have a stake in biotech, fungicides and pesticides, each with its own crop sciences division. Monsanto, meanwhile, is a leader in the genetic engineering field.

It's not just for eating anymore

When you think of corn, what initially comes to mind is probably something edible: creamy corn on the cob dripping with golden butter, crisp, salty corn chips or sweet sodas. It's unlikely that you would consider postage stamps, aspirin or imitation silk as corn derivatives, but all of these goods are manufactured using corn byproducts. Archer Daniels Midland is one of the

Visit Vault at **www.vault.com** for insider company profiles, expert advice, career message boards, expert resume reviews, the Vault Job Board and more.

VAULT CAREER LIBRARY 109

largest agricultural processors in the world, turning oilseeds (like soybeans), corn, wheat and nuts into food products like flour, sweeteners and emulsifiers, as well as plant-derived wood preservatives, industrial starches (which become everything from wallboard to glue) and ethanol. Its competitor in the realm of corn-derived sweeteners and starches is Corn Products International. Bunge is the world's largest processor of oilseeds, turning them into such products as biofuels, livestock meal and mayonnaise, while Cargill is a highly diversified agricultural products processor, making such items as soy waxes, vitamins, pharmaceutical coatings, flavoring agents, dairy and meat products.

An enormous range of jobs is required to keep these companies humming. Grain mills and processing plants need supervisors and staff, while commodities merchants are needed to buy and sell grain, cocoa and other articles of commerce to ensure a consistent supply. Logistics experts get the stuff from where it is to where it's going; veterinarians, nutritionists and chemists synthesize new compounds for the nutrition of animals and people; and chemists come up with coloring and flavoring agents and new uses for agricultural byproducts. Along with the usual jobs in HR, sales and IT, lawyers and MBAs are needed to keep good business practices and make sure everyone plays by the rules.

Not exactly *American Pastoral*

You're in for a shock if "agriculture" brings to mind amber waves of grain and fruited plains. Rather, agribusiness is as tech-focused and cutting-edge as every other industry these days. Steroids, hormones and antibiotics, for example, are routinely administered to U.S. meat and dairy animals. Steroids up the rate at which meat animals transform feed into muscle, while hormones, when administered through slow-release pellets implanted in the animal's ear, cause it to gain weight and, in cows, improve milk production. Hormones are also applied to fruits and vegetables. In order to ship fruit long distances, it must be picked before it is fully ripe to withstand the trip. Once it reaches its destination, it is treated with ethylene, the chemical which, in nature, causes fruits to ripen.

Antibiotics are given to animals to cure illnesses—a frequent occurrence when stock is kept in close conditions and fed an unnatural diet. Modern poultry flocks, for instance, are so large that sick animals frequently cannot be isolated, so producers treat all the birds that may have come into contact with the infected individual by adding antibiotics to their drinking water. Feed lot-fattened, corn-fed cattle must be given antibiotics, too, lest the distress caused their digestive tracts by eating corn kill them. Antibiotics are more widely used in subtherapeutic doses, or doses not large enough to cure an infection, a practice that encourages the proliferation of antibiotic-resistant bacteria (much as with a human who takes antibiotics at the first sign of every sniffle). Without competition, resistant bacteria can spread rapidly throughout a population and subsequently be transferred to people who eat raw or undercooked meat.

Begun, this clone war has

Beyond antibiotics and hormones, recent biotech advances have become major issues in the agriculture industry. While farmers have been selecting crops for higher yield, greater disease resistance, better flavor and other desirable qualities for the last 12,000-odd years, we are now able to manipulate individual genes in order to express specific traits. Genetic engineering has produced Golden Rice, designed to accumulate vitamin A—insufficient quantities of which can cause blindness and even death in children—in the edible portion of the grain, a boon for cultures in which rice is the staple crop and a varied diet unassured.

Researchers are looking into growing oral vaccines for hepatitis B and HIV in tomatoes and potatoes, a less expensive method than traditional vaccine production, which would make large-scale vaccination of the populations of poorer countries possible. Genetic tinkering has produced plants such as Monsanto's Roundup Ready corn, canola, soybeans and cotton, and Bayer CropScience's Liberty Link corn, which are, respectively, resistant to the proprietary herbicides Roundup and Liberty. Today, nearly all soy and half of the corn grown in the U.S. is genetically modified, as is 75 percent of cotton.

Scientists are also beginning to explore these methods for use on animals, seeking to increase egg and milk production, change fat content and speed maturity. Genetically modified varieties of catfish and tilapia, designed to grow faster, are already for sale in some countries, while bulls are being cloned in order to improve the breeding stock of cattle. Pet fish implanted with genes that produce luminescent proteins have been available for purchase since 2003.

However, such tinkering has spawned a number of advocacy groups that fear unforeseen consequences. Many groups argue that direct genetic manipulation could produce harmful side effects that simple hybridization and crossbreeding would not, while others warn that herbicide residue might remain in the tissues of resistant plant varieties, or that engineered genes might cross into wild plant populations. Entire nations have gotten in on the act, too: Nigeria, Zambia and Zimbabwe have refused or plan to refuse shipments of genetically modified corn.

The organic green giant

Consumers, motivated by concerns about the above, as well as factory farming, animal cruelty and the health of the environment, are increasingly demanding organic, ethically-treated, free-range, and antibiotic- and hormone- free food products. And apparently they are willing to pay the premium price: in 2005, organic accounted for 2.5 percent of all retail foods sold, while sales of organic meats increased 55 percent and condiments and dairy increased nearly a quarter. Demand for organic milk products outstripped supply by 10 percent that year.

Many businesses are taking advantage of this surge in organic interest. The supermarket chain Whole Foods, started in 1980 and one of the more popular purveyors of organic produce, has the highest profit margin per square foot of any grocery store. At the other end of the spectrum, Wal-Mart began offering organic products in 2006. While such produce's widespread availability will certainly have tangible benefits for the environment and for customers, there are some drawbacks. Faced with price competition, retailers will inevitably demand lower prices from organic farmers, which could put them out of business. In addition, though organic produce can be sourced from foreign countries—China, for instance—regulations stipulating what organic means are certain to differ from country to country, or could even be absent altogether.

But it's not just other countries' organic farming practices (or lack thereof) that have the potential to make waves. Organic farming was the subject of a June 2005 U.S. federal court ruling that demands stricter standards for organic food—standards that many fear will slow industry growth. Consumer advocates were pleased with the ruling (which banned synthetic ingredients in products labeled organic and requires dairy farmers to feed cows 100 percent organic feed), though the organic dairy industry says the regulations will make it more expensive to convert to organic from conventional feed, and will potentially discourage farmers from becoming organic. Consumer groups reject this argument, and claim the ruling will increase the integrity of the organic label and create a steady increase in the strength of standards. (In 2006, though, a rider was attached to the agricultural appropriations bill that loosened regulations concerning the use of non-organic ingredients in products sold as organic.)

From farmhand to finance

The agriculture industry is exceptionally diverse when you consider the number of different segments it encompasses. Operations include fish hatcheries, apple orchards, flower nurseries, slaughterhouses and more. Farm workers (who account for 90 percent of industry employees) require minimal training, but inspectors must have a relevant college degree or valid experience. Managers include farm and ranch owners, as well as those who operate ripening facilities or cold storage. Agricultural graders sort products, such as fruits and eggs, and inspectors evaluate the cleanliness of processing facilities. These professionals generally require both an agriculture degree and a background in the field.

Agronomists (researchers in the many disciplines involving agriculture) start at the bachelor degree level, and many have doctorates to perform "pure" research. Commodities brokers, who manage business deals and trade in futures, have their own specialty within the industry. The Bureau of Labor Statistics (BLS) expects that growing farms and more efficient machinery

Visit Vault at **www.vault.com** for insider company profiles, expert advice, career message boards, expert resume reviews, the Vault Job Board and more.

VAULT CAREER LIBRARY

111

means that there will be fewer such jobs in the future. However, small-scale farming, especially of the organic variety, is expected to grow. Additional growth sectors are the agricultural science and engineering industries. Agricultural scientists devise new food-processing methods, study soil and animal management, and frequently consult for the government or food processing companies. Agricultural engineers design farm equipment for increased efficiency and reduced environmental impact. Depending on the career path they wish to pursue, these people generally have advanced degrees. The BLS reports that these industries are expected to grow by 14 percent between 2004 and 2014.

Vault Q&A: Bettye Hill, Archer Daniels Midland Company (ADM)

As Director of Compliance in Employment in the Office of Compliance and Ethics at Archer Daniels Midland Company (ADM), Bettye Hill is responsible for ensuring that the agriculture leader is compliant with a wide variety of standards when it comes to employment. The owner of a bachelors degree with a concentration in management from Southwest Texas State in San Marcos, Hill collected a wide variety of educational and career experience before arriving at ADM. Her educational background includes an MBA, a JD and an LLM; her career path has been similarly wide-ranging, and includes HR positions in the insurance and grocery industries as well as running her own private law practice. She took some time out to speak with Vault about her current position.

Vault: Can you explain what your office's main responsibilities are?

Hill: The Office of Compliance and Ethics oversees ADM's operations and employees to ensure that as a company we act with integrity. We perform compliance audits and also investigate complaints. Some of the compliance issues we look at could very well be things that are regulated—that is, legal regulations—but they're also best practices, too.

We also develop policies and guidelines, implement and review training programs and interact with government entities on government inquiries, for example, the Department of Labor. We manage the affirmative action plans of the company.

We also interact with ADM locations outside the United States to ensure that we're compliant with the labor laws for those particular countries.

There's also government-required reporting that we make sure we file (for example, the EEO-1 report), which is a required report related to equal opportunity.

Vault: Of your many degrees, which do you think is most relevant to your current position?

Hill: Obviously the bachelors degree is necessary without any others. I am able to utilize my MBA and law degree in this position.

Vault: In what way do you use your MBA?

Hill: I would say it provides me with the ability to make decisions from a much broader business perspective because it enhances my critical and strategic thinking. This comes into play with strategic long-term planning—looking at what strategic processes you have to have in place to get the desired end result. The MBA gives me the skills I need to align what I am doing to the business objectives of the company.

Vault: Can you give me an example of what this means on a day-to-day basis?

Hill: Let's take as an example training needs. We would make an assessment of what those needs are, then we would determine how best to provide the training that is needed.

That includes all the business considerations that are required when providing the training, including frequency, and how the training would be provided—by this, I mean the medium—the cost of the training, and which people will receive it. All of this has to be determined once you identify the need.

Vault: And how would you say your law degree comes into play?

Hill: We certainly assist management with questions they may have on employment, such as the Fair Labor Standards Act, FMLA and so on. We deal with employment law every day.

Vault: Having worked in a variety of industries, how would you say working in the agriculture industry compares?

Hill: It's an industry you can be proud to be a part of. You know it's an industry that deals with the necessities of life, food, feed, fuel and industrial products. I think it's a great industry from that standpoint.

Vault: How would you characterize the corporate culture at ADM?

Hill: I think at ADM you have an opportunity to work with colleagues that are bright, definitely driven and committed to ADM's continued success.

Visit Vault at **www.vault.com** for insider company profiles, expert advice, career message boards, expert resume reviews, the Vault Job Board and more.

V∧ULT CAREER LIBRARY 113

Agriculture Employer Directory

Plum Creek Timber Company

99 Third Ave, Suite 4300
Seattle, WA 98104-4096

Recruiting Contact:
Phone: 206-467-3600
E-mail: careers@plumcreek.com
www.plumcreek.com

Job Search Website:
www.jobsearch.org/seeker/jobsearch/keyword
Search by the following keyword and location
parameters: Keyword: Plum Creek, Location: National

Plum Creek is the United States' largest private landowner with over 8 million acres of land and growing. An S&P 500 company, Plum Creek has revenues over $1.5 billion, offices in 18 states, and various positions in forestry, real estate, land management, manufacturing, accounting, human resources, and legal.

We have a collaborative, team-centric, execution oriented culture focused on delivery and strive for a good balance between career and personal life, and between cutting edge and proven technology. Plum Creek's substantial growth has created many unique career opportunities. You'll be able to build a rewarding and successful career, while enjoying the low-key atmosphere that makes life in our tight-knit communities a happy and warm place to live and visit.

Plum Creek wants to attract and keep the best people-the team who drives our success. That is why we offer superior performers opportunities for compensation that is in the top 25% for our marketplace. Benefits packages consists of a comprehensive range of benefits including Health care, Health and Dependent Daycare Funds, Life and Disability protection, Saving and Retirements benefits, Paid Vacation, Relocation, and more.

Our Resources group including scientists, nursery managers, foresters, and other experts operate under the Sustainable Forestry Initiative (SFI) principles to guide all aspects of our approach to forest management and to the procurement of wood. Resources capitalized and reached revenues over $760 million dollars in 2006. Their approach to forestry incorporates the perpetual growing and harvesting of trees with the protection of wildlife, plants, soil, and water quality.

Archer Daniels Midland Company (ADM)

4666 Faries Pkwy.
Decatur, IL 62525
Phone: (217) 424-5200
Fax: (217) 424-6196
Toll Free: (800) 637-5843
www.admworld.com

Bunge Limited

2 Church St.
Hamilton, HM 11, Bermuda
Phone: 914-684-2800
www.bunge.com

Cargill

15407 McGinty Rd. West
Wayzata, MN 55391
Phone: (952) 742-7575
Fax: (952) 742-7393
www.cargill.com

ConAgra Foods, Inc.

1 ConAgra Dr.
Omaha, NE 68102-5001
Phone: (402) 595-4000
Fax: (402) 595-4707
www.conagra.com

Corn Products International, Inc.

5 Westbrook Corporate Center
Westchester, IL 60154
Phone: (708) 551-2600
Fax: (708) 551-2570
Toll Free: (800) 443-2746
www.cornproducts.com

Perdue Farms Incorporated

31149 Old Ocean City Rd.
Salisbury, MD 21804
Phone: (410) 543-3000
Fax: (410) 543-3292
www.perdue.com

Pilgrim's Pride Corporation

4845 US Hwy. 271 North
Pittsburg, TX 75686-0093
Phone: (903) 855-1000
Fax: (903) 856-7505
www.pilgrimspride.com

Smithfield Foods, Inc.

200 Commerce St.
Smithfield, VA 23430
Phone: (757) 365-3000
Fax: (757) 365-3017
www.smithfieldfoods.com

Tyson Foods, Inc.

2210 W. Oaklawn Dr.
Springdale, AR 72762-6999
Phone: (479) 290-4000
Fax: (479) 290-4061
www.tysonfoodsinc.com

Airlines

Airline Industry Overview

A volatile industry

The airline industry consists of companies that move people and cargo with planes. The International Air Transport Association (IATA) claims that this $450 billion worldwide industry stimulates 8 percent of global GDP through tourism, shipping and business travel. But despite its enormous contribution to world commerce, the industry has historically gone through dizzying booms and alarming busts as it reacts to changes in regulation and the economy. Currently, airlines are still trying to dig themselves out of the hole caused by September 11. IATA says the imposition of security measures since then has cost the industry an average of $5 billion per year. Spats with labor unions, troubles with underfinanced pensions, high jet fuel prices and a string of bankruptcies, from which some carriers were still emerging as late as 2006, have caused further havoc. Nevertheless, *The Economist* thinks that once these issues have been resolved (no easy task), the airlines will be in a position to expand.

Cleared for takeoff

The airline industry took to the skies (pun intended) following the Wright brothers' first successful flight in 1905. As with many new technologies, airplanes were first used extensively in a war—namely, World War I, for reconnaissance, bombing and aerial combat. Following the war, when the U.S. found itself with a surplus of military aircraft and pilots with not much to do, the postal service opted in 1918 to use them to start a transcontinental air mail service, which ran from New York to San Francisco. To keep costs down, 12 spur routes were spun off to independent contractors—thus were the familiar friendly sky-flying companies of American Airlines, United Airlines, TWA and Northwest born.

Passenger flights did not become a reality until Ford introduced a 12-seat plane, which made carrying people potentially profitable. Pan American Airways, the first airline with international destinations, was founded in 1927, with other airlines adding international routes in the 1940s. Remarkably, airlines remained generally profitable during the Great Depression. Following that period, World War II brought many advances to the civilian air transport sector. Innovations initially intended for bombers made passenger planes larger, faster, able to carry heavier payloads and to fly at higher altitudes. The 1970s saw the introduction of supersonic air travel with the advent of the Concorde—which is now defunct.

Big trouble for the Big Six

Since September 11, Congress has given well over $20 billion to the airline industry in the form of reimbursements for losses incurred while planes were grounded following the attacks, monetary help for new passenger and plane security requirements, and pension funding relief. But many of the industry's major players were forced to shoulder massive debt loads to continue operating, on top of debt they had been accumulating since even before the terrorist attacks. Of the "Big Six"—the *grandes dames* of the American airline industry, United, US Airways, American, Northwest, Continental and Delta—all but two, Continental and American, have been forced to file for Chapter 11. Smaller airlines including Great Plains, Hawaiian, Midway, National, Sun Country and Vanguard have also shown up in bankruptcy court.

Airline aid

Though passenger confidence continued to grow in the years following the terrorist attacks, and an improved economy bodes well for the travel industry as a whole, the industry's red ink continues to flow: according to a June 2004 Senate report, the industry carried combined debts of more than $100 billion as of that year, with much of it due by 2006. As such, major

Visit Vault at **www.vault.com** for insider company profiles, expert advice, career message boards, expert resume reviews, the Vault Job Board and more.

VAULT CAREER LIBRARY 115

carriers continue to lobby the feds for financial support in the form of subsidies and loans. Delta and Northwest are currently pleading with members of Congress to pass legislation allowing the airlines to stretch their multi-billion dollar pension payments over a 25-year period. As it stands now, Northwest would contribute $900 million in pensions in 2006, while Delta would give up $500 million—amounts neither airline can afford. In order to force lawmakers into passing the bill, Delta and Northwest are threatening to terminate pension plans that cover a combined 86,000 employees—a potential political disaster for members of Congress.

Looking up?

After industry profits reached a nadir in 2001 and 2002, business—if not profit—is showing signs of recovery. According to the IATA, a stronger world economy saw passenger traffic rise by 7 percent between 2005 and 2006, and air freight experienced a 5 percent gain. In order to accommodate this increased demand for air travel, and to lower their fuel expenditures, airlines are snapping up new, more fuel-efficient planes. The IATA predicts losses for 2006 will be in the $3 billion range (which, though not great, is lower than the $5 billion lost in 2005). Assuming oil prices stabilize, the industry should be back in the black in 2007.

The industry is being kept in the red by a combination of factors more complex that the Bernoulli effect. Air carriers were hit hard by rising fuel costs, with jet fuel prices exceeding $90 per barrel. Industry players estimate that if oil prices stay high, airlines will pay $21 billion more for fuel in 2006 than they did in the previous year. Labor disputes and underfinanced pensions have also been expensive problems for many carriers, at the same time as savvy consumers have been taking advantage of such services as Expedia and Orbitz to grab the lowest fares. Some carriers are playing to the budget travel crowd. Southwest just introduced a program called Ding which causes the customer's computer to make noise when low fares to specified destinations are released.

Overall, costs associated with air travel dropped significantly over the past year, as a result of price competition and attempts to keep ticket prices low despite high fuel costs. Industry belt-tightening seems to be working. The IATA reports that the industry break-even fuel price went from $22 per barrel in 2003 to $50 per barrel in 2005, though with crude trading at nearly twice the break-even price, it seems that airlines may still have a ways to go.

A global network

Around the world, many airlines still are heavily subsidized—or owned outright—by their home nations. While this has been a successful setup for many, others haven't been so lucky—Swissair and Belgium's airline, Sabena, both crumbled when their respective governments couldn't keep up with demands for subsidies. Global alliances have been formed between subsidized international and U.S. carriers to avoid some regulatory issues and to maximize profits by sharing resources, including routes and marketing strategies. Well-known alliances include Oneworld, an alliance between American Airlines and British Airways, and SkyTeam, a partnership made up of Delta Air Lines, Air France and AeroMexico. Such partnerships aren't always successful—an alliance between Dutch carrier KLM and Alitalia fell apart, for instance, after the Italian airline had trouble securing funding from its government patrons.

Partnerships aside, the airline industry remains remarkably competitive, and in today's tough climate, it's everyone for themselves. The only major merger between top airlines in the past few years was the early 2004 acquisition of KLM by Air France. Tight regulatory controls in the U.S. make it tough for major domestic carriers to merge, even if the companies involved were healthy enough to consider doing so. A plan to join United Airlines and US Airways was the last such proposal to be floated, and it was shot down due to antitrust regulations. The US Airways name showed up again in merger talks, linked to America West for $1.5 billion, and the two companies made it official in September 2005. Despite the mergers, size is no guarantee of profit. Four of the Big Six have gone into bankruptcy since 2001, while smaller Southwest has maintained its profitability, largely by an aggressive program of hedging fuel prices.

Going regional

Regional airlines, which benefit from smaller, newer jets and lower operating costs than the domestic giants, have gained ground in recent years, becoming the fastest-growing segment of the airline market. Approximately 25 to 30 regional, or commuter, carriers operate in the industry today, according to the Bureau of Labor Statistics. Recent statistics from the Regional Airline Association reveal that one in five domestic airline passengers travel on a regional airline, and that the regional fleet makes up one third of the U.S. commercial airline fleet on the whole. The big carriers have taken notice, and many now have controlling interests in newer regional airlines—Delta controls Delta Express, Atlantic Southeast and Comair, for instance, while American has American Eagle. The trend is reflected in Europe, too. Both globally and domestically, regional airlines benefit from such partnerships as alliances with major carriers allow the upstart regionals access to major airport hubs. In some cases, however, regional and low-budget airlines have skirted the hub question altogether by choosing to operate out of slightly out-of-the-way airports—Southwest's use of Islip airport, in a suburb of New York, and JetBlue's adoption of Long Beach, near Los Angeles, are two examples. And in other cases, regional airlines have decided to spread their wings and join the burgeoning low-cost boom.

The budget boom

The budget airline sector—consisting of top performers like Southwest Airlines and JetBlue, plus a growing number of upstarts—has gotten a good deal of attention lately. But budget flight isn't a new phenomenon in the industry—in fact, Southwest has been around since 1971. The difference is in the branding and public acceptance of these carriers, fueled in part by Southwest's customer-centric approach, and by customers' reduced service expectations post-September 11. Expanded routes have helped, too—where once low-budget carriers limited their flights to relatively short hauls in regional markets, today's top discount airlines regularly offer cross-country, and even international, flights. The budget carrier phenomenon has rocked Europe, too, where more than 50 low-cost carriers were in operation in 2004, compared to just four in 1999. European customers have warmed up to the budget boom as well. British-based easyJet increased its passenger flow more than eight-fold between 1999 and 2004, while low-cost carrier Ryanair, operating out of Ireland, ranked as one of the top performers in the industry worldwide, second in market capitalization only to Southwest as of mid-2004, according to Yahoo! Finance.

Some of the larger airlines have decided to take advantage of the low-cost boom, such as United's Ted and Delta's Song, but to not much avail; Song, in fact, was reabsorbed into Delta in 2006, three years after its first plane took off. Despite Song's failure, airlines around the world have realized that there just aren't as many passengers willing to pay for five-star air travel these days—at least, not enough to make these services profitable for most carriers. The demise of the Concorde, in 2003, was seen by many analysts as yet another indication of this trend. Instead, consumers prefer to pick and choose their perks. An in-flight cocktail on JetBlue will cost you the same, but XM radio and satellite TV is free. Charging for amenities that previously came gratis allows carriers to keep ticket prices low, yet still turn a profit.

Cutting costs

Above all, cost savings are seen as key to the success of low-budget carriers. One way air carriers measure their fiscal health is through cost per available seat mile (or CASM), a complex formula involving airplane capacity, operating costs, route lengths and other factors. Whereas American Airlines spends about 9.4 cents for each seat on each mile flown, budget competitors like Southwest and JetBlue lighten their loads with CASMs of 7.6 cents and 6.4 cents, respectively, according to an MSNBC article from December 2003. Those pennies add up over time, and so-called "legacy" carriers are under pressure to pinch them ever harder. But with more liberal work rules and a less-senior workforce overall, low-cost carriers beat their established rivals in terms of labor costs.

Visit Vault at www.vault.com for insider company profiles, expert advice, career message boards, expert resume reviews, the Vault Job Board and more.

VAULT CAREER LIBRARY   117

Investing in a dream(liner)

Major carriers hope to save money in the future by investing in new planes that offer a lower cost of ownership and operation. In early 2004, Boeing got the go-ahead from Japan's Al Nippon Airlines to begin work on a new 787 Dreamliner passenger jet, which promises fuel savings of up to 20 percent—other carriers' orders are expected to follow. Meanwhile, Airbus, the French firm and Boeing's rival for No. 1 aircraft maker in the world, unveiled a brand new high-scale jumbo jet, the A380, at the start of 2005 at a gala event during the Le Bourget air show in Toulouse, France. Designed to comfortably seat 555, the A380 rocked the airline industry and represented a joint effort with France, Britain, Germany and Spain, all of whom contributed to the 10-year, $13 billion program that designed the plane. The double-decker leviathan, the largest plane ever built, boasts a 262-foot wingspan and extra space companies can use to install bedrooms, gyms, bars and lounges. The conservation end, though, is where the A380 packs its biggest punch: its carbon fiber components and fuel-efficient technology are estimated to match or exceed Boeing's 20 percent fuel savings, and slash cost per passenger. Delivery of the planes has already been delayed six months by technical issues.

Other cost-cutting measures in the airline industry overall include streamlining fleets and retiring older planes; cancelling unprofitable routes; greater efficiency in procurement processes involving suppliers; and slashing commissions once paid regularly to middlemen such as travel agencies. Many see technological advancements as their great hope—according to a January 2004 *BusinessWeek* article, Continental hopes to save $500 million annually in coming years partly by investing in Web-based check-in systems and wireless bag tracking.

Labor pains

According to the Bureau of Labor Statistics (BLS), labor costs make up roughly 38 percent of many airlines' operating costs—that's around 40 cents for every dollar spent by an air carrier. Passenger safety regulations, a workforce made up of highly specialized and rarely cross-trained professionals, half of whom are unionized, make it tough for airlines to trim costs from their labor budgets. One way they've done this is by cutting workforces to the bare bones. Following September 11, Continental Airlines and US Airways were the first to make dramatic cuts, laying off about 20 percent of their respective workforces and paring flight schedules. Most other carriers followed suit.

Industry employment is largely at the mercy of the economy, though the BLS expects jobs to increase somewhat independently due to a growing population and greater demand for air travel. The BLS predicts employment growth initially in low-cost and local carriers, with larger airlines following the trend as they cut costs post-bankruptcy.

There are several different categories of employment within the airline industry: flight attendants and customer service personnel, ground crews and pilots. The latter category represent some of the most highly-paid workers in the country, and so competition for these jobs is understandably intense. (Not as much for flight attendants, customer service personnel and ground crews.) The more FAA licenses a pilot has—that is, the more flying time he has on complex, modern equipment—the more in demand his services will be. For this reason, military-trained pilots are particularly desirable; however, recent military actions mean they are in short supply.

Civilians can learn to fly at a private flight school and gain experience on progressively larger aircraft; they may work their way up from private jets to regional carriers and from there to the larger airlines. Initially, a newly hired pilot will be a flight engineer or co-pilot, assisting the captain with communications with control towers, instrument readings and flight duties. Work assignments for flight attendants and pilots are frequently given on a seniority basis, with the most senior employees having the pick of the litter. New hires, therefore, must be prepared to receive less desirable assignments initially.

Airlines Employer Directory

Alaska Air Group
19300 Pacific Highway South
Seattle, WA 98188
Phone: (206) 392-5040
Fax: (206) 433-3379
www.alaska-air.com

American Airlines
4333 Amon Carter Boulevard
Fort Worth, TX 76155
Phone: (817) 963-1234
Fax: (817) 967-9641
www.aa.com

British Airways
Waterside, Harmondsworth
London, UB7 0GB
United Kingdom
Phone: +44-08708509850
Fax: +44-20-8759-4314
www.ba.com

Continental Airlines, Inc.
1600 Smith Street
Houston, TX 77002
Phone: (713) 324-5000
www.continental.com

Delta Air Lines, Inc.
P.O. Box 20706
Atlanta, GA 30320-6001
Phone: (404) 715-2600
Fax: (404) 715-5042
www.delta.com

JetBlue
118-29 Queens Boulevard
Forest Hills, NY 11375
Phone: (718) 709-3026
www.jetblue.com

Northwest Airlines Corporation
2700 Lone Oak Parkway
Eagan, MN 55121
Phone: (612) 726-2111
Fax: (612) 726-7123
www.nwa.com

Southwest Airlines
2702 Love Field Drive
Dallas, TX 75235
Phone: (214) 792-4000
Fax: (214) 792-5015
www.southwest.com

US Airways Group, Inc.
2345 Crystal Drive
Arlington, VA 22227
Phone: (703) 872-7000
Fax: (703) 872-5134
www.usairways.com

Visit Vault at **www.vault.com** for insider company profiles, expert advice,
career message boards, expert resume reviews, the Vault Job Board and more.

VAULT CAREER LIBRARY   119

Architecture and Interior Design

The Architecture Career Path

Much like interior design companies, architectural firms often have specialties: residential, commercial or institutional. Residential architects plan all manner of private residences, including multi-family residential buildings, such as condominiums or semi-attached dwellings. Commercial architects design public spaces, such as office buildings and country clubs. Institutional architects work on structures such as public libraries and municipal buildings. Some firms include in-house services such as structural, mechanical and electrical engineering, or design-related services like landscape and interior design. Depending on the size and geographic location of the firm, work may focus only on one area or cover all three. Company size varies widely—the number of employees ranges anywhere from one person to over 100, but the average is nine or ten people. Since most people have limited knowledge of the construction process, they'll enlist an architect as the first step in developing a new residence or public building. A successful architect, like an interior designer, pays careful attention to the wants and needs of his client, turning ideas into tangible drawings and offering assistance in many aspects of the project, including site studies, securing planning and zoning approvals, and helping to select a contractor.

Clients select architectural firms in the same manner they choose a designer, gathering names from friends and associates who have developed similar projects, through publications such as *Architectural Digest* and researching which architects designed the buildings or homes they admire. They can also contact the American Institute of Architects (AIA) for lists of local architects. Many design publications list architects as resources, and architects also self-promote in trade publications. As in any industry, certain icons are so well known that they can be very selective about projects they accept. Some current well-known architects include Frank Gehry, Michael Graves and Richard Meier. One of Meier's recent famous works is the Getty Center in Los Angeles. Two of Gehry's latest notable structures are the Guggenheim Museum Bilbao in Spain and The Walt Disney Concert Hall in Los Angeles. Graves' list of projects is numerous, encompassing everything from private residences to civic buildings. Some examples are Disney corporate headquarters in Burbank, Calif., the headquarters and training center for the Philadelphia Eagles and a building on the University of Virginia campus. The number of famous architects taking on residential projects has increased; for example, Daniel Libeskind (architect of the master plan for the new World Trade Center site) is working on a residential tower in Denver, and Frank Gehry is developing ideas for a luxury tower in Manhattan. The phenomenon of prominent architects working on residential projects is not entirely new; after all, famed architect Frank Lloyd Wright is often most remembered for his private dwellings such as Fallingwater, a residential home in Bear Run, Penn. One reason architects take on private residences is the increased level of creativity those projects engender. As Richard Meier has said, "Individuals aren't afraid to take risks. You don't get that level of collaboration with many corporate clients."

Architects are usually brought on board shortly after the land or existing property has been acquired, ultimately selected based on some combination of price, qualification and personal fit. Owners usually interview several prospective applicants, getting a chance to see examples of the firms' work and how they organize projects for completion. The interview also provides an opportunity for potential clients to interact with the person or people who will be working on the job before committing to anything. Many firms, too, exercise their own judgment, careful not to take every opportunity that crosses their path. As one principal of a mid-size architectural firm says; "We have made a concerted effort to filter our client base so that we don't accept projects from potential clients who we sense may not be a good fit."

Architecture jobs

Depending on the size of the firm, positions vary. At smaller firms, job descriptions and responsibilities tend to overlap, as each person is expected to wear more than one hat. A small to mid-size firm (four to 10 people) tends to offer the following positions:

Visit Vault at **www.vault.com** for insider company profiles, expert advice, career message boards, expert resume reviews, the Vault Job Board and more.

VAULT CAREER LIBRARY   121

Administrative: This position focuses on providing administrative support and office management: filing, answering phones, scheduling, ordering—anything that helps the office run smoothly. Administrative positions require no background in architecture and provide a good way for a person with an interest in architecture to safely test the waters and observe the actual operations of an architecture firm.

Draftsperson: There are often two categories within this title, junior and senior, differentiated by level of experience and responsibility. A draftsperson drafts the drawing for a project, directed by the project architect or project manager. She should have the requisite degree in architecture, but is not necessarily licensed, and she should have a solid understanding of computer aided design (CAD) in addition to good hand-drawing and hand-lettering skills. A wide range of experiences is acceptable for this position.

Job captain: This person coordinates and works on the drawings for a project. She organizes and updates the drawings and directs staff as necessary. A job captain has a degree in architecture but is not necessarily licensed. She should have a minimum of about five years' work experience.

Project manager: The person in this position is responsible for day-to-day management, coordination of staff on projects, scheduling of tasks and consultant coordination. This job requires educational and work experience similar to what a job captain requires.

Project architect: A project architect is responsible for the overall supervision of the project: design and coordination of details for the drawings, consultation coordination, decision making for field issues, etc. (in small offices some responsibilities overlap with the project managers). Production of specifications (what types of materials are to be used) and overall review of project documents are also responsibilities of a project architect. This position requires licensing in the state of employment. Attaining this position typically requires ten years of work experience.

Principal or partner: This person runs the firm. Some firms with more than one head person have a design principal or partner and a business partner. At others, the principal might do everything: design, marketing, overall administrative and strategic planning, client contact and meetings, project scheduling and administration and business planning.

Salaries and corporate culture

Similarly to interior design, architecture is often misunderstood, and as a result, glamorized. Some top architects have the opportunity to work on famous buildings and landmarks, and express great creativity. But there are scores of others working on much more mundane projects, and not being well-compensated either. In fact, architecture careers have a reputation for being underpaid, particularly relative to the amount of education required. Asked to describe a drawback to her job, one architect says, "The pay, in comparison to other professions such as law and medicine, tends to be lower."

Salary ranges in a small to medium-size firm are usually anywhere from $30,000 for lower-level positions to $80,000 for positions higher up the food chain. Employees at larger firms can make more money, and certainly, well-known architects can command more also. Average architectural salaries range from $25,000 to $80,000, depending on a person's experience and the size of the company they work for. Partners can earn well into six figures, particularly at large firms. Salary.com states the national average for architectural salaries as $36,715 on the low end, $54,522 for the middle bracket and $69,276 on the high end.

Though architecture is known for long hours and late nights, this is more accurate at some firms than others. Some firms maintain fairly stable nine-to-five, forty-hour work weeks, while others are more stressful. Hours worked often depend on the type of projects the firm undertakes and the deadlines it agrees to; some companies take on publicly funded or other institutional projects and face contract provisions that require absolute deadlines on certain phases of the process. This requires the architect to meet deadlines, no matter the overtime involved.

Corporate culture varies depending on the size of the firm, larger leaning toward more conservative and hierarchical, smaller ones usually allowing greater freedom. Architecture certainly allows for more creativity than professions such as banking or accounting, but it is still business-focused and requires one to turn an artistic vision into something useful and functional. Asked if architecture is creative, one architect responded, "I would say yes, but not in the same way school is creative. Clients generally don't give us free rein and some firms also separate their staff into design and production groups, the former being more freely creative on a conceptual level and the latter being more technical. The production staff figures out how to build what the design staff creates."

Like fashion, entertainment and other creative professions, certain industry stars glamorize the profession and create misunderstanding about the reality of working in the business. The Michael Graveses and I. M. Peis (architect of Hancock Place, the tallest building in Boston, not to mention the controversial Louvre Pyramid) of the world are rare; much more common are architects who love their job but work on average projects and receive average paychecks.

Pay fluctuates depending on firm size and an architect's area of specialization. Small to mid-size firms offer greater freedom in terms of creativity and structure, but generally do not compensate employees as well. Unlike interior design, architecture is more of a necessity than a luxury. Any person or company that needs to create a structure has to enlist the help of an architect, so clients don't tend to have as much expendable income across the board as those enlisting interior decorators. Perks include travel and social invitations; architects attend many of the same events frequented by interior designers and other professionals in the design arena. Although architects may not need to be as image-conscious as their interior design colleagues, they still must maintain knowledge of trends and culture. Appearing knowledgeable and speaking eloquently on historical architecture and famous buildings is essential. Being published in trade magazines is extremely helpful for raising awareness about a particular firm and the talented individuals it employs.

Employment options

Architects are not limited to working only at traditional architectural firms. The AIA provides a list of the many options available within four main categories: corporate architecture, public architecture, facility management and "other options." Corporate architects are employed within the retail, office, manufacturing, medical and hospitality industries, and there are numerous job choices available at such companies, ranging from entry-level planners to high-level executives. Public architects work for government agencies from federal to local levels. The government recruits architects to serve on capital projects planning, design and construction programs; the architect may be a direct government employee or hired as a consultant. Projects might include civic buildings, government offices, military facilities, courts and research facilities. Facility management uses architects to integrate architecture, engineering and environmental sciences for public and private corporations, architecture and consulting firms. Facilities management, as explained by the Facility Management Association of Australia, "coordinates the strategic and operational management of facilities in public and private sector organizations. They range from those making very high-level decisions within an organization and contributing to strategic planning, to those managing the operations of the facilities. Facility managers are key decision-makers in the areas of communications, utilities, maintenance and other workplace services. They often control the spending in these areas and are responsible for the outcomes." In terms of "other" career options, architects can serve as writers, critics and educators. For instance, Michael Graves served as an architecture professor at Princeton for nearly forty years, and Robert A.M. Stern is the dean of the Yale School of Architecture.

Visit Vault at **www.vault.com** for insider company profiles, expert advice, career message boards, expert resume reviews, the Vault Job Board and more.

VAULT CAREER LIBRARY   **123**

Interior Design Basics

Designer or decorator?

The terms interior designer and interior decorator are often used interchangeably by both design industry professionals and laypeople, however, the difference between the two is distinct and important. An interior designer is likely to be offended if referred to as a decorator, but a decorator probably won't correct you if mistaken for a designer.

The primary distinction between the two is that a designer has more responsibility and is formally trained and educated, whereas a decorator may be self-taught and have no formal schooling. Designers, who have been trained in many areas, including drafting, space planning, furniture design and history, ergonomics and business practices, are involved in all facets of a project. They are expected to have in-depth knowledge of safety and building codes and many construction-related issues. On the other hand, a decorator tends to be limited to working primarily with surface decorations like paint, furnishings and fabrics. Numerous designers and decorators practice interior design, with decorators primarily concentrating on residential design and designers more evenly dispersed through residential and contract design. In an *Architectural Digest* interview, interior designer Mariette Himes Gomez explains, "I hate to generalize, and I don't want to set up stereotypes, but decorators usually are individuals who prefer to reupholster and do new draperies and pick out furniture." On the other hand, Gomez describes her interior design practice as "coordinat[ing] our services with an architect from the time the building is under construction."

The role of a designer

Interior designers are hired to plan the interiors, and to some extent, exteriors of private homes, hotels, restaurants, cruise ships, hospitals, offices and countless other spaces. They work with clients, contractors, architects and any number of specialists to create functional and pleasing living and working environments. They make decisions about flooring materials, wall and ceiling paints and treatments, lighting, window treatments, appliances, furnishings and accessories.

Good taste and visuals are only a part of the elements a designer must consider when creating a space. Designers must also address functionality and compliance with safety codes and standards. Educated interior designers should be aware of how all these components relate to codes and guidelines and ensure they are in compliance with regulations.

Designers must have a wide range of skills. While creativity is probably the most widely acknowledged asset, designers must also have the ability to multitask and work effectively on several projects at one time; time management and organizational abilities are key. Designers must also be effective communicators, able to work with clients, contractors, architects and vendors, to name a few. As Betty Sherrill, president of legendary design firm McMillen, Inc., says, "Part decorator, part architect, the interior designer today must have a head for business and budgets, as well as a command of materials and marketing."

Interior Design Accreditations

Accreditations and education

In almost every state, there is more than one accredited interior design education program. The Foundation for Interior Design Education Research (FIDER) posts a list of accredited programs on its web site (www.fider.org). In New York, there are nine FIDER-approved programs, the most notable being the Pratt Institute in Brooklyn. Parsons is not FIDER accredited, but it does have a considerable reputation in the field. The number of accredited programs available in a geographic region depends on the size of the state, as well as the profile of design there. Well-known design hubs such as California (Los

Angeles and San Francisco) and Illinois (Chicago) have twelve and six programs respectively, but smaller states without a real design hub, such as Iowa and Arkansas, each have one. According to ASID, FIDER estimates that there were nearly 17,000 students enrolled in FIDER-accredited professional interior design programs as of December 2003.

Formal schooling

The need for formal schooling in interior design is debatable. According to the American Society of Interior Designers, at least 50 percent of all practicing designers in the United States have completed two or more years of college or vocational training; 40-45 percent have completed a four-year college program. Of the four-year college graduates, 40 percent received a degree in interior design. The remaining 60 percent have degrees in architecture, fine arts, liberal arts, industrial design, education and business administration, among other subjects. Depending on whether you are interested in contract or residential design, the requirements will vary. Residential design is less likely to require formal schooling and a specific background, whereas contract design is more restrictive, often necessitating a design degree. There are many, many successful residential decorators (who might call themselves designers, depending on their location) who have absolutely no formal schooling in design. However, many of these individuals have other outstanding characteristics and qualities that have made them a success. They probably have a very strong work ethic, outstanding taste and an eye for beauty. They most likely have very strong people skills. They probably have excellent presentation skills and are well versed in the art of sales. "Design isn't so much about decorating as sales. You have to sell yourself, your image, your ideas and the products," says one top residential designer.

Young would-be designers have plenty of options. With some serious networking and hard work you can probably get in the door in a support position at a residential design firm and work your way up from there, taking night courses in design to increase your pace up the ladder. If you are switching careers and don't have years to spend climbing the corporate ladder, a degree or at least certificate in design is very beneficial. Having a degree will open you up to working at both residential and commercial firms and will get you a better position than someone with zero design education—but you will definitely still have to put in many years of hard work to get to head designer. Going out on your own is usually not an option for most brand new design graduates or those with little concrete experience. Most clients will want to see a portfolio of a designer's work, which won't add up to much if a designer only has school projects or pictures of her own living room to show.

The main thing to keep in mind is that interior design is not the glamorous job it may appear to be. If you envision days spent shopping for fabrics and picking out furnishings, that's really only about ten percent of the job. "Be prepared to work very hard when you first start out," says one designer. "A lot will be expected of you and you will need to pay your dues. Be very sure that this is what you want to do. Design, particularly if you work for one of the big firms, is not always as creative or glamorous as you might think. It is a business and it is about business. On the other hand, if you are good, there are great opportunities out there."

Licensing

The field of interior design is still evolving, and what designates an interior designer varies by location. ASID provides a list (www.asid.org/design_basics/proessional_credentials/reg_law_agencies _state.asp) of requirements by state. Twenty-two states, as well as the District of Columbia, have some regulations regarding what qualifications an interior designer must meet. Other states not on that list either don't have any requirements or are in the process of defining them. It's important to make sure you know the requirements for the state where you intend to practice. It is also important to remember that decorators (as opposed to designers) do not have to meet the same requirements. Currently, designation requirements are still under debate in many localities. For example, the October 2004 issue of *Interior Design* details the efforts of Ruth Lynford, the legislative chair of Interior Designers for Legislation in New York, encouraging a bill that would reserve the title of interior designer "for those who meet certain educational and professional qualifications and pass an examination on fire, safety and building codes." (Anyone practicing for 15 years or more would have been able to apply for an exemption.) After

Visit Vault at **www.vault.com** for insider company profiles, expert advice, career message boards, expert resume reviews, the Vault Job Board and more.

VAULT CAREER LIBRARY 125

two years, the bill was finally passed, only to be overturned by the governor. Only time will tell how successful future legislative measures will be.

States that do register and license designers typically require some combination of education and work experience, and possibly passing a qualifying exam. The most popular exam is offered by the National Council for Interior Design Qualification (NCIDQ). This organization, founded in the early 1970s, was created to establish the necessary qualifications for designating a professional interior designer. The NCIDQ administers a qualifying exam that entitles successful candidates to become certified in interior design and a professional member in interior design-related organizations such as the American Society of Interior Designers (ASID). The exam tests knowledge of safety and health issues, space planning, historical styles, fabric selection and math. Requirements for taking the NCIDQ are: four to five years of interior design education plus two years of full-time work experience in interior design, or three years of interior design education plus three years of full-time work experience in interior design, or two years of interior design education plus four years of full-time work experience in interior design.

Membership in ASID or other professional groups such as the International Interior Design Association (IIDA), while not necessary to function in the industry, does hold weight and can be beneficial in acquiring clients. These organizations have various types of memberships, such as student, professional, allied and industry. They provide opportunities for networking and further education in addition to being great sources of information. ASID has 42 chapters throughout North America. To become a professional member, an interior designer must have passed the NCIDQ exam in addition to having a course of accredited education or relevant work experience. Allied members are not required to have passed the NCIDQ exam but must either have acquired a four- or five-year bachelor's degree in interior design or architecture, or two- or three-year degree or certificate in interior design, or six years of full-time work in interior design or architecture. The ASID web site (www.asid.org) provides its members valuable information for networking and industry information. It even has an area for posting resumes and searching for candidates.

It is imperative for designers in contract design to be licensed. In this portion of the industry, designers work primarily on large commercial properties such as hotels, resorts and cruise ships, and it's critical that designers in these areas have knowledge of safety regulations and codes. In residential design, it is not as important, since the design space is mostly private and not required to meet such stringent regulations.

Just as the American Bar Association (ABA) reviews and accredits educational programs for the legal profession, the interior design industry has The Foundation for Interior Design Education Research. FIDER was established in 1970 to develop standards for interior design education. It is responsible for accrediting interior design programs and ensuring a program meets the qualifications of the industry. Attending a FIDER-approved school is not required to practice interior design or to take the NCIDQ, but the accreditation suggests that the institution and its graduates are concerned with meeting industry standards. FIDER provides a list of its approved programs by state. Whether to pursue a formal degree in interior design or to take a more general approach is an important decision that will affect future employment. If you're interested in pursuing a career in commercial or hospitality design, it's highly advisable to complete a formal degree. According to a recent interior design graduate of Parsons School of Design in New York City, her first job with a hospitality firm would not have been possible without such a degree. In fact, her firm would not have even contemplated her resume without the requisite design degree.

On the other hand, if residential design is more appealing, then a less traditional approach is acceptable. Many employees and even principals at well-recognized design firms hold no formal qualifications in interior design. It is not unusual for highly successful residential interior designers (or decorators) to have no formal background in the field; instead, they often hold degrees in art history, architecture or fine arts. If a degree is the chosen path, there are several methods for acquiring it. Many schools offer a bachelor of interior design (BID) or bachelor of fine art with a concentration in interior design (BFA). Others provide associates degrees and continuing education courses, which are also a means of gaining some formal training.

Some schools also offer interior architecture degrees. These are architecturally based degrees with an emphasis on interior design, but they are not exact substitutes for an interior design education.

One residential interior designer who attended Parsons School of Design says that she finds her formal training and education in the field to be a huge asset. "It trained me how to think a certain way and be aware of all the elements that go into making great design," she says.

A typical curriculum for a degree in interior design varies according to program. Associate and certificate programs are less time-consuming, and therefore more concentrated.

If you are already enrolled in a school that does not offer a program in interior design, your next best alternative is to take courses in the arts, both studio and history classes. Education in art history is the backbone of many noncertified designers and decorators. Drawing and sculpture, or whatever art courses appeal to you, can only benefit your visual growth and understanding. Other recommended areas of study are business and marketing. As Rhonda Layton, an interior designer and business owner, says, "Interior design is about 90 percent networking, marketing, selling, knowing the right people and this little thing called chutzpah, 7 percent paperwork and 3 percent design."

A Day in the Life: Design Assistant

8:00 a.m.: Arrive at the office before the rest of the staff, brew coffee and ensure the office is in order. Wash dishes left over from yesterday's client meeting.

8:30 a.m.: Check voicemail and e-mail for messages. Review calendar for day's appointments and call for confirmations. Adjust schedule as necessary and print revised schedule for head designer.

9:00 a.m.: Other employees arrive. Operate switchboard for all incoming calls and take messages for staff who are unavailable. Field calls from sales representatives requesting appointments with designers. Interface with clients and vendors.

10:00 a.m.: Speak with the head designer. Receive instructions on several tasks, such as picking up fabric samples from design center, contacting dealers regarding memo items (pieces on loan for display only) for a client meeting, dictation of a letter for a potential client that must be messengered by noon.

11:00 a.m.: Work on projects assigned by head designer while continually operating switchboard. Letter is first priority; complete it and give to head designer to proof. Contact dealers regarding memo items and arrange shipment with local delivery service.

12:00 p.m.: Send revised letter to potential client. Once messenger arrives, escape for lunch. Pick up fabric samples while picking up lunch—a reprieve from the switchboard for at least an hour. Visit several fabric houses and leave design center loaded down with bags. Pick up lunch for yourself and other office mates at nearby café.

1:30 p.m.: Check voicemail and e-mail for messages while you were out. Open and sort mail. Address envelopes for bookkeeper. Prepare office for client meeting at 2:30. Run up the street to purchase a new orchid for entryway. Brew more coffee and tea. Ensure conference room is organized and clean. Gather any last minute information head designer needs for meeting.

2:30 p.m.: Show clients to conference room, offer drinks and snacks. Work on additional projects other staff members have requested: errands, scheduling of appointments, shipments of furniture. Keep track of money in meters and ensure clients do not get parking tickets while in meeting.

Visit Vault at **www.vault.com** for insider company profiles, expert advice, career message boards, expert resume reviews, the Vault Job Board and more.

VAULT CAREER LIBRARY   **127**

4:00 p.m.: Clients leave. Clean conference room, wash dishes. Empty trash throughout office. Return calls on behalf of designer and schedule additional appointments for remainder of week.

5:00 p.m.: Since there is nothing urgent to complete, you get to leave on time!

Architecture and Interior Design Employer Directory

AECOM Technology Corporation
555 S. Flower St., Ste. 3700
Los Angeles, CA 90071-2300
Phone: (213) 593-8000
Fax: (213) 593-8730
www.aecom.com

M. Arthur Gensler Jr. & Associates, Inc.
2 Harrison St., Ste. 400
San Francisco, CA 94105
Phone: (415) 433-3700
Fax: (415) 836-4599
www.gensler.com

Arquitectonica
801 Brickell Avenue
Suite 1100
Miami, FL 33131
Phone: (305) 372-1812
Fax: (305) 372-1175
www.arquitectonica.com

BHDP Architecture
302 W. 3rd Street, Ste. 500
Cincinnati, OH 45202
Phone: (513) 271-1634
Fax: (513) 271-7017
www.bhdp.com

Cesar Pelli & Associates Architects
1056 Chapel Street
New Haven, CT 06510
Phone: (203) 777-2515
Fax: (203) 787-2856
www.cesar-pelli.com

Costas Kondylis and Partners LLP
31 West 27 Street
New York, NY 10001
Phone: (212) 725-4655
Fax: (212) 725-3441
www.kondylis.com

Foster and Partners
Riverside Three
22 Hester Road
London, SW11 4AN
United Kingdom
Phone: +44 (0)20.7738.0455
Fax: +44 (0)20.7738.1107
www.fosterandpartners.com

Fox & Fowle Architects, P.C.
22 West 19th Street
New York, NY 10011
Phone: (212) 627-1700
Fax: (212) 463-8716
www.foxfowle.com

Gensler
2 Harrison Street, Suite 400
San Francisco, CA 94105
Phone: (415) 433-3700
Fax: (415) 836-4599
www.gensler.com

H+L Architecture
1621 18th Street
Suite 110
Denver, CO 80202
Phone: (303) 295-1792
Fax: (303) 292-6437

HOK Group, Inc.
211 N. Broadway, Ste. 600
St. Louis, MO 63102
Phone: (314) 421-2000
Fax: (314) 421-2152
www.hok.com

Kohn Pedersen Fox Associates
111 West 57th Street
New York, NY 10019
Phone: (212) 977-6500
Fax: (212) 956-2526
www.kpf.com

NBBJ
111 S. Jackson St.
Seattle, WA 98104
Phone: (206) 223-5555
Fax: (206) 621-2300
www.nbbj.com

NB Design Group
1932 First Avenue, Suite 926
Seattle, WA 98101
Phone: (206) 441-7754
Fax: (206) 728-2341
www.nbdesigngroup.net

Morphosis Architects
2041 Colorado Avenue
Santa Monica, CA 90404
Phone: (310) 453-2247
Fax: (310) 829-3270
www.morphosis.net

RTKL Associates Inc.
901 S. Bond St.
Baltimore, MD 21231
Phone: (410) 528-8600
Fax: (410) 385-2455
www.rtkl.com

Skidmore Owings & Merrill LLP
224 S. Michigan Ave
Ste. 1000
Chicago, IL 60604
Phone: (312) 554-9090
Fax: (312) 360-4545
www.som.com

Visit Vault at **www.vault.com** for insider company profiles, expert advice,
career message boards, expert resume reviews, the Vault Job Board and more.

VAULT CAREER LIBRARY   **129**

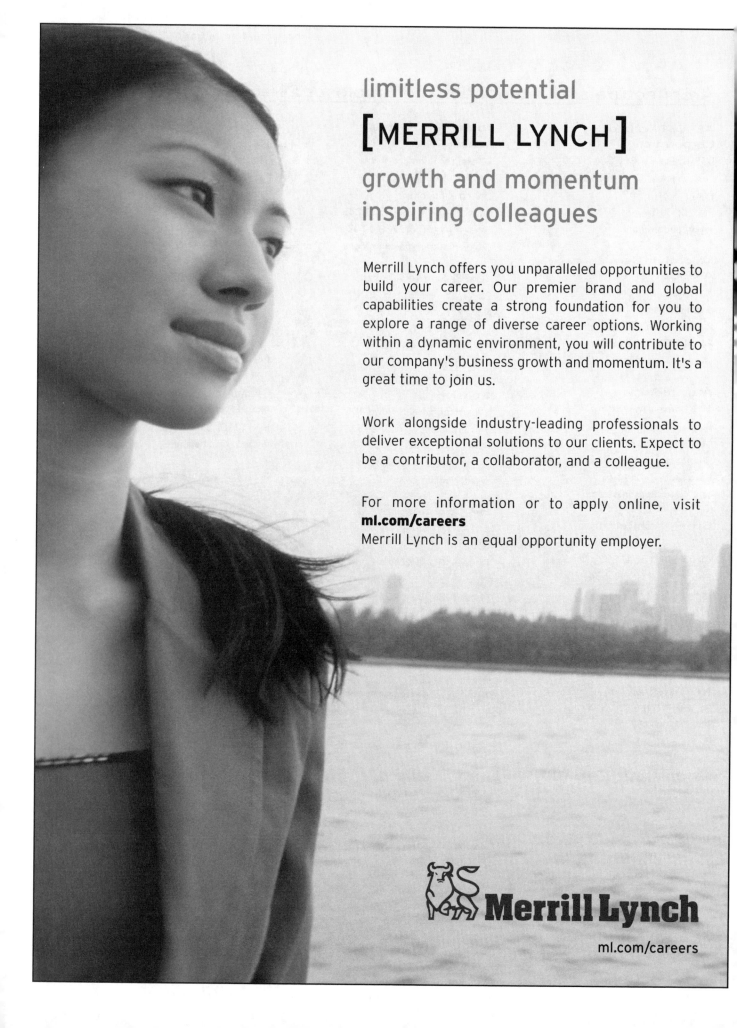

Banking

Investment Banking

Investment banking is the business of raising money for companies. Companies need capital in order to grow their business; they turn to investment banks to sell securities to investors—either public or private—to raise this capital. These securities come in the form of stocks or bonds.

Generally, an investment bank is comprised of the following areas:

Corporate finance

The bread and butter of a traditional investment bank, corporate finance generally performs two different functions: 1) mergers and acquisitions advisory, and 2) underwriting. On the mergers and acquisitions (M&A) advising side of corporate finance, bankers assist in negotiating and structuring a merger between two companies. If, for example, a company wants to buy another firm, then an investment bank will help finalize the purchase price, structure the deal and generally ensure a smooth transaction. The underwriting function within corporate finance involves raising capital for a client. In the investment-banking world, capital can be raised by selling either stocks or bonds to investors.

Sales

Sales is another core component of the investment bank. Salespeople take the form of the classic retail broker, the institutional salesperson, or the private client service representative. Brokers develop relationships with individual investors and sell stocks and stock advice to the average Joe. Institutional salespeople develop business relationships with large institutional investors, who manage large groups of assets, like pension funds or mutual funds. Private Client Service (PCS) representatives lie somewhere between retail brokers and institutional salespeople, providing brokerage and money management services for extremely wealthy individuals. Salespeople make money through commissions on trades made through their firms.

Trading

Traders also provide a vital role for the investment bank by facilitating the buying and selling of stock, bonds or other securities, either by carrying an inventory of securities for sale or by executing a given trade for a client. Traders deal with transactions large and small and provide liquidity (the ability to buy and sell securities) for the market. (This is often called making a market.) Traders make money by purchasing securities and selling them at a slightly higher price. This price differential is called the "bid-ask spread."

Research

Research analysts follow stocks and bonds and make recommendations on whether to buy, sell or hold those securities. Stock analysts (known as equity analysts) typically focus on one industry and will cover up to 20 companies' stocks at any given time. Some research analysts work on the fixed-income side and will cover a particular segment, such as high-yield bonds or U.S. Treasury bonds. Salespeople within the I-bank use research published by analysts to convince their clients to buy or sell securities through their firm. Corporate finance bankers rely on research analysts to be experts in the industry in which they are working. Reputable research analysts can generate substantial corporate finance business and substantial trading activity, and thus are an integral part of any investment bank.

Visit Vault at **www.vault.com** for insider company profiles, expert advice, career message boards, expert resume reviews, the Vault Job Board and more.

VAULT CAREER LIBRARY 131

Syndicate

The hub of the investment banking wheel, syndicate provides a vital link between salespeople and corporate finance. Syndicate facilitates the placing of securities in a public offering, a knock-down, drag-out affair between and among buyers of offerings and the investment banks managing the process. In a corporate or municipal debt deal, syndicate also determines the allocation of bonds.

Commercial Banking

"Neither a borrower nor a lender be," Polonius advises Laertes in *Hamlet*. Good thing commercial banks haven't taken Shakespearean bromides to heart. (It didn't get Polonius anywhere, either.) Commercial banks, unlike investment banks, generally act as lenders, putting forth their own money to support businesses, as opposed to investment advisors who rely on other folks— buyers of stocks and bonds—to pony up cash. This distinction, enshrined by fundamental banking laws in place since the 1930s, has led to noticeable cultural differences (exaggerated by stereotype) between commercial and investment bankers.

Commercial bankers (deservedly or not) have a reputation for being less aggressive, more risk-averse and simply not as mean as investment bankers. Commercial bankers also don't command the eye-popping salaries and elite prestige that I-bankers receive.

There is a basis for the stereotype. Commercial banks carefully screen borrowers because the banks are investing huge sums of their own money in companies that must remain healthy enough to make regular loan payments for decades. Investment bankers, on the other hand, can make their fortunes in one day by skimming off some of the money raised in a stock offering or invested into an acquisition. While a borrower's subsequent business decline can damage a commercial bank's bottom line, a stock that plummets after an offering has no effect on the investment bank that managed its IPO.

We'll take your money

Commercial bankers make money by their legal charter to take deposits from businesses and consumers. To gain the confidence of these depositors, commercial banks offer government-sponsored guarantees on these deposits on amounts up to $100,000. But to get FDIC guarantees, commercial banks must follow a myriad of regulations (and hire regulators to manage them). Many of these guidelines were set up in the Glass-Steagall Act of 1933, which was meant to separate the activities of commercial and investment banks. Glass-Steagall included a restriction on the sale of stocks and bonds (investment banks, which could not take deposits, were exempt from banking laws and free to offer more speculative securities offerings). Deregulation—especially the Financial Services Modernization Act of 1999—and consolidation in the banking industry over the past decade have weakened these traditional barriers.

The lending train

The typical commercial banking process is fairly straightforward. The lending cycle starts with consumers depositing savings or businesses depositing sales proceeds at the bank. The bank, in turn, puts aside a relatively small portion of the money for withdrawals and to pay for possible loan defaults. It then loans the rest of the money to companies in need of capital to pay for, say, a new factory or an overseas venture. A commercial bank's customers can range from the dry cleaner on the corner to a multinational conglomerate. For very large clients, several commercial banks may band together to issue "syndicated loans" of truly staggering sizes.

Commercial banks lend money at interest rates that are largely determined by the Federal Reserve Board (currently governed by the bespectacled Alan Greenspan). Along with lending money that they have on deposit from clients, commercial banks lend out money that they have received from the Fed. The Fed loans out money to commercial banks, that in turn lend it to bank customers in a variety of forms—standard loans, mortgages and so on. Besides its ability to set a baseline interest rate for all loans, the Fed also uses its lending power to equalize the economy. To prevent inflation, the Fed raises the interest rate it charges for the money it loans to banks, slowing down the circulation of money and the growth of the economy. To encourage economic growth, the Fed will lower the interest rate it charges banks.

Making money by moving money

Take a moment to consider how a bank makes its money. Commercial banks in the U.S. earn 5 to 14 percent interest on most of their loans. As commercial banks typically only pay depositors 1 percent—if anything—on checking accounts and 2 to 3 percent on savings accounts, they make a tremendous amount of money in the difference between the cost of their funds (1 percent for checking account deposits) and the return on the funds they loan (5 to 14 percent).

Corporate Finance

Stuffy bankers?

The stereotype of the corporate finance department is stuffy, arrogant (white and male) MBAs who frequent golf courses and talk on cell phones nonstop. While this is increasingly less true, corporate finance remains the most white-shoe department in the typical investment bank. The atmosphere in corporate finance is, unlike that in sales and trading, often quiet and reserved. Junior bankers sit separated by cubicles, quietly crunching numbers.

Depending on the firm, corporate finance can also be a tough place to work, with unforgiving bankers and expectations through the roof. Although decreasing, stories of analyst abuse abound, and some bankers come down hard on new analysts to scare and intimidate them. The lifestyle for corporate finance professionals can be a killer. In fact, many corporate finance workers find that they literally dedicate their lives to the job. Social life suffers, free time disappears and stress multiplies. It is not uncommon to find analysts and associates wearing rumpled pants and wrinkled shirts, exhibiting the wear and tear of all-nighters. Fortunately, these long hours pay remarkable dividends in the form of six-figure salaries and huge year-end bonuses.

Personality-wise, bankers tend to be highly intelligent, motivated and not lacking in confidence. Money is important to the bankers, and many anticipate working for just a few years to earn as much as possible before finding less demanding work. Analysts and associates tend also to be ambitious, intelligent and pedigreed. If you happen to be going into an analyst or associate position, make sure you check your ego at the door but don't be afraid to ask penetrating questions about deals and what is required of you.

The deal team

Investment bankers generally work in deal teams which, depending on the size of a deal, vary somewhat in makeup. In this chapter we will provide an overview of the roles and lifestyles of the positions in corporate finance, from analyst to managing director. (Often, a person in corporate finance is generally called an I-banker.) Because the titles and roles really do not differ significantly between underwriting to M&A, we have included both in this explanation. In fact, at most smaller firms, underwriting and transaction advisory are not separated, and bankers typically pitch whatever business they can scout out within their industry sector.

Visit Vault at **www.vault.com** for insider company profiles, expert advice, career message boards, expert resume reviews, the Vault Job Board and more.

VAULT CAREER LIBRARY 133

At M&T Bank, we understand that you want more than just a job.

M&T Bank can help you make the most of your ambition and abilities. As one of the best performing banks in the country, we've fostered a diverse, challenging and professional environment where you'll find exceptional growth opportunities and a team-oriented culture.

M&T's **Management Development Program** represents our strong commitment to developing new managers. This unique program for recent college graduates involves a full year of formal training designed to develop technical and leadership skills. Immediately, you'll be able to present your individual strengths to high-profile group projects. We are looking for students from all majors to discover the opportunities in a wide range of divisions throughout the organization.

Find out what it's like to work for one of the strongest and most highly regarded regional banks in the country. For more information about our Management Development Program, visit our website at www.mandtbank.com/campus. An equal opportunity employer M/F/D/V.

Understanding what's important.®

Analysts

Analysts are the grunts of the corporate finance world. They often toil endlessly with little thanks, little pay (when figured on an hourly basis), and barely enough free time to sleep four hours a night. Typically hired directly out of top undergraduate universities, this crop of bright, highly motivated kids does the financial modeling and basic entry-level duties associated with any corporate finance deal.

Modeling every night until 2 a.m. and not having much of a social life proves to be unbearable for many an analyst and after two years many leave the industry. Unfortunately, most bankers recognize the transient nature of analysts, and work them hard to get the most out of them that they can. The unfortunate analyst that screws up or talks back too much may never get quality work, spending his days bored until 11 p.m. waiting for work to come, stressing even more than the busy analyst. These are the analysts that do not get called to work on live transactions, and do menial work or just put together pitchbooks all the time.

When it comes to pay, much depends on whether the analyst is in New York or not. In the City, salary often begins for first-year analysts at $45,000 to $55,000 per year, with an annual bonus of approximately $30,000. While this seems to be a lot for a 22-year-old with just an undergrad degree, it's not a great deal if you consider per-hour compensation. At most firms, analysts also get dinner every night for free if they work late, and have little time to spend their income, often meaning fat checking and savings accounts and ample fodder to fund business school or law school down the road. At regional firms, pay typically is 20 percent less than that of their New York counterparts. Worth noting, though, is the fact that at regional firms hours are often less, and the cost of living is much lower. Be wary, however, of the small regional firm or branch office of a Wall Street firm that pays at the low end of the scale and still shackles analysts to their cubicles. While the salary generally does not improve much for second-year analysts, the bonus can double for those second-years who demonstrate high performance. At this level, bonuses depend mostly on an analyst's contribution, attitude and work ethic, as opposed to the volume of business generated by the bankers with whom he or she works.

Institutional Sales and Trading (S&T)

The war zone

If you've ever been to an investment banking trading floor, you've witnessed the chaos. It's usually a lot of swearing, yelling and flashing computer screens: a pressure cooker of stress. Sometimes the floor is a quiet rumble of activity, but when the market takes a nosedive, panic ensues and the volume kicks up a notch. Traders must rely on their market instincts, and salespeople yell for bids when the market tumbles. Deciding what to buy or sell, and at what price, is difficult when millions of dollars are at stake.

However, salespeople and traders work much more reasonable hours than research analysts or corporate finance bankers. Rarely does a salesperson or trader venture into the office on a Saturday or Sunday; the trading floor is completely devoid of life on weekends. Any corporate finance analyst who has crossed a trading floor on a Saturday will tell you that the only noises to be heard on the floor are the clocks ticking every minute and the whir of the air conditioner.

Visit Vault at **www.vault.com** for insider company profiles, expert advice, career message boards, expert resume reviews, the Vault Job Board and more.

VAULT CAREER LIBRARY   135

Shop Talk

Here's a quick example of how a salesperson and a trader interact on an emerging market bond trade.

SALESPERSON: Receives a call from a buy-side firm (say, a large mutual fund). The buy-side firm wishes to sell $10 million of a particular Mexican Par government-issued bond (denominated in U.S. dollars). The emerging markets bond salesperson, seated next to the emerging markets traders, stands up in his chair and yells to the relevant trader, "Give me a bid on $10 million Mex Par, six and a quarter, nineteens."

TRADER: "I got 'em at 73 and an eighth."

Translation: I am willing to buy them at a price of $73.125 per $100 of face value. As mentioned, the $10 million represents amount of par value the client wanted to sell, meaning the trader will buy the bonds, paying 73.125 percent of $10 million plus accrued interest (to factor in interest earned between interest payments).

SALESPERSON: "Can't you do any better than that?"

Translation: Please buy at a higher price, as I will get a higher commission.

TRADER: "That's the best I can do. The market is falling right now. You want to sell?"

SALESPERSON: "Done. $10 million."

S&T: A symbiotic relationship?

Institutional sales and trading are highly dependent on one another. The propaganda that you read in glossy firm brochures portrays those in sales and trading as a shiny, happy integrated team environment of professionals working for the clients' interests. While often that is true, salespeople and traders frequently clash, disagree and bicker.

Simply put, salespeople provide the clients for traders, and traders provide the products for sales. Traders would have nobody to trade for without sales, but sales would have nothing to sell without traders. Understanding how a trader makes money and how a salesperson makes money should explain how conflicts can arise.

Traders make money by selling high and buying low (this difference is called the spread). They are buying stocks or bonds for clients, and these clients filter in through sales. A trader faced with a buy order for a buy-side firm couldn't care less about the performance of the securities once they are sold. He or she just cares about making the spread. In a sell trade, this means selling at the highest price possible. In a buy trade, this means buying at the lowest price possible.

The salesperson, however, has a different incentive. The total return on the trade often determines the money a salesperson makes, so he wants the trader to sell at a low price. The salesperson also wants to be able to offer the client a better price than competing firms in order to get the trade and earn a commission. This of course leads to many interesting situations, and at the extreme, salespeople and traders who eye one another suspiciously.

The personalities

Salespeople possess remarkable communication skills, including outgoing personalities and a smoothness not often seen in traders. Traders sometimes call them bullshit artists while salespeople counter by calling traders quant guys with no personality. Traders are tough, quick and often consider themselves smarter than salespeople. The salespeople probably know better how to have fun, but the traders win the prize for mental sharpness and the ability to handle stress.

Research

If you have a brokerage account, you have likely been given access to research on stocks that you asked about. This research was probably written by an investment bank's research department.

To the outsider, it seems that research analysts spend their time in a quiet room poring over numbers, calling companies and writing research reports. The truth is an entirely different story, involving quite a bit of selling on the phone and on the road. Analysts produce research ideas, hand them to associates and assistants, and then man the phone talking to buy-side stock/bond pickers, company managers and internal salespeople. They become the managers of research reports and the experts on their industries to the outside world. Thus, while the lifestyle of the research analyst would initially appear to resemble that of a statistician, it often comes closer to that of a diplomat or salesperson.

The Players

Research assistants

The bottom-level number crunchers in research, research assistants generally begin with no industry or market expertise. They come from solid undergraduate schools and performed well there, but initially get stuck with mundane research tasks, such as digging up information and editing/formatting reports. Research assistants also take over the spreadsheet modeling functions required by the analyst. Travel is limited for the budding research assistant, as it usually does not make financial sense to send more than the research analyst to meetings with company officials or money managers.

Research associates

Burdened with numbers and deadlines, the research associate often feels like a cross between a statistician and a corporate finance analyst. Long hours, weekends in the office and number-crunching sum up the routine of the associate. However, compared to analyst and associate analogues in corporate finance, the research associate works fewer hours, often makes it home at a reasonable time, and works less on the weekend. Unfortunately, the associate is required to be present and accounted for at 7:30 a.m., when most morning meetings take place.

Mirroring the corporate finance analyst and associate positions, research associates can be bright, motivated kids directly out of top undergraduate universities. Or, at firms dedicated to hiring MBAs in research, the research associate role is the entry-level position once the MBA has been earned.

A talented research associate can earn much in the way of responsibility. For example, the research associate may field phone calls from smaller "B" accounts (i.e., smaller money managers) and companies less important to the analyst. (The analyst handles the relationships with the biggest buy-siders, best clients and top salespeople.) When it comes to writing reports, some analysts give free reign to associates in writing. Also, research associates focus on one industry and typically work for only one full-fledged research analyst. This structure helps research associates delve deeper into the aspects of one industry group and enables them to work closely with a senior-level research analyst.

To start, research assistants/associates out of undergraduate schools typically get paid similarly to the corporate finance analyst right out of college. After one or two years, the compensation varies dramatically, depending on performance and the success of the analysts in the industry group as well as the associate's contribution. For the MBA research associate, the compensation is similar to I-banking associates: as of this writing, $80,000 salaries with $30,000 signing bonuses, plus a $30,000 year-end bonus, are typical.

Visit Vault at www.vault.com for insider company profiles, expert advice, career message boards, expert resume reviews, the Vault Job Board and more.

VAULT CAREER LIBRARY   137

citigroup

"I work with a fantastic team of people comprising a huge variety of skills and experience. The diversity within the group makes for an excellent team, one in which we are all working together to help one another achieve our goals."

PAULA SHEEHAN, ANALYST

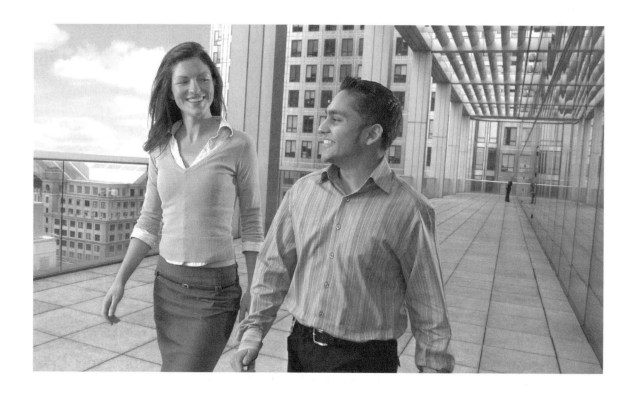

Global Banking

Global Capital Markets

Global Transaction Services

Global Corporate Services

Citigroup Investment Research

The Citigroup Private Bank

Working at Citigroup means being part of a team that is making history in the financial services world. If this appeals to you, come see us. We're looking forward to meeting you.

apply online at
www.oncampus.citigroup.com

It All Depends on the Analyst

Insiders stress that the research associate's contribution entirely depends on the particular analyst. Good analysts (from the perspective of the associate) encourage responsibility and handoff a significant amount of work. Others communicate poorly, maintain rigid control and don't trust their assistants and associates to do much more than the most mundane tasks.

Being stuck with a mediocre analyst can make your job miserable. If you are considering an entry-level position in research, you should carefully evaluate the research analyst you will work with, as this person will have a huge impact on your job experience.

Note that in research, the job titles for analyst and associate have switched. In corporate finance, one begins as an analyst, and is promoted to associate post-MBA. In research, one begins as a research associate, and ultimately is promoted to the research analyst title.

Research analysts

The research analyst, especially in equity, is truly a guru. Analysts follow particular industries, recommend stocks to buy and sell, and convince salespeople and buy-siders why they or their clients should or should not invest in Company XYZ. The road to becoming an analyst is either paved with solid industry experience, or through the research assistant/associate path.

Full-fledged analyst positions are difficult to come by. The skills required to succeed as an analyst include a firm grasp of the industry and dynamics of stock picking, and the sales skills required to convince investors and insiders alike why a stock is such an excellent buy. An analyst lacking in either area will simply not become the next *II*-rated star (that is, an analyst highly rated by the annual *Institutional Investor* poll).

Research analysts spend considerable time talking on the phone to investors, salespeople and traders, pitching buy and sell ideas or simply discussing industry or company trends. Everyone tries to get the research analyst's ear, to ask for advice or (as we will discuss in-depth later) to pressure him or her to change a rating or initiate coverage of a particular stock. Analysts also travel regularly, visiting buy-siders or big money managers and companies in their field. Indirectly, they are trying to generate trading business with money managers, research ideas from companies or trying to build a reputation in the industry. All in all, analysts must be able to quickly and convincingly pitch an idea, and defend it thoroughly when the time comes.

In this atmosphere, research analysts must scrutinize every company that they maintain under coverage. Any news or company announcements will spur a deluge of phone calls to the analyst, with questions ranging from the big picture to the tiniest of details. They also must maintain a handle on an extremely important aspect of any company—the numbers. Inaccurate earnings estimates, especially when they are far from the mark, reflect poorly on the analyst. Why didn't an analyst know the company stock was going to come out with such low earnings? Or, why didn't the research analyst know that industry growth was slowing down? The analyst is responsible for staying on top of these things.

Compensation packages for research analysts run the gamut. Some *II*-rated star analysts in hot industries command multimillion dollar annual packages, especially during bull markets. Most banks figure their compensation for analysts with formulas that are usually incomprehensible to even the research analysts. The factors that go into analyst compensation typically include a mix of the following:

• The performance of stocks under coverage (meaning that if their stocks perform like the analyst predicts, they get paid well).

• Trading activity within the firm of stocks under coverage.

• Corporate finance business revenue of companies in their industry.

• Performance evaluations of the research analyst by superiors.

Visit Vault at **www.vault.com** for insider company profiles, expert advice, career message boards, expert resume reviews, the Vault Job Board and more.

VAULT CAREER LIBRARY   139

• *Institutional Investor* rankings (Once a research analyst finds himself listed as an *II*-ranked analyst, the first stop is into his boss's office to renegotiate his annual package.)

Note: As they progress in their careers, research analysts receive titles similar to investment bankers, namely VP (Vice President), SVP (Senior Vice President) and ultimately MD (Managing Director). However, the tasks of a research analyst tend to remain somewhat consistent once the analyst level is reached, with perhaps more research selling and traveling involved at the most senior levels, and more oversight of a group of more junior analysts.

The *Institutional Investor* (*II*) Ratings Scorecard

Institutional Investor is a monthly magazine publication that, among other things, rates research analysts. The importance of the *II* ratings to investment banks and even many institutional investors cannot be overstated. Most industry watchers believe and follow the ratings as if they were gospel.

How do the ratings work? Essentially, *II* utilizes a formula to determine the best research analysts on Wall Street, surveys industry professionals and publishes their rankings annually. Note the bias, however, toward research analysts at bulge bracket firms in these ratings. *II*'s formula essentially involves surveys of "directors of research, chief investment officers, portfolio managers and buy-side analysts at the major money management institutions around the world." Major money managers deal primarily with large investment banks for their trading needs and a portion of their research needs.

In 2000 Merrill Lynch and Morgan Stanley split the top spot in the *II* rankings. Both firms had 55 analysts rated including 22 and 12 first-teamers, respectively. Merrill Lynch had held the top spot alone for the two previous years while Morgan Stanley shot up from No. 3. Salomon Smith Barney came in third with 46 All-Americans, followed by Credit Suisse First Boston (38). Donaldson Lufkin & Jenrette (now a part of Credit Suisse First Boston) and Goldman Sachs were tied for fifth with 35 All-Americans.

The Product

Industry research reports

To establish oneself as a knowledgeable analyst, many researchers begin by writing and issuing an industry piece. For example, an industry research report on the oil and gas sector might discuss issues such as commodity prices, the general outlook for the sector and valuations of companies in the industry.

The time required to generate an industry piece depends on the length of the report, the complexity of the industry and how important it is to show expertise to investors and management teams in the industry. For completely new industries for new analysts, a full six months or more is allotted to enable the analyst to fully understand the industry and develop a thorough report. Once it is printed, salespeople will use an industry research report to get up to speed and learn about a particular segment.

Touted as industry gospel, industry research reports take substantial time to produce and earn the firm nothing except awareness that the investment bank follows an industry and has expertise in that industry. However, the brand equity built by an industry piece can be substantial and make corporate finance banker cold-calling a much easier process.

Company specific research reports

Once an analyst's industry piece has been written and digested by the investment community, the analyst focuses on publishing research reports on specific companies. To create a well-rounded research universe, research analysts will typically write on the top industry players, as well as several smaller players in the industry. One of the most critical roles of an equity research analyst is to make future earnings estimates for the companies he or she covers. (The average earnings estimate of all analysts covering a company is called the "consensus" estimate.) Company-specific reports fall into three categories: initiation of coverage, updates and rating changes.

Initiation of coverage: This is exactly what it sounds like. These reports indicate that an analyst has not previously written research or covered the particular company. Usually an initiation of coverage report includes substantial information about the business, a detailed forecast model and risk factors inherent in the business.

Update: When a stock moves, news/earnings are released or the analyst meets with management, an update report is put out. Often one-pagers, updates provide quick information important to current movements in the stock or will raise or lower earnings estimates.

Change of rating: Whenever an I-bank alters its rating on a stock (we will discuss these ratings later), a report is issued. These reports vary in length from one to five pages. Reasons for a downgrade include: lower than expected earnings, forecasts for diminished industry or firm growth, management departures, problems integrating a merger, or even overpriced stocks. Reasons for an upgrade include: better than expected earnings, new management, stock repurchases or beneficial industry trends.

Conflict of Interest

It is crucial to note whether an investment bank has provided corporate finance services to the company under coverage. Usually at the end of a research piece, a footnote will indicate whether this is the case. If so, investors should be careful to understand the inherent conflict of interest and bias that the research report contains. Often covering a company's stock (and covering it with optimistic ratings) will ensure corporate finance business, such as a manager role in equity offerings, M&A advisory services and so on.

Market commentary

Analysts usually cover a particular (small) universe of stocks, but some analysts, called market strategists, survey and report on market conditions as a whole. Most large banks publish market commentary reports on a daily basis (sometimes even several within a day), augmented with weekly, monthly and quarterly reviews. Included in such reports is information on the performance of stocks in major market indices in the U.S., major markets worldwide, and in various sectors—such as transportation, technology and energy—in the U.S. Some of these commentaries offer forecasts for the markets or for particular sectors. Naturally, economic data is paramount to stock market performance overall and thus pervades market commentaries.

Economic commentary

Similar to a market commentary, economic reports are also published periodically and cover economic indicators and trends. These reports are often stuffed with graphs of macroeconomic factors such as GDP, inflation, interest rates, consumer spending, new home sales, import/export data, etc. They provide useful information regarding government fiscal and monetary policy, and often link to fixed income reports. Often the same market strategist writes both the economic commentaries and the market commentaries for a firm.

Fixed income commentary

Analysts covering the fixed income markets publish periodic reports on the debt markets. Often tied to the economic commentaries, fixed income market reports comment on the performance of various fixed income instruments including U.S. government securities, mortgages, corporate bonds, commodity prices and other specialized fixed income securities. The five-point scale for rating stocks is ubiquitous in banking, but the definitions that banks refer to do not accurately measure what the analyst believes. The following scale reflects the general consensus on stock ratings, but keep in mind that these

Visit Vault at **www.vault.com** for insider company profiles, expert advice, career message boards, expert resume reviews, the Vault Job Board and more.

V^ULT CAREER LIBRARY 141

Banking Employer Directory

BMO Capital Markets

111 W. Monroe
Chicago, IL 60603

Recruiting Contact:
Phone: 866.377.1866
E-mail: campusrecruiting@bmo.com
www.bmocm.com/aboutus/campusrecruiting/

Undergraduate schools BMO recruits from:

Brown; Columbia; Cornell, DePauw, Emory, University of Indiana, Northwestern University, Notre Dame, New York University, Rice, University of Chicago, University of Illinois, University of Iowa, University of Michigan, University of Texas, University of Wisconsin, Villanova

BMO Capital Markets is a leading, full-service North American financial services provider offering equity and debt underwriting, corporate lending and project financing, merger and acquisitions advisory services, merchant banking, securitization, treasury and market risk management, debt and equity research and institutional sales and trading. BMO Capital Markets has offices in 26 locations around the world, including 14 in North America.

BMO Capital Markets is a member of BMO Financial Group (NYSE, TSX: BMO), one of the largest diversified financial services providers in North America with more than $268 billion in total assets and 34,000 employees as of January 31, 2006.

Citigroup Corporate and Investment Banking

388 Greenwich Street
New York, New York 10013
Recruiting Contact Phon: 212-816-6000
www.oncampus.citigroup.com

global corporate &
investment banking group

Citigroup Corporate and Investment Banking is a full service investment banking and securities brokerage firm, providing a complete range of financial advisory, research and capital raising services to corporations, governments and individuals. Citigroup (NYSE: C) and its affiliates, have a reach that spans over 100 countries and territories. This enables us to offer a unique combination of local market insight, as well as the expertise necessary for today's global economy.

What we give you is the chance to gain invaluable experience, leverage the insights of multicultural backgrounds and broaden your experience through global working relationships and a wide variety of work opportunities.

Undergraduate schools Citigroup recruits from:

Babson; Barnard; Baruch; Berkeley; Boston College; Brown; Cal Poly; Carnegie Mellon; Chicago; Columbia; Cornell; Dartmouth; Duke; Emory; Fordham; Georgetown; Georgia Tech; Harvard; Holy Cross; Howard; Illinois; Johns Hopkins; Lehigh; Miami; Michigan; MIT; Morehouse; Northwestern; Notre Dame; NYU; UPenn; Princeton; Rutgers; Spelman; Stanford; Stevens; St. Johns; Stony Brook; Texas A&M; Tufts; UCLA; UNC; U Texas at Austin; UVA; USC; UWO; Villanova; Wake Forest; Yale

Banking Employer Directory, cont.

Credit Suisse

11 Madison Avenue
10th Floor
New York, New York 10010

Recruiting Contacts:
Candace Kohl
Undergraduate Campus Relationship Manager
Phone: 212-325-3655

Christine Zinser
Undergraduate Campus Relationship Manager
Phone: 212-538-2954

www.credit-suisse.com/standout
E-mail: uscampus.recruiting@credit-suisse.com

Undergraduate schools Credit Suisse recruits from:
We recruit from top undergraduate programs. For more information, please visit our website: www.credit-suisse.com/standout

As one of the world's leading banks, Credit Suisse provides its clients with investment banking, private banking and asset management services worldwide. Credit Suisse offers advisory services, comprehensive solutions and innovative products to companies, institutional clients and high-net-worth private clients globally, as well as retail clients in Switzerland. Credit Suisse is active in over 50 countries and employs approximately 40,000 people. Credit Suisse's parent company, Credit Suisse Group, is a leading global financial services company headquartered in Zurich. Credit Suisse Group's registered shares (CSGN) are listed in Switzerland and, in the form of American Depositary Shares (CSR), in New York.

Goldman, Sachs & Co.

85 Broad Street
New York, NY 10004
Recruiting Contact Phone: 212-902-1000
www.gs.com/careers

Goldman Sachs is a leading global investment banking, securities and investment management firm that provides a wide range of services worldwide to a substantial and diversified client base that includes corporations, financial institutions, governments and high net worth individuals. Founded in 1869, it is one of the oldest and largest investment banking firms. The firm is headquartered in New York and maintains offices in London, Frankfurt, Tokyo, Hong Kong and other major financial centers around the world. Please visit our Careers site for information about applying online and our recruiting process.

Undergraduate schools Goldman recruits from:
The following is a list of our primary cross-divisional target schools. The firm also hires from a number of additional schools on a divisional basis, and welcomes online applications from all colleges and universities.

Barnard; UC Berkeley, Brown University; Carnegie Mellon; University of Chicago; Columbia University, Cornell University; Dartmouth College; Duke University; Emory University; Georgetown University; Hampton University; Harvard University; Howard University; Indiana University; University of Michigan, MIT, Morehouse College, University of North Carolina Northwestern University, University of Notre Dame; New York University; Princeton University, Rutgers University; Spelman College, Stanford University; University of Texas - Austin; UCLA; USC; University of Pennyslvania; Vanderbilt University; University of Virigina; Wellesley College; Yale University

Visit Vault at **www.vault.com** for insider company profiles, expert advice, career message boards, expert resume reviews, the Vault Job Board and more.

V∧ULT CAREER LIBRARY   **143**

Banking Employer Directory, cont.

M&T Bank Corporation

One M&T Plaza
11th Floor
Buffalo, N.Y. 14203

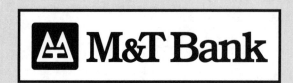

Recruiting Contact:
Phone: (716) 842-5445
www.mandtbank.com/campus

Undergraduate schools M&T recruits from:
Amherst; Bowdoin; Brown; Carnegie Mellon; Canisius; Colgate; Columbia; Cornell; Dartmouth; George Washington; Georgetown; Hampton; Harvard; Howard; Ithaca; Johns Hopkins; Lafayette; Morehouse; Mt. Holyoke; Niagara; Penn State; Princeton; RIT; Smith; Spelman; Swarthmore; SUNY Binghamton; SUNY Geneseo; Syracuse; University at Buffalo; University at Maryland; University of Notre Dame; University of Pennsylvania; University of Rochester; University of Virginia; Vassar; Wellesley; Williams; Yale

M&T Bank Corporation is one of the 20 largest commercial bank holding companies in the U.S., with over $56 billion in assets as of June 30, 2006.

As one of the most respected regional banks in the country, M&T Bank is recognized for financial strength and stability built on our belief that we succeed when our employees, customers and communities do. We are proud of our record of civic and charitable support and our employees' leadership and volunteerism.

We work hard to understand what's important to our customers and to create a supportive, inclusive culture and work environment where employees can succeed personally and professionally.

Merrill Lynch

250 Vesey Street
4 World Financial Center
New York, New York 10080
www.ml.com/careers

Merrill Lynch is one of the world's leading wealth management, capital markets and advisory companies, with offices in 37 countries and territories and total client assets of approximately $1.5 trillion.

Merrill Lynch has two core businesses - Global Private Client and Global Markets & Investment Banking Group offering a range of services for private clients, small businesses, and institutions and corporations.

range of asset classes and serves as a strategic advisor to corporations, governments, institutions and individuals worldwide.

> **Corporate Snapshot**
> **Founded:** 1914 (Charles E. Merrill & Co)
> **Employees:** 55,300
> **Q3 2006 Net Revenue:** $9.9 billion
> **Total Client Assets:** Approx. $1.5 trillion
> **Total Stockholders' Equity:** $38.9 bn
> **Fortune 500:** Ranked No.34
> **Stock Symbol:** MER
> **Global Markets:** 37 countries.
>
> *As of quarter-end, Q3 2006.*

Merrill Lynch owns just under half of BlackRock, one of the world's largest publicly traded investment management companies with approximately $1 trillion in assets under management.

We're growing our business by helping clients grow theirs.
Our client relationships are among our greatest competitive assets. We deepen and enrich these relationships through disciplined growth, innovation, and seamless execution.

Schools Merrill recruits from
Merrill recruiters from a variety of top tier undergraduate schools.

Banking Employer Directory, cont.

SunTrust Banks, Inc.

303 Peachtree St. NE
Atlanta, GA 30308
www.suntrust.com/campus

Undergraduate schools SunTrust recruits from:
Clemson; Duke; Emory; Florida A&M; Florida International; Florida State; Georgia Tech; Howard; James Madison; Rollins; Spelman; Tennessee State; University of Central Florida; University of Florida; University of Georgia; University of Miami; University of Maryland; UNC-Chapel Hill; University of Richmond; University of South Florida; UT-Knoxville; University of Virginia; Vanderbilt; Virginia Commonwealth; Virginia Tech; Wake Forest; Washington & Lee.

Please view our Campus Recruiting Calendar on suntrust.com/campus.

SunTrust is one of the nation's largest financial institutions. We operate an extensive distribution network in Florida, Georgia, Maryland, North Carolina, South Carolina, Tennessee, Virginia, and the District of Columbia, and also serve customers in selected markets nationally. Primary businesses include deposit, credit, trust and investment services. Through various subsidiaries SunTrust provides credit cards, mortgage banking, insurance, brokerage, and capital market services.

SunTrust makes a significant investment in the training and development of its employees. Our internship and full-time Training Program positions provide a solid platform on which to build your career. Visit suntrust.com/campus to learn more about our opportunities.

Wachovia Corporation

301 South College Street
Suite 4000, One Wachovia Center
Charlotte, NC 28288
Wachovia.com/careers

Allen & Co.
711 Fifth Avenue
9th Floor
New York, NY 10022
Phone: (212) 832-8000
Fax: (212) 832-8023

Bank of America
100 North Tryon Street
Charlotte, NC 28255
Phone: (704) 388-2547
Fax: (704) 386-6699
www.bofa.com

Bank of America, Global Corporate & Investment Banking Division
9 West 57th Street
New York, NY 10019
Phone: (212) 583-8900
100 N. Tryon Street
Charlotte, NC 28255
Phone: (800) 432-1000
www.bankofamerica.com

Bank of New York
1 Wall Street
New York, NY 10286
Tel: (212) 495-1784
Fax: (212) 809-9528
www.bankofny.com

Barclays Capital
5 The North Colonnade
Canary Wharf
London, E14 4BB
United Kingdom
Phone: +44-20-7623-2323

200 Park Avenue
New York, NY 10166
Phone: (212) 412-4000
www.barcap.com

Bear Stearns
383 Madison Avenue
New York, NY 10179
Phone: (212) 272-2000
Fax: (212) 272-4785
www.bearstearns.com

Visit Vault at **www.vault.com** for insider company profiles, expert advice, career message boards, expert resume reviews, the Vault Job Board and more.

VAULT CAREER LIBRARY   **145**

Banking Employer Directory, cont.

The Blackstone Group
345 Park Avenue
New York, NY 10154
Phone: (212) 583-5000
Fax: (212) 583-5712
www.blackstone.com

Brown Brothers Harriman
& Co.
140 Broadway
New York, NY 10015-1101
Phone: (212) 483-1818
Fax: (212) 493-8545
www.bbh.com

CIBC World Markets
300 Madison Avenue
New York, NY 10017
Phone: (212) 856-4000
www.cibcwm.com

Citigroup Inc.
399 Park Avenue
New York, NY 10043
Phone: (800) 285-3000
Fax: (212) 793-3946
www.citigroup.com

Citigroup Corporate and Investment Banking
388 Greenwich Street
New York, NY 10013
Phone: (212) 816-6000
www.citigroupcib.com

Citizens Financial Group
One Citizens Plaza
Providence, RI 02930
www.citizensbank.com

Cowen and Company, LLC
1221 Avenue of the Americas
New York, NY 10020
Phone: (646) 562-1000
Fax: (646) 562-1741
www.cowen.com

Deutsche Bank
60 Wall Street
New York, NY 10005
Phone: (212) 250-2500
www.db.com

Dresdner Kleinwort
1301 Avenue of the Americas
New York, NY 10019
Phone: (212) 969-2700
www.dresdnerkleinwort.com

Evercore Partners
55 East 52nd Street
43rd Floor
New York, NY 10055
Phone: (212) 857-3100
Fax: (212) 857-3101
www.evercore.com

Friedman, Billings, Ramsey Group
1001 19th Street North
Arlington, VA 22209
Phone: (703) 312-9500
Fax: (703) 312-9501
www.fbr.com

Gleacher Partners
660 Madison Avenue
19th Floor
New York, NY 10021
Phone: (212) 418-4200
Fax: (212) 752-2711
www.gleacher.com

Greenhill & Co.
300 Park Avenue
New York, NY 10022
Phone: (212) 389-1500
www.greenhill-co.com

HSBC Holdings
8 Canada Square
London, UK E14 5HQ
Phone: +44-020-7991-8888
Fax: +44-020-7992-4880
www.hsbc.com

Houlihan Lokey Howard & Zukin
1930 Century Park West
Los Angeles, CA 90067
Phone: (310) 553-8871
Fax: (310) 553-2173
www.hlhz.com

Jefferies & Company, Inc.
520 Madison Avenue
12th Floor
New York, NY 10022
Phone: (212) 284-2550
www.jefferies.com

JPMorgan
270 Park Avenue
New York, NY 10017
Phone: (212) 270-6000
Fax: (212) 270-2613
www.jpmorgan.com

Keefe, Bruyette & Woods
The Equitable Building
787 Seventh Avenue, 4th Floor
New York, NY 10019
Phone: (212) 887-7777
www.kbw.com

LaSalle Bank Corporation
135 S. LaSalle Street
Chicago, Illinois 60603
Phone: (312) 904-2000
www.lasallebank.com

Lazard
30 Rockefeller Plaza
New York, NY, 10020
Phone: (212) 632-6000
www.lazard.com

Lehman Brothers
745 Seventh Avenue
New York, NY 10019
Phone: (212) 526-7000
Fax: (212) 526-8766
www.lehman.com

Macquarie Group
125 West 55th Street
New York, NY 10019
Phone: (212) 231-1000
Fax: (212) 231-1010
www.macquarie.com/us

Banking Employer Directory, cont.

Morgan Keegan

Morgan Keegan Tower

50 Front Street, 17th Floor

Memphis, TN 38103

Phone: (901) 524-4100

Fax: (901) 579-4406

www.morgankeegan.com

Morgan Stanley

1585 Broadway

New York, NY 10036

Phone: (212) 761-4000

Fax: (212) 762-0575

www.morganstanley.com

Nomura Holdings

2 World Financial Center

Building B

New York, NY 10281-1198

Phone: (212) 667-9300

Fax: (212) 667-1058

www.nomura.com

Peter J. Solomon Company

520 Madison Avenue

New York, NY 10022

Phone: (212) 508-1600

Fax: (212) 508-1633

www.pjsc.com

Piper Jaffray & Co.

800 Nicollet Mall

Suite 800

Minneapolis, MN 55402-7020

Phone: (612) 303-6000

Fax: (612) 303-8199

www.piperjaffray.com

Raymond James Financial

880 Carillon Parkway

St. Petersburg, FL 33716

Phone: (727) 567-1000

Fax: (727) 567-5529

www.rjf.com

RBC Capital Markets

Royal Bank Plaza

200 Bay Street

Toronto, Ontario, M5J 2W7

Phone: (416) 842-2000

Fax: (416) 842-8033

One Liberty Plaza

165 Broadway

New York, NY 10006

Phone: (212) 858-7000

www.rbccm.com

Robert W. Baird & Co. (Baird)

777 East Wisconsin Avenue

Milwaukee, WI 53202

Phone: (414) 765-3500

Fax: (414) 765-3633

www.rwbaird.com

Rothschild North America

1251 Avenue of the Americas

51st Floor

New York, NY 10020

Phone: (212) 403-3500

Fax: (212) 403-3501

www.rothschild.com

Sandler O'Neill + Partners, L.P.

919 Third Avenue

6th Floor

New York, NY 10022

Phone: (212) 466-7800

www.sandleroneill.com

Thomas Weisel Partners

One Montgomery Street

San Francisco, CA 94104

Phone: (415) 364-2500

Fax: (415) 364-2695

www.tweisel.com

UBS Investment Bank

299 Park Avenue

New York, NY 10171

Phone: (212) 821-3000

677 Washington Boulevard

Stamford, CT 06901

Phone: (203) 719-3000

www.ibb.ubs.com

Wachovia

301 S. College Street

Suite 400

Charlotte, NC 28288

Phone: (704) 374-6161

Fax: (704) 383-0996

www.wachovia.com

Wells Fargo

420 Montgomery Street

San Francisco, CA 94163

Phone: (800) 411-4932

Fax: (415) 677-9075

www.wellsfargo.com

William Blair & Company

222 West Adams Street

Chicago, IL 60606

Phone: (312) 236-1600

Fax: (312) 368-9418

www.williamblair.com

WR Hambrecht + Co

539 Bryant Street

Suite 100

San Francisco, CA 94107

Phone: (415) 551-8600

Fax: (415) 551-8686

www.wrhambrecht.com

Visit Vault at **www.vault.com** for insider company profiles, expert advice, career message boards, expert resume reviews, the Vault Job Board and more.

VAULT CAREER LIBRARY

147

The only way people should be labeled.

that was easy.℠

Consumer Products/Marketing

Consumer Products/Marketing Industry Overview

It's all goods

Encompassing everything from dish soap to automobiles, the consumer products industry is a vast empire made up of the multitude of material products available to customers, stretching across dozens of related industries. To get a handle on the market, analysts often divide it into two categories, durable and non-durable goods. As the names imply, the former comprises items with (relative) staying power, like cars, home furnishings, jewelry and electronics. The latter category includes more ephemeral merchandise, with a life expectancy of fewer than three years, like clothing, personal care items, and office and cleaning supplies. Others break the industry down into products that are staples and those that are discretionary—the difference between what consumers need and what they'd like to have.

Considerable consumption

The numbers are staggering: spending on consumer products accounts for two-thirds of the volume of trade in the economy, and yearly spending by U.S. shoppers on consumables hovers around $7 trillion. And that doesn't count the increased presence of U.S.-made consumer products in the farthest reaches of the globe: as American and European markets become increasingly saturated and competitive, manufacturers of consumer products are turning toward new markets, especially in hot spots like India, China and Russia.

Ask for it by name

The consumer products era began in earnest during the mid-19th century, when industrialization enabled the swift and economical production of identical things in quantity. There is no market without consumers, and a convenient effect of the Industrial Revolution was the creation of an urban middle class that had enough disposable income and time to spend shopping. Location constraints were lifted as rail networks expanded across the country, allowing vast amounts of goods to be sent wherever there was a market for them. Producers, meanwhile, had to compete with trusted local manufacturers, and so began to rely on advertising and packaging to catch shoppers' interest and loyalty.

Brands are critical to the success of those that make consumer products. The cultivation of a set of (hopefully warm and fuzzy) emotions in the consumer towards a product leads to brand loyalty and profits. And in a marketplace where producers may be selling functionally identical items, brands cause consumers to reach for things for which they have the strongest positive associations—that make them feel as if they were getting good quality and value for their money. This process happens even if the branded item costs more than a generic version. Perhaps the first indicator of the value of brands occurred in 1988 when Phillip Morris purchased Kraft for six times what the company was worth. It wasn't the company Philip Morris was purchasing; rather it was the value of people's emotions about Velveeta.

A lot in store

Most consumer products companies are Fortune 500 mainstays that control a supermarket's worth of brands. Proctor & Gamble, the world's largest household products firm, would like you to start each day by brushing your teeth with Crest; washing your hair with Herbal Essences shampoo; then applying, if you desire, an Olay moisturizer, followed by a Cover Girl lipstick. Then you can treat yourself to a cup of Folger's before you wash your clothes in Tide; your dishes with Dawn; your kitchen floor with Mr. Clean; use Swiffer in the living room to remove hair from your Iams-fed dog; and spritz your furniture with Febreeze. (For the sake of brevity, the other 290-odd brands the company controls will be glossed over.)

Visit Vault at **www.vault.com** for insider company profiles, expert advice, career message boards, expert resume reviews, the Vault Job Board and more.

VAULT CAREER LIBRARY   149

On the other hand, Britain-based industry giant Unilever, with a large international presence, would like you to start each day by washing up with Dove or Lifebuoy soap, followed up by moisturizing with Pond's. For breakfast they offer Lipton tea and toast with Country Crock margarine; for lunch there's a sandwich with Hellman's mayonnaise or Amora mustard; and for dinner there are Bertolli skillet dinners accompanied by Bird's Eye frozen vegetables and Knorr dried seasonings; dessert is a Heart brand ice cream; and so on and so forth for this company's 400 brands. Other leaders in the non-durables sector are Johnson & Johnson, Kimberly-Clark and Colgate-Palmolive. The foods giants are Nestle, Kraft and suds suppliers Anheuser-Busch, InBev and Molson Coors.

In the durable goods sector, Whirlpool leads the U.S. appliance pack, while abroad, consumers choose worldwide leader Electrolux for their dishwashing, refrigerating and vacuuming needs. Other leading home appliance manufacturers are GE and OSRAM. Cars are frequently cited as the classic example of durable goods, and Americans usually choose Toyota, GM and Ford to drive the country's high- and byways.

The buying game

With the $57 billion dollar blockbuster merger of Procter & Gamble with Gillette in January 2005, the consumer products industry saw two of its biggest companies become one. Also at the start of 2005, Adolph Coors Co. merged with Molson Inc. to create the world's fifth-largest brewer in a $3.4 billion deal. Whirlpool made a new version of the washer-dryer combo when they picked up competitor Maytag in March 2006 for $2.6 billion.

Keep up the goods work

The challenge for consumer products companies is getting the right quantity of the right product to the right consumer at the right time at the right price. If any of these factors is out of whack, the business can kiss a portion of its profits goodbye. While each company organizes their people in a slightly different manner, there are six principal areas in which consumer products companies hire. Firstly, they need a product to sell, and so they have product development departments. Secondly, the products need to be made from something, so there is a purchasing department to source materials. Thirdly, there needs to be a demand for the product, so some companies have marketing and branding teams in-house. Fourthly, there is a customer relations group that solicits buyers for the product, and also does market research to find the best market and price point for the item. Fifthly, the logistics team ensures that the right quantity of the product gets to the right place on time. Finally, there is a compliment of lawyers who specialize in IP law to protect the company from infringement; in addition, there are departments for HR and IT to keep everything moving smoothly.

Demand for people in the consumer products industry is likely to grow in the next decade. A wobbly and increasingly competitive domestic economy notwithstanding, the nascent markets of India and China have an enormous appetite for consumer goods, and provide ample opportunities for growth.

Marketing and Brand Managers

What is a marketer? The allure of brand management

Marketing encompasses a wide variety of meanings and activities. Some marketing positions are very close to sales, while others set overarching marketing strategy. What marketing positions have in common is the sense of ownership over the product or service, as well as the drive to understand customer needs and desires and translate those into some kind of marketing communication, advertising campaign or sales effort. The manager of product or service marketing is called the brand manager—he or she is the ruler of that marketing universe.

Careers within the marketing/branding arena are high profile. The business world is now realizing that strong brands and solid marketing programs drive shareholder value, and that companies can no longer make fundamental strategy decisions without truly understanding how to market a product. Today's business challenges—the quest for company growth, industry consolidation and deregulation, economic webs, and the emergency of new channels and technologies—make marketers even more valuable.

The titles of brand manager, product manager and, to a lesser extent, marketing manager are often used to describe the same function—some companies use one title, others use another. Marketing managers tend to be used in industries other than consumer packaged goods; product managers are often used in tech industries. "Brand management" implies more complete supervision of a product. The typical brand management framework gives a brand "group" or "team"—generally comprised of several assistant brand or assistant marketing managers and one supervising brand manager—responsibility for all matters relevant to their product or products. Whether this responsibility is in fact complete depends somewhat on the size of the company relative to the number of brands it has, the location of the brand group, and most importantly on the company's attitude toward marketing.

How important is the individual brand manager?

Consider the company to determine the level of brand manager responsibility. The first factor: the size of the company relative to its number of brands. For a company with hundreds of different brands—Nabisco, for example—brand managers, or even assistant brand managers, may have a great deal of power over a specific brand. At companies with a few core products, brand managers will focus on narrower aspects of a brand. As one recently hired assistant brand manager at Coca-Cola comments: "They're not going to take an MBA and say, 'Okay, you're in charge of Sprite.'" Brand managers at such companies will instead be focused on marketing to a particular demographic or geographic group, or perhaps handling one aspect of the product's consumption (plastic bottles, cases of aluminum cans and so forth).

International brand managers have historically held more sway than managers in the company's home market, but keep in mind that the daily tasks of international brand managers often lean more toward questions of operations, rather than questions of strategy or marketing. ("How much should we produce?" or "How is our distribution network affecting sales?" rather than "What do we want our brand identity to be?") International brand management is sometimes split into two positions. Global brand managers are more strategic, concentrating on issues such as protecting brand equity and developing product offerings that can be rolled out into subsidiaries. Local brand managers are more tactical. Local managers focus on executing global plans that are delivered to them, and tweak them for local consumers. Also know that with the increasing trend toward globalization and the truly global presence of certain brands, companies have sought to impose more centralization and tighter controls on the marketing of those brands from country to country. In the past, individual country managers have had more discretion and leeway to make decisions about a brand's packaging, advertising, etc. Now, companies have established tighter guidelines on what can be done with regard to a brand around the world, with the goal of protecting and enhancing the value of the brand, and ensuring a consistent product and message worldwide.

Finally, consumer products companies place varying levels of importance on their brand or marketing departments. Some, such as the Ford Motor Company, are driven as much by financial analyses of production costs or operations considerations as by marketing. The level of emphasis on finance or operations matters at a firm will influence not only the independence and authority of marketing managers, but also potential marketing career paths. At some companies, marketing is the training ground for general management. At General Mills, marketing is considered so important that employees in other functions who show promise are plucked from their positions and put into the department.

Visit Vault at **www.vault.com** for insider company profiles, expert advice, career message boards, expert resume reviews, the Vault Job Board and more.

VAULT CAREER LIBRARY   **151**

Careers in Marketing

Taking charge of a brand involves tackling many diverse job functions—and different subspecialties. Decide where you'd like your main concentration to lie.

Brand management

In a typical brand management organizational structure, positions are developed around responsibility for a particular product rather than a specific functional expertise (i.e., you're an assistant brand manager for Cheerios). This structure enables you to be the "master of all trades," acquiring an expertise in areas such as manufacturing, sales, research and development, and communications. In brand management, the marketing function is responsible for key general management decisions such as long-term business strategy, pricing, product development direction and, in some cases, profit and loss responsibility. Brand management offers a terrific way to learn intensively about a particular product category (you could be a recognized expert on tampons!) and to manage the responsibility of running a business and influencing its performance.

The core of brand work is brand strategy. Brand managers must decide how to increase market share, which markets and demographic groups to target, and what types of advertising and special promotions to use. And at the very heart of brand strategy is identifying a product's "brand identity." Brand groups then figure out how to exploit brand strategy, or, in some cases, how to change it. PepsiCo's Mountain Dew has built its popularity among youth as a high-caffeine beverage into a "brand identity" of cutting-edge bravado that has boosted market share, while the Banana Republic chain underwent a transformation from an outdoor adventure store that sold actual army-navy surplus to an upscale, chic clothing store. In both cases, the brands have benefited from a shift in brand identity, and consequently, a shift in their market. Brand identity is normally created and confirmed through traditional print, radio and TV advertising. Advertising is usually produced by outside agencies, although brand insiders determine the emphasis and target of the advertising.

Some liken a brand manager to a hub at the center of a hub and spoke system, with the spokes going out to departments like finance, sales, manufacturing, R&D, etc. It is the brand manager's job to influence the performance of those groups—over whom he or she has no direct authority—in order to optimize the performance of his or her brand or product line.

Advertising

If you enjoy watching commercials more than television programs, then consider the advertising side of marketing. As an account executive, your role is to serve as a liaison between your brand management client and the departments within your agency. Account executives manage the creative production process from beginning to end, from researching what benefits a product offers, to writing the strategy for a typical commercial. Account executives must also handle matters such as briefing the creative department on how to execute the advertising strategies, working with the media department to buy ad time or space and determining how to spend the marketing budget for advertising. (Will potential consumers be best reached via TV, outdoor billboards, print or radio—or through a general saturation campaign?) Along with managing the creative process, account executives at ad agencies are increasingly becoming strategic experts in utilizing traditional media, digital media, direct marketing and other services.

Direct marketing

Ever wonder who is responsible for making those coupons you receive in the mail? Or the Saab videotape you've received every two years since you bought your car in 1993? You can thank direct marketers. Direct marketers are masters in one-to-one marketing. They assemble databases of individual consumers who fit within their target market, go after them with a personal approach, and manage the production process from strategy inception to out-the-door distribution.

Direct marketers have two main objectives: to stay in touch with their current consumer base and to try to generate more business by finding individuals who fit a target set of criteria but are not currently using their particular product. For instance, if you've ever checked out of the supermarket and got a coupon for Advil after buying a bottle of Tylenol, chances are a direct marketer is trying to convince you to switch brands by offering you a monetary incentive.

It's important to note that direct marketing isn't just done through snail mail. It operates in multiple media such as the Web, telemarketing and in-store promotions. Direct marketers have a powerful new tool in their arsenal—the Internet. Marketers are able to track the online habits and behavior of customers. They can then serve up customized banner advertisements that are much more likely to be relevant to them. Many consumers have agreed to receive promotional offers on certain subjects—marketers can then send them targeted e-mail messages that allow for much easier access to purchase or action (clicking on a link, for example) than a conventional mail direct marketing programs.

Affiliate/property marketing

If you're working with a major brand company like Nike, Disney, Pepsi or L'Oreal, chances are you'll do a lot of cross-promotion, or "affiliate marketing." For instance, Nike has marketing relationships with the NBA, NFL and a variety of individual athletes and athletic teams. Disney has a strong relationship with McDonald's; cute toys from the entertainment company's latest flick are often packaged with McDonald's Happy Meals upon the release of each new movie. L'Oreal works with celebrities like Heather Locklear and sponsors events such as the annual Academy Awards.

Marketers must manage the relationship between any two entities. If Disney wants to promote the cartoon du jour with McDonald's, or Pepsi wants to make sure that all Six Flags theme parks have a Pepsi Ride, then marketers need to ensure both parties get what they need out of the deal and stay true to their own brand images.

Price marketing/sales forecasting

Pricing is largely driven by market pressure. Most people, for example, won't pay more than $2 for a hamburger in a fast food restaurant. On the other hand, brand managers always have some pricing leeway that can greatly affect market share and profitability. An increase of a nickel in the price of a product sold by the millions can make huge differences in revenue—assuming the price rise doesn't cause equivalent millions less of the products to be sold. Brand managers need to figure out the optimal pricing strategy for their product, though it's not always a case of making the most money. Sometimes it makes more sense to win market share while taking lower profits. How do brand managers justify their prices? Through extensive research. Paper towels, for example, may be much more price-sensitive than a luxury item like engagement rings or smoked salmon.

Brand and marketing managers don't always have free reign over pricing. At some companies, such as those that sell largely through mail order, or those with complex pricing systems, pricing and promotional offers may be limited to what the operational sales system can handle. Explains one marketing manager at a long-distance phone company (an industry with notoriously tangled pricing plans): "It's very easy to offer something to the customer. It's very difficult to implement that in the computer system."

Another large part of the general management duties of brand managers is forecasting product sales. This means not only keeping track of sales trends pertaining to one's product, but anticipating responses to marketing campaigns and product launches or changes. The forecasts are used to determine production levels. Once a year, brand groups draw up budgets for their production, advertising and promotion costs, try to convince the finance folks that they absolutely need that amount, get less than they ask for, and then rework their budgets to fit the given budget. As one international brand manager at one of the world's biggest consumer goods companies puts it: "You don't determine the production and then get that budget; you get the budget, and then determine the production."

Visit Vault at www.vault.com for insider company profiles, expert advice, career message boards, expert resume reviews, the Vault Job Board and more.

VAULT CAREER LIBRARY 153

WHO SAID YOU CAN'T SURVIVE ON PIZZA?

Domino's Pizza recognizes that to be "best-in-class" and maintain our position as the world leader in the pizza delivery industry, we need to have exceptional leaders. We have developed a rotational program (called People Pipeline) to develop future corporate business leaders at Domino's.

THE PEOPLE PIPELINE PROGRAM PROVIDES:
- Big picture perspective of the business
- Rotational assignments that include travel and relocation with exposure to multiple business units
- Executive exposure - regular meetings with our executive vice presidents
- A mentor relationship to aid in your development
- Ongoing training and development

ACCOLADES OF THE PROGRAM:
- Recognized in The Guide to Best Entry-level Jobs by the *Princeton Review*
- Received "The Future of the Leader Award" by *Paragon Leadership International*

REQUIREMENTS OF PROGRAM:
- Bachelors degree
- Less than 5 years of professional work experience, excluding internships or positions held while attending college
- Proven leadership experience
- Ability to relocate

For more about this opportunity, please email recruiter3@dominos.com. Please type VAPPL in the subject line for reference.

CORPORATE LEADERSHIP OPPORTUNITIES

High-tech marketing

Not everyone markets applesauce for a living. Many people choose to enter the world of high tech marketing because they want to work with products and technologies that reshape and improve the world around us. These marketers feel that they would rather change the way a person interacts with the world in a sophisticated way, rather than spend time understanding what hair color teenagers find most appealing. High tech marketers spend much of their time understanding research and development issues, and working on new product launches.

Technology companies like Intel, Dell and Microsoft have recognized the power of branding and are utilizing traditional marketing tactics more and more. Amazon's extensive marketing campaign in 1998 helped brand that company in the mind of consumers still new to e-commerce as the company to purchase books (and other products) online. Intel became perhaps the first semiconductor company readily identifiable to the public through its heavily branded "bunny people." Marketing in the high tech world will continue to grow in importance over the next decade, as technology companies become more consumer-oriented (see Microsoft's X-Box). Marketing a service or software product versus a more tangible product is a bit different. It may be more challenging to understand how consumers relate to the product. Inventory and distribution issues may be tracked differently.

Market research

If you are an analytical person who likes numbers and analysis, and enjoys tracking consumer behavior, then market research may be the field for you. A product is much more effective when a company understands the consumer it is targeting. That's where market researchers come in. They employ a variety of different qualitative and quantitative research techniques to understand consumers. Surveys, tracking systems, focus groups, satisfaction monitors, psychographic and demographic models, and trial/repurchase estimations are all methods researchers use to understand how consumers relate to their products. Researchers who find that consumers associate lemon scents with cleanliness, for example, may suggest that cleansers could drive up sales by adding a lemon aroma.

Public relations

Public relations professionals manage company communications and relations with the outside world. You can work for an internal PR firm (large companies have their own departments that manage the public relations for all of their brands) or you can work for a PR agency and be placed on a brand account. Public relations executives write public releases to local and national publications and develop ideas that will increase the "buzz" surrounding their brand. Some PR firms have excellent reputations for pulling off "stunts" that get their products in the news and increase their brand recognition. Public relations executives may also be forced to defend a brand in the face of public scrutiny—such as the Tylenol brand during the rash of poisonings in the 1980s. While event-driven functions like press releases and stunts are significant, perhaps the most important function of a PR professional is to establish strong relationships with media representatives and to persuade them to cover an interesting story about the company they represent.

Marketing consulting

Although most well-known consulting firms are known for their expertise in general strategy, many consulting firms now hire industry or functional experts that focus on marketing issues. These firms need people with expertise in the areas of branding, market research, continuous relationship marketing, pricing strategy and business-to-business marketing—they tend to hire people with previous marketing experience and value consultants who have been successful marketing managers and have lived through the full range of business issues from the inside. McKinsey and Monitor are two general strategy firms that have begun to hire marketing specialists. Other boutique marketing consulting firms, such as Kurt Salmon, focus on certain

Visit Vault at **www.vault.com** for insider company profiles, expert advice, career message boards, expert resume reviews, the Vault Job Board and more.

VAULT CAREER LIBRARY 155

product categories like beverages, health care, and retail. All major ad agencies are also attempting to reinvent themselves as marketing partners focused on marketing strategy beyond simple advertising.

What is a Brand?

Marketing analysis is primarily concerned with identifying a market, understanding it and developing a product to fill a need in the market. (There are of course, other logistical details, such as understanding what is required to make the product profitable.)

But a product is just a physical object or service. A brand, on the other hand, is a product that has consistent emotional and function benefits attached to it. Products are interchangeable—a brand builds value. Brands engage the consumer, inspire an emotional reaction and are consistent in their appearance. What attributes create brands?

Consistent strategy

Products that are constantly changing their strategies/market positions will never hold a consistent place in the consumer's mind. Owning a piece of the consumer's mind makes a brand a brand. When you think of a coffee shop, you now think of Starbucks—that's because Starbucks is a successful brand.

Consistent appearance

What do people think of visually when they think of your brand? Everyone knows Nike's logo—an elegant, high-speed swoosh.

Positioning

Good brands must stand for different things than their category competitors. Volvo cars, for example, are associated with safety, while Corvettes stand for sporty speed, and Saturns for value and good customer service.

Connection with target audience

A brand must build an emotional connection with the consumers who use it. The consumer must feel that there are no substitutes in the marketplace. Consumers may choose Pepsi or Coke in a blind taste test—but that "preference" has little to do with the drink they actually buy in the supermarket.

Top 12 Ways to Revitalize a Brand

Despite the fact that product categories are becoming more complex every day and marketing budgets are down, brand managers are constantly feeling pressure to increase sales, profits and market share. This list is adapted from an article in *Brandweek* and provides excellent examples of how companies improved the marketing of brand name products.

1. Create new usage occasions. (Wednesday is Prince Spaghetti Day; Orange juice is not just for breakfast anymore.)

2. Find customers outside your existing target group. (The Bank for Kids; Gillette for Her product line; and Pert for Kids shampoo.)

3. Discover a new way of using the product. (Lipton Recipe Soup Mix; Baking Soda can be used as toothpaste; Jell-O pudding can be used as cake filling; Comet Disinfecting Powder not only cleans surfaces in your house, but also is great to use on old garden tools and old sneakers.)

4. Position your product as the one used by professionals and experts. (Chapstick and Picabo Street; Tide and its "professional launderettes.")

5. Tell a compelling story about your product's origins. (Jack Daniels; Nantucket Nectars; Ben & Jerry's.)

6. Create a jingle that relates to your product's unique feature. (Heinz ketchup's "Anticipation"; Wisk's "Ring around the Collar"; Alka Seltzer's "Plop, Plop, Fizz, Fizz.")

7. Develop a new delivery vehicle or packaging convenience. (Lysol Toilet Bowl Cleaner's "Angle Neck"; the Colgate "Pump.")

8. Create a character to personify your product, ingredient or attribute. (Post's California Raisins; Kraft's Cheesasaurus; Dow's Scrubbing Bubbles.)

9. Use media vehicles in a new way. (P&G created the "soap opera" to advertise their brands; the "Got Milk" campaign effectively uses mouth-watering billboards; newspapers as a means of distributing product samples.)

10. Look for effective tie-ins/partnerships. (United Airlines serving Starbucks Coffee; McDonald's distributing Disney toys; Gillette distributing razors at Boston Red Sox baseball games.)

11. Promote your product as benign addiction. (Lay's "Bet You Can't Eat Just One"; Snackwell's "Won't be able to say no.")

12. Become a reason for family and friends togetherness. (M&M's Make Friends; Kodak Golden Moments; McDonald's after the big baseball game; "Celebrate the Moments of Your Life" with Folgers.)

Visit Vault at **www.vault.com** for insider company profiles, expert advice, career message boards, expert resume reviews, the Vault Job Board and more.

VAULT CAREER LIBRARY   157

Consumer Products/Marketing Employer Directory

Domino's Pizza, LLC

30 Frank Lloyd Wright Drive
Ann Arbor, Michigan 48106
www.dominos.com
Recruiting Contact E-mail: Recruiter3@dominos.com

Founded as a single store in 1960, Domino's Pizza stands as the recognized world leader in pizza delivery. From the beginning, we have been dedicated to the best service, quality products and delivery excellence.

Each day, more than 1 million customers enjoy hot, delicious Domino's Pizza products on six continents, where we operate more than 8,000 stores in over 50 countries, all dedicated to providing great tasting pizza delivered directly to your door.

At Domino's, we recognize that the best way to ensure the success of the company is to first ensure the satisfaction of our team members.

Undergraduate schools Domino's recruits from:

Michigan State University, Western Michigan University, Central Michigan University, Howard University (primary schools)

Multiple other schools for job postings, interviewing, etc.

L'Oréal

575 Fifth Avenue
New York, New York 10017
Recruiting Contact Phone: 212-818-1500
www.lorealusa.com

Undergraduate schools L'Oreal recruits from:

L'Oreal has an on-campus presence at several schools including: Babson; Brown; Columbia; New York University; University of Pennsylvania;

We do however consider students from all undergraduate universities and students from schools where we don't have a presence should apply on-line. Go to lorealusa.com

The L'Oréal Management Development Program is designed for students graduating with a bachelor's degree who want to pursue a career in Marketing, Sales, Finance, Information Systems, Logistics, Manufacturing or Research and Development. This rotational program is designed to give you the opportunity to gain exposure and hone your skills through hands-on assignments. It puts a strong emphasis on professional development through formal training held at our Management Development Center and individual check-points with members of the HR community.

L'Oréal USA offers a formal internship program consisting of three main elements (1) The day to day functional job assignment (2) A business related project to be completed and presented to management (3) Educational and Professional Development sessions.

Consumer Products/Marketing Employer Directory, cont.

Procter & Gamble

1 P&G Plaza
Cincinnati, Ohio 45202

Recruiting Contact:
Phone: 1-888-486-7691
E-mail: careers.im@pg.com
www.pg.com/careers

Undergraduate schools P&G recruits from:
Various Schools throughout the United States.

Three billion times a day, P&G brands touch the lives of people around the world. Our company has one of the strongest portfolios of trusted, quality, including Pampers®, Tide®, Ariel®, Always®, Whisper®, Pantene®, Mach3®, Bounty®, Dawn®, Pringles®, Folgers®, Charmin®, Downy®, Lenor®, Iams®, Crest®, Oral-B®, Actonel®, Duracell®, Olay®, Head & Shoulders®, Wella, Gillette®, and Braun. The P&G community consists of almost 140,000 employees working in almost 80 countries worldwide.

P&G embraces the principles of personal integrity, respect for the individual and doing what's right for the long term. We recognize our consumers, brands and employees as the pillars of our business.

3M Company

3M Center
St. Paul, MN 55144
Phone: 651-733-1110
Fax: 651-736-2133
www.mmm.com

Alberto-Culver Company

2525 Armitage Ave.
Melrose Park, IL 60160
Phone: (708) 450-3000
Fax: (708) 450-3354
www.alberto.com

Altria Group Inc.

120 Park Avenue
New York, NY 10017
Phone: (917) 663-5000
Fax: (917) 663-2167
www.altria.com

Anheuser-Busch Companies, Inc.

1 Busch Place
St. Louis, MO 63118
Phone: (314) 577-2000
Fax: (314) 577-2900
www.anheuser-busch.com

Avon Products, Inc.

1345 Avenue of the Americas
New York, NY 10105-0196
Phone: (212) 282-5000
Fax: (212) 282-6049
www.avoncompany.com

Black & Decker

701 E. Joppa Road
Towson, MD 21286
Phone: (410) 716-3900
Fax: (410) 716-2933
www.bdk.com

Bose Corp.

The Mountain
Framingham, MA 01701
Phone: (508) 879-7330
Fax: (508) 766-7543
www.bose.com

Canon U.S.A., Inc.

1 Canon Plaza
Lake Success, NY 11042
Phone: (516) 328-5000
Fax: (516) 328-5069
www.usa.canon.com

Clorox Company

1221 Broadway
Oakland, CA 94612-1888
Phone: (510) 271-7000
Fax: (510) 832-1463
www.clorox.com

Coca-Cola Company, The

1 Coca-Cola Plaza
Atlanta, GA 30313-2499
Phone: (404) 676-2121
Fax: (404) 676-6792
www.cocacola.com

Colgate-Palmolive

300 Park Avenue
New York, NY 10022
Phone: (212) 310-2000
Fax: (212) 310-2475
www.colgate.com

ConAgra Foods Inc.

1 ConAgra Drive
Omaha, Nebraska 68102
Phone: (402) 595-4000
Fax: (402) 595-4707
www.conagra.com

Visit Vault at **www.vault.com** for insider company profiles, expert advice, career message boards, expert resume reviews, the Vault Job Board and more.

VAULT CAREER LIBRARY   **159**

Consumer Products/Marketing Employer Directory, cont.

Dial Corporation
15501 N. Dial Blvd.
Scottsdale, AZ 85260-1619
Phone: (480) 754-3425
Fax: (480) 754-1098
www.dialcorp.com

Dole Food Company, Inc.
1 Dole Drive
Westlake Village, CA 91362
Phone: (818) 879-6600
Fax: (818) 879-6615
www.dole.com

Eastman Kodak Company
343 State Street
Rochester, NY 14650
Phone: (585) 724-4000
www.kodak.com

The Estée Lauder Companies
767 Fifth Avenue
New York, NY 10153
Phone: (212) 572-4200
Fax: (212) 572-6633
www.elcompanies.com

General Mills
1 General Mills Blvd.
Minneapolis, MN 55426
Phone: (763) 764-7600
Fax: (763) 764-7384
www.generalmills.com

The Gillette Company
Prudential Tower Building
Boston, MA 02199
Phone: (617) 421-7000
Fax: (617) 421-7123
www.gillette.com

The Goodyear Tire & Rubber Company
1144 E. Market Street
Akron, OH 44316-0001
Phone: (330) 796-2121
Fax: (330) 796-2222
www.goodyear.com

Hallmark Cards, Inc.
2501 McGee Street
Kansas City, MO 64108
Phone: (816) 274-5111
Fax: (816) 274-5061
www.hallmark.com

Hasbro, Inc.
1027 Newport Avenue
Pawtucket, RI 02862
Phone: (401) 431-8697
Fax: (401) 431-8535
www.hasbro.com

Hershey Foods, Inc.
100 Crystal A Drive
Hershey, PA 17033
Phone: (717) 534-6799
Fax: (717) 534-6760
www.hersheys.com

HJ Heinz
600 Grant St.
Pittsburgh, PA 15219
Phone: (412) 456-5700
Fax: (412) 456-6128
www.heinz.com

Hormel Foods
One Hormel Place
Austin, MN 55912-3680
Phone: (507) 437-5611
Fax: (507) 437-5129
www.hormel.com

Johnson & Johnson
1 Johnson & Johnson Plaza
New Brunswick, NJ 08933
Phone: (732) 524-0400
Fax: (732) 524-3300
www.jnj.com

Kimberly-Clark Corporation
351 Phelps Drive
Irving, TX 75038
Phone: (972) 281-1200
Fax: (972) 281-1490
www.kimberly-clark.com

Kraft Foods Inc.
Three Lakes Drive
Northfield, IL 60093
Phone: (847) 646-2000
Fax: (847) 646-6005
www.kraft.com

Land O'Lakes
4001 Lexington Avenue North
Arden Hills, MN 55126
Phone: (651) 481-2222
Fax: (651) 481-2000
www.landolakesinc.com

Liz Claiborne, Inc.
1441 Broadway
New York, NY 10018
Phone: (212) 354-4900
Fax: (212) 626-3416
www.lizclaiborne.com

L'Oréal
41, rue Martre
92117 Clichy, France
Phone: +33-1-47-56-70-00
Fax: +33-1-47-56-80-02
www.loreal.com

LVMH Moët Hennessy Louis Vuitton SA
22 avenue Montaigne
75008 Paris, France
Phone: +33-1-44-13-22-22
Fax: +33-1-44-13-21-19
www.lvmh.com

Mary Kay, Inc.
16251 Dallas Parkway
Addison, TX 75001
Phone: (972) 687-6300
Fax: (972) 687-1611
www.marykay.com

Mattel, Inc.
333 Continental Blvd.
El Segundo, CA 90245-5012
Phone: (310) 252-2000
Fax: (310) 252-2180
www.mattel.com

Consumer Products/Marketing Employer Directory, cont.

Molson Coors Brewing Company
311 10th Street
Golden, CO 80401-0030
Phone: (303) 279-6565
Fax: (303) 277-6246
www.molsoncoors.com

Nestlé USA
800 N. Brand Blvd.
Glendale, CA 91203
Phone: (818) 549-6000
Fax: (818) 549-6952
www.nestleusa.com

Newell Rubbermaid Inc.
10 B Glenlake Pkwy., Suite 600
Atlanta, GA 30328
Phone: (770) 407-3800
Fax: (770) 407-3970
www.newellrubbermaid.com

NIKE, Inc.
1 Bowerman Drive
Beaverton, OR 97005-6453
Phone: (503) 671-6453
Fax: (503) 671-6300
www.nike.com

PepsiCo, Inc.
700 Anderson Hill Rd
Purchase, NY 10577-1444
Phone: (914) 253-2000
Fax: (914) 253-2070
www.pepsico.com

Revlon, Inc.
237 Park Avenue
New York, NY 10017
Phone: (212) 527-4000
Fax: (212) 527-4995
www.revloninc.com

Sara Lee Corporation
3 First National Plaza
Chicago, IL 60602-4260
Phone: (312) 726-2600
Fax: (312) 726-3712
www.saralee.com

S.C. Johnson & Son, Inc.
1525 Howe Street
Racine, WI 53403-5011
Phone: (262) 260-2000
Fax: (262) 260-6004
www.scjohnson.com

Smithfield Foods
200 Commerce Street
Smithfield, VA 23430
Phone: (757) 365-3000
Fax: (757) 365-3017
www.smithfieldfoods.com/home.asp

Sony Corporation
7-35, Kitashinagawa, 6-chome,
Shinagawa-ku
Tokyo, 141-0001, Japan
Phone: +81-3-5448-2111
Fax: +81-3-5448-2244
www.sony.net

Stanley Works
1000 Stanley Dr.
New Britain, CT 06053
Phone: (860) 225-5111
Fax: (860) 827-3987
www.stanleyworks.com

Unilever
Unilever House
Blackfriars
London, UK EC4P 4BQ
United Kingdom
Phone: +44-20-7822-5252
Fax: +44-20-7822-6191
www.unilever.com

Whirlpool Corporation
2000 N. M-63
Benton Harbor, MI 49022-2692
Phone: (269) 923-5000
Fax: (269) 923-5443
www.whirlpoolcorp.com

Visit Vault at **www.vault.com** for insider company profiles, expert advice,
career message boards, expert resume reviews, the Vault Job Board and more.

VAULT CAREER LIBRARY   **161**

Energy/Oil & Gas

What is the Energy Sector?

The energy sector produces, converts and distributes fuels for heat, light and propulsion. Oil, natural gas and coal are burned to make heat and electricity. Wind, flowing water and sunlight are converted into electricity. Oil is refined to propel cars, planes and industrial machines. And to achieve these things, the companies who are producing, transporting, converting and distributing these energy sources are supported by a variety of service firms, investors, equipment providers, and government regulators.

There is a great divide in the energy sector between the oil and gas "side" and the electricity "side," each of which accounts for about half of the business jobs across the sector. "Oil and gas" refers to the exploration for, and extraction and processing of oil and natural gas. In contrast, the electric power business revolves around converting fuel to electricity in power plants and distributing that electricity to consumers. The economics of the two fields, and the regulations that govern them, are quite distinct. Generally, people make their energy careers in one camp or the other, without too much crossover. Natural gas is one arena that bridges the oil and gas versus electricity divide—it is extracted from the earth together with oil, and is also a primary fuel for generating electricity.

When people refer to the "energy sector," they can actually mean: electric power, oil and gas, or both together. We're taking a broad view of the industry, covering upstream (exploration), midstream (refining) and downstream (distribution and sales) oil and gas activities, electric power generation and transmission, equipment manufacturing, regulatory oversight and lending to, investing in and advising companies involved in the sector.

Just how big is the industry that comprises all those diverse activities? Companies in the energy sector take in nearly $1 trillion in revenue annually, out of the $17 trillion earned by all U.S. businesses. Energy-related businesses employ about 2.5 million people, or 2 percent of the U.S. workforce—far more than banking, high tech or telecommunications. Energy companies as a whole employ a high percentage of production workers (the people who drive local utility repair trucks, laborers on oil rigs and gas station attendants), compared to other industries; of the 2.5 million energy jobs in the U.S., about 90 percent of them are blue-collar jobs or technical positions. The subject of this book is the one-quarter-million energy-related business jobs out there: the business analysts, finance associates, marketing managers, economic modelers and operations consultants, to name a few roles.

Energy sector positions capture about 2 percent of new MBA graduates, an amount roughly proportional to the industry's size. In contrast, the investment banking and investment management sectors together capture 40 percent of graduates, and consulting absorbs another 20 percent. Even the significantly smaller high tech industry takes on three times the number of new MBAs as does the energy sector. What this means for you as a job seeker is that the energy sector is not as dominated by people with graduate business degrees as some other popular arenas. There is plenty of opportunity for smart, well-trained college graduates to rise through the ranks without necessarily going back to school.

Industry History

It's shocking to think that the Middle East, which is such a perpetual focus of U.S. foreign policy, has not always been the center of the energy world. In fact, oil was only discovered in the region in the 1950s. Only some two decades later, demand for oil had skyrocketed in tandem with the new supply, and a cartel had been formed that controlled world prices tightly enough to cause a severe economic crisis in the U.S.

How long ago did contemporary methods of generating heat, light and work come into being? Compared to the information technology sector, you might say that the energy sector is an old industry. However, compared to the majority of industries

Visit Vault at **www.vault.com** for insider company profiles, expert advice, career message boards, expert resume reviews, the Vault Job Board and more.

V/ULT CAREER LIBRARY **163**

that make up our economy—banking, publishing, construction, manufacturing, to name a few—the energy sector as we know it is a recent development. (See chart "History of Energy Production" on the next page)

After spending hundreds of thousands of years burning wood to heat our caves and then our houses, wood eventually became scarce and expensive, and humans discovered the slow-burning heat of coal. The Chinese figured out the benefits of coal in the 100s A.D., followed by the Europeans during the Middle Ages. Access to coal quickly became a European geopolitical issue so volatile that it sparked bitter conflicts between Germany and France, who battled for centuries over Alsace and the coal-rich Saar Valley.

At first, people burned coal to heat the air directly, but in the 1800s coal-fired radiant hot water heating systems proliferated, relegating the sooty mess coal created to the basement. In the early 20th century, a natural gas pipeline system started to be laid, allowing homes to burn a far cleaner fuel to heat either the air or water for radiators. Europe, with limited natural gas deposits, turned to oil-fired radiant hot water heating once oil became readily available in the early 1900s. After World War II, when electricity became more reliable and far cheaper, houses were eventually built with all-electric heating systems, particularly in Europe.

Not only was burning wood our earliest heating source, it was also our first source of artificial light. Lighting became a little more constant when animal fat-based candles were developed in about 3000 B.C., followed closely by liquid animal fat and plant oil lamps (think Aladdin's lamp, or the oil lamps lighting ancient Biblical temples). Around the world, evenings were lit by flickering flames until the turn of the 19th century, when coal gas lighting was first introduced to affluent homes and public sidewalks. In the mid-1800s, when petroleum oil was discovered and drilled in the U.S., it was refined into kerosene to produce a higher-quality oil lamp for the masses.

The revolution in lighting was, of course, electric light. Electricity was first produced in the mid-1800s, but was only used to power industrial machinery at first. When practical incandescent lightbulbs were commercialized in the 1880s, indoor electric lighting quickly spread around the world.

Where did the electricity to power the lightbulb come from? The first electric power plant was a coal-fired steam turbine generator built in 1880. However, after the success of the first hydroelectric power plant at Niagara Falls in 1895, reliable, clean hydropower provided most of the electricity in the U.S. in the first half of the 20th century. As electricity demand grew, many coal plants were built, and some countries developed geothermal power infrastructure (using steam from deep in the earth to drive turbines). Natural gas-fueled power plants first entered the mix after World War II, when the pipeline infrastructure was robust enough to provide a constant fuel source. In 1957, the first nuclear reactor started operation. In recent decades, commercial solar power, windpower and fuel cells reappeared, after having been first developed experimentally in the 19th century.

In contrast to the late 19th century revolution in indoor lighting, the watershed years in harnessing energy to do work occurred far earlier. After relying for thousands of years on waterwheels, windmills and sails to turn gears and propel objects (and before that on animals and our own brute strength), humankind saw the development of the steam engine at the turn of the 18th century. These external combustion engines used wood or coal to boil water into steam, which turned gears that ran factories, drove trains and ultimately spawned the Industrial Revolution. Ironically, factories operating such relatively sophisticated machinery in 1750 would have been lit only by smoky oil lamps and heated by sooty coal stoves.

With the advent of electric generation in the mid-1800s came electric and battery-powered motors (in which the batteries were charged by electricity) that drove industrial machinery of all types. Even before electricity was applied to lighting, it was used to drive the very first cars—a design that effectively fell by the wayside until 1997, when Toyota introduced a commercial hybrid electric car. The commercial development of oil-fired internal combustion engines in the late 1800s allowed cars to go faster and farther, initiating our society's seemingly insatiable appetite for petroleum.

By the early 1900s, most people in the industrial world had access to clean, radiant indoor heating and constant, bright indoor incandescent electric lighting. They drove gasoline-powered cars with internal combustion engines, and had run their factories with powerful steam turbines for nearly two centuries. Oil and natural gas wells across the U.S. and Europe were pumping in earnest, and major new deposits were soon to be discovered in the Middle East.

Since then, the major methods by which we produce heat, light and work have not materially changed. The history of the energy sector since the mid-1900s has been a story of technological advancements in efficiency and environmental impact reduction, as the industry transformed from a low tech, heavy-manufacturing identity to one that is fast-paced, cutting-edge and very high tech.

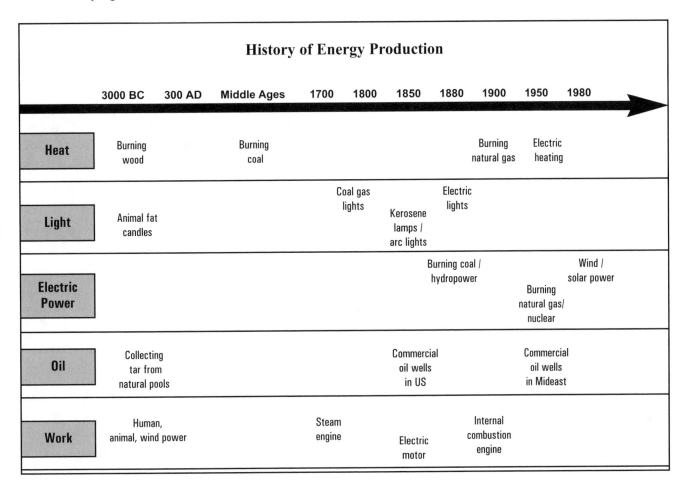

History of Energy Production

	3000 BC	300 AD	Middle Ages	1700	1800	1850	1880	1900	1950	1980
Heat	Burning wood		Burning coal					Burning natural gas	Electric heating	
Light	Animal fat candles				Coal gas lights	Kerosene lamps / arc lights	Electric lights			
Electric Power						Burning coal / hydropower		Burning natural gas/ nuclear		Wind / solar power
Oil	Collecting tar from natural pools					Commercial oil wells in US		Commercial oil wells in Mideast		
Work	Human, animal, wind power			Steam engine		Electric motor	Internal combustion engine			

Technology Frontiers

People in the energy sector are passionate about the high tech nature of their industry. Although the basic process of gathering fuels and burning them to produce electricity, light, heat and work is fairly set, how efficient that process is and how much pollution it generates are the subjects of some pretty hard-core science and revolutionary changes.

In order to be a compelling job candidate, it helps to be knowledgeable and passionate about new technologies appearing on the horizon. Below are just a handful of examples of the cutting-edge research and development happening in different parts of the energy world:

• One company has developed a very low tech alchemy to turn pollution into fuel: letting algae "eat" NOx (nitrogen oxide) and CO_2 (carbon dioxide) emissions from fossil plants. Algae thrive on these abundant feedstocks in power plant exhaust streams—pollution is reduced, the algae grows and can later be dried and burned as fuel.

Visit Vault at **www.vault.com** for insider company profiles, expert advice, career message boards, expert resume reviews, the Vault Job Board and more.

VAULT CAREER LIBRARY   **165**

- An important emerging power plant pollution-control technology involves burning fuel without using a flame. The recently-commercialized Xonon combustor turns natural gas into energy by bringing it into contact with a catalyst. In flameless combustion, no NOx is formed at all, thus preventing smog and acid rain.

- High-temperature superconducting transmission lines are currently in testing. Traditional copper wires cause enough resistance to lose some 10 percent of the electricity they carry. Superconducting niobium-titanium alloy wires cooled by a tiny liquid nitrogen core eliminate line losses and thus effectively increase our electricity supply.

- We have used the principal of piezoelectricity for decades to generate electricity from motion. Certain types of miniature crystals spontaneously generate a high-voltage current when moved—portable gas grill lighters that don't use a flint work in this way. Now companies are looking into more advanced applications, like using piezoelectric generators embedded in the sole of a soldier's boot to power battlefield equipment.

- Did you know there's a gasoline-powered car with a fuel efficiency of 10,000 MPG? Such impressive efficiency comes from using a tiny, one-cylinder engine with little internal resistance, thin hard tires and a super-light car body to reduce road friction, a bubble-shaped aerodynamic design and a lightweight child driver on a smooth and level indoor track. While these extreme design elements may not be practical for commercial vehicles, fuel efficiency R&D (research and development) is an active and promising space.

- Data transmission over electrical wires is a little-known, older technology that is finding exciting new applications. The current in an electrical wire can also carry data—street lights have been remotely controlled this way for decades, and in the past few years home automation via the wires in the wall has proliferated. (Did you know that you can turn your dishwasher on from your computer at work?) Companies have recently started marketing modems that send and receive more complex data over power lines: Internet access, voice and video.

- Battery technology is one of the real stumbling blocks of technological innovation these days—how much does it help you to have a supercomputer the size of a pad of paper if it dies after being unplugged for two hours? Companies are bringing better rechargeable lithium ion batteries to market, and actively developing laptops and cell phones powered by fuel cells with mini onboard tanks of hydrogen or methanol fuel.

- If you think wireless electricity is impossible, think again! We will soon be seeing desk surfaces and other furniture manufactured with embedded electrical chips—when you put a portable device down on the surface, the chip activates and recharges your laptop, phone, television, blender, razor, vacuum cleaner ... or whatever. Less realistically, people have also thought about wireless electricity in the form of "space solar power," in which huge solar-paneled satellites would collect energy from the sun and beam it to earth in the form of radio frequencies, which would then be converted into electricity.

- Bringing the fabled hydrogen economy to reality requires an inexpensive source of free hydrogen. Development-stage hydrogen production techniques include harnessing the sun to release hydrogen from pure sugar, and using high-temperature catalysis (rather than energy-intensive electrolysis) to split water into H2 and O2.

Energy Career Opportunities

In order to pursue a job in the energy sector, your first decision is what type of position you want—in other words, what functional role you want to play. Your function has a lot more impact on the nature of your job than does the type of company in which you work.

You can have a wide variety of business jobs in the energy sector:

- Asset development

- Corporate finance

- Quantitative analytics, risk management

- Trading, energy marketing

- Investment analysis

- Consulting

- Business development

- Banking

- Strategy and planning

- Economics and policy analysis

Different companies can have widely varying names by which they refer to these roles. For example, "marketing" in one company involves advertising and product promotion, whereas "marketing" in another can mean commodities trading. Similarly, "business development" can be more akin to sales in one company, or synonymous with strategic planning in another.

What Type of Company?

Job functions and company types intersect in numerous ways—for example, you can do corporate finance in a large oil company or with a small fuel cell manufacturer, or choose between asset development and trading within a given utility. (See chart "Employer Types by Job Function" on page 185.) Below, we have summarized the characteristics of each of the major energy sector employer types:

Oil companies

Oil companies engage in exploration and production of oil ("upstream" activities), oil transportation and refining ("midstream"), and petroleum product wholesale and retail distribution ("downstream"). The largest companies, known as the "majors," are vertically integrated, with business operations along the entire spectrum from exploration to gas stations. Smaller oil companies, known as "independents," are often exclusively involved in exploration and production. Upstream is considered the glamorous place to be, where all the big decisions are made. Upstream jobs also involve heavy international work, with many employees sent off to new postings around the world every three years or so. We should also note that E&P businesses are fairly similar in nature among oil companies and companies mining other natural resources like uranium or coal—moving among these types of firms during a career can be a logical path.

The majors are known for excellent rotational training programs, and a fair number of people take advantage of those programs and then jump over to independents for good salaries. Oil companies pay well in general, but jobs are not necessarily as stable as one might think. When oil prices drop, company operating profits are dramatically impacted, and layoffs are fairly common. American oil jobs are overwhelmingly concentrated in Houston. International hot spots include London, Calgary and the Middle East.

Some oil companies focus exclusively on midstream and downstream activities. They operate refineries to distill crude oil into its many commercially useful petroleum derivatives, like gasoline, jet fuel, solvents and asphalt. Refineries are, in theory, built to last 40 years, but some have been around for as long as 80 years. That means that new refineries are rarely built, and the refinery business is mostly about managing the razor-thin margins between purchased crude oil inputs and revenue from refined product outputs.

Visit Vault at **www.vault.com** for insider company profiles, expert advice, career message boards, expert resume reviews, the Vault Job Board and more.

VAULT CAREER LIBRARY   167

Oil services companies

Oil services companies provide a very wide range of outsourced operational support to oil companies, such as owning and renting out oil rigs, conducting seismic testing and transporting equipment. The fortunes of these companies follow the price of oil: when oil is expensive, oil companies drill a lot and make a lot of money, so business volume and revenue increase for their oil services contractors. Working for an oil services company probably means working in Texas or internationally, and can feel very much like working for an oil company, given the similarity in issues and activities.

Pipeline operators

Pipeline operators own and manage tens of thousands of miles of petroleum products and natural gas pipelines. Many of them also operate oil intake terminals, engage in commodities trading and energy marketing, and own natural gas storage facilities or petroleum refineries as well. Unlike the major oil companies, pipeline operation companies are not household names—nonetheless, the largest ones take in several billion in annual revenue, comparable to the scale of a medium-sized oil company.

Utilities

Utilities are, by definition, located all over the country ... everyone has to get their electricity and gas from somewhere, of course. However, as a result of massive consolidation among utility holding companies, the corporate offices for your local utility may not necessarily be that local. There are presently about 50 investor-owned utilities in the country, but industry insiders predict that in a few years mergers may leave us with as few as 10. The "graying" of the utility industry is a well-documented trend; 60 percent of current utility employees are expected to retire by 2015—meaning there's lots of opportunity today for young job seekers.

"Utility" is actually a loose term that we use to succinctly refer to gas utilities and all types of power generation companies: investor-owned utilities, government-owned utilities, municipal power companies, rural electric co-ops and independent power producers (IPPs) or non-utility generators (NUGs). Utilities differ greatly in terms of their lines of business: some have sold off most of their generation assets and are primarily distribution companies with power lines as their primary assets. Others may own large amounts of regulated power plants, and may also own non-utility generators or individual independent power plants. As the electricity market fell apart starting in 2001, most IPPs sold off their assets piecemeal to large utility holding companies or financial institutions.

Transmission grid operators

Transmission grid operators, known as independent system operators (ISO) or regional transmission operators (RTO), provide a power generation dispatch function to a regional electricity market. They don't own the transmission lines, but coordinate how much power is generated when and where, such that supply and demand are equal at every moment. This is an extremely complex process, and necessitates the analytical skills of electrical engineers and other generally quantitative and analytical operations staff.

Equipment manufacturers

Equipment manufacturers make turbines, boilers, compressors, pollution control devices, well drilling and pipeline construction equipment, software control systems, pumps and industrial batteries. Many of them also provide engineering services and construction/installation of their equipment. The major gas turbine manufacturers, for example, also offer engineering, procurement and construction of entire power plants. Oil-related equipment makers are often characterized as "oil services" firms. The equipment manufacturers in the energy industry are not particularly concentrated in one geographic area, though of course many of the oil business-oriented ones have major offices in Texas.

Investment funds

Investment funds are a diverse bunch: mutual funds, private equity funds, and hedge funds. As a whole, the investment fund world is fairly concentrated in Boston, New York and San Francisco, but there are small funds dotted all over the country as well.

Mutual funds hire stock analysts primarily out of MBA programs to track, value and recommend stocks in a particular sector (e.g. energy, natural resources, consumer products) to the fund managers. However, there are a lot of other finance-related positions inside these massive firms where undergrads are sought after as well.

The number of hedge funds in the U.S. has been growing at a phenomenal rate in the past few years, but they are still notoriously difficult places to get jobs. Hedge funds often hire people out of investment banking analyst programs. They tend to not hire people out of the mutual fund world, given that their valuation approach is so different, their investing horizon is so much shorter, and their orientation many times is towards short-selling as well as buying stocks. While some hedge funds may focus exclusively on energy, most are generalist and opportunistic with respect to their target sectors.

Private equity funds invest money in private (i.e. not publicly traded) companies, often also obtaining operating influence through a seat on the portfolio company's board of directors. As a result, an analyst's work at a private equity fund is vastly different from that at a mutual fund or hedge fund. You are not following the stock market or incorporating market perception issues into your valuations and recommendations; instead, you are taking a hard look at specific operating issues, identifying concrete areas where the portfolio company can lower costs or enhance revenue. A few private equity firms specialize in energy investing, and many more do occasional deals in the energy space as part of a broader technology or manufacturing focus. Private equity firms hire just a few people straight out of college or MBA programs, and many others from the ranks of investment banking alumni.

Banks

Banks are primarily involved in lending money to companies, but they also have their own trading operations, private wealth management and investment analysis groups. Commercial and investment banks arrange for loans to energy companies, as well as syndicate loans (i.e. find other people to lend the money) for them. Investment banks manage IPOs, and mergers and acquisitions (M&A) activities as well. The banking world is overwhelmingly centered in New York (and London), with some smaller branches in Chicago and San Francisco.

Consulting firms

Consulting firms offer rich opportunities for those interested in the energy industry. Consulting on business issues (rather than information technology or technical, scientific issues) is done at three types of firms: management consultancies, risk consulting groups and economic consulting shops. Consulting firms are often interested in hiring people with good functional skills rather than requiring specific industry expertise and provide a broad exposure to energy sector business issues, as well as good training. Business consulting firm offices are located in most major cities, but much of the energy sector staff may be located in Houston, Washington, D.C. and New York.

Nonprofit groups

Nonprofit groups are tax-exempt corporations (pursuant to IRS code 501(c)3) engaged in issue advocacy or public interest research. Advocacy groups may focus on developing grassroots support for public policy changes, publicizing public interest issues or problems through direct actions, or working to influence politicians to enact or change legislation. Most of the energy-related advocacy groups focus on environmental topics, though some also cover corporate financial responsibility and investor protection issues. Think tanks are public policy research institutes, staffed mainly by PhDs who generate research

Visit Vault at **www.vault.com** for insider company profiles, expert advice,
career message boards, expert resume reviews, the Vault Job Board and more.

VAULT CAREER LIBRARY   **169**

and opinion papers to inform the public, policy-makers and media on current issues. Interestingly, the think tank is primarily a U.S. phenomenon, although the concept is slowly catching on in other countries. Some think tanks are independent and nonpartisan, whereas some take on an explicit advocacy role. Nonprofits are funded by individual donations and grants from foundations, and accordingly a substantial portion of their staffs are dedicated to fundraising. Most energy nonprofits are based in Washington, D.C., where they have access to the federal political process, but many of them have small regional offices or grassroots workers spread out across the country.

Government agencies

Government agencies at the federal and state levels regulate the energy markets and define public energy and environmental policy. Federal agencies are mostly located in Washington, D.C., and each state has staff in the state capital. Jobs can include policy analysis, research project management or management of subcontractors. The energy agencies tend to hire people with environmental or engineering backgrounds, and are lately following a policy of hiring people with general business and management education and experience.

Energy services firms

Energy services firms help companies (in any sector) reduce their energy costs. Working for an energy services firm is similar in many respects to consulting—except that you go much further down the path of implementation. Typically, an energy services firm first conducts an energy audit to understand where a company spends money on energy: electricity, heat and industrial processes. Then, the firm actually implements energy-saving measures "inside the fence" of the client company. This can involve investments and activities such as putting lightbulbs on motion sensors, upgrading the HVAC (heating, ventilation, air conditioning) system, negotiating better rates with the utility suppliers, or developing a cogeneration power plant adjacent to the factory. Often, the energy services firm receives payment for these services in the form of a share in the net energy cost savings to the client. These firms are located across the country, with a few of the largest clustered in Boston.

Employer Types by Job Function

Job Function	Possible Employer Types
Asset Development	Utility; Oil Company; Pipeline Operator; Energy Services Firm
Corporate Finance	Utility; Pipeline Operator; Oil Company; Equipment Manufacturer
Quantitative Analytics, Risk Management	Utility; Oil Company; Transmission Grid Operator; Pipeline Operator; Investment Fund; Bank
Trading, Energy Marketing	Utility; Oil Company; Pipeline Operator; Investment Fund; Bank
Investment Analysis	Investment Fund; Bank
Consulting	Consulting Firm; Oil Services Company
Business Development	Equipment Manufacturer; Utility; Oil Services Company; Pipeline Operator; Energy Services Firm
Banking	Bank
Strategy and Planning	Utility; Oil Company; Pipeline Operator; Oil Services Company; Equipment Manufacturer
Economic and Policy Analysis	Government Agency; Nonprofit Group; Consulting Firm

Visit Vault at **www.vault.com** for insider company profiles, expert advice, career message boards, expert resume reviews, the Vault Job Board and more.

VAULT CAREER LIBRARY   171

Energy/Oil & Gas Employer Directory

Plum Creek Timber Company

99 Third Ave, Suite 4300
Seattle, WA 98104-4096

Recruiting Contact:
Phone: 206-467-3600
E-mail: careers@plumcreek.com
www.plumcreek.com

Job Search Website:
www.jobsearch.org/seeker/jobsearch/keyword
Search by the following keyword and location
parameters: Keyword: Plum Creek, Location: National

Plum Creek is the United States' largest private landowner with over 8 million acres of land and growing. An S&P 500 company, Plum Creek has revenues over $1.5 billion, offices in 18 states, and various positions in forestry, real estate, land management, manufacturing, accounting, human resources, and legal.

We have a collaborative, team-centric, execution oriented culture focused on delivery and strive for a good balance between career and personal life, and between cutting edge and proven technology. Plum Creek's substantial growth has created many unique career opportunities. You'll be able to build a rewarding and successful career, while enjoying the low-key atmosphere that makes life in our tight-knit communities a happy and warm place to live and visit.

Plum Creek wants to attract and keep the best people-the team who drives our success. That is why we offer superior performers opportunities for compensation that is in the top 25% for our marketplace. Benefits packages consists of a comprehensive range of benefits including Health care, Health and Dependent Daycare Funds, Life and Disability protection, Saving and Retirements benefits, Paid Vacation, Relocation, and more.

With extensive ownership in oil and gas producing regions of the southern states and the Appalachian basin. We enter into royalty leases for these assets with high-quality exploration and production companies and work closely with our lessees on surface management, access and other operating related issues.

Plum Creek actively explores and leases land that contains mineral and construction material reserves throughout our ownership which include industrial minerals such as titanium, bromine, and kaolin, as well as construction aggregates including sand, gravel, dimension and monumental stone, and landscape rock. We work closely with our lessees to evaluate geological opportunities, permitting, zoning, wetlands mitigation and final reclamation efforts. As the largest land owner in the US, we are looking for entrepreneurial individuals to capitalize on these resources and strengthen our natural resources business.

Allegheny Energy, Inc.
800 Cabin Hill Drive
Greensburg, PA 15601
Phone: (724) 837-3000
www.alleghenyenergy.com

Alliant Energy Corporation
4902 N. Biltmore Lane
Madison, WI 53718
Phone: (608) 458-3311
Fax: (608) 458-4824
www.alliantenergy.com

American Electric Power Company, Inc.
1 Riverside Plaza
Columbus, OH 43215
Phone: (614) 716-1000
Fax: (614) 716-1823
www.aep.com

Anadarko Petroleum Corporation
1201 Lake Robbins Drive
The Woodlands, TX 77380
Phone: (832) 636-1000
Fax: (832) 636-8220
www.anadarko.com

Aquila, Inc.
20 W. 9th Street
Kansas City, MO 64105
Phone: (816) 421-6600
Fax: (816) 467-3591
www.aquila.com

Atmos Energy Corporation
3 Lincoln Centre
5430 LBJ Freeway
Suite 1800
Dallas, TX 75240
Phone: (972) 934-9227
Fax: (972) 855-3040
www.atmosenergy.com

Energy/Oil & Gas Employer Directory, cont.

Baker Hughes Incorporated
3900 Essex Lane
Suite 1200
Houston, TX 77027
Phone: (713) 439-8600
Fax: (713) 439-8699
www.bakerhughes.com

BP p.l.c.
1 St. James's Square
London SW1Y 4PD
United Kingdom
Phone: +44-20-7496-4000
Fax: +44-20-7496-4630
www.bp.com

British Nuclear Fuels plc
1100 Daresbury Park
Warrington WA4 4GB
United Kingdom
Phone: +44-1925-832-000
Fax: +44-1925-822-711
www.bnfl.com

Calpine Corporation
50 W. San Fernando Street
San Jose, CA 95113
Phone: (408) 995-5115
Fax: (408) 995-0505
www.calpine.com

CenterPoint Energy Inc.
1111 Louisiana Street
Houston, TX 77002
Phone: (713) 207-1111
Fax: (713) 207-3169
www.centerpointenergy.com

Chevron Corporation
6001 Bollinger Canyon Rd.
San Ramon, CA 94583
Phone: (925) 842-1000
Fax: (925) 842-3530
www.chevron.com

ConocoPhillips Company
600 N. Dairy Ashford Road
Houston, TX 77079
Phone: (281) 293-1000
Fax: (281) 293-2819
www.conocophillips.com

Consolidated Edison Inc.
4 Irving Place
New York, NY 10003
Phone: (212) 460-4600
Fax: (212) 982-7816
www.conedison.com

Crown Central LLC
1 North Charles Street
Baltimore, MD 21201
Phone: (410) 539-7400
Fax: (410) 659-4747
www.crowncentral.com

Devon Energy Corporation
20 N. Broadway
Oklahoma City, OK 73102-8260
Phone: (405) 235-3611
Fax: (405) 552-4550
www.devonenergy.com

Duke Energy Corporation
526 S. Church Street
Charlotte, NC 28202-1803
Phone: (704) 594-6200
Fax: (704) 382-3814
www.duke-energy.com

Dynegy Inc.
1000 Louisiana Street
Suite 5800
Houston, TX 77002
Phone: (713) 507-6400
www.dynegy.com

Edison International
2244 Walnut Grove Avenue
Rosemead, CA 91770
Phone: (626) 302-2222
Fax: (626) 302-2517
www.edison.com

El Paso Corporation
1001 Louisiana Street
Houston, TX 77002
Phone: (713) 420-2600
Fax: (713) 420-4417
www.elpaso.com

Entergy Corporation
639 Loyola Avenue
New Orleans, LA 70113
Phone: (504) 576-4000
Fax: (504) 576-4428
www.entergy.com

Exelon Corporation
10 S. Dearborn Street
37th Floor
Chicago, IL 60680-5379
Phone: (800) 483-2220
Fax: (312) 394-7945
www.exeloncorp.com

Exxon Mobil Corporation
5959 Las Colinas Boulevard
Irving, TX 75039
Phone: (972) 444-1000
Fax: (972) 444-1350
www.exxon.mobil.com

FirstEnergy Corp.
76 S. Main Street
Akron, OH 44308
Phone: (800) 633-4766
Fax: (330) 384-3866
www.firstenergycorp.com

Foster Wheeler Ltd.
Perryville Corporate Park
Clinton, NJ 08809-4000
Phone: (908) 730-4000
Fax: (908) 730-5315
www.fwc.com

GE Energy
4200 Wildwood Parkway
Atlanta, GA 30339
Phone: (678) 844-6000
Fax: (678) 844-6690
www.ge.com/energy

Gulf Oil Limited Partnership
90 Everett Avenue
Chelsea, MA 02150
Phone: (617) 889-9000
Fax: (617) 884-0637
www.gulfoil.com

Visit Vault at www.vault.com for insider company profiles, expert advice,
career message boards, expert resume reviews, the Vault Job Board and more.

VAULT CAREER LIBRARY   173

Energy/Oil & Gas Employer Directory, cont.

Halliburton Company
5 Houston Center, 1401 McKinney
Suite 2400
Houston, TX 77010
Phone: (713) 759-2600
Fax: (713) 759-2635
www.halliburton.com

Hess Corporation
1185 Avenue of the Americas
New York, NY 10036
Phone: (212) 997-8500
Fax: (212) 536-8593
www.hess.com

Koch Industries Inc.
4111 E. 37th Street North
Wichita, KS 67220
Phone: (316) 828-5500
Fax: (316) 828-5739
www.kochind.com

Marathon Oil Corporation
5555 San Felipe Road
Houston, TX 77056-2723
Phone: (713) 629-6600
Fax: (713) 296-2952
www.marathon.com

Occidental Petroleum Corporation
10889 Wilshire Boulevard
Los Angeles, CA 90024
Phone: (310) 208-8800
Fax: (310) 443-6690
www.oxy.com

Pacific Gas & Electric Company
77 Beale Street
San Francisco, CA 94177
Phone: (415) 973-7000
Fax: (415) 267-7268
www.pge.com

PNM Resources, Inc.
Alvarado Square
Albuquerque, NM 87158
Phone: (505) 241-2700
Fax: (505) 241-2367
www.pnmresources.com

PPL Corporation
2 N. 9th Street
Allentown, PA 18101
Phone: (610) 774-5151
Fax: (610) 774-4198
www.pplweb.com

Public Service Enterprise Group Incorporated
80 Park Plaza, Suite 3
Newark, NJ 07102
Phone: (973) 430-7000
Fax: (973) 824-7056
www.pseg.com

The REC Group
REC ASA
Veritasveien 14
N-1323 Høvik
Norway
Phone: +47 67 81 52 50
www.asimi.com

Reliant Energy, Inc.
1000 Main Street
Houston, TX 77002
Phone: (713) 497-3000
Fax: (713) 488-5925
www.reliant.com

Schlumberger Limited
300 Schlumberger Drive
Sugar Land, TX 77478
Phone: (212) 350-9400
Fax: (212) 350-9457
www.slb.com

Scottish Power plc
1 Atlantic Quay
Glasgow G2 8SP
Phone: +44-141-248-8200
Fax: +44-141-248-8300
www.scottishpower.plc.uk

Sempra Energy
101 Ash Street
San Diego, CA 92101
Phone: (619) 696-2000
Fax: (619) 696-2374
www.sempra.com

Shell Oil Company
1 Shell Plaza
910 Louisana Street
Houston, TX 77002
Phone: (713) 241-6161
Fax: (713) 241-4044
www.shellus.com

Southern Company
270 Peachtree Street NW
Atlanta, GA 30303
Phone: (404) 506-5000
Fax: (404) 0455
www.southernco.com

Southwest Gas Corporation
5241 Spring Mountain Road
Las Vegas, NV 89193
Phone: (702) 876-7011
Fax: (702) 364-3180
www.swgas.com

Star Gas Partners, L.P.
2187 Atlantic Street
Stamford, CT 06902
Phone: (203) 328-7310
Fax: (203) 328-7422
www.star-gas.com

Sunoco, Inc.
10 Penn Center
1801 Market Street
Philadelphia, PA 19103-1699
Phone: (215) 977-3000
Fax: (215) 977-3409
www.sunocoinc.com

TXU Corp.
1601 Bryan Street
Dallas, TX 75201
Phone: (214) 812-4600
Fax: (214) 812-7077
www.txucorp.com

Energy/Oil & Gas Employer Directory, cont.

USEC Inc.
6903 Rockledge Drive
Bethesda, MD 20817
Phone: (301) 564-3200
Fax: (301) 564-3201
www.usec.com

Valero Energy Corporation
1 Valero Way
San Antonio, TX 78249
Phone: (210) 345-2000
Fax: (210) 345-2646
www.valero.com

Vectren Corporation
1 Vectren Square
Evansville, IN 47708
Phone: (812) 491-4000
Fax: (812) 491-4706
www.vectren.com

Weatherford International
515 Post Oak Boulevard, Suite 600
Houston, TX 77207
Phone: (713) 693-4000
Fax: (713) 693-4323
www.weatherford.com

Westar Energy
818 S. Kansas Avenue
Topeka, Kansas 66612
Phone: (785) 575-6300
www.wr.com

The Williams Companies
One Williams Center
Tulsa, OK 74172
Phone: (918) 573 2000
Fax: (918) 573 6714
www.williams.com

WPS Resources Corporation
700 North Adams Street
Green Bay, WI 54301
Phone: (920) 433-4901
Fax: (920) 433-1526
www.wpsr.com

Xcel Energy
800 Nicollet Mall
Minneapolis, MN 55402
Phone: (612) 330-5500
Fax: (612) 330-2900
www.xcelenergy.com

Visit Vault at **www.vault.com** for insider company profiles, expert advice,
career message boards, expert resume reviews, the Vault Job Board and more.

VAULT CAREER LIBRARY   175

Use the Internet's
MOST TARGETED
job search tools.

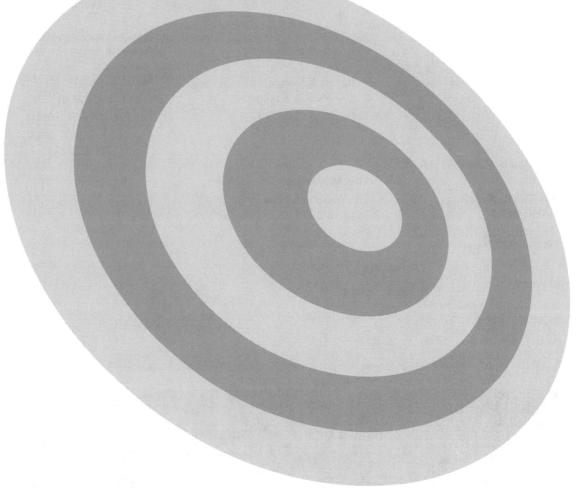

Vault Job Board

Target your search by industry, function, and experience level,
and find the job openings that you want.

VaultMatch Resume Database

Vault takes match-making to the next level: post your resume
and customize your search by industry, function, experience
and more. We'll match job listings with your interests and
criteria and e-mail them directly to your in-box.

Engineering

Overview of Engineering Careers

They're everywhere!

Engineers are involved in any industry where a product is made, designed or repaired. They design software, create and develop mechanical systems, improve civil infrastructure, design and develop aircraft and spacecraft and evaluate industrial systems. Engineering is the art of applying scientific and mathematical principles, experience and judgment to design, build and repair a technical product or system to meet a specific need.

In good company

Engineering has a long and storied history—after all, who do you think figured out how to build the Pyramids or send men to the moon? Its ranks are also filled with such historical luminaries as Leonardo Da Vinci, Thomas Edison and Henry Ford.

Wide variety of work

The five largest fields of engineering are chemical, civil, electrical, industrial and mechanical engineering. There are also many more specialized engineering fields, including nuclear, biomedical, aerospace and environmental engineering. Professional societies recognize more than 25 engineering specialties, and new ones continue to develop along with advances in science and technology. Engineers are problem solvers, and if you're considering a career in engineering, it's probably because you have a love of math and science and have a knack for dissecting complex mechanical or logistical problems.

Specialized knowledge

A fundamental aspect of engineering is the practical application of scientific or mechanical knowledge. A civil engineer, for example, might be assigned a project to build or improve roads and bridges, dams and irrigation systems, water treatment processes or public transportation systems. Civil engineers also test buildings to make sure they are structurally sound, particularly large institutional ones. The term "civil engineering" essentially indicates projects related to public works; the work itself may involve principles of mechanical engineering, electrical engineering or other specialized fields.

Making it, and making it work

Manufacturers employ engineers to design and develop products such as consumer and industrial electronics, fabricated metals, machine tools, chemical compounds, transportation equipment, aircraft, communication equipment and space vehicles. Engineers also develop the production processes necessary to create those products, from designing the machinery to designing the factories where the machinery is operated.

Other avenues

With so many separate disciplines within the engineering field, it's not surprising that there is some overlap. Some of the most common fields of engineering are:

Visit Vault at **www.vault.com** for insider company profiles, expert advice, career message boards, expert resume reviews, the Vault Job Board and more.

VAULT CAREER LIBRARY 177

Electrical engineering

As members of the largest engineering field, electrical engineers deal with anything from power systems and transmission, circuitry and communication, to industrial robots, microprocessors and digital broadcasting. They might also design circuit boards for audio equipment, broadcast systems for cell phones and television or power stations and citywide electric-utility services. Other projects might include radar and navigation systems, electric motors, machinery controls, lighting and wiring in buildings, automobiles and aircraft.

Software engineering (programming), Web engineering, IT engineering

Software engineers (also called programmers) create programs for use on various computer platforms such as Windows, Macintosh or Unix. Web engineers are essentially programmers who develop applications specifically for the Web. Specialists in information technology (IT) focus on creating and maintaining information networks, often within companies or government agencies. IT engineers make sure that networks stay secure and run smoothly, both within an office (known as a local area network, or LAN) and between remote locations (known as a wide area network, or WAN).

Mechanical engineering

Mechanical engineers create, develop and run manufacturing systems, engines, pipelines, robots, refrigeration equipment and other mechanical tools. Mechanical engineers focus on how machines work by researching, developing, designing, manufacturing and testing tools, engines, machines and other mechanical devices. They work on power-producing machines such as electric generators, internal combustion engines, and steam and gas turbines. They also develop power-using machines such as refrigeration and airconditioning equipment, machine tools, material handling systems, elevators and escalators, industrial production equipment and robots used in manufacturing.

Mechanical engineers work in many industries, and their job varies by industry and function. Some specialties include applied mechanics; computer-aided design and manufacturing; energy systems; pressure vessels and piping; and heating, refrigeration, and airconditioning systems. Mechanical engineering is one of the broadest engineering disciplines. Mechanical engineers may work in production operations in manufacturing or agriculture, maintenance or technical sales; many are administrators or managers.

Chemical engineering

It is true that chemical engineers are comfortable with chemistry, but they do much more with this knowledge than just make chemicals. In fact, the term "chemical engineer" is not even intended to describe the type of work a chemical engineer performs. Instead it is meant to reveal what makes the field different from the other branches of engineering. Chemical engineers apply the principles of chemistry and engineering to solve problems involving the production or use of chemicals, building a bridge between science and manufacturing.

The knowledge and duties of chemical engineers overlap many fields. They apply principles of chemistry, physics, mathematics, and mechanical and electrical engineering. They frequently specialize in a particular operation such as oxidation or polymerization. Others specialize in a particular area, such as pollution control or the production of specific products such as fertilizers and pesticides, automotive plastics or chlorine bleach. They must be aware of all aspects of chemical manufacturing and how it affects the environment, the safety of workers and customers. Because chemical engineers use computer technology to optimize all phases of research and production, they need to understand how to apply computer skills to process analysis, automated control systems and statistical quality control.

Environmental engineering

Using the principles of biology and chemistry, environmental engineers develop methods to solve problems related to the environment. They are involved in water and air pollution control, recycling, waste disposal and public health issues. Environmental engineers conduct hazardous-waste management studies, evaluate the significance of the hazard, offer analysis on treatment and containment and develop regulations to prevent mishaps. They design municipal sewage and industrial wastewater systems. They analyze scientific data, research controversial projects and perform quality control checks. Many environmental engineers work as consultants, helping their clients comply with regulations and clean up hazardous sites, including brownfields, which are abandoned urban or industrial sites that may contain environmental hazards.

Careers in Electrical Engineering

America's dependence on electronics is so great that most people can't get through a day without using a product that has a microcontroller or other electronic circuitry. And this is all part of electrical engineering. Digital alarm clocks, automotive controls, computer networks, TVs, cell phones and MP3 players were all designed in large part by clever people who studied electronic engineering in college. Indeed, many of the products we take for granted today, from the smallest chip to the large supercomputers that help predict weather, stemmed from the minds of electronic engineers who wanted to build something new and different.

From ideas that range from seemingly crazy to really nifty to just plain useful, engineers come up with working products. Marketing people might come up with concepts and software developers play an important role in design, but engineering is where it all begins. The digital revolution that's changing the world wouldn't be possible without it—electronic engineers are developing the hardware that is truly changing the world.

Entering this fast-paced field requires an inquisitive mind, and an ability to understand difficult technical principles that are often mathematically based. A creative bent and the ability to analyze problems from different angles also help. If you have these traits, you'll find that you'll always be challenged by a career as an electrical engineer and particularly by the fast rate of technical change.

There are a number of other beneficial paybacks for those who choose electrical engineering. Electronic engineers earn good salaries while getting to work with interesting technologies. And because many products require electronic technologies, it's fairly easy to find a field you can understand and enjoy.

On the downside, staying abreast of technology in a global economy is a challenge. Technologists must keep up to date so they don't lose their job to cheaper offshore workers. The impact of international competition from low wage countries is being hotly debated throughout the electronics industry.

The scoop

Since electronic engineers are the men and women responsible for developing concepts for new technologies, they play an integral part in the digital revolution. Among other advances, electrical engineers made the Internet a vehicle for communicating freely to people anywhere on Earth. They devised techniques for sending data, the methods for making sure everything gets to its destination. They designed the PCs, servers and other equipment that let people see images from around the globe in a matter of seconds.

When people talk about smart appliances, smart phones and other so-called smart products, they're unknowingly complimenting the intelligent people who made those products. Electrical engineers are responsible for making cell phones small enough to fit in your pocket, and they also figured out how to put cameras into a mobile phone that can last for hours without recharging.

Visit Vault at **www.vault.com** for insider company profiles, expert advice,
career message boards, expert resume reviews, the Vault Job Board and more.

VAULT CAREER LIBRARY **179**

But electrical engineers have been changing the world for most of the 20th century. The term electronics didn't exist at the dawn of the 1900s. But the engineers of the day quickly realized that the science of moving electrons had enough potential to have its own name.

Some history

During the first half of the 1900s, engineers made radios with tubes (glass enclosures surrounding large, fragile electronic circuits, often assembled by hand). The first TVs also had many tubes besides the picture tube, which is still widely used as the television's screen. These tubes were so large and bulky that Eniac, the first real digital computer, weighed thirty tons when it started churning data in 1944.

The stage for the era of electronics was set by research scientists at Bell Labs, who did the work of electrical engineers, even though many didn't hold what was then a new degree. In 1947, Bell researchers figured out how to make a transistor, which became the basic building block of the silicon chips now used in millions of products.

In the 1950s, a transistor radio the size of a cigarette pack was a marvel. Today, there are literally millions of transistors on a chip. The size benefits of digital electronics over tubes are obvious: for example, compare the bulky cathode ray tube computer screens that have been used for decades to the sleek flat panel displays of today. The CRT, which is also the technology used for conventional television screens, is the last of the tube technologies to become obsolete, falling victim to replacements that were developed by electronic engineers.

This act of replacement is a mainstay of engineering. The nature of the field involves tinkering—looking at something and figuring out how to make a better version. Whether an engineer is looking at equipment on a factory floor, in an airplane or in his office, he's likely to take the shell off a product, see how it works and then come up with something better.

This kind of tinkering forms the basis for new technologies. The scope is staggering—everything from compact disk players, airbags and antilock braking systems, to computer networks and calculators derive from new technologies developed by electrical engineers who thought there was a better way to do something.

The history of electronics is loaded with people who had a novel idea and then worked diligently to bring their products to life. Hewlett Packard was started by a couple of guys working in a garage, where they created a novel instrument first used by sound engineers making Disney's *Fantasia*.

Decades later, an HP engineer worked nights to come up with a new product that contained a new technology—some referred to this product as a personal computer. Steve Wozniak wasn't the first to make an affordable computer, but he helped found Apple Computers, the first company to make computers available to the average family.

There are many other companies that have significantly impacted the electronics industry; as a matter of fact, electrical engineers at IBM have led the country in patents for decades, providing breakthrough after breakthrough. And engineers at Texas Instruments invented the integrated circuit—commonly known as a microchip—and also popularized compact calculators.

Electrical Engineering Employment Opportunities

Electrical engineering is an exploding field. If you have an electronic engineering degree, it's hard to think of a field that provides more choices. The boom of smart equipment has created many jobs for engineers, and the push to come up with the next new thing keeps engineers busy across many fields. Cars, trains, robots and refrigerators all have electronic controls; even lightbulbs and dog collars now employ electronic components.

Among the largest employers of electrical engineers are computer, telecommunications and consumer electronics companies. These fields are pretty much the domain of electrical engineer, though a few mechanical engineers are needed for package design. There are almost always job openings at the giants within these fields, such as IBM, Motorola, Cisco, Sharp, Qualcomm, Texas Instruments and Dell. These huge corporations employ hundreds of engineers at their home offices, but many also have remote engineering sites scattered around the country.

Most major corporations also have international offices. Though there is some chance for transferring overseas, the bulk of engineers in a region tend to be from that area.

Finally, there are a number of smaller companies that produce many different types of basic computing and telecommunications equipment.

The mainstays

The majority of electrical engineers go into what might be considered traditional job categories (if anything can be considered traditional in an industry that really didn't start to mature until 1981, when the first IBM PC was introduced).

The declining costs of electronics mean chips and systems will continuously find new applications. As computer chips become cheaper, clever electrical engineers can design electronic controls that are cheaper than mechanical switches.

And that's bound to continue. Semiconductor manufacturers make exponentially more chips every year. Though the first microchip was made by Texas Instruments' Jack Kirby in 1958, it wasn't until 1994 that worldwide sales cracked $100 billion. In the following six years, the industry matched growth that had previously taken 36 years, as sales surpassed $200 billion in 2000, according to the Semiconductor Industries Association.

Common appliances like refrigerators and stoves have benefited from plenty of electrical technologies, but it's only been in recent years that they have incorporated electronic components like microcontrollers. Today, it's possible to buy a refrigerator that links to the Internet and uses bar code readers to determine whether it's time to buy milk or mustard.

Diverse industries

While this kind of growth creates many new job opportunities, job growth doesn't rise at nearly the same rate as market shipments. Corporations contend there aren't enough skilled engineers, and many are hiring engineers from foreign countries or contracting with designers abroad.

Nevertheless, the industry has not suffered a decline in the number of jobs worldwide. That's partly because the electronics industry is predicated on providing new, improved products in increasingly shorter development cycles. In some industries, like those of mobile phones and PCs, new products come out every few months, making older products obsolete in a hurry. Throughout the electronics industry, more than half of a company's revenue typically comes from products that were introduced within the past 18 months.

All these products require some level of design expertise. Complex products obviously require skilled engineers who understand leading-edge technologies, but someone has to design even the simplest products. New electrical engineers can often find a home with companies that need some design expertise for these simpler products.

But engineers can ply their craft in many different fields. Many engineers start out in conventional areas of electronics, but remain on the lookout for openings in fields that particularly interest them. Guitar amplifiers, race cars and medical instruments all have electronic components. Trains and planes make extensive use of electronic controls. A few lucky engineers are able to blend their hobbies, whether that's music or racing, with their career.

Visit Vault at **www.vault.com** for insider company profiles, expert advice, career message boards, expert resume reviews, the Vault Job Board and more.

VAULT CAREER LIBRARY   **181**

Not everyone wants to combine their hobby and their job. Sometimes that takes the fun out of things. But for those who do, it is a possibility, as electronics is an area that holds almost unlimited career opportunities for engineers who want to work in areas that might be considered "out of the mainstream."

While the dominant firms in many fields are well known, there are far more opportunities at the hundreds of smaller firms around the country. Throughout the electronics industry, there are often customers who want something a bit different from what mainstream companies can provide. Smaller companies can carve out a niche in these specialized areas, which are often too minor for large corporations to address. Most of these so-called contract design houses have fewer than 50 engineers.

Civil Engineering Careers

What is civil engineering?

Civil engineering is just one of many types of engineering, which includes chemical, computer/software, mechanical, electrical, agricultural, aerospace, biomedical/bioengineering, mining, systems, engineering management, nuclear, and industrial. Unlike other forms of engineering, civil engineering deals with the practical aspects of everyday life. Because there are a range of design and technology issues within the civil field, programs of study in civil engineering tend to incorporate information from other areas to develop engineering solutions. In this sense, programs of study in civil engineering tend to be more comprehensive than those of other engineering fields.

As defined by the American Society of Civil Engineers (ASCE), "Civil engineering is about community service, development, and improvement. It involves the conception, planning, design, construction, and operation of facilities essential to modern life, ranging from transit systems to offshore structures to space satellites. Civil engineers are problem solvers, meeting the challenges of pollution, traffic congestion, drinking water and energy needs, urban redevelopment, and community planning."

The word civil is derived from the Latin word civilis, which derives from civis, or citizen. Engineering is defined by the Accreditation Board for Engineering and Technology (ABET) as "the profession in which a knowledge of the mathematical and natural sciences gained by study, experience, and practice is applied with judgment to develop ways to utilize economically the materials and forces of nature for the benefit of mankind.." Thus, civil engineering is applying learned scientific knowledge to the creation of processes, information, technology, and solutions that make everyday life easier for the average citizen, meaning all of us. It is a profession that significantly affects the life of our global environment.

Examples of civil engineering: past and present

Traditionally civil engineering is most often associated with roads, bridges, buildings, and dams. But civil engineering has always been a major facet of society and culture. Examples of civil engineering designs abound throughout history, from the construction of pyramids in ancient Egypt, to the Parthenon in Athens, to the Great Wall of China. And in the relatively short history of the United States, great civil engineering has characterized our most distinguished national treasures. From highways to skyscrapers, great feats have been achieved within the field in the past one hundred and fifty years.

Transportation didn't become a major issue in the United States until automobiles were commercially available. Roads that were once designed for horses and buggies were insufficient for modern cars. In 1908, the first concrete road was laid in Detroit, Michigan, which was to become the home of automobile manufacturing, and some thirty years later the Federal Interstate Highway System was created and eventually authorized in 1956. This highway system, originally named "The Dwight D. Eisenhower System of Interstate and Defense Highways," is comprised of 42,700 miles of interconnecting roads. Though modern roads were crucial for effective transportation, structurally sound bridges were also necessary. As industry grew, the need for wider and stronger bridges to accommodate railroad commerce and increased traffic forced engineering methods to change. The Romans constructed magnificent stone bridges throughout the European empire, some of which are still in use. But it was not until the Industrial Revolution that bridge construction changed dramatically. With new materials such as iron, bridge design became more technologically advanced. In the 20th century, steel and concrete became the materials of choice for bridges. One of the best examples of this is the Golden Gate Bridge, which was completed in 1937.

The incredible architectural achievements of the early 20th century caused civil engineering to begin to attract greater recognition than its sister fields. The Woolworth Building, the Sears Tower, and the Chrysler Building exemplified these modern architectural designs, and the public became fascinated with these larger-than-life structures that combined art and engineering. The collective American imagination was also captured during the building of the concrete Hoover Dam in 1931. In the midst of the Great Depression, flooding and water shortages affected the adjoining area. Not only were thousands of jobs provided, but a major hydroelectric innovation was created to address irrigation, power and water supply needs in the neighboring area.

Civil Engineering in Detail

All basic engineering studies begin at the same point, with general courses in math and science. But for those who choose to pursue civil engineering, a specialty area needs to be determined. There are six major disciplines: structural, geotechnical, environmental, transportation, water resources, and construction. Though the disciplines are related, the differences are significant enough that a civil engineering degree with a specialization in structures does not mean you are qualified to design a water treatment facility.

Structural

A structural engineer focuses on the design and analysis of structures, such as buildings and bridges, to determine how well these structures will hold up to various environmental factors including earthquakes, hurricanes, and excessive wind. Structural engineering research has focused on developing technology to protect buildings during earthquakes, of critical concern since there were over 30,000 reports of seismic activity worldwide in 2003. If a structure is badly designed it will eventually fail, which could potentially harm to the people who live or work in or around it. In 1940, the original Tacoma Narrows Bridge in Washington collapsed, as excessive winds created vibrations and caused the steel and concrete bridge to give way, as if it was made from rubber. More recently, the 9/11 terrorist attacks on the World Trade Center raised questions about the structural integrity of the Twin Towers. Because the towers collapsed, numerous investigations were launched to find out how and why.

Other structural projects on which an engineer might focus are amusement park rides, sporting arenas, even the International Space Station. Many people are confused about the difference between architecture and structural engineering, particularly the role each plays in the construction of commercial and residential projects. Though the architect may provide artistic elements to the structure, the engineer makes sure it can stand. Structural engineers are also learned in the properties and behavior of the various materials used in construction, such as steel, concrete, aluminum, timber, and plastics. Without the work of structural engineers, how we travel, where we work, and even how we entertain ourselves would be vastly different.

Geotechnical

Geological engineering incorporates science and technology to create projects and solve problems relating to geology. Geology is more than the study of rocks and volcanoes, and geotechnical engineering requires knowledge of not only geology, but chemistry, physics, and earth science as well. Technology involving the Earth and its natural resources has an effect on a global scale. Some components of geotechnical engineering are soil mechanics, earthquake engineering, foundation engineering, coastal and offshore engineering, rock mechanics, applied seismology, petroleum engineering, drilling, and

Visit Vault at **www.vault.com** for insider company profiles, expert advice, career message boards, expert resume reviews, the Vault Job Board and more.

VAULT CAREER LIBRARY   **183**

hydrogeology. Construction projects involve tunnels, pipelines, mines, levees, embankments, stable slopes and structural foundations. The engineer must also consider soil conditions in all of these scenarios, as if the soil is unsuitable the project might not succeed. In turn, during environmental disasters, soil remediation is developed by geotechnical engineers. Petrolatum, natural gas, and mineral exploration are all major industries involved in geotechnical engineering. The necessary analysis involved in geotechnical engineering requires extensive field tests and laboratory work..

Environmental

Environmental protection has become a significant problem in the last thirty years or so. As the public has become increasingly aware of environmentalism and pollution, the development of technology to preserve and improve the environment has become necessary. Environmental engineering analyzes environmental problems and develops solutions to those problems. This discipline combines the study of environmental science, mathematics, atmospheric science, biology, hydrology, chemistry, and engineering technology. Improving air and water quality, locating and treating underground water sources, solid waste management, rehabilitating contaminated industrial and residential areas, and treating non-hazardous and hazardous substances, are all tasks undertaken by environmental engineers. Providing safe drinking water, reducing air emissions, understanding global warming, and treating waste water are all critical to a safe and clean environment. Because environmental problems are so widespread, this specialty is essential to several industries, and in some cases the work of an environmental engineer may overlap with that of a geotechnical or water resource engineer.

Water resources

The average human male body is composed of 60 percent water. Water comprises 70 to 75 percent of the Earth's surface. In short, water is one of our most essential natural resources. However, it is also once of the most threatened. Water scarcity is not a new phenomenon; over two thousand years have passed since the times of Biblical droughts and the availability of clean water continues to be a concern. A water resource engineer finds ways to improve the quality and quantity of water and water sources. Hydrology, meteorology, fluid dynamics, and environmental science all play a part in water resources engineering. These specialists concentrate on flood and storm water analysis, wetland protection, groundwater remediation, water supply planning and management, wastewater treatment, and beach erosion control. In 1999, North Carolina experienced some of the worst flooding in its history. The force of Hurricane Floyd decimated entire towns; jobs were lost and forty-eight people died. Water resource engineers are trained to assess flood risk and develop technology to prevent flooding. Knowledge of water quality and groundwater modeling, remote sensing of precipitation, and awareness of how pollutants travel in surface and groundwater is essential to this field. The design, construction and maintenance of canals, dams, pumping stations, and water storage and treatment facilities are all responsibilities of water resource engineers. Many university programs in environmental engineering incorporate water resources as a subcategory.

Construction

Every single civil engineering project involves construction; a structure needs to be erected, a tunnel needs to be dug, a road needs to be laid, a treatment plant needs to be built. Construction engineers manage these projects. Once a given project is designed by an engineer of the appropriate specialty, the construction engineer will oversee day to day responsibilities. Once a contractor is awarded a project, they assign the construction engineer to the project site. This engineer then works with various engineers involved in the project design, such as electrical, structural, chemical, or geotechnical engineers. The construction engineer is also responsible for implementing and maintaining the project schedule and the budget, incorporating their technical and managerial knowledge to bring the project to a successful close. Construction engineers have the most complete understanding of construction projects, and have strong command of various engineering disciplines not just their own.. The construction industry is one of the largest in the world'a present day example would be the rebuilding of Iraq, most of which is being carried out by American corporations. According to the Coalition Provisional Authority Iraq Program

Management Office (PMO), as of the time of publication, almost forty contracts had been awarded in the 2004 fiscal year alone. This field is also known as engineering management.

Transportation

Getting stuck in a traffic jam may not be the highlight of your day; nor is waiting for a train after you missed an earlier one. The development of an efficient and reliable transportation system is crucial in maintaining a functioning society, and daily movement, whether by car, bus, train, airplane, boat, or truck, can either adversely or constructively affect commerce. Transportation engineers are responsible for designing, constructing, and maintaining highways, railways, airfields, and ports. Besides researching and improving traffic control, these engineers develop new methods of transportation and find ways to improve mass transportation. Some of their research also includes pedestrian accidents. In Japan and some Western European countries, transportation innovations have vastly improved life in those areas; the Eurostar is a prefect example. This high-speed train provides travel between the United Kingdom and continental Europe, cutting down on travel time at speeds upwards of 186 mph. Transportation engineers also plan and maintain pipelines for gas, water, and oil.

Vault Q&A: Jay Wilkins, BASF's Rotational Development Program

After graduating with a degree in chemical engineering from the University of Texas at Austin, in December 2004, Jay Wilkins admittedly had "no idea" what type of engineering position he wanted to pursue. He ended up joining BASF's Professional Development Program (PDP) for chemical engineers, which gave him the opportunity to work and gain experience in several different positions.

Vault: How did you find out about BASF's PDP program?

Wilkins: BASF posted on the career site through the engineering center at my school.

Vault: Did you know what sort of engineering position you were looking for when you graduated and started the program?

Wilkins: I really had no idea. That's what I think is so great about this program. When I came out of school, I really didn't know what kind of chemical engineering career I wanted to pursue. For example, there's process engineering, project engineering, product development, operations engineering, instrumentation, control systems engineering, environmental health and safety, and many other derivatives. In addition to the various job functions, there are also many different industries in which to perform them. Just within BASF alone, there are divisions for polymers, agricultural products such as fertilizers and pesticides, cosmetics, catalysts, inorganics, nutritional products, coatings and textures, textiles, pharmaceuticals, and many other chemical groups such as oxo-alcohols and specialty amines.

What I really liked about the rotational program is that not only did you get experience in several different job functions, but also in several different industries within the same company. By the time I got done with the program, I knew exactly what I wanted to do and where I wanted to do it.

When I went through the program, there were three six-month assignments, since then, it's been changed to two nine-month assignments. I rolled off the program a month ago.

Vault: So where did you start out?

Wilkins: I started out as an operations engineer in Port Arthur, Texas. There, I was dealing with issues in the plant on a day-to-day basis -- solving problems that arose in the plant and implementing small capital projects. For example, I designed and implemented a control loop to regulate the concentration in a furnace feed line. I also monitored the performance of over 300 process safety valves in order to determine which ones were leaking into the flare header.

Visit Vault at **www.vault.com** for insider company profiles, expert advice, career message boards, expert resume reviews, the Vault Job Board and more.

VAULT CAREER LIBRARY **185**

The Port Arthur site is a chemical plant. It produces ethelyne, propylene, and other chemical derivatives. It's the largest steam cracker in the world. A steam cracker takes long chains of hydrocarbons and heats them up, "cracking" the chains and forming double bonds.

Vault: Where did you go next?

Wilkins: My second rotation was at a smaller site, a manufacturing plant in Sparta, Tennessee in the upper Cumberland Mountains. It was a site that produced performance polymers or hard plastics. Every brand of hand tool, such as Black and Decker, DeWalt, and Bosch, uses plastics from the Sparta BASF site.

Sparta was a manufacturing site rather than a chemical plant. It was very different from the Port Arthur site. For example, there weren't as many engineers on-site in Sparta. As a PDP participant at that site, I got to experience a combination of process, operations, and product engineering. In a smaller site, you wear many hats, because there are not 10 to 12 engineers with all different job functions. There's just a handful of engineers and all share duties. As a result, I had a lot of responsibility and opportunity to do a lot of capital projects, day-to-day improvement projects, and also some design work. It was a good chance to do lots of different things within the same job.

Vault: So where are you now?

Wilkins: Geismar, Louisiana. It's a town close to Baton Rouge. I recently accepted a permanent position here, but it was also my third rotational assignment.

I picked this position because I really enjoyed the work I was doing during my assignment. When it was time to roll off of the program, I applied to an open position here.

It's a process engineering position, which is a bit different from operations and project engineering. It's more design work, working on projects that are a long time in the future, even a couple years off. I'm doing a lot of sizing and simulation work. It's a lot of what I like to call pencil and paper engineering. It's similar to the type of engineering you do in school.

Vault: What sort of products are you working on?

Wilkins: Geismar is our largest North American site, and is a very large chemical plant. It's almost what you would call seven or eight chemical plants in one. So at this site we make many chemicals -- we make specialty amines, polyalcohols, ethylene oxide, isocyanates, aniline, diols, surfactants, and a few others. As a PDP I was working mostly on projects in ethylene oxide and TDI, which is an isocyanate used for foams that go into products such as seat cushions.

Vault: Did you get to choose your rotations?

Wilkins: The first assignment was chosen for me when I signed up for the program. PDP participants are placed depending on business needs. Halfway through my first assignment, I was able to choose the second one. BASF has a database set up and there's a list of job openings for PDP participants only. I checked the database the other day and there were 50-60 openings all over the company.

You basically apply to whichever positions you are interested in, and it's a first-come, first serve basis. Assignments must be at different sites. The process begins three months before your rotation ends, and you usually go through a phone interview.

Vault: Was your relocation paid for?

Wilkins: Everything that is associated with the move is paid for, including a house-hunting trip.

Vault: Is there much communication among the different employees in the program?

Wilkins: We have teleconferences about once a month to discuss what each PDP participant is working on and maintain contact with all participants.

A lot of times, it's just more of keeping details straight, hearing about what other people are doing in the sites and their roles, and hearing about other assignments so you can make the decision about whether you want to rotate to that assignment.

Vault: Is there a formal mentor program set up?

Wilkins: With this program, at your first site you have a mentor that's assigned to you, basically to kind of guide you along. Usually it's somebody that's not in your department.

Vault: How often did you meet with your mentor?

Wilkins: Really as often as I wanted to. I knew where his office was, and we'd talk maybe about once every other week. We'd try to have lunch every two weeks.

Also, it's remarkable how many people you come across that graduated from the program. These former PDP participants can relate to where you're at; they've been in your shoes, and you can always ask them questions. It's good to have so many engineers around you that have gone through the same program.

Visit Vault at **www.vault.com** for insider company profiles, expert advice, career message boards, expert resume reviews, the Vault Job Board and more.

VAULT CAREER LIBRARY   **187**

Engineering Employer Directory

ARCADIS G&M

630 Plaza Drive, Suite 200
Highlands Ranch, Colorado 80129
Recruiting Contact Phone: 720-344-3500
www.arcadis-us.com

Undergraduate schools ARCADIS recruits from:

Arizona State University ; University of Arizona ; University of California - Berkeley; University of Central Florida; CO School of Mines; Colorado State University; Georgia Tech; Michigan Tech; University of Nebraska; North Carolina State University; Penn State University; Purdue; Rensselaer Polytechnic Institute ; University of South Florida ; Stanford; Texas A&M; University of Texas,; University of Puerto Rico; Valparaiso University; Virginia Tech

ARCADIS is a global engineering company specializing in consulting and implementation services for environment, infrastructure, and facilities. We execute more than 10,000 projects annually throughout the world, enhancing the sustainable quality of life through the services we provide.

Our culture is based on entrepreneurship, openness and agility; we look for professionals who are innovative, have strong work ethics, positive attitudes and like to have fun with their work and colleagues. We provide mentoring and career opportunities to advance within our company.

Applicable degree programs and opportunities would include civil engineers, environmental engineers, geologists, hydrogeologists, construction management, and more.

Parsons

100 West Walnut Street
Pasadena, CA 91124

Recruiting Contact:
Phone: 626.440.4047
E-mail: Collegehires.parsons@parsons.com
www.parsonsjobs.com

Undergraduate schools Parsons recruits from:

Cal Poly Pomona; Cal Poly SLO; Drexel; Georgia Tech; Miami University; MIT; NC A&T; Notre Dame; Penn State; Stanford; Texas A&M; UC Berkeley; Univ. of WA, Seattle; University of Hawaii; USC (So Cal);

Founded in 1944, Parsons is one of the largest 100% employee-owned engineering and construction companies in the United States, with revenues exceeding $2.9 billion in 2004. Parsons provides facility and infrastructure solutions through superior program management and technology-based approaches. Our ability to plan, design, construct, and operate diverse facilities and infrastructure systems has satisfied both government and industrial clients' needs for over 60 years. Our 11,500 employee-owners, located worldwide, team with customers and stakeholders while providing dependable services. We measure our success one project at a time by exceeding expectations and satisfying our customers.

We are committed to continually enhancing our organizational capability by attracting, retaining and developing exceptional talent. Our results-oriented and collaborative team environment encourages the development of creative solutions to the most challenging engineering, scientific, logistics, and construction issues.

COMPREHENSIVE BENEFITS AND COMPETITIVE SALARY:
Parsons offers a competitive compensation and benefits package which includes medical, dental, vision, and life insurance; tuition reimbursement program; credit union membership; Employee Stock Ownership Plan, 401(k) plan, career development, and more. EOE/M/F/D/V. Diversity candidates are encouraged to apply.

Engineering Employer Directory, cont.

Agilent Technologies, Inc.
395 Page Mill Rd.
Palo Alto, CA 94306
Phone: (650) 752-5000
Fax: (650) 752-5633
Toll Free: (877) 424-4536
www.agilent.com

Bechtel Group, Inc.
50 Beale St.
San Francisco, CA 94105-1895
Phone: (415) 768-1234
Fax: (415) 768-9038
www.bechtel.com

The Boeing Company
100 N. Riverside Plaza
Chicago, IL 60606-1596
Phone: (312) 544-2000
Fax: (312) 544-2082
www.boeing.com

CH2M HILL Companies, Ltd.
9191 S. Jamaica St.
Englewood, CO 80112
Phone: (303) 771-0900
Fax: (720) 286-9250
www.ch2m.com

Chevron Corporation
6001 Bollinger Canyon Rd.
San Ramon, CA 94583
Phone: (925) 842-1000
Fax: (925) 842-3530
www.chevron.com
ConocoPhillips
600 N. Dairy Ashford Rd.
Houston, TX 77079
Phone: (281) 293-1000
Fax: (281) 293-2819
www.conocophillips.com

Fluor Corporation
Las Colinas Blvd.
Irving, TX 75039
Phone: 469-398-7000
Fax: 498-398-7255
www.fluor.com

Foster Wheeler Ltd.
Perryville Corporate Park
Clinton, NJ 08809-4000
Phone: (908) 730-4000
Fax: (908) 730-5315
www.fwc.com

General Dynamics Corporation
2941 Fairview Park Dr., Ste. 100
Falls Church, VA 22042
Phone: (703) 876-3000
Fax: (703) 876-3125
www.gendyn.com

Halliburton Company
5 Houston Center, 1401 McKinney,
Ste. 2400
Houston, TX 77010
Phone: (713) 759-2600
Fax: (713) 759-2635
www.halliburton.com

Honeywell
Honeywell International Inc.
101 Columbia Road
Morristown, NJ 07962
Phone: (973) 455-2000
Fax: (973) 455-4807
www.honeywell.com

Kimley-Horn and Associates, Inc.
3001 Weston Pkwy.
Cary, NC 27513
Phone: (919) 677-2000
Fax: (919) 677-2050
www.kimley-horn.com

Lockheed Martin Corporation
6801 Rockledge Dr.
Bethesda, MD 20817
Phone: (301) 897-6000
Fax: (301) 897-6704
www.lockheedmartin.com

Northrop Grumman Corporation
1840 Century Park East
Los Angeles, CA 90067-2199
Phone: (310) 553-6262
Fax: (310) 553-2076
www.northgrum.com

Raytheon Company
870 Winter St.
Waltham, MA 02451
Phone: (781) 522-3000
Fax: (781) 522-3001
www.raytheon.com

Rockwell Collins
400 Collins Road N.E.
Cedar Rapids, IA 52498
Phone: (319) 295-1000
Fax: (319) 295-5429
www.rockwellcollins.com

Siemens AG
Wittelsbacherplatz 2
D-80333 Munich
Germany
Phone: +49-89 636-00
Fax: +49-89 636-52 000
www.siemens.com

Symbol Technologies
1 Symbol Plaza
Holtsville, NY 11742-1300
Phone: (631) 738-2400
Fax: (631) 738-5990
Toll Free: (800) 722-6234
www.symbol.com

Visit Vault at **www.vault.com** for insider company profiles, expert advice,
career message boards, expert resume reviews, the Vault Job Board and more.

VAULT CAREER LIBRARY 189

Fashion

Do you thrill to the thought that gray might—just might—be the new black? Do you tire of fashion trends before they even hit the stores? Then a career in fashion could be the right choice for you. Those who truly love the field say that the perks—fabulous clothes, exposure to famous people and brands, extraordinary diversity, awareness of upcoming trends and cool job status—are worth the struggle. Still, fashion is not all glitz and glamour. Even more than talent, an understanding of the industry is what lands the job.

Even though the fashion industry is difficult to break into, opportunities abound there—creative jobs in design and marketing; retail sales and buying positions; corporate careers in finance, planning and distribution.

Yet whether you are seeking a place on the catwalk or in the haute couture clubhouse, the fashion business is just that—a business. Insiders from all over the fashion world say that their jobs are high on stress and low on pay. Moreover, insiders conclude, people are often judged as much on looks as on performance. With its rigorous hours, capricious culture and wobbly corporate ladder, the fashion industry certainly isn't for everybody. Yet for a dedicated minority, there is no more exciting and inspiring place. Lecturing at a forum hosted by the Fashion Group Foundation, designer Isaac Mizrahi characterized fashion this way: "I hope you all adore what you're doing. It's really got to be this obsession. You have to love cloth. You have to love chalk. You have to love pins. You do it because you love to do it, and can't stop doing it."

Designers create and produce garments, textiles and accessories. Some have formal training and some do not. Almost all designers begin as assistant designers for a few years and eventually become designers. In a large company, a designer may move up the ladder to be a design director. A design director manages the designers from each group. For example, at a company like Bebe, there may be a designer for each group (such as dresses, suits, knits and denim), but a design director will coordinate the efforts of all the designers so the brand presents a cohesive image. Product development usually refers to retailers that develop their own product in conjunction with manufacturers. Product development differs from design in that it usually doesn't require as many technical skills. In fact, product developers may work with designers from other companies to create products for their own brand.

Fashion Design Jobs

Assistant Designer: Helps the designer create new designs. May help with sketches and research.

Designer: Creates plans for clothes that fit the image, season and price point of the brand.

Assistant Technical Designer: Assists designer or technical designer in all aspects of quality and fit procedures. Must have strong computer skills.

Technical Designer: Follows design direction to develop garments through technical sketches, specific measurements for garments, receiving and reviewing samples and sketching and measuring garments for technical packages.

Sample Pattern Maker: Translates designers' sketches into wearable works of art by draping and making patterns to create sample garments. Almost all patternmakers draft patterns on computers.

Textile Designer: Creates textiles by using various fibers and knitting or weaving techniques for industries ranging from apparel to upholstery.

Visit Vault at **www.vault.com** for insider company profiles, expert advice, career message boards, expert resume reviews, the Vault Job Board and more.

VAULT CAREER LIBRARY 191

The Scoop on Design Careers

Most fashion experts would agree that design, one of fashion's most competitive and exciting fields, requires technical and art training, leadership, ingenuity, highly developed patternmaking skills and a keen understanding of the aesthetic as well as the practical and cost-effective. Design also calls for absolute dedication. Some of the most successful designers refer to their vocation as an "obsession" or a "way of life." Given the hardships, designers have to be crazy about what they do. How else would they be able to survive the grueling hours, low entry-level pay and lack of success guarantees?

The first step toward becoming a designer is reconsidering your decision. Our insiders say there is no shame in being a realist: "Fashion students often come in bright-eyed and idealistic. They think they are ready for the hard work and difficult hours so long as they can have the glamour too. What they don't realize is that very, very few designers hit it big." Aspiring designers also err when it comes to focus. "You have to think about what consumers really want," advises another source. "It's vital to know the realities of the job market. Pay attention to what people are going to buy rather than what you want to create." And it never hurts to look at your other options. "Students don't know that there are a hundred other jobs in fashion besides design," says an insider from a New York fashion school. "There are trim buyers, pattern makers, sample makers, quality control experts and fashion consultants. Often, these jobs are not only better-paying, they are 100 percent more secure."

For those who have listened to the naysayers and still want to be designers, the advice is—go for it. Insiders from such famous New York City fashion schools as Pratt, Parsons and FIT all concede that someone has to be the next Donna Karan or Calvin Klein. Why not you? If you think you have the guts, the talent and the backbone, "go global and go for the top," declares one enthusiastic source.

The climb may take some time, however. "It's very rare for a young fashion designer to set up his own label immediately after graduation," confesses a source. In reality, most graduates will spend five or more years working for a designer, gaining experience, earning a reputation and making contacts. Some fashion professionals will even start a design career outside of the industry in order to break into the field. Internships at major fashion houses or other jobs, like pattern work or retail, can sometimes launch you into design. The bottom line: don't be too hasty. Think of each job as a stepping stone in your career—so that you will always know what options you have.

Our Survey Says: Fashion Industry Culture

Image

In the fashion industry, your image is an important factor in your career. In some fields, such as modeling, a certain "type" is required. In other fields, such as public relations, good looks are preferred. Evidence of fashion's obsession with appearance is everywhere. Many retail employees must sport the clothing of their company. Designers serve as walking examples of their work. Even employees at fashion magazines "dress accordingly." Appearance is more important for fashion professionals who interact with the public and who work for high-end employers. (If you work in finance or planning, your dress matters less. And if you work at Kohl's versus Bloomingdale's, being "fashionable" is not as important.)

The "beauty prerequisite" is a source of pride, but also of contention. "You're often judged by what you wear and what you look like," says a designer who specializes in women's couture. Noverto Gonzalez, who worked as an assistant buyer at Saks Fifth Avenue says, "You have to represent whom you work for. The industry can be pretentious. They look at your shoes, bag and watch to check out the label." Certainly, appearance alone probably won't make or break a fashion career. Most fashion employers are looking for traditional skills and abilities. Nevertheless, in the fashion industry appearance may count more than it does in other industries.

Read the magazines and follow celebrities if you want to keep up with the latest trends. Consider magazine staples like *Vogue*, *Harper's Bazaar* and *W*. You may also want to look at the French, English or Spanish editions of these magazines.

Do good and be beautiful

Fashion is home to glamour, beautiful people and of course, celebrities. Everyone knows the name of at least one supermodel; most people could name quite a few more. In fashion, namedropping and networking are the norm. But another common, if less known, aspect of the fashion world is philanthropy. "Philanthropy," designer Kenneth Cole said at a fashion charity event, "has been part of our corporate culture from the beginning."

This warm-and-fuzzy consciousness isn't simply motivated by the heart: the wallet has something to do with it. Specifically, mixing philanthropy with commerce is a sales tool called cause-related marketing. Since public service is an ideal conduit for sales, many famous designers embrace one cause or another. However, these causes are often as changeable as the industry itself. Points out one fashion insider: "Fashion may embrace fur-wearing one day and protest it the next. Its loyalties are superficial." There are drawbacks to here-today-gone-tomorrow activism. Nevertheless, public service organizations can benefit by the media attention given to "fashionable causes."

Melting pot

The glass ceiling is not much of a problem in an industry where "women outnumber men." "Race is rarely, if ever, an issue" and "a large number of the men in design are gay," says an insider at an upscale department store. In fact, an insider at The Gap is happy to report, "Gender and ethnicity are just not an issue." In almost all aspects of the industry, the pervasion of different cultures, races, religious faiths and sexual orientations is common. "I expected to see a lot of white upperclass yuppies," remarks one J. Crew insider, "but this wasn't what I envisioned. The proverbial New York City melting pot boils over into the [J. Crew] corporate office."

L'Oreal is one brand that prides itself on its international flavor. In fact, it boasts that many of its employees are multilingual. Nike is also sound in the diversity department. At this company, different ethnic groups gather for "informal meetings." One member of the company's "Hispanic caucus" finds Nike "a fun place to meet other Latinos and network." Of course, not all employees are content with their company's heterogeneity. At companies like Lands End and L.L. Bean, some employees complain of a lack of diversity. But others argue that the predominately white demographics simply reflect the surrounding communities. "Maine and Wisconsin are not exactly known for large mixes of ethnic communities," says one. "It would follow that the minority headcount is proportional to the community and state." An Asian-American L.L. Bean insider agrees, "I have always felt that the employee makeup simply reflects the general population [in Maine]." As production continues to grow overseas, fashion industry employees are becoming more accustomed to a global marketplace. Companies may buy their fabric from Korea, cut and sew in Sri Lanka, pack and ship in Hong Kong, warehouse in the U.S. and sell in Canada and Mexico.

While the fashion industry is one of the most ethnically diverse around, insiders still complain of "a herd mentality." Complains one: "At my last job, everyone had a blonde bob. Fortunately, my new job is more diverse. It doesn't seem that race or sexuality is that important—it's all about how you look. Class and style are what are most important." Speaking of blondes, one celebrity dresser "can't wait to dress Gwyneth Paltrow." Why? "Because everyone wants to dress her!" He continues, "I enjoy meeting celebrities on a personal level, although not everything about my job is glamorous. It's not glamorous running around buying shoes at the last minute and sitting around a seating chart at 3 a.m., guessing who will be happy sitting next to each other." An assistant designer agrees that the industry is, at best, unpredictable. "I'm not doing what I thought I'd be doing," she says. "There are some people [in this industry] with high profile jobs, but most of us end up working for other famous people."

Visit Vault at **www.vault.com** for insider company profiles, expert advice, career message boards, expert resume reviews, the Vault Job Board and more.

VAULT CAREER LIBRARY   193

Networking

Ask around the fashion industry and you'll find people who dreamed of working there all their lives and people who stumbled into their positions by chance. One associate designer maintains, "To get into the creative end of the industry, you need a proper education. You need to study design. Technical people such as buyers and inventory planners, on the other hand, are more likely to have 'fallen' into their jobs." No matter how they got there, however, fashion professionals admit that having industry contacts is often more important than having talent. "To find a job," reveals an employee from Federated, "it's important to use the people you know. I found my first job through contacts, the next by sending an exploratory note and the third was luck—I got it out of a newspaper advertisement. I'd say my first job was the easiest to find."

While many people—and fashion students in particular—might feel dismayed by this need to know the "right people," one insider says worry is unnecessary. "Students often think they cannot make connections while confined within college walls," says a career counselor from a top New York fashion school. "This is a myth. Connections is just another word for relationships. You have relationships with other students, professors, career counselors, the school administration and many others. At fashion schools, most of the teachers have previous experience in the fashion industry." What does that mean? An acquaintance at your school or workplace might already have valuable job information!

It all comes down to networking. To find the right fashion job for you, it is necessary to discuss your job search with the people you know—and with the people they know. Ask questions, inquire about openings and request informational interviews. Fashion students should attend as many college-sponsored events as possible and seek relevant internships. After a fashion internship has ended, they should keep in touch with their managers. A fashion career counselor confirms, "Those who serve as intern advisors often grow very fond of their interns. They want to know that you've graduated; they want to help and advise you."

Internships

Most fashion internships are in design, marketing and production—and unpaid. Like the entertainment industry, actual education isn't as important as work experience. You will need some education to get in the door, but after that your resume or connections will get you farther. If you want to go into fashion or retail, get an internship or even a part-time job in sales or merchandising to get started. Each experience on your resume will help land a better internship or full-time job the next time. Although some internships are posted in the trade papers, many internship searches are self-directed because many are never publicized. If the position is at a popular company or designer, the internship will never be posted since everyone will want it on his or her resume.

Make sure to express your desire to learn and help the company—even if you think your level of responsibility is not as high as you would like. Once you are in the company, you can find out about other positions before they may even be open. Build your resume, and you can get the interviews and introductions. Of course, your initial job in the fashion industry may not pay well. There are several options here—you work to get the experience or to learn enough to start your own business. If you are thinking of the latter, take any experience you can. It will pay off later.

Day in a Life: Assistant Product Manager, Federated Merchandising Group

Noverto Gonzales graduated from the University of North Texas with a BA in Merchandising in 1999. His first summer internship was at JC Penney in Texas. It was a ten-week program: five weeks as assistant department manager on the retail floor and five weeks as an assistant buyer. He knew he wanted to live in New York City, so the summer before he graduated, Noverto landed another internship in the city. He was offered an internship at Barney's and Saks Fifth Avenue but chose the one at Saks since a salary came with it. The Barney's internship paid a small stipend at the end of the summer. His New York City job search was entirely self-directed.

After graduation, he was offered a position at JC Penney (in Texas) and Saks Fifth Avenue. JC Penney was very supportive and knew he wanted to go to New York. He began his career as an assistant buyer at Saks Fifth Avenue Catalog. He moved on to Federated as an assistant product manager. Federated operates Bloomingdale's, Macy's West and East, Goldsmith's, The Bon Marche, Burdines, Lazarus and Rich's department stores. At the Federated Merchandising Group, he worked with other product managers, buyers, the design team and the technical design team. Federated Merchandising Group, a division of Federated Department Stores, is responsible for the conceptualization, design, sourcing and marketing of private brands which are exclusive to Macy's, Rich's, Lazarus, Goldsmith's, The Bon Marche, Burdines and Bloomingdale's. These private labels include: INC, Style & Co., Alfani, Tools of the Trade, Charter Club, JM Collection, Tasso Elba, Club Room and Greendog.

Noverto Gonzalez's Day

9:00 a.m.: Get into office and check e-mail. Our overseas office in Turkey has left me some notes. Update production time and action plans. The approvals for fit samples, lap dips and trims are managed by product development. For example, if our designer doesn't like a button on a sample, we have to find a replacement.

10:30 a.m.: Fit model comes in. We have fittings three times a week. I keep a "Fit" book and take notes of things that were changed. The designer and assistant designer are also in the meeting.

11:30 a.m.: I go back to my office to update the open purchase orders. If the parameters of the order change, I have to update it and make sure the legal documents are correct as well. Some of essential information is color, style number, vendor, country of origin, first cost and landed cost. I also deal with quota issues.

12:30 p.m.: Get back to the office and work on design samples. Go over current season sales and look through styles and colors. Look at different types of bodies or fabrication. Often, I have to address costing issues. If we want our cost of production to be something specific, like $5, we might have to negotiate with our vendors. Or we would look at the price of a set and then increase the price of the pant and decrease the shirt. Every year we are pressured to reduce cost from last year.

2:00 p.m.: Grab a quick and late lunch.

2:30 p.m.: Attend line development meeting. We're always working on three seasons at once. Develop fall, go into meeting for holiday and check spring production calendar. The seasons Federated followed were fall, holiday, spring and summer.

4:00 p.m.: Check e-mail and update my calendar. Once a week, I track all shipments. I reconcile the shipping logs, purchase orders and sales. If the shipment does not have a corresponding receipt number, I ask someone in the D.C. (distribution center) or e-mail a vendor and ask for proof of shipment.

5:30 p.m.: Track advertising samples. These samples are used for our ads. The buyers request ad samples.

6:00 p.m.: Go home!

Noverto comments: "My favorite part of the industry is working with fashion forecasting offices. You know what's going on next year. The ironic thing is that there are so many trends but most things end up looking the same! Every company does similar things. The worst part of the industry is that it is pretentious. You always have to stay on top. If something doesn't sell then you're responsible for it."

Visit Vault at **www.vault.com** for insider company profiles, expert advice, career message boards, expert resume reviews, the Vault Job Board and more.

VAULT CAREER LIBRARY   195

Day in a Life: Dress Buyer, Victoria's Secret Catalog

Sylvia Dundon graduated from the Fashion Institute of Technology with a BA in Marketing (concentration Merchandising Management) and an AAS in Buying and Merchandising in December 1998. It took two years to obtain her AAS and another three years for her BA since she was working at the Gap and Victoria's Secret while she was attending school. She began her career as an assistant buyer at Victoria's Secret Catalog and later was promoted to associate buyer.

Sylvia Dundon's Day

9:00 a.m.: Check e-mail and voice mail. Prioritize who gets called back first based on what time zone they're in.

9:30 a.m.: Check sales on computer—especially dress sales for the items I bought most recently. If the catalog just dropped (that is, was sent out), wait a few days for the sales to hit. Work with the planner. ("At Victoria's Secret, the planner is the buyer's partner. The planner executes the actual purchase order, financial planning, stock models and markdowns.")

10:30 a.m.: Decide how to allocate five pages of the catalog. For example, how many dresses should I feature per page? Do I think I'll sell more dresses with three per page or should I focus on one large picture of a single dress? I have to justify my decisions to management and work with the merchandise manager. Some of my decisions are based on what sold in the catalog last year.

11:30 a.m.: Sample fitting. Go to the fit room and work with your technical specialist and fit model. The fit model tries on samples and we make sure the garment is the right specifications and fit. If the garment is not correct, we send our corrections to the vendor. A sample garment usually goes through one to three rounds of corrections.

12:00 p.m.: Layout and film review. I go visit the creative department and look at a layout of our catalog. The point is to review the actual photography and layout (for colors). If the color of the garment is wrong, I cut a swatch from the garment as a sample so the creative dept. can fix the photo to match. If the skirt in the photo is too long, they can fix the length, too. If everything looks great, I just approve the layout.

12:45 p.m.: Run out to buy a sandwich so I can eat at my desk and check voice mail.

2:00 p.m.: Roll out my sample rack. Send out samples for a photo shoot. Work with in-house model for shoot samples to make sure they fit and look right according to Victoria's Secret standards.

3:00 p.m.: Meet a few vendors. I cut a few fabric swatches for product development. Sometimes I go out into the market or vendor showrooms to look at their lines. If I really like something, I will ask them to send samples for me the next day.

4:00 p.m.: Go to a fashion forecast meeting. This meeting includes both the fashion and design departments and is intended to make sure that we're all aware of the trends and direction that Victoria's Secret wants to take that season. Even though we're buying different categories (dresses, shirts, etc.), we all want to have the same mindset. I also see slide shows of samples bought in Europe. All the buyers get to see the main themes for the season—which include a color palette and the general trends.

6:00 p.m.: Address production issues. Approve a button or lab dip. The lap dip is the color intended for production. Quite often, the manufacturer hasn't produced the correct color, so I have to ask them to do another lab dip.

7:00 p.m.: Address the e-mails I didn't get to during the day. Go home!

Fahion Employer Directory

Abercrombie & Fitch Co.
6301 Fitch Path
New Albany, OH 43054
Phone: (614) 283-6500
Fax: (614) 283-6710
www.abercrombie.com

Ann Taylor Stores Corporation
100 Ann Taylor Drive
P.O. Box 571650
Taylorsville, UT 84157-1650
Phone: (212) 541-3300
Fax: (212) 541-3379
www.anntaylor.com

The Body Shop International PLC
Watersmead
Littlehampton
West Sussex BN17 6LS
United Kingdom
Phone: +44-1-903-731-500
www.the-body-shop.com

Chanel S.A.
135, Avenue Charles de Gaulle
92521 Neuilly-sur-Seine Cedex
France
Phone: +33-1-46-43-40-00
www.chanel.com

Dolce & Gabbana SPA
Via Santa Cecilia, 7
20122 Milan
Italy
Phone: +39-02-77-42-71
www.dolcegabbana.it

Donna Karan International Inc.
550 Seventh Avenue
New York, NY 10018
Phone: (212) 789-1500
Fax: (212) 921-3526
www.donnakaran.com

Eddie Bauer, Inc.
15010 NE 36th St.
Redmond, WA 98052
Phone: (425) 755-6100
Fax: (425) 755-7696
www.eddiebauer.com

Estee Lauder Companies Inc.
767 Fifth Ave.
New York, NY 10153-0023
Phone: (212) 572-4200
Fax: (212) 572-6633
www.elcompanies.com

Federated Department Stores
7 West Seventh Street
Cincinnati, OH 45202
Phone: (513) 579-7000
Fax: (513) 579-7555
www.federated-fds.com

Gap Inc.
One Harrison Street
San Francisco, CA 94105
Phone: (415) 427-2000
Fax: (650) 874-7828
www.gapinc.com

Guess?, Inc.
1444 S. Alameda St.
Los Angeles, CA 90021
Phone: (213) 765-3100
Phone: (213) 744-7838
www.guess.com

J. Crew Group Inc.
770 Broadway
New York, NY 10003
Phone: (212) 209-2500
Fax: (212) 209-2666
www.jcrew.com

Tommy Hilfiger
25 West 39th St., 14th Floor
New York, NY 10018
www.tommy.com

Kenneth Cole Productions, Inc.
603 West 50th St.
New York, NY 10019
Phone: (212) 265-1500
Fax: (212) 830-7422
www.kennethcole.com

L'Oreal USA
575 5th Ave.
New York, NY 10017
Phone: (212) 818-1500
Fax: (212) 984-4999
www.lorealusa.com

Levi Strauss & Co.
1155 Battery St.
San Francisco, CA 94111
Phone: (415) 501-6000
Fax: (415) 501-7112
www.levistrauss.com

Limited Brands
3 Limited Parkway
Columbus, OH 43216
Phone: (614) 415-7000
Fax: (614) 415-7440
www.limited.com

Nike, Inc.
One Bowerman Drive
Beaverton, OR 97005-6453
Phone: (503) 671-6453
Fax: (503) 671-6300
www.nikebiz.com

Nordstrom, Inc.
1617 Sixth Ave.
Seattle, WA 98101-1742
Phone: (206) 628-2111
Fax: (206) 628-1795
www.nordstrom.com

Pacific Sunwear of California, Inc.
3450 E. Miraloma Ave.
Anaheim, CA 92806-2101
Phone: (714) 414-4000
Fax: (714) 414-4251
www.pacsun.com

OshKosh b'Gosh, Inc.
112 Otter Ave.
Oshkosh, WI 54901
Phone: (920) 231-8800
Fax: (920) 231-8621
www.oshkoshbgosh.com

Polo Ralph Lauren Corporation
650 Madison Avenue
New York, NY 10022
Phone: (212) 318-7000
Fax: (212) 888-5780
www.polo.com

Reebok International Ltd.
1895 J. W. Foster Blvd.
Canton, MA 02021
Phone: (781) 401-5000
Fax: (781) 401-7402
www.reebok.com

Revlon, Inc.
237 Park Ave.
New York, NY 10017
Phone: (212) 527-4000
Fax: (212) 527-4995
www.revloninc.com

Visit Vault at www.vault.com for insider company profiles, expert advice, career message boards, expert resume reviews, the Vault Job Board and more.

VAULT CAREER LIBRARY   197

Isn't it time for a Quiet Conversation™ about your future?

The result could be the opportunity to build your own financial services practice. Visit www.nmfn.com for more information.

Northwestern Mutual
FINANCIAL NETWORK®

It's time for a Quiet Conversation.™

Financial Services and Insurance

Brokerage Services

Sales is a core area of most securities firms, comprising the vast majority of people and relationships and accounting for a substantial portion of revenue. Securities salespeople can take the form of a classic retail broker, an institutional salesperson, or a private wealth manager. Retail brokers develop relationships with individual investors and sell securities and advice to the average Joe. Institutional salespeople sell securities to and develop business relationships with large institutional investors—those that manage large groups of assets such as pension funds or mutual funds. Lying somewhere in between retail brokers and institutional salespeople are private wealth managers, who provide brokerage and money management services for extremely wealthy individuals, typically defined as those with more than $1 million in liquid assets Instead of private wealth manager, some financial services firms use the term private client service (PCS) representative to denote salespeople to the wealthy. However, PCS rep is being used more and more frequently to define the type of business done by retail brokers. All salespeople, no matter who they're selling to, make money through commissions on trades made through their firms.

Retail brokers/PCS representative

In addition to PCS representative, some firms call them account executives, others call them financial advisors, and still others give them the financial consultant moniker. Regardless of the official designation, firms are still referring to your classic retail broker. The broker's job involves managing the account portfolios for individual investors—usually called retail investors. Brokers charge a commission on any stock trade and also give advice to their clients regarding stocks to buy or sell and when to buy or sell them. To get into the business, retail brokers must have an undergraduate degree and demonstrated sales skills. The Series 7 and Series 63 examinations are also required before selling commences. Having connections to people with money offers a tremendous advantage for a starting broker.

Slowing down but no signs of stopping

Typically, where the equities markets go, the brokerage industry follows, which means the brokerage industry is alive and well, if not kicking as strongly as it was a few years ago. In 2005, after enjoying two straight years of solid gains, the major stock indices slowed. The Dow Jones Industrial Average even decreased slightly by 0.61 percent during the year, after rising 3.15 percent in 2004 and 25 percent in 2003. The S&P 500 only increased 3 percent in 2005, after rising 9 percent in 2004 and 26 percent in 2003. And the Nasdaq Composite Index rose 1.4 percent in 2005, following an 8.6 percent increase in 2004 and 50 percent rise in 2003.

In 2006, though, the markets began picking up steam again. Through mid-April, the DJIA had risen 3.9 percent, the S&P 500 had increased 3.4 percent and the Nasdaq Composite had shot up 5.7 percent. As a result of the steady though modest gains in the equity markets in the past two years, some of the top retail brokerage firms have continued to cash in. In 2005, Merrill Lynch's brokerage unit boosted net revenue by 10 percent, pretax earnings by 16 percent and total assets in brokerage accounts by 8 percent. And in the first quarter of 2006, Merrill's brokerage unit increased net revenue by 13 percent versus the same period a year earlier. Morgan Stanley, meanwhile, increased retail brokerage net revenue by 6 percent in 2005 and total client assets increased by 2 percent, though the firm did show a decline in retail brokerage pretax income.

Visit Vault at **www.vault.com** for insider company profiles, expert advice, career message boards, expert resume reviews, the Vault Job Board and more.

VAULT CAREER LIBRARY   199

A Day in the Life: Credit Analyst

Looking for a job with high visibility, lots of responsibility, variety, market impact, and access to the highest levels of company management? Consider working as a credit analyst for one of the major rating agencies such as Standard & Poor's, Moody's Investors Service, or Fitch Ratings. Rating agency analysts are responsible for issuing opinions incorporating letter grades regarding the creditworthiness of a variety of types of debt issuers. A company's credit rating determines the interest cost it pays on its debt. Clients, known as issuers, range from industrial companies, to municipalities and states, to sovereign governments, financial institutions, and mutual funds, the newest focus of ratings.

Analysts usually require an MBA or other graduate degree along with expertise in a particular industry. Alternatively, many ratings analysts begin their careers working as commercial bank lenders. Good writing, communication, and financial analysis skills are also important. Other key attributes for aspiring analysts are an ability to juggle multiple tasks, maintain composure under stress and a keen interest in financial markets.

Analysts at major rating agencies interact with senior company management, sell-side and buy-side analysts, other members of the investor community, and the press. In corporate finance, analysts are responsible for surveying a list of companies within a specific industry sector. They monitor companies' operating performance in order to anticipate and/or respond to changes that effect their creditworthiness: which is defined as the ability and willingness to pay. Analysts issue press releases, meet with company management, interact with investment and commercial bankers, tour company facilities, attend analyst briefings, respond to investor and press calls, and publish industry and company-specific articles.

The work can be quite stressful because it involves managing the often optimistic expectations of issuers and their bankers, and at times delivering bad news in the form of "negative rating surprises." But overall, it can be extremely rewarding. It is interesting, challenging, and critically important to financial markets.

Wondering where people go from there? Given the high visibility of the position, particularly for analysts working in dynamic, growing industries, the skill set analysts develop is highly valued. Working as an analyst can be an entry into many exciting career paths: investment banker, buy-side or sell-side analyst, portfolio manager, or even a position in industry.

Given the nature of the work, an analyst's activities can vary considerably from day to day. However, there are certain aspects of the position that are fairly typical. Below is a brief description of what a day in the life of a ratings analyst can be like.

The Rating Game: A Day in the Life

8:45 a.m.: Arrive at the office. Scan *The Wall Street Journal* while waiting for computer to boot up. Breathe a sigh of relief that there are no major articles on any of my companies. Check voicemail. Good, Brite Lite Leisure's treasurer finally got back to me on my question about their capital spending plans.

9:10 a.m.: Computer is up. Dial into news wire service. Run search on my list of 34 companies. Fortunately I subscribe to an alert service which allows me to run just one search to see what's happening with my companies. Make a mental note to put in calls to the chief financial officers of two of my companies to follow up on recent news releases.

10:10 a.m.: Dial into replay of earnings conference call for Acme Entertainment. I prefer to listen to the replays rather than the live calls, because then I can rewind in case I miss something. I will definitely need to put out a press release, as the company has just announced a major acquisition during the call. Wish again that management would give me advance warning about these things.

11:00 a.m.: Attend rating committee for casino operator. The vote is a close one with four of the analysts on the credit committee voting for a low investment grade rating of "BBB-" and three voting for a high speculative grade rating of "BB+". It is always interesting to attend these committees, because I get to learn more about a different industry segment. Also since most of the companies I follow are speculative grade or "high yield" companies, sending in on other committees helps me understand the different analytical challenges investment grade issuers pose. This is one way the company ensures consistency in the rating process across groups.

12:00 p.m.: Draft press release announcing credit downgrade on Acme Entertainment. Review with boss. Make minor changes based on her comments. Hold quick committee with other members of industry group to make sure they are in agreement with rating action. I prefer to get the release ready to go before I call the company so that I can send it out as soon as possible after we talk. Preferably before I begin to get calls from investors based on news of the acquisition.

2:00 p.m.: Press release is finally done. I've spoken to the CFO to deliver the news. Luckily, he anticipated the move and was not argumentative about it. Our group editor has just sent the release out over the newswires and I have a copy of the final version. Grab a quick lunch and finish reading the *Journal* before calls begin to come in about the rating downgrade.

3:30 p.m.: Check newswires again. Go through faxes. It's a slow news day. Update spreadsheets for three of my companies that announced quarterly earnings today. It looks like I may have to draft another release based on some of these numbers.

4:30 p.m.: Take a quick walk over to my friend Susan's cubicle to see how her day is going. Trade notes about what deals we're working on. Make plans to have lunch sometime later in the week.

5:00 p.m.: Finally a few minutes of quiet—until I remember I need to begin my industry article since I am behind on publishing goals for the year. I need to think of a good title for it; I want something that will grab the reader and focus my ideas.

5:15 p.m.: Call from investment banker regarding potential new issuer. Who says the market is cooling? This is my second new deal this month! Get him to give me a quick overview of the company. Then discuss timing—the company wants a fast turnaround since their roadshow starts in two weeks—and size of deal, explain rating process.

6:00 p.m.: Have a brief discussion with department manager about my ideas for potential articles. Also, update her on new deals that are coming in.

6:15 p.m.: Review my calendar for tomorrow. I need to be in a little early to go over materials for my 10 a.m. management meeting.

6:30 p.m.: Get stuff ready to head to the gym. On second thought, maybe I'll take my friend up on her offer for dinner.

Credit Card Services

Issuing credit cards is one of the most common ways in which financial services firms provide credit to individuals. Via the credit card, firms provide individuals with the funds required to purchase goods and services, and in return, individuals repay the full balance at a later date, or make payments on an installment basis. Via the debit card, people avoid debt by withdrawing the purchase amount from their bank accounts and transferring it to the seller. Though you're most likely familiar with how credit and debit cards work, you might not be familiar with just how large the card industry is today. According to the *Nilson Report*, more than 1.9 trillion credit or debit cards were circulating worldwide at the beginning of 2004; in the U.S., more than 847 million cards were in circulation. In 2005, American Express, Discover, MasterCard and Visa branded credit and debit cards generated $2.14 trillion in purchase volume, credit cards accounting for $1.75 trillion in purchases and debit cards for $872 billion. The two largest branded cards, Visa and MasterCard, increased circulation by a combined 68.6 million in 2005, rising to 862.5 million outstanding. Credit cards still make up the majority of the market, but debit cards are gaining traction. In 2005, of total cards in circulation, 31 percent were debit cards, up from 29 percent in 2004. The most popular card is the Visa credit, followed by MasterCard credit, then Visa debit, American Express credit, MasterCard debit and Discover credit. According to the *Nilson Report*, in 2005, the average U.S. household had 12.7 payment cards.

Visit Vault at **www.vault.com** for insider company profiles, expert advice, career message boards, expert resume reviews, the Vault Job Board and more.

VAULT CAREER LIBRARY 201

Integrity. Objectivity. Independence.

{If these values appeal to you, then speak to us.}

Standard & Poor's is the world's foremost provider of independent credit ratings, indices, risk evaluation, investment research, data and valuations. An essential part of the world's financial infrastructure, Standard & Poor's has played a leading role for more than 140 years in providing investors with the independent benchmarks they need to feel more confident about their investment and financial decisions.

Undergraduate opportunities are available in two of Standard & Poor's core businesses, Corporate Value Consulting (CVC) and Ratings.

Associate

Standard & Poor's Corporate Value Consulting (CVC) offers a collaborative approach to quantifying underlying tangible and intangible assets for clients involved in an acquisition, divestiture, restructuring, recapitalization, tax appeal, or shareholder buyout.

Research Assistant

Standard & Poor's Ratings business is comprised of: Corporate & Government Ratings (includes bank and insurance ratings) and Structured Finance Ratings, which pioneer the development of new analytical criteria for a broad spectrum of financial instruments.

Preferred candidate(s) will have a bachelor's degree in finance, accounting, economics, engineering or related discipline. Excellent analytical and oral/written communication skills are essential. The ability to work with financial models and data is required for the Research Assistant positions.

To learn more about these opportunities, please visit our website at **www.standardandpoors.com/careers**

YOUR CONFIDENCE IS SHOWING.
YOU'VE GOT STANDARD & POOR'S

STANDARD
&POOR'S

www.standardandpoors.com

Heavy metal

The credit card traces its roots back to 1914 when Western Union began doling out metal cards, called "metal money," which gave preferred customers interest-free, deferred-payment privileges. Ten years later, General Petroleum Corporation issued the first metal money for gasoline and automotive services, and by the late 1930s, department stores, communication companies, travel and delivery companies had all began to introduce such cards. Then, companies issued the cards, processed the transactions and collected the debts from the customer. The popularity of these cards grew until the beginning of World War II, when "Regulation W" restricted the use of cards and, as a result, stalled their growth.

After the war, though, cards were back on track. Modes of travel were more advanced and more accessible, and more people were beginning to buy expensive modern conveniences such as kitchen appliances and washing machines. As a result, the credit card boomed in popularity, as consumers could pay for these things on credit that otherwise they couldn't afford to buy with cash.

Charge-it

In 1951, New York's Franklin National Bank created a credit system called Charge-It, which was very similar to the modern credit card. Charge-It allowed consumers to make purchases at local retail establishments, with the retailer obtaining authorization from the bank and then closing the sale. At a later date, the bank would reimburse the retailer and then collect the debt from the consumer. Acting upon the success of Franklin's Charge-It, other banks soon began introducing similar cards. Banks found that cardholders liked the convenience and credit line that cards offered, and retailers discovered that credit card customers usually spent more than if they had to pay with cash. Additionally, retailers found that handling bank-issued cards was less costly than maintaining its own credit card program.

Also in the 1950s, the Diner's Club charge card was created. This card, which gave users 60 days to make repayment, was the first to allow consumers to pay for goods and services from a variety of retailers. Another 1950s credit card milestone was the BankAmericard, created by California's Bank of America. The BankAmericard was the first "revolving credit" card—it gave cardholders the option to pay their debts in whole, or in monthly minimum payments while the issuers charged interest on the remaining balances.

The association and the Master

Bank of America continued its credit card innovations in the 1960s with the introduction of the bank card association. In 1965, Bank of America began issuing licensing agreements that allowed other banks to issue BankAmericards. To compete with the BankAmericard, four banks from California formed the Western States Bankcard Association and introduced the MasterCharge. By 1969, most credit cards had been converted to either the MasterCharge (which changed its name to MasterCard in 1979) or the BankAmericard (which was renamed Visa in 1977).

Cutting the cost of transaction processing and decreasing credit card fraud were the next innovations introduced to the industry. Electronic authorizations, begun in the early 1970s, allowed merchants to approve transactions 24 hours a day. By the end of the decade, magnetic strips on the back of credit cards allowed retailers to swipe the customer's credit card through a dial up terminal, which accessed the issuing bank card holder's information. This process gave authorizations and processed settlement agreements in a mater of minutes. In the 1980s, the ATM (Automatic Teller Machine) began to surface, giving cardholders 24-hour access to cash.

The debut of the debit, the climb of the cobrand

The 1990s saw the debit card rise in popularity. The debit card grew from accounting for 274 million transactions in 1990 to 8.15 billion transactions in 2002. The 1990s also witnessed the surge of cobranded and affinity cards, which match up a

Visit Vault at www.vault.com for insider company profiles, expert advice, career message boards, expert resume reviews, the Vault Job Board and more.

VAULT CAREER LIBRARY   203

credit card company with a retailer to offer discounts for using the card (think Citibank's AAdvantage cards and American Express' Mileage Rewards program). Although cobranded cards took a dip in the late 1990s—according to some industry experts, this was because issuers had exhausted the most lucrative partners—they've recently returned in full force. Consider that in 2003 alone, MBNA (now a part of Bank of America), struck some 400 new deals with various companies such as Merrill Lynch, Royal Caribbean and Air Canada. Additionally, it renewed deals with another 1,400 organizations, including the National Football League and the University of Michigan. And in 2004, MBNA signed agreements with numerous other companies and organizations such as A.G. Edwards & Sons, the Massachusetts Institute of Technology, Arsenal Football Club (U.K.), Starwood Hotels and Resorts, and Charles Schwab.

And then there were four

In September 2003, a federal court upheld a lower court ruling that cost credit card powerhouses Visa and MasterCard a combined $3 billion. The court found Visa and MasterCard rules preventing the companies' member banks from also issuing American Express and Morgan Stanley's Discover cards to be illegal and harmful to competition. MasterCard was forced to pay $2 billion in damages and Visa paid $1 billion.

In October 2004, the U.S. Supreme Court decided not to hear Visa and MasterCard's appeal in the government's antitrust suit against them, effectively ending the two companies' rules that have prevented banks from issuing cards on rival networks. As a result, Amex and Discover became free to partner with the thousands of banks that issue Visa and MasterCard, which should allow Amex and Discover to gain ground on the two credit powerhouses that, together, control about 79 percent of the U.S. credit card market (as of August 2004).

Upon the initial ruling in September 2003, Amex CEO Kenneth I. Chenault said, "We plan to add more partnerships with other issuers on a selective basis, ensuring they are a strategic fit for our brand and can drive more high-spending customers to the merchants on our network." In 2004, David W. Nelms, chairman and CEO of Morgan Stanley's Discover Financial Services unit, told *BusinessWeek* that the ruling "will create competition in our industry for the first time."

That competition is expected to be intense, say insiders. According to *BusinessWeek*, U.S. consumers use cash or checks to pay for about 59 percent of their $8.2 trillion in transactions each year. That leaves $4.8 trillion in cash outlays for credit card companies to capture. The *Nilson Report* estimates that debit- and credit-card spending will grow 13 percent a year from 2005 to 2008. "You're talking about the most profitable retail banking product in the world," *Nilson* publisher David Robertson told *BusinessWeek* in August 2004. "The competition among the titans is going to be fierce." He added, "They are already clobbering each other."

Re-Discovering the possibilities

In the midst of Morgan Stanley's great personnel exodus of March 2005, the firm announced plans to spin off its Discover credit-card unit. The reason for the plan, according to former Morgan Stanley CEO Philip Purcell, was Discover "will be more properly valued as a stand-alone entity" than as a piece of Morgan Stanley. Soon after the announcement, analysts began estimating the Street value of the huge credit card unit. The range fell anywhere between $9 billion and $16 billion. Analysts also disagreed over whether or not the spin-off would maximize shareholder value.

However, new Morgan Stanley CEO John Mack's first big move at the helm, after taking over the reins in mid-2005, was to reverse course on the Discover business. "Discover is not only a strong business, but also an attractive asset for Morgan Stanley," Mack said in a statement. "It is a unique, successful franchise with growth opportunities that gives Morgan Stanley a consistent stream of stable, high-quality earnings and substantial cash flow, diversifies the company's earnings and broadens our scale and capital base."

In 2004, the numbers certainly supported Mack's statement. Discover delivered record before-tax earnings of $1.27 billion in 2004, representing 19 percent of Morgan Stanley's total before-tax earnings. In January 2005, Discover aquired the fast-growing PULSE debit network, which had more than 4,100 financial institution customers. The unit also recently formed a partnership with China UnionPay, China's largest payment network with 800 million cards, and new partnerships with GE Consumer Credit mean that the Discover Network can offer Wal-Mart- and Sam's Club-branded cards. In its 2005 fiscal year, though, Discover's net revenue and pre-tax income declined, by 2 percent and 25 percent, respectively.

The big buy

In June 2005, BofA went big again, following its $49-billion purchase of FleetBoston Financial in 2003 with the announcement that it would acquire credit card behemoth MBNA in a deal worth $35 billion. The purchase made Bank of America one of the largest card issuers in the U.S., with $143 billion in managed outstanding balances and 40 million active accounts. Bank of America added more than 20 million new customer accounts as well as affinity relationships with more than 5,000 partner organizations and financial institutions. Bank of America also expects to achieve overall expense efficiencies of $850 million after-tax, which would be fully realized in 2007, and anticipates a restructuring charge of $1.25 billion after-tax. Cost reductions will come from a range of sources, including laying off 6,000 employees.

The big IPO

At the end of August 2005, MasterCard, which became a private share corporate in 2002, announced that it plans to become a publicly traded company. It will launch an IPO sometime in 2006, and adopt new corporate governance and an open ownership structure that will include the appointment of a new board of directors, comprised mostly of independent directors, and the establishment of a charitable foundation. Under the new corporate governance and ownership structure, MasterCard's current shareholders, approximately 1,400 financial institutions worldwide, are expected to retain a 41 percent equity interest in MasterCard through their ownership of non-voting Class B common stock. In addition, existing shareholders will receive Class M common stock that will have no economic rights but will provide them with certain rights, including the right to elect several directors from financial institutions around the world. The deal is estimated to eclipse Google's $1.92 billion IPO in 2004, as analysts estimate that MasterCard could raise up to $2.45 billion in the offering, for which Goldman Sachs is acting as the lead underwriter.

No contact credit

"Contactless" cards and finger-swiping systems are the latest advances in the world of plastic purchasing. By the end of 2005, banks had issued 3.5 million debit and credit cards that do not need to be run through machines but simply scanned via radar-like beams. Already, these cards can be used at retailers like McDonald's, 7-Eleven and CVS. And by the end of 2006, banks are expected to have issued 25 million contactless debit and credit cards, according to the *Nilson Report*. Other than not having to run the cards through a machine, a benefit is for purchases less than $25, a signature isn't required.

Another no contact credit payment system is now in place: the pay-by-finger system. All you have to do is press your finger (its print) against a device, enter some personal information, such as your phone number, on a keypad and your payment is made; fingerprints are linked up with credit or debit cards. The system is already in place at hundreds of U.S. supermarkets such as Albertsons and Piggly Wiggly.

Visit Vault at **www.vault.com** for insider company profiles, expert advice, career message boards, expert resume reviews, the Vault Job Board and more.

VAULT CAREER LIBRARY   **205**

Insurance

Risky business

The insurance industry is a multi-trillion-dollar market dealing in risk. In exchange for a premium, insurers promise to compensate individuals and businesses for future losses, thus taking on the risk of personal injury, death, damage to property, unexpected financial disaster and just about any other misfortune you can name. According to the Insurance Information Institute (III), in 2004 the industry contributed over $269 million (2.3 percent) to the U.S. GDP.

The insurance industry is commonly divided into categories such as life/health and property/casualty. Life dominates the mix, making up about 60 percent of all premiums. The bigger categories can be subdivided into smaller groups; property, for instance, may cover homeowner's, renter's, auto and boat policies, while health is made up of subsets including disability and long-term care.

These days, though, you can find insurance for just about anything: weddings, bar mitzvahs, the chance of weather ruining a vacation—even policies for pets, a $160 million market in 2005, with growth of a quarter expected in 2006, according to research firm Packaged Facts. Even insurance companies themselves can be insured against extraordinary losses, by companies specializing in reinsurance. Celebrity policies always get a lot of press: though rumors that Jennifer Lopez had insured her famous asset (sorry) for $1 billion proved to be unfounded, other such policies do indeed exist. In fact, the phrase "million dollar legs" comes from Betty Grable's policy for that amount (a similar policy is held by TV's Mary Hart); other notable contemporary policies include Bruce Springsteen's voice, reportedly covered at around $6 million.

The world's top five

Though the United States is, on average, ahead of the rest of the world in terms of insurance coverage, insurance is a truly global industry. Ranked by 2005 revenue data from the III, the top five U.S. insurance companies are American International Group (AIG), Berkshire Hathaway, State Farm, Allstate and Hartford Financial Services. Other leaders abroad include Germany's Allianz, France's AXA, the Netherlands' ING, England's Lloyd's and Italy's Assicurazioni Generali. Other leading American insurers include Travelers, Nationwide, Loews, Progressive and Chubb.

And consolidation is the name of the game—Hoover's reports that the top ten property/casualty insurers account for nearly half of all premiums written. Perhaps the most notable example of the mania for mergers and acquisitions in the industry was the $82 billion merger in 1998 between Citicorp and the Travelers Group, which created Citigroup. Some insurance companies have also begun to reconfigure themselves from mutual insurers, or those owned by policyholders (e.g., State Farm), to stock insurers, or those held by shareholders (e.g., Allstate). This process, known as "demutualization," promises to raise even more capital for insurance companies to indulge in more acquisitions.

Insurance investigations

Of late, life at the top for a number of insurance heavyweights has been less than perfect. An investigation by federal and state prosecutors into AIG's accounting practices revealed accounting problems that forced the company to reduce reported profits by nearly $4 billion over five years, largely the fault of former CEO Maurice Greenberg and former CFO Howard Smith. Greenberg, personally picked by AIG founder Cornelius Vander Starr to steer the company, stepped down from his post in March 2005 after nearly four decades on the job. That May, New York State Attorney General Eliot Spitzer filed a complaint against AIG, Greenberg and Smith, over accusations of securities fraud, common law fraud and a number of violations of insurance and securities laws.

Additional investigations are popping up. In May 2005, Chubb received a subpoena from federal prosecutors investigating its use of nontraditional insurance that could artificially boost financial results. The announcement came on the heels of a November 2004 statement that Spitzer's office, in an investigation into bid-rigging practices between insurance brokers and insurers, requested information from Chubb, along with a number of other companies. At that point, executives at AIG had already pleaded guilty to such practices. And in June 2005, Allstate agreed to pay $34 million in restitution and fines to settle claims from California insurance regulators, who had accused the company of overcharging on a quarter of a million policies over a five-year period. In July 2005, Marsh & McLennan was accused of manipulating bids and receiving kickbacks for funneling business, but settled with New York State later that year for $850 million. The following year, the company was again facing a lawsuit, this time based on securities fraud and bid rigging.

Though the headlines have mostly come from major corporations, the ripple effects of such negative press have leaked across the entire industry. As a case in point, the FBI launched a nationwide review of insurance practices at more than 7,000 companies in May 2005, looking for problems in accounting patterns similar to those found at AIG. According to a report in *The New York Times* that same month, many industry officials were surprised at the review, while others said it was "premature" for the bureau to associate AIG's cooking of its books with the industry as a whole.

Branching out

The last quarter-century has seen a shift in the industry away from life insurance toward annuity products, focusing on managing investment risk rather than the (obviously inevitable) risk of mortality. With increasing deregulation in the U.S. and Japan, these insurers are moving ever closer to competition with financial services firms. Indeed, the business of the insurance industry doesn't end with insurance. The world's top companies have broadened their array of financial services to include investment management, annuities, securities, mutual funds, health care management, employee benefits and administration, real estate brokerage and even consumer banking. The move towards financial services follows the 1999 repeal of the Glass-Steagall Act, which barred insurance companies, banks and brokerages from entering each other's industries, and the Gramm Leach-Bliley Act of 1999, which further defined permissible acts for financial holding companies. Now insurance companies are free to partner with commercial banks, securities firms and other financial entities.

At the speed of the Internet

Like many other industries, the insurance market has been transformed in recent years by the Internet. Traditionally, insurance products have been distributed by independent agents (businesspeople paid on commission) or by exclusive agents (paid employees). But insurers who sell over the Web reap the benefits of lower sales costs and customer service expenses, along with a more expedient way of getting information to consumers. Though few insurers have moved to 100 percent online vending of their policies, the vast majority have found it helpful to provide quotes on their web sites.

A new threat

The September 11 terrorist attacks sent shockwaves through the insurance industry, not only costing insurers roughly $23.5 billion in property-related losses and $40 billion in other associated claims, but also causing insurers and reinsurers to take a hard look at how they would handle the risks associated with possible future terrorist acts. The Terrorism Risk Insurance Act (TRIA), signed into law by President Bush in November 2002, aimed to deal with the nearly incalculable risk posed by this threat. Among other things, the law defined a terrorism-related event as one with a minimum of $5 million in damages, along with providing for the sharing of risk between private insurers and the federal government over a three-year period, with each participating company responsible for paying a deductible before federal assistance is available. If losses are incurred above the insurer's deductible (much as with an individual who must undergo a costly operation), the government is obliged to pay

Visit Vault at **www.vault.com** for insider company profiles, expert advice, career message boards, expert resume reviews, the Vault Job Board and more.

VAULT CAREER LIBRARY   **207**

90 percent. While the measure met with much grumbling from all parties involved, for the most part the industry acknowledged that the plan at least allows for the potential risk to insurers from terrorism-related disasters to be quantified.

TRIA was extended for two years in December 2005. However, provisions of the extension reduced the government's exposure, putting more of the burden on private insurers. The act mandates increases in the amount of damage an event must cause before the government steps in over the life of the bill—in 2006 a terrorist act must cause $50 million in damage to be certified as such, and in 2007 the deductible doubles to $100 million.

When disaster strikes

Despite the catastrophic destruction of September 11, the nation's most costly insurance incidents come straight from the Mother Nature. The hurricane season of 2004, during which a succession of four hurricanes battered the Southeast, racked up insured property losses estimated at $22.9 billion, exceeding the property damage incurred on September 11 by $3 billion. Florida lawmakers passed a bill that December that eliminated multiple hurricane deductibles as of May 2005. The 2004 season also brought on more than two million separate insurance claims, a number far greater than the 750,000 filed following 1992's Hurricane Andrew. For the full year 2004, insured catastrophe losses (including tornadoes, hurricanes, terrorism, winter storms, earthquakes, wind/hail/flood and fire) were estimated at a record $27.5 billion.

The 2004 hurricane season, however, pales in comparison to 2005's, the most active in recorded history, and during which 15 hurricanes formed in the Atlantic. The most destructive of these was Katrina, a category 3 storm which devastated New Orleans and the Gulf Coast at the end of August, causing $100 billion in damages, twice that done by Andrew. More than 1 million claims were filed against some $40 billion of insured property. Hurricanes Rita and Wilma, which reached category 5, also damaged the Gulf Coast and South Florida, respectively. Insurers fear that cyclical weather patterns—as well as, many believe, global warming—augur an increase in hurricane numbers and severity.

Insurance companies are, unsurprisingly, doing what they can to mitigate the risks of future hurricane seasons. National Oceanic and Atmospheric Administration (NOAA) predictions, released in May 2006, indicate an 80 percent chance of an "above normal" hurricane season with particularly strong storms, including four to six storms of category 3 or higher. In order to prevent losses of the sort that attended the hyperactive 2005 season, insurers such as Allstate are refusing to insure or renew policies on houses in coastal regions. Instead, companies are concentrating on wooing policyholders in the Midwest, which is less prone to natural disasters (tornadoes notwithstanding). The insurers that still write policies for coastal regions are charging higher premiums—*The Economist* reports that they have surged 200 percent in some areas. Updated disaster prediction models and higher reinsurance rates are blamed for these significant price jumps.

Fraud: the $100 billion challenge

Another industry issue is fraud—not the kind perpetrated by rogue executives, but rather the kind done by Joe Q. Public, which costs an estimated $85 to $120 billion per year, according to the III. The institute's data shows that in 2004 property/casualty insurance fraud cost the industry $30 billion, while auto insurance fraud racked up $14 billion in false claims. Topping the cake is health care fraud, which costs the nation a whopping $95 billion on an annual basis, according to some estimates. Fraud comes in two flavors, "hard" and "soft," with hard fraud being a deliberate invention or staging of an accident, fire or other type of insured loss to reap the coverage. Soft fraud, meanwhile, covers policyholders' and claimants' exaggeration of legitimate claims, such as when victims of burglaries overstate the value and amount of lost property, or when car accident claimants pad damage claims in order to cover their deductibles.

Unhealthy healthcare

Medical malpractice is another hot topic. Health insurers generally get a bad rap from the public: in 2005, only 9 percent of those polled thought that health insurance companies were "generally honest and trustworthy," and only 5 percent of respondents thought that HMOs had similar qualities. (Only tobacco and oil companies were rated as less trustworthy.) The media and politicians (neither of which the public considers very trustworthy, for that matter) give plenty of air time to horror stories about managed care companies slighting critically ill patients, and insurers refusing to cover necessary treatments or technologies. Is this reputation deserved? It depends on who you ask, but the industry has its own battles in health care— for example, it sees medical malpractice claims, which have skyrocketed in recent years, as a true crisis. Indeed, according to the III, some insurers have quit writing malpractice policies entirely rather than shoulder the risk (the median malpractice award in 2001, the latest year for which this figure is available, was $1 million). Insurance company Farmers, which racked up more than $100 million in malpractice-related losses in 2003, announced, not surprisingly, that it would get out of the malpractice game.

A July 2005 study by the Center for Justice and Democracy, a group against tort reform, found that malpractice rates had increased 120 percent between 2000 and 2004, while the amount of money paid in claims increased by a paltry 5.7 percent, and the surpluses collected by insurers increased by 33 percent. Researchers culled data from annual statements filed with state insurance departments from the nation's 15 biggest medical malpractice insurers. Insurers blasted the study's methodology, claiming it failed to take into account additional costs insurers face, such as underwriting. The Physician Insurers Association of America (PIAA) reports an average wait time of four and a half years between the time an accident occurs and the time a claim is paid, a lapse which forces companies to collect premiums "based on future cost expectations."

PIAA president Lawrence Smarr called the study a "meaningless comparison no respectable actuary would consider." Connecticut Attorney General Richard Blumenthal asked the National Association of Insurance Commissioners to review the study, indicating that such disparate numbers warranted "the need for more much tougher and aggressive oversight to prevent and punish profiteering." Jay Angoff, a former state insurance commissioner of Missouri, agreed: "In recent years, medical malpractice hasn't been unprofitable … it's been phenomenally profitable." In the meantime, the Bush administration is working to cap malpractice damages in an effort to drive down health care costs (and, more than likely, please the formidable medical lobby).

The whole(sale) story

In a curious twist, Costco Wholesale Corp., the largest wholesale club operator in the U.S., announced the start of a pilot program in July 2005 designed to offer individual health insurance policies to California shoppers maintaining "executive membership" status. The company says the program is geared toward people who cannot get group insurance, such as the jobless or owners of family businesses. For now, Costco insurance is only available in the Golden State, as representatives for the company say spreading insurance to its 18 million members nationwide is most likely unfeasible. Though most analysts say the plan will likely have little effect on the 45 million uninsured Americans from coast to coast, some have suggested that discounters like Costco may spur growth in locally based, low-premium niche plans. Meanwhile, insurance brokers are quietly wondering if Costco's wholesale plan could have ramifications of Wal-Mart-like proportions on brokerage firms. Glenn Melnick, director of the USC Center for Health Financing, Policy and Management, claims that low-priced health products have the potential to "really shake up the market," thus forcing insurers to develop more low-cost products.

Working in insurance

According to the U.S. Bureau of Labor Statistics (BLS), the insurance industry employed 2.3 million people in 2004, the most recent year for which full statistics are available. Of these employees, 62 percent worked for insurance carriers; 27 percent

Visit Vault at **www.vault.com** for insider company profiles, expert advice, career message boards, expert resume reviews, the Vault Job Board and more.

VAULT CAREER LIBRARY   209

for agencies, brokerages and other employers; and the balance of the workforce was made up of the self-employed, generally as sales agents.

Most insurance agents specialize in life and health insurance, or property and casualty insurance. But a growing number of "multi-line" agents sell all lines of insurance. An increasing number of agents also work for banking institutions, non-depository institutions, or security and commodity brokers. Medical, financial and health insurance are among the fastest-growing industry sectors.

Common jobs in the industry include claims adjusters, appraisers, examiners and investigators; marketing and sales managers; customer service representatives; insurance sales agents; underwriters; lawyers; computer systems analysts; computer programmers; and computer support specialists. Data provided by the BLS suggests that though corporate downsizing and changes in business practices will limit growth in the industry over the next few years, a number of job openings are expected as older workers leave or retire.

Actuary

Actuaries are vicarious risk-takers. They calculate risk by analyzing statistics and, based on their analysis, make decisions regarding pricing and investment strategies. Some actuaries work in the financial services industry, but seven out of 10 are employed in the insurance industry. Whatever the industry, actuaries decide whether a venture is financially sound.

Actuaries in the insurance industry calculate the probability that there will be a return on their investment. To do this, they consider probabilities of death, dismemberment, disability, or property loss. Actuaries are the reason teenagers driving sports cars pay such prohibitively high premiums. Actuaries ensure that insurance prices will enable the company to pay all claims and expenses and that the price yields a profit. Their keen mathematical skills and analytical abilities are a boon in investing, classifying risk, planning pensions, managing credit and pricing corporate offerings. Once they reach upper-level management positions, actuaries are often called upon to determine and implement complex company policies. Actuaries also often testify in court to verify the loss incurred by a policyholder who has been disabled or killed and in divorce cases as to the current value of pension benefits. Actuaries may also appear before public agencies to contest legislation that affects their businesses. These professionals also work as independent consultants who are hired by insurance companies, corporations, hospitals, labor unions and health care providers for their advice. Due to the breadth of topics they may work on, it is important for the actuary to keep current with many different industries and fields.

Actuaries earn competitive salaries from the time they start and are paid for every hour of credit that they earn from "actuarial exams." Actuaries spend up to eight months a year studying for these exams, which test everything from specific knowledge (casualty insurance, life insurance, pension services) to linear algebra, probability, calculus, statistics, risk theory and actuarial mathematics. Actuaries are pressured to complete the entire series of examinations as soon as possible in order to advance in the field. The first set of exams brings the actuary to the associate level and takes four to six years to complete. Preparation for the exam requires hours of study outside of work, dramatically impacting the personal and social lives of potential actuaries. Actuaries can spend up to 10 years or more taking exams and studying to reach the title of fellowship, particularly if they stop along the way to get married and have families. The long hours required to gain titles and prestige in the actuarial field do not go unrewarded—starting salaries are very high and continue to climb for more experienced actuaries.

Financial Services and Insurance Employer Directory

Northwestern Mutual Financial Network

720 E Wisconsin Ave
Milwaukee, WI 53202-4797

Recruiting Contact:
Phone: 414 271 1444
E-mail: tammybrudnicki@northwesternmutual.com
www.nmfn.com

Undergraduate schools Northwestern Mutual recruits from:
Nationwide

NORTHWESTERN MUTUAL FINANCIAL NETWORK....

has been named a "Top 10 Internship" in America's Top Internships by the Princeton Review eight consecutive times since 1996 and named America's 2000 Top Sales Force co-winner (with Cisco Systems) by Sales & Marketing Management Magazine. The Internship Program provides career opportunity to college students who want to "test drive" a career in sales. Financial Representative positions are also available. Reps provide guidance and innovative solutions to clients to develop a customized plan that meets long-term financial goals. The position is an opportunity to build your own business while providing financial security for your clients.

Standard & Poor's

55 Water Street	1221 Avenue of the Americas
New York, NY 10041	New York, NY 10020
Phone: (212) 438-2000	Phone: (212) 512-1000

www.standardandpoors.com/careers

Schools Standard & Poor's recruits from

Columbia; Boston College; NYU; USC; UCLA; Berkeley; Stanford; U Texas-Austin, U. of Chicago; U. Michigan; LSU; Indiana; U Wisconsin-Madison; U. of Illinois; Lehigh; Cornell; Harvbard; MIT; Wharton; CUNY-Baruch; Villanova; Emory; Penn St.; UNC-Chapel Hill; Florida; St. Josephs; U. of South Carolina; UVA; Howard; Spelman; Morehouse; Hampton

Aetna Inc.

151 Farmington Avenue
Hartford, CT 06156
Phone: (860) 273-0123
Fax: (860) 273-3971
www.aetna.com

AFLAC Inc.

1932 Wynnton Road
Columbus, GA 31999
Phone: (706) 323-3431
Fax: (706) 324-6330
www.aflac.com

A.G. Edwards & Sons

One North Jefferson Ave.
St. Louis, MO 63103
Phone: (314) 955-3000
Fax: (314) 955-5402
www.agedwards.com

The Allstate Corporation

2775 Sanders Road
Northbrook, IL 60062
Phone: (847) 402-5000
Toll Free: (800) 574-3553
Fax: (847) 326-7519
www.allstate.com

American International Group, Inc.

70 Pine Street
New York, NY 10270
Phone: (212) 770-7000
www.aig.com

American Express

World Financial Center
200 Vesey St.
New York, NY 10285
Phone: (212) 640-2000
www.americanexpress.com

Visit Vault at **www.vault.com** for insider company profiles, expert advice, career message boards, expert resume reviews, the Vault Job Board and more.

VAULT CAREER LIBRARY

211

Financial Services and Insurance Employer Directory, cont.

AON Corporation
Aon Center
200 E. Randolph Street
Chicago, IL 60601
Phone: (312) 381-1000
Fax: (312) 381-6032
www.aon.com

Blue Cross and Blue Shield Association
225 N. Michigan Avenue
Chicago, IL 60601
Phone: (312) 297-6000
Fax: (312) 297-6609
www.bcbs.com

Capital One Financial
1680 Capital One Dr.
McLean, VA 22012
Phone: (703) 720-1000
Fax: (703) 205-1755
www.capitalone.com

Charles Schwab
101 Montgomery Street
San Francisco, CA 94104
Phone: (415) 627-7000
Fax: (415) 636-5970
www.schwab.com

Chubb Corporation
15 Mountain View Road
Warren, NJ 07059
Phone: (908) 903-2000
Fax: (908) 903-2027
www.chubb.com

CIGNA Corporation
1 Liberty Place
Philadelphia, PA 19192
Phone: (215) 761-1000
Fax: (215) 761-5515
www.cigna.com

CIT Group
1211 Avenue of the Americas
New York, NY 10036
Phone: (212) 536-1211
www.cit.com

Conseco, Inc.
11825 N. Pennsylvania Street
Carmel, IN 46032
Phone: (317) 817-6100
Fax: (317) 817-2847
www.conseco.com

Countrywide Financial
4500 Park Granada
Calabasas, CA 91302
Phone: (818) 225-3000
Fax: (818) 304-5979
www.countrywide.com

E*TRADE FINANCIAL Corp.
135 East 57th Street
New York, NY 10022
Phone: (646) 521-4300
Fax: (650) 842-2552
www.etrade.com

Edward Jones
12555 Manchester Road
Des Peres, MO 63131
Phone: (314) 515-2000
Fax: (314) 515-2622
www.edwardjones.com

Equitable Life Assurance Society, The
Warwick Court
Paternoster Square
London EC4M 7DX
United Kingdom
Phone: +44 (0)20 7489-6400
Fax: +44 (0)20 7489-6404
www.equitable.co.uk

Erie Indemnity Company
100 Erie Insurance Place
Erie, PA 16530
Phone: (814) 870-2000
Fax: (814) 870-3126
www.erie-insurance.com

Fannie Mae
3900 Wisconsin Ave., NW
Washington, DC 20016-2892
Phone: (202) 752-7000
Fax: (202) 752-4447
www.fanniemae.com

Federated Investors Inc.
Federated Investors Tower
1001 Liberty Avenue
Pittsburgh, PA 15222-3779
Phone: (412) 288-1900
Fax: (412) 288-6823
FederatedInvestors.com

Fitch Ratings
1 State Street Plaza
New York, NY 10004
Phone: (212) 908-0500
Fax: (212) 480-4435
www.fitchratings.com

Freddie Mac
8200 Jones Branch Drive
McLean, VA 22102-3100
Phone: (703) 903-2000
Fax: (703) 903-2759
www.freddiemac.com

GE Commercial Finance/GE Consumer Finance/GE Asset Management
260 Long Ridge Road
Stamford, CT 06927
Phone: (203) 357-4000
Fax: (203) 357-6489
www.gecommercialfinance.com

GEICO
1 GEICO Plaza
Washington, DC 20076
Phone: (301) 986-3000
HR Toll Free: (800) 824-5404
Fax: (301) 986-3092
www.geico.com

Financial Services and Insurance Employer Directory, cont.

Golden West Financial
1901 Harrison Street
Oakland, CA 94612
Phone: (510) 446-3420
Fax: (510) 446-4259
www.gdw.com

Guardian Life Insurance Company of America, The
7 Hanover Square
New York, NY 10004
Phone: (212) 598-8000
Fax: (212) 919-2170
www.guardianlife.com

The Hartford Financial Services Group, Inc.
Hartford Plaza
690 Asylum Avenue
Hartford, CT 06115
Phone: (860) 547-5000
Fax: (860) 547-2680
www.thehartford.com

Hilb, Rogal & Hobbs Company
4951 Lake Brook Drive, Suite 500
Glen Allen, VA 23060
Phone: (804) 747-6500
Fax: (804) 747-6046
www.hrh.com

ING Insurance Americas
5780 Powers Ferry Rd. NW
Atlanta, GA 30327-4390
Phone: (770) 980-5100
Fax: (770) 980-3301
www.ing-usa.com

John Hancock Financial Service, Inc.
John Hancock Place
Boston, MA 02117
Phone: (617) 572-6000
Fax: (617) 572-9799
www.johnhancock.com

Legg Mason
100 Light Street
Baltimore, MD 21202-1099
Phone: (410) 539-0000
Fax: (410) 454-4923
www.leggmason.com

Liberty Mutual Holding Company Inc.
175 Berkeley Street
Boston, MA 02116
Phone: (617) 357-9500
Fax: (617) 350-7648
www.libertymutual.com

Lincoln Financial Group
100 N. Greene Street
Greensboro, NC 27401
Phone: (336) 691-3000
Fax: (336) 691-3938
www.jpfinancial.com

Marsh Inc.
1166 Avenue of the Americas
New York, NY 10036
Phone: (212) 345-5000
Fax: (212) 345-4838
www.marsh.com

Massachusetts Mutual Life Insurance Company
1295 State Street
Springfield, MA 01111
Phone: (413) 788-8411
Fax: (413) 744-6005
www.massmutual.com

MasterCard International
2000 Purchase St.
Purchase, NY 10577
Phone: (914) 249-2000
Fax: (914) 249-4206
www.mastercard.com

Mellon Financial
1 Mellon Center
Pittsburgh, PA 15258
Phone: (412) 234-5000
Fax: (412) 234-9495
www.mellon.com

MetLife, Inc.
200 Park Avenue
New York, NY 10166
Phone: (212) 578-2211
Fax: (212) 578-3320
www.metlife.com

Moody's
99 Church St.
New York, NY 10007
Phone: (212) 553-0300
Fax: (212) 553-7194
www.moodys.com

Morgan Keegan & Company
Morgan Keegan Tower
50 Front St., 17th Floor
Memphis, TN 38103
Phone: (901) 524-4100
www.morgankeegan.com

Mutual of Omaha Insurance Company
Mutual of Omaha Plaza
Omaha, NE 68175
Phone: (402) 342-7600
Fax: (402) 351-2775
www.mutualofomaha.com

Nationwide Mutual Insurance Company
1 Nationwide Plaza
Columbus, OH 43215
Phone: (614) 249-7111
Fax: (614) 249-7705
www.nationwide.com

New York Life Insurance Company
51 Madison Avenue
New York, NY 10010
Phone: (212) 576-7000
Fax: (212) 576-8145
www.newyorklife.com

Visit Vault at **www.vault.com** for insider company profiles, expert advice, career message boards, expert resume reviews, the Vault Job Board and more.

VAULT CAREER LIBRARY   213

Financial Services and Insurance Employer Directory, cont.

Northwestern Mutual

Corporate Headquarters:

720 East Wisconsin Avenue

Milwaukee, WI 53202-4797

Phone: (414) 271-1444

Fax: (414) 665-9702

www.nmfn.com

Oxford Health Plans, LLC

48 Monroe Turnpike

Trumbull, CT 06611

Phone: (203) 459-6000

Fax: (203) 755-3962

www.oxhp.com

Physicians Mutual Insurance Company

2600 Dodge Street

Omaha, NE 68131

Phone: (402) 633-1000

Fax: (402) 633-1096

www.physiciansmutual.com

The Principal Financial Group

711 High Street

Des Moines, IA 50932

Phone: (515) 247-5111

Fax: (515) 246-5475

www.principal.com

The Progressive Corporation

6300 Wilson Mills Road

Mayfield Village, OH 44143

Phone: (440) 461-5000

Fax: (440) 603-4420

www.progressive.com

Prudential Financial

751 Broad Street

Newark, NJ 07102-3777

Phone: (973) 802-6000

Fax: (973) 802-4479

www.prudential.com

Raymond James Financial

880 Carillon Parkway

St. Petersburg, FL 33716

Phone: (727) 567-1000

Fax: (727) 567-5529

www.rjf.com

Sallie Mae

12061 Bluemont Way

Reston, VA 20190

Phone: (703) 810-3000

Fax: (703) 810-7053

www.salliemae.com

The St. Paul Travelers Companies, Inc.

385 Washington Street

St. Paul, MN 55102

Phone: (651) 310-7911

Fax: (651) 310-3386

www.stpaultravelers.com

State Farm Mutual Automobile Insurance Company

1 State Farm Plaza

Bloomington, IL 61710

Phone: (309) 766-2311

Fax: (309) 766-3621

www.statefarm.com

State Street Corporation

State Street Financial Center

One Lincoln Street

Boston, MA 02111

Phone: (617) 786-3000

www.statestreet.com

TD Ameritrade

4211 South 102nd Street

Omaha, NE 68127

Phone: (402) 331-7856

Fax: (402) 597-7789

www.amtd.com

Thrivent Financial for Lutherans

625 4th Avenue South

Minneapolis, MN 55415

Phone: (800) 847-4836

www.thrivent.com

UnitedHealth Group Incorporated

UnitedHealth Group Center

9900 Bren Road East

Minnetonka, MN 55343

Phone: (952) 936-1300

Fax: (952) 936-7430

www.unitedhealthgroup.com

Unitrin, Inc.

1 E. Wacker Drive

Chicago, IL 60601

Phone: (312) 661-4600

Fax: (312) 494-6995

www.unitrin.com

UnumProvident Corporation

1 Fountain Square

Chattanooga, TN 37402

Phone: (423) 755-1011

Fax: (423) 755-3962

www.unumprovident.com

Visa USA

P.O. Box 194607

San Francisco, CA 94119

Phone: (415) 932-2100

Fax: (415) 932-2529

www.usa.visa.com

WellPoint, Inc.

120 Monument Circle

Indianapolis, IN 46204

Phone: (317) 488-6000

Fax: (317) 488-6028

www.wellpoint.com

W.R. Berkley Corporation

475 Steamboat Road

Greenwich, CT 06830

Phone: (203) 629-3000

Fax: (203) 769-4098

www.wrbc.com

This section was excerpted from the *Vault Guide to the Top Financial Services Employers* and the *Vault Guide to the Top Insurance Employers*. Get the inside scoop on finance careers with Vault:

- **Vault Guides:** *Vault Guide to the the Top Financial Services Employers, Vault Guide to the Top Insurance Employers, Vault Guide to Finance Interviews*

- **Vault Employee Surveys:** Vault's exclusive employee surveys for American Express, Charles Schwab, Capital One, GEICO, Nationwide, Northwestern Mutual and other top financial services and insurance employers

- **Employer Research:** Company snapshots providing business descriptions and the latest news on top financial services employers

- **Career Services:** Vault Resume and Cover Letter Reviews, rated the "Top Choice" by *The Wall Street Journal* for resume makeovers

Go to www.vault.com/finance

or ask your bookstore or librarian for other Vault titles.

Visit Vault at **www.vault.com** for insider company profiles, expert advice, career message boards, expert resume reviews, the Vault Job Board and more.

VAULT CAREER LIBRARY   **215**

Department of the Navy
Financial Management Trainee Program

153 Ellyson Avenue, Suite A
Pensacola, FL 32508-5245

Telephone: 850-452-3783/85   Fax: 850-452-3821   Internet Address: www.navyfmip.com

Navy's Financial Management Civilian Careers is a 28-month program of professional development through academic and on-the-job training. Emphasis is on practical work experience supplemented by academic training. Through a series of rotational work assignments within the organization's geographic area and one out-of-area assignment – each employee gains necessary professional competence.

Of more than 200,000 civilians employed at Navy and Marine Corps locations throughout the world, more than 7,600 work in financial management. To provide a continuous, well-trained, motivated, and mobile financial management work force, the Navy recruits, hires, and trains eligible civilians as analysts, accountants and auditors.

Employees are placed at Navy or Marine Corps locations called "home ports" and are managed throughout the two year training program by the Financial Management Intern Program Office.

Expertise/Education sought: All Majors; Business, Finance, Economics; Accounting

Entry-Level Positions Available: Analysts, Accountants, and Auditors

The Program

Home port financial managers guide employees through On-the-Job (OJT) training assignments that are outlined in the Individual Development Plan (IDP). The OJT consists of rotational training assignments in all areas of financial management and periodic academic training. Rotational assignments are typically at the home port and other local sites, with one out-of-town assignment during the second year of training.

Employees are promoted non-competitively with satisfactory performance. Most begin at the GS-7 pay grade and complete the program at the GS-11 pay grade - an increase of approximately $15,000 in two years!

Typical Financial Management Functions

❖ Formulating budget estimates in support of program objectives and priorities; presenting and justifying budget requests; developing plans for allocating resources; monitoring program execution; reviewing and analyzing funding documents; conducting comparative analyses to examine trends; reviewing budget policy and statutes to ensure compliance.

❖ Reviewing and interpreting accounting and financial management policy, procedures, standards and statutes to ensure compliance; monitoring and examining accounts, specific appropriations or financial records for account status and reporting requirements; and verifying accounts documentation.

❖ Planning and conducting performance and financial reviews of major programs and entities to evaluate the reliability, efficiency and effectiveness of the organization; making recommendations based on findings that identify cost savings through improved operations; and following up on recommendations to ensure implementation.

Benefits

Competitive Salary; Flexible Hours; Generous Leave Benefits for Family Care; Holidays, Vacation and Personal Illness leave; A portable Retirement Plan with Tax-Deferred Savings and government matching funds options; Choice of Health Care plans; Life Insurance; and Tuition Assistance.

U.S. Citizenship Required   *An Equal Opportunity Employer*

Government and Politics

Life on Capitol Hill

Behind the headlines on any given day in the nation's capital there are a thousand sub-plots taking form: the Member of Congress and her staff working at breakneck pace to prepare a bill to reform Federal education programs; a last minute compromise to pass a key piece of legislation; a House member positioning himself for a run for even higher office; a reporter about to break a big story about a new scandal. The environment is continually changing, and the confluence of national politics, local interests, ambitions and personal agendas creates a sense of constant flux and excitement.

In any position on Capitol Hill, an employee's first responsibility is ultimately to serve the interests of his Member (and his or her constituents). And all of the 535 total Members of Congress have very distinct interests. Some love the national spotlight, and spend what seems to be a majority of the their time before a news camera (or in search of one). Others are masters of the legislative process and use their position to propose and advance legislation. Many style themselves as hometown heroes who keep a low profile and focus on directing federal benefits to their districts.

Despite their style, certain elements mentioned above will be true of all Members of Congress: all will attempt to direct federal resources to their districts and attend to their constituents needs; all will use the media to communicate their messages and build (or repair) their images; and all will be involved in the legislative process to some degree, either as legislative technicians, advocates or simply as voters.

Each Member of Congress also has his or her own distinct management style. The organization of a Member's office greatly reflects the individual personality and goals of the Member. Some offices are very formal, requiring business attire at all times, while others are less traditional. Some Members are very hands-on in running their offices, while others delegate much of the decision-making to their senior staff. Some have track records of keeping loyal staff, while others turn over staff on a championship pace. All of these factors—and many more—contribute to the pace of life on Capitol Hill.

Why Capitol Hill?

If you ask Hill staffers why they choose to work on Capitol Hill, you will get a number of different answers. Most, however, will express some common themes: they want to work on issues that they believe in; they want the opportunity to serve their country; and they enjoy using the skills needed to succeed on the Hill and pace of life it requires.

"One of the most exciting aspects of working on the Hill is the opportunity to participate in the workings of our democracy," says one Senate staffer. "The prestige of the place is nice, but for me the real satisfaction comes from knowing that the work we do makes a difference in the lives of real people."

A former House staffer stresses the opportunity to work on a variety of issues as one of the prime benefits of working for Congress. "I can't think of anywhere else where you can work on so many different issues in the course of the day. It's perfect for people who are curious about a lot of things and enjoy the intellectual challenge of understanding multiple issues and putting that knowledge to use on a day-to-day basis."

Another staffer, while acknowledging the benefits of working for Congress, says that the lifestyle will not be for everyone. "Things move very fast on the Hill. If you can't keep up, or you can't—for lack of a better term—multitask, you will probably not be happy here in the long run. This is a place for high energy people who get charged up from going into work every day not knowing exactly what to expect."

Working on the Hill can provide unique experiences that very few other positions afford, including international travel, the opportunity to work with national media and the opportunity to be involved in shaping history.

Visit Vault at **www.vault.com** for insider company profiles, expert advice, career message boards, expert resume reviews, the Vault Job Board and more.

VAULT CAREER LIBRARY   217

"One of the greatest experiences was seeing a piece of legislation that my boss was active in passing signed into law," relates one staffer. "Looking back on that bill today, it is clear that it has helped small businesses to grow and provide good jobs for a lot of people in our district and across the country."

The opportunity for travel, both domestically and internationally, is also cited as a benefit of working on the Hill, particularly for higher-level staffers. "Many organizations sponsor fact finding trips both here in the United States and abroad," says one staffer. "These travel opportunities allowed me to gain a better understanding on a lot of key issues."

Considering Working on the Hill?

If your considering working on the Hill, you should make sure you know what you're getting into. Here, we give you a quick self-assessment test to see if a career on Capitol Hill seems like a good fit for you.

The Hill is probably for you if:

- You like excitement and the idea that every day can bring something different.

- You enjoy following public affairs and reading the newspaper.

- You like talking about politics ... a lot.

- You don't mind starting off paying your dues by answering the phone, writing letters and taking calls from angry constituents.

- You don't care what your work space looks like, so long as you have a desk and a computer.

- You work well under pressure.

The Hill is probably not for you if:

- You'd rather be doing anything other than talking about politics.

- You prefer stable, predictable environments.

- You don't like talking to random people during the course of your day.

- You want the security of a distinct career path.

- You don't like long, unpredictable hours.

Capitol Hill Internships

Some of the most powerful people in Washington have never run for office, yet they command as much power as many of Members of Congress. And many of them began their careers answering phones or writing letters as interns on Capitol Hill.

Traditionally seen as the starting point to a career in government and politics, Capitol Hill offices are flooded with resumes every year from undergraduates eager to gain experience and contacts to begin their ascent to Washington power broker. Internships are available in the personal offices of Members of Congress—both Senators and Representatives. Additionally, Committees on both the House and Senate side offer internships.

"Interning is the best way to get your foot in the door," said one former intern who used the experience to find a full-time position. "The minute I walked in on the first day of my internship, I knew that I wanted to work on Capitol Hill. The office was buzzing with activity, the televisions were tuned to the House floor, and everyone in the office was young and dedicated. Interning allows you to experience the excitement of Capitol Hill and build the skills and contacts you will need to start a career."

There are two important considerations to make in applying for internships on Capitol Hill: where you want to work and what you want to do. Most of the internships offered by Congress will be with Members' personal offices. The Congressional committees and House and Senate leadership offices all offer internship opportunities as well. The following descriptions provide some of the differences and advantages of each type of internship.

Personal offices

Personal offices of both Senators and Members of the U.S. House of Representatives reflect the individual personality and management style of the Members. Representatives' Washington, DC offices usually employ eight to 10 employees. Senators' Washington offices are much larger in terms of employees and the staff sizes are based on the population of the state each Senator represents.

In general, House offices will feel more intimate (some might say cramped) than the Senate offices. In the House, interns generally work on a variety of topics, depending where the staff feels their skills can be best utilized. Due to their larger staffs, Senate offices may be able to provide a greater degree of specialization in an area of interest to the intern, such as the legislative process or media relations. Despite these differences, much of the experience will be the same regardless whether one chooses the House or Senate; answering the phone, responding to constituent inquiries, processing requests for flags flown over the U.S. Capitol, and helping visitors are all part and parcel of the intern experience.

In applying for internships, students should definitely consider the Members of Congress that represent their home towns and their college's or university's location. To find information on a Member of Congress, including an internship application, visit the Member's personal web site. Web sites for House Members can be accessed at www.house.gov and Senators sites can be found at www.senate.gov.

Committees

The Committees of the U.S. Congress offer internships. The Committees are where much of the legislative process takes place. Internships with a committee provide the opportunity to learn about specific areas of legislation (e.g. tax policy or the annual appropriations process) and to dig deeper into the legislative process than a similar internship in a Member's personal office. Since Committee staffs do not answer to constituents as Members' staffs do, interns will spend much less time writing letters. However, they most likely will not get the same level of interaction with a Member of Congress and the senior staff as interns do in a personal office.

Leadership offices

The Republican and Democrat members of the House and Senate elect leaders to organize their parties, set their agendas, count votes, and communicate their messages. The top elected leaders in each party are given separate offices and staffs to carry out their responsibilities. These leadership offices are another source of Capitol Hill internships for students. Since there are fewer leadership offices and staff members, and since members of the leadership enjoy high profile positions, internships with these offices will be very competitive.

Visit Vault at **www.vault.com** for insider company profiles, expert advice, career message boards, expert resume reviews, the Vault Job Board and more.

VAULT CAREER LIBRARY   219

Outside the Washington Beltway

While most students focus on internships inside the Beltway, there are opportunities where they live and study to build experience and make contacts. One of the best ways to become involved in the process is to volunteer for a political campaign. Closely contested Senate and House races require an army of unpaid labor to help achieve a victory on Election Day. Volunteers will often have the opportunity to work closely with the candidate and his or her top campaign staff. Moreover, a victory by their candidate provides a ready-made path to an internship or position on Capitol Hill. Contacting the appropriate local or national party committees can help turn up races that need assistance.

Additionally, many Members of Congress offer internships in their district offices. While the work focuses more on constituent aid than on the legislative process, the schedule may be more flexible to accommodate school hours and the experience could provide entry into the Washington, D.C. office after graduation.

When to intern

The busiest time in Washington for interns is during the summer. The streets of Washington literally seem to be teeming with undergraduates. Summer internships provide a good opportunity to network with other interns and enjoy a wide range of social activities. Furthermore, Congress tends to be very busy during the early summer months of June and July. Congress takes an August recess during Washington's hottest month, and the pace of life slows down greatly on the Hill and across the city. Internships at times other than the summer can be a very good option since there will be fewer interns and more work to go around. Often, they are combined with college programs for credit. However, students should work to ensure that Congress is in session while they are in Washington; interning during November and December of an election year will greatly reduce the value of the experience since Congress rarely has any official activities scheduled during this time.

Advocacy Organizations

For students more interested in a cause than a specific political agenda, or for those students who want to broaden their Washington, D.C. experience beyond Capitol Hill, nearly every organization and every cause is represented in some form or another within the nation's capital. Many of these are large organizations that provide internships for students. However, please be aware that internships will vary from organization to organization: some will be well structured, others less so; many will offer pay or stipends, but many more will not; some will be smaller organizations while others will be larger and more bureaucratic. It is imperative for students to do their research.

While the list of advocates within Washington is too numerous to cover in great detail, there are many organizations on the right, left and even in the center that students may wish to explore.

For example, students interested in the issue of gun control could apply for internships on either side of the debate, depending on their philosophy, and still work with some of the most influential organizations in Washington. The National Rifle Association and the Brady Campaign to Prevent Gun Violence both offer legislative internships in their Washington-area headquarters.

Students interested in environmental issues should consider the liberal-leaning World Wildlife Federation or Sierra Club, while those who favor a conservative philosophy on the environment could look into opportunities with a think tank or the Council of Environmental Republican Advocacy or a business organization.

There are many organizations that are also non-partisan, and that represent a professional group or other point of view. For example, the American Medical Association represents the interests of doctors before Congress and works closely with members of both parties.

Please note that it is very common for organizations with distinct agendas on both the left and the right to describe themselves as "non-partisan." While this is true in a legal sense, the fact is that many of these organizations do favor the left or the right in their activities. Students who aren't sure about an organization's true nature should cast a critical eye on its issue advocacy efforts, board of directors, and web site to determine its true leanings.

For a comprehensive list of advocacy organizations in Washington, as well as White House and Congressional staff, corporate offices and trade associations, check out the *Capitol Source*, which is published by the National Journal Group. It is available in Washington area bookstores and can be ordered online at www.njdc.com/about/capitolsource.

Examples of advocacy organizations

While many advocacy organizations are legally non-partisan, their politics can be considered different shades of liberal, conservative, or middle of the road. Below are some examples of various types of advocacy organizations and their ideological leanings.

American Heart Association: While headquarters in Dallas, the American Heart Association, like many medical groups, maintains an advocacy office in Washington, D.C. to lobby for greater research funding and promote legislation that encourages healthy lifestyles, such as anti-tobacco measures. It is considered a moderate organization. www.americanheart.org

AARP: The nation's leading seniors organization is also one of the most influential advocates in the nation's capital, making its presence felt on a number of high profile issues, including Social Security, Medicare, and health care issues. It is generally considered a moderate organization. www.aarp.org

Brady Campaign to Prevent Gun Violence: The Brady Campaign, named after the former White House press secretary wounded during the attempted assassination of President Ronald Reagan, works to enact gun control laws and regulation through grassroots organization and campaign support to similar-minded candidates. It is considered a liberal organization. www.bradycampaign.org

Citizens for a Sound Economy: CSE fights for lower taxes, less government and fewer regulations. It recruits and trains grass roots activists across the country to influence the economic agenda on the national, state and local levels. It is considered a conservative organization. www.cse.org

Christian Coalition: The Christian Coalition supports policies on the federal, state and local levels that reflect its moral values. Examples include opposition to abortion and gambling, and support for lower taxes, among many social and economic issues. It is considered a conservative organization. www.cc.org

Concord Coalition: The Concord Coalition advocates for fiscal responsibility while ensuring Social Security, Medicare and Medicaid remain secure. It was founded by the late former Senator Paul Tsongas (D-MA) and former Senator Warren Rudman (R-NH) and is considered a moderate organization. www.concordcoaltion.org

National Resources Defense Council: The NRDC supports environmental protections and engages in advocacy on issues ranging from global warming to nuclear waste. It is considered a liberal organization. www.nrdc.org

National Rifle Association: The National Rifle Association provides an array of services to gun owners and is a well-known legislative advocate in the nation's capital. The NRA opposes legislation that regulates gun ownership and supports candidates that agree with its positions on gun issues. It is considered a conservative organization. www.nra.org

Common Cause: Common Cause is a strong proponent of campaign finance reform and actively lobbies to reduce the amount of money in the political process. It is considered a liberal organization. www.commoncause.org

Visit Vault at **www.vault.com** for insider company profiles, expert advice, career message boards, expert resume reviews, the Vault Job Board and more.

VAULT CAREER LIBRARY   221

The Staff Assistant

If you are coming out of an undergraduate program, or are a recent graduate, and want to start your career on the Hill, your first position will most likely be as a staff assistant (or possibly as a legislative correspondent).

The staff assistant role is viewed as the traditional entry-level position for those with little to no Capitol Hill or legislative experience. It is not glamorous, and the pay is low, but it does provide the first important entrée to Capitol Hill.

The primary responsibilities of the staff assistant tend more toward administrative work. On the surface, a staff assistant is often seen as a glorified, college educated receptionist. As a staff assistant, you will usually be the first person a visitor sees upon entering the office. Your responsibilities include greeting guests, arranging tours of the Capitol, opening and sorting the mail, and answering the phone.

However, as a staff assistant, you will also have the opportunity to assist the more senior staff in a variety of areas and learn the ropes on Capitol Hill. As you learn the fundamentals of your position, you will have more time to put your education to use. Staff assistants often have the chance to work with legislative assistants to research legislation and other issues, take on special projects for the chief of staff, or help the press secretary by proofreading speeches and organizing media lists.

Moreover, the position of staff assistant reinforces one of the foremost truisms of work in Washington: proximity to power is key. As a staff assistant, you will perform many mundane tasks. You will be paid far less than you could command in an entry-level position elsewhere. You will also work directly for a Member of Congress and position yourself for far more interesting jobs in the future. Therefore, newcomers to Washington are hungry for an entry-level spot on Capitol Hill. It is the proximity that provides experience and opens doors to bigger opportunities.

"Getting started on the Hill means lots of time doing stuff they didn't teach you in college, like answering the phones and spending a lot of time dealing with constituents. But I wouldn't give up this job for anything. A lot of my friends off the Hill make more money, but in the long run my time on the Hill will open a lot more doors for me down the road," says one staff assistant.

"Working as a staff assistant is both frustrating and exciting," another explains. "Frustrating because some of the work can be tedious and some of the people you deal with can be quite rude. It's exciting because our office moves so fast. The Senator is very involved on many high profile issues and is always being asked to appear on television. I've been able to meet many high profile Washington dignitaries and leaders."

The Foreign Service

The Foreign Service is often the first thing that comes to mind when people think of a global career. And unlike many of the other opportunities covered in this book, a Foreign Service career is indeed that—a career. Joining the Foreign Service means accepting a professional (and personal) life spent overseas, with constant rotations every few years. It can be very rewarding, exciting and occasionally glamorous work.

While the salary generally does not match what you can make in the private sector, generous allowance perks and subsidies help make up the difference. For example, there is a hardship "bonus" for postings in difficult areas of the world, up to 25 percent above your base salary. One Foreign Service Officer commented on the pay: "There's a lot of internal grumbling about the salary, but it's really not that bad. When you look at the remuneration, you have to look at the whole package, including subsidized housing and unlimited access to American military exchanges and the American-priced foodstuffs."

Applicants enter the Foreign Service in one of five career tracks: Management Affairs, Consular Affairs, Economic Affairs, Political Affairs and Public Diplomacy. Which career track you enter as a beginning FSO (Foreign Service Officer) will influence the nature of your assignments and your career, and there is little crossover between the tracks once you have made your decision. FSOs often undergo intensive training before being posted to their first overseas assignment, including, in some cases, up to two years full-time language study. Check out www.state.gov for more information on the application procedure, and also www.afsa.org, the American Foreign Service Organization, for more information on what life is like in the Foreign Service.

Qualifications

While potential FSOs come from all backgrounds, being accepted is extremely competitive—roughly 40,000 applicants apply for the Foreign Service exam every year, only about 400 are eventually accepted. If you are serious about joining the Foreign Service, be prepared to do your homework!

The exam is offered once a year, and studying for it can be a grueling exercise. Successfully completing the exam (and then the subsequent oral interviews) requires extensive and intensive knowledge of U.S. and world history, international relations and major political issues. Says one foreign service officer who joined in the mid 1990s: "The applicants who do best on the test are those who have literally spent a lifetime preparing for it: They're naturally interested in foreign affairs and world events, have often done their degree in that area, and have followed the news their whole life. This type of background will be invaluable." Check out www.state.gov for more information on the exam, study hints and guides.

Potential FSOs come from a wide variety of backgrounds, and knowledge of a foreign language is not required (though it will make you a more attractive candidate). In addition to deep knowledge of world affairs, the State Department looks for personal characteristics and traits that will best represent America overseas.

Uppers and downers

The Foreign Service is an excellent training ground and a superior way to see the world. With the world a constantly changing place and an increasingly wide array of international issues—think medical, environmental, social and religious, as well as economic and political—on the agenda, the Foreign Service can provide an exciting and stimulating career path.

The lifestyle and constant rotations have a downside, too, and that is the impact on your personal life. While picking up and exploring a new city and a new job every few years can be exciting in your twenties, the lack of stability can be more problematic as you get older. Having a spouse or partner who is willing to rotate with you is a plus. The State Department is gradually lengthening the time of each rotation, expanding the average to three or four years.

Visit Vault at www.vault.com for insider company profiles, expert advice, career message boards, expert resume reviews, the Vault Job Board and more.

VAULT CAREER LIBRARY   223

Government and Politics Employer Directory

Central Intelligence Agency
P.O. Box 4090
Reston, VA 20195
Phone: (703) 482-0677
www.cia.gov

Drug Enforcement Administration
2401 Jefferson Davis Highway
Alexandria, VA 22301
Phone: (202) 307-1000
www.dea.gov

Environmental Protection Agency
1200 Pennsylvania Ave., NW
Washington, DC 20460
Phone: (202) 272-0167
www.epa.gov

Federal Aviation Administration
800 Independence Ave. SW
Room 908
Washington, DC 20591
Phone: (202) 267-3883
Fax: (202) 267-5039
www.faa.gov

Federal Communications Commission
445 12th St. SW
Washington, DC 20554
Phone: (888) 225-5322
Fax: (202) 418-0232
www.fcc.gov

Federal Emergency Management Agency
500 C Street, SW
Washington, DC 20472
Phone: (202) 566-1600
www.fema.gov

Federal Reserve Board
20th St. and Constitution Ave., NW
Washington, DC 20551
Phone: (202) 452-3000
www.federalreserve.gov

Federal Trade Commission
600 Pennsylvania Ave, N.W.
Washington, DC 20580
Phone: (202) 326-2222
Fax: (202) 326-3197
www.ftc.gov

General Services Administration
1800 F Street, NW
Washington, DC 20405
Phone: (202) 501-0800
www.gsa.gov

Nat. Institute of Standards and Tech.
100 Bureau Drive
Gaithersburg, MD 20899
Phone: (301) 975-6478
www.nist.gov

National Labor Relations Board
Franklin Court Building, Suite 5530
1099 14th Street
Washington, DC 20570
Phone: (202) 273-1960
www.nlrb.gov

National Park Service
1849 C Street, NW
Washington, DC 20240
Phone: (202) 208-6843
Fax: (202) 219-0910
www.nps.gov

Nuclear Regulatory Commission
11545-11555 Rockville Pike
Rockville, MD 20852
Phone: (301) 415-8200
www.nrc.gov

Occupational Safety and Health Administration
200 Constitution Ave., NW
Washington, D.C. 20210
Phone: (202) 208-8663
www.osha.gov

RAND Corporation
1776 Main Street.
Santa Monica, CA 90401
Phone: (310) 393-0411
Fax: (310) 393-4818
www.rand.org

Securities and Exchange Commission
450 5th St. NW
Washington, DC 20549
Phone: (202) 942-8088
Fax: (202) 942-9659
www.sec.gov

Social Security Administration
6401 Security Blvd.
Baltimore, MD 21235-0001
Phone: (800) 772-1213
www.ssa.gov

United Nations
1st Ave. at 46th Street
New York, NY 10017
Phone: (212) 963-1234
Fax: (212) 963-3133
www.un.org

U.S. Air Force
1480 Air Force Pentagon
Washington, DC 20330
Phone: (800) 423-USAF
www.airforce.com

U.S. Air Force Judge Advocate General
1420 Air Force Pentagon
Washington, DC 20330
Phone: (800) JAG-USAF
www.jagusaf.hq.af.mil

U.S. Census Bureau
4700 Silver Hill Road
Washington, DC 20233-0001
Phone: (301) 763-4636
Fax: (301) 457-3670
www.census.gov

Government and Politics Employer Directory, cont.

U.S. Department of Agriculture

1400 Independence Avenue
SW Washington, DC 20250-0003
Phone: (202) 720-2791
Fax: (202) 720-5043
www.usda.gov

U.S. Department of Commerce

1401 Constitution Avenue NW
Washington, DC 20230
Phone: (202) 482-2000
www.commerce.gov

U.S. Department of Defense

The Pentagon
Washington, DC 20301
Phone: (703) 428-0711
www.defenselink.mil

U.S. Department of Education

400 Maryland Ave., SW
Washington, DC 20202-0498
Phone: (800) 872-5327
www.ed.gov

U.S. Department of Energy

1000 Independence Ave., SW
Washington, DC 20585
Phone: (800) 342-5363
Fax: (202) 586-4403
www.energy.gov

U.S. Department of Health and Human Services

200 Independence Avenue, SW
Washington, DC 20201
Phone: (202) 619-0257
www.hhs.gov

U.S. Department of Homeland Security

245 Murray Drive
Washington, DC 20528
Phone: (202) 282-8000
Fax: (202) 282-8404
www.dhs.gov

U.S. Department of Housing and Urban Development

451 7th Street SW
Washington, DC 20410
Phone: (202) 708-1112
www.hud.gov

U.S. Department of the Interior

1849 C Street NW
Washington, DC 20240
Phone: (202) 208-3100
www.interior.gov

U.S. Department of Justice

950 Pennsylvania Avenue NW
Washington, DC 20530-0001
Phone: (202) 353-1555
www.justice.gov

U.S. Department of Labor

200 Constitution Ave., NW
Washington, DC 20210
Phone: (202) 693-6000
Fax: (202) 693-6111
www.dol.gov

U.S. Department of State

2201 C Street NW
Washington, DC 20520
Phone: 202-647-4000
www.state.gov

U.S. Department of the Treasury

1500 Pennsylvania Ave., NW
Washington, DC 20220
Phone: (202) 622-1260
Fax: (202) 622-6415
www.treasury.gov

White House, The

New Executive Office Building
Washington, DC 20503
Phone: (202) 395-5892
www.whitehouse.gov

Visit Vault at **www.vault.com** for insider company profiles, expert advice, career message boards, expert resume reviews, the Vault Job Board and more.

VAULT CAREER LIBRARY   225

This section on health care careers was excerpted from the *Vault Guide to the Top Health Care Employers* and the *Vault Career Guide to Physical Therapy*. Get the inside scoop on finance careers with Vault:

- **Vault Guides:** *Vault Guide to the Top Health Care Employers, Vault Insider Guide to Medical School Admissions, Vault Career Guide to Physical Therapy, Vault Career Guide to Nursing, Vault Career Guide to Pharmaceutical Sales and Marketing*

- **Vault Employee Surveys:** Vault's exclusive employee surveys for Medtronic, HCA, UnitedHealth Group, Boston Scientific and other top health care employers

- **Employer Research:** Company snapshots providing business descriptions and the latest news on top health care employers

- **Career Services:** Vault Resume and Cover Letter Reviews, rated the "Top Choice" by *The Wall Street Journal* for resume makeovers

Go to www.vault.com/health

or ask your bookstore or librarian for other Vault titles.

Health Care

Health Care Industry Overview

An industry in flux

You can't live with it and you can't live without it—this pretty much sums up the attitude many Americans have toward today's health care industry, which is made up of a variety of providers of patient care, including hospitals, nursing homes and physicians, as well as those who help coordinate, manage and pay for that care, like HMOs and other health insurers. It's no secret that the sector is a volatile one: despite making up nearly 15 percent of the nation's gross domestic product (GDP)—U.S. health care spending totaled $1.8 trillion in 2004, more than $6,000 per capita—the industry has had a tough time figuring out how to turn a profit in such a way that benefits both providers and patients. One reason for this is that the industry's growth rate has consistently outpaced that of the overall economy in recent years. Economists predict health care spending will make up 18.7 percent of the country's GDP in 2014, a percentage considered unsustainable by many analysts. It is estimated that the public sector will pay for nearly half of all health spending in the U.S. by that year—not a healthy number.

Having a senior moment

According to the American Association of Retired Persons (AARP), by the year 2050 seniors will outnumber children for the first time ever. With approximately one million people turning age 60 each month worldwide, the phenomenon known as "global aging" promises to have a profound effect on the demand for and delivery of health care services. This shift is sparking interest in all issues affecting senior health, from preventative care to programs promoting home care and assisted living as alternatives to the oft-dreaded nursing home option.

Creaky Medicare

The United States' aging population is also putting pressure on the nation's reimbursement system for seniors and low-income patients. The Medicaid program is funded by the federal government but administered by the states, serving low-income individuals who do not have access to health care through their employers, while the Medicare program serves people over the age of 65. Because of this, the federal government looms large in health care. In fact, ranked by sales, the government's own Centers for Medicare & Medicaid Services (CMS) ranks No. 1 in the industry. Around 40 million Americans are eligible for Medicare coverage, more than twice as many as when the program was first established in 1966 under President Johnson. In 2005, Medicare spending came to $330 billion. Expenditures from the program are expected to be 3.2 percent of GDP in 2006, rising to 11 percent of GDP by 2008.

Claims are submitted by health care providers through carriers, companies that have contracted with the government to serve as middlemen in the payment process. After the patient navigates a tricky set of rules governing coverage, these claims are either accepted or denied by the contractors. Top Medicare contractors include private not-for-profit BlueCross BlueShield organizations in a number of states, plus other companies such as publicly-held Aetna and Humana. Shareholders of these companies have seen their stock climb as seniors sign up in droves for prescription drug coverage, driving up profits.

The Medicare program, perennially the subject of reform packages in Congress, has long been a political hot potato. The Bush administration has made several attempts to tweak the program, with mixed results. The revised Medicare drug plan, known as Medicare Part D, which came into effect in 2006, provided seniors with a flurry of plan options provided by various insurance companies. But the byzantine regulations introduced by the plan options left many seniors confused and worried they were not getting the coverage they needed.

Visit Vault at **www.vault.com** for insider company profiles, expert advice, career message boards, expert resume reviews, the Vault Job Board and more.

VAULT CAREER LIBRARY 227

New regulations, introduced in July 2006 and set to take effect in 2007, will rejigger the rates at which Medicare compensates hospitals and physicians for various procedures. Compensation for surgeries, such as hip and knee replacements and various cardiac procedures, will be cut by as much as a third. In response, the American Medical Association (AMA) has announced that if compensation for Medicare patients is reduced, physicians will be forced to restrict the number of such cases they can handle. This legislation represents the opening salvo in a series of laws that will try to rein in Medicare spending by 34 percent over the next nine years. Further economic fallout may include hospitals seeking higher reimbursement from insurance companies, which will then raise premiums, further increasing the cost of healthcare.

Flying without a net

The rest of the population—those who aren't eligible for Medicare or Medicaid, some 86 percent—either have to buy private insurance on their own, get it at discounted rates through an employer, or just go without and hope for the best. An alarming number of Americans, including many children, are in the latter category—15 percent of the population at last count, or some 44 million people.

What's more, this number, along with the number of those who must purchase insurance on their own, may well grow. Health care costs have continued to rise, at three times the rate of inflation by some estimates, and employers are increasingly unwilling or unable to pay to insure their employees. An April 2005 report by the *Health Affairs Policy Journal* predicted that the number of non-elderly uninsured Americans will grow to 56 million by 2013. Not only do these people risk financial ruin when faced with unexpected medical emergencies, they're also less likely to rely on routine visits to doctors, dentists and the like to maintain good health, thereby preventing more serious conditions down the line. Reports also indicate that health care is more expensive overall for the uninsured. For example, some hospitals bill uninsured clients a higher rate for the same procedures provided to those with health coverage, since big insurance companies are able to negotiate discounts with providers, and uninsured individuals are more likely to default on their payments due to bankruptcy.

The situation isn't so rosy for consumers fortunate enough to have coverage, either. Private health insurance companies paid for 35 percent of the total health care expenditures in the U.S. in 2002, or nearly $550 billion. But as the cost of providing health care coverage continues to rise, many employers are finding they can no longer afford this benefit, and are passing more of the costs on to employees in the form of higher premiums and stingier reimbursement plans. In an effort to remedy this situation, the AMA is currently at work on a plan that mixes private and public sector financing to benefit the uninsured and improve quality of care and patient choice, with features like tax credits for the purchase of insurance and a wide range of affordable insurance options.

Unmanageable care

Managed care, which arose in the 1980s and 1990s as a response to rampant inflation in health care costs, has changed the face of the industry. Under these managed care systems, insurers realized that they could rein in costs by establishing networks of providers who participate in a health maintenance organization (HMO), which in turn covers a host of insured patients' needs. But in order for the reimbursement to be profitable, health care providers have to curb their own costs. This includes keeping strict limits on the amount of time they spend with patients to maximize the number of appointments they can squeeze in during a day—leading to the hour-in-the-waiting-room, five-minutes-in-the-exam-room doctor visits many Americans experience today. Top managed care companies include Anthem, HealthNet and UnitedHealth Group.

As illustrated by Hollywood dramas, prime-time news programs, and even the 2000 Gore presidential campaign, the public largely sees HMOs as stingy and heartless, willing to deny—via an impenetrable system of rules and limits—society's neediest members basic procedures that are deemed too costly or unnecessary. For their part, managed care organizations argue that without these limits, the cost of health care would rise for everyone in the network (and society at large), nullifying the benefits of such a system. Meanwhile, the government has gotten into the managed care game, allowing patients to participate in its "Medicare+Choice" program, which also operates under the provider network philosophy.

The doctor will see you now

At the other end of the spectrum, consumers who can flash the cash increasingly are turning to "concierge" or "boutique" physician practices. These private practices offer the attentive, personal and thorough care associated with the pre-HMO days of house calls and Norman Rockwell paintings-for a price. Patients shell out an annual fee up front that can range from several hundred to tens of thousands of dollars to join an exclusive roster of clients seen by a participating internist. So rather than scrambling to see up to 30 patients a day (as in a typical managed care practice), boutique physicians can limit their number of cases to a select handful. Some of these practices charge for appointments above and beyond the annual fee (which is just a sort of retainer for their services), while some accommodate reimbursement by health plans for things like specialized tests. As health care costs skyrocket and patients grow frustrated with insurance plans and the quality of managed care, these practices are becoming more popular-and profitable-business options for those doctors who don't see exclusive care for the well-off as an ethical dilemma.

The quest for reform

Every time campaign season rolls around, the health care crisis gets a lot of buzz-but since Hilary Clinton's attempt to create a universal coverage plan was shot down early in her husband's tenure, few mainstream candidates have been willing to outline a specific, coherent reform strategy. In fact, rejection of sweeping health care reform is somewhat of a tradition in the U.S., going back to the days when President Truman stumbled in the 1940s after introducing a universal coverage proposal. In addition, according to an April 2004 *BusinessWeek* article, of those citizens who actually get out and vote each season, a large majority (92 percent in 2000) have health insurance anyway, so it doesn't necessarily pay for politicians to run on fixing the problem of the uninsured. So while many reformers say a "single-payer plan"-one in which the government assumes administration of all health care costs-is the only reasonable way to tame the coverage dragon, it may be a while before a viable plan takes shape.

Liability looms

Another type of reform that gets plenty of congressional buzz is in the area of medical malpractice liability, which the powerful AMA has made its top priority. The association has taken to identifying states that are in a "medical liability crisis" owing to exploding insurance premiums and their effect-providers limiting or halting certain services because of liability risks. As of July 2006, there were 22 states on the AMA's list. One such state, Massachusetts, is a case in point: according to Massachusetts Medical Society research, 50 percent of the state's neurosurgeons, 41 percent of orthopedic surgeons and 36 percent of general surgeons had been forced to limit their scopes of practice due to insurmountable medical liability costs.

The Bush administration said an end to "junk lawsuits" was one of its primary goals for the president's second term, calling for "medical liability reform that will reduce health care costs and make sure patients have the doctors and care they need." In the early months following his January 2005 inauguration, Congress passed Bush-backed legislation to restrain class-action lawsuits and overhaul bankruptcy laws. However, Bush's influence has not fared as well for the "med-mal" bill, which was passed through the House but not the Senate. Bush's proposal would have limited to $250,000 the amount a health provider could be required to pay a patient for "pain and suffering" beyond actual cost of medical services; the proposal also provided for payout of judgments over time instead of in a lump sum.

It's a seemingly unending loop: multi-million-dollar judgments against providers, brought by a solid industry of trial lawyers devoted to representing mistreated patients, make headlines regularly. These judgments then cause liability insurers to panic,

Visit Vault at **www.vault.com** for insider company profiles, expert advice, career message boards, expert resume reviews, the Vault Job Board and more.

VAULT CAREER LIBRARY   **229**

with many refusing to cover health care providers at all. As such, the insurers who have stayed in the medical liability market charge a premium providers increasingly can't afford to pay.

For lawmakers, the issue is a tough one: how do you set a cap on the amount a plaintiff can receive for the preventable death of a loved one? Patient advocates frame the issue as a David-versus-Goliath scenario, charging that the monolithic medical community wants to limit consumers' rights to sue providers for poor care. Meanwhile, as the industry waits for the federal government to come up with a solution, states have begun to tackle the issue themselves, setting their own limits on the amount of money a malpractice judgment can reap for the plaintiff. Voters in the state of Texas, which was listed on the AMA's liability list, recently approved a constitutional amendment capping awards for non-economic damages at $250,000. (Similar measures are in place in West Virginia and Ohio.) Though these states' actions are a far cry from the national reform physicians and insurers desire, it is a start in a definitive—if not right—direction.

Hot hospitals

In 2005, $616 billion was spent on care in hospitals. Growing demand for hospital services, along with higher rates from private insurers, have led to an increase in capital expended in this area. Among the approximately 6,100 hospitals in the U.S., a few tower over the rest. Each year, *U.S. News & World Report* publishes a ranking of the nation's top hospitals, surveying doctors around the country about hospitals' reputations in 17 medical specialties as well as other factors like staffing, morbidity rates and technology. In 2006, the magazine's list named Baltimore's Johns Hopkins Hospital No. 1 overall—a position the institution has held for 16 years running. The Mayo Clinic came in second, followed by the Cleveland Clinic and Massachusetts General.

In 2005, the government launched www.hospitalcompare.hhs.gov, which compares nearly 4,200 hospitals that volunteered data in 17 different areas related to heart attacks, heart failure and pneumonia in an effort to help physicians and patients see how hospitals nationwide compare in terms of quality of care. Federal officials plan to use the site as a model for future efforts to publicize hospital results and assess Medicare participants, which they hope will lead to quality improvements within practices.

The Fall of the House of Tenet

Tenet Healthcare, the nation's second-largest hospital chain, provides a cautionary tale about the perils of doing business in the health care industry. The company, with 98 acute care hospitals and numerous other facilities nationwide, has been the subject of federal investigations into the way it handled Medicare payments over the last few years. Charles Grassley, chair of the Senate Finance Committee, has said that Tenet "appears to be a corporation that is ethically and morally bankrupt." In May 2003, beleaguered CEO Jeffrey Barbakow stepped down after 10 years of heading the firm. The company paid a record settlement amount of $375 million in 1994 for alleged kickbacks and bribes to doctors as inducements to refer patients to its psychiatric hospitals. Tenet made headlines again 10 years later as it began talking to the feds about a possible $1 billion settlement to end an investigation into charges it performed unnecessary heart surgeries on patients. In August 2006, Tenet agreed to settle with the DOJ for $725 million, as well as $175 million in Medicare payments.

Another headline-grabbing health care scandal involves HealthSouth, the nation's largest provider of physical rehab, outpatient surgery and diagnostic services. In 2003, the Securities and Exchange Commission hit the company with charges of cooking the books, accusing the company and its founder and CEO, Richard Scrushy, of overstating earnings by $1.4 billion since 1999. While Scrushy got off scot-free, his former CFO, Aaron Beam, was sentenced to three months in prison and $285,000 in fines. In July 2006, another higher-up in the company, Weston Smith, was fined $7 million and sentenced to over 2 years in prison for his involvement in securities law violations. Word on the street is that the company will soon spin off its outpatient rehabilitation and surgery units.

The dreaded "home"

The term "nursing home" strikes fear in the hearts of many Americans, largely due to media reports detailing abuse and unsanitary conditions at many facilities (but also because of consumers' first-hand experiences with these institutions.) The nation's nursing homes—also sometimes called "skilled nursing facilities" (SNFs) or "long-term care facilities"—have traveled a rocky road in recent years. Indeed, their crisis helps illustrate larger trends in the health care industry as a whole, particularly among providers that, like nursing homes, rely heavily on federal and state dollars to reimburse them for the cost of patient care. By 2001, nine of the top nursing home corporations in the country, including top names like Genesis Health Ventures, Kindred Healthcare, Sun Healthcare Systems and Mariner Post-Acute Networks, had gone through bankruptcy court, saddled with hundreds of millions in debt.

What brought these billion-dollar companies to this low point, when they have such a steady stream of consumers desperate for their services? For one thing, many long-term care facilities overextended their debt burdens in the 1990s, investing in rehab facilities and other ancillary services that promised big (some would say inflated) paybacks from Medicare. Then Medicare struck back, as Congress passed the Balanced Budget Act of 1997, which, among other things, sought to reduce federal health care spending by instituting entirely new payment systems for major health entities like nursing homes, home care agencies, hospitals and doctors. Under the old system, providers were basically paid a fixed amount, or fee, for each service they provided to Medicare patients. Fair enough, but patient advocates and Congress began to worry that nursing home clients were receiving a bit too much care—excessive and unnecessary therapy services, for instance—simply because facilities could make more money by providing and charging the feds for it. Under the BBA, Congress mandated a new "prospective payment system" (PPS) that set up strict guidelines for how long-term care facilities were to be reimbursed for care provided to Medicare and Medicaid patients. Under PPS, facilities are basically paid a fixed per diem for a patient's care depending on the severity of her needs (or "acuity level"), which is determined using a host of intricate rules. The system also set certain limits, or "caps," on services such as rehab, under which Medicare would only pay a fixed amount per patient annually.

The combination of leftover debt and poor financial management, plummeting federal dollars and skyrocketing liability insurance due to high-profile malpractice judgments—plus a host of other factors like low staffing due to undesirable working conditions and a higher acuity level among the patient population—sent, by some estimates, at least 10 percent of the nursing home industry into Chapter 11 by 2001. Most of the nursing home giants have recovered and are learning to adjust to the new payment system, but the situation provided a valuable lesson to other health care providers, like rehab hospitals, whose new Medicare PPS systems took effect after the long-term care revamp had done its damage. Congress, acknowledging that it may have been a bit enthusiastic with the red ink, also kicked in some million-dollar concessions to boost reimbursements after intense industry lobbying.

Others, however, weren't so lucky: many providers of those once high-paying ancillary services, like physical therapy, were forced to close their doors in the aftermath of PPS. Home health care providers, also highly dependent on Medicare and Medicaid payments, weathered a similar crisis under their own new payment system—and, like their counterparts, managed to eke out some financial givebacks from Congress during the past few years.

CDHC—the new wave of care?

One plan for health care that has generated a buzz in the Bush administration is the idea of "consumer-driven health care," or CDHC. The idea is simple: if consumers can control their own health care spending, providers and insurers will be forced to compete for business, thus (hopefully) increasing quality of care while driving down costs. At the crux of CDHC are health savings accounts (HSAs), or tax-free accounts offered along with low-cost, high-deductible insurance plans. Either employee or employer (or both) stow away a certain amount of money in the HSA each year, which consumers can spend on virtually any health treatment or medication they want; whatever is unused remains in the account for any future health-related expenses.

Visit Vault at www.vault.com for insider company profiles, expert advice, career message boards, expert resume reviews, the Vault Job Board and more.

VAULT CAREER LIBRARY   231

Early forms of CDHC have shown up in a number of employer health care plans, including Sara Lee and Aetna, and benefits consultancy Mercer expects 73 percent of companies to add HSAs to their benefits offerings by 2006. Advocates for CDHC plans use the example of cosmetic surgery: since consumers must pay for procedures completely out of pocket, they almost always find the best care at the lowest price. Since 1998, the average price of a tummy tuck has risen 19 percent, only slightly higher than inflation, and far below the 49 percent rise in per capita spending on health care for the same period. Opponents of the plan suggest that employers will use CDHC as a cover to drive up health care costs, further the divide between the quality of care received by the rich and the poor. What CDHC plans do not take into account is that the bulk of the cost of health care spending is not from overconsumption of medical care by people who can afford it, but rather from treating people with chronic conditions such as diabetes, which require thousands of dollars per year to manage.

Becoming the biggest

According to Philip Pfrang, the national director of Life Sciences and Health Care at Deloitte & Touche's Mergers & Acquisition Services practice, M&A activity among managed care companies is alive and well as regional firms try to expand their brands to reach more U.S. workers both at home and abroad. Pfrang likens the managed care sector of health care to the pharmaceutical business, which has seen a select few companies emerge as large organizations through acquisitions. The hospital sector has also seen its fair share of venture/mergers recently, as competitive pressures in the industry increase.

WellPoint, today's largest leading health plan, gained its No. 1 ranking through a 2004 merger with Anthem worth $16.4 billion. Humana, the third-largest HMO in the nation, nearly became the top provider back in 1998, but failed to complete a merger with UnitedHealth, which chose instead to grow through its own acquisitions, including the 2002 purchase of AmeriChoice and the 2003 buyout of Mid-Atlantic Medical Services, worth $2.95 billion. One merger that proved to be a huge success was the 1997 combination of Beckman Instruments and the Coulter Corporation. The resulting company, Beckman Coulter, is currently one of the world's largest providers of instrument systems and products for laboratory work. Additionally, Coventry Health Care, among the largest HMO providers nationwide, was formed in 1998 through Coventry Corporation's acquisition of the Principal Financial Group's health care unit.

Sometimes, in the health care industry, reinvention can be an equally powerful tool to gaining market share. A number of the top companies in health care today survived bankruptcy scandals during the 1990s and re-emerged as successful businesses. Kindred, one of the nation's largest health care providers, was formerly Vencor; Caremark Rx, one of the nation's largest pharmaceutical services providers, used to be a division of the now-defunct MedPartners; and DaVita, the country's largest independent provider of dialysis services, was once Total Renal Care Holdings.

Other top companies in health care today include Cardinal Health, one of the largest wholesalers of pharmaceutical products and surgical supplies; HCA, one of the largest hospital operators in the U.S.; and Medtronic, one of the world's leading medical technology companies. More recent merger activity in the sector includes Boston Scientific's 2006 acquisition of Guidant, a medical devices manufacturer. As part of the deal, Guidant's vascular and endovascular divisions were spun off to Abbott Laboratories.

Where the jobs are

In spite of its daunting complexity, the health care industry has one big upside: it's a reliable producer of jobs. The healt0h services industry, the largest of all industries in 2004, as categorized by the Bureau of Labor Statistics (BLS), employed nearly 13 million people that year. Of the 20 occupations the BLS projects to grow the fastest in coming years, eight are in health services. Furthermore, of new jobs that will be created by 2014, about 19 percent, or some 3.6 million, will be in health services, more than in any other industry. The Labor Department predicts an increase of 22.2 percent in nursing jobs by 2014, while physician's assistant jobs will grow by 54 percent, occupational therapist positions by 33 percent and home care opportunities by 66 percent. Fitness trainers and dental hygienists are also expected to be popular professions.

While the suggestion of working in the health care industry may conjure visions of crushing med school debt and grueling internships, in fact the majority of jobs in the sector require less than four years of college education. Graduates of one- and two-year certification programs, for example, can work as medical records and health information technicians. Service occupations abound, including medical and dental assistants, nursing and home health aides and facility cleaning jobs. The BLS predicts particularly strong growth in jobs outside of the inpatient hospital sector, such as medical assistants and home health aides. There is a constant clamor for more nurses, too, as facilities face growing regulatory pressure to meet mandatory staffing levels.

Physical Therapy Careers

What is physical therapy?

Physical therapy is a growing profession with four areas of practice: examination of individuals with impairment, functional limitation, and disability; treatment of impairment and functional limitation through therapeutic intervention which includes exercise, patient education, and application of modalities; consultation; and research. Physical therapists evaluate ill or injured persons to determine what functional limitations are present. For example, a young man who suffers from spinal cord injury will have strength and flexibility limitations in various muscle groups depending on the level of injury. A young woman with multiple sclerosis may have functional limitations in balance and coordination. Initial evaluations performed by the physical therapist include measurements on a wide battery of abilities.

Physical therapists measure an individual's capability in domains including strength, endurance, flexibility, coordination, balance, gait, skin integrity, and ability to perform simple activities of daily living. After initial evaluation of a patient, the physical therapist will identify a set of problems with physical function and assess how these problems may best be approached through exercise, massage or a modality (treatment applications other than exercise, such as hot/cold packs, ultrasound (healing through deep sound technique), or electrical stimulation).

Physical therapists today also act as consultants through their knowledge of exercise, and those in clinical and academic settings are also involved in research projects to determine whether the treatment interventions they are currently using are grounded in theory and to determine how best to improve upon interventions. In today's health care arena, physical therapists must be patient advocates; that is, balance the dual roles of providing expert information to patients on all types of disease and injuries, allowing the patient to play an active role in choosing options for treatment.

Physical therapists work in a variety of settings, including acute care hospitals, rehabilitation centers, fitness centers, nursing homes, schools and private practice.

Acute care

The acute care setting is fast-paced and requires the physical therapist to work as a member of an interdisciplinary team which may include a social worker, doctor, nurse, occupational therapist and speech therapist. As a member of the acute care team, the physical therapist sees patients immediately after acute injury and illness, and often evaluates patients before and after surgery. For instance, an 85-year-old woman suffering from a fracture to the hip may require a total hip replacement. The therapist must evaluate this patient's strength, range of motion, balance and coordination after the injury, before surgery and after surgery. Exercise intervention would be cautious and determined by level of pain and flexibility limitations.

Rehabilitation

Rehabilitation centers focus on returning patients to a way of life that most resembles what life was like prior to injury. Physical therapists will often see patients every day, or three times a week, and work over a period of three months or more

Visit Vault at **www.vault.com** for insider company profiles, expert advice, career message boards, expert resume reviews, the Vault Job Board and more.

V∧ULT CAREER LIBRARY   **233**

to enable a spinal cord-injured patient to be able to move from a bed to a chair, or to enable a brain-injured patient to walk 200 feet without falling.

Fitness

When a physical therapist works in a fitness center, his focus is on exercise, either as prevention to illness or as a way to maintain a healthy lifestyle. A physical therapist may also evaluate and treat minor sports injuries that occur as a result of excessive or ill-advised exercise. The fitness center therapist may work with persons with or without disabilities who wish to stay healthy through exercise.

Nursing home

A physical therapist working in a nursing home or skilled nursing facility (SNF) needs to be comfortable with and skilled at working with the old, severely disabled, and terminally ill population. The major difference for the physical therapist working in the nursing home or skilled nursing facility is that the patients he or she sees will not be discharged to home. They will stay at the respective facility their whole lives, and this difference can take an emotional toll on the physical therapist as patients often suffer from depression.

Schools

A physical therapist working in the school system sees the very young client versus the very old. In the United States, and some other parts of the world, children with disabilities are integrated into schools with the non-disabled. The disabled pediatric population needs the services of physical therapists, occupational therapists and often speech therapists. The physical therapist working in the public schools works a September to June schedule with summers off, and daily working hours often vary. School systems also require that a physical therapist work as a member of a interdisciplinary team (teacher, parent, student, physical therapist, occupational therapist and speech therapist), but the therapist will have more autonomy than the hierarchy of an acute care hospital allows.

Evaluation by physical therapists

When a physical therapist evaluates a patient (regardless of whether she is working in a direct access or non-direct access state), evaluation is divided into two parts. There is a subjective portion of the evaluation, in which the therapist listens to the patient's history and story of injury or illness, and there is an objective portion, where the therapist conducts a series of tests for strength, flexibility, balance, coordination, skin integrity and more. Physical therapists learn not only to be compassionate and attentive listeners but also to be acute observers of physical strengths and deficits. She is looking to connect a deficit in an area such as strength or balance with a "functional" deficit; in other words, a deficit on a quantitative test is connected to what portion of the patient's physical function and quality of life is being affected. Once limitations are found, the physical therapist writes down, or "documents" baseline measures and later compares these with how far the client progressed or improved with treatment.

Academics and clinicians in the field of physical therapy are focused on providing treatment guided by empirical evidence. Compared to the fields of psychology and medicine, for example, the emphasis on empirical evidence to justify treatment is more recent in physical therapy. Progressive resistive exercise (exercise using increasing amount of weight resistance with a specified number of repetitions) has been used to strengthen musculature for at least a century, and consistent systematic reviews of randomized clinical trials to determine whether progressive resistive exercise strengthens muscles more effectively than no exercise have only been conducted in physical therapy over the past 20 years. In today's health care environment, students and practicing physical therapists demand evidence supporting the proven effects of treatments they are using and that such treatments can be verified with published research. Students entering the field of physical therapy today will encounter colleagues who have published, taught, developed a clinical expertise niche or done a little of it all. The possibilities in the field are endless. Today the American Physical Therapy Association urges all practicing physical therapists to enroll in continuing education classes to keep skills up to date and with a scientific edge. Most professionals do so gladly and are often reimbursed by the sites/programs at which they work.

Physical therapy educational programs strive to provide students with as much about what it is like to have a disability, injury or illness as possible. PT students not only study the anatomy and physiology of the human body but participate in discussions and courses centering around the psychosocial needs of persons with disabilities. PT programs include sections on the legal ramifications of being disabled and PTs in and out of school must stay up to date on all aspects of health care policy and how it affects their patients through continuing education, referred journals and the media.

Physical therapists must promote the power of exercise, both aerobic and anaerobic. Aerobic exercise (riding a bike for 15 minutes or more, vigorous walking for 30 minutes, running for 10 minutes, swimming) increases circulation to the heart, improves lung capacity and increases endurance for greater periods of exercise. An individual recovering from a heart attack or stroke with the proper precautions will benefit greatly from aerobic exercise as improved circulation, cardiovascular health and aerobic endurance has been proven to protect against future heart attacks or strokes. Aerobic exercise is beneficial to all ages and for many illnesses. (Currently there is an obesity epidemic among America's children and aerobic exercise is directly linked to a healthy weight in children.) Anaerobic exercise is exercise of shorter duration where the emphasis is on force output versus sustained activity. Examples of anaerobic exercise would be a bench press of less than 3 repetitions, jumping from a standing position in basketball, or a wrestler pinning an opponent down in less than three minutes. Anaerobic exercise challenges muscles to their ultimate force output and stretches fibers to increase muscle bulk. Physical therapists use anaerobic exercise to increase muscle strength in patients who are weakened through many different illnesses and injury.

Physical therapists "prescribe" exercise for infants, children, young and older adults, and considered to be very old (85 and up). Public health experts today are calling on physical therapists for advice and consultation on all types of morbidity epidemics such as childhood obesity, cardiovascular disease and osteoporosis, so in many cases, physical therapists can augment clinical practice (clinical practice is defined as the evaluation and treatment of patients in need of physical therapy services) with private consultation to companies, non-profit organizations or schools. Aside from knowing "how much and what kind" of exercise to prescribe, physical therapists should also know all contraindications (when NOT to prescribe) exercise.

Physical therapists use their hands to work, called "manual therapy" in PT vernacular. All physical therapists have the ability to do manual therapy and are schooled in different techniques of massage and mobilization (moving soft tissue and bones manually). However, some physical therapists find career tracks that take them away from direct contact with the patient. Physical therapists who become teachers and administrators will be less adept at manual therapy techniques because of lack of daily practice than those who evaluate and treat patients for a living. Some physical therapists become famous because of the effectiveness of their manual skills. Ted Corbitt is a renowned manual therapist who gained a national reputation over more than 25 years at the International Center for the Disabled in New York. A long-distance runner, he also created the idea for the New York City marathon with Fred Lebow.

Manual therapy includes techniques for stretching, strengthening, and reducing pain. Physical therapists may use massage as a manual technique for reduction of pain. Techniques include effleurage, a massage technique from Sweden in which broad strokes are used to increase circulation throughout the body; acupressure, which identifies trigger points through deep pressure; and friction massage, quick, brisk movements in the direction opposite fibers' alignment to interrupt neuronal pain signals and increase circulation. Depending on the type of injury, a therapist may choose effleurage to relax tense musculature throughout the body, trigger point massage to release a specific tight muscle (the trapezius, for example, is often tight due to poor posture), or friction massage for an injury like a sprained ankle, in which specific massage at the site of pain can compliment rest, ice and elevation. Physical therapists also perform mobilization techniques, a method by which tissue is moved to reduce pain. There are four grades of mobilization (1-4) from most gentle to more forceful pressure. PTs also perform myofascial treatment (moving the fascia of the body to reduce pain) without instruments, only hands. Myofascial treatment has been proven to be very effective with chronic pain patients. Craniosacral therapy is another type of manual

Visit Vault at **www.vault.com** for insider company profiles, expert advice, career message boards, expert resume reviews, the Vault Job Board and more.

VAULT CAREER LIBRARY   235

treatment in which the cranium (the skull) and the sacrum (the portion of the backbone between the coccyx and the low back) are mobilized and massaged to relieve pain. Craniosacral therapy is effective in reduction of migraine headaches, arthritic pain and many types of chronic pain.

When physical therapists are not treating patients with manual therapy or exercise they may be providing so-called "modality" treatments, which include use of whirlpools, paraffin treatments (hot wax), electrical stimulation, or ultrasound (healing by sound waves). Whirlpool treatment may be used to clean wounds after injury, and also helps decrease swelling. Paraffin is often used for the hands and feet, to relieve arthritis-related joint pain. Electrical stimulation is often used after a neurological injury, such as stroke, to stimulate nerve action potential and regain movement. Ultrasound is used to decrease pain and increase circulation after any injury, and the theory is that sound waves make this possible.

Physical therapists also provide their patients with advice about their physical problems, providing tips for reducing physical stress and strain, options for exercise once at home, as well as counsel on postural alignment, healthy work environments, even the right shoes.

As physical therapy moves from requiring a Master's degree to a Clinical Doctorate, physical therapists are performing not only evaluation, but functional physical diagnosis, as a doctor would. In the past, physical therapists were only expected to evaluate and treat patients, but the increasing number of clinical doctorates in the field is elevating those therapists' role in the treatment process.

Not all personnel in the field of physical therapy are licensed to evaluate and treat patients. The two professional rungs in the field of physical therapy are the physical therapist and the physical therapist assistant. A physical therapist assistant (PTA) is an individual who completes a two-year associate degree undergraduate program and is able to provide treatment only, under the direction of a physical therapist; a PTA is not licensed to evaluate patients. Non-professional personnel include physical therapy aides, who provide set-up, maintenance of treatment area and scheduling services.

To help individuals achieve maximum functional capabilities in order to continue to live as full a life as possible, physical therapists set short term and long term goals at the time of evaluation for all patients. An example of a short-term goal for a patient with a low back injury may be to decrease the pain level from a level of 9/10 (extreme pain) to 7/10 (moderate-high level pain). An example of a long-term goal for a patient with low back injury may be to have the patient be able to return to work or school. Physical therapists are trained to write all goals as measurable items, primarily because insurance companies reimburse objective and quantifiable measures. It's important to look for places of employment that allow enough time for documentation of these goals and other note-writing. Increasingly, due to managed care, the complexity of federal and non-federal insurance rules and patient liability issues, there is more and more paperwork required by all professionals working with patients. Daily duties for the physical therapist involve not only evaluating and treating patients but also writing down all findings and treatment in measurable terms carefully and consistently. A good place of employment allows the physical therapist enough time for note-writing so that the copious paperwork stays under control and the therapist does not have to stay late after hours to keep up with it. Many places of employment now encourage PTs to input data into a computer, thus saving time for the therapist and standardizing note-writing across the organization.

While typical diagnoses physical therapists evaluate and treat include orthopedic injuries such as bone fractures or muscle strains/sprains, neurological conditions such as stroke and spinal cord injury, cardiovascular conditions including asthma, and heart conditions, physical therapists treat conditions that affect a myriad of systems in the body. And people often have more than one problem at a time, which is referred to as a dual diagnosis. Increasingly, patients are more knowledgeable about medical conditions largely because of Internet access, so physical therapists often evaluate patients who have researched their own condition. This means that the PT sometimes has to spend time reeducating the patient with accurate information about physical therapy procedures, so it's critical that the PT have a love of life-long learning to stay abreast of all the changes in health care treatments.

Health Care Employer Directory

Aetna Inc.
151 Farmington Ave.
Hartford, CT 06156
Phone: (860) 273-0123
Fax: (860) 273-3971
Toll Free: (800) 872-3862
www.aetna.com

Amerigroup Corporation
4425 Corporation Lane
Virginia Beach, VA 23462
Phone: (757) 490-6900
Fax: (757) 490-7152
www.amerigrp.com

Applera Corporation
301 Merritt 7
Norwalk, CT 06851-1070
Phone: (203) 840-2000
Fax: (203) 840-2312
www.applera.com

Beckman Coulter, Inc.
4300 N. Harbor Blvd.
Fullerton, CA 92834-3100
Phone: (714) 871-4848
Fax: (714) 773-8283
www.beckman.com

Beverly Healthcare
1000 Beverly Way
Fort Smith, AR 72919
Phone: (479) 201-2000
Fax: (479) 201-1101
www.beverlyhealthcare.com

Boston Scientific Corporation
1 Boston Scientific Place
Natick, MA 01760-1537
Phone: (508) 650-8000
Fax: (508) 647-2393
www.bostonscientific.com

Caremark Rx, Inc.
211 Commerce Street, Suite 800
Nashville, TN 37201
Phone: (615) 743-6600
Fax: (205) 733-9780
www.caremark.com

CIGNA
1 Liberty Place
Philadelphia, PA 19192-1550
Phone: (215) 761-1000
Fax: (215) 761-5515
www.cigna.com

Community Health Systems, Inc.
155 Franklin Road, Ste. 400
Brentwood, TN 37027-4600
Phone: (615) 373-9600
Fax: (615) 371-1068
www.chs.net

Coventry Health Care, Inc.
6705 Rockledge Drive
Suite 900
Bethesda, MD 20817
Phone: (301) 581-0600
Fax: (301) 493-0731
www.cvty.com

DaVita, Inc.
601 Hawaii Street
El Segundo, CA 90245
Phone: (310) 536-2400
Fax: (310) 536-2675
www.davita.com

Express Scripts, Inc.
13900 Riverport Drive
Maryland Heights, MO 63043
Phone: (314) 770-1666
Fax: (314) 702-7037
www.express-scripts.com

Fresenius Medical Care AG
Else-Kröner-Straße 1
61346 Bad Homburg, Germany
Phone: +49-6172-608-0
Fax: +49-6172-608-2488
www.fmc-ag.com

Guidant Corporation
111 Monument Circle, 29th Floor
Indianapolis, IN 46204
Phone: (317) 971-2000
Fax: (317) 971-2040
www.guidant.com

HCA, Inc.
1 Park Plaza
Nashville, TN 37203
Phone: (615) 344-9551
Fax: (615) 344-2266
www.hcahealthcare.com

Health Management Associates, Inc.
5811 Pelican Bay Blvd., Suite 500
Naples, FL 34108-2710
Phone: (239) 598-3131
Fax: (239) 598-2705
www.hma-corp.com

Health Net, Inc.
21650 Oxnard Street
Woodland Hills, CA 91367
Phone: (818) 676-6000
Fax: (818) 676-8591
www.healthnet.com

HealthSouth Corporation
1 HealthSouth Pkwy.
Birmingham, AL 35243
Phone: (205) 967-7116
Fax: (205) 969-6889
www.healthsouth.com

Hillenbrand Industries, Inc.
700 State Route 46 East
Batesville, IN 47006-8835
Phone: (812) 934-7000
Fax: (812) 934-7371
www.hillenbrand.com

Humana Inc.
The Humana Building
500 W. Main Street
Louisville, KY 40202
Phone: (502) 580-1000
Fax: (502) 580-3677
www.humana.com

Kaiser Permanente
1 Kaiser Plaza, Suite 2600
Oakland, CA 94612-3673
Phone: (510) 271-5800
Fax: (510) 267-7524
www.kaiserpermanente.org

Visit Vault at **www.vault.com** for insider company profiles, expert advice, career message boards, expert resume reviews, the Vault Job Board and more.

VAULT CAREER LIBRARY   **237**

Health Care Employer Directory, cont.

Kindred Health Care
680 S. 4th Street
Louisville, KY 40202-2412
Phone: (502) 596-7300
Fax: (502) 596-4170
www.kindredhealthcare.com

Laboratory Corporation of America
358 S. Main Street
Burlington, NC 27215
Phone: (336) 229-1127
Fax: (336) 436-1205
www.labcorp.com

Magellan Health Services, Inc.
16 Munson Road
Farmington, CT 06032
Phone: (860) 507-1900
Fax: (410) 953-5200
www.magellanhealth.com

Manor Care, Inc.
333 N. Summit Street
Toledo, OH 43604-2617
Phone: (419) 252-5500
Fax: (419) 252-5596
www.hcr-manorcare.com

Mariner Health Care, Inc.
1 Ravinia Dr., Ste. 1500
Atlanta, GA 30346
Phone: (678) 443-7000
Fax: (770) 393-8054
www.marinerhealth.com

Medco Health Solutions
100 Parsons Pond Drive
Franklin Lakes, NJ 07417-2604
Phone: (201) 269-3400
Fax: (201) 269-1109
www.medco.com

Medical Mutual of Ohio
2060 E. 9th Street
Cleveland, OH 44115-1300
Phone: (216) 687-7000
Fax: (216) 687-6044
www.mmoh.com

Medtronic, Inc.
710 Medtronic Pkwy. NE
Minneapolis, MN 55432-5604
Phone: (763) 514-4000
Fax: (763) 514-4879
www.medtronic.com

NeighborCare, Inc.
601 East Pratt Street, 3rd Floor
Baltimore, MD 21202
Phone: (410) 528-7300
Fax: (410) 528-7473
www.neighborcare.com

PacifiCare Life and Health Insurance Company
5995 Plaza Drive
Cypress, CA 90630
Phone: (714) 952-1121
Fax: (714) 226-3581
www.pacificare.com

Quest Diagnostics Incorporated
1 Malcolm Avenue
Teterboro, NJ 07608
Phone: (201) 393-5000
Fax: (201) 462-4715
www.questdiagnostics.com

Sierra Health Services, Inc.
2724 N. Tenaya Way
Las Vegas, NV 89128
Phone: (702) 242-7000
Fax: (702) 242-9711
www.sierrahealth.com

St. Jude Medical, Inc.
1 Lillehei Plaza
St. Paul, MN 55117-9983
Phone: (651) 483-2000
Fax: (651) 482-8318
www.sjm.com

Stryker Corporation
2725 Fairfield Road
Kalamazoo, MI 49002
Phone: (269) 385-2600
Fax: (269) 385-1062
www.strykercorp.com

Sun Healthcare Group, Inc.
18831 Von Karman, Ste. 400
Irvine, CA 92612
Phone: (949) 255-7100
Fax: (949) 255-7054
www.sunh.com

Tenet Healthcare
13737 Noel Road
Dallas, TX 75240
Phone: (469) 893-2200
Fax: (469) 893-8600
www.tenethealth.com

UnitedHealth Group Inc.
UnitedHealth Group Center
9900 Bren Road East
Minnetonka, MN 55343
Phone: (952) 936-1300
Fax: (952) 936-7430
www.unitedhealthgroup.com

Universal Health Services
Universal Corporate Center
367 S. Gulph Road
King of Prussia, PA 19406-0958
Phone: (610) 768-3300
Fax: (610) 768-3336
www.uhsinc.com

WellChoice, Inc.
11 W. 42nd Street
New York, NY 10036
Phone: (212) 476-7800
Fax: (212) 476-1281
www.wellchoice.com

WellPoint, Inc.
120 Monument Circle
Indianapolis, IN 46204
Phone: (317) 488-6000
Fax: (317) 488-6028
www.wellpoint.com

High Tech

The Scope of High Tech Careers

There are certainly many companies that can be considered "technology" companies because the products or services they produced involve computers, software or networking systems. Prominent examples include Microsoft, IBM, Cisco Systems and Dell Computer. But technology careers also extend beyond high tech industries. IT is integral in most businesses, and its definition is continually being redefined. Although most jobseekers know that IT involves widespread technologies, few trying to enter the field probably know just which technologies or which jobs it encompasses.

Authorities describing IT demonstrate how widespread yet "blurry" the field is. First of all, "There is not a government-wide definition of who is classified as an information technology worker," says Roger Moncarz, an economist for the U.S. Bureau of Labor Statistics. "There's a wide sampling of estimates out there, for exactly how to define an information technology worker."

Moncarz continues, "Based on our definition of information technology workers, and based on government occupational surveys, we come up with 3.3 million to 3.5 million IT workers in America. The Information Technology Association of America (ITAA), in their recently released study, says there are 10.4 million IT workers. So there's wide discrepancy."

Regardless of who may define it, one thing is certain: IT is everywhere. Offices large and small must maintain, utilize, and upgrade IT infrastructures to be effective in the marketplace. Because of the ubiquitous and demanding nature of the technology, IT jobs run the gamut from entry-level, low-tech positions to tech-savvy engineering managers.

Information technology (IT) is a huge, ever-changing field. It encompasses the products and services necessary to store, convert, and deliver information electronically. This includes the entire computer infrastructure of an organization: computer hardware, packaged software, computer system architecture, documents outlining technical procedures, many other computer-related products and lots and lots of people.

Computers and IT continue to have an explosive impact of on life and business. More than ever, companies must rapidly evolve, incorporating new technologies into their daily operations to remain competitive. From one-man sales companies to international medical labs, almost every type of business utilizes an IT infrastructure to run, to expand, and occasionally, to simply comply with the law.

IT is essential to business because it allows people to communicate faster, more efficiently, and with more capabilities than older technologies. A lone costume maker in Illinois can suddenly turn her enterprise into an international business by putting up a web site. A corporate executive can instantaneously deliver vital information to associates in Japan, South Africa and England through the power of a secure network. A student whose laptop gets stolen can immediately retrieve all of his lost information from a backup database server. A doctor can use a computer program that makes all of his patients' correspondences and information secure from prying eyes. There is power in IT.

Since technology issues are so critical to a company's health, a significant portion of business is involved with IT. In fact, one in every 14 jobs in America is an IT or IT-related position. IT careers cover a broad range of businesses, skill paths, office sizes and backgrounds.

Visit Vault at **www.vault.com** for insider company profiles, expert advice, career message boards, expert resume reviews, the Vault Job Board and more.

VAULT CAREER LIBRARY   239

Categories of Tech Professionals

Let's take a look at three major categories of workers: hardware, software and support personnel.

Hardware

Hardware-oriented workers create and maintain electronic communications infrastructures. They build computers, which both businesses and home users buy. They also build large computers called servers, which mostly businesses buy. When businesses buy computers and servers, company hardware employees set up the computers, connecting them to each other and the server. This way, all of the computers have a common set of resources available to them, and all of the computers can communicate with each other. Hardware employees are often the ones who decide the architecture of the computer clusters and the resources they contain.

Software

Software employees create programs that use and manipulate computer infrastructures. Through typing code and commands into the computers, they design the software interfaces between people and hardware. They also use those interfaces to create utilities and applications that perform specific tasks like tracking business records.

Nowadays, they build systems for the Internet and other networks. They make sure that information flows efficiently between computers within an organization, or to and from a web site. At the same time, they keep the information safe, making sure that only authorized people can access sensitive information.

Support

The hardware and software infrastructures at most companies are so large and complex, that separate departments must plan them and support them. Support role employees include people in customer care, leadership and managerial roles, and testing departments. Analysts and managers decide the future of business IT infrastructures. Constantly examining new technology and how it can make business more effective, they weigh the costs and benefits to buying new hardware or modifying existing systems. Quality assurance testers make sure that the systems perform as they were designed and planned. Performing tests and discovering the limits of the systems make sure that the infrastructure investments are worth the cost and effort in the long run. Customer, sales and user support people make sure that company employees know how to use the systems, and that the systems are in good working order. They also help customers use the software, information or hardware that the company distributes.

Tech workers = nerds?

When people think of IT workers, especially programmers and engineers, they often think of the ultimate nerd. They may get images of the lone man with a five o'clock shadow, messy hair and a pocket protector, sitting in a dark room and staring at a computer screen all day and night. Or, they may get an image of the espresso junkie who rides a Razor Scooter in the office, playing foosball and starting Nerf gun fights all day long. These stereotypes of IT are becoming less true.

The IT field has come to resemble traditional corporate culture more than it did during the dot-com heyday. IT employees must be able to communicate well and work sensitively with others, they must travel for some jobs, and they must deal with all sorts of environments to succeed.

Instead of wearing pocket protectors and bad hair, most successful tech workers know how to present themselves professionally to managers and non-tech departments. Increasingly, even programmers need to communicate constantly with analysts, business development offices, and other corporate departments.

Rather than work odd hours and obsess over minor code details, successful engineers know how to prioritize their tasks and follow project requirements efficiently. They need to be around during regular business hours in order to coordinate with business departments. They may work long hours, but that is usually to keep up with tight deadlines born from tighter budgets.

In a nutshell, many IT departments no longer have the time or money to accommodate the stereotypical nerd. While some tech offices still have foosball tables and video games in the office, the number of such offices has been dwindling for years. Companies have been downsizing, and employees have had to take on multiple roles. Workers simply cannot afford the time to fool around in the office, much less gain a reputation of doing so. Companies cannot afford to have departments full of antisocial geeks, since so much of business depends on smooth interdepartmental communication. Many companies have even engaged in efforts to make their tech employees more sociable and stronger communicators.

Contrary to the stereotypes, IT employees must often face a workplace higher in stress, higher in its demands and lacking in diversity.

Common Positions for Recent College Grads

Entry-level network employees

Desktop support or customer service workers (more specific information on these positions below) do the most basic network maintenance. These workers sit at their desks, receiving phone calls or emails from people who need help using any of the company's software or hardware. Specifically in the network capacity, they provide end user support for network-based applications and perform routine network repairs. Desktop support workers who work exclusively with network matters may be referred to as LAN support workers, or network maintenance workers. These support workers only deal with client machines and cables; they do not touch the server.

If people phone in and report network problems, like if an employee's client computer can no longer communicate with the network, the desktop or LAN support worker recommends solutions to the problem over the phone, such as reconfiguring the client operating system to detect the network. If that does not help, the support worker schedules and performs repairs on the client hardware and software. Such repairs can include tightening loose network cables attached to the client machines, installing more RAM on client machines, or reinstalling client application software. They also go all around the office configuring the individual client computers to communicate with the network.

Entry-level network employees make about $29,000 to $40,000 a year. They usually work regular 40-hour workweeks, although they must work after hours or weekends if the network requires maintenance or repairs at those times. These workers should know the common concepts and procedures of network repair and upkeep, but they usually rely on existing guidelines and instructions, reporting to a project leader or more senior LAN support worker.

In time, which can be as short as a year, the support worker can prove enough network competence and knowledge to become a junior network or systems administrator.

Visit Vault at **www.vault.com** for insider company profiles, expert advice, career message boards, expert resume reviews, the Vault Job Board and more.

V∧ULT CAREER LIBRARY 241

Junior administrators

Junior administrators are task-oriented employees who do basic server work. They do not research, gather data from managers or make planning decisions. Instead, they perform specific tasks given to them by senior admins. However, although they are junior, these admins do not tool with end-user applications or client machine operating systems. Those duties still belong to desktop support personnel. At the junior level, a lot of network and systems duties overlap.

Junior network administrators do basic network configuration and basic network maintenance, such as opening or closing server ports as needed. They also do a lot of the network monitoring. The computer programs that monitor networks produce warning messages if network problems arise, so junior administrators must watch for these messages.

"The junior sys admin also does basic configuration and maintenance," says Greg Land, a junior systems administrator for HotJobs.com. "If there's some kind of network problem, they might replace server memory modules, or replace server CPU's." Also, if the senior system adminstrator determines that a certain amount of server resources need to be allocated for something like company e-mail, the junior system adminstrator configures the server software accordingly.

With experience and demonstrated competence here comes seniority. Within about two to four years, junior adminstrator can attain senior ranks. Both salary and responsibilities increase substantially here. While junior administrators are task-oriented, senior admins are project oriented.

Junior software engineers

A recent college graduate with little experience could get a job as a junior software engineer. Inexperienced software engineers usually start off supporting existing software. They review and analyze the results of software tests, and they help to implement software by installing the programs or applications. They also debug and modify programs according to the direction of senior engineers.

They sit at their desks, in cubicles or in rooms of several engineers, typing on computer screens that are full of text windows. They use various utilities to graphically map out program designs, and they use many purely text interfaces to install or modify their software projects. Rather than developing entire software packages, they create small dependency programs or functions that the main programs use. Beginner developers may make $55,000 to $87,750 per year.

Good analytical and problem-solving skills are necessary for success here. And, at this point, their biggest asset is programming know-how. There are a lot of parts to the job, all of which involve sitting in front of a computer screen: aiding with small portions of program design, debugging existing portions of software, installing programs or dependencies, documenting and mapping programs, etc. These engineers may look like the typical nerd, with bad hair and five o'clock shadows, spending most of their time at text screens and cavorting with other like-minded engineers. Deadlines can be insanely demanding, and software engineers often work over 40 hours a week and on weekends.

Support specialists

Computer support specialists, or technical support specialists/workers, or customer service representatives, or helpdesk workers/technicians provide technical assistance to users over the phone or via e-mail. Using diagnostic programs, they help customers or fellow employees troubleshoot and repair their hardware or software. Support specialists also help users install hardware and software.

These workers sit at their desks taking calls and answering emails all day from people having problems using company hardware or software. More technically trained workers go around the office helping users install or repair their client computers. Other experienced ones may take more complicated technical calls from customers. "It's helpful for people entering IT to have experience in helpdesk, because it gives them exposure to a wide variety of issues on any level of an IT product," says Anthony Dickerson, a technical support worker from a proprietary banking software company.

Helpdesk positions also help technical people get used to dealing with customers and building professional relationships. In addition to that, helpdesk often teaches people to stay calm in bad situations. For example, Ingrid Johanns worked in technical support for a health care company. She relates, "The software guys were working on a system that would make automatic calls to patients, to remind them to do something (do an exercise, go to an appointment, etc.). And they screwed up. The system accidentally called people at two in the morning, and it would not stop calling until the recipient had listened to the message fully. Very bad. And my job at the time, being in customer support ... well, they had me call all the patients and apologize for the call. I wanted to kill those software guys. It was their fault—they should have made those TOTALLY AWKWARD calls. Anyway, you really learn how to call people and talk with them about anything. You get over that awkward feeling really fast by overdosing on awkwardness."

Support specialists must often help people who do not know much about computers, and they must typically answer questions that the product manuals often do not. Thus, specialists must communicate carefully with users to diagnose problems and to walk the users through solutions. Good communication skills are paramount to advancement here. Good analytical and problem solving skills are also essential.

Support specialists get different types of questions at different types of companies. Workers at a hardware sales company may get questions about how to manually configure computer components. Workers at an e-commerce site may get questions about how to access personal information through the company's web site.

Specialists also need to understand the various stresses that each business will offer. For instance, specialists at a financial web site may get many frantic phone calls from customers worried about their money. "I've had a customer service job at a credit card company for clients, and I've done customer service at a medical insurance group, Blue Cross/Blue Shield" says Dara Sanderson, who now works at WebMD. "Both of them were different. The one at Blue Cross/Blue Shield was a little less frantic, but the questions you got were more important because you're dealing with people's health. Both of them were the type of job that could be very tedious, and there are days when you would dread having to deal with people. But neither were mentally very difficult to handle though."

Usually, helpdesk workers only need to work 40 hours a week, although customer service offices must often operate 24 hours a day. Thus, they may work evenings or weekends if the company provides support over extended hours. Also, overtime work may be necessary when unexpected technical problems arise.

Visit Vault at **www.vault.com** for insider company profiles, expert advice, career message boards, expert resume reviews, the Vault Job Board and more.

VAULT CAREER LIBRARY   243

High Tech Employer Directory

Plum Creek Timber Company

99 Third Ave, Suite 4300
Seattle, WA 98104-4096

Recruiting Contact:
Phone: 206-467-3600
E-mail: careers@plumcreek.com
www.plumcreek.com

Job Search Website:
www.jobsearch.org/seeker/jobsearch/keyword
Search by the following keyword and location parameters: Keyword: Plum Creek, Location: National

Plum Creek is the United States' largest private landowner with over 8 million acres of land and growing. An S&P 500 company, Plum Creek has revenues over $1.5 billion, offices in 18 states, and various positions in forestry, real estate, land management, manufacturing, accounting, human resources, and legal.

We have a collaborative, team-centric, execution oriented culture focused on delivery and strive for a good balance between career and personal life, and between cutting edge and proven technology. Plum Creek's substantial growth has created many unique career opportunities. You'll be able to build a rewarding and successful career, while enjoying the low-key atmosphere that makes life in our tight-knit communities a happy and warm place to live and visit.

Plum Creek wants to attract and keep the best people-the team who drives our success. That is why we offer superior performers opportunities for compensation that is in the top 25% for our marketplace. Benefits packages consists of a comprehensive range of benefits including Health care, Health and Dependent Daycare Funds, Life and Disability protection, Saving and Retirements benefits, Paid Vacation, Relocation, and more.

Our IT department collaborates closely with the businesses to deliver cutting edge technology solutions that add business value, to migrate to a new technology stack based upon Microsoft technologies, and to mature our delivery processes around IT best practices. Over 60 members of our advanced IT team are lucky enough to call the Flathead Valley in Montana home, while other members are in beautiful Athens, GA and Seattle, WA. We are consistently building and integrating hot new technologies focused upon Sharepoint, .NET, ESRI based GIS technologies, and complex data migrations, which continues to test and challenge our employees within this paradigm of new

3Com

350 Campus Drive
Marlborough, MA 01752-3064
Phone: (508) 323-5000
Fax: (508) 323-1111
www.3com.com

Advanced Micro Devices, Inc.

One AMD Place
P.O. Box 3453
Sunnyvale, CA 94088-3453
Phone: (408) 749-4000
Fax: (508) 323-1111
www.amd.com

Agilent Technologies

395 Page Mill Road
Palo Alto, CA 94306
Phone: (650) 752-5000
Fax: (650) 752-5300
www.agilent.com

Analog Deivces, Inc.

1 Technology Way
Norwood, MA 02062-9106
Phone: (781) 329-4700
Fax: (781) 461-3638
www.analog.com

Apple Computer, Inc.

1 Infinite Loop
Cupertino, CA 95014
Phone: (408) 996-1010
Fax: (408) 974-2113
www.apple.com

Applied Materials, Inc.

3050 Bowers Avenue
Santa Clara, CA 95054-8039
Phone: (408) 727-5555
Fax: (408) 748-9943
www.appliedmaterials.com

Ariba Inc.

807 11th Avenue
Sunnyvale, CA 94089
Phone: (650) 390-1000
Fax: (650) 390-1100
www.ariba.com

Boeing Company, The

100 N. Riverside Plaza
Chicago, IL 60606-2609
Phone: (312) 544-2000
Fax: (312) 544-2082
www.boeing.com

Bose Corp.

The Mountain
Framingham, MA 01701
Phone: (508) 879-7330
Fax: (508) 766-7543
www.bose.com

High Tech Employer Directory, cont.

Cisco Systems, Inc.
170 West Tasman Drive
San Jose, CA 95134
Phone: (408) 526-4000
www.cisco.com

**Computer Associates
International, Inc.**
1 Computer Associates Plaza
Islandia, NY 11749
Phone: (631) 342-6000
Fax: (631) 342-5329
www.ca.com

Compuware Corporation
1 Campus Martius
Detroit, MI 48266-5099
Phone: (313) 227-7300
Fax: (248) 737-7108
www.compuware.com

**Cypress Semiconductor
Corporation**
3901 N. 1st Street
San Jose, CA 95134-1599
Phone: (408) 943-2600
Fax: (408) 943-6841
www.cypress.com

Dell Inc.
One Dell Way
Round Rock, TX 78682
Phone: (512) 338-4400
Fax: (512) 728-3653
www.dell.com

EMC Corporation
176 South Street
Hopkinton, MA 01748
Phone: (508) 435-1000
Toll Free: (877) 362-6973
Fax: (508) 497-6912
www.emc.com

Gateway, Inc.
7565 Irvine Center Drive
Irvine, CA 92618
Phone: (949) 471-7000
Fax: (949) 471-7041
www.gateway.com

Hewlett-Packard Company
3000 Hanover Street
Palo Alto, CA 94304
Phone: (650) 857-1501
Fax: (650) 857-5518
www.hp.com

Intel Corporation
2200 Mission College Blvd
Santa Clara, CA 95052
Phone: (408) 765-8080
Fax: (408) 765-9904
www.intel.com

**International Business
Machines Corporation (IBM)**
New Orchard Road
Armonk, NY 10504
Phone: (914) 499-1900
Fax: (914) 765-7382
www.ibm.com

Intuit Inc.
2632 Marine Way
Mountain View, CA 94043
Phone: (650) 944-6000
Fax: (650) 944-3699
www.intuit.com

LSI Logic Corporation
1621 Barber Lane
Milpitas, CA 95035
Phone: (408) 433-8000
Fax: (408) 954-3220
www.lsilogic.com

Microsoft Corporation
1 Microsoft Way
Redmond, WA 98052-6399
Phone: (425) 882-8080
Fax: (425) 936-7329
www.microsoft.com

Motorola, Inc.
1303 E. Algonquin Road
Schaumburg, IL 60196
Phone: (847) 576-5000
Fax: (847) 576-5372
www.motorola.com

NCR Corporation
1700 S. Patterson Blvd.
Dayton, OH 45479
Phone: (937) 445-5000
Toll Free: (800) 225-5627
Fax: (937) 445-1682
www.ncr.com

Oracle Corporation
500 Oracle Parkway
Redwood City, CA 94065
Phone: (650) 506-7000
Fax: (650) 506-7200
www.oracle.com

Rockwell Collins
400 Collins Road N.E.
Cedar Rapids, IA 52498
Phone: (319) 295-1000
Fax: (319) 295-5429
www.rockwellcollins.com

SAP Aktiengesellschaft
Dietmar Hopp Allee 16
69190 Walldorf
Germany
Phone: +49-6227-7-47474
Toll Free: (800) 225-5627
Fax: +49-6227-7-57575
www.sap.com

**Science Applications
International Corporation
(SAIC)**
10260 Campus Point Drive
San Diego, CA 92121
Phone: (858) 826-6000
Fax: (858) 826-6800
www.saic.com

Siebel Systems, Inc.
2207 Bridgepointe Pkwy.
San Mateo, CA 94404
Phone: (650) 295-5000
Fax: (650) 295-5111
www.siebel.com

Visit Vault at www.vault.com for insider company profiles, expert advice,
career message boards, expert resume reviews, the Vault Job Board and more.

VAULT CAREER LIBRARY   245

High Tech Employer Directory, cont.

Siemens AG, Inc.
Wittelsbacherplatz 2
D-80333 Munich, Germany
Phone: +49-89 636-00
Fax: +49-89 636-52 000
www.siemens.com

Sony Corporation
7-35, Kitashinagawa, 6-chome,
Shinagawa-ku
Tokyo, 141-0001
Japan
Phone: +81-3-5448-2111
Fax: +81-3-5448-2244
www.sony.net

Sun Microsystems, Inc.
4150 Network Circle
Santa Clara, CA 95054
Phone: (650) 960-1300
Fax: (408) 276-3804
www.sun.com

Sybase Inc.
1 Sybase Drive
Dublin, CA 94568
Phone: (925) 236-5000
Fax: (925) 236-4321
www.sybase.com

Symantec Corporation
20330 Stevens Creek Blvd.
Cupertino, CA 95014-2132
Phone: (408) 517-8000
Fax: (408) 253-3968
www.symantec.com

Texas Instruments Incorporated
12500 TI Blvd.
Dallas, TX 75266-4136
Phone: (972) 995-2011
Toll Free: (800) 336-5236
Fax: (972) 995-4360
www.ti.com

Unisys Corporation
Unisys Way
Blue Bell, PA 19424
Phone: (215) 986-4011
Fax: (215) 986-2312
www.unisys.com

Xerox Corporation
800 Long Ridge Road
Stamford, CT 06904
Phone: (203) 968-3000
Fax: (203) 968-3218
www.xerox.com

Hospitality and Tourism

Hospitality and Tourism Industry Overview

Hospitality's broad scope

The hospitality and tourism industry is made up of a variety of interconnected sectors, including lodging (everything from roadside motels to luxury resorts), recreational activities (theme parks, cruises and the like), rental cars and food services. All of these sectors work in tandem with the transportation industry to bring consumers to the destinations where they'll spend money on the local goods and services. In the industry, this is known as an "upstream" effect: the more likely travelers are to board a plane to get somewhere, for instance, the more in demand the hospitality and tourism industry's services become. According to the World Tourism Association, worldwide spending by vacationers was $682 billion in 2005—more than $2 billion per day.

Because of the relationship between tourism, hospitality and transportation, the after-effects of the September 11 attacks, along with other turmoil overseas, had a chilling effect on the industry from 2001 through 2003. The subsequent dip in the economy also led to slashed budgets for business travel, the bread and butter of the lodging and rental car sectors. But recently, a variety of factors—including a perception that the economy is improving, increased confidence about security and lower-cost plane fares—have led to an overall rebound. PKF Hospitality Research predicts that hotel revenue (along with costs, unfortunately) would be up for the fourth consecutive year in 2007.Even high gas prices haven't managed to dampen travelers' wanderlust. According to a survey conducted by AAA, 1.2 percent more people will take a trip of 50 miles or more over the weekend of July 4, 2006 than did the year before. The Travel Industry Association (TIA) forecasted in May 2006 that the average trip would cost $1,000, but they also noted travelers would economize on food and hotels in order to reduce the sting of high prices at the pump.

Checking into hotels

In 2004, according to the Bureau of Labor Statistics (BLS), nearly 62,000 establishments—including upscale hotels, RV parks, motels, resorts, casino hotels, bed and breakfasts and boarding houses—provided overnight accommodation in America, employing 1.8 million wage and salary workers in the process. Two thirds of these workers were employed in service occupations such as housekeeping and food prep.

Hotels fall into five basic categories: commercial, resort, residential, extended-stay and casino, with some commercial hotels classified as conference facilities, featuring spaces designed to accommodate large-scale meetings and events. In recent years, the industry has seen the most growth in extended-stay properties, accommodating guests for visits of five nights or longer. By eliminating traditional services like lobby facilities, 24-hour staff and daily housekeeping, the sector has been able to reap profits. Average revenue per available room (known in the trade as RevPAR) increased 8.2 percent in 2005 to $57.29.

Top hotel corporations include Marriott International, Starwood and Intercontinental. Another hospitality giant is Cendant, considered the world's largest hotel franchiser, with Days Inn, Super 8 and other brands under its roof. In July 2006 Cendant's board voted to divide the company into four parts. Its travel booking services would become Travelport; the Cendant name will be attached to the company that controls the Avis and Budget car rental firms; and the hotels and time shares will be owned by Wyndham Worldwide. Realogy was created to take over the company's real estate functions.

Inhospitable climate

If you've had a bad customer service experience in the hospitality and tourism industry, you're not alone—and the industry itself is taking notice. The industry has struggled for some time with human resource issues, and "the current bad situation

Visit Vault at **www.vault.com** for insider company profiles, expert advice, career message boards, expert resume reviews, the Vault Job Board and more.

VAULT CAREER LIBRARY 247

is worsening," says the International Society of Hospitality Consultants (ISHC). The ISHC frets about the way the "spirit of hospitality is deteriorating," with guest services compromised by staff reductions, high turnover and poorly trained workers. Recent news indicates things are looking up, however: the American Hotel and Lodging Association (AHLA) reported in 2006 that hotel consumer satisfaction had improved by nearly 3 percent over the previous year.

Labor issues also continue to dog the industry. As hotels compete with other sectors like retail and fast food for unskilled and semi-skilled labor, costs are rising, and workers are becoming increasingly demanding of benefits. In addition, for a sector that relied heavily on an immigrant labor population, post-September 11 border tightening has also put strain on the industry. But, according to the ISHC, the challenge which will most affect the lodging industry in 2006 is higher operating costs, especially those associated with labor and fuel, which have certainly taken a bite out of revenue. Hoteliers must also contend with rising insurance premiums (especially in areas prone to natural disasters such as hurricanes), escalated competition between accommodations, stiffer "brand standards" and the rising cost of construction and renovation.

The wired customer

Hotels, along with nearly every other portion of the hospitality and tourism industry, are adjusting to the increased presence of the Internet in travel planning and spending. Industry analysts predict that 60 percent of travel bookings will be made online by 2008. According to a TIA survey, online bookings in 2005 were up 25 percent over 2004, with consumers preferring the comforting glow of their computer screen to waiting on hold (telephone bookings down 16 percent), or, heaven forbid, leaving the house (travel agent bookings were down to a mere 4 percent). The Internet has had the effect of empowering customers, allowing them to comparison shop for the best deals through so-called "e-mediaries" like Expedia, Orbitz and Travelocity, all of which sell rooms and other travel services such as rental cars, often at discounted rates. Consumers' ability to compare prices before booking has created downward pressure on room rates, which, according to the ISHC, will continue to affect hotels' profitability. The flip side to this situation is that, while online hotel and transportation bookings allow customers to compare prices, travelers who book online have a tendency to be profligate with their pinched pennies once they arrive at their destination: the TIA reports that in 2005 online bookers spent more and participated in more activities while on vacation than those who arranged their trips by phone.

Global distribution

At the same time, hotels are becoming more reliant on electronic database systems and the Internet to book rooms. Indeed, across the industry, electronic distribution—an online means of allowing travel agencies, consolidators, consumers and other bookers to access available rooms, rental cars, flights and even golf course tee times—has become the norm. This trend stems from the Global Distribution System (GDS) and Internet Distribution System (IDS) models that form the inner machinery of the travel industry. There are four main GDSs, or booking systems, in the world, allowing access to bookings for airlines, car rentals, hotels and cruise reservations. Known by different names in various parts of the world, the GDSs are familiar to American travel bookers as Amadeus, Galileo (a subsidiary of Travelport), Sabre and Worldspan.

The GDS sector arose in the 1960s as a means for airlines to keep track of their schedules, seat availability and prices. Formed by airline leaders such as American (which founded Sabre), the GDSs were installed in travel agencies in the 1970s, marking one of the first successful business-to-business e-commerce ventures. A few decades later, e-commerce travel sites like Expedia and Travelocity, using Sabre and other GDS systems as their information engines, made travel booking available to the connected masses. In addition, the more than 500,000 travel agents operating worldwide now have a wealth of electronic methods to plug into and shop from. This means that few entities that want to survive in hospitality and tourism can afford to be shut out of these systems.

To be represented on a GDS, a hotel or hotel chain has to select a method of branding, as either a private label chain, part of a larger marketing brand or as one of a collective group of similar properties. In any case, according to the Hotel Electronic

Distribution Network Association (HEDNA), cost per booking for hotels through a GDS or IDS is cheaper than any other distribution method, including bookings made directly through the property.

De-commissioning agencies

But ironically, what started off as a tool to help travel agents access and sell travel to consumers has now led to the steady erosion of the travel agency sector itself, as empowered consumers no longer need to rely on a middleman to purchase airline tickets and even travel packages. The agency industry is dominated by traditional retailers of travel like American Express, Carlson Wagonlit and Navigant. But e-retailer Expedia's position as the 2006 market leader illustrates the agencies' plight. Airlines, once a steady source of income for travel agencies, also have caught on to the diminishing agency trend. Beginning in the mid-1990s, major air carriers, after decades of providing at least a 10 percent commission to agents on sales, slashed or eliminated these commissions entirely. The loss of income drove some agencies out of business, while others consolidated. According to the BLS, the number of travel agents in the U.S. was just under 89,000 in 2005, while the agency reported a number around 100,000 in 2004. Associations such as the American Society of Travel Agents insist that the industry can continue to thrive by providing the extra attention to detail, insider knowledge and customer service that consumers crave.

Feeding the masses

In the vast lodging and recreation territory, there has to be a way to deliver food and other sundries to guests cheaply and efficiently. That's where companies which specialize in outsourcing come in. With a revenue of more than €11.68 billion in 2005, French company Sodexho is a powerhouse in providing outsourced food and services to hospitality facilities (as well as a host of other institutions from nursing homes to elementary schools). It ranks fourth in market capitalization among all players in the restaurant industry, coming in behind McDonald's, Starbucks and Yum! Brands. Another global contender is Aramark, which in 2001 purchased ServiceMaster Management Services and boosted revenues to more than $10 billion in 2005. Aramark scored a huge contract in 2004 to provide food services for the Olympic Village at the Summer Games in Athens, its 13th time providing such services at the competition.

Tours of duty

The good thing about hospitality and tourism is that there's almost always a job to be found. In the US, the travel and tourism industry is expected to contribute 10.5 percent to the GDP and 10 percent of jobs in 2006, according to the World Travel & Tourism Council. The BLS further reports that jobs in accommodation and food services as a whole are expected to increase 17 percent between 2004 and 2014. There are a wide variety of jobs in the industry for people of all skill sets and education levels, and high turnover in the industry means they have a wide availability. Most entry-level jobs in hotels require little training. Housekeeper and janitor positions require the least training and education and fewest opportunities for advancement, though they can be attractive to people who might want seasonal or temporary work. Those who work in guest services, as a host or hostess or desk clerk, can advance to supervisory positions with sufficient experience. Completion of a program in hotel management will lead to more rapid advancement. Hotels may also need people in the food service industry, such as chefs and restaurant staff if they have a restaurant in-house. Hospitality involves 24-hour service, and low seniority may mean working night and weekend shifts, at least initially. Travel agents need at least a high school diploma, good sales, research, and computer skills; though a BA in geography or travel services helps. Currently, 13 states require travel agents to be certified.

Visit Vault at www.vault.com for insider company profiles, expert advice, career message boards, expert resume reviews, the Vault Job Board and more.

VAULT CAREER LIBRARY   249

Hospitality Careers

It isn't easy working in the hospitality industry—guests can be rude, the holiday rush is nightmarish and employees work seven days a week. Hotel workers must put the needs of their guests first and maintain a sunny and accommodating disposition at all times—not easy when you have been working for 12 hours on Christmas Day without a break. However, the perks in the business are such that hospitality workers put up with the disadvantages of the industry.

It takes a team

Every member of a hotel staff, from housekeeping to the hotel manager, is responsible for the seamless operation of the establishment. At smaller hotels and motels, the responsibility for overseeing rooms, food and beverage service, registration and overall management can fall on the shoulders of a single manager.

Large hotels, such as The Plaza in New York, employ hundreds of workers. To start, the general manager may be aided by a staff of assistant managers, each with his or her own department to supervise. The hotel manager sets the establishment's standards of operation (within the owners' or executives' guidelines); it is the job of the assistant managers to see that these are executed adroitly. The general manager sets room rates, allocates funds to departments, approves expenditures and establishes standards for service that employees in housekeeping, decor, food quality and banquet operations must offer to guests. Many hotels have resident managers, who live in the hotel and are on hand 24 hours a day for guests and staff (though they usually work a standard eight-hour day).

The housekeeping staff is responsible for maintaining banquet, meeting and guest rooms—right down to the mints on the pillows—and ensuring that public areas are clean, orderly and well-kept. Almost all hotels also have food and beverage managers on hand to supervise hotel restaurants, bars, banquet rooms and room service. These employees plan menus and direct food presentation and preparation. Hotels employ a long list of support staff in various areas, including accountants, entertainers, maintenance workers, security officers, gardeners and everything in between. The behind-the-scenes services consist of sales, administration and marketing personnel.

You're working late

Although hotel staff, managers in particular, officially work eight-hour days, the jobs almost invariably require overtime. And since hotels require 24-hour service, shifts can vary and sometimes be very hectic. In the hospitality industry, details are of the utmost importance and last-minute preparations and crisis aversion are par for the course. As compensation, however, hotel employees get paid sick leave and vacation, as well as full benefits (especially if they work for large corporations) and discounted or free food. Many hotels also offer free or cheap housing within the hotel itself to some employees, such as the resident manager.

Although in the past, most hotel managers have been hired from food and beverage, front desk, housekeeping and sales positions without formal education, employers now give hiring preference to individuals with degrees in hotel and restaurant management. Internships and part-time jobs also give a step up when it comes to getting hired for a management-track position. Graduates of hotel or restaurant management programs usually start as trainee assistant managers or at least advance to such positions quickly. New hotels without formal on-the-job training programs often prefer experienced personnel for higher-level positions.

The majority of the jobs in the industry (more than 60 percent) are in service and administrative support. Large hotel and motel chains offer better opportunities for advancement than small, independently owned establishments and offer transfers to other hotels or motels in the chain. Hotel personnel are encouraged (and are in some cases required) to move around to different hotels several times in their careers.

Travel Agent

Overview

A travel agent is a harried traveler's best friend. Amateurs who have attempted to arrange their own airfare, hotel accommodations, or vacation schedule know that can be frustrating and fruitless without the insider savvy of a travel agent. But travel agents don't just book reservations. They give advice, weather forecasts and restaurant suggestions too.

The training required to become a travel agent is highly specialized; many agents have certifications from six- to 12-week college or continuing education courses. Even with their training and indispensability to their clients, travel agents aren't very well paid. Airlines have "capped" the commissions which they used to pay travel agents to a flat rate for fares over $500; previously an agent received 10 percent of the total fare, regardless of the price. It's not as if travel agents have a light work schedule, either. They often stay at their desks until at least 7 p.m., or later if a client should call with a missed flight or a lost passport. Travel agents generally choose their career path out of a love of travel and customer satisfaction, rather than expectations of fame and wealth.

There is, however, a wealth of job opportunities for travel agents—right now, anyway. This is something that is never stable for agents entering the job market, since the travel industry is easily upset by economic fluctuations and international political crises.

Career path

Some colleges offer four-year degrees in travel and tourism, while others have courses that relate to the industry. While a college degree is not required to become a travel agent, some employers prefer agents to have a background in computer science, geography, communications, or foreign languages. Courses in accounting and business management are also a wise investment, as many agents consider starting their own agencies. Six- to 12-week programs offered at community colleges and continuing education programs are comprehensive and are usually sufficient training for beginning travel agents. Some agents start as reservation clerks or receptionists in agencies, advance to office manager or other managerial positions and eventually move on to become full-fledged agents. Agents in larger firms often specialize by type of travel (leisure vs. business), or by destination (The Galapogos Islands vs. Iceland).

Travel agents who wish to advance quickly can take advanced courses from the Institute of Certified Travel Agents. Upon completion of the courses, an agent becomes a certified travel counselor. The American Society of Travel Agents (ASTA) offers a correspondence course as well. These certifications can be helpful for those wishing to start their own businesses, as is gaining formal supplier or corporation approval (airlines, ship lines, and rail lines), since approval is necessary before travel agents are authorized to receive commissions. Certain states also require some form of registration or certification of retail sellers of travel services.

Vault Q&A: Nancy Vu, Manager of Field Employment & Recruiting Hilton Hotels

In 2005, Hilton Hotels relaunched its management training program, called the Leader-In-Training (LIT) program. In its first year, the company hired 28 recent graduates for the program. Nancy Vu, Manager of Field Employment & Recruiting at Hilton Hotels, took time out from her schedule to talk with Vault from Hilton's corporate headquarters in California.

Vault: I understand that this is a new, or relaunched, management training program. Tell me about the genesis of the program.

Visit Vault at **www.vault.com** for insider company profiles, expert advice, career message boards, expert resume reviews, the Vault Job Board and more.

VAULT CAREER LIBRARY 251

Vu: We started in 1999, when Hilton Hotels Corporation acquired Promus Hotels Company, we acquired four new hotel brands—Doubletree, Embassy Suites Hotels, Hampton and Homewood Suites by Hilton—and thousands of additional team members. Prior to the acquisition, we had a management development program called the HPDP [Hilton Professional Development Program] in place. After the merger we reviewed the program and realized that it really catered to just the Hilton brand, so we had to implement a new program that worked with all of the brands.

Vault: How long was HPDP around?

Vu: Since about 1988. We have directors and VP who came through that program and are still with us.

Vault: So what's new about this program?

Vu: What we've done is taken a look at that old program, and looked at how we can revamp it so we can tie together the various properties, so that if someone's a trainee at a Hilton or a Doubletree, they could eventually become a manager at a Doubletree or any other brand.

Vault: How does the program work?

Vu: It's a six- to eight-month program. We have six different tracks: Sales, Food & Beverage, Revenue Management, Front Office, Housekeeping, and Human Resources.

Each trainee is assigned to a training hotel—and this hotel could be a Doubletree, a Hilton or an Embassy. The first three to four months is general rotation in the hotel. A new team member goes through 11 or 12 different areas of the hotel—every major department is covered including property operations, finance, human resources, engineering, banquets and others.

Vault: What happens after that initial period of rotations?

Vu: The last three to four months, they spend in their area of specialization in the same hotel. After that, they are placed in an entry-level management position. So if you're on the sales track, you'll be a sales manager.

Vault: Do the employees stay with the hotel they were at?

Vu: More than likely they'll end up staying in their training hotel, but if not, they'll stay in their region. [Hilton has six geographic regions: Northeast, Southeast, Central, West, Hawaii and Focus Service & International.]

Vault: How do you place the trainees?

Vu: The SVP of Operations looks for areas of need in hotels, and then we try to find a win-win situation, where the hotel need matches with the candidate's area of interest. For example, the Hilton New York has a revenue management trainee and a front office trainee this year. So again, using the Hilton New York example we looked for students specifically interested in the Northeast, and specifically interested in sales or front office. We don't want to put them in a track where they don't want to be.

Vault: What are the requirements for the program?

Vu: You have to have a minimum 2.8 GPA and you have to be enrolled in the hotel program at your college or university. We recruited at 16 schools this past year.

Vault: Why do you have the trainees go through the initial rotation period?

Vu: If you're going to become a general manager one day you're going to have to understand all the different departments and functions. The more well rounded you are in understanding all of operations, the better you're going to be as a general manager or any executive level position. We want them to understand how each department links to one another.

Our front office people stay in very close contact with sales, our sales stay in very close contact with revenue management. There's so much interaction within each of the departments—engineering/maintenance are in close contact with housekeeping, because they are the team members who are actually in contact with our customers. We want our trainees to get their feet wet in all these areas. That way they have a better understanding of what goes on in the rest of the hotel.

That said, not everybody [that goes through the program] wants to become a general manager. Some students go through this training program find they love working in other aspects of the hotel. For example, someone who has an affinity for the front office could start as a Director of Front Office at a 200-room hotel and work their way up to Director of Front Office at a 1,200-room hotel.

Vault: Is there an orientation that starts the program?

Vu: We held a kick-off meeting in mid-June with all of the trainees where they had an opportunity to meet with each other and start building a network that will serve as a support group while they're in the program. Also, there are many executive committee members at corporate headquarters that attended the meeting and offered support and advice.

Vault: Is there any classroom training as part of the program?

Vu: We conducted a few training courses during the orientation. Within the program itself, in addition to whatever training they have on the job, they are required to attend or participate in specific training courses.

Vault: What sort of courses are these?

Vu: There are diversity training programs, safety training and others. We have those training requirements for any manager that joins Hilton. And if we're grooming people in this program to be managers, then it's our expectation that they're going to take these training courses during their training. Also, as part of the program, they're required to do a project. They thought they were done with projects after graduating, but no.

Vault: What sort of projects do they work on?

Vu: It's determined by what department they work in. For example, in Sales, maybe they'd be asked to participate in a sales blitz, a promotion where you're improving the hotel's visibility among all your clients or potential clients. For Food and Beverage it could be creating a brand new menu item for the restaurant.

Visit Vault at **www.vault.com** for insider company profiles, expert advice, career message boards, expert resume reviews, the Vault Job Board and more.

VAULT CAREER LIBRARY

253

Hospitality and Tourism Employer Directory

Sodexho

200 Continental Drive
Suite 400
Newark, DE 19713
www.sodexhousa.com

Undergraduate schools Sodexho recruits from:

University of Central Florida; San Diego State University - Imperial Valley Campus; California State Polytechnic University; North Carolina Central University; University of Maryland - Eastern Shore; Brigham Young University; Howard University; San Francisco State University (Assc Member); Culinary Institute of America; Kendall College; Lexington College; Purdue University; Michigan State University; Morgan State University; Widener University; Indiana University of Pennsylvania; New Mexico State University; University of Memphis; Trident Technical College; Massachusetts Maritime; University of Massachusetts; Johnson & Wales-Providence; Johnson & Wales - Charlotte; University of Wisconsin - Stout; Kansas State University; Mercyhurst College; Penn State University; University of Houston; Tuskegee University

Sodexho is the leading food and facilities management services company in North America and a member of Sodexho Alliance. Every day more than 120,000 Sodexho employees work to improve the quality of daily life for our clients and customers all over the U.S. and Canada. Sodexho Inc. offers innovative outsourcing solutions to more than 6,000 corporations, health care, long term care and retirement centers, schools, college campuses, military and remote sites throughout North America. Sodexho USA proudly serves as the official food service provider for the US Marine Corps.

Accor

2, rue de la Mare Neuve
91021 Évry Cedex, France
Phone: +33-1-69-36-80-80
www.accor.com

Aramark Corporation

ARAMARK Tower, 1101 Market St.
Philadelphia, PA 19107-2988
Phone: (215) 238-3000
Fax: (215) 238-3333
www.aramark.com

Budget Rent A Car System, Inc.

6 Sylvan Way
Parsippany, NJ 07054
Phone: (973) 496-3500
Fax:(973) 496-7999
www.budget.com

Carlson Companies, Inc.

701 Carlson Parkway
Minnetonka, MN 55305
Phone: (763) 212-1000
Fax: (763) 212-2219
www.carlson.com

Carnival Corporation

3655 N.W. 87th Ave.
Miami, FL 33178-2428
Phone: (305) 599-2600
Fax: (305) 406-4700
www.carnivalcorp.com

Cendant Corporation

9 W. 57th St.
New York, NY 10019
Phone: (212) 413-1800
Fax: (212) 413-1918
www.cendant.com

Cintas Corporation

6800 Cintas Blvd.
Cincinnati, OH 45262-5737
Phone: (513) 459-1200
Fax: (513) 573-4130
www.cintas-corp.com

Compass Group

Compass House, Guildford Street
Chertsey
Surrey KT16 9BQ
United Kingdom
Phone: +44-1932-573-000
www.compass-group.com

Enterprise Rent-A-Car Company

600 Corporate Park Dr.
St. Louis, MO 63105
Phone: (314) 512-5000
Fax: (314) 512-4706
www.enterprise.com

The Hertz Corporation

225 Brae Blvd.
Park Ridge, NJ 07656-0713
Phone: (201) 307-2000
Fax: (201) 307-2644
www.hertz.com

Hospitality and Tourism Employer Directory, cont.

Hilton Hotels Corporation

9336 Civic Center Dr.

Beverly Hills, CA 90210

Phone: (310) 278-4321

Fax: (310) 205-7678

www.hilton.com

Hyatt Corporation

200 W. Madison St.

Chicago, IL 60606

Phone: (312) 750-1234

Fax: (312) 750-8550

www.hyatt.com

InterActiveCorp

152 W. 57th St.

New York, NY 10019

Phone: (212) 314-7300

Fax: (212) 314-7309

www.iac.com

InterContinental Hotels Group PLC

67 Alma Rd.

Windsor

SL4 3HD

United Kingdom

Phone: +44-1753-410-100

Fax: +44-1753-410-101

www.ihgplc.com

Kohler Co.

444 Highland Dr.

Kohler, WI 53044

Phone: (920) 457-4441

Fax: (920) 457 1271

www.kohlerco.com

Royal Caribbean Cruises Ltd.

1050 Caribbean Way

Miami, FL 33132

Phone: (305) 539-6000

Fax: (305) 374-7354

www.rccl.com

Starwood Hotels & Resorts Worldwide, Inc.

1111 Westchester Ave.

White Plains, NY 10604

Phone: (914) 640-8100

Fax:(914) 640-8310

www.starwood.com

Vanguard Car Rental USA, Inc.

200 S. Andrews Ave.

Fort Lauderdale, FL 33301

Phone: (954) 320-4000

Fax: (954) 320-4456

www.vanguardcar.com

Visit Vault at **www.vault.com** for insider company profiles, expert advice, career message boards, expert resume reviews, the Vault Job Board and more.

VAULT CAREER LIBRARY

255

Human Resources

Every organization has people, which means every organization needs Human Resources (HR) professionals. HR helps manage and develop the people in an organization. Sometimes called "Personnel" or "Talent Management," HR is the function in charge of an organization's employees, which includes finding and hiring employees, helping them grow and learn in the organization, and managing the process when an employee leaves. Human Resources takes care of people from the time they're interested in the organization to long after they leave.

The History of Human Resources

Now a thriving, growing profession, Human Resources wasn't always a key part of most organizations—if at all. Until the early 1900s, all human resources functions were typically handled by the workers themselves or their bosses (often called master craftsmen). As more workers were needed, master craftsmen would just go out and find them (talk about the birth of recruiting!)

When the 1900s brought inventions and changes in the workplace, like machines that automated production, human resources began to take shape. The addition of machines made factories run more quickly and smoothly, but also meant that the workers had to learn how to use them, and forced factory managers to introduce rules and procedures on the factory floor.

Frederick Taylor, a businessman and researcher, first introduced the concept of scientific management. Taylor's theory took workplace rules and procedures one step further, declaring that there was only one best way to do a job. He spent years collecting data on the tasks making up specific jobs and then researching the workers who performed each small task. Workers who performed well, following tasks to the letter, remained employed and were paid well. Those who didn't were among the first to hear "you're fired."

Taylor's research was the first to increase worker productivity, but his robotic approach didn't prove to be an effective management tool. Still, his work showed the importance of managing workers to increase a company's success. While Taylor's work focused more on company success than that of the worker, it propelled many companies to begin to personalize the workplace, anticipating the first appearance of HR. One of the earliest HR roles was that of a welfare secretary whose role was to look out for the welfare of the workers. An ancestor of what's now called a Benefits Manager, welfare secretaries created libraries and recreation areas in the workplace as well as primitive medical and health programs.

But HR really took shape in the 1930s when a company called Western Electric asked a team of researchers to figure out how to increase workers' productivity at one of their plants in Chicago. The Hawthorne Studies, taking their name after the targeted plant, set out to determine whether changing the lighting in the plant could help the employees work faster. What they found instead was how important it was for plant managers to pay attention to the workers, reward them for a good job and make sure they were satisfied. The idea of happy workers being productive workers took hold and still remains true today. If a company wants to perform well, it has to create and manage a content workforce. HR plays a critical role in making sure that happens.

The Hawthorne Studies fueled the study of worker behavior in organizations, and what was called behavioral science. The growth of behavioral science as a field studied how jobs and the workplace affect workers and how workers affect the performance of a company.

The study of behavioral science reinforced the importance of welfare secretaries. The secretaries' jobs became more and more complex as governments introduced labor laws to keep up with the changing workplace. These laws, restricting the rights of both employers and employees, required the welfare secretaries to keep paper records of employees and their activities. One of the first human resources laws, the Fair Labor Standards Act (FLSA) created a minimum wage, set rules for child labor and required employers to treat employees fairly in regards to wage and hours worked.

Visit Vault at www.vault.com for insider company profiles, expert advice, career message boards, expert resume reviews, the Vault Job Board and more.

VAULT CAREER LIBRARY   257

In many industries, workers also began organizing into unions—groups of workers banding together to lobby for rights in the workplace. New laws around union activity also required companies and welfare secretaries to understand and comply with the laws.

Many companies began hiring multiple welfare secretaries—one responsible for hiring employees, another responsible for employee benefits and perhaps another to train employees on the factory floors. These specialty areas evolved into the specialty areas of the Human Resources profession today.

Human Resources Today

Today, human resources is essential to the success of business. The level of importance HR holds does differ from organization to organization, but businesses consistently rely on HR professionals to help them through high-growth times and periods of turmoil. Regardless of how successful (or not) an organization is, there is always a need for HR staff. The welfare secretary title may be long gone, but the idea of having Human Resources professionals focus on specific areas of managing and developing a company's workers has remained. Now, in most organizations, there are HR professionals who focus specifically on hiring, training, benefits, labor relations, health and safety and more.

While it's important to like working with and wanting to help people to be successful in HR, that's definitely not the only skill or attribute you need to be a successful HR professional. HR is about creating systems, processes and environments where employees perform better and are satisfied, and there are many different career paths and opportunities in the profession. For example, HR professionals can take center stage as a recruiter or trainer. In these roles, you're interacting with people all day long, whether conducting interviews or running a training course. But HR professionals can also serve behind the scenes, administering payroll, tracking HR metrics (statistics about company workers) or running an organization's Human Resource Information System (HRIS), technical databases where all employee data is stored and managed.

While HR continues to grow as a function, in many companies it does not carry the importance or value of its colleagues in finance, sales or marketing. Know that as satisfying as an HR career can be, the profession still struggles to gain respect in many places.

What Do HR Professionals Do?

Typical HR responsibilities are focused in major areas such as recruiting and staffing, compensation and benefits, training and learning, labor and employee relations, and organization development. Most HR professionals have experience in one or more of these specialty areas. These areas all deal with helping employees in an organization perform more effectively and satisfactorily on the job.

Recruiting and staffing

You're either in or you're out. When an employee leaves and a job opens up or new jobs are created, HR is usually in charge of the process. Recruiting and staffing is one of the largest areas of HR. Recruiters start the process—working with specific departments to write job descriptions and understand what skills and abilities the new employee should have. Then they're off and running—responsible for finding candidates, determining who might be a good fit, conducting interviews and making job offers. While recruiters involve department employees in the process to interview and make the hiring decisions, it's the recruiters who are usually in charge of finding the talent, managing interview scheduling, negotiating offers and making sure departments have all the information they need to make the best hiring decisions possible.

While recruiters work to find and hire the talent, staffing experts determine who should go where. They strategize with different departments to anticipate hiring needs and help determine where a new employee might best fit in an organization.

Staffing professionals are heavily relied on in high-growth companies to make sure the company is prepared to hire enough new employees to grow the company, and that employees are in the right positions.

Recruiting and staffing professionals are also called upon to help an organization market to prospective employees. This can include creating and managing recruiting events, designing marketing pieces such as company brochures and commercials, and staffing career fairs to educate prospective employees about open opportunities. Many organizations also have recruiting and staffing professionals dedicated to working with universities. These roles are focused on finding talent on undergraduate and graduate school campuses and can include a great deal of travel and campus presentations.

Compensation and benefits

Finding talent is important, but employees also have to be paid. HR, specifically compensation and benefits professionals, are in charge of making sure new employees are given an appropriate salary and benefits, and current employees continually receive their salary and benefits.

Compensation experts focus on the money. This includes processing regular payroll (making sure that the check is in the mail) and payroll changes, including raises and tax changes. Compensation experts also work closely with an organization's finance department to ensure salaries stay within each department's budget, as well as conducting and researching salary surveys to make sure they're paying the going rate.

Benefits professionals also have to make sure employees are taken care of—they specialize in helping employees with medical and other company benefits. This may include teaching new employees about their medical plan choices, implementing and managing the plans offered by the company, and managing the cost of benefits for the company.

Compensation and benefits professionals are also often tasked with communicating salary and benefits information to employees. This may include marketing and promoting new benefits offerings to a company or managing an company's Open Enrollment Period—a brief period of time where employees can change medical plans and other benefit options.

One-on-one counseling may also be part of the job. If an employee leaves an organization, the benefits manager may counsel the employee on access to health insurance available after departure. Employees also often seek guidance on understanding their compensation packages, making changes to employment tax forms or managing a difficult medical insurance claim.

Training and learning

Part teacher, part manager, part leader—that's a training professional. Helping employees become oriented to a new job or company is just one of the many responsibilities of training and learning professionals. Sometimes called training, or learning and development, it's helping both new and tenured employees develop and grow as professionals both on and off the job.

Training and learning professionals are typically responsible for running programs designed to educate and develop employees. This can include programs for an entire employee population, such as new hire orientation or ethics training, but also includes more specialized programs for different groups of workers within a company, like online training courses, in-class instruction or on-the-job training.

Training managers, for example, are called upon to do everything from registering and tracking training courses, to developing new courses and evaluating the effectiveness of training programs after they happen. This may include designing surveys or determining if newly trained employees perform better than they did before the training. They also may be responsible for providing information to employees on training classes and programs outside the company.

In some organizations, training and learning professionals actually deliver the training courses. They might create a presentation skills course and then send trainers on the road to teach the new course to employees around the country. Since it's often cheaper to train current employees rather than hire new ones, training and learning is becoming increasingly

Visit Vault at www.vault.com for insider company profiles, expert advice, career message boards, expert resume reviews, the Vault Job Board and more.

VAULT CAREER LIBRARY   259

important in the business world. A company's strong commitment to training and development is also a boost to its workers' morale.

Labor and employee relations

Just like welfare secretaries responded to new laws in the early 1900s, labor and employee relations professionals ensure that anything dealing with employee contracts, rights, responsibilities and complaints is taken care of right quick.

Labor relations is a function typically found in companies whose employees are members of unions. Labor Relations professionals are called upon to deal directly with unions, doing everything from interpreting current union contracts to negotiating new ones. They also analyze and monitor union activity and work with unions during organizing campaigns—the time when unions recruit new members.

Employee relations professionals need to be familiar and comfortable with the law; they are also responsible for equal employment opportunity and affirmative action programs. For government agencies or companies that do work for the government, this may include creating reports to demonstrate a company is complying with the law and making an effort to hire and retain employees from underrepresented ethnicities. Other key responsibilities may include counseling or conflict resolution within an organization, helping employees who are dealing with disagreements in the workplace or have issues preventing them from doing their jobs.

Labor and employee relations is not found in every human resources department. Organizations that don't have government contracts or unionized employees may rely on outside attorneys or consultants to deal with any legal issues or employee conflicts that arise.

Organization development (OD)

While developing employees is important, perhaps just as important is developing an organization. A relatively new field, organization development focuses on evaluating how a company is structured and how employees work together to see where improvements can be made. Also referred to as organization effectiveness, this might include helping to restructure the chain of command in a department to helping employees cope with a major change, such as the introduction of a new company-wide technical system.

OD professionals are experts in understanding behavior and psychology. They often act as internal consultants, helping their fellow employees understand how a new company program might affect the employees' behavior.

They often work closely with Training Professionals to address development needs for the company. OD Professionals may develop company-wide team-building activities or introduce new programs for leadership development.

OD specialists often manage the performance review process, making sure that employees are evaluated and moved within the organization based on how well they're working. OD Specialists may also help companies develop succession plans (determining who is in line to be the next person in a leadership position, such as CEO or CFO) and mentoring programs, making sure less experienced employees can learn from their more experienced comrades. OD professionals may also be called upon to help an employee address individual issues through executive coaching, or a department address a leadership or performance challenge.

Less common OD work may include coaching or career development. Coaches, common at the executive level, help employees overcome poor teamwork or management skills. Many large firms are hiring external coaches, or creating coaching functions in order to help valuable employees deal with singular issues that may prevent them from being promoted.

Health and safety

Factory machines, hazardous chemicals and construction sites are all potentially dangerous situations for workers. This is where Health and Safety Professionals come in. One of the oldest HR specialties, Health and Safety professionals are responsible for ensuring a safe working environment for all workers—this is more of an issue in industries with risky work settings such as manufacturing, healthcare and construction. While all organizations must protect the safety of their employees while at work, it is more complicated in industries that have worksites beyond a typical office environment.

One of the major components of the role of a Health and Safety Professional is to be proactive—assessing a work environment to anticipate where the dangers might be and correcting them before an injury occurs. This might include periodic tours of a work site, or research into the latest workplace safety options.

Health and Safety Professionals are also responsible for reacting to issues, concerns or problems related to the workplace environment. They might handle a complaint from a worker about a dangerous factory machine or an on-site injury. They work closely with compensation and benefits professionals to handle any injuries and determine how to prevent future injuries from occurring.

Working with an organization's legal team and employee law specialists is also part of the role. Health and Safety Professionals are responsible for following Federal and State rules governing workplace safety including, in some industries, submitting reports that demonstrate a company's compliance with the law.

Why HR?

While HR professionals have varying degrees of interaction with an organization's employees, all HR people can enjoy the satisfaction of knowing that the work they do has a direct impact on people every day. HR professionals like helping employees navigate through tough problems and get back to normal on the job. Whether it's helping an employee overcome a performance problem or fix an expensive and stressful medical claim, there is an inherent satisfaction in these types of tasks.

They also enjoy the ability to interact with different groups of people; HR professionals may be working with employees in many different parts of the company. Organization development specialists may act like internal consultants helping different departments in a company work better together. This means they might be working with a sales team one week and a product design team the next. So there is a ton of variety in their day-to-day tasks.

In his role at Bank of America, Phil Skeath likes the diversity of projects. "Each time I am on a new project," he says, "I find myself identifying general concepts I learned in my educational experience, adapting them, and applying them to a specific issue in the Bank."

They also like contributing to the business and bottom line. For example, one of the most common issues CFOs are facing in 2005 (according to *CFO Magazine*) is the rising cost of healthcare. HR and benefits professionals who analyze how to lower these costs can save a company millions of dollars. Talk about making an impact.

Why not?

For most HR professionals, the positives of working in HR (such as extending a job offer to a very excited job candidate) are enough to outweigh the drawbacks (in the opposite category, downsizing or laying off employees). Otherwise, they wouldn't be there in the first place. But no job is perfect. Even rock stars have to deal with annoying paparazzi and screaming fans. While it's highly unlikely you'll be chased by reporters working in HR, you may be chased by unhappy employees. One of the toughest things about working in HR is providing a service many employees take for granted. No one says "thanks HR" every time they get a paycheck. But if something goes wrong, if employees don't get paid, if benefits disappear or new employees aren't trained properly, you may end up with a mailbox full of angry callers to contend with.

Visit Vault at www.vault.com for insider company profiles, expert advice, career message boards, expert resume reviews, the Vault Job Board and more.

VAULT CAREER LIBRARY 261

Like many professions, starting out in HR you may also have your fair share of administrative work. Many HR careers may begin with processing paperwork for new employees, or entering and maintaining resumes in an online database. This might seem like menial work, especially if you've just received a college degree, but don't walk away too quickly. These roles, while tedious, provide a great learning opportunity and a chance to prove you're ready for more responsibilities.

HR also suffers from some common misconceptions, like being a touchy-feely profession or being female-dominated; we'll go into some of these misconceptions and how to deal with them later in this guide.

Ready to help your colleagues and organization perform better? Before you determine what type of HR role you might best be cast in, it's important to understand that HR as a function isn't the same in every organization.

Human Resource Management (HRM)

Human Resource Management (HRM) is the set of traditional HR activities that manage or support the people in the organization, and every working organization has to have at least one person responsible for HRM. The major areas of HRM include:

- Recruiting and Staffing
- Compensation and Benefits
- Labor and Employee Relations
- Health and Safety

In HRM roles, professionals need to keep the HR motor humming and wheels turning. Imagine if you stopped receiving your paycheck or if your company stopped recruiting altogether. HRM functions are key to keeping organizations running smoothly, and HRM professionals are responsible for preventing any interruption in services that employees expect.

HRM professionals are also responsible to the organization as a whole. Running all of these processes can cost a lot of money, and it is up to HRM professionals to make decisions that help save the company money and make sure employees are well-served. In each of the major areas of HRM, professionals are continually evaluating processes and implementing new programs and systems to better serve the organization. Examples include:

- Recruiting and Staffing: recruiting management systems (RMS) or applicant tracking systems (ATS) are the latest trend in electronically managing the influx of resumes during busy recruiting times. These systems save organizations money by streamlining the recruiting process and requiring fewer staff members to manage employee records.

- Labor and Employee Relations: legal training for managers on topics such as sexual harassment and workplace law is becoming more and more common, in order to proactively reduce lawsuits related to workplace behavior.

- Health and Safety: while injuries at plants and hazardous sites are common, HR professionals are also recognizing the increase in office injuries; many Health and Safety professionals are introducing ergonomically correct office furniture. While these fancy chairs and glare-reducing computer screens may be expensive, such nvestments can prevent future injuries and their associated costs.

- Compensation and Benefits: benefits outsourcing is a popular way to reduce costs and responsibility for an organization. Some Compensation and Benefits professionals work with outside vendors to manage programs such as an employee stock purchase plan. Since these outside vendors already have the expertise and systems in place to manage these programs, it saves the company the expense of creating them from scratch.

Companies such as The Home Depot are well known for their HR practices, and are consistently looking for ways to ease and automate the function in order to serve customers, and ultimately the organization, better. The Home Depot has become more recently renowned for creatively recruiting veterans who have recently finished their military careers. Since advertising on online job boards can be expensive, finding new channels to recruit prospective employees is an important way to save valuable recruiting dollars.

As a Human Resources VP for a consulting firm professes, improving the way employees are served is an important part of the job. "In the last five years, over 75% of our HR transactions have been automated to better serve our customers. We created a company Intranet and put our benefits elections process online as well as all of our employee policies and procedures. No more paper!"

HRM professionals are also often charged with reporting HR's return on investment (ROI) to the company through tracking HR metrics (statistics on how a company's employees are performing) and demonstrating the value HR brings to the company. Compensation and benefits professionals might track how much employees are spending on healthcare costs and seek ways to reduce them. On the other hand, an employee relations professional might track statistics on how many minorities are employed in an organization for an affirmative action report. Measuring such activity is important for HRM professionals to show their commitment to an organization's bottom line.

HR management professionals must continually be thinking about ways to better serve and save a company money at the same time.

Common Human Resource Management (HRM) Roles

Common HRM roles include:

- Compensation Manager
- Senior Recruiter
- Health and Safety Manager
- Employment Lawyer
- Labor Relations Specialist
- Benefits Specialist
- HR Generalist

Human Resource Development (HRD)

Human Resource Development (HRD) is the second part (albeit much smaller) of the HR world. If HRM professionals are keeping the wheels turning smoothly, HRD professionals are helping them turn faster and better. Human Resource Development refers to the activities in an organization that help develop and grow employees. Many organizations simply refer to HRD as training or learning and development but in reality, it's much more than that. HRD includes:

- Training and learning
- Organization development, which includes:
  - Succession planning (determining who is next in line for a CEO or other senior job)
  - Coaching (helping employees overcome on-the-job problems)
  - Performance management (those pesky performance reviews)

HRD is the area of HR that is growing most quickly as organizations recognize the need to go way beyond simply managing their workforce. While smaller organizations often have HR Generalists assume the responsibility for training alongside other HR tasks, large companies such as Medtronic, Bank of America and Texas Instruments have entire functions devoted to subsets of HRD such as organization development.

"Organization development is a key part of Human Resources," says Phil Skeath, a performance improvement consultant at Bank of America. "We are business partners who support our line managers' needs, but we are also an integral part in driving the company's strategy."

Visit Vault at **www.vault.com** for insider company profiles, expert advice, career message boards, expert resume reviews, the Vault Job Board and more.

VAULT CAREER LIBRARY   **263**

HRD professionals may be responsible for a certain subset of the workforce (such as training the sales force), or may serve as internal consultants working on projects as they arise, such as helping to restructure a department or working on the succession plan for an entire division. Other HRD responsibilities include employee performance evaluations, training new employees, and helping companies deal with change as the result of a new program, technology, merger or acquisition.

HRD careers are growing every year. Training and development is one area in which the Bureau of Labor Statistics (BLS) predicts growth in 2005 and beyond. This is due not only to how complex jobs are becoming, but also the aging of the workforce, and the many changes in technology requiring more and more training and development programs for workers. What does this mean for HR professionals? HRD might well be an increasingly popular career path.

Because HRD is not only growing, but is structured very differently from organization to organization, if you see HRD as a viable career path, it's important to research where it fits in specific companies. Organizations that only have a training and learning function may not see as much value in HRD as a company that has a specific organization development function.

Human Resources Employer Directory

Buck Consultants
One Pennsylvania Plaza
New York, NY 10119
Phone: (212) 330-1000
Fax: (212) 695-4184
www.buckconsultants.com

ADP TotalSource Group
10200 Sunset Drive
Miami, FL 33173
Phone: (305) 630-1000
Fax: (305) 630-2006
www.adptotalsource.com

Adecco SA
Sägereistrasse 10
8152 Glattbrugg
Switzerland
Phone: + 41 44 878 8888
Fax: + 41 44 829 8888
www.adecco.com

Convergys
201 E. 4th Street
Cincinnati, OH 45202
Phone: (513) 723-7000
Fax: (513) 421-8624
www.convergys.com

Hay Group
The Wanamaker Building
100 Penn Square East
Philadelphia, PA 19107
Phone: (215) 861-2000
Fax: (215) 861-2111
www.haygroup.com

Hewitt Associates
100 Half Day Road
Lincolnshire, IL 60069
Phone: (847) 295-5000
Fax: (847) 295-7634
www.hewitt.com

Kelly Services, Inc.
999 W. Big Beaver Road
Troy, MI 48084
Phone: (248) 362-4444
Fax: (248) 244-4360
www.kellyservices.com

Manpower Inc.
5301 N. Ironwood Road
Milwaukee, WI 53217
Phone: (414) 961-1000
Fax: (414) 906-7985
www.manpower.com

Mercer Human Resource Consulting
1166 Avenue of the Americas
New York, NY 10036
Phone: (212) 345-7000
Fax: (212) 345-7414
www.mercerHR.com

Paychex, Inc.
911 Panorama Trail South
Rochester, NY 14625-2396
Phone: (585) 385-6666
Fax: (585) 383-3428
www.paychex.com

Robert Half International Inc.
2884 Sand Hill Road
Menlo Park, CA 94025
Phone: (650) 234-6000
Fax: (650) 234-6999
www.rhii.com

Spherion
2050 Spectrum Blvd.
Fort Lauderdale, FL 33309
Phone: (954) 308-7600
Fax: (954) 308-7666
www.spherion.com

Towers Perrin
263 Tresser Blvd.
Stamford, CT 06901
Phone: (203) 326-5400
www.towersperrin.com

Watson Wyatt Worldwide
901 North Glebe Road
Arlington, VA 22203
Phone: (703) 258-8000
Fax: (703) 258-8585
www.watsonwyatt.com

Visit Vault at **www.vault.com** for insider company profiles, expert advice,
career message boards, expert resume reviews, the Vault Job Board and more.

VAULT CAREER LIBRARY

265

Investment Management

How many industries can you think of that impact households all over the world? Very few. That is one of the many exciting aspects of the asset management industry—more people than ever before are planning for their future financial needs, and as a result, the industry is more visible and important than ever. The asset management community seeks to preserve and grow capital for individuals and institutional investors alike.

Investment management vs. asset management

A quick note about the terms **investment management** and **asset management**: these terms are often used interchangeably. They refer to the same practice—the professional management of assets through investment. Investment management is used a bit more often when referring to the activity or career (i.e., "I'm an investment manager" or "That firm is gaining a lot of business in investment management"), whereas "asset management" is used more with reference to the industry itself (i.e., "The asset management industry").

More stability

Because of the stability of cash flows generated by the industry, investment management provides a relatively stable career when compared to some other financial services positions (most notably investment banking). Investment management firms are generally paid a set fee as a percentage of assets under management. (The fee structure varies, and sometimes is both an asset-centered fee plus a performance fee, especially for institutional investors.) Still, even when investment management fees involve a performance incentive, the business is much less cyclical than cousins like investment banking. Banking fees depend on transactions. When banking activities such as IPOs and M&A transactions dry up, so do fees for investment banks, which translates into layoffs of bankers. In contrast, assets are quite simply always being invested.

History

To better understand why asset management has become such a critical component of the broader financial services industry, we must first become acquainted with its formation and history.

The beginnings of a separate industry

While the informal process of managing money has been around since the beginning of the 20th century, the industry did not begin to mature until the early 1970s. Prior to that time, investment management was completely relationship-based. Assignments to manage assets grew out of relationships that banks and insurance companies already had with institutions—primarily companies or municipal organizations with employee pension funds—that had funds to invest. (A pension fund is set up as an employee benefit. Employers commit to a certain level of payment to retired employees each year and must manage their funds to meet these obligations. Organizations with large pools of assets to invest are called institutional investors.)

These asset managers were chosen in an unstructured way—assignments grew organically out of pre-existing relationships, rather than through a formal request for proposal and bidding process. The actual practice of investment management was also unstructured. At the time, asset managers might simply pick 50 stocks they thought were good investments—there was not nearly as much analysis on managing risk or organizing a fund around a specific category or style. (Examples of different investment categories include small cap stocks and large cap stocks. We will explore the different investment categories and styles in a later chapter.) Finally, the assets that were managed at the time were primarily pension funds. Mutual funds had yet to become broadly popular.

Visit Vault at **www.vault.com** for insider company profiles, expert advice, career message boards, expert resume reviews, the Vault Job Board and more.

VAULT CAREER LIBRARY   267

ERISA, 401(k) plans and specialist firms

The two catalysts for change in the industry were: 1) the broad realization that demographic trends would cause the U.S. government's retirement system (Social Security) to be underfunded, which made individuals more concerned with their retirement savings, and 2) the creation of ERISA (the Employment Retirement Income Security Act) in 1974, which gave employees incentives to save for retirement privately through 401(k) plans. (401(k) plans allow employees to save pre-tax earnings for their retirement.) These elements prompted an increased focus on long-term savings by individual investors and the formation of what can be described as a private pension fund market.

These fundamental changes created the opportunity for professional groups of money managers to form "specialist" firms to manage individual and institutional assets. Throughout the 1970s and early 1980s, these small firms specialized in one or two investment styles (for example, core equities or fixed income investing).

During this period, the investment industry became fragmented and competitive. This competition added extra dimensions to the asset management industry. Investment skills, of course, remained critical. However, relationship building and the professional presentation of money management teams also began to become significant.

The rise of the mutual fund

In the early to mid 1980s, driven by the ERISA laws, the mutual fund came into vogue. While mutual funds had been around for decades, they were only used by financially sophisticated investors who paid a lot of attention to their investments. However, investor sophistication increased with the advent of modern portfolio theory (the set of tools developed to quantitatively analyze the management of a portfolio; see sidebar on next page). Asset management firms began heavily marketing mutual funds as a safe and smart investment tool, pitching to individual investors the virtues of diversification and other benefits of investing in mutual funds. With more and more employers shifting retirement savings responsibilities from pension funds to the employees themselves, the 401(k) market grew rapidly. Consequently, consumer demand for new mutual fund products exploded (mutual funds are the preferred choice in most 401(k) portfolios). Many specialists responded by expanding their product offerings and focusing more on the marketing of their new services and capabilities.

Modern Portfolio Theory

Modern Portfolio Theory (MPT) was born in 1952 when University of Chicago economics student Harry Markowitz published his doctoral thesis, "Portfolio Selection," in the *Journal of Finance*. Markowitz, who won the Nobel Prize in economics in 1990 for his research and its far-reaching effects, provided the framework for what is now known as Modern Portfolio Theory. MPT quantifies the benefits of diversification, looking at how investors create portfolios in order to optimize market risk against expected returns. Markowitz, assuming all investors are risk averse, proposed that investors, when choosing a security to add to their portfolio, should not base their decision on the amount of risk that an individual security has, but rather on how that security contributes to the overall risk of the portfolio. To do this, Markowitz considered how securities move in relation to one another under similar circumstances. This is called "correlation," which measures how much two securities fluctuate in price relative to each other. Taking all this into account, investors can create "efficient portfolios," ones with the highest expected returns for a given level of risk.

Consolidation and globalization

The dominant themes of the industry in the 1990s were consolidation and globalization. As many former specialists rapidly expanded, brand recognition and advanced distribution channels (through brokers or other sales vehicles) became key success factors for asset management companies. Massive global commercial and investment banks entered the industry, taking business away from many specialist firms. Also, mutual fund rating agencies such as Lipper (founded in 1973, now a part of Reuters) and Morningstar (founded in Chicago in 1984) increased investor awareness of portfolio performance. These rating agencies publish reports on fund performance and rate funds on scales such as Morningstar's 4-star rating system.

These factors led to a shakeout period of consolidation. From 1995 to 2001, approximately 150 mergers took place, creating well-established and formidable players such as Capital Group and Citigroup. As opposed to specialist firms, these large financial services firms provide asset management products that run the gamut: mutual funds, pension funds, management for high-net-worth individuals, etc. While many excellent specialist firms continue to operate today, they are not the driving force that they once were.

Buy-side vs. Sell-side

If you've ever spoken with investment professionals, you've probably heard them talk about the "buy-side" and the "sell-side." What do these terms mean and how do the two sides of the Street interact with one another?

What's the difference?

Simply stated, the buy-side refers to the asset managers who represent individual and institutional investors. The buy-side purchases investment products with the goal of increasing its assets. The sell-side refers to the functions of an investment bank. Specifically, this includes investment bankers, traders and research analysts. Sell-side professionals issue, recommend, trade and "sell" securities for the investors on the buy-side to "buy." The sell-side can be thought of primarily as a facilitator of buy-side investments—the sell-side makes money not through a growth in value of the investment, but through fees and commissions for these facilitating services. In this chapter, we'll take a brief look at the types of jobs on each "side." The rest of the book will look at the buy-side in detail.

Jobs on the Buy-side

Buy-side firms are structured in a far less formal manner than sell-side firms. Consequently, career paths are more flexible and job descriptions vary more from one firm to another. In general, buy-side firms have a three-segment professional staff consisting of:

• Portfolio managers who invest money on behalf of clients

• Research analysts who provide portfolio managers with potential investment recommendations

• Marketing and sales professionals who distribute the investment products to individual and institutional investors

When beginning your career on the buy-side, you typically will start as an assistant or associate in one of these three areas.

Visit Vault at **www.vault.com** for insider company profiles, expert advice, career message boards, expert resume reviews, the Vault Job Board and more.

V/\ULT CAREER LIBRARY   **269**

Professional Positions in Asset Management

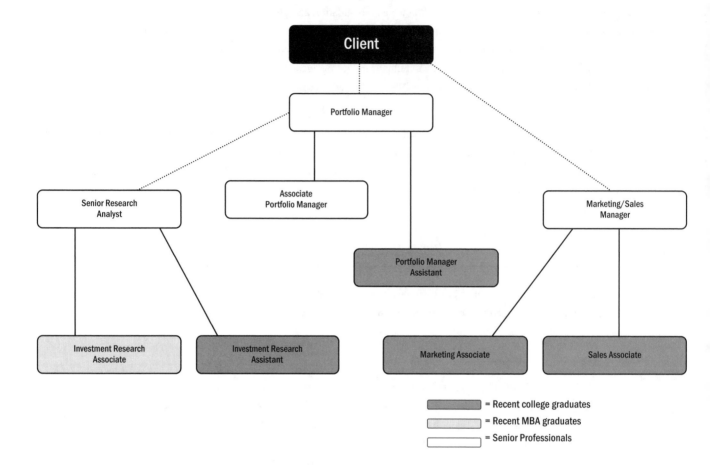

Portfolio Manager Assistant

In general, portfolio manager assistants screen for potential investments, monitor portfolio characteristics, and assist in client relations. Recent college graduates typically will spend two to four years in this role before returning to business school or migrating to a role in the investment research department.

This position varies among the firms in the industry, and the role itself differs depending on which segment of the firm you work in—mutual fund, institutional or high-net-worth. For instance, high-net-worth portfolio assistants spend more time working with clients, while institutional assistants spend more time monitoring and analyzing portfolios. Regardless, the general assignment focuses on supporting the portfolio manager.

Portfolio manager assistants are often instrumental in the process of screening for potential investments. Using the general strategy of the investment product—such as market-capitalization, earnings growth, valuation multiples or industry—the assistant screens all available stocks in the market (about 10,000) to identify the smaller list that meets the portfolio's criteria. The screened list for an active portfolio varies, but typically ranges between 100 and 300 securities. Portfolio manager assistants then gather additional research for the portfolio manager to begin the process of fundamentally analyzing the potential investment.

Once investments are made, portfolio manager assistants are responsible for monitoring the reconciliation of the trades. In this role, they work with the operations staff to assure that the portfolio is properly updated and performance records are accurate. Most firms have separate operations departments that reconcile trades and produce monthly client reports. However, many of the smaller firms require their portfolio assistants to perform the operations function as well. You should be aware of this, and clarify the exact job responsibilities when applying and interviewing for the job.

Portfolio assistants also participate in the process of client service, although the proportion of time spent in this area depends on the type of client being served. For instance, an assistant to a mutual fund portfolio manager would spend very little time on client service. Institutional and high-net-worth portfolio managers have fewer clients and they meet with them once or twice a year. Intermittently, their clients require vast and detailed investment reports and market commentaries. While marketing helps prepare these formal presentations, the portfolio manager assistant plays a crucial role in collecting economic and market data for the investment commentary and portfolio analysis sections of the report.

The position requires a person who understands capital markets, is capable of meeting deadlines and enjoys working on multiple projects simultaneously. The downside is that the reporting and operational components of the job have a quick learning curve and then become repetitive. Furthermore, it is not the best place to learn how to really value companies. Rather, you are being exposed to the years of experience that the portfolio manager possesses. Most important, portfolio manager assistants receive the benefit of seeing a broad picture of investing money across several industries, whereas research assistants typically get exposure to one component or sector. All in all, in the right setting, the position is a great introduction to the industry and a worthwhile apprenticeship to pursue.

Portfolio Manager Assistant Uppers and Downers

Uppers	Downers
• Broad exposure to the industry	• Less formal training process
• Reasonable working hours	• Some operations work
• Direct exposure to portfolio managers	• Repetitive assignments

Investment Research Assistant

Investment research assistants work with senior research analysts to help in developing investment recommendations to portfolio managers. Recent college graduates will spend, on average, two to four years in this role before returning to business school. However, some of the most successful assistants are often promoted directly to research associate (most of these fast-trackers will have completed their CFA while working as an assistant).

The investment research assistant is responsible for helping to monitor the industry and changes within companies covered in the industry, and for updating financial models accordingly. Assistants collect data for industry data services, company conference calls and surveys. For instance, in the previous Apple Computer example, the assistant would be collecting data about consumer demand and input prices for semiconductors. Additionally, the assistant provides support to the senior analyst in the construction of recommendation reports sent out to the portfolio managers. Specifically, the assistant updates charts and modifies numerical sections of the report.

While some of the work is routine and the hours are long, assistants are sitting next to, and learning from, the intellectual capital of the firm. A good analyst will teach you the ropes, including the intangibles behind analyzing companies, financial valuation and industry knowledge.

Visit Vault at **www.vault.com** for insider company profiles, expert advice, career message boards, expert resume reviews, the Vault Job Board and more.

VAULT CAREER LIBRARY   271

The role of investment research assistant requires a high level of quantitative knowledge. Primarily, a basic working knowledge of accounting, financial markets, financial analysis and statistics is needed for this position. Aside from a strong quantitative background, research assistants need to be detail oriented, analytical problem solvers, diligent, and superior communicators. Generally, firms are looking for finance or accounting majors for these jobs, but engineers and science majors are also coveted for technology and health care related industries.

Investment Research Assistant Uppers and Downers

Uppers	Downers
• Great quantitative experience • Most portfolio managers were once in research • Gain industry expertise • Pays well • Typically a collegial environment	• Long hours (60+ hours/week) • Lots of independent time in front of the computer • Repetitive assignments

Marketing and Sales

Increasingly, as the industry grows and matures, investment management companies are focusing on professional marketing and sales as a point of differentiation—especially on the institutional side of the business.

Traditionally, marketing and sales have been more or less an afterthought: much of the marketing and sales work was performed by investment professionals. This is no longer the case, however, and firms are increasingly building teams of dedicated marketing and sales professionals.

Because sales and marketing professionals are typically required to be fluent in all of the investment products, these positions create a great opportunity to learn about the various investment styles that clients demand. This area is a great career opportunity for those who are interested in asset management but don't want to be the investment decision maker.

If your goal is to use sales and marketing as a stepping stone to the investment side, make it a point to network early on with investment professionals and prove yourself at your current job before making it known that you want to make the switch, and work toward developing the quantitative skills needed for the investment positions.

Below is a broad description of the positions that exist in the institutional marketing and sales segment.

Marketing or Sales Associates

Marketing and sales associates are typically recent college graduates. The positions are quite similar, although they are traditionally segmented by different types of organization.

Marketing associates assist in creating portfolio review presentations and in developing promotional presentations for potential new clients. They are traditionally segmented by investment product type such as equity or fixed income.

Sales associates assist in answering RFPs (request for proposals) issued by institutions seeking to hire new investment managers. Additionally, associates assist senior client servicing officials in maintaining and expanding client relationships. Sales associates are traditionally segmented by client type—public pension funds, corporate pension funds, endowments and foundations.

Marketing or Sales Associate Uppers and Downers

Uppers	Downers
• Broad knowledge of all of the investment products in the marketplace • Great professional atmosphere for people that like the industry, but don't want to be the investment decision maker • Less hierarchical career path than the investment side • More entry-level jobs than the investment side • Lots of client interaction	• Difficult to jump to the investment side • Limited focus on building quantitative skills • Repetitive assignments

Visit Vault at **www.vault.com** for insider company profiles, expert advice, career message boards, expert resume reviews, the Vault Job Board and more.

V∧ULT CAREER LIBRARY   273

Investment Management Employer Directory

Advest
90 State House Sq.
Hartford, CT 06103
Phone: (860) 509-1000; (800)
243-8115
Fax: (860) 509-3849
www.advest.com

AIG Global Investment Group
175 Water Street
New York, NY 10038
Phone: (212) 458-2000
Fax: (212) 458-2200
www.aiggig.com

AIM Investments
11 Greenway Plaza, Suite 100
Houston, TX 77046
Phone: (713) 626-1919; (800) 959-
4246
Fax: (713) 993-9890
www.aiminvestments.com

Alliance Capital Management
1345 Avenue of the Americas
New York, NY 10105
Phone: (212) 969-1000
Fax: (212) 969-2229
www.alliancecapital.com

**Allianz Global Investors of
America L.P.**
888 San Clemente Dr.
Suite 100
Newport Beach, CA 92660
Phone: (949) 219-2200
Fax: (949) 219-3949

**American Century
Investments**
4500 Main Street
Suite 1500
Kansas City, MO 64111
Phone: (816) 531-5575
Fax: (816) 340-7962
www.americancentury.com

AMVESCAP
30 Finsbury Square
London
EC2A 1AG, United Kingdom
Phone: 44-20-7638-0731
Fax: 44-20-7065-3962
www.amvescap.com

BlackRock
40 East 52nd Street
New York, NY 10022
Phone: (212) 810-5300
www.blackrock.com

CalPERS
Lincoln Plaza
400 Q Street
Sacramento, CA 95814
Phone: (916) 326-3000
Fax: (916) 558-4001
www.calpers.ca.gov

**Credit Suisse Asset
Management (CSAM)**
466 Lexington Avenue
New York, NY 10017
Phone: (212) 875-3500
Fax: (646) 658-0728
us.csam.com

D.E. Shaw & Co., L.P.
120 West 45th Street
39th Floor, Tower 45
New York, NY 10036
Phone: (212) 478-0000
Fax: (212) 478-0100
www.deshaw.com

Dreyfus Corporation
200 Park Ave.
New York, NY 10166
Phone: (212) 922-6000
Fax: (212) 922-7533
www.dreyfus.com

Evergreen Investments
200 Berkeley Street
Boston, MA 02116
Phone: (617) 210-3200
www.evergreeninvestments.com

Fidelity Investments
82 Devonshire St.
Boston, MA 02109
Phone: (617) 563-7000
Fax: (617) 476-6150
www.fidelity.com

Franklin Resources
One Franklin Parkway
Bldg. 970, 1st Floor
San Mateo CA 94403
Phone: (650) 312-2000
www.franklintempleton.com

GAMCO Investors, Inc.
One Corporate Center
Rye, NY 10580-1422
Phone: (914) 921-5100
Fax: (914) 921-5392
www.gabelli.com

Janus Capital Group
151 Detroit Street
Denver, CO 80206
Phone: (303) 333-3863
Fax: (303) 336-7497
www.janus.com

MFS Investment Management
500 Boylston Street
Boston, MA 02116
Phone: (617) 954-5000
Fax: (617) 954-6620
www.mfs.com

Nuveen Investments
333 West Wacker Drive
Chicago, IL 60606
Phone: (312) 917-7700
Fax: (312) 917-8049
www.nuveen.com

Investment Management Employer Directory, cont.

Pequot Capital Management
500 Nyala Farm Road
Westport, CT 06880
Phone: (203) 429-2200
Fax: (203) 429-2400
www.pequotcap.com

PIMCO
840 Newport Center Dr.
Newport Beach, CA 92660
Phone: (949) 720-6000
Fax: (949) 720-1376
www.pimco.com

Putnam Investments
1 Post Office Square
Boston, MA 02109
Phone: (617) 292-1000
www.putnaminvestments.com

Schroder Investment Management North America
875 Third Avenue
22nd Floor
New York, NY 10022-6225
Tel: (212) 641-3830
Fax: (212) 641-3985
www.schroders.com/us

TIAA-CREF
730 Third Avenue
New York, NY 10017
Phone: (212) 490-9000
Fax: (212) 916-4840
www.tiaa-cref.org

T. Rowe Price
100 E. Pratt St.
Baltimore, MD 21202
Phone: (410) 345-2000
Fax: (410) 752-3477
www.troweprice.com

The Vanguard Group
100 Vanguard Blvd.
Malvern, PA 19355
Phone: (610) 669-1000
Fax: (610) 669-6605
www.vanguard.com

Wellington Management
75 State Street
Boston, MA 02109
Phone: (617) 951-5000
Fax: (617) 951-5250
www.wellington.com

Visit Vault at **www.vault.com** for insider company profiles, expert advice, career message boards, expert resume reviews, the Vault Job Board and more.

VAULT CAREER LIBRARY 275

Journalism

Newspapers

Newspapers were the first great mass medium, uniting local communities in ways they had never been before. Benjamin Franklin was one of the first newspaper moguls in America. He shrewdly controlled both the production and distribution of his newspaper, *The Pennsylvania Gazette*. He was a printer, and wrote many of the articles himself under various pen names. He also served as postmaster, overseeing the delivery of his own newspaper. By the time of the American Revolution, there were 37 newspapers with a combined weekly circulation of just 5,000 copies in the 13 colonies.

Newspapers would give birth to other great titans like William Randolph Hearst, whose "yellow journalism" was believed to have helped ignite the Spanish-American War; Joseph Pulitzer, journalist and publisher for whom the most coveted prize in journalism is named; Adolph Ochs, publisher of *The New York Times*, who coined the phrase, "All the News That's Fit to Print;" Katharine Graham, Chairman & CEO of The Washington Post Company, one of the most powerful women the newspaper industry has ever seen.

Newspapers enjoyed their height more than 70 years ago and have been in decline ever since, due to rising production costs, the introduction of electronic mediums, and changing reading habits. They still play a vital role as "watchdogs" in many local communities, as well as providing a "public record" in an increasingly cluttered media landscape.

What makes newspapers unique?

In addition to its mobility and relatively low price, the most voracious readers of newspapers would say it is the serendipity of the newspaper that makes it special above all other media. It's the surprise of coming across a story that you might not otherwise find, let alone read, that makes newspapers a treasure.

Today's web surfers would say the Internet has developed its own version of serendipity, drawing them deeper and deeper into a virtual world, almost as if you needed to leave a trail of cheese to find your way back out. Thankfully, the "mouse" can lead the way!

What attracts people to work for a newspaper?

Those who are drawn to newspaper work, whether as a journalist or a sales account executive, relish the idea of serving a local community. Most enjoy the unpredictable nature of the business. Every day is truly different. Many newspaper employees are very independent, goal-driven and enjoy the pressure of meeting deadlines. Newspapers also provide an environment in which you are constantly meeting new people, as well as learning new facts and ideas.

Many journalists are attracted to newspapers because of the opportunity to build strong ties and reliable sources in local communities, something few journalists in other media are able to do. Print journalists also enjoy the challenge of using words alone to connect with the community they serve. They weave together facts, bits of information and quotes to tell a story, all without the aid of video or sound.

Is a Career in Newspapers for You?

Lifestyle

If you desire a career in which every day is different, than working for a newspaper will be right up your alley. Of course, the hours are long and few pursue a career in journalism in hopes of becoming wealthy. Don't worry, you won't starve. Once your career hits its stride, you should make a comfortable living. Entry-level pay is definitely low, but this is the period of your career where you want to focus on gaining experience and honing your journalism skills, or on the business side, your sales skills.

Visit Vault at **www.vault.com** for insider company profiles, expert advice, career message boards, expert resume reviews, the Vault Job Board and more.

VAULT CAREER LIBRARY   **277**

The hours are long and irregular. News doesn't just happen from 9 a.m. to 5 p.m.; the Internet has now made news available on demand to consumers at any time they want. Newspapers have been adjusting to this new phenomenon as the Internet grows in influence. Increasingly, newspapers are becoming sensitive to work/life balance issues; offering part-time work, job sharing and work-at-home options.

Each day can be a roller coaster ride from covering a high profile event to the run-of-the-mill story you felt like you've done a thousand times. There is also enormous satisfaction in having your name in print, and in knowing that you are providing information that can positively impact the lives of the community you are serving.

Desired skills & traits

Tenacity: Whether your motivation is to meet a deadline, to beat the competition or to break a story, persistence in getting the story and its facts straight is crucial to becoming a successful journalist.

Communication Skills: Strong verbal and written talents are at the very heart of newsgathering and reporting. Listening is often an understated skill, but crucial. Once facts have been gathered, reporting involves putting them into perspective to capture all sides of a story.

Attention to Detail: Otherwise overlooked bits of information have compromised numerous journalism careers, as has recently occurred at *The New York Times* and the BBC. Every bit of information must be scrutinized. Organizational skills are also a must to maintain sources, to meet deadlines and to keep on top of ongoing news situations.

People Skills: Journalists may be regarded as wordsmiths, but their profession can also be viewed as managing networks of relationships. How you relate to your co-workers, the community and your sources will vastly influence the quality of your stories. Empathy and persuasiveness go hand in hand when forging strong professional relationships.

Magazines

Magazines were the first true national media in America. Newspapers had been a predominantly local medium, but magazines were the first to unite people across the country with the help of the U.S. Postal system as the means of distribution. Magazines edified and entertained people from coast to coast with interests in homemaking, hunting, politics, and hundreds of other topics and hobbies.

By 1900, there were over 5,500 magazines in circulation. According to the Magazine Publishers of America, there are now well over 17,000 titles. Magazines like *Cosmopolitan*, *Atlantic Monthly* and *The Saturday Evening Post* became media fixtures in the American home by the middle of the last century. In 1923 the term "newsmagazine" was coined, with the launch of *Time*, by Henry Luce and Briton Hadden. Today magazines are facing rising production and distribution costs. Many in the industry believe their survival lies in targeting smaller niche audiences.

What makes magazines unique?

The longer format of magazines allows writers to go deeper into stories or provide more detailed information about a specific topic, whereas newspapers typically offer the latest headlines of the day. Magazines unite people with common interests like fishing, crafts, gardening or automobiles. In some instances, magazines are saved to be used as reference material in the home or office. For example, many amateur chefs and food enthusiasts save their copies of *Bon Appetit*, *Cooking Light* or *Food & Wine* for the recipes and cooking tips they find within their pages. While magazines are just as portable as newspapers, they are more likely to be passed around and shared with others, reaching a larger audience beyond just their subscription and newsstand circulation.

What attracts people to work for a magazine?

Overall, there are more aesthetic considerations in the development of a magazine than for a newspaper. Magazines have a personality all their own. Newspapers, on the other hand, are literally black and white, offering few frills beyond getting out the news of the day.

On the content side, many journalists savor the opportunity to sink their teeth into just one story or to stick to a specific content area. For photographers, there are far more creative opportunities in magazines than in newspapers, where photography is primarily limited to capturing images of news as it happens.

On the business side, magazines offer the opportunity to develop direct marketing campaigns to target niche audiences, rather than the one-size-fits-all marketing strategies of broadcast television. Sponsorships are also more focused on national advertisers, rather than local ones, as is common among newspapers.

Is a Career In Magazines for You?

Lifestyle

Stability is not necessarily a feature of working in magazines. Pay is very low as you start out, so it is necessary to move around a lot in order to increase your salary. Increasingly, many jobs in magazines are becoming freelance, especially on the content side, for writers, photographers, designers and illustrators.

The hours can also be crazy, especially when you are trying to meet a deadline, but working for a magazine can be very exciting. Since there always seems to be a new magazine being launched, you will be invited to many different parties. There are some people lucky enough (depending on how you look at it) to plan these posh events as their full-time jobs. As you gain responsibility, there is the potential for travel as well.

Desired skills & traits

Research: Due to their longer format and less frequent publication, magazines place a different emphasis on research than do newspapers. Not only is it important to get the facts straight, but far more detailed knowledge of subject matter is required. Research in newspapers tends to be broader, in magazines it's inclined to be more focused.

Writing: A distinct writing style is necessary to capture the brand and personality of the magazine. A more personalized style also guides readers through longer stories commonly found in magazines. On the flip side, there are many magazine features that now require highly creative and "punchy" copy for features that offer readers quick pops of information.

Expertise: As magazines become more and more niche oriented, it is helpful to bring a unique area of expertise to the table, even for more general publications like *Time* or *Newsweek*. Many writers and reporters for magazines are increasingly freelance, so it is important to begin building a knowledge base in a particular area like health, business or entertainment. As a result, you can write for any magazine, rather than limiting yourself to one magazine title.

Business Skills: In such a highly competitive marketplace, where most newly launched magazines fail within the first year, business skills are crucial. Understanding demographic research, database management and direct marketing are a must. Even on the creative side, it doesn't hurt to understand the basics of business and how to better connect with your target audience.

Entrepreneurial Spirit: Last year, over 400 new titles were launched in the U.S. While established titles may not champion the entrepreneurial spirit, start-up magazines definitely do. A "can-do" attitude, good organizational skills, creativity and the ability to solve problems are all welcome traits in helping to establish a new magazine title.

Visit Vault at **www.vault.com** for insider company profiles, expert advice, career message boards, expert resume reviews, the Vault Job Board and more.

VAULT CAREER LIBRARY   279

TV News

Broadcast television burst forth in the late 1940s, growing out of the tradition of broadcast radio. In fact, it was first regarded as "radio with pictures." It soon developed into a form all its own. It brought groundbreaking events into millions of Americans' living rooms, from Edward R. Murrow's look at the life of migrant workers to Walter Cronkite reporting from the middle of the Vietnam war zone to the live-television assassination of Lee Harvey Oswald by Jack Ruby.

Since its birth over 60 years ago, television news has grown to become the voice of local communities throughout America, and national broadcasts have helped make our vast country seem smaller. Over the last two decades, the emergence of cable television, led by the pioneering efforts of Ted Turner's CNN in 1980, has grown to deliver news 24/7.

What makes television news unique?

Broadcast television has enabled interview subjects to share their story in their own words. Sometimes moving images speak for themselves without the aid of a professional journalist's words. Broadcast stories have made us swell with pride, shed a tear or bust a gut. Television has enabled a mass audience to witness history first hand—to view news as it happens.

Through the years, television journalism has provided Hollywood with inspiration, ranging from dramas like Broadcast News to revealing looks at the industry based on true stories, like The Insider, to comedies like Anchorman. Why are Americans so fascinated by television news? For the same reason so many people pursue a career in this business—the combination of the star power generated by a visual broadcast medium and the ability of video journalism to capture the raw emotion of a story.

What attracts people to work in television news?

Many television journalists love the rush of reporting live news events and being able to share those images with viewers at home. Video enables journalists to capture the sights, sounds and details of a moment like no other medium.

Most news broadcasts are live, adding to the pressure of the environment and the immediacy with which news is delivered to a mass audience. Television news shares many of the same characteristics of other journalistic disciplines, but it is perceived as the most glamorous. At the national level, your work can be shared with a larger audience than newspapers, magazines or radio can attract.

Network/Cable News Track

Producing

Production Assistant: An entry-level position performing administrative duties that vary from company to company and even from show to show. Median salary: $20,000

Broadcast Associate: In charge of gathering basic elements for a broadcast, including archival footage and research for producers. Median salary: $25,000

Booker: Focused on booking guests to be interviewed for live broadcasts. This position is common in cable news, as well as morning broadcasts that have a lot of live guests. Median salary: $40,000

Assistant or Associate Producer: Depending on the size of the organization, an assistant producer is junior to an associate producer, but they both perform similar functions. Responsibilities include setting up interviews, research, arranging and sometimes supervising shoots and gathering other elements required for a piece. Median salary: $45,000

Segment Producer: In charge of one portion of a broadcast, generally in between two blocks of commercials. Median salary: $45,000

Web Producer: An increasingly important part of each broadcast and news organization, overseeing the production of various web pages dedicated to a particular show or a specific topic area. Median salary: $30,000

Show Producer: Performs similar functions as a producer at the local level. Show producers generally work in cable news and oversee the rundown, script and elements for a show. Median salary: $50,000

Field Producer or Producer: Oversees the logistics of producing a story or elements for a piece in the field. After seeking approval of the executive producer for a story, they oversee its entire process, from developing an outline to identifying interview subjects to setting up interviews for correspondents; many times they even conduct the interviews themselves. Median salary: $60,000

Senior Producer: Works with producers to develop story ideas and to provide editorial guidance and suggestions.

Executive Producer: Oversees an entire broadcast. Responsibilities include setting budgets, helping to arrange high-profile interviews, developing story ideas and providing overall editorial direction for the broadcast.

National or Foreign Editor: Function is similar to that of an assignment editor. Keeps an eye on developing stories on national or international scene. Also coordinates the necessary resources for the coverage of domestic or foreign news events.

Senior Executive Producer: Within large news organizations, a Senior Executive Producer manages the overall brand of a show, particularly when there are multiple broadcasts under the same name, like 60 Minutes or Dateline. Determines potential revenue opportunities, provides editorial guidance and steers the overall promotion of the broadcast.

Vice President: Oversees a specific operational area, like newsgathering, or a daypart, like primetime broadcasts.

President: Head of the news operation, providing overall editorial, financial and brand direction for organization.

On air

Correspondent: Functions much the same as reporters do at the local level, but they have a producer assigned to them, helping them put their video package together. They will write the script, but the producer gathers the elements. In cable news, they will also perform several live shots throughout the progression of a developing story.

For magazine shows or "soft news," correspondents conduct interviews and write the script for their piece. Stories for magazine shows can run as long as ten minutes, while packages for a hard news broadcast, like the evening news, run only about one and a half minutes. Median salary: $125,000

Anchor: As with local broadcasts, the anchor is the central figure of a show, introducing all the stories and correspondents. They will also conduct interviews on the set and sometimes in the field. Salary: Varies, depending on the reach of the broadcast.

Local Television News Track

Assignment desk

Desk Assistant: An entry-level position at a local station on the assignment desk. Works with assignment editor to answer phones, read the wires, listen to the police and fire department scanners, as well as help coordinate photographers and reporters in the field. Median salary: $20,000

Assignment Editor: Manages the assignment desk. Generally there is a dayside assignment editor and a nightside assignment editor. Many stations also have an assignment editor to cover the overnight hours and to help prepare for the early morning

Visit Vault at www.vault.com for insider company profiles, expert advice, career message boards, expert resume reviews, the Vault Job Board and more.

VAULT CAREER LIBRARY 281

newscasts. They pitch story ideas, assign reporters and photographers to stories and gather research to help with the development of stories. Median salary: $30,000

Producing

Production Assistant: Another entry-level position to help with administrative tasks and to provide additional support to the assignment desk, reporters, producers, photographers and editors. Median salary: $20,000

Associate Producer: After a year or so spent in an entry-level position, this is the next step on the road to becoming a producer. Works with producer(s) on one or two assigned newscasts, the 5 p.m. and 6 p.m. news, for example. Asked to write "readers," copy read by the anchor with no video, as well as introductions for reporter packages. May also edit video on a nonlinear editing system. Median salary: $22,000

Producer: Generally oversees one broadcast, sometimes two. Develops the "rundown," a document that determines the order of the stories in the newscasts and makes sure the entire newscast runs on time. Writes the opening headlines and some readers. Constantly monitors wires and assignment desk for breaking news, as well as the latest developments for existing stories. Median salary: $26,000

Executive Producer: Oversees all newscasts. Depending on the market, there may also be a Senior Producer who works with the Executive Producer. Works to make sure lead story is consistent throughout all newscasts. Works with producers to maintain editorial and production standards, as articulated by the station. Median salary: $49,000

Assistant News Director: Works with news director to manage entire newsgathering and production operation. Median salary: $55,000

News Director: Oversees all aspects of news gathering operation, from editorial to production to graphics, making sure the look and feel of all newscasts is consistent with the editorial standards and overall vision of the station. Median salary: $65,000

Photographer: The actual collection of video is gathered by photographers, or "photogs." Many photographers learn their trade on the job or receive Special training at a trade school. Like on-air talent and producers, they also move around the country to build their career.

Increasingly, more and more photogs are also wearing the editor's hat, due to shrinking budgets and new technologies that make it even easier to edit. Most photogs at local stations already edit a reporter's package, either back at the station or in a live truck (a vehicle used to broadcast from remote locations). Median salary: $24,000

On air

The "face" of the newsgathering operation is the reporters and anchors of each station, also referred to as "the talent." Becoming an on-air reporter or anchor is very tough. Most people will start out as a general assignment reporter in a very small market and will move around the country every one to two years, jumping to larger markets with better financial compensation.

Some will also have to work less coveted schedules like overnights and weekends just to start building their career and demo tape. It is no longer uncommon for reporters to start out as "video journalists" or VJs. These reporters are virtual one-man bands. They use digital video cameras and laptop editing software, shooting and editing their own video, in addition to producing and writing their own story.

Median salary for reporters: $26,000
Median salary for anchors: $48,000

Meteorologist or Weatherman: Meteorologists possess a degree in meteorology or atmospheric science, whereas some weathermen do not. Much of today's weather forecasting is left to high-powered computers that offer various models to predict the weather. Weather is one of the most popular segments of local broadcasts. There are both on-air and producing opportunities in weather. Beyond television stations, there are also opportunities on cable at The Weather Channel and local 24/7 weather channels, as well as weather service companies like AccuWeather or WeatherCentral.

Sportscaster or Sports Anchor: In some cases, a station's lead sports anchor is also referred to as the sports director. There is a growing emphasis within some local television stations on reducing their sports staff and delegating coverage of sports to the news staff, as a result of increasing competition from sports cable networks and web sites. Alternatively, there are more and more opportunities to work in sports cable television, as well as for professional sports organizations and leagues that have recently launched their own networks.

Radio News

Radio was the first electronic mass medium, bringing live news events as they happened into millions of homes for the first time. Still unsure of its impact, Orson Welles duped millions of listeners into thinking Martians were invading earth in 1938. Charles Collingwood, Eric Sevareid and Edward R. Murrow brought millions of Americans to the front lines of war, sending back live reports from Europe during World War II.

Radio was quickly adopted by Americans: 90 percent of homes owned one by 1930. In that year, radio personality Lowell Thomas gave birth to radio news when he began reading the news on air. At first, newspapers tried to fight this trend, citing copyright laws, but they were eventually overruled when the courts determined that no one could own the news, and the factual content was part of the public domain. The Golden Age of radio was eclipsed by the advent of television in the 1950s, forcing it to reinvent itself from the primary electronic medium for news and entertainment into a local medium for news, talk and music.

What makes radio unique?

Radio is a mass medium, but it creates a one-on-one relationship between the announcer and the listener. The listener is allowed to visualize a story for themselves, becoming absorbed in their own imagination as they are guided by a storyteller. For this reason, radio has been often referred to as "the theater of the mind."

Radio is probably the least expensive of all media to consume, thereby truly reaching out to a mass audience. The phenomenon of talk radio also promotes a diversity of voices and allows the average man or woman the opportunity to be heard in a public forum. The unique features of radio provide insight in to what is on the minds of Americans. It's no surprise that radio talk show hosts are regularly interviewed by television broadcasters when major news events like the attacks of September 11th occur, in order to understand the common person's perspective.

What attracts people to work in radio?

Like newspapers, every day is different and there is a focus on serving local communities. Radio provides a more personal connection to the audience than print. The nature of the medium promotes a sense of immediacy—getting reaction from the community as news happens. Of course, if you have a voice like velvet, it certainly won't hurt your chances of landing an on-air gig!

On the business side, radio offers a similar opportunity to that of newspapers, in working with local sponsors. Radio also enables advertisers to target niche audiences, and offers greater flexibility to refine their marketing messages than they can in

Visit Vault at **www.vault.com** for insider company profiles, expert advice,
career message boards, expert resume reviews, the Vault Job Board and more.

VAULT CAREER LIBRARY 283

print. Once an ad hits the presses, there's no turning back, but it is technically possible to change a radio spot throughout the course of the day.

Career Track

Content track

The primary function of the editorial staff is to gather and report the news. Each morning, they have a meeting to pitch story ideas and to assign resources to stories to be covered that day. They monitor wires, call on their sources and read a variety of print media to find stories.

Much of the content in radio is interview-driven, and because there are no visual elements, a premium is placed on telling a story through the written word. Anchors conduct interviews in the studio by phone, live on the air, with a newsmaker like a local politician, civic leader or another member of the community. Reporters will conduct interviews as part of their stories and will also collect sound bites from "Man on the Street" (MOS) interviews to be used in taped stories or as part of live interview segments.

Desk Assistant: For those just getting their start in radio, desk assistants are a "jack of all trades," helping to research stories, set up interviews and even write copy for news readers. Generally, most start out at smaller stations, where there is an opportunity to gain more hands-on experience than at a station in a larger market. Median salary: $20,000

Writer: Writes copy for announcers and anchors, as well as introductions for packages produced by reporters. Once again, at smaller stations with fewer resources, anchors most likely write much of their own scripts. Median salary: $23,000

Producer: More likely found at larger stations, producers develop the rundown for live broadcasts and book interviews for live interview broadcasts or talk shows. Median salary: $26,000

Assignment Editor: Cruises the wires, the fire department and police scanners and consults community sources, looking for stories or breaking news like fires and shootings. The assignment editor will also help write certain stories, particularly those from the wires, as well as copy to introduce reporter packages. Median salary: $25,000

Reporter: Goes out into the community to investigate leads and news tips, gathers information for stories and conducts interviews. Once a reporter has gathered all the elements for his story, he writes a script and produces his package or segment. Reporters also report live from news events. Median salary: $26,000

Anchors: Monitors the wires for stories, writes copy, introduces stories by reporters, provides perspective for breaking news, conducts live interviews and delivers the news to the community of listeners. Median salary: $25,000

Host: Similar to an anchor, but generally associated with a live broadcast made up of in-studio interviews or call-ins from listeners.

Commentators: Provide opinions or editorials about news events or issues facing a local community.

Assistant News Director: Manages day-to-day news gathering and production operations. Median salary: $25,000

News Director: Provides editorial direction for the station, develops budgets and oversees the assignment of resources for news coverage. Median salary: $31,000

General Manager: Provides overall leadership for editorial, sales and promotion for a station. Median salary: Varies widely depending on the size of the station and market.

Journalism Employer Directory

Newspaper Publishers

A.H. Belo Corp.
400 S. Record St.
Dallas, TX 75202-4841
Phone: 214-977-6606
Web: www.belo.com

Advance Publications
950 Fingerboard Rd.
Staten Island, NY 10305
Phone: 212-286-2860
Web: www.advance.net

Cox Newspapers
6205 Peachtree Dunwoody Rd.
Atlanta, GA 30328
Phone: 678-645-0000
Web: www.coxnews.com/cox

Dow Jones & Company
1 World Financial Center
200 Liberty St.
New York, NY 10281
Phone: 212-416-2000
Web: www.dj.com

Freedom Communications
17666 Fitch Ave.
Irvine, CA 92614-6022
Phone: 949-253-2300
Web: www.freedom.com

Gannett Co.
7950 Jones Branch Dr.
McLean, VA 22107-0910
Phone: 703-854-6000
Web: www.gannett.com

Hearst Newspapers
959 8th Ave.
New York, NY 10019
Phone: 212-649-2000
Web: www.hearst.com/newspapers

Knight-Ridder
50 W. San Fernando St., Ste. 1500
San Jose, CA 95113
Phone: 408-938-7700
Web: www.kri.com

Media General
333 E. Franklin St.
Richmond, VA 23219
Phone: 804-649-6000
Web: www.mediageneral.com

MediaNews Group
1560 Broadway, Ste. 2100
Denver, CO 80202
Phone: 303-563-6360
Web: www.medianewsgroup.com

The E.W. Scripps Company
312 Walnut St.
Cincinnati, OH 45202
Phone: 513-977-3000
Web: www.scripps.com

The New York Times Company
229 West 43rd St.
New York, NY 10036
Phone: 212-556-1234
Web: www.nytco.com

The Washington Post Company
1150 15th St. NW
Washington, DC 20071
Phone: 202-334-6000

Tribune Co.
435 N. Michigan Ave.
Chicago, IL 60611
Phone: 312-222-9100
Web: www.tribune.com

Magazine Publishers

AMI, American Media Inc.
One Park Avenue
10th Floor
New York, NY 10016
Phone: 212-545-4800

American Express Publishing Corporation
1120 Avenue of the Americas
New York, NY 10036
Phone: 212-382-5600
Web: www.amexpub.com

Condé Nast Publications
4 Times Square, 17th Floor
New York, NY 10036
Phone: 212-286-2860
Web: www.condenast.com
Owns: Allure, Vogue, Wired, Glamour, GQ, The New Yorker, Vanity Fair, Lucky

Crain Communications
1155 Gratiot Ave.
Detroit, MI 48207-2997
Phone: 313-446-6000
Web: www.crain.com
Owns: Advertising Age, AutoWeek, TelevisionWeek

Forbes Inc.
60 5th Ave.
New York, NY10011
Phone: 212-620-2200
Web: www.forbesinc.com

Gruner + Jahr AG & Co. (U.S. Office)
375 Lexington Ave., 10th Floor
New York, NY 10017
Phone: 212-499-2000
Web: www.guj.de

Hachette Filipacchi Médias (U.S. Office)
1633 Broadway, 45th Floor
New York, NY 10019
Phone: 212-767- 5322
Web: www.hachette-filipacchi.com
Owns: Elle, Car & Driver, American Photo, Women's Day

Visit Vault at **www.vault.com** for insider company profiles, expert advice, career message boards, expert resume reviews, the Vault Job Board and more.

VAULT CAREER LIBRARY 285

Journalism Employer Directory, cont.

Hearst Magazines
959 8th Ave.
New York, NY 10019
Phone: 212-649-2000
Web: www.hearst.com/magazines
Owns: Cosmopolitan, Good
Housekeeping, Town & Country, O,
The Oprah Magazine, Esquire, Popular
Mechanics

McGraw-Hill Companies
1221 Avenue of the Americas
New York, NY 10020
Phone: 212-512-2000
Web: www.mcgraw-hill.com
Owns: BusinessWeek

Meredith Corporation
1716 Locust St.
Des Moines, IA 50309-3023
Phone: 515-284-3000
Web: www.meredith.com
Owns: Better Homes and Gardens,
Ladies' Home Journal, MORE

National Geographic Society
1145 17th St. NW
Washington, DC 20036-4688
Phone: 202-857-7000
Web: www.nationalgeographic.com
Owns: National Geographic

PRIMEDIA
745 5th Ave.
New York, NY 10151
Phone: 212-745-0100
Web: www.primedia.com
Owns: Motor Trend, Soap Opera
Digest

Rodale
33 East Minor Street
Emmaus, PA 18098
Phone: 610-967-5171
Web: rodale.com
Owns: Men's Health, Organic Living,
Organic Style, Men's Health

The Washington Post Company
1150 15th St. NW
Washington, DC 20071
Phone: 202-334-6000
Web: www.washpostco.com
Owns: Newsweek

Time, Inc.
1271 Avenue of the Americas
New York, NY 10020-1393
Phone: 212-522-1212
Web: www.timeinc.com
Owns: Time, Entertainment Weekly,
People, Sports Illustrated, Fortune

U.S. News & World Reports
1050 Thomas Jefferson St. NW
Washington, DC 20007-3837
Phone: 202-955-2000
Web: www.usnews.com
Owns: U.S. News & World Reports

Wenner Media
1290 Avenue of the Americas
New York, NY 10104-0298
Phone: 212-484-1616
Owns: Rolling Stone, Men's Journal,
US Weekly

TV News Companies

ABC News
77 West 66th St.
New York, NY 10023
Phone: 212-456-6200
Web: www.abcnews.com

CBS News
524 West 57th St.
New York, NY 10019
Phone: 212-975-4321
Web: www.cbsnews.com

CNBC
1 CNBC Plaza
Englewood Cliffs, NJ 07632
Phone: 201-735-2622
Web: moneycentral.msn.com

CNN
1 CNN Center
Atlanta, GA 30303
Phone: 404-827-1500
Web: www.cnn.com

Fox News Channel
1211 Avenue of the Americas
New York, NY 10036
Phone: 212-301-3000
Web: www.foxnews.com

MSNBC
1 MSNBC Plaza
Secaucus, NJ 07094
Phone: 201-583-5000
Web: www.msnbc.com

NBC News
30 Rockefeller Plaza
New York, NY 10112
Phone: 212-664-4444
Web: www.msnbc.com

PBS
1320 Braddock Pl
Alexandria, VA 22314-1692
Phone: 703-739-5000
Web: www.pbs.org

The Weather Channel
300 Interstate North Parkway
Atlanta, GA 30339
Phone: 770-226-2609
Web: www.weather.com

Radio News Companies

ABC, Inc.
77 W. 66th St.
New York, NY 10023-6298
Phone: 212-456-7777
Web: www.abcradio.com

Bloomberg Radio
499 Park Ave.
New York, NY 10022
Phone: 212-318-2000
Web: www.bloomberg.com/radio/

Journalism Employer Directory, cont.

Citadel Broadcasting
7201 W. Lake Mead Blvd., Ste. 400
Las Vegas, NV 89128
Phone: 702-804-5200
Web: www.citadelbroadcasting.com

**Clear Channel
Communications**
200 E. Basse Rd.
San Antonio, TX 78209
Phone: 210-822-2828
Web: www.clearchannel.com

Fox Radio
6205 Peachtree Dunwoody Rd.
Atlanta, GA 30328
Phone: 678-645-0000
Web: www.coxradio.com

Cumulus Media
3535 Piedmont Rd., Bldg. 14, Fl. 14
Atlanta, GA 30305
Phone: 404-949-0700
Web: www.cumulus.com

Emmis Communications
40 Monument Circle, Ste. 700
Indianapolis, IN 46204
Phone: 317-266-0100
Web: www.emmis.com

Entercom Communications
401 City Ave., Ste. 409
Bala Cynwyd, PA 19004
Phone: 610-660-5610
Web: www.entercom.com

Fisher Communications
100 4th Ave. North, Ste. 440
Seattle, WA 98109
Phone: 206-404-7000
Web: www.fsci.com

Infinity Broadcasting
1515 Broadway, 46th Floor
New York, NY 10036
Phone: 212-846-3939
Web: www.infinityradio.com

National Public Radio
635 Massachusetts Ave. NW
Washington, DC 20001-3753
Phone: 202-513-2000
Web: www.npr.org

Westwood One
40 West 57th St.
New York, NY 10019
Phone: 212-641-2000
Web: www.westwoodone.com

Visit Vault at **www.vault.com** for insider company profiles, expert advice,
career message boards, expert resume reviews, the Vault Job Board and more.

V∧ULT CAREER LIBRARY   287

COMMUNITY STARTS HERE.

Orrick prides itself on service to the community. We view it as our responsibility, as fundamental to the way we work as a firm, and as individuals.

Our community responsibility is fueled by individual passion. We reach out and respond in areas with the greatest need and where we can make the greatest impact. Arts and education. Legal services and community building. Our efforts go well beyond financial assistance, providing leadership, legal counsel, and volunteer support as well.

To discover more about Orrick and our Community Responsibility efforts, please visit www.orrick.com/community.

ORRICK

HONG KONG   LONDON   MILAN   MOSCOW   PARIS   ROME   TAIPEI   TOKYO
NEW YORK   SAN FRANCISCO   SILICON VALLEY   LOS ANGELES   WASHINGTON DC   SACRAMENTO   PACIFIC NORTHWEST   ORANGE COUNTY
WWW.ORRICK.COM

Law/Paralegal

Corporate Law Basics

What is corporate law?

Corporate law is the law of corporations. A corporation is an artificial legal entity, typically chartered by a state and formed in order to operate a business. Once chartered, the corporation is completely separate from its owners, is liable for its own debts and must pay its own taxes.

But many lawyers deal with corporations, and not all of them call themselves corporate lawyers. In fact, at this point, you might not have a clear idea of the differences among a litigator who works in-house for a corporation, a tax lawyer who advises corporations from the vantage point of a law firm and a corporate lawyer. If you watch too much television, you might believe that lawyers represent clients on deals one day and head to the courtroom for high-profile litigation the next. This is highly unusual in the real practice of law. While both litigators and corporate lawyers deal with corporations, they do so in very different ways.

Litigation vs. transactional law

One of the basic divisions in the practice of law is between litigation and corporate, or transactional, law. Litigation attorneys, or litigators, deal with the judicial process, with civil disputes or criminal cases that are headed to court. In the realm of criminal law, they are prosecutors, public defenders or private defense attorneys. Those attorneys who handle conflicts between individuals, whether over personal injuries, domestic disputes or other matters, are civil trial lawyers. Commercial litigators are trial attorneys whose clients include corporations and businesses.

Note that being a litigator doesn't automatically put you in a courtroom. Public defenders may indeed be in court every week. But litigators who work on corporate or commercial matters might never go to court. They serve their clients by filing motions and briefs and settling conflicts without actually going to trial.

It's a myth that everyone who wants to be a lawyer wants to spend time in a courtroom. Many people don't have any interest in criminal law or personal injury. Some would rather contribute to the creation of a business venture than participate in its breakdown. Some lawyers don't care to write the (many) documents that must be submitted to court. Attorneys who facilitate transactions in the fields of corporate or tax law, intellectual property or employee benefits are considered transactional lawyers. In the world of business, transactional lawyers try to set up deals in a way that will avoid litigation and make clear the rights and responsibilities of all parties in the event that something does go wrong.

The difference between corporate law and commercial litigation is simple. Corporate lawyers build transactions or deals, and litigators deal with transactions gone wrong, whether through the judicial system or through alternative methods of dispute resolution like mediation or arbitration.

Transactional law and corporate lawyers

So, what is a corporate lawyer? Basically, corporate lawyers advise businesses on their legal obligations, rights and responsibilities. People who call themselves corporate lawyers are usually corporate generalists, lawyers who provide advice on how to structure a business and evaluate ventures and who coordinate with specialists, like tax lawyers, employee benefits lawyers and real estate attorneys (who are all transactional lawyers), to serve the sophisticated needs of their corporate clients.

While corporate attorneys may provide day-to-day advice to their clients, most of their work, at least in larger law firms, is transactional in nature. In fact, some firms use the terms "transactional" and "corporate" interchangeably when describing

Visit Vault at **www.vault.com** for insider company profiles, expert advice, career message boards, expert resume reviews, the Vault Job Board and more.

V∧ULT CAREER LIBRARY   **289**

areas of practice. Corporate lawyers structure transactions, draft documents, review other lawyers' agreements, negotiate deals, attend meetings and make calls toward those ends. A corporate lawyer ensures that the provisions of an agreement are clear, unambiguous and won't cause problems for their client in the future. Corporate attorneys also advise on the duties and responsibilities of corporate officers, directors and insiders.

There are many varieties of corporate law practice, and not all corporate lawyers do the same kind of work. Moreover, not all firms categorize corporate practice in the same way. For example, some firms might have separate practice groups for antitrust or mergers & acquisitions, while others include them within their corporate department. The following list, while not exhaustive, outlines some of the areas in which corporate attorneys might spend their time.

Areas of Corporate Practice

Corporate formation, governance and operation

A corporation is a legal entity created through the laws of its state of incorporation. Individual states make laws relating to the creation, organization and dissolution of corporations. The law treats a corporation as a legal "person" that has the standing to sue and be sued, and is distinct from its stockholders. The legal independence of a corporation prevents shareholders from being personally liable for corporate debts. The legal person status of corporations gives the business perpetual life; the death (or, in today's climate, discrediting) of an official or a major stockholder does not alter the corporation's structure, even if it affects the stock price.

A corporate lawyer can help a client create, organize or dissolve a business entity. To form a corporation, an attorney drafts articles of incorporation, which document the creation of the company and specify the management of internal affairs. Most states require a corporation to have bylaws defining the roles of officers of the company. Corporate lawyers also deal with business entities in the forms of partnerships, limited liability companies, limited liability partnerships and business trusts; each form has its own set of legal rights and responsibilities, organizational structure and tax burdens. Attorneys help their clients decide which of these legal forms is best suited for the business they want to run and the relationships the principals want to build with each other.

A corporate lawyer who helps a client form a company might later be called upon for other legal advice related to the start-up or management of the business, like reviewing a lease for office space or equipment, or drafting employment contracts, non-disclosure and non-compete agreements. Corporate lawyers might research aspects of employment law or environmental law or consult with another attorney who specializes in that field. Business executives also seek advice from corporate attorneys on the rights and responsibilities of corporate directors and officers.

Mergers & acquisitions

One major corporate practice area is mergers and acquisitions ("M&A"). Through acquiring (buying) or merging with another company, a business might add property, production facilities or a brand name. A merger or acquisition might also work to neutralize a competitor in the same field. Corporate attorneys provide legal counsel about proposed transactions. To help evaluate a proposed venture, a corporate lawyer (who typically relies on a team of corporate lawyers) reviews all of the company's key assets and liabilities, meaning financial statements, employment agreements, real estate holdings, intellectual property holdings and any current, pending or likely litigation. This is called due diligence. The corporate lawyer can then assess the situation and raise specific issues with the client—for example, who's responsible for the Environmental Protection Agency investigation of that piece of property the company owns? What happens to the employees of the target company or to the stock options of the company's directors?

Corporate lawyers consult with their clients about these questions and together lawyer and client determine which parties should accept current or potential liabilities. The lawyers then draft the merger or acquisition agreement and negotiate in detail the terms of each party's rights, responsibilities and liabilities.

Venture capital

In a venture capital practice, a lawyer works on private and public financings and day-to-day counseling. This means they help new businesses find money for their ventures, organize their operations and maintain their legal and business structures after formation. In venture capital, as in any corporate law position dealing with emerging companies, lawyers help build and expand businesses. Their responsibilities can include general corporate work, like drafting articles of incorporation and other documents, as well as technology licensing, financing, and mergers & acquisitions.

Some lawyers find this type of work less confrontational than M&A practice because the client is working with other parties toward a common goal. Sometimes, in mergers & acquisitions, the parties see the process as a zero-sum game in which each must get the best deal no matter how it may affect future relations with the other company. This is especially the case in hostile acquisitions.

Project finance

The development and construction of power plants, oil refineries, industrial plants, pipelines, mines, telecommunications networks and facilities and transportation systems involve the cooperation of many different entities, many different lawyers and extremely large sums of money. Project finance attorneys specialize in these deals. They form a project entity, a corporation, partnership or other legal entity that will exist for the term of the project, and they draft power purchase agreements and construction contracts and negotiate financial terms with lenders and investors.

Corporate securities

Some corporate lawyers specialize in corporate securities law. On a federal level, the Securities Act of 1933 requires companies who sell securities to the public to register with the federal government. Corporations must follow certain protocols regarding disclosure of information to shareholders and investors depending on the size of the corporation and the type of investor. If shares of a company's stock are traded on a public stock exchange, the company has to file detailed reports with the Securities and Exchange Commission and distribute parts of those reports (the prospectus) to shareholders. The Securities Act of 1934 addresses the obligations of companies traded on a national stock exchange.

To ensure the companies remain in accordance with these laws, corporate attorneys prepare reports for initial public offerings, yearly and quarterly disclosures, and special disclosures whenever something happens that might affect the price of the stock, like impending litigation, government investigation or disappointing financial results. Even if you don't specialize in corporate securities law, the issuance of stock and the creation and distribution of the reports are subject to a whole host of rules with which corporate lawyers must be familiar.

Intellectual property

Corporate lawyers often advise their clients on intellectual property matters. Intellectual property law can include research and analysis of trade secret issues, patent and trademark licensing and protection, software licensing and copyright law.

Visit Vault at www.vault.com for insider company profiles, expert advice, career message boards, expert resume reviews, the Vault Job Board and more.

VAULT CAREER LIBRARY   291

the people behind the deals

Barbara Brown, Partner and Chair
Paul Hastings' Washington, DC Office

Paul *Hastings*

#2 – Best in Labor & Employment
#3 – Best in Real Estate

#30 – Overall in Prestige
#1 – Labor & Employment – Partner Ranking

Barbara Brown was named by *Washingtonian* magazine as one of the 50 best lawyers in Washington, DC and has been hailed as the leading employment lawyer for the region by Chambers USA. This is no surprise. We know that the best talent achieves the best results.

One of 45 female partners at Paul Hastings, Barbara's success is strengthened by a collegial environment that crosses practices and borders, allowing our attorneys to meet the needs of our clients in legal areas as diverse as employment law, corporate, litigation, real estate and tax.

Spanning 17 offices, seven countries and three continents, Paul Hastings provides businesses with sophisticated and innovative solutions for their largest legal matters and most complex transactions, no matter where they operate in the world.

Non-legal roles

Business clients frequently look to their lawyers for advice directly related to the operation of their business but only tangentially related to the law, such as how to deal with special interest groups, how to respond to concerns about product safety, whether to fire an executive, how to plan for the possibility of adverse media coverage, how to create a business plan, how to cope with a serious ethical lapse, whether to close a factory and what kind of compensation plans should be offered to employees.

A Day in the Life: Junior Corporate Associate

Here's a look at a day in the life of a junior corporate associate at a medium-sized firm.

8:30 am: Arrive at the office and proceed directly to an internal training session covering an aspect of the year-end reporting process. This training is part of a six-session series presented by the firm every year to prepare the associates for the upcoming reporting season.

10:00 am: Return to office to pick up file on a private biotechnology client and hurry to a meeting with a senior associate. At the meeting, discuss the list of names and addresses of the client's stockholders (mailing list), which I reviewed the day before in preparation for a Section 228 Notice of Action Taken mailing. Point out to the senior associate which addresses are missing and ask her to obtain these from the client. She also suggests where to look for additional information regarding stockholder addresses.

10:30 am: Discuss the upcoming Section 228 Notice of Action Taken with my assistant. This particular mailing will be to nearly one hundred stockholders. You have found that if you discuss upcoming large projects with your assistant in advance, she is more likely to clear her schedule of other work and help you complete the project in a timely manner.

10:35 am: Take a few minutes to check e-mails from the night before. Most of them discuss various due diligence issues that have been uncovered during document review for a merger. (I am working on a team with a mid-level associate and a partner on a merger of our client with and into another biotechnology company.)

10:50 am: Briefly review estimated corporate tax forms from California that need to be forwarded to another client. Draft a cover letter to the client to accompany the tax forms and instructions.

11:15 am: Meet with the mid-level associate to discuss various merger diligence issues and the "to-do" list for the day.

11:30 am: Proofread the cover letter to be sent with the tax forms and instructions and send the packet to the client.

11:40 am: At the request of the mid-level associate, call opposing counsel to discuss a new diligence question. Take notes of discussion. Copy a few documents from the master diligence file for the review of the mid-level associate and bring the copies to her office.

12:10 p.m.: Eat lunch in office. Organize e-mails from the previous day while eating. Moving e-mails from the Inbox into client-related folders helps you to locate relevant messages quickly.

1:00 p.m.: Revise the mailing list for the Section 228 mailing to incorporate new information provided by the senior associate. Find additional information in a closing binder that the senior associate provided during the morning meeting. Check the mailing list against the stock ledgers to ensure that all stockholders are accounted for. Give the list to assistant so that she can get an early start on preparing mailing labels.

Visit Vault at **www.vault.com** for insider company profiles, expert advice, career message boards, expert resume reviews, the Vault Job Board and more.

VAULT CAREER LIBRARY   **293**

Litigation Basics

What is litigation?

Litigation is always in the news—from the controversial landmark abortion case, Roe v. Wade, to the O.J. Simpson trials, to the environmental class action lawsuits portrayed in the films Erin Brockovich and A Civil Action. A litigation is a legal proceeding between two or more parties. A litigator is a lawyer who represents a party in litigation. Because litigation is an adversarial proceeding between opposing parties, most of a litigator's job involves preparing for trial, even if a negotiated settlement is the ultimate goal.

In cases where parties have contracted to resolve their disputes out of court, a mediator can be hired to find an amicable compromise between the parties. This mediation (or, in some cases, arbitration) reduces the number of cases that go to trial so the already crowded courts are not completely overwhelmed.

Criminal proceedings

There are two kinds of litigation: civil and criminal. When someone breaks a state or federal law, he commits an offense against society. The government, on behalf of the community, begins a criminal proceeding to hold the offender responsible. A criminal litigation is therefore between the government and the accused, or defendant. The government is represented by a prosecutor, typically a district attorney (for state prosecutions) or a federal prosecutor (for federal crimes). The defendant is represented by either a private criminal attorney or a public defender appointed by the state. (Occasionally, usually against the advice of both his lawyer and the judge, a defendant chooses to represent himself, or acts pro se.)

Most states divide crimes into misdemeanors and felonies. A misdemeanor is any offense that results in less than one year of jail time. Petty theft, possession of a small amount of drugs, or breaking and entering is some examples of misdemeanors. Many misdemeanors can result in a fine or instead of jail time. Felonies are more serious offenses that virtually always result in prison terms of more than one year and may include a fine as well as incarceration. Murder, racketeering, rape and kidnapping are all felony offenses. In some states, serious felonies, such as the murder of a policeman or murder with premeditation, are capital offenses, in which cases a criminal defendant might face the death penalty. A person accused of a crime is presumed innocent until proven guilty beyond a reasonable doubt.

Civil actions

A civil action encompasses virtually any non-criminal court proceeding. It can be a private action between two citizens, a proceeding by one person against the state, a suit by an individual against a corporation or any combination thereof. The party bringing the suit, known as the plaintiff or petitioner, usually is seeking a sum of money (damages) from another party (the defendant or respondent) to compensate her for a claimed injury or loss. Sometimes the remedy sought involves not money but performance; one party wants the court to compel another either to do something he is obligated to do or to stop doing something that is injurious to one bringing suit. In a civil action, the case turns not on the defendant's guilt but on the issue of liability—a party is found either liable or not liable. The burden of proof required to establish liability in a civil suit is generally a lower threshold than the "guilt beyond a reasonable doubt" required in a criminal trial.

In the case of both criminal and civil litigation, the parties may never actually make it to court; they might come to a mutual compromise before the trial date. Parties to a civil suit might reach a financial agreement or other settlement, while the prosecution and defense in a criminal case might agree to a plea bargain, under which a prosecutor offers a reduced charge or sentence in exchange for the defendant's plea of guilt.

Lawsuits and Trials

A lawsuit is filed at the trial level. A trial might be in front of a jury or just a judge (known as a bench trial). In criminal actions, a defendant has the right to a speedy trial. There is no such right for parties in civil cases, and many civil actions go on for years. Most litigation will never even reach a courtroom—the parties might settle, one side might withdraw from the suit or a judge might dismiss the case before trial.

A trial entails everything you see on television: a judge, a jury, a variety of evidence, opposing lawyers and two parties. During the trial, the jury considers questions of fact: Did Mr. Hughes kill his wife? Was the car crash an accident? Was XYZ Company negligent in manufacturing faulty women's lingerie? Did the wire in the plaintiff's bra actually cause the injury she claims it did? The jury is there to decide these questions, using only the evidence presented in court. Before and during the course of the trial, there are also questions of law to be addressed by the judge: Should photos of Mr. Hughes' bedroom be allowed into evidence? Is the testimony of XYZ's chief designer admissible? Should the fact that juror number three slept through the testimony result in a mistrial?

The judge decides questions of law, usually after both parties have presented their arguments. In making her decision, the judge relies on previous case law and the relevant rules of civil and criminal procedure. (You can see questions of law being decided on Law & Order and The Practice when the lawyers meet the judge in chambers before trial, usually to request that she exclude a piece of the prosecutor's evidence for one reason or another. In real life, before making such a decision the judge would review lengthy written memoranda from all lawyers involved).

When the trial is over, the losing party often has the opportunity to appeal the decision to an appellate court. The role of the appeals court is not to second-guess the jury's or judge's rulings on the facts; at the appellate level, only questions of law can be reviewed. The appellate court hears from both sides to decide, essentially, if the trial was conducted properly. If the appeals court concludes that a question of law was not properly decided by the trial judge, it can reverse or overturn the lower court's decision—essentially negating it—or it can remand the case, asking the lower court to reconsider the case in light of the appellate court's opinion. A reversal is often followed by a remand. In the case of Mr. Hughes' murder trial, an appellate court would not decide whether or not Mr. Hughes killed his wife—the jury already concluded that he did—but it can find that the photos of his bedrrom were improperly admitted into evidence. The court might then overturn the guilty verdict and remand the case back to the lower court for a new trial in which the jury will not be able to consider those photographs as evidence.

An appellate court is rarely seen on television, but the decisions of appeals courts are very important, not only to the parties involved but to future litigants in the same jurisdiction.

A Day in the Life: Corporate Litigation Associate

9:30 a.m.: Arrive at work. Get coffee, make small talk with officemate, and check e-mails .and phone messages with secretary.

10:15 a.m.: Return phone calls and emails. Call senior associate with question regarding yesterday's research issue. Call duplicating to check on document review on white-collar crime case, and put them in contact with paralegal assigned to the case.

10:40 a.m.: Go down to document review room. There are 70 boxes of documents here, but some are out being copied. Review documents with fellow associates, looking for relevant issues.

12:30 p.m.: Associate lunch in conference room. Lunch/training session is about witness interviews. Take notes and eat roast beef sandwiches. Schmooze with fellow associates about who's working for the most demanding partner.

Visit Vault at **www.vault.com** for insider company profiles, expert advice, career message boards, expert resume reviews, the Vault Job Board and more.

VAULT CAREER LIBRARY   295

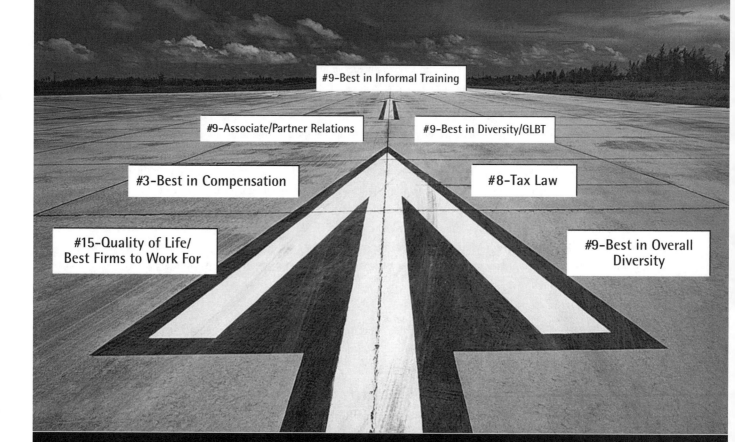

1:50 p.m.: Return to office. Check e-mails and continue with yesterday's research issue about statute of limitations in federal court for securities fraud cases. Spend most of the time researching the issue on Westlaw and Lexis-Nexis.

4:00 p.m.: Take a break from the computer and go down to the document review room. Go through witness statements, expert testimony, product promotional materials, statistical data and internal memos to look for evidence of intent.

5:15 p.m.: Return to office and prepare for meeting with partner and rest of team.

5:30 p.m.: Meeting with partner and rest of team. Meeting goes long, but the focus of the research has now changed. Partner would like a memo in 48 hours on this new research issue. Update partner on document review and duplicating process.

6:30 p.m.: Speak with senior associate about organization and approach of new memo and how to research new issue. Check with document review room on duplications of documents. Plan out how much more needs to be done and talk with paralegal about organizing document review.

7:30 p.m.: If you're feeling really motivated, you can go back to the document review room. Otherwise, leave for home, knowing it will be waiting for you tomorrow!

A Day in the Life: Assistant District Attorney

9:00 a.m.: Arrive at office, check e-mails and get files and paperwork for court.

10:00 a.m.: Arrive at court for multiple issues, including an arraignment for a burglary case, hearings for drug possession cases, money laundering case and attempted murder case. Speak with court clerks while clients arrive and judge hears various issues.

12:15 p.m.: Meet opposing counsel for plea bargain agreement for drug possession case.

1:00 p.m.: Quick lunch at desk, looking over emails and phone calls. Wait for witness to show up at 2:00.

2:00 p.m.: Witness doesn't show. Work on research for motion on attempted murder case involving Fourth Amendment right of seizure.

3:00 p.m.: Brief interview with police officers on felony assault case.

3:30 p.m.: Witness for 2:00 finally shows up with father and sister. Conduct fact-finding issue on domestic violence case. Witness recants some testimony and father pressures her not to testify against her husband, leaving ADA uncertain as to strength of case.

4:45 p.m.: Contact court clerks regarding hearing status of various cases.

5:10 p.m.: Review documents for money laundering and call witnesses and corporate officers for interviews in the next few days.

6:15 p.m.: Head home.

Visit Vault at **www.vault.com** for insider company profiles, expert advice,
career message boards, expert resume reviews, the Vault Job Board and more.

V/\ULT CAREER LIBRARY   **297**

Paralegal

A mixed lot

From freshly graduated English BAs to document-drafting veterans with training and certification, paralegals are really something of a mixed lot. Some have formal training, while others do not. Some have one of many certifications, while others have none. Paralegals, or legal assistants as they are sometimes called, come from a great variety of backgrounds and perform a wide range of tasks. As a result, compensation and working conditions vary to a large degree. Further complicating matters is that, while some legal assistants find they enjoy their paralegal careers, many others aspire to law degrees.

Swimming in paper

Generally speaking, much of what paralegals do involves the large mounds of paperwork generated by legal work. Legal assistants may find themselves sifting through these documents, organizing them, analyzing them, or even drafting them. In addition, paralegals perform research and prepare reports based upon their findings. To do this, paralegals must have a good understanding of legal terminology and good research skills. When permitted by law, paralegals involved with community service sometimes even represent clients at administrative hearings. In short, paralegals can do everything a lawyer does, except the "practice of law": presenting cases in court, setting legal fees and giving legal advice. Paralegals are free to do just about anything else, which is good if it involves using the brain, but numbing if it involves rote clerical work.

Varying pay

Pay for legal assistants reflects the great variety of the work performed. Entry-level workers do not enjoy high salaries, but with increased experience and education, compensation becomes healthier. Paralegals in major metropolitan areas tend to earn more money than those in smaller locales. Similarly, working for a large law firm means higher pay. Major firms may also have perks in the way of bonuses, extra vacation time, and tickets to sports events and the like. At any rate, paralegals can almost always count on hefty overtime hours at the rate of time and a half to boost salaries.

Some feel that obtaining a certification or a degree in paralegal studies can lead to greater compensation and responsibility. Two certifications are available to those in the profession, the Certified Legal Assistant exam (CLA) and the Paralegal Advanced Competency Exam (PACE). The two-day CLA exam is offered by the National Association of Legal Assistants three times a year. The PACE exam is affiliated with the National Federation of Paralegal Associations and is administered throughout the year by an independent agency. Once either of these certifications has been obtained, a paralegal may use the title Registered Paralegal (PR).

In addition to certification exams, many paralegal training programs are available (some are run through colleges and universities, while others are independent). Most of these degrees are either two- or four-year programs. Correspondence courses, which have grown increasingly popular due to the Internet, are also an option. Degrees recognized by the American Bar Association and the American Association for Paralegal Education tend to be the most reputable.

Law/Paralegal Employer Directory

Akin Gump Strauss Hauer & Feld LLP
Robert S. Strauss Building
1333 New Hampshire Avenue, NW
Washington, DC 20036-1564
Phone: (202) 887-4000
www.akingump.com

Arnold & Porter LLP
555 Twelfth Street, NW
Washington, DC 20004-1206
Phone: (202) 942-5000
www.arnoldporter.com

Baker & McKenzie
One Prudential Plaza
130 East Randolph Drive, Suite 2500
Chicago, IL 60601
Phone: (312) 861-8000
www.bakernet.com

Baker Botts L.L.P.
One Shell Plaza
910 Louisiana
Houston, TX 77002-4995
Phone: (713) 229-1234
www.bakerbotts.com

Boies, Schiller & Flexner LLP
570 Lexington Avenue, 16th Floor
New York, NY 10022
Phone: (212) 446-2300
www.bsfllp.com

Cadwalader, Wickersham & Taft LLP
One World Financial Center
New York, NY 10281
Phone: (212) 504-6000
www.cadwalader.com

Cleary Gottlieb Steen & Hamilton LLP
One Liberty Plaza
New York, NY 10006
Phone: (212) 225-2000

2000 Pennsylvania Avenue, NW
Washington, DC 20006
Phone: (202) 974-1500
www.cgsh.com

Clifford Chance US LLP
31 West 52nd Street
New York, NY 10019
Phone: (212) 878-8000
www.cliffordchance.com

William P. Rogers Building
2001 K Street NW
Washington, DC 20006
Phone: (202) 912-5000

Covington & Burling LLP
1201 Pennsylvania Avenue, NW
Washington, DC 20004-2401
Phone: (202) 662-6000
www.cov.com

Cravath, Swaine & Moore LLP
Worldwide Plaza
825 Eighth Avenue
New York, NY 10019-7475
Phone: (212) 474-1000
www.cravath.com

Davis Polk & Wardwell
450 Lexington Avenue
New York NY 10017
Phone: (212) 450-4000
www.davispolk.com

Debevoise & Plimpton LLP
919 Third Avenue
New York, NY 10022
Phone: (212) 909-6000
www.debevoise.com

Dewey Ballantine LLP
1301 Avenue of the Americas
New York, NY 10019
Phone: (212) 259-8000
www.deweyballantine.com

DLA Piper Rudnick Gray Cary US LLP
1200 19th Street, NW
Washington, DC 20036-2412
Phone: (202) 861-3900
www.dlapiper.com

Freshfields Bruckhaus Deringer
520 Madison Avenue
New York, NY 10022
Phone: (212) 277-4000

701 Pennsylvania Avenue NW, Suite 600
Washington, DC 20004
Phone: (202) 777-4500

65 Fleet Street
London EC4Y 1HS
Phone: +44 20-7936-4000
www.freshfields.com

Fried, Frank, Harris, Shriver & Jacobson LLP
One New York Plaza
New York, NY 10004-1980
Phone: (212) 859-8000
www.friedfrank.com

Fulbright & Jaworski L.L.P.
Fulbright Tower
1301 McKinney, Suite 5100
Houston, TX 77010-3095
Phone: (713) 651-5151
www.fulbright.com

Gibson, Dunn & Crutcher LLP
333 South Grand Avenue
Los Angeles, CA 90071-3197
Phone: (213) 229-7000
www.gibsondunn.com

Jenner & Block LLP
One IBM Plaza
Chicago, IL 60611-7603
Phone: (312) 222-9350
www.jenner.com

Jones Day
51 Louisiana Avenue, NW
Washington, DC 20001-2113
www.jonesday.com

Hogan & Hartson LLP
555 Thirteenth Street, NW
Washington, DC 20004-1109
Phone: (202) 637-5600
www.hhlaw.com

Visit Vault at **www.vault.com** for insider company profiles, expert advice, career message boards, expert resume reviews, the Vault Job Board and more.

VAULT CAREER LIBRARY   299

Law/Paralegal Employer Directory, cont.

King & Spalding LLP
1180 Peachtree Street N.E.
Atlanta, GA 30309-3521
Phone: (404) 572-4600
www.kslaw.com

Kirkland & Ellis LLP
Aon Center
200 East Randolph Drive
Chicago, IL 60601
Phone: (312) 861-2000
www.kirkland.com

Latham & Watkins LLP
633 West Fifth Street, Suite 4000
Los Angeles, CA 90071
Phone: (213) 485-1234
www.lw.com

Linklaters
One Silk Street
London, EC2Y 8HQ
Phone: 44 20 7456 2000

1345 Avenue of the Americas
New York, NY 10105
Phone: (212) 903-9000
www.linklaters.com

Mayer, Brown, Rowe & Maw LLP
71 South Wacker Drive
Chicago, IL 60606
Phone: (312) 782-0600
www.mayerbrownrowe.com

McDermott, Will & Emery
227 West Monroe
Chicago, IL 60606-5096
Phone: (312) 372-2000
www.mwe.com

Milbank, Tweed, Hadley & McCloy LLP
One Chase Manhattan Plaza
New York, NY 10005
Phone: (212) 530-5000
www.milbank.com

Morgan, Lewis & Bockius LLP
1701 Market Street
Philadelphia, PA 19103-2921
Phone: (215) 963-5000
www.morganlewis.com

Morrison & Foerster LLP
425 Market Street
San Francisco, CA 94105-2482
Phone: (415) 268-7000
www.MoFo.com

O'Melveny & Myers LLP
400 South Hope Street
Los Angeles, CA 90071-2899
Phone: (213) 430-6000
www.omm.com

Orrick, Herrington & Sutcliffe LLP
666 Fifth Avenue
New York, NY 10103-001
Phone: (212) 506-5000

The Orrick Building
405 Howard Street
San Francisco, CA 94105
Phone: (415) 773-5700
www.orrick.com

Paul, Hastings, Janofsky & Walker LLP
Paul Hastings Tower
515 South Flower Street, 25th Floor
Los Angeles, CA 90071
Phone: (213) 683-6000
www.paulhastings.com

Paul, Weiss, Rifkind, Wharton & Garrison LLP
1285 Avenue of the Americas
New York, NY 10019
Phone: (212) 373-3000
www.paulweiss.com

Pillsbury Winthrop Shaw Pittman LLP
1540 Broadway
New York, NY 10026
Phone: (212) 858-1000

50 Fremont Street
San Francisco, CA 94105
Phone: (415) 983-1000

2300 N Street, NW
Washington, DC 20037
Phone: (202) 663-8000
www.pillsburylaw.com

Proskauer Rose LLP
1585 Broadway
New York, NY 10036
Phone: (212) 969-3000
www.proskauer.com

Ropes & Gray LLP
One International Place
Boston, MA 02110-2624
Phone: (617) 951-7000
www.ropesgray.com

Shearman & Sterling LLP
599 Lexington Avenue
New York, NY 10022
Phone: (212) 848-4000
www.shearman.com

Sidley Austin LLP
One South Dearborn
Chicago, IL 60603
Phone: (312) 853-7000

787 Seventh Avenue
New York, NY 10019
Phone: (212) 839-5300
www.sidley.com

Simpson Thacher & Bartlett LLP
425 Lexington Avenue
New York, NY 10017
Phone: (212) 455-2000
www.simpsonthacher.com

Law/Paralegal Employer Directory, cont.

Skadden, Arps, Slate, Meagher & Flom LLP and Affiliates
Four Times Square
New York, NY 10036
Phone: (212) 735-3000
www.skadden.com

Sullivan & Cromwell LLP
125 Broad Street
New York, NY 10004
Phone: (212) 558-4000
www.sullcrom.com

Wachtell, Lipton, Rosen & Katz
51 West 52nd Street
New York, NY 10019-6150
Phone: (212) 403-1000
www.wlrk.com

Weil, Gotshal & Manges LLP
767 Fifth Avenue
New York, NY 10153
Phone: (212) 310-8000
www.weil.com

White & Case LLP
1155 Avenue of the Americas
New York, NY 10036
Phone: (212) 819-8200
www.whitecase.com

Williams & Connolly LLP
The Edward Bennett Williams Building
725 12th Street, NW
Washington, DC 20005
Phone: (202) 434-5000
www.wc.com

Willkie Farr & Gallagher LLP
The Equitable Center
787 Seventh Avenue
New York, NY 10019-6099
Phone: (212) 728-8000
www.willkie.com

Wilmer Cutler Pickering Hale and Dorr LLP
1875 Pennsylvania Avenue, NW
Washington, DC 20006
Phone: (202) 663-6000

60 State Street
Boston, MA 02109
Phone: (617) 526-6000
www.wilmerhale.com

Wilson Sonsini Goodrich & Rosati
650 Page Mill Road
Palo Alto, CA 94304-1050
Phone: (650) 493-9300
www.wsgr.com

Winston & Strawn LLP
35 West Wacker Drive
Chicago, IL 60601
Phone: (312) 558-5600
www.winston.com

Visit Vault at **www.vault.com** for insider company profiles, expert advice, career message boards, expert resume reviews, the Vault Job Board and more.

VAULT CAREER LIBRARY   **301**

Appreciation·
Achievement·Being·
Belonging·Becoming·
Development·Diversity·
Enhancement·Enjoyment·
Positive Experiences·
People·Friends·Family·
Flexibility·Freedom·Fulfillment·
Happiness·Health·Hopes·Identity·
Improvement·Integrity·
Knowledge·Nurture·
Opportunities·Opinions·
Satisfaction·Security·
Truth·Dreams

Quality of Life

What is your definition of QUALITY of life? At The Gallup Organization, you'll work in a culture that SUPPORTS you not just professionally, but personally. Whether your PASSION is building new business, managing consulting projects, or assisting executives, you'll have the OPPORTUNITY to do what you do BEST every day. We'll help you discover your TALENTS and build STRENGTHS.

How do we know that life is BETTER at Gallup? **A recent survey by Vault.com of 2,500 consultants ranks Gallup #1 in corporate culture.** At Gallup, we offer more than just a job — we offer you a FUTURE.

GALLUP

www.gallup.com/careers

BUILD
YOUR
FUTURE

Management Consulting

What is Consulting?

A giant industry, a moving target

Consulting, in the business context, means the giving of advice for pay. Consultants offer their advice and skill in solving problems, and are hired by companies who need the expertise and outside perspective that consultants possess. Some consulting firms specialize in giving advice on management and strategy, while others are known as technology specialists. Some concentrate on a specific industry area, like financial services or retail, and still others are more like gigantic one-stop shops with divisions that dispense advice on everything from top-level strategy, to choosing training software, to saving money on paper clips.

But consulting firms have one thing in common: they run on the power of their people. The only product consulting firms ultimately have to offer is their ability to make problems go away. As a consultant, you are that problem-solver.

Not the kind of consulting we mean

As a standalone term, "consulting" lacks real meaning. In a sense, everyone's a consultant. Have you ever been asked by a friend, "Do I look good in orange?" Then you've been consulted about your color sense. There are thousands upon thousands of independent consultants who peddle their expertise and advice on everything from retrieving data from computers to cat astrology. There are also fashion consultants, image consultants, and wedding consultants. For the purposes of this section, we are going to use the term "consulting" to refer specifically to management consulting.

Management consulting firms sell business advisory services to the leaders of corporations, governments, and non-profit organizations. Typical concentrations in consulting include strategy, IT, HR, finance, and operations. Types of problems in consulting include pricing, marketing, new product strategy, IT implementation, or government policy. Finally, consulting firms sell services in virtually any industry, such as pharmaceuticals, consumer packaged goods, or energy.

Firms can be organized or broken up according to topic, type of problem, or industry. For example, a firm might focus on strategy problems only, but in virtually any industry. Bain & Company is an example of one such firm. Another firm might focus on a specific industry, but advise on nearly any type of issue. Mercer Oliver Wyman, which focuses on the financial services industry, is an example of this type of firm. Many of the larger firms have a "matrix" organization, with industry practice groups but also functional practice groups. And some firms are extremely specialized. For example, a firm might have only two employees, both focusing solely on competitive analysis in the telecommunications industry. All of these are examples of management consulting.

Caveats about consulting

All this might sound great, but before we go on, we should address some common misconceptions about consulting.

- **Implementation**—You might be thinking, "All consultants do is figure out problems at companies and explain them. Awesome. I'm going to be making great money for doing something really easy." Unfortunately, that's not true. Spotting a client's problems is a mere fraction of the battle. (Most people with a fair amount of common sense and an outsider's perspective can identify a client's problems. And in many cases, clients also understand where the problems lie.)

  The job of the consultant, therefore, isn't just about knowing what's wrong. It's about figuring out how to make it right. Even finding the solution isn't the end of the story. Consultants must make sure the solution isn't too expensive or impractical to implement. (Many consulting firms have what's called an 80 percent rule: It's better to put in place a solution

Visit Vault at **www.vault.com** for insider company profiles, expert advice, career message boards, expert resume reviews, the Vault Job Board and more.

VAULT CAREER LIBRARY   303

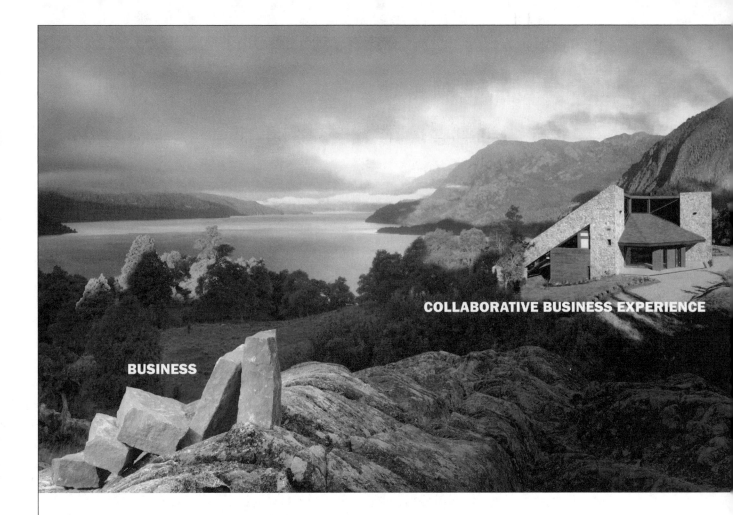

BUSINESS

COLLABORATIVE BUSINESS EXPERIENCE

TOGETHER. When a single word makes all the difference.

Transforming your enterprise – whether you're making big or small changes – is never easy. Experience has shown us that if we define measurable objectives and set realistic schedules **together,** build joint teams, and above all, anticipate and mitigate risks **together,** then we improve our chances. Add to that motivation and commitment of over 60,000 people around the world and the knowledge and experience we share with you daily, and the result is faster, and more tangible success that lasts.

Together. One word that captures the difference between typical business practice and Capgemini's unique branded approach to delivering Consulting, Technology and Outsourcing Services - the Collaborative Business Experience.

Let's create a Collaborative Business Experience – together.

CONSULTING.TECHNOLOGY.OUTSOURCING

www.us.capgemini.com

that takes care of 80 percent of the problem than to strive for a perfect solution that can't be put into place.) A corollary to this is the 80/20 rule: 80 percent of a problem can be solved in 20 percent of the time. Consultants must also get buy-in from the clients. Not only does bureaucracy often make implementation tough, but consultants must also convince individual client employees to help them make solutions work. It's tough to solve problems—and that's why clients hire consultants.

- **Glamour**—Consulting can indeed be exciting and high profile, but this is the exception, not the rule. Chances are, you won't be sitting across from the CEO at your next project kick-off, and you probably won't be staying in four-star hotels in the coolest cities in the world (though both are possible). Depending on the industry and location of your client's business, your environment might be a mid-range hotel in a small city, and you might be working with the senior vice president of one of the company's many business units.

- **Prestige**—Consulting is widely thought of as a prestigious career among business circles, particularly MBAs. But you should realize that in contrast to work in investment banking, your work in consulting will probably never get mentioned in *The Wall Street Journal*. Very few consulting firms are publicly recognized for the help they give.

As a result, few people outside of the industry really understand what consulting is. In fact, a running joke about consulting is that no one can explain it, no matter how hard or many times one tries. If you want a job you can explain to your grandmother, consulting isn't for you. Most "civilians" won't have heard of your firm—unless it has been involved in a scandal, that is.

- **Income**—The salary looks attractive on paper, but remember, it's not easy money. Divide your salary over the (large) number of hours, and the pay per hour isn't much better than other business careers.

So what does a consultant actually do, anyway?

Most "non-consultants" are mystified by the actual job and its day-to-day responsibilities. There are good reasons why this is so. While you're used to giving advice and solving problems, you may not understand how this translates into a career path. The problem is compounded because consultants tend to use a very distinctive vocabulary. You may not know what your skill set is, or how not to boil the ocean, or what the heck consultants mean when they talk about helicoptering. In addition, many consulting firms have their own specific philosophies and problem-attacking frameworks, which only raise the level of jargon.

The short answer is that you will be working on projects of varying lengths at varying sites for different clients. What you do will depend on your seniority, experience, phase of the project and your company. If you are a partner, you are selling work most of the time, whereas if you have a recent MBA degree, you are probably overseeing a couple of entry-level consultants doing research. For the most part, we'll describe the job that entry-level and mid-level (MBA or the equivalent) consultants do. Generally, projects follow the pitching/research/analysis/report writing cycle.

Depending where you are in the project lifecycle, here are some of the things you could be doing:

Pitching

- Helping to sell and market the firm (preparing documents and researching prospective clients in preparation for sales calls)

- Helping to write the proposal

- Presenting a sales pitch to a prospective client (usually with PowerPoint, Microsoft's presentation software)

Research

- Performing secondary research on the client and its industry using investment banking reports and other research sources (these include Bloomberg, OneSource, Hoover's Online, Yahoo! News and SEC filings)

Visit Vault at **www.vault.com** for insider company profiles, expert advice, career message boards, expert resume reviews, the Vault Job Board and more.

VAULT CAREER LIBRARY 305

a different kind of rating agency

Fitch Ratings is a leading global rating agency, committed to providing the world's credit markets with accurate, timely, and prospective credit opinions. Built on a foundation of organic growth and strategic acquisitions, Fitch Ratings has grown rapidly during the past decade, gaining market presence throughout the world and across all fixed income markets. Fitch Ratings is dual-headquartered in New York and London, operating offices and joint ventures in more than 50 locations and covering entities in more than 90 countries. Fitch Ratings is a majority-owned subsidiary of Fimalac, S.A., an international business support services group headquartered in Paris, France.

Analytical Positions

Entry-level analysts are key contributors to all analytical departments: Structured Finance, Corporate Finance, Public Finance, Credit Products, and Credit Policy. If you join Fitch, you will:

> Provide support to lead analysts on new issue ratings or transaction performance reviews.
> Gather and analyze financial statements, as well as the latest industry, regulatory, and economic information.
> Develop an understanding of legal and accounting issues affecting securities.
> Run computer models and spreadsheet-based applications to evaluate credit risk and cash flow coverage.
> Present analysis or transaction reviews at rating committee meetings.
> Develop an ability to differentiate among rating categories.
> Be involved in drafting rating affirmations or other rating actions.
> Write research reports and press releases.
> Adopt Fitch style: a high-level of service to our clients and a team-oriented approach to ratings analysis.

Candidates Must Possess :

> BA/BS degree.
> Ability to apply advanced mathematical concepts.
> Excellent verbal and written communication skills.
> Proficiency in Microsoft Word/Excel®.
> Knowledge of Access® and Bloomberg a plus.

For more information about career opportunities, please log on to *www.fitchratings.com* and visit the "Careers at Fitch" section of our website.

Summer Internships available
Equal Opportunity Employer

www.fitchratings.com

- Interviewing the client's customers to gather viewpoints on the company

- Checking your firm's data banks for previous studies that it has done in the industry or with the client, and speaking to the project leads about their insights on the firm

- Facilitating a weekly client team discussion about the client company's business issues

Analysis

- Building Excel discounted cash flow (DCF) and/or other quantitative financial models

- Analyzing the gathered data and the model for insights

- Helping to generate recommendations

Reporting

- Preparing the final presentation (typically a "deck" of PowerPoint slides, though some firms write up longer reports in Microsoft Word format)

- Helping to present the findings and recommendations to the client

Implementation

- Acting as a project manager for the implementation of your strategy, if your firm is typically active during the implementation phase of a project

- Executing the coding, systems integration, and testing of the recommended system, if you work for an IT consulting practice

- Documenting the team's work after the project is over

Administration

- Working on internal company research when your firm has no projects for you. (Being unstaffed is referred to as being "on the beach," a pleasant name for what is often a tedious time.)

- Filling out weekly time tracking and expense reports

Keep in mind that the analysis phase—usually the most interesting part—is probably the shortest part of any assignment. Consultants staffed on projects typically do a lot of research, financial analysis, Excel model building and presentation. You will attend lots of meetings in your quest to find the data, create the process and meet the people who will help you resolve the issues you've been hired to address. And, when you're not staffed, you will spend time "on the beach" doing research on prospective clients and helping with marketing efforts. (It's called "on the beach" because the time when you're not staffed on a paid engagement is usually less frenetic—though not always so!) Consulting firms spend a lot of time acquiring the work, and depending on how the firm is structured or how the economy is doing, you could spend significant amounts of time working on proposals. For you, this usually means lots of research, which is then elucidated on the omnipresent PowerPoint slides.

To some extent, though, the boundaries of the job are virtually limitless. Each project carries with it a new task, a new spreadsheet configuration, a new type of sales conference, or an entirely new way of thinking about business. To top it all off, you often must travel to your work assignment and work long hours in a pressurized environment. It's not easy.

Visit Vault at **www.vault.com** for insider company profiles, expert advice, career message boards, expert resume reviews, the Vault Job Board and more.

VAULT CAREER LIBRARY   **307**

diverse people

working together

People are our greatest asset. We recognize that it takes exceptional individuals with different talents and perspectives to team creatively and develop the innovative solutions our clients expect. To learn more about how you can realize your full potential as a member of our team of leading global consultants, visit www.boozallen.com.

Booz Allen Hamilton is the one firm that helps clients solve their toughest problems, works in true partnership with clients, and delivers results that endure.

Booz | Allen | Hamilton

Consulting Skill Sets

Consultants focus their energies in a wide variety of practice areas and industries. Their individual jobs, from a macro level, are as different as one could imagine. While a supply chain consultant advises a client about lead times in their production facility, another consultant is creating a training protocol for a new software package. What could be more different?

Despite the big picture differences, however, consultants' day-to-day skill sets are, by necessity, very similar. (Before we go any further: by skill set, we mean "your desirable attributes and skills that contribute value as a consultant." Skill set is a handy, abbreviated way to refer to same.)

Before we talk about the skill sets, keep in mind that there is a big difference between the job now and the job six to eight years from now, if and when you are a partner. We are going to talk about whether you would like the job now, but you should think about whether this might be a good long-term career for you. Is your goal to see it through to partner? If you would rather have an interesting job for six years, you just have to know you have the qualities to be a good consultant and manager. To be a partner, you have to be a persuasive salesperson. You will spend nearly 100 percent of your time selling expensive services to companies who don't think they need help. Your pay and job security will depend on your ability to make those sales.

Do you have the following characteristics in your skill set?

- **Do you work well in teams?** Consultants don't work alone. Not only do they frequently brainstorm with other consultants, but they also often work with employees at the client company, or even with consultants from other companies hired by the client. Consultants also frequently attend meetings and interview potential information sources. If you're the sort of person who prefers to work alone in quiet environments, you will not enjoy being a consultant.

- **Do you multi-task well?** Not only can consulting assignments be frenetic, but consultants are often staffed on more than one assignment. Superior organizational skills and a good sense of prioritization are your friends. Would your friends describe you as a really busy person who's involved in a ton of activities, and still able to keep your personal life on track?

- **Speaking of friends, do you like talking to people?** Do you find yourself getting into interesting conversations over lunch and dinner? If you consider yourself a true introvert and find that speaking to people all day saps your energy, you will likely find consulting quite enervating. On the other hand, if you truly relish meetings, talking to experts, explaining your viewpoints, cajoling others to cooperate with you and making impromptu presentations, you've got some valuable talents in your consulting skill set.

- **Did you love school?** Did you really like going to class and doing your homework? There's a high correlation between academic curiosity and enjoyment of consulting.

- **Are you comfortable with math?** Consulting firms don't expect you to be a math professor, but you should be comfortable with figures, as well as commonly used programs like Excel, Access and PowerPoint. If you hate math, you will hate consulting. On a related note, you should also relish and be good at analysis and thinking creatively. Consultants have a term, now infiltrating popular culture, called "out of the box thinking." This means the ability to find solutions that are "outside the box"—not constrained by commonly accepted facts.

- **Are you willing to work 70, even 80 hours a week?** Consultants must fulfill client expectations. If you must work 80 hours a week to meet client expectations, then that will be your fate. If you have commitments outside work, for example, you may find consulting hours difficult. Even if you have no major commitments outside work, understand what such a schedule means to you. Try working from 8 a.m. to 10 p.m. one day. Now imagine doing so five days a week for months on end.

Visit Vault at **www.vault.com** for insider company profiles, expert advice, career message boards, expert resume reviews, the Vault Job Board and more.

VAULT CAREER LIBRARY   309

EXPERIENCE. SUCCESS.

INVEST IN YOURSELF

You've invested a lot to get to where you are today. Now join a company that invests in you. As a global, $14.6 billion, Fortune 500® provider of IT services, CSC rewards your talent with the resources you need to grow your career. The result? Exceptional career mobility, and the chance to learn from 78,000 colleagues worldwide.

At CSC, we build and deploy mission-critical technologies that help our clients achieve and maintain strategic advantage. Whether helping to put the space shuttle in orbit, suppressing forest fires in California or seeking gaps in IT security, you'll find a culture of collaboration and innovation dedicated to making sure you have the skills to succeed. Here, you can explore different projects, learn new skills and create a career that matches your needs.

CSC currently has opportunities for highly-motivated, academically strong candidates who are seeking careers that constantly offer new challenges. If you want to make a career in technology – its development, its deployment, or its practical application – join CSC. To learn more, **visit www.csc.com** or **http://careers.csc.com**.

An Equal Opportunity Employer M/F/D/V.

EXPERIENCE. RESULTS.

CSC.COM   CONSULTING   SYSTEMS INTEGRATION   OUTSOURCING

• **Last, but certainly not least, are you willing to travel frequently?** (See the next section for a discussion of travel in consulting.)

Be truthful. If you can't answer most of these points with a resounding "yes," consulting is most likely not for you. The point is not just to get the job, but also to know what you're getting into—and to truly want to be a consultant.

The traveling salesman problem

A lot of people go into the consulting field with the notion that travel is fun. "Traveling four days a week? No problem! My last vacation to Italy was a blast!" However, many soon find the traveling consultant's life to be a nightmare. Many consultants leave the field solely because of travel requirements.

Here's what we mean by consulting travel. Different consulting firms have different travel models, but there are two basic ones:

• A number of consulting firms (the larger ones) spend four days on the client site. This means traveling to the destination city Monday morning, spending three nights in a hotel near the client site, and flying home late Thursday night. (This will, of course, vary, depending on client preference and flight times.) The same firms often try to staff "regionally" to reduce flying time for consultants.

• The other popular travel model is to go to the client site "as needed." This generally means traveling at the beginning of the project for a few days, at the end of the project for the presentation, and a couple of times during the project. There is less regularity and predictability with this travel model, but there is also less overall time on the road.

Here are some variations of these travel modes that pop up frequently:

• International projects involve a longer-term stay on the client site. (Flying consultants to and from the home country every week can get expensive.) For example, the consultant might stay two or three weeks on or near the client site (the client might put you up in a corporate apartment instead of a hotel to save costs) and then go home for a week, repeating the process until the end of the project.

• Then, there is the "local" project that is really a long commute into a suburb, sometimes involving up to two hours in a car. Examples of this include consulting to Motorola (based in not-so-convenient Schaumburg, IL) while living in Chicago, or consulting to a Silicon Valley client while living in San Francisco. In these cases, you might opt to stay at a local hotel after working late, instead of taking the long drive home. This is not very different from non-local travel, and it can be more grueling, due to the car commute.

You need to ask yourself a number of questions to see if you are travel-phobic. For example, when you pack to go on vacation, do you stress about it? Do you always underpack or overpack? Do you hate flying? Do you hate to drive? Do you mind sleeping in hotel rooms for long periods of time? Are you comfortable with the idea of traveling to remote cities and staying there for three or four nights every week for 10 weeks? If you're married, do you mind being away from your spouse (and children if you have them) for up to three nights a week? Does your family mind? Will your spouse understand and not hold it against you if you have to cancel your anniversary dinner because the client wants you to stay a day later? If you and your spouse both travel for work, who will take care of the pets? Does the idea of managing your weekly finances and to-do lists from the road bother you?

If these questions make your stomach churn, look for consulting companies that promise a more stable work environment. For example, if you work in financial consulting and live in New York City, most of your clients may be local. But because consulting firms don't always have the luxury of choosing their clients, they can't guarantee that you won't travel. Moreover, many large companies build their corporate campus where they can find cost-effective space, often in the suburbs or large corporate parks. (If you absolutely can not travel, some of the largest consulting firms, such as Accenture, have certain business units that can guarantee a non-traveling schedule. Ask.)

Visit Vault at **www.vault.com** for insider company profiles, expert advice, career message boards, expert resume reviews, the Vault Job Board and more.

V/\ULT CAREER LIBRARY   **311**

Note that travel is common in the consulting field, but not all consultants travel. And not all clients expect you to be on site all the time. It absolutely depends on the firm's travel model, industry, your location, and most importantly, your project.

Who Hires Consultants, and Why?

Corporations, governments, and non-profit institutions hire consultants for a number of reasons. Every consulting project springs from a client's need for help, or at least the kind of help that short-term, internal hiring can't solve. Some clients, for example, need to overhaul their entire IT infrastructure, yet they're out of touch with the latest back-end systems or don't have the staff resources for such a large project. Other clients may be merging, but lack any experience with post-merger staffing procedures, and need a neutral party to mediate. Some clients may need an outsider's perspective on a plant shutdown. Perhaps a client wants to bring in extra industry knowledge.

Consultants get hired for political reasons too. Launching big projects can be very cumbersome, particularly at Fortune 500 companies,. In order for a single dollar to be spent on such a project, most companies require senior executive approval. And without a major consultancy's brand name attached to the project, approval can be hard to get. But once a consulting firm steps into the picture, everyone involved has plausible deniability in the event that the project fails. There is an old adage: "No one ever got fired for hiring McKinsey" (or a similarly prestigious consulting firm.) Some clients still adhere to this as a rule of thumb.

Second, even if a giant project gets the green light, there's no guaranteeing it will be implemented. The reason? Simple bureaucratic inertia. Senior executives lose interest. Direct reports move on to other issues. In short, companies lose their focus. (An insider at a large private global corporation reports that steps from a major consulting report from 1996 were approved but, as of September 2002, had not yet been implemented.) By bringing in consultants to oversee large projects, companies ensure that someone is always watching the ball. In many cases, the correct solution may be quite evident to many, but having it confirmed by an outside party makes implementing a plan easier politically.

In the era of downsizing, consultants have another political use. Companies with an itch to fire a percentage of their workforce often like to bring in consultants. When the consultants recommend a workforce reduction, the company can fire at will, blaming their hired guns for the downsizing.

For some types of consulting (particularly outsourcing or IT), consultants are actually a form of cost-effective labor. It costs the firm less money to hire some outsiders to help them with a project, rather than hire some folks full-time at the expense of a competitive salary and benefits package. Consultants may also get the job done faster, not because they are necessarily better, but because the company might not get away with forcing regular employees to adhere to a compressed time frame by staying late hours. By definition, consultants are hired to work not at the pace of the corporation but at a differently prescribed pace. A contingency performance basis makes this an even better deal for the client.

Whatever the reasons for hiring consultants, they're bound to be compelling—because, even despite the cost-effectiveness argument in some cases, consultants are very costly on average. Given travel expenses, hotel bills, and actual project fees, hourly prices for consultants can easily climb into the $500 per hour range.

The worker behind the curtain

Consultants are a back-room breed of professional. In joint projects with their clients, they do much of the work and can expect none of the recognition. All consultants must deliver bottom-line value, and often spend countless hours huddled in cramped spaces to do just that. If you do a great job, chances are your client will thank you, but you may never hear about it again. In some cases, you will leave your project before its completion and may never know whether it succeeded or failed.

If you enjoy recognition and completion, you will want to consider the type of consulting firm you join. Does your firm have a history of repeat business? If so, you will have a better chance of seeing the client through different projects and business cycles; you may even work with the same client on different engagements. (Marakon Associates, for example, boasts that 90 percent of its work comes from engagements with previous clients.) Other firms might offer a methodology that isn't as repeatable. If your firm focuses solely on competitive analysis studies, chances are good that, if your client stays in the same industry, you won't need to sell that service to them again.

Economic consulting firms like Charles River Associates and the Brattle Group often help law firms with litigation support, including research, economic analysis, and testimonies. This can be very interesting work, and since you're supporting one side or the other of a public dispute, you will certainly know how the fruits of your labor will turn out. Depending on the size of the dispute, so might everyone else who follows the business news.

Another example is M&A consulting. Some firms, like L.E.K. Consulting, have practice areas specifically focused on due diligence, company analysis, and transaction support. The bad news is that on such projects, you are subject to the even longer and more erratic hours suffered by other M&A professionals. On the bright side, you will eventually read in The Wall Street Journal about any triumph enjoyed by your client. Your firm may not be mentioned, but at least you will be able to see the results of your hard work become a reality. (It'll also be easier for you to transition to other financial work in the future, if that is your wish.)

So, think about the level of recognition and completion you need for your work, and look for a firm that does the type of work that suits that level. If you find that you require higher levels of recognition and completion than any type of consulting can offer, then you may want to look into other professions.

Training for Consultants

A career in consulting is attractive for many reasons, but few of these are as important to jobseekers as the amount of training they will receive. Unlike industries such as consumer products or pharmaceuticals, where companies funnel investment dollars into product design and research & development, the consulting industry's largest expenditure (apart from staff salaries and overhead) is training. Every year, consulting firms allocate as much as 20 percent of their revenues to internal training programs, and consultants reap the benefits. It is not uncommon for a consultant to spend four to eight weeks per year attending firm-sponsored classes, taking computer-based training programs (CBTs), and studying industry-related literature to improve their performance on the job.

The training requirements in consulting are, by any measure, extensive, and employees who hail from top-ranked schools and prestigious firms find the ongoing skill development not only to be personally satisfying, but also valuable. Headhunters and recruiters for Fortune 500 companies realize how much training consultants receive, and they are willing to pay top dollar for people who have spent considerable time developing their skills.

Orientation training

Over the course of their careers, consultants will encounter two general categories of training: orientation and ongoing training. Orientation training begins soon after new hires walk in the door and greet their assigned human resource representatives. In large firms, most of the orientation training actually occurs in a distant location: after new hires fill out reams of paperwork at their home office, they board a plane and fly to the firm's massive training campus. Once they check into their assigned rooms, attend a welcome meeting, and spend some time getting to know their "classmates" from around the world, they begin a program that will last anywhere from one to four weeks, depending on the firm.

Orientation training is notoriously rigorous and exhausting. New hires spend most of their days working in teams, meeting with firm executives who pose as clients, attending lectures, learning computer code and completing CBTs. Consulting firms

Visit Vault at www.vault.com for insider company profiles, expert advice, career message boards, expert resume reviews, the Vault Job Board and more.

VAULT CAREER LIBRARY   313

spend millions of dollars each year to prepare new hires for their first few projects and they make sure that, by the end of the training, employees understand just how strenuous consulting can be. Consulting firms do budget in time for rest and relaxation, but such time pales in comparison to the hard work and countless hours of team-based learning. Regardless, most new consultants, despite feeling worn out at the end of each day, find the experience very gratifying. Orientation training may be a rude awakening, but it offers many perks. Where else can recent college graduates work with people from around the world, build lasting friendships, and be paid large sums of money to attend class?

Ongoing training

Once consultants get acclimated to living in hotels and working with clients, training requirements re-emerge as part of their ongoing development. Every year experienced consultants complete a curriculum of computer training, industry-specific seminars, management workshops and a host of other training programs designed to complement on-the-job learning.

Aside from making consultants better at what they do, ongoing training also functions as a tool to gauge how ready employees are for promotion. Indeed, many firms will not promote an employee unless he first completes the required curriculum for that particular year. Consultants, therefore, have a two-part incentive for completing their ongoing training requirements. Not only do they hope to become better consultants, but they want very much to rise through the ranks, make more money and have greater responsibility.

Management Consulting Employer Directory

Booz Allen Hamilton

8283 Greensboro Drive
McLean, Virginia 22102
www.boozallen.com

Undergraduate schools Booz Allen recruits from:

Carnegie Mellon; Columbia; Georgetown; Howard; Maryland; Michigan; MIT; Northwestern; Penn; Penn St.; Rice; SMU; Virginia; Virginia Tech

Booz Allen Hamilton is a global strategy consulting firm. We work with our clients-senior executives of Fortune 500 companies and public sector agencies-to transform their organizations and their industries with our combination of strategy, technology, operations, and change management consulting capabilities. Undergraduate hires typically work with clients in primarily analytical roles on strategy-based transformation projects.

Capgemini

Five Times Square
New York, NY 10036
www.us.capgemini.com/careers

Capgemini, one of the world's foremost providers of Consulting, Technology and Outsourcing services, assists clients via the Collaborative Business Experience. CBE is designed to help our clients achieve better, faster, more sustainable results through seamless access to our network of world-leading technology partners and collaboration-focused methods and tools. We help clients implement growth strategies, leverage technology, and thrive through the power of collaboration. Capgemini employs approximately 61,000 people worldwide and reported 2005 global revenues of 6,954 million euros.

Computer Sciences Corporation

Corporate Headquarters
2100 East Grand Ave.
El Segundo, CA 90245
http://careers.csc.com

Visit Vault at **www.vault.com** for insider company profiles, expert advice, career message boards, expert resume reviews, the Vault Job Board and more.

VAULT CAREER LIBRARY   315

Management Consulting Employer Directory, cont.

Gallup

901 F Street
Washington, DC 20004
Recruiting Contact Phone: 888-288-8595
www.gallup.com/collegerecruiting

GALLUP

Recruiter contacts are located at www.gallup.com/collegerecruiting

Undergraduate schools Gallup recruits from:
Gallup recruits at a number of colleges and universities across the US and Internationally. To see if Gallup recruits at your school, please contact your recruiter at www.gallup.com/collegerecruiting

Gallup Consulting is very different from most consulting firms. While other firms provide services in traditional disciplines like cost reduction, building or re-engineering processes and systems, or mergers and acquisitions, we help companies drive true organic growth — revenue and profit increase from continuing operations. Our consultants are trusted advisors to many of the world's leading companies. Our approach enables us to identify, develop, and implement solutions that align with our clients' visions and strategies.

Accenture
1345 Avenue of the Americas
New York, NY 10105
Phone: (917) 452-4400
Fax: (917) 527-5387
www.accenture.com

The Advisory Board Company
2445 M Street, NW
Washington, DC 20037
Phone: (202) 266-5600
Fax: (202) 266-5600
www.advisoryboardcompany.com

Analysis Group, Inc.
111 Huntington Avenue, 10th Floor
Boston, MA 02199
Phone: (617) 425-8000
Fax: (617) 425-8001
www.analysisgroup.com

Arthur D. Little
68 Fargo Street
Boston, MA 02210
Phone: (617) 443-0309
Fax: (617) 443-0166
www.adlittle-us.com

A.T. Kearney
222 West Adams Street
Chicago, IL 60606
Phone: (312) 648-0111
www.atkearney.com

Bain & Company
131 Dartmouth Street
Boston, MA 02116
Phone: (617) 572-2000
Fax: (617) 572-2427
www.bain.com

BearingPoint
1676 International Drive
McLean, VA 22102
Phone: (703) 747-3000
Fax: (703) 747-8500
www.bearingpoint.com

Booz Allen Hamilton
8283 Greensboro Drive
McLean, VA 22102
Phone: (703) 902-5000
Fax: (703) 902-3333
www.boozallen.com

Boston Consulting Group
Exchange Place
31st Floor
Boston, MA 02109
Phone: (617) 973-1200
Fax: (617) 973-1339
www.bcg.com

Cambridge Associates LLC
100 Summer Street
Boston, MA 02110
Phone: (617) 457-7500
Fax: (617) 457-7501
www.cambridgeassociates.com

Capgemini
750 Seventh Avenue
Suite 1800
New York, NY 10019
Phone: (212) 314-8000
Fax: (212) 314-8001
www.us.capgemini.com

Cornerstone Research
599 Lexington Avenue, 43rd Floor
New York, NY 10022-7642
Phone: (212) 605-5000
Fax: (212) 759-3045

1000 El Camino Real, Suite 250
Menlo Park, CA 94025-4327
Phone: (650) 853-1660
Fax: (650) 324-9204
www.cornerstone.com

Management Consulting Employer Directory, cont.

Corporate Executive Board
2000 Pennsylvania Avenue, NW
Suite 6000
Washington, DC 20006
Phone: (202) 777-5000
Fax: (202) 777-5100
www.executiveboard.com

CRA International
John Hancock Tower
200 Clarendon Street, T-33
Boston, MA 02116
Phone: (617) 425-3000
Fax: (617) 425-3132
www.crai.com

Dean & Company
8065 Leesburg Pike, Suite 500
Vienna, VA 22182
Phone: (703) 506-3900
Fax: (703) 506-3905
www.dean.com

Deloitte Consulting LLP
1633 Broadway, 35th Floor
New York, NY 10019
Phone: (212) 492-4500
Fax: (212) 492-4743
www.deloitte.com

Diamond Management & Technology Consultants, Inc.
John Hancock Center
875 North Michigan Avenue
Suite 3000
Chicago, IL 60611
Phone: (312) 255-5000
Fax: (312) 255-6000
www.diamondconsultants.com

First Manhattan Consulting Group
90 Park Avenue, 18th Floor
New York, NY 10016
Phone: (212) 557-0500
www.fmcg.com

FTI Consulting
500 East Pratt Street
Suite 1400
Baltimore 21202
Phone: (410) 951-4800
Fax: (410) 951-4895
www.fticonsulting.com

Gallup Consulting
901 F Street, NW
Washington, DC 20004
Phone: (877) 242-5587
Toll Free: (202) 715-3030
Fax: (202) 715-3041
www.gallup.com

Gartner, Inc.
56 Top Gallant Road
Stamford, CT 06904
Phone: (203) 964-0096
www.gartner.com

Giuliani Partners LLC
5 Times Square
New York, NY 10036
Phone: (212)931-7300
Fax: (212) 931-7310
www.giulianipartners.com

Hewitt Associates
100 Half Day Road
Lincolnshire, IL 60069
Phone: (847) 295-5000
Fax: (847) 295-7634
www.hewitt.com

Huron Consulting Group
550 West Van Buren
Chicago, IL 60607
Phone: (312) 583-8700
Toll Free: (866) 229-8700
Fax: (312) 583-8701
www.huronconsultinggroup.com

IBM Global Business Services
New Orchard Road
Armonk, New York 10504
Phone: (914) 499-1900
Fax: (914) 765-7382
www-1.ibm.com/services/

Katzenbach Partners LLC
381 Park Avenue South
Fifth Floor
New York, NY 10016
Phone: (212) 213-5505
Fax: (212) 213-5024
www.katzenbach.com

Kurt Salmon Associates
1355 Peachtree Street, NE
Suite 900
Atlanta, GA 30309
Phone: (404) 892-0321
Fax: (404) 898-9590
www.kurtsalmon.com

LECG
2000 Powell Street, Suite 600
Emeryville, CA 94608
Phone: (510) 985-6700
Fax: (510) 653-9898
www.lecg.com

L.E.K. Consulting
28 State Street
16th Floor
Boston, MA 02109
Phone: (617) 951-9500
Fax: (617) 951-9392
www.lek.com

Mars & Co
124 Mason Street
Greenwich, CT 06830
Phone: (203) 629-9292
Fax: (203) 629-9432
www.marsandco.com

Marakon Associates
245 Park Avenue
44th Floor
New York, NY 10167
Phone: (212) 377-5000
Fax: (212) 377-6000
www.marakon.com

Visit Vault at **www.vault.com** for insider company profiles, expert advice,
career message boards, expert resume reviews, the Vault Job Board and more.

VAULT CAREER LIBRARY 317

Management Consulting Employer Directory, cont.

McKinsey & Company
55 East 52nd Street
New York, NY 10022
Phone: (212) 446-7000
Fax: (212) 446-8575
www.mckinsey.com

Mercer Human Resource Consulting
1166 Avenue of the Americas
New York, NY 10036
Phone: (212) 345-7000
Fax: (212) 345-7414
www.mercerHR.com

Mercer Management Consulting
1166 Avenue of the Americas
32nd Floor
New York, NY 10036
Phone: (212) 345-8000
Fax: (212) 345-8075
www.mercermc.com

Mercer Oliver Wyman
99 Park Avenue, 5th Floor
New York, NY 10016
Phone: (212) 541-8100
Fax: (212) 541-8957/8958
www.merceroliverwyman.com

Monitor Group
Two Canal Park
Cambridge, MA 02141
Phone: (617) 252-2000
Fax: (617) 252-2100
www.monitor.com

Mitchell Madison Group
17 State Street, 22nd Floor
New York, NY 10004
Phone: (212) 605-0141
Fax: (212) 605-0142
www.mitchellmadison.com

Navigant Consulting, Inc.
615 North Wabash Avenue
Chicago, IL 60611
Phone: (312) 573-5600
Fax: (312) 573-5678

www.navigantconsulting.com

NERA Economic Consulting
50 Main Street, 14th Floor
White Plains, NY 10606
Phone: (914) 448-4000
Fax: (914) 448-4040
www.nera.com

OC&C Strategy Consultants
244 Madison Avenue, Fourth Floor
New York, NY 10016
Phone: (646) 479-7127
www.occstrategy.com

PA Consulting Group
4601 North Fairfax Drive
Suite 600
Arlington, VA 22203
Phone: (571) 227-9000
Fax: (571) 227-9001
123 Buckingham Palace Road
London
SW1W 9SR
United Kingdom
Phone: +44 20 7730 9000
Fax: +44 20 7333 5050
www.paconsulting.com

The Parthenon Group
200 State Street, 14th Floor
Boston, MA 02109
Phone: (617) 478-2550
Fax: (617) 478-2555
www.parthenon.com

PRTM
1050 Winter Street
Suite 3000
Waltham, MA 02451
Phone: (781) 434-1200
Fax: (781) 647-2804
444 Castro Street
Suite 600
Mountain View, CA 94041
Phone: (650) 967-2900
Fax: (650) 967-6367
www.prtm.com

Putnam Associates
25 Burlington Mall Road
Burlington, MA 01803
Phone: (781) 273-5480
Fax: (781) 273-5484
putassoc.com

Roland Berger Strategy Consultants
HighLight Towers
Mies-van-der-Rohe-Straße 6
80807 Munich
Germany
Phone: +49 89 9230-0
Fax: +49 89 9230-8202
www.rolandberger.com

Stern Stewart & Co.
780 Third Avenue, 6th Floor
New York, NY 10017
Phone: (212) 261-0600
Fax: (212) 581-6420
www.sternstewart.com

Strategic Decisions Group
735 Emerson Street
Palo Alto, CA 94301
Phone: (650) 475-4400
Fax: (650) 475-4401
www.sdg.com

Towers Perrin
263 Tresser Blvd.
Stamford, CT 06901
Phone: (203) 326-5400
www.towersperrin.com

Watson Wyatt Worldwide
901 North Glebe Road
Arlington, VA 22203
Phone: (703) 258-8000
Fax: (703) 258-8585
www.watsonwyatt.com

ZS Associates
1800 Sherman Avenue, 7th Floor
Evanston, IL 60201
Phone: (888) 972-4173
Fax: (888) 972-7329
www.zsassociates.com

Do you have an interview coming up with a consulting firm?

Unsure how to handle a case interview?

Vault Live Case Interview Prep

Vault's consulting experts bring you a new service to help you prepare for interviews with consulting firms. We'll help you prepare for that all-important case interview with a 30-minute mock interview and a 30-minute question and answer session with our consulting expert over the telephone.

A Vault consulting expert will put you through a real case used by the major consulting firms. You will be given the case at your appointment and will be asked to explain it, dissect it, and give a rationale for your responses.

The prep session will cover:

- Case strategies for attacking different case types
- Case frameworks, including Value Chain Analysis and Value Drivers Frameworks
- Market sizing cases
- A representative business strategy case (for example, a market-entry case)
- And more!

For more information go to
www.vault.com/consulting

> the most trusted name in career information™

Manufacturing

Manufacturing Industry Overview

This engine's humming right along

America's manufacturing industry is a powerful engine driving the nation's economy, making up 11 percent of employment and 12 percent of the US gross domestic product (GDP) in 2005. In the past decade, the industry contributed 22 percent of the country's economic growth, or 28 percent with the addition of software production. Through a phenomenon known as the multiplier effect, manufacturing actually creates economic output in other industries by using intermediate goods and services in its production process—so that, according to the Department of Commerce, every $1 of a manufacturing product sold to a final user creates an additional $1.43 in intermediate economic output. The U.S. continues to lead the world in many manufacturing sectors, including automobiles, aerospace, steel, telecommunications and consumer goods; it also maintains the lead in exports of manufactured products. Manufacturing and exporting goods is critical to maintaining a strong currency and economy, so it's no wonder economists pay close attention to manufacturing stats and figures.

Beginning in 2000, following a boom that spanned most of the 20th century, manufacturing employment has been declining, most sharply during the 2001-2003 economic downturn. Despite the economy's general resurgence from 2003 to 2005, industry employment has, according to the Bureau of Labor Statistics (BLS), only begun to level off. A number of circumstances led to the slump, including increased oil and energy prices, more efficient and less manpower-intensive production methods (productivity increased 5 percent between 2004 and 2005) and a strong U.S. dollar, which weakened the export trade.

Auto manufacturing for the people

Manufacturing has long been closely tied to automobile production—indeed, a Michigan assembly line may be what many people think of when they hear the word "manufacturing." In 2004, the latest year for which BLS data is available, the auto sector accounted for about 1.1 million jobs. For the most part, the U.S. was able to ward off the competitive threat from Japanese companies that surfaced in the early 1990s by improving product line quality domestically—though a bullish Wall Street environment and Asian economic weakness also helped. The so-called "Big Three" automakers—General Motors, DaimlerChrysler and Ford—claimed about 57 percent of the U.S. passenger car market in 2005, though American-made staples like the Ford Excursion and Chevy Tahoe have witnessed an ongoing decline in sales of nearly 20 percent for the first half of 2005. The main culprits in the auto industry slump include the rise in gas prices to record-high levels per gallon and the rapidly increasing price of steel per ton, which, according to data from *Purchase* magazine, more than doubled from $260 in May 2003 to $535 in May 2005.

Since big-ticket purchases like cars are closely tied to consumer confidence, the terrorist attacks of September 11 and the resulting economic turmoil forced carmakers to offer customers heavy discounts (such as the zero-percent financing campaign initiated by GM) and cash-back incentives to keep inventory moving. In the summer of 2005, the Big Three even announced promotions to offer vehicles at the same rate employees pay, thousands of dollars below the sticker price, to boost lagging sales. Capacity has also been slashed to bring inventories in line with reduced demand, leading to an unhealthy combination of diminished productivity and weak prices. All of this has led to major job cuts, as well as negative ripple effects for related sectors like steel companies.

Though the auto industry has attempted to rebound by revamping cars to meet consumer demand for items like SUVs and, in contrast, fuel-efficient hybrid vehicles, analysts warn that U.S. companies need to look to the East again as Asian markets improve and manufacturers like Toyota and Honda pick up the pace. To pique public interest, automotive companies are increasingly combining with major electronics manufacturers to provide a variety of in-vehicle add-ons like satellite radio,

Visit Vault at **www.vault.com** for insider company profiles, expert advice, career message boards, expert resume reviews, the Vault Job Board and more.

VAULT CAREER LIBRARY 321

crash avoidance systems and iPods; the percentage of electronic content in automobiles is expected to increase to 40 percent by 2010. At the same time, though, such developments also increase automotive warranty costs and vehicle recalls.

Vehicle manufacturing is also coming from a new source—automakers such as BMW, Honda, Hyundai and Toyota have moved manufacturing plants to the Southeast U.S. In the past 20 years, these companies have quietly cut down on imports and increased domestic production by seven times—in fact, 2005 was the first year that Japanese carmakers made more cars abroad than domestically. The Association of International Automobile Manufacturers estimates that by 2009 these foreign automakers will have invested $3.3 billion and have hired 10,000 additional workers. Despite this, according to Ward's, auto production in the light vehicle category is down 3 percent from 2005.

Steely resolve

Steel, demand for which has been bolstered by the developing economies of India and China (which was responsible for 30 percent of the world's demand in 2005), is another U.S. manufacturing mainstay. In addition, the destruction caused by hurricanes Katrina and Rita destroyed many steel structures in the Southeast, such as bridges, barges and oil rigs, which need to be replaced or extensively repaired. The steel market hasn't always been so strong, however. Prices in 2002 were low, with seven companies controlling nearly half of American steel production. A spate of bankruptcies and acquisitions, along with rising prices and increased efficiency, revived the industry. According to Roland Berger Strategy Consultants, steel prices have increased more than 150 percent between 2003 and 2005. Now, three companies—Mittal, U.S. Steel and Nucor—supply 55 percent of the American steel market.

All roads lead to tech

Electronics manufacturing covers companies engaged in manufacturing, among other things, power distribution equipment, communications devices, semiconductors, industrial electronics and household appliances. Above all, the sector plays a vital role in a number of other industries, including telecommunications, medical and automotive; electronics demand is thus inextricably tied to the rise and fall of dependent industries. Innovative new consumer products and advancing digital technology are also opening up new markets and avenues of revenue. Despite this, the BLS expects that employment in this sector will decrease by 7 percent over the 2004-2014 period due to increased efficiency and jobs being moved overseas.

Flying the friendly skies

Aerospace also contributes significantly to U.S. manufacturing. In the commercial sphere, airplane manufacturing is dominated by Boeing and European rival Airbus. These companies and others, like Lockheed Martin, Northrop Grumman and Raytheon, also are involved in the production of military aircraft, missiles and space equipment. The commercial airline sector saw a severe downturn following September 11, but the past few years have seen a rebound. By the end of 2004, aerospace sales, orders, exports and employment had all increased significantly. The trend continued in 2005 with increases across all sectors of the industry, according to the Aerospace Industries Association (AIA). Sales increased 9.2 percent in 2005, and the AIA's predictions for 2006 are healthy. The BLS expects the airline manufacturing sector to grow by 8 percent over from 2004 to 2014.

Manu's got a chemical love

Chemical manufacturing is an important segment of the manufacturing industry, producing solvents, dyes, soaps, bleaches and plastics for use in factories and at home. The hurricanes of 2004 and 2005 hurt this segment by destroying a number of factories in the Southeast, and high oil prices drove up the cost of many petrochemical-derived products. This has resulted in decreased revenues along with an increased drive toward mergers and acquisitions. Notable deals include Dow Chemical's purchase of Union Carbide and Valspar's purchase of Lilly Industries. One area of chemical manufacturing that is picking up steam is the specialty chemicals sector, which has been boosted by the recent strength of the housing market. Nevertheless, the BLS expects employment within the chemical manufacturing segment of the manufacturing industry to decline by 14 percent between 2004 and 2014, due to increased efficiency, production outsourcing and more stringent regulation, among other factors.

Manufacturing grab-bag

Other manufacturing sectors include plastics, textiles, apparel, rubber, minerals and forestry, which holds claim to roughly 7 percent of all U.S. manufacturing output. Here again, employment figures have plummeted in recent years due to a convergence of unfavorable economic conditions and changes in demand due to the new "paperless" business environment as well as manufacturing techniques for furniture and cabinetry that use less wood. But the industry currently is expecting solid profits due to the increasing demand for lumber that's being driven by the rise in housing and construction activity, especially in the hurricane-damaged Southeast. The good news may not last long, though: a softening housing market would lead to a decline in demand for lumber. Additionally, environmentalists have come out swinging against the industry in recent years, primarily through campaigns to protect old growth forests.

A shifting—but optimistic—outlook

Like many industries, manufacturing has seen a steady push toward technologies that promise greater efficiency and productivity while reducing the need for manpower. It's likely that many of the factory jobs lost since the beginning of the century will never return, signaling a fundamental shift in the industry as a whole. The BLS predicts total manufacturing employment will decrease by 0.6 percent through 2014. Statistics from the Labor Department released in July 2005 showed a decline in manufacturing jobs for the fourth straight month, leaving employment at 14.27 million—a 55-year low. Motor vehicle production accounted for 18,000 of 24,000 jobs lost overall that June.

A shift also has taken place in the makeup of the industry. According to the National Association of Manufacturers (NAM), chemicals, industrial machinery and equipment, and electronics are the three largest manufacturing sectors today, making up a third of the industry's gross domestic product. Fifty years ago, the three largest sectors were food, primary metals and motor vehicles.

But despite the impression of general decline the industry might give, the job market is remarkably vibrant. According to a 2005 survey done by Deloitte with NAM, 90 percent of employers in the industry reported a demand for skilled workers, and 65 percent needed scientists and engineers. The manufacturing job market should also continue to move in the job seeker's favor as members of the Baby Boom generation begin to retire.

What is the Supply Chain?

Suppliers and vendors

A simple definition of supply chain is the network of vendors that provides materials for a company's products, but in reality, the supply chain is more complicated. There is a stream of flows from supplier to supplier until a product reaches an end user. For example, oil is rigged from the ground, sent to a refinery, plastic is made, an injection molding shop buys plastic pellets, makes plastics components, ships the components to a customer, the customer assembles the plastic parts into their machine, and then sells the machine to their customer. The further away from the customer, the farther "upstream" a supplier is considered to be.

Visit Vault at **www.vault.com** for insider company profiles, expert advice, career message boards, expert resume reviews, the Vault Job Board and more.

V/\ULT CAREER LIBRARY 323

The network of vendors in a supply chain often includes tiered suppliers (meaning a company does not receive materials directly from the supplier, but is involved in getting materials or parts from an upstream supplier to a downstream supplier). The more complex a product, the more significant the upstream supplier's roles are. From a supply chain manager's perspective, his suppliers are primarily responsible for managing their own supply chain but he should have some involvement.

Oftentimes, a manufacturing facility acts as a supplier to a downstream manufacturing facility. For example, a company could have their manufacturing plant in the U.S. and their assembly plant in Mexico. The U.S. plant would be considered an internal supplier, since it's part of the same company. The transportation of materials throughout the supply chain is often called logistics. This includes air, land, and sea shipping as well as customs processing to allow materials to cross borders. The supply chain does not end until the product reaches the consumer. For this reason, distribution centers, distributors, and wholesalers are all part of the supply chain. It is not rare for a supply chain to involve a dozen parties.

The relationship between a supplier and a manufacturing company is not as simple as a supply chain manager ordering parts and the supplier shipping them. There are continuous flows between the supplier and the customer. Figure X below shows these flows in chronological order from top to bottom. (Note that this figure is for an already established supplier and material.) In the case of a new supplier, a supplier audit (a verification that a supplier has the potential to meet the manufacturer's needs) should be conducted first to determine if the supplier is appropriate for the work.

In the case of new material, the customer must first supply the anticipated number of units required, along with all of the drawings and specifications, to the supplier to get a quotation of unit price and lead time. After the quotes are received and a supplier is chosen, a purchase order should be done for the setup costs and samples. Setup costs can be a few hundred to hundreds of thousands of dollars (mostly tooling costs). A supply chain manager should always present the setup costs along with the piece price quote when working with engineers (so manufacturing methods are not specified solely on unit cost). For example, making a simple part by thermoforming would cost about $50 each, whereas making it by injection molding would cost $5 each. However, injection molding requires a $10,000 mold. If you only need 20 pieces annually, you are better off using thermoforming.

Depending on whether prototypes or the component have already been made or not, the samples ordered may be just to verify the ability of the supplier to make the parts, or to verify the design of the finished product. In other words, the supplier may fabricate a part correctly, but a manufacturer's engineering department may determine that the part needs to be redesigned. This would start the process over. Once samples have been approved, the flow of Figure X can be followed.

A manufacturing company has to furnish a forecast (usually annually) so the supplier can then go through his supply chain and make sure that all the materials needed (i.e. material, lubricant, machine capacity, labor resources) for the component the supplier provides will be available. A manufacturer then issues a purchase order, which serves as a commitment to purchase a defined number of units. A purchase order must have terms and conditions accompanying it to protect your company. Usually, a customer will not want to receive the entire forecast amount at once. Instead, a manufacturer could issue multiple purchase orders throughout the year, or do what is called a blanket purchase order for a large amount and then make releases against that purchase order for small amounts when they actually want it.

For example, a company uses 1,000 rods of aluminum in a year. They may lock into a price for the entire year (the price of aluminum changes daily), but not take delivery of all 1,000 rods at once. Instead, the supply chain manager would request economic order quantity (EOQ) releases. An EOQ is the optimal balance between taking delivery for the entire 1,000 rods at once and paying for material that will not be used for months, and paying transportation, inspection, and transaction costs for receiving frequent smaller shipments. The formula for EOQ is

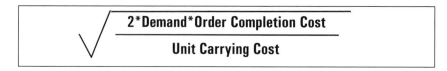

$$\sqrt{\frac{2*Demand*Order\ Completion\ Cost}{Unit\ Carrying\ Cost}}$$

where the Order Completion Cost is the total cost of placing the purchase order, paying for a setup at the vendor (if applicable), and paying the transportation and in-house handling to get the components to the production floor. The unit carrying cost is the cost of holding inventory (insurance, warehouse lease, shrinkage costs, security, cost of capital, etc.)

Customers can do releases to the supplier at specific time intervals or specific inventory intervals. With inventory intervals, when a customer gets to a certain number of rods left, they would issue a release for the next shipment of rods.

A supplier should send a confirmation to the customer acknowledging they have received the purchase order and agreed to the terms and conditions described therein. The supplier sends the material per the purchase order and then sends an invoice for the amount shipped. Once the goods have been accepted by the customer, a payment is sent to the supplier equal to the amount of the invoice.

OEM suppliers

There are basically three types of suppliers. In the first, or most conventional scenario, a company provides a design for what they want the supplier to furnish and the supplier makes it to the company's specifications. The second is the Original Equipment Manufacturer (OEM) supplier. In this case, the company does not specify the design for a custom product, but in fact buys a product that the supplier sells to many customers. These products are called off-the-shelf (a screw is an example of a component that is usually purchased as an off-the-shelf product rather than being custom designed).

Contract manufacturers

Contract manufacturers are the third type of suppliers, in which formal contracts between the supplier (the contract manufacturer) and your manufacturing company are relied upon. The contract manufacturer purchases or makes all of the components, assembles the product, tests it, and ships the finished product either directly to the customer or to a warehouse. Companies that want to get out of the manufacturing aspect of their products turn to contract manufacturers. The supply chain manager finds suitable contract manufacturers and manages the relationship after a contract has been signed. A company has to put a huge amount of trust into the contract manufacturer, since the customer does not have the same level of visibility or

Visit Vault at **www.vault.com** for insider company profiles, expert advice, career message boards, expert resume reviews, the Vault Job Board and more.

V/\ULT CAREER LIBRARY   **325**

control over the manufacturing of the product as they do when they are making the product themselves. Contract manufacturing is an option in almost every industry from food processing to semiconductors.

Freight forwarders and transportation providers

Transportation providers and freight forwarders are also controlled by a supply chain management practitioner. Transportation providers pick up product from one location and deliver them to another. Obviously, it is very costly to pick up some cargo in Los Angeles and drive it all the way to New York for delivery. For this reason, these companies consolidate shipments from different places in a departing hub (whether it be a port, a warehouse, or an airport), send them to an arriving hub, and then deliver them to their final destination. It is quite common for a transportation provider to hand off a shipment to another company to carry out some or all of the transportation. This is called subcontracting or third party carriers. Specialty transportation providers also exist (i.e. for transporting explosive materials, refrigerated cargo, etc.). Some manufacturing companies have traffic, transportation, or logistics departments that take care of most of this work so a supply chain manager can concentrate on suppliers only.

Freight forwarders specialize in transportation across borders. They coordinate the paperwork, book the space with a transportation provider, and track the goods from pickup to delivery. Because of the complexity of customs requirements, tariff codes, and language barriers for different countries, it is better to have freight forwarders involved if a company is dealing with more than a few countries or commodities.

Supply Chain Careers

Supply chain management occupations

Below are brief summaries of the duties for supply chain management occupations. Not every organization will have all of these positions and the duties of the positions will not be limited to those described here.

Buyer: Buyers do purchasing just like supply chain managers. The difference is that supply chain managers buy parts and materials for the company's products, whereas buyers purchase everything else. Some examples of items that buyers procure are desktop computers, office supplies, and hand tools.

Planner: A planner takes the forecast from marketing/sales and breaks that into a build schedule of what products should be built and when they should be built to meet inventory goals. Planners also work with supply chain managers to control inventory of parts and materials.

Purchasing Administrative Assistant: A purchasing administrative assistant takes care of the filing of paperwork for the purchasing department. S/he will also coordinate travel arrangements.

Logistics Manager: A logistics manager is responsible for the traffic of goods coming to and going from the factory. This encompasses air, land, and ocean traffic, both domestic and international.

Supply Chain Engineer: A supply chain engineer works on technical issues with the supplier. This involves working with suppliers to improve their quality, helping them to analyze failures, and developing new products.

Commodity Manager: A commodity manager is similar to a supply chain manager. Some companies separate the ownership of parts and materials for the supply chain managers by product line. For example, if a company makes binoculars, telescopes, cameras, and microscopes, and they have four supply chain managers, they might assign one supply chain manager for each product family. Another approach is to distribute the work by commodity. One supply chain manager would be responsible for the optics on all of the product families and one supply chain manager would be responsible for the plastic parts on all of the product families. When this is the case, the supply chain managers can be called commodity managers.

Receiving Inspector: A receiving inspector is responsible for checking the quality of the parts and materials that come from the vendor before they get moved to the production floor for consumption and before the supplier gets paid. There are statistics charts that define the number of samples from a shipment that need to be checked to meet the desired confidence level that the entire lot received is acceptable, so a receiving inspector does not check 100% of the incoming items.

Procurement Manager: A procurement manager is in charge of the buyers and supply chain managers. The procurement manager sets the goals for the department and provides a level of escalation when a supply chain manager is having trouble managing a supplier.

Receiving Coordinator: The receiving coordinator processes the parts and materials delivered. This includes doing a receiving transaction in ERP, moving the parts to their location, and making sure the paperwork the supplier sends matches what was received.

Receiving Supervisor: The receiving supervisor is responsible for the receiving department. Besides supervising receiving department workers, the receiving supervisor is in charge of creating and improving department processes.

Accounts Payable Coordinator: The accounts payable coordinator works in the accounting department and processes the invoices from the suppliers. After verifying the invoices match what was actually received, the accounts payable coordinator sends a payment to the supplier.

Visit Vault at **www.vault.com** for insider company profiles, expert advice, career message boards, expert resume reviews, the Vault Job Board and more.

VΛULT CAREER LIBRARY   **327**

Manufacturing Employer Directory

Pulte Homes, Inc.

100 Bloomfield Hills Parkway, Suite 300
Bloomfield Hills, Michigan 48304
Recruiting Contact Phone: 248-647-2750
www.pulte.com

Undergraduate schools Pulte recruits from:
Check out our 2007 Campus Schedule at careers.pulte.com!

Simply stated, when you work at Pulte Homes your career experience is the way it should be. If you are looking for a company that values innovation, leadership, diversity, entrepreneurial spirit, flexibility and hard work, then Pulte Homes is the 'home' for you! Pulte Homes Inc., is the largest Home Builder in America with over $14.7 Billion in revenues and over 14,000 employees building a diversified portfolio of residential structures ranging from high-rise urban lofts to multi-million dollar mansions to resort-style communities.

Forget the idea of having to wait in line for a promotion or climbing an endless corporate ladder, at Pulte, YOU take control of your career and path the way for your future success! Pulte has a small, family-like, fun culture, backed by a powerhouse FORTUNE 150 ranking. We realize that it is our employees who give us our competitive advantage so we strongly believe in developing the most diverse and brightest talent in America. Pulte offers competitive paid internships and full time positions in the fields of Sales and Marketing, Customer Relations, Construction Operation Management, Information Technology and Mortgage Banking. Join Pulte, a company that is changing the rules to create an employment experience of a lifetime!

Why is Pulte the best employer for new college grads? See what our college recruits have to say!:
"The training was incredible and all the employees were happy to go out of there way to insure that I was not only obtaining the best knowledge, but feeling very comfortable and most of all, having fun!!!"

—Trevor P., Bowling Green State Grad 2005

3M
3M Center
St. Paul, MN 55144
Phone: (651) 733-1110
Fax: (651) 736-2133
www.mmm.com

ABB Ltd.
Affolternstrasse 44
8050 Zurich, Switzerland
Phone: +41-43-317-7111
Fax: +41-43-317-4420
www.abb.com

Alcoa, Inc.
201 Isabella Street
Pittsburgh, PA 15212-5858
Phone: (412) 553-4545
Fax: (412) 553-4498
www.alcoa.com

Applied Materials, Inc.
3050 Bowers Avenue
Santa Clara, CA 95054-8039
Phone: (408) 727-5555
Fax: (408) 748-9943
www.appliedmaterials.com

BASF
Carl-Bosch Street 38
67056 Ludwigshafen, Germany
Phone: +49-621-60-0
Fax: +49-621-60-42525
www.basf.com

Bayerische Motoren Werke (BMW)
Petuelring 130
D-80788 Munich, Germany
Phone: +49-89-382-0
Fax: +49-89-382-2-44-18
www.bmwgroup.com

The Boeing Company
100 N. Riverside Plaza
Chicago, IL 60606-2609
Phone: (312) 544-2000
Fax: (312) 544-2082
www.boeing.com

Boise Cascade, LLC
1111 W. Jefferson Street
P.O. Box 50
Boise, ID 83728-0001
Phone: (208) 384-6161
Fax: (208) 384-7189
www.bc.com

Caterpillar, Inc.
100 NE Adams Street
Peoria, IL 61629
Phone: (309) 675-1000
Fax: (309) 675-1182
www.cat.com

Manufacturing Employer Directory, cont.

DaimlerChrysler

Epplestrasse 225

70546 Stuttgart, Germany

Phone: +49-711-17-0

Fax: +49-711-17-94022

1000 Chrysler Drive

Auburn Hills, Michigan 48326-2766

Phone: (248) 512-5420

Fax: (248) 512-4885

www.daimlerchrysler.com

Dana Corporation

4500 Dorr Street

Toledo, OH 43615

Phone: (419) 535-4500

Fax: (419) 535-4643

www.dana.com

Deere & Company

One John Deere Place

Moline, IL 61265

Phone: (309) 765-8000

Fax: (309) 765-5671

www.johndeere.com

The Dow Chemical Company

2030 Dow Center

Midland, MI 48674

Phone: (989) 636-1000

Fax: (989) 636-3518

www.dow.com

E.I. DuPont De Nemours and Company

1007 Market Street

Wilmington, DE 19898

Phone: (302) 774-1000

Fax: (302) 999-4399

www.dupont.com

Eaton Corporation

Eaton Center

1111 Superior Avenue

Cleveland, OH 44114-2584

Phone: (216) 523-5000

Fax: (216) 523-4787

www.eaton.com

Federal-Mogul Corporation

26555 Northwestern Highway

Southfield, MI 48034

Phone: (248) 354-7700

Fax: (248) 354-8950

www.federal-mogul.com

Ford Motor Company

1 American Road

Dearborn, MI 48126-2798

Phone: (313) 322-3000

Fax: (313) 845-6073

www.ford.com

GE Advanced Materials

1 Plastics Avenue

Pittsfield, MA 01201

Phone: (413) 448-7110

Fax: (413) 448-7465

www.geadvancedmaterials.com

General Dynamics Corp.

3190 Fairview Park Drive

Falls Church, VA 22042-4523

Phone: (703) 876-3000

Fax: (703) 876-3125

www.gendyn.com

General Motors

300 Renaissance Center

Detroit, MI 48265-3000

Phone: (313) 556-5000

Fax: (248) 696-7300

www.gm.com

Georgia-Pacific Corporation

133 Peachtree Street, NE

Atlanta, GA 30303

Phone: (404) 652-4000

Fax: (404) 230-1674

www.gp.com

Honeywell International Inc.

101 Columbia Road

Morristown, NJ 07962-1219

Phone: (973) 455-2000

Fax: (973) 455-4807

www.honeywell.com

Ingersoll-Rand Company Limited

Clarendon House

2 Church Street

Hamilton, HM 11, Bermuda

Phone: (441) 295-2838

www.irco.com

International Paper Company

400 Atlantic St.

Stamford, CT 06921

Phone: (800) 223-1268

Fax: (203) 541-8200

www.ipaper.com

ITT Industries, Inc.

4 W. Red Oak Lane

White Plains, NY 10604

Phone: (914) 641-2000

Fax: (914) 696-2950

www.ittind.com

Johnson Controls

5757 N. Green Bay Avenue

Milwaukee, WI 53201

Phone: (414) 524-1200

Fax: (414) 524-2077

www.johnsoncontrols.com

Lockheed Martin Corporation

6801 Rockledge Drive

Bethesda, MD 20817-1877

Phone: (301) 897-6000

Fax: (301) 897-6704

www.lockheedmartin.com

Newell Rubbermaid Inc.

10 B Glenlake Pkwy., Suite 600

Atlanta, GA 30328

Phone: (770) 407-3800

Fax: (770) 407-3970

www.newellrubbermaid.com

Northrop Grumman Corporation

1840 Century Park East

Los Angeles, CA 90067-2199

Phone: (310) 553-6262

Fax: (310) 553-2076

www.northgrum.com

Visit Vault at **www.vault.com** for insider company profiles, expert advice, career message boards, expert resume reviews, the Vault Job Board and more.

VAULT CAREER LIBRARY

329

Manufacturing Employer Directory, cont.

PPG Industries, Inc.
1 PPG Place
Pittsburgh, PA 15272
Phone: (412) 434-3131
Fax: (412) 434-2448
www.ppg.com

Raytheon Company
870 Winter Street
Waltham, MA 02451-1449
Phone: (781) 522-3000
Fax: (781) 522-3001
www.raytheon.com

Smurfit-Stone Container Corporation
150 N. Michigan Ave.
Chicago, IL 60601
Phone: (312) 346-6600
Fax: (312) 580-2272
www.smurfit-stone.com

Solectron Corporation
777 Gibraltar Drive
Milpitas, CA 95035
Phone: (408) 957-8500
Fax: (408) 957-6056
www.solectron.com

Thermo Electron Corporation
81 Wyman Street
Waltham, MA 02454-9046
Phone: (781) 622-1000
Fax: (781) 622-1207
www.thermo.com

Toyota Motor Company
1, Toyota-cho
Toyota City, Aichi Prefecture 471-8571, Japan
Phone: +81-565-28-2121
Fax: +81-565-23-5800
www.toyota.co.jp (Worldwide)
www.toyota.com (North America)

United States Steel Corporation
600 Grant Street
Pittsburgh, PA 15219-2800
Phone: (412) 433-1121
Fax: (412) 433-5733
www.ussteel.com

United Technologies
One Financial Plaza
Hartford, CT 06103
Phone: (860) 728-7000
Fax: (860) 728-7979
www.utc.com

Weyerhaeuser Company
33663 Weyerhaeuser Way South
Federal Way, WA 98063-9777
Phone: (253) 924-2345
Fax: (253) 924-2685
www.weyerhaeuser.com

© 2006 Vault Inc.

Media and Entertainment

The Industry

The media universe is dotted with veritable galaxies of companies—from multi-billion dollar diversified conglomerates to small, independent movie studios and production facilities. High school dropouts and PhDs in philosophy, MBAs and computer programmers, septuagenarians and twentysomethings, all work cheek by jowl to bring to life creative endeavors, to grow sustainable billion-dollar franchises like Batman and Harry Potter, and to create new ways to keep the American public entertained and spending money on leisure.

There are two broad subcategories within media and entertainment: creative and business. The creative side actually makes the products or content and has four major areas: motion pictures, television, publishing and music. The business side sells the content, ensures that everything is legal and helps the business grow. The business encompasses the corporate high-level strategy groups, the divisions (a.k.a. business units) that work in the trenches of a specific operation and the standard overarching business functions evident in every company (e.g. accounting, legal, human resources, IT).

First and foremost, entertainment and media industries start with creative content. Everything else stems from this.

Motion pictures

Movies are by far the biggest segment of the media and entertainment industry, not only because of their prominence within the American cultural landscape, but also because of a successful motion picture's ability to sell products in other enormously profitable places as well (also known as ancillary revenue streams)—home video, international distribution, TV rights and so on. Each of the eight major film studios releases about 20 to 30 films each year, with the average studio release costing about $30 million. Studios are typically broken down into two functional components, the business side and the creative side.

The creative side is the where the movies are actually made. There are a few key divisions on the creative side of the movie business:

- **Development:** The key players in the development stage are producers, screenwriters, agents and studio executives. Production companies, the "homes" of producers, start with a script. Every year, these companies are delivered hundreds of scripts (mostly unsolicited) from famous, semi-famous and unknown writers. The executives at each of the production companies then sort through the scripts (written by both new and established screenwriters), negotiate with agents to purchase interesting ones, and then bring together key players (e.g. a director, lead actors, other producers) who will commit to starring in or making the film if a studio finances it. A studio is then "pitched" the idea and if the film is approved, the film then gets a "green light" to go into production. The latter stage of development is also often called pre-production.

- **Pre-production:** This is everything that happens to get a movie rolling just before filming starts—location scouting, and the casting and hiring of the crew, for instance.

- **Production:** Once a movie is "green lit," production starts. To use an analogy, if the screenplay is the blueprint, production is when the movie is built by the cast and crew. Filming sometimes happens on a soundstage on a film studio's property, but often it occurs "on location," at an out-of-studio venue.

Top Studios

- Disney
- Dreamworks SKG
- MGM/UA
- Paramount
- Sony/Columbia
- Universal
- Warner Brothers
- 20th Century Fox

Top "Indie" Studios

- Artisan
- Fine Line/New Line
- Fox Searchlight
- Miramax
- Sony Pictures Classics
- USA Films

Visit Vault at **www.vault.com** for insider company profiles, expert advice, career message boards, expert resume reviews, the Vault Job Board and more.

VAULT CAREER LIBRARY   331

- **Post-Production:** After all the raw footage has been filmed, it is taken to an editing studio, where professional film editors and the director work together with sound effects artists and special effects wizards (if necessary) to pull a movie together. This is also the stage when music, titles and credits are added and when the film preview (called a "trailer" in industry-speak) is created and sent to movie theaters.

Vital in the movie business is the relationship that studios have with movie theaters, or exhibitors, as they are called in the industry. Exhibitors decide which movies they will show and often split marketing costs with theaters. Because of the 1948 antitrust ruling that divorced theaters from studios, the power of studios weakened. Multiplexes (cinema theaters with multiple screens) then came into the picture, taking advantage of the separation from studios to release many different types of movies, contributing to the proliferation of movie niches and independent films produced on small budgets.

The other side of filmmaking is the business side, which deals with ancillary revenue streams and creative vehicles (e.g., theme parks, licensed products, home video) that come after the filmmaking process. These are often completely separate businesses that employ different media for dissemination (e.g., stores, third party distributors like McDonald's, the Internet). Because many of the most successful movies of all time are franchises (Star Wars, Indiana Jones, Lord of the Rings), the business side works to exploit the enormous revenue opportunities that come with leveraging those properties. As the business side has come to generate billions of dollars in recent years, movie studios have grown into diversified conglomerates with many different business arms. The main divisions are:

- **Home video:** Tapes and DVDs are the second phase of a movie's life cycle, bringing films into the homes of consumers after its life in the box office has run its course.

- **Consumer products:** All filmed properties and characters with commercial appeal are further exploited by other companies that pay licensing fees for the rights to use images and names.

- **Retail:** Virtually all major film studios sell customized items directly to customers either through stores, catalogs or direct mail, some in larger endeavors than others (e.g. The Disney Stores, Warner Brothers Studio Stores).

- **Theme parks:** Large destination parks (e.g. Disneyland, Universal Studios) provide the opportunity to further leverage a film's appeal to consumers in an exciting, live-action setting.

Television

With televisions in the homes of over 99% of the U.S. population, TV is arguably the most powerful media vehicle in the entertainment industry. Deregulation of cable companies and increased bandwidth in distribution (with digital cable) has further increased the options of television networks. This has resulted in a glut of channels targeting ever-narrower niches (e.g. golf, cooking, independent movies).

This growth, however, has resulted in the popularity of several successful cable channels eroding the once dominant share of the networks (ABC, CBS, NBC). Success stories include ESPN, E!, Lifetime, USA and MTV. One result of all this change is the growth in career opportunities for people considering television careers.

Top TV Networks	
ABC	USA
NBC	ESPN
CBS	A&E
Fox	CNN
PBS	TNT
TBS	Nickelodeon
Discovery	Lifetime

The TV industry is structured somewhat differently from film. One of the key difference is that TV is full of sales and marketing positions, since most networks make money on advertising. (If a show is particularly successful, it can make even more money by being sold into syndication (e.g., Law & Order), by being made into a movie (e.g., The X-Files) or by launching spin-offs (e.g., Cheers launching Frasier). Typically, the network does not make much money from these types of deals; the winners are usually the creators of the show and the production company that originally produced the show. Advertising, therefore, is all the more critical for networks.

Here are some key divisions of television networks:

- **Development:** The television industry parallels the film industry in that scripts for new television shows are constantly sought out and studied in the hopes of creating the next Friends or ER. Job positions within TV development are typically divided into the different types of programming that appears on TV—sitcoms, dramas, miniseries, specials and daytime. Network executives are "pitched" ideas by production companies and writers. If the executive likes an idea, a "green light" is given for the show's pilot, the introductory episode. If the pilot is successful, it then becomes a series.

- **Production:** Because television typically calls for shorter production cycles, television studios are often fully equipped soundstages where TV shows are filmed and edited and where final cuts are put into post-production.

- **Programming:** Once a show is on the air, it is watched carefully to see how it performs. Programming executives closely monitor Nielsen ratings, provide comments on scripts to develop shows with the most promising audience appeal, reconfigure schedules to improve performances and cut shows when they fail to build a loyal audience. Shows may be kept when their ratings are low but they attract the desirable 18- to 34-year-old audience.

- **Network affiliates:** While the bulk of ad revenues come in at the national level, the major networks have bodies of network affiliates throughout the country that have individual sales forces that sell local advertising, which comprises most of the remaining portion of overall company revenues. In addition to ad sales, affiliates also manage some content creation, primarily local news production.

Music

The music industry has several components—there are divisions that discover new artists, there are those that develop and produce music with mass appeal, and there are the promoters and marketers. And now, in the age of the Internet, there are lots of people hired to make sure that the record labels do not get fleeced by music freeloaders who find ways to acquire and disseminate the product for free, or to figure out how to create profitable businesses distributing or marketing music through the Internet.

While the music industry is enormous, and one of the most globally-significant parts of the entertainment industry because music is so universal and ubiquitous, the threat of its erosion due to Internet piracy concerns poses a serious threat to the growth of new artists and revenue opportunities.

That said, for job seekers, the most promising opportunities continue to be in A&R, distribution and marketing.

> **Big 5 Record Labels**
> - BMG (Arista, Jive Records, RCA)
> - EMI-Capitol (Virgin)
> - Sony (Columbia, Epic)
> - Universal (MCA, Polygram)
> - Warner (Warner Brothers, Elektra, Atlantic)

- **A&R:** These are the talent scouts that listen to demo tapes, attend shows, travel and keep their ear to the ground to understand new trends and to uncover fresh voices that best bring those trends to life.

- **Production:** Once an act has been signed onto a record label, the producers perfect the music to make it commercially palatable for radio stations, critics and consumers. The packaging of the CD and creation of the artist image is also finalized in this stage.

- **PR/Marketing:** This is the group that toils to get airplay on radio stations, gets the music video shot and hopefully aired, leverages television and press coverage and puts the artist in the public eye. Arbitron ratings, essentially Nielsen ratings for radio, let both radio stations and record labels know what consumers are listening to, what is working and what is most popular.

- **Distribution:** This group specifically deals with getting the CDs into record stores and venues where consumers can purchase them.

Visit Vault at www.vault.com for insider company profiles, expert advice, career message boards, expert resume reviews, the Vault Job Board and more.

VAULT CAREER LIBRARY   333

- **Concerts:** Concerts and live performances that are able to attract large numbers of consumers are increasingly underwritten by large corporate sponsors to defray expenses (e.g., Pepsi sponsoring a Britney Spears concert tour).

The biggest media companies (i.e. AOL Time Warner, Viacom, The Walt Disney Company) span across all of these industries (and then some). The chart on the next page shows roughly how these large organizations are structured.

Media Conglomerate Relationships

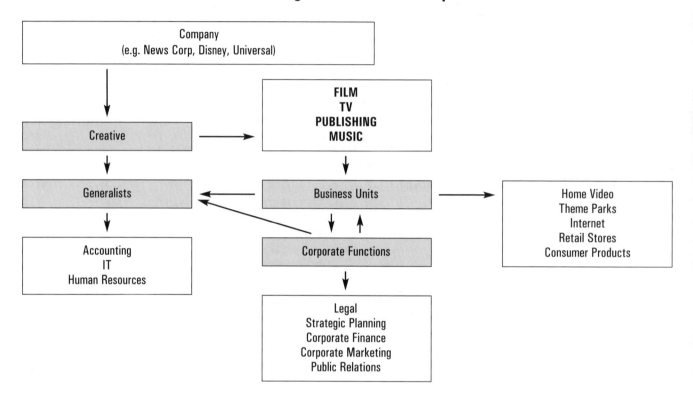

The Big Conundrums

In choosing to enter the entertainment industry, there are several personal decisions that you need to carefully consider. There are no "right" answers. Starting a career in entertainment often calls for steadfast commitment and patience. Some of these decisions involve location, others involve education, still others involve the line of business one can pursue.

New York or Los Angeles?

Most entertainment companies are situated on either the East or West Coast, and that is, by and large, where most newcomers end up. "You definitely want to start in New York or Los Angeles—it's where all the action is," were the words of one record label executive at Virgin. Los Angeles has the development and distribution arms of all the major film and television studios as well as many of the top offices of music labels as well. New York has the balance of the music business, as well as some television (MTV and Nickelodeon for example) and almost 90 percent of all the publishing powerhouses.

Increasingly though, the media and entertainment industry offers opportunities beyond New York and L.A. There are now far more businesses located in other parts of the United States and the world, especially as production costs soar in New York and L.A. Canada is increasingly popular with movie studios, and Vancouver and Toronto both have thriving arts communities. Likewise, the concentration of software engineers in Silicon Valley makes it the home of many special effects companies. Cable networks are increasingly located away from major cities, and shows are often shot in studios in smaller cities like Atlanta and New Orleans. In fact, the most music production outside of New York and Los Angeles occurs in Nashville, the home of the ever-popular country music genre.

Creative or business?

While the creative side of the entertainment business is often considered more interesting because it is what encourages creativity (and because it is the side that holds the best parties with all the famous celebrities), the compensation is lower, the career trajectory is less certain and the work, especially initially, can be demeaning. Assistants often work 12 hours a day, endure being yelled at regularly and must often trek around town every morning to fetch their boss' coffee, dry-cleaned clothes and children.

The business side, on the other hand, is generally regarded as less exciting. There is a fair amount of showmanship even in this part of the business (there was one such businessman who was legendary for keeping his "director-level" business card after being promoted to VP in the hopes that others would believe him to be a film director), but for the most part the path is more predictable, performance is rewarded and the pay is more generous. The tradeoff is, of course, that the positions are not glamorous and the hours are often just as long. "You always feel like you are on the periphery of where the action really is," laments one executive who works in a studio's home video division.

The choice is certainly a difficult one. Success is often not transferable. There are occasionally tales of the studio accountant who transitioned to be a TV producer, but in general, very few make lateral moves, especially since the work required to build up a creative resume is very different than for a business resume, and vice versa.

The role of education

The role of education in the success of Hollywood players remains an enigma. Insiders often say that their degree was worthless in landing their job. In general, the creative side does not reward MBAs. On the business side, however, a graduate degree is often a critical success factor. Furthermore, entrée into the business side of entertainment comes to many only because of an MBA—there are executive training programs at many top media companies (e.g. Bertelsmann, Sony, Disney, Random House) that recruit at many leading business schools. While these are competitive and coveted positions, there is enough to go around for the truly committed. One recent MBA graduate from a top program said, "I just moved to Los Angeles without a job and had interviews with everyone I knew for a month straight—informationals, job interviews, anyone who would talk to me." She eventually landed a promising manager-level position in television distribution.

On the creative side, there are a slew of hot directors and other moviemakers that hail from the ranks of the film school elite— New York University, the American Film Institute, UCLA, USC and others. While these schools offer strong alumni networks and thorough training, they are costly investments. In addition to the annual tuition of the program, there is the additional expense of creating one's final project—a film that will likely cost at least $20,000. There are many success stories of talented people who saved money by taking classes at local community colleges, rented cheap equipment and made their way to festivals like Sundance.

Choosing an industry

The decision on what industry to pursue depends on one's interests and passions. The industries are all similar—personalities drive the business, egos are enormous, attitudes are bad and expectations are high. There are important differences, however. Film and TV generally allow more transition between the two (writers, actors, directors, even producers switch between the two media), but for the most part, it is much harder to transition out of music or publishing.

The key questions to ask yourself:

Visit Vault at **www.vault.com** for insider company profiles, expert advice, career message boards, expert resume reviews, the Vault Job Board and more.

VAULT CAREER LIBRARY   335

- What medium do you prefer? Do you really love music? Are you a big film buff? Do you read 20 magazines a month?

- Do you enjoy the artistic or business dimension of a project?

- Can you handle working on a project for several years (as is common in the film and music industries) or do you prefer projects that have shorter production cycles (which you will find in television and magazine publishing)?

- Would you enjoy working with a set team (the creative department of a film studio) or setting up projects with new people (as on the production side of filmmaking)?

- Where do you know more people? Where could you leverage a personal or alumni network?

- Where do you want to live? Do you like city living? Do you mind driving or do you prefer walking?

Remember that there are the inevitable sub-specializations, much like a lawyer who focuses on criminal litigation or a doctor who is a radiologist. Music executives, for instance, are known for the genre of music they produce, and film producers are normally associated with a certain type of film.

Creative Assistants

While widely regarded as the bottom, the legendary dregs of the pool, the creative assistant (CA) position is the starting point for any career launch into the creative side of the industry. Cynics say assistants are there to feed the egos of self-important creative executives, but others assert that it is a rite of passage to the brotherhood (and sisterhood) of entertainment, not to mention a good training ground for the next generation of creative executives.

The typical job of a creative assistant is to do everything from fetching coffee to kids from one's boss' day care, answering hundreds of calls on a daily basis and making dinner reservations for one's manager, to occasionally, if there is time, reading scripts and writing coverage.

Survival Skills for Assistants

Being an assistant is the first rung up the entertainment ladder. Here are some tips for getting and keeping these jobs—and setting yourself up to move up beyond the assistant level.

Getting in

While assistants are the proverbial low men on the creative totem pole, they are nonetheless difficult positions to land because there are a fixed number of spots and openings are rare. A position becomes available only when people are promoted, fired or quit. Furthermore, it is the starting place for everyone, so the competition is quite tough. Even experienced business executives with MBAs who want to transition to the creative side are unable to avoid becoming a CA. Throughout the media and entertainment world are countless former attorneys, accountants and other aspiring professionals.

The most popular way of breaking into an assistant position is through referrals. Others break in through cold calls. Still others penetrate the ranks by making friends with other assistants and then patiently trolling for the next job opening. Some CAs migrate from a low-status boss to a higher-status boss, remaining in the assistant ranks for many years.

The interview

The interview for an assistant position is usually intended to assess one's humility, modesty and overall industriousness. There will be the inevitable questions that inquire into one's general tolerance in gruntwork. Often, it takes the form of the following question: "But you're overqualified for this job—won't you get bored?" Beware. The point of the question is to question your dedication to tiring, detailed work. A good answer will showcase your intelligence while pointing out that you are not only capable, but eager, willing and very able to execute even the most menial of tasks with alacrity and aplomb. Typical tasks that are the domain of assistants are answering phones, running errands and accepting a less-than-ideal lifestyle. You need to persuade your interviewer, who is unlikely to be the person you will work for (Hollywood types often prefer to forego meeting with the "little people"), that you will do anything and everything that's asked and required of you, and then some. You will be told about your benefits (few to none) and your pay. Do not flinch or waver in any way. It will be construed as a sign of weakness!

Occasionally, an interviewer will ask you for your "coverage," which is essentially a synopsis and analysis of a script. Assistants are sometimes entrusted with the responsibility of writing coverage on scripts, and any previous experience writing such coverage can prove to one's advantage. If you don't have any coverage experience, an interviewer will sometimes give you a script and ask that you provide your written comments on it.

Managing your boss

The position of assistant encompasses such duties as secretary, butler, chauffer, mother and confidante. For all the books ever written on management skills, they are all but irrelevant in the entertainment industry. Rarely will you aggregate a larger group of individuals who care less about developing others. One executive described the junior ranks as "suckling on the teats of wolves."

The most important traits of successful assistants are:

- *Flexibility.* Many assistants are required to juggle and reprioritize their own lives in order to accommodate their managers. One assistant tells of missing a flight for a vacation because the manager called inquiring about some small bit of information that the assistant was supposed to have had.

- *Patience.* Many assistants report countless evenings of waiting around in the office long after the boss had left to a leisure dinner with "business partners." Many managers often tell their underlings to wait until they they are told to go home. Usually the request is legitimized by the (flimsy) guise of receiving a phone call that must be immediately patched through.

- *Resourcefulness.* Often, it is the assistant's responsibility to unearth obscure tidbits of information or to seek out some difficult-to-find object. Whether it reservations at 8 p.m. on a Friday night for the most popular restaurant in town or a rare edition, out-of-print book, assistants are often expected to find ways to make difficult things happen.

- *Indulgence.* The assistant is also expected to be kind and proactive—remembering birthdays and special occasions, congratulating successes and commiserating failures. The best assistants are known for anticipating special requests, accommodating the quirks of their managers, before the manager asks. "I'll try to get my boss his favorite latte every morning if he's unable to pick one up for himself," says one assistant at a prominent Hollywood talent agency.

- *Eagerness.* Cheerfulness and a positive attitude, even in the face of adversity, is vital in the profession. The grumpy are quickly replaced with those more eager and willing.

Making the most of low wages

Assistants make anywhere from $20,000 per year to above $45,000. Usually, the higher paid assistants are in the coveted positions of working at a studio in a unionized position. The majority of assistants earn a salary near the lower end of the spectrum. In order to sustain a viable lifestyle, most assistants resort to the usual manners of making ends meet—sharing living expenses with roommates in modest neighborhoods, limiting indulgences on food (ordering in on the company's dime whenever possible), cutting back expenses on clothing and entertainment, investing in cheap transport, borrowing funds from

Visit Vault at **www.vault.com** for insider company profiles, expert advice, career message boards, expert resume reviews, the Vault Job Board and more.

VAULT CAREER LIBRARY   **337**

parents. Despite the low salaries, there are often perks to the profession that should not be overlooked. Many assistants manage to alleviate some of their expenses on staples like dry cleaning by leveraging the generous expense accounts of their managers. Others engage in supplementary income sources, such as teaching on weekends, in order to increase their cash flow.

Getting promoted

If you stick it out long enough in a CA job, you'll probably move up The hard part is waiting it out, often over the course of several years, sacrificing late nights, while making the right connections and waiting for a lucky break. While there are things that can be done—meeting lots of people, keeping your ears and eyes open to opportunities, jumping to a lesser-known company in order to make a transition out of the assistant ranks— promotion ultimately boils down to timing, persistence and good fortune. Good assistants quickly learn to build networks with other assistants, to share information on what's hot in order to give their bosses the extra edge, to religiously listen in on phone calls and to constantly look out for their own best interests.

Media/Entertainment Employer Directory

ABC, Inc.
77 W. 66th Street
New York, NY 10023-6298
Phone: (212) 456-7777
Fax: (212) 456-1424
www.abc.go.com

Bertelsmann AG
Carl-Bertelsmann-Strasse 270
D-33311 Gütersloh, Germany
Phone: +49-5241-80-0
Fax: +49-5241-80-9662
www.bertelsmann.com

Black Entertainment Television
One BET Plaza
1235 W. Street, NE
Washington, DC 20018
Phone: (202) 608-2000
Fax: (202) 608-2589
www.bet.com

Bloomberg L.P.
499 Park Avenue
New York, NY 10022
Phone: (212) 318-2000
Fax: (917) 369-5000
www.bloomberg.com

Creative Artists Agency
9830 Wilshire Blvd.
Beverly Hills, CA 90212-1825
Phone: (310) 288-4545
Fax: (310) 288-4800
www.caa.com

CBS, Inc.
51 W. 52nd Street
New York, NY 10019
Phone: (212) 975-4321
Fax: (212) 975-4516
www.cbs.com

Clear Channel Communications
200 E. Basse Road
San Antonio, TX 78209
Phone: (210) 822-2828
Fax: (210) 822-2299
www.clearchannel.com

CNN News Group
1 CNN Center
Atlanta, GA 30303
Phone: (404) 827-1500
Fax: (404) 827-2437
www.cnn.com

Comcast Corporation
1500 Market Street
Philadelphia, PA 19102-2148
Phone: (215) 665-1700
Fax: (215) 981-7790
www.comcast.com

Cox Communications, Inc.
1400 Lake Hearn Drive
Atlanta, GA 30319
Phone: (404) 843-5000
Fax: (404) 843-5975
www.cox.com

Discovery Communications, Inc.
1 Discovery Place
Silver Spring, MD 20910
Phone: (240) 662-2000
Fax: (240) 662-1868
www.discovery.com

Dow Jones & Company, Inc.
1 World Financial Center
200 Liberty Street
New York, NY 10281
Phone: (212) 416-2000
Fax: (212) 416-4348
www.dj.com

DreamWorks SKG L.L.C.
1000 Flower Street
Glendale, CA 91201
Phone: (818) 733-7000
Fax: (818) 695-7574
www.dreamworks.com

Fox Entertainment Group
1211 Avenue of the Americas
New York, NY 10036
Phone: (212) 852-7111
Fax: (212) 852-7145
www.fox.com

Gannett Company, Inc.
7950 Jones Branch Drive
McLean, VA 22107-0910
Phone: (703) 854-6000
Fax: (703) 854-2046
www.gannett.com

HarperCollins Publishers, Inc.
10 E. 53rd Street
New York, NY 10022
Phone: (212) 207-7000
Fax: (212) 207-7145
www.harpercollins.com

Home Box Office (HBO)
1100 Avenue of the Americas
New York, NY 10036
Phone: (212) 512-1000
Fax: (212) 512-1182
www.hbo.com

Houghton Mifflin Company
222 Berkeley St.
Boston, MA 02116-3764
Phone: (617) 351-5000
Fax: (617) 351-1105
www.hmco.com

International Data Group
1 Exeter Plaza, 15th Floor
Boston, MA 02116-2851
Phone: (617) 534-1200
Fax: (617) 423-0240
www.idg.com

John Wiley & Sons, Inc.
111 River St.
Hoboken, NJ 07030
Phone: (201) 748-6000
Fax: (201) 748-6008
www.wiley.com

Liberty Media
12300 Liberty Blvd.
Englewood, CO 80112
Phone: (720) 875-5400
Fax: (720) 875-7469
www.libertymedia.com

Visit Vault at **www.vault.com** for insider company profiles, expert advice, career message boards, expert resume reviews, the Vault Job Board and more.

VAULT CAREER LIBRARY

339

Media/Entertainment Employer Directory, cont.

Martha Stewart Living Omnimedia, Inc.
11 W. 42nd Street
New York, NY 10036
Phone: (212) 827-8000
Fax: (212) 827-8204
www.marthastewart.com

The McGraw-Hill Companies, Inc.
1221 Avenue of the Americas
New York, NY 10020
Phone: (212) 512-2000
Fax: (212) 512-3840
www.mcgraw-hill.com

Metro-Goldwyn-Mayer Inc.
10250 Constellation Blvd.
Los Angeles, CA 90067
Phone: (310) 449-3000
Fax: (310) 449-8857
www.mgm.com

National Public Radio, Inc.
635 Massachusetts Avenue NW
Washington, DC 20001-3753
Phone: (202) 513-2000
Fax: (202) 513-3329
www.npr.org

News Corporation
1211 Avenue of the Americas
8th Floor
New York, NY 10036
Phone: (212) 852-7017
Fax: (212) 852-7145
www.newscorp.com

Paramount Pictures
5555 Melrose Avenue
Hollywood, CA 90038
Phone: (323) 956-5000
Fax: (323) 862-1204
www.paramount.com

Pearson PLC
80 Strand
London
WC2R ORL
United Kingdom
Phone: +44-20-7010-2000
Fax: +44-20-7010-6060
www.pearson.com

Penguin Group
80 Strand
London
WC2R ORL
United Kingdom
Phone: +44-2070103396
Fax: +44-2070106642
www.penguin.com

Pixar Animation Studios
1200 Park Avenue
Emeryville, CA 94608
Phone: (510) 752-3000
Fax: (510) 752-3151
www.pixar.com

Primedia
745 Fifth Avenue
New York, NY 10151
Phone: (212) 745-0100
Fax: (212) 745-0121
www.primedia.com

Reed Elsevier PLC
1-3 Strand
London
WC2N 5JR, United Kingdom
Phone: +44-20-7930-7077
Fax: +44-20-7166 5799
www.reedelsevier.com

Reed Elsevier NV
Raderweg 29
1043 NX Amsterdam
The Netherlands
Phone: +31 20 485 2222
Fax: +31 20 618 0325

Reuters Group PLC
85 Fleet Street
London
EC4P 4AJ, United Kingdom
Phone: +44-20-7250-1122
Fax: +44-20-7542-4064
www.reuters.com

Scholastic Corporation
557 Broadway
New York, NY 10012
Phone: (212) 343-6100
Fax: (212) 343-6934
www.scholasticinc.com

Simon & Schuster, Inc.
1230 Avenue of the Americas
New York, NY 10020
Phone: (212) 698-7000
Fax: (212) 698-7099
www.simonsays.com

SourceMedia
One State Street Plaza
27th Floor
New York, NY 10004
Phone: (212) 803.8200
www.sourcemedia.com

Time Warner
1 Time Warner Center
New York, NY 10019
Phone: (212) 484-8000
Fax: (212) 489-6183
www.timewarner.com

USA Network, Inc.
152 West 57th Street
New York, New York 10019
Phone: (212) 314-7300
Fax: (212) 314-7309
www.usanetwork.com

Viacom Inc.
1515 Broadway
New York, NY 10036
Phone: (212) 258-6000
Fax: (212) 258-6464
www.viacom.com

Vivendi Universal
42 avenue de Friedland
75380 Paris Cedex 08
France
Phone: +33-1-71-71-10-00
Fax: +33-1-71-71-10-01
www.vivendiuniversal.com

W.W. Norton & Company
500 5th Avenue
New York, NY 10110
Phone: (212) 354-5500
Fax: (212) 869-0856
www.wwnorton.com

Nonprofit

Imagine what it might be like to say:

"Today at work I helped to provide a safe place for 100 teens in my community to go after school to receive tutoring and homework assistance."

"This year at work I raised a million and a half dollars to fund a program that promotes better early education for young children."

"Throughout the course of my career I helped to clean up my city's most depressed neighborhoods and developed hundreds of new affordable homes for disadvantaged families."

If being able to do this type of work in the course of your career appeals to you, you may want to consider a career in the nonprofit/philanthropy world. It won't be easy going, though. In recent years, and especially since the September 11 terrorist attacks, the U.S. has seen a jump in its number of registered charitable organizations. All of these organizations are in need of strong leaders as many in the sector are concerned that our country is not prepared to financially support this recent influx of newly registered charities. It is clear that only the strongest and savviest organizations are certain to survive.

This need for more and better trained nonprofit administrators is fueling the development of many well respected degree programs at universities and colleges nationwide. At the same time, more people, particularly college age and recent graduates are showing an interest in pursuing a career in nonprofit administration.

The rewards can be quite satisfying for professionals who succeed. Such positions come with, at times, a tremendous amount of prestige and respect, interactions with a broad array of people from all class levels and at executive levels, a satisfying salary. Many organizations represent the lifeblood of their communities and are in the daily eye of the local, sometimes national, public and media.

Nonprofit Uppers and Downers

Uppers

Many of the positive aspects of working in a nonprofit/philanthropy career apply to many different organizations.

- The work a nonprofit staff member goes beyond simply executing a role in the general pursuit of making someone more money, or as much money as possible. The job that a staff member does can positively impact the lives of sometimes thousands of people, or change or improve some negative aspect of our society for future generations, or create new, affordable homes for disadvantaged families, or teach a mentally disabled person a trade and help him achieve financial independence. Nothing can measure up to the feeling at the end of the day when you realize that every call you made, letter you wrote, bill you reconciled, staff meeting you sat through, paper you filed, or decision you made could benefit someone who needs your organization's help.

- Non-profits are generally more family-friendly than the corporate world. Many are more casual, offer better vacation and work hours, and have a more liberal approach to lifestyle choices. However this is not universal—so check before making the assumption.

- Because there are never enough people to do the work, working in a nonprofit can give you the opportunity to a variety of tasks outside your job description.

Visit Vault at **www.vault.com** for insider company profiles, expert advice, career message boards, expert resume reviews, the Vault Job Board and more.

VAULT CAREER LIBRARY   341

Downers

Downers in nonprofit careers tend to depend on the organization. Common negatives include:

- Staff members often do the equivalent of more than one person's job for often lower salaries (overstaffed and underpaid)

- There are few, if any, company perks of the sort offered by employers in the corporate world (gym memberships, entertainment tickets, etc.). Perhaps more importantly, in recent years, standard benefit packages (health care plans, etc.) have also been shrinking.

- Success is often difficult to determine. For example, say a local advocacy organization implements a community education campaign promoting parents to read more to their children. Is it possible to truly achieve an accurate determination of the campaign's success and to what degree parent behavior changed? Quite possibly, there is simply not enough funding that would be needed to design a community survey, or, at best, conduct adequate focus groups.

- Success is often tied to bringing in money/fundraising. While you may reap greater satisfaction from working at an organization whose overriding goal is not to make money, don't think that you're escaping the importance of money altogether.

- Working at certain nonprofits can mean continually seeing unhappy, indigent people—or worse. For example, employees at women's domestic abuse shelters see a steady daily stream of battered women and their children. The shelter's staff often faces depression and burnout.

- High academic standards—many nonprofits require a Master's degree, and some require PhDs for senior positions. Many also require hands on experience with target beneficiaries before being taken seriously.

Many Choices

While work in the nonprofit world includes can be characterized in certain general ways such as the ones above, the sector is hugely diverse, both in terms of types of organizations, and types of positions available. Nonprofits can be huge organizations, employing thousands of paid workers coordinated through a well-defined organizational structure (for example, regional chapters). They can just as easily be tiny—many nonprofits are comprised of only a paid executive director and volunteers.

Moreover, the missions of nonprofits vary widely. The type of organization most commonly associated with the term "nonprofit" is the community-based organization, frequently referred to as a "CBO." CBOs represent a tremendously important group of service providers, implementing their programs on the "front lines" of direct service. These organizations are seen as diligent, tireless workers, often responding to very basic, unmet needs that exist within a community. Typical examples of CBOs would be homeless shelters, "meals-on-wheels" programs and job placement nonprofits.

CBOs aren't the only type of nonprofit, of course. Other types include nonprofit arts/culture organizations (e.g., the Whitney Museum of Art, the Goodman Theater in Chicago), advocacy/social policy research organizations (e.g., Children's Defense Fund, Mothers Against Drunk Driving), scientific research organizations (RAND and the CATO Institute), international (e.g., Save the Children, UNICEF), and foundations that fund the nonprofit world (e.g., Pew Charitable Trust, the Ford Foundation).

Finally, there are many different roles within the nonprofit world. The way to best understand these is to understand the executives who head up these functions. The most prominent include the executive director (basically, the CEO of a nonprofit), the director of development (who oversees fundraising), the director of programming/project director (who has hands-on responsibility for designing the nonprofits programs and services), the director of public relations & marketing/communications (who oversees relationships with the press and reports to donors). Working with these executives are staff workers and volunteers, as well as employees of different organizations working with the nonprofit, usually as a source of funding. (For example, employees of philanthropic foundations or government agencies work with nonprofits their organizations help fund.)

Nonprofit Doesn't Mean Money Doesn't Matter

Today's nonprofit organization is a very different institution than it was only a decade ago. In a nutshell, the nonprofit corporate culture has become more professional. An increased emphasis on efficient management have enhanced the sector's approach to program implementation or problem solving through the development of better, more cost-effective strategies for providing services. Just as importantly, nonprofit organizations have also greatly improved their approach to cultivating and accessing stronger financial support. Many unpredictable variables impact our national economy and subsequently philanthropic donations to nonprofits. The nonprofit/philanthropy field is learning how to protect itself from financial fluctuations.

One common approach to this challenge is to diversify funding sources. An extreme example of this is a church in Jamaica, NY that is running and staffing its own charter bus company, essentially running its own for-profit venture and "donating" the income to the church's operational funds. More commonly, however, nonprofits are branching out into other areas of service in hopes of attracting new donors. This is programmatically justified as a way of making a more comprehensive impact on a single area of service or issue.

Other nonprofits are developing entirely new competencies in hopes of introducing the organization to an entirely new pool of supporters. One example of this is an early education advocacy group, Child Care Action Campaign, which has served as a facilitator and communicator of research and best practices for 20 years. Recently, however, it developed and implemented an early literacy childcare provider training program, sending trainers out into neighborhoods to teach providers how to encourage literacy with the young children in their care. This decision was responsible for nearly $300,000 in new support from donors who only fund "direct service" programs (nonprofits that work directly with those it seeks to serve, rather than just training workers who work with them or conducting research), essentially opening a door to a new revenue stream. In this instance, the organization jumped into community or direct service while continuing its work in advocacy and research.

Development Work and Organizations

From large development organizations and banks such as the IMF and the World Bank funding giant multi-decade projects, to small NGOs (non-governmental organizations) organizing grass-roots projects, to volunteer agencies providing everything from fence builders to business consultants, global development has become a huge industry.

There is a wide range of opportunities under the "development" umbrella, and just as wide a variety of people working in this industry. Development gurus range from top-level senior executives to junior volunteers straight out of college. Opportunities run from micro-finance to building bridges, from environmental work to helping democracy take hold in remote corners of the world. Many development organizations focus on economic development and financial skills. While there are certainly still opportunities to help villagers build houses, more and more opportunities focus on small business development, nurturing local entrepreneurship and providing sustainable business skills.

Types of "development" organizations

Development is such a broad term, but the following groups of organizations are generally included under this umbrella:

- Public multinationals: Huge organizations like the UN, the World Bank, and the ADB (Asian Development Bank).

Visit Vault at www.vault.com for insider company profiles, expert advice, career message boards, expert resume reviews, the Vault Job Board and more.

VAULT CAREER LIBRARY 343

- Multinational NGOs: Large non-government organizations, such as Amnesty International, CARE, Doctors without Borders and the World Wildlife Fund (WWF)

- Smaller NGOs: Hundreds of locally based, often grassroots organizations devoted often to one particular issue or problem, be it women's health, micro-finance or political education.

- Volunteer organizations: Organizations that rely on volunteers, though they may pay a stipend.

There are also private companies involved in development work and branches of private companies that work as a non-profit on development-related issues. For example, many of the major consulting and tax consulting companies have arms dedicated to the issues of development, privatization and economic development. Their clients are mainly governments and the public multinationals.

Volunteering for development work

Volunteering is often the first step for many people to get involved in development work, though volunteering can be an attractive option even if you don't envision a long-term career in development. Volunteering, either on a long-term (up to two years) or short-term (a few months) basis is a great way to experience another culture while making a difference.

There are thousands of volunteer opportunities out there, offering you the chance to get involved in whatever your particular passion or geographic preference is. The most famous organization for Americans is the Peace Corps, but there are numerous other organizations and agencies that offer opportunities for committed volunteers.

Most volunteer assignments are just that: volunteer, meaning you won't be drawing a salary. In some cases, though, you may draw a stipend. A stipend is a living allowance to cover basic necessities, so that while you might not be saving any money, you won't be out of pocket either. Some programs will cover airfare and housing. When evaluating whether or not volunteering is feasible for you, consider loan-forgiveness—many universities have loan-forgiveness programs for graduates who choose to work in the nonprofit sector.

Many volunteer opportunities require you to pay the organization for the opportunity to volunteer. Think seriously about these types of opportunities, especially for "volunteer" programs that are for teaching English. While it is great to have the support these programs offer, you could easily be paid for doing the same work.

A Day in the Life: Peace Corps Volunteer, Senegal

Mark is a Peace Corps Volunteer in Senegal, West Africa.

6:30 a.m.: Thwunk! Thwunk! The sound has been creeping into my sleep for about an hour now, and I finally wake up and acknowledge it. Outside my hut, the women of the village have been up since pounding millet.

7:15 a.m.: I dress—no shower now, but one later. With no electricity or running water, a shower in the morning would be a luxury. Plus, I know I'm going to get dirty today, so what's the point?

7:45 a.m.: Time for a leisurely breakfast in the family compound. We all sleep in our own huts, and meet in the middle for meals and socializing. I sit on a raised dais and drink the local coffee—bitter but good. As I drink, I think about what I have to do today: the upcoming meeting, the state of my motorcycle—do I have enough gas?

8:00 a.m.: I wave goodbye to my host family—the men are heading out to the fields and the women are cooking or going out on water runs. I hop on my motorcycle—with 50 villages in my area of responsibility, good, reliable transport is a major concern. Luckily this little guy hasn't let me down yet.

8:30 a.m.: I drive along the dusty roads and wave to the occasional villager I see. After two years here, they all know me, and I know most of them.

9:15 a.m.: I arrive at my target village, dusty and hot. Even though it's still relatively early, the sun seems impossibly high in the sky, like it's been every day. Senegal is one of the hottest places on earth. Sometimes, I feel like I spend every day just sweating.

9:30 a.m.: The women of the village are slowly gathering in one of the central compounds around me. Today is our fifth meeting, and we're actually going to get started on the project we've been talking about for two months now: planting a fruit orchard. The women will use the fruit to supplement their family's diets, or to sell for some surplus cash at the market.

10:00 a.m.: All the women have finally arrived. Time is a different concept here: having everyone together an hour after the meeting was scheduled is actually great. Heck, I was even 10 minutes late! I explain what we're going to be doing today, and then we all head down to the field that's designated to be the orchard.

10:45 a.m.: We're hard at work in the future orchard, carefully preparing the fruit seedlings in little bags of soil and lining them up in the ground. As we work, the women chatter and tease me. They all want to know when I'm going to bring my girlfriend to live in the compound. The fact that I don't have a girlfriend doesn't seem to stop them! They also ask about my family, and tell me about theirs.

12:00 p.m.: A good morning's work, and time to get out of the sun. I have lunch at one of the compounds and share news with the men of my host family. Then a short nap, a quick play with some of the smaller kids, and then it's time to be off. I'll be back next month when the seedlings start to sprout.

1:30 p.m.: I head towards the nearest town, realizing I've actually got a free afternoon. This is a rarity—with the number of villages I'm responsible for, I usually have two or even three meetings in a given day. This is good—I've got some shopping to do, not to mention getting some more gas for the motorcycle...

2:30 p.m.: Fuda is the central town around here, a hub for all the villages in the area. I wander through the market, picking out some vegetables for my family. They don't receive a stipend for hosting me, so I try to help out in other ways. Buying some vegetables to add to the family's cooking budget and (I've got to admit—bring some changes in my diet!) is a good way to help out.

3:30 p.m.: Potatoes, tomatoes, onions, a couple of delicious looking oranges, gas for my motorcycle and a new shirt for myself. All in order. I've still got time and some energy, so I stop by a local bar. I hope to see one or both of the other Peace Corps volunteers that serve in the area, but I'm out of luck.

4:00 p.m.: I down a local beer—like the coffee it's bitter but good! I chat with the owners of the bar and a couple of men who have sought refuge on the cool patio. They all know me by now, and after studying the local language fairly intensively during my first year I'm now comfortable enough to talk about anything.

4:30 p.m.: No more beer, I have a long drive ahead of me back to my village. I leave a note for the other PCs, telling them I'll be back on Saturday, and telling them to look for me. Then it's back on the motorcycle and the dusty roads.

6:00 p.m.: My favorite time of the day. The work is over, I've had my shower, and the heat is slipping away as the sun starts to set. All around the village people are drifting between compounds, talking and catching up on the news of the day. We have plenty of visitors over at our house. I relax on our dais in the middle of the compound, trying to forget about the busy day I have ahead of me tomorrow. It'll take care of itself.

8:00 p.m.: Supper is prepared by my 8 year old "niece," who is just learning to cook. Tonight it's chicken and a rice mixture we eat with our hands. The sun is setting now, and after eating we lie back on the dais, staring up at the sky. We talk about astronomy and the stars, then listen to the BBC on the radio for a while. After, we discuss international politics and the state of the world. The villagers are very interested in the world outside, and since I've come to live here I've become much more

Visit Vault at **www.vault.com** for insider company profiles, expert advice, career message boards, expert resume reviews, the Vault Job Board and more.

VAULT CAREER LIBRARY   345

aware of world events too. Funny to think that in a tiny village on the edge of Africa the people are more informed than in some of the biggest cities back home.

10:00 p.m.: My host dad wakes me gently. I've drifted off to sleep outside on the dais, and now it's time to go to my hut and my real bed.

Grant Writers

According to the perception perpetuated by the often money-strapped nonprofit community, the grant writer is the one person who can keep the organization afloat, or at least allow staff to embark on that next exciting project. However far from the truth this may be—and in fact it is, since foundation grants account for only 12 percent of all charitable giving in the United States—the myth persists each time a sizable grant is awarded to an organization.

True-life, fairy-tale stories about life-saving (or organization-saving) grants abound. Richard Linklater received a $2,300 grant from a Texas-based nonprofit supporting independent film to complete Slackers, the film that established his career. On the other end of the scale, Conservation International—one of the largest conservation organizations in the world—received a $261 million grant from the Betty and Gordon Moore Foundation for a range of special projects to protect biological diversity worldwide; this is the largest grant ever awarded to an environmental group. Such stories of a single grant that makes a dream project possible only lend power to a certain mythology around grant fundraising.

So who gives out these grants? For the most part, the primary focus of institutional fundraising is foundations, which are in fact another kind of legally recognized nonprofit organization established for the purpose of distributing funds to worthy causes. Like other nonprofits, foundations will have a governing board, usually known as the board of trustees, and an executive director or president, all of whom are usually involved in making decision about who to fund.

So what do grant writers do every day? Whether they work as in-house grant writers or freelancers, grant writers aren't just writers, they're also correspondents, researchers, financial managers, and active participants in the program side of nonprofits.

And when they finally sit down to write the grant proposal they bring everything together to make sure it best represents the nonprofit program.

There is much more to the grant-writing profession than cranking out well-written grant proposals. There are four fundamental, ongoing responsibilities of a grant writer:

• Writing or managing the process of writing grant proposals and reports on current grants.

• Identifying prospective foundation, corporate, and government grant makers and devising strategies for initiating or strengthening relationships with these funders.

• Maintaining regular correspondence and contact with current and prospective funders.

• Maintaining a calendar of proposal submission and reporting deadlines and coordinating staff involvement in meeting those deadlines.

These activities fall under the rubric of institutional fundraising, referring to the range of institutions that give grants—foundations, corporations, and government agencies.

Asker of the hard questions

The grant writer is often the first person to document all aspects of a program or project and therefore plays an important role in helping flesh out that program. It is often the grant writer who asks the most difficult questions about the program, knowing that the grant maker will ask the same tough questions. The grant writer is therefore a crucial player in program planning for the organization, and can often lead this process.

Unlike other fundraisers (particularly major gift and planned giving officers), grant writers are less likely to work directly with funders, although there are opportunities to interact with staff at foundations, government agencies, and corporations with grant-making programs. Most of the time, grant writers collaborate closely with a nonprofit's leadership—primarily the executive director, but also with other managers—and with program staff on building relationships with foundations and corporations.

Most foundation officers want to hear the inside scoop on any issue from those on the front lines, or they want the executive director to show up for a meeting to demonstrate how important the foundation is to the grant-seeking organization. The grant writer is therefore scheduling meetings with foundations (depending on the size of the nonprofit, this administrative task may be delegated to the executive director's assistant or to a development coordinator) and helps staff prepare for these meetings, rather than attending them.

The grant writer also drafts most correspondence to grant makers, from thank you notes to informal updates on program activities. A good grant writer is also reminding program staff to regularly send information on to funders, from news articles in which the nonprofit is cited, to legislation that a program person helped draft.

Researcher

Research is another key activity. In addition to interviewing program staff, grant writers are on the Internet, reviewing news articles on the issues on which the nonprofit focuses and on grant makers' activities. Grant writers are often asked to provide detailed briefings to the executive director on potential funders, including information on current assets, stock prices of corporations with foundations, latest grants awarded, staff changes at the foundation, and any intelligence on grant makers' program planning processes.

A good grant writer will also work with the executive director on any pitch for a new project, whether on paper or for a meeting with a foundation officer. In this capacity, the grant writer coaches the executive director or program staff on buzz words or jargon that will strike a chord with a particular foundation's staff (capacity building, leveraging funds, and partnerships are popular terms among foundations, for example), and on how to position a project as strongly matching the foundation's interests.

Financial manager

A grant writer is also a financial manager of sorts, working closely with a nonprofit's accountant or director of administration to develop budgets for projects and programs, and also with program staff on how they spend grants. At larger nonprofits, a finance department may produce financial documents for grant makers and employ a grants manager to oversee expenditures to grants; but more often than not, the grants writer is as knowledgeable as the organization's leadership and financial officers

A Day in the Life of an In-house Grant Writer

This is the day in the life of a fictional grant writer who works for a $5 million regional nonprofit organization with a mission to expand respite care services for families with mentally ill children.

9:00 a.m.: Come into the office, turn on the computer in your cubicle, and scan your e-mail. The executive director has sent a message asking for the latest stock report for a well known retail company. He is meeting tomorrow with the company's owner, who has an autistic child and who recently established a small family foundation with a focus on improving services for the mentally ill.

Visit Vault at **www.vault.com** for insider company profiles, expert advice, career message boards, expert resume reviews, the Vault Job Board and more.

VAULT CAREER LIBRARY **347**

9:15 a.m.: Search the MSN Money website for the monthly closing prices of the retail company's stock. You print a chart of stock prices, an article announcing a recent stock split, and the foundation's proposal submission guidelines posted on the foundation's website. You consult with your boss, the director of development, on what additional information to provide. She suggests that you remind the executive director that he was going to speak with the company's owner not only about a personal gift, but also about approaching the foundation to fund a new project, a website for families needing respite care for mentally ill children. You dash off a quick note to the executive director to accompany the packet you have pulled together.

10:15 a.m.: Start on your main project for the day: a draft proposal to a large foundation describing your organization's biggest, most complex program: a statewide outreach and education initiative for low-income families with mentally ill children. You have a lot of questions about how a new lecture series at local community centers will build upon a number of outreach events the organization sponsored last year, including a poorly attended lecture series at local libraries. You review your notes from a recent meeting with program staff, and call the director of community outreach to discuss how these new lectures will be different from the previous ones and how she hopes to encourage greater attendance.

12:30 p.m.: Run out and grab some lunch from the deli across the street. You bring it back to your desk so that you can continue to work through the proposal draft.

1:30 p.m.: Look up at the clock and see that you have a half-hour to finish preparing for the monthly meeting of the public policy team. You finalize a short presentation on the status of existing foundation funding for a campaign to lobby the state legislature for greater health care coverage for respite care. You add a summary of the history, interests, and submission deadlines for three foundations you and the director of development have identified from prospect research. You stick your head into your boss's office to see if she will be joining the meeting. She is on the phone with the chair of the board discussing the elements of the next fundraising report and presentation to for the next board meeting. You quickly make a note to yourself to provide her with a quick summary of grants that have come in this month.

2:00 p.m.: Join the policy meeting. The director of public policy starts a discussion about whether to partner with a regional mental health center with strong connections to state officials. You remind the team that one of the foundations you have identified as a prospect is also funding the center. You also ask a number of questions about this partnership and how the two organizations would work together to engage officials at the state's department of mental health.

3:15 p.m.: Return to your desk and resume drafting the proposal. You complete the section on the lecture series and turn your attention to creating the budget. You recall a conversation in the hallway with the director of administration, who mentioned that rent would be going up next year. You call the director to figure out if you should adjust the percentage added to the program expenses for overhead.

4:30 p.m.: Finish a draft of the budget and e-mail it to the program director and the director of administration for review. The executive director calls to thank you for the stock information and to ask what he should highlight about the new project in his meeting tomorrow. You go over with him the overall structure of the website and remind him that there will be a chat room devoted to parents with autistic children.

5:15 p.m.: Turn your attention back to the draft proposal. People are starting to leave the office, so it's quieting down. You figure if you can plow through another 45 minutes, you can complete the draft.

6:05 p.m.: Look up from a completed draft and see that it is time to go. You quickly look over the draft and see that there are a lot of questions highlighted in yellow. You decide to review it one more time tomorrow before sending it out to program staff for comment. Your boss is still around and you ask if she wants to see the draft before or after program staff have reviewed it. She opts for after the program staff review and asks that you flag for her any remaining program questions that remain unanswered. You turn off the computer.

6:15 p.m.: Just as you are about to head out the door, the executive director calls again. The program officer at another large foundation contacted him. She said that she reviewed our proposal describing the health care coverage campaign and is recommending to the foundation's board an increase in funding by $50,000. The executive director complements you on your work on the proposal, adding that he can now hire a new outreach person to enlist psychiatrists and pediatricians in the campaign. You make a note to write a thank you to the foundation officer tomorrow. As you close the door, you think about asking your boss to hire a freelance grant writer to help with three proposals due next month.

Visit Vault at **www.vault.com** for insider company profiles, expert advice, career message boards, expert resume reviews, the Vault Job Board and more.

VAULT CAREER LIBRARY **349**

Nonprofit Employer Directory

American Cancer Society, Inc.
1599 Clifton Rd. NE
Atlanta, GA 30345
Phone: (404) 320-3333
Fax: (404) 982-3677
www.cancer.org

American Civil Liberties Union
125 Broad St., 18th Fl.
New York, NY 10004-2400
Phone: (212) 549-2500
Fax: (212) 549-2646
www.aclu.org

American Heart Association
7272 Greenville Ave.
Dallas, TX 75231-4596
Phone: (800) 242-8721
Fax: (214) 706-1191
www.americanheart.org

American Red Cross
2025 E St., NW
Washington, DC 20006
Phone: (202) 303-4498
Fax: (202) 942-2024
www.redcross.org

Human Rights First
333 Seventh Avenue
13th Floor
New York, NY 10001-5004
Phone: (212) 845 5200
www.humanrightsfirst.org

Legal Aid Society, The
199 Water St.
New York, NY 10038
Phone: (212) 577-3300
Fax: (212) 635-3581
www.legal-aid.org

Teach For America
315 West 36th Street
6th Floor
New York, NY 10018
Phone: (212) 279-2080
Fax: (212) 279-2081
www.teachforamerica.com

Pharmaceuticals and Biotech

What's in a Name: Big Pharma, Big Biotech and Biopharma?

Strictly speaking, the term "pharmaceuticals" refers to medicines composed of small, synthetically produced molecules, which are sold by large, fully integrated drug manufacturers. The largest of these players—companies like Pfizer, GlaxoSmithKline and Merck—as well as a handful of others are referred to as "Big Pharma" because they are huge research, development and manufacturing concerns with subsidiaries all over the globe. Indeed, Big Pharma is where over 50 percent of the industry's sales are generated. Big Pharma is responsible for all of those television commercials urging us to contact our doctors if we suspect we suffer from everything ranging from acid reflux disease to social anxiety disorder. Yet despite life-saving, cancer-fighting drugs and significant corporate philanthropy, Big Pharma's recent product recalls and safety testing troubles (Vioxx and Celebrex) have made it the industry we've come to love to hate.

Most biotechs are small, research-oriented companies dedicated to applying genetics to curing a multitude of heartbreaking diseases, ranging from Alzheimer's to multiple sclerosis. A handful of companies—such as Amgen, Genentech and Chiron—have broken through the rest of the pack to become "fully integrated" like their Big Pharma cousins. The term "fully integrated" means that they manufacture as well as sell their own products. These "products" are proteins, which need to be injected since they are very large molecules compared to the synthetic molecules Big Pharma sells. The largest biotechs are actually mid-sized pharmaceutical companies in the way they function and are sometimes called "Big Biotech."

As for the largest Big Pharma players, most are either gobbling up small biotechs through outright acquisitions or, alternatively, entering into licensing agreements. This has been happening over the last decade, and is likely to continue throughout the rest of this decade, since it is increasingly difficult to find innovative new drugs through traditional science. In fact, innovation is the industry's biggest current challenge. Companies are using acquisitions and alliances to round out their product pipelines and meet investor expectations. Big drug manufacturers can now claim to research, manufacture and sell both synthetics and biologics. What this means to you is that you should include the largest biotechs as well as the largest traditional pharmaceuticals when planning a marketing career. That's good news since it increases the number of players and potential employers.

What you should keep in mind, however, is that the marketing models around which traditional pharmaceuticals and biotechs are developed are complementary. Pharmaceutical companies are generally organized around the "blockbuster" model, i.e., they derive most of their sales and profits from a handful of broadly acting drugs, which are mass-marketed to a broad patient population by a network of sales representatives, or "detail" people. This is the same model that brought Vioxx to the market and it is increasingly under attack. By industry consensus, a "blockbuster" is a drug whose annual revenue reaches or exceeds $1 billion. The biotech firms, on the other hand, tend to be organized around smaller franchises, i.e., their products are targeted to small patient populations with rare genetic diseases. Their biologics are sold by specialty sales representatives, who often have a relatively high degree of scientific knowledge. Because of this focus, biotech products are often referred to as specialty pharmaceuticals. To complicate matters, some biologics reach blockbuster status with respect to their revenue, since they are usually much more expensive than therapeutics. Considering that some biologics cost $10,000 per patient per year, you would need a mere 100,000 patients to reach $1 billion in revenue. Compare this to the millions of patients who ingest small molecule drugs like Prozac or Viagra.

Because this transition is ongoing, the dividing line between the two industries will continue to blur. That leaves us with the problem of how to refer to the emerging industry. Some people use the term "Biopharma" to include both types of products.

The Global Biopharmaceutical Industry

The global industry is dominated by three major market segments: North America is the largest and comprises 49 percent of the total market, Europe is second with some 28 percent, and Japan third at 11 percent in 2003 sales. Although these

Visit Vault at **www.vault.com** for insider company profiles, expert advice, career message boards, expert resume reviews, the Vault Job Board and more.

VAULT CAREER LIBRARY 353

combined markets account for 78 percent of global sales, the remaining emerging market segments—other Asian countries, Africa, and Australia and Latin America—are growing rapidly.

Although the industry is dominated by a handful of super-large companies, the global industry is actually highly fragmented. Over 2,000 pharmaceutical and biotech companies exist worldwide. In the top tier are the large, multinational companies that dominate the market or Big Pharma. In the middle tier are the specialty companies. Many large companies have tended to absorb second-tier companies before they can grow enough to pose a competitive threat. That trend has a contracting effect on the number of firms. The opposite happens on the third and lowest tier, which is composed of an ever increasing group of start-ups mostly focused on discovery research.

According to IMS Health, Inc., a health care research and information company, as recently as 1998, the global pharmaceutical market was valued at $280 billion. By 2003, total global sales had grown 9 percent over 2002 levels to $492 billion or nearly half a trillion dollars! This figure was derived from retail sales in major global markets. This astonishing growth over a five-year period reflects the increasing role pharmaceuticals are taking as first-line treatment options in many disease conditions in the developed world.

Economic activity is concentrated in both products and therapeutic areas. As we noted, most of the industry's revenue is based on mega-sales of blockbuster products, i.e., those that generate at least $1 billion in sales. In 2000, the 20 highest selling drugs generated a collective sales revenue of $100 billion or roughly 50 percent of total sales of the top 500 drugs. In 2002, 58 products each generated sales over $1 billion. Reflecting the stress-ridden, developed world's disease vulnerabilities, the most profitable products treated heart disease, gastric distress, mood and mental disorders, and inflammatory conditions.

The U.S. pharmaceutical industry

The U.S. pharmaceutical industry is comprised of approximately 100 companies, according to the Pharmaceutical Research and Manufacturers of America (PhRMA), a leading industry trade and lobbying organization. This does not include biotech companies, which number approximately 325 publicly traded companies, with hundreds more private, discovery research oriented firms. The U.S. drug market is concentrated—the top 10 largest companies accounted for 60 percent of total retail sales in 2003, according to IMS Health, Inc.

The U.S. not only has the largest pharmaceutical market in the world but also the only one without government controls. That characteristic has major consequences on drug pricing, innovation and R&D investment. Standard & Poor's expects the U.S. to continue to be the largest of the top 10 pharmaceutical markets for the foreseeable future as well as the fastest growing.

Although pharmaceutical companies are scattered throughout the continental United States, the industry is geographically concentrated in the Mid-Atlantic states (New York, New Jersey and Pennsylvania) and on the West Coast in California. A handful of companies can also be found in Massachusetts, Illinois and North Carolina. New Jersey is the heart of the industry and has by far the largest number of companies within a single state.

Departments in a Biotech Company

Biotech companies focused on health care applications contain all the major departments of conventional pharmaceutical companies—R&D, operations, quality control, clinical research, business development, and finance and administration. In fact, the top 10 biotech companies are essentially mid-cap pharmaceutical companies. Each department houses several functional groups, or specific, logically related areas of activity.

As you think about a career in the pharmaceuticals and biotech industry, it is useful to identify the general area(s) where your primary interests and aptitudes lie. Let's take a look at the different departments in a biopharma company.

Research and development

The research and development (R&D) department is responsible for discovering promising drug candidates. The three major functions include discovery research, bioinformatics and animal sciences. The discovery research function involves performing experiments that identify either targets on the cell or potential drug candidates. The animal sciences function provides cell cultures, grows microorganisms and manages the care of animals used in discovery research. The extensive data generated from experiments is analyzed with the help of the bioinformatics function, which assists discovery research in identifying the most biologically active compounds.

Operations

The operations department is responsible for making commercial quantities of a candidate drug available. Once a promising drug candidate has been identified, the process/product development function determines how to "scale up" quantities of a product to make enough available for clinical trials, since laboratory-size quantities are usually very small. When a product emerges from clinical trials successfully, the manufacturing and production function creates the final product—complete with packaging and labeling—that we see on pharmacist and drugstore shelves. Also housed under the operations umbrella is the environmental health and safety function, which assesses the environmental impact of a potential product.

Clinical research

Once a drug candidate emerges from R&D, the clinical research department takes over and becomes responsible for shepherding the drug through the FDA approval process. The clinical research function sets up and manages the clinical trials needed to determine a drug's safety and effectiveness or "efficacy." The regulatory affairs function ensures that all FDA reporting requirements are completed and submitted in a timely manner. Finally, the medical affairs/drug information function is responsible for overseeing all the information related to a drug candidate.

Quality

The quality department has groups focusing on quality control, quality assurance and validation. These groups ensure that products are manufactured along rigorous, consistent standards of quality. This usually means that well-defined and documented procedures are followed when producing a product either for clinical trials or as an end product.

Finance and administration

The finance and administration department contains these two functional areas as well as information systems and legal. All activities relating to the financial management of the company, its legal relationships to investors, creditors and employees are housed in this department. The company-wide computer systems—separate from computing specifically directed at analyzing research data—are also managed here.

Business development

The business development group is typically responsible for identifying prospective new alliance partners and managing existing alliances. The marketing function studies markets, identifies target customer bases, and sets pricing and promotion strategy. Sales actually meets with potential customers in the field—usually specialist physicians in targeted areas of specialization (e.g., cardiologists, endocrinologists, urologists, etc.)

Visit Vault at **www.vault.com** for insider company profiles, expert advice, career message boards, expert resume reviews, the Vault Job Board and more.

VAULT CAREER LIBRARY   355

Project management

Finally, many biotech companies also have a separate project management department, which is responsible for ensuring that work requiring the collaboration of several internal departments is discharged smoothly and efficiently. This department oversees special projects that don't naturally fit into any of the traditional formal functions but that require cross-functional collaboration.

To Lab or Not To Lab?

Given the breadth of choices, you might well wonder how to focus your own career aspirations. You may be turned on by science while in college enough to earn a major in a scientific discipline but not be sure you want to make research your life-long career. That's fine, as long as you have a sense of how to manage the critical early years of professional experience. To get a wide-angle view of the major career paths available, we have found it helpful to think in terms of two fundamental paths: laboratory research oriented and non-laboratory research oriented. Within each path are several different career tracks, discussed later.

Laboratory research-oriented career paths are found in the research and development (R&D) department. This area is also called "discovery research" because the work involves finding new processes, drugs and technologies. These careers involve "bench work," referring to a laboratory bench, where scientists set up experiments to generate data. In biotech research, two other areas—bioinformatics and animal sciences—are especially tightly integrated.

Non-research oriented career paths include everything else. Several functions—operations, manufacturing and quality—have an engineering bent and primarily focus on the applications of science. Others, like clinical research, include all the jobs needed to set up and manage clinical trials and oversee submissions to regulatory agencies. Note that the "clinical research" function includes all the jobs needed to set up and manage clinical trials. They are put here rather than in the research-oriented path since they require knowledge of medicine and occur in clinical settings—such as hospitals or clinics. Still others are business-oriented and include support functions, such as finance, administration, legal, IT, business development and sales/marketing. Finally many companies have a project management function to help coordinate projects that overlap among several internal functions.

The common denominator is that careers in most of these functions require at least an undergraduate foundation in a life science. This includes the more generic business functions. Many careers require advanced training in science in addition to education in a functional area. For example, attorneys specializing in intellectual property often also have a PhD in a life science. Business development people typically have either a bachelor's or a master's in a scientific area in addition to an MBA. The industry sets these educational prerequisites for employment outside the lab because a thorough grounding in the vocabulary of genetics, an orientation to the basic concepts behind the products, and a familiarity with the issues and challenges facing the industry are necessary to get people effectively on the same page. The bottom line is this: If you are up and coming in the educational system, you are joining a limited pool of qualified talent competing for the available jobs. That's good news if most of your career is still ahead of you.

Laboratory Research Careers

Within a lab context, you can choose from three career paths: discovery research, bioinformatics and animal sciences.

Discovery research

Since biotech is still in its infancy, most jobs in biotech companies, especially the smaller ones, are in discovery research. Discovery researchers can range from protein chemists to geneticists to biochemists to many other disciplines in the life sciences. There are jobs at all levels. With a bachelor's degree, you can get an entry-level job as a research associate and work for several years, though you will need an advanced degree for more senior jobs. Most responsible positions, however, require a PhD. You can definitely break into the industry after undergraduate studies. Entry-level research positions will get your feet wet and give you a chance to experience the culture of research first-hand before committing yourself to advanced studies.

Animal science specialists

Instead of using chemicals the way traditional pharmaceutical chemists do, discovery research scientists use cells, which have to be obtained from animals, then cultivated, separated and utilized in special facilities. Discovery researchers rely on veterinarians and other animal science specialists. They grow cultures, make and purify DNA, and help conduct the earliest phases of testing, when a drug's safety is determined via animal testing.

Bioinformatics

Since nearly all experimental setups are computerized and reams of data are generated with each experiment, the results of biotech experiments are analyzed by specialists who straddle the fence between the biological sciences and information technology. These data analysts are called bioinformatics professionals and comprise some of the most sought-after employees in the industry. They help discovery researchers identify those molecular structures that have the most favorable response profile, and thus the most promising drug candidates.

Bioinformatics has three realms of activity: you can create databases to store and manage large biological data sets, you can develop algorithms and statistics to determine the relationships among the components of these datasets, or you can use these tools to either analyze or interpret biological data—e.g., DNA, RNA or protein sequences, protein structures, gene expression profiles, or biochemical pathways.

Non-Laboratory Research Careers

As discussed previously, non-laboratory research careers in biotech encompass a large range of functions, including engineering, careers in medical and clinical settings, administrative/support functions, and sales and marketing.

Engineering careers

Engineering careers have a strong practical application. Where discovery research scientists identify potential drug candidates, engineers are more concerned with figuring out first, how to ensure that enough material is available for clinical testing, and second, how to manufacture an approved drug. Engineering careers require a great capacity for precision, order, defined processes and a need to see tangible results after a day's work. If you like your work to be exact and practical, engineering-related careers may be just the thing.

Visit Vault at **www.vault.com** for insider company profiles, expert advice, career message boards, expert resume reviews, the Vault Job Board and more.

VAULT CAREER LIBRARY   **357**

Four career paths exist in engineering: process/product development, manufacturing, environmental health and safety, and quality. The first three functions are usually grouped together under the operations department. Although engineering-related, the quality department is usually a separate function in the organization, regardless of its size, probably because its mandate requires independent judgment.

Process/product development

Process/product development engineers ensure that the first goal is achieved. They need to understand how a product's input ingredients behave when relatively larger quantities of the product are needed. It turns out that problems come up when scaling up quantities. Think of it as having to take your grandma's favorite recipe for chocolate cake, that comfortably serves eight, and increasing it by an order of magnitude—now you need to make cake for 80. Chances are the mixer, pans and ovens used to make the eight-serving cake will not be able to handle the new cake. For that, you'll need industrial size equipment; you may have to adjust the oven temperature and time for baking; you may even need to substitute some ingredients that don't behave quite the same way. These are the types of adjustments process engineers need to explore to make larger batches of materials available for testing. Most entry-level positions require a bachelor's degree and at least some industry exposure, which you can get with a well-placed internship or co-op program while still in college.

Manufacturing

Where process development careers have an investigative component, manufacturing careers are plant-based and focused on producing FDA-approved products for end consumers. Plant managers oversee this task through very strict standards of consistency and quality that have been codified and adopted industry-wide. Among the many different types of tasks and procedures performed are fermentation, protein purification, solvent extraction, tissue culture, preparation of bulk solutions, non-critical aseptic fills of buffers, filling and labeling of vials under sterile and non-sterile conditions, large-scale bioreactor operations, critical small- or large-volume sterile fills and aseptic manipulation of cell cultures.

To qualify for jobs, even at entry level, employers expect some familiarity with terms such as GMP, GLP and cGMP. Manufacturing of biotech products requires expensive facilities because the end products are often proteins, which are bigger and harder to produce than the small molecules that make up conventional drugs. You must be able to run complex equipment and ensure that procedures are followed and standards are maintained throughout the manufacturing process.

Environmental health and safety

Fully developed companies also maintain an environmental health and safety group to assess the impact of a product on the environment and ensure that any toxic by-products of research or manufacturing are properly disposed. Environmental engineers test and monitor air and water quality, investigate the health effects of potential toxins, dispose of regular as well as hazardous wastes, develop procedures to control pollution and give input on how to manage the land around a facility. This task becomes especially important in industrial applications of biotechnology, where chemical spills can have devastating effects on the environment if they are not contained quickly. Keeping up and complying with environmental regulations also falls under this group. Environmental engineers prepare permit applications, perform regulatory reviews, inspect the operations at the company's facilities and participate in environmental audits.

Quality

Careers in the quality function focus on developing and implementing standards, methods and procedures to inspect, test and evaluate the precision, accuracy, efficacy and reliability of a company's products. These support tasks ensure that the company's submissions to the FDA as well as the products bought by consumers adhere to industry standards. In a tightly regulated industry with a significant potential for liability if a product is defective, careers in the quality function help ensure the safety of the consuming public.

Medical and clinical setting careers

When a product has been demonstrated to be safe in animals—that is, it's passed Phase 1 testing—it is ready to be tested on a small sample of humans and be submitted as a candidate for a new drug to the FDA. These activities occur in clinical settings, involve interpretation of massive amounts of clinical data and require extensive documentation to the regulatory body. Two basic paths exist: clinical research and regulatory affairs. Jobs in these functions are usually grouped together in most companies.

Clinical research

First, let's clarify the term "research" in clinical research. Clinical researchers are physicians, nurses and data management professionals who administer and interpret the reactions of patients who have been enrolled in clinical trials. Often, these patients suffer from the disease condition targeted and need to pass a set of qualification criteria set by physician specialists, who must ensure that their overall health status is sufficiently stable to participate in testing the drug candidate. Once a drug is administered to an enrolled patient, the latter is carefully monitored for reactions to the drug. These include desired effects and other "adverse" or undesired effects. Both sets of data are captured manually and electronically. Sometimes, manual data has to be transferred to electronic form. All data eventually becomes housed in databases, where physicians and database managers interpret the overall effects of the drug on the total population of patients enrolled in the study. These activities thus constitute research in a clinical setting using clinical data.

Medical knowledge at all levels is required for careers in clinical research—physicians identify prospective patients and interpret clinical data; nurses administer drug candidates and help monitor patient reactions; even database specialists need to have some understanding of the type of data the medical professionals generate in order to collaborate with physicians in interpreting it. With the hundreds of biotech drug candidates in the pipeline, clinical research jobs are expected to continue to be plentiful.

Regulatory affairs

Regulatory affairs is the other clinically oriented track. Jobs in this function involve dealing with all aspects of the regulatory environment surrounding drug approval, including submitting new drug applications (NDAs), preparing submissions to the FDA summarizing clinical trial results, keeping up with legislation affecting regulatory policy, ensuring the drug company meets new regulations and working with the marketing function to make sure the message sent to consumers is consistent with federal compliance requirements. Careers in this function often require extensive reading and writing skills, as well as enthusiasm toward activities that protect both the company and the consuming public.

Administrative and support function careers

Biotech companies have a myriad of other careers that support the R&D and clinical testing functions. Typically, the finance and administration department houses these career paths: finance, administration, information systems, legal and facilities management. Although most companies have a separate project management function, the essence of this group is administrative and that's why we are including it here.

Finance

Although entry-level jobs in the finance function often don't require industry-specific experience, the more senior positions usually ask for exposure to the biopharmaceutical environment. Accounting positions fall into this function. Jobs are available at all levels, including analysts, managers, directors and vice presidents. Increasingly, understanding how licensing deals work and how to initiate and implement mergers and acquisitions is essential for finance jobs in the biotech industry. Furthermore, leaders in finance play key roles in obtaining the financing needed to run the many small research-oriented biotech companies. To fulfill this mission, they need to have understanding of the company's core technology and be able to communicate its potential value to private equity investors and venture capital firms.

Visit Vault at www.vault.com for insider company profiles, expert advice, career message boards, expert resume reviews, the Vault Job Board and more.

VAULT CAREER LIBRARY   359

Administration

Administrative support includes administrative assistants, human resource professionals, safety managers, librarians and external relations officers. In the larger firms, the latter comprise of public relations specialists, who deal with the media; investor relations specialists, who deal with Wall Street investment houses and the financial press; and government relations specialists, who represent the company to government committees and stay abreast of important legislation. Since some aspects of biotech research remain controversial, the specialists in this last function play the special role of advocate for their companies.

Information systems

The information systems function is responsible for the company's computing and networking equipment, as opposed to the specialized equipment used by the bioinformatics group in discovery research. There are jobs for programmers, analysts, network specialists, cyber-security experts, and web site developers and site maintenance personnel. As a company grows, it needs more sophisticated software to maintain its human resource function, in order to keep up with employee benefits, compensation and training data. Working collaboratively with the HR manager, the IS department determines what hardware and software to acquire, installs it and ensures it is properly maintained.

Legal

You probably understand that biotech companies need lawyers to keep the company on the right side of the law. But if you think there's one generic biotech lawyer, think again. With alliances, partnerships, regulations (U.S. and international), patents, trademarks, labor laws, benefits plans, and mergers and acquisitions to keep up with, lawyers come in several varieties: patent/intellectual property (IP) attorneys, labor/employment law attorneys and contract attorneys. Patent/intellectual property attorneys are entrusted with protecting the innovations generated by discovery researchers. The most important ingredient here is that the IP attorney "speak the same language" as researchers; thus, many companies require advanced science as well as legal education. Labor/employment law attorneys look after the company's human resources policies and ensure that hiring practices adhere to federal labor law. Contract attorneys help draft agreements that business development people enter into with alliance partners, participate in negotiations and review terms of contracts involving the selling of the company or the acquisition of other companies.

Facilities management

In discussing facilities management jobs, first we should define what this means in biotech. In this context, they refer to the facility that houses the company—as opposed to the facilities housing animals used in experimentation. This career track requires some understanding of real estate, leases, zoning requirements, etc., as well as the specific needs of the company. Many companies need clean rooms and other areas in which to house special equipment. Nearly all need facilities that are wired to support powerful computing, networking and other data transfer equipment.

Project management

While project management is more a function than a career path, it is possible to manage projects as a career. The key here is to be able to work with lots of different types of people, be very organized and be able to push back to meet deadlines when necessary. Project managers make significant contributions when members of different functional groups need to come together around a task, usually getting a drug candidate into clinical trials or launching a product. It's not so much that functional specialists (scientists, marketers, regulators) are not cooperative; rather, each function has its own mandate and its own criteria for reward. A project manager can make a unique contribution by ensuring that each function has its say without tilting the company's resources (time, money, etc.) too much in any single direction.

Sales and marketing careers

Career paths in this function include sales, marketing, new business development and alliance management.

Sales and marketing careers in biotech are going through enormous changes due to several factors: Differences in drug pricing across different geographical areas are becoming increasingly important political issues; biotech drugs typically have smaller sales forces that have very high levels of product knowledge; marketing, at least in the U.S., is increasingly directed toward the consumer, as opposed to the physician; and consumers are clamoring for the government and insurers to pick up at least part of the cost of prescription drug costs. Beyond this complex web of economic forces, lies the business development function, which is itself composed of finding new business partners and managing existing alliances. Finding your way through this terrain largely depends on your skills set and preferences—where you experience satisfaction and where you get frustrated.

Sales and Marketing

Most companies consider sales and marketing to be one function, but with two basic areas of activity. Within the sales function, you can typically find three career tracks: field sales, sales management, and managed markets. A fourth track, sales training, is closely associated with sales and is distinct from the broader training and development function, which is usually associated with human resource departments. Sales training groups bridge the sales and marketing function: in some companies, they are considered part of marketing support, and hence part of the marketing function. The main point, however, is that all companies that have field sales forces have rigorous sales training departments.

Within the marketing function are two main areas of activity: marketing management and marketing support. The latter is actually composed of several distinct groups, some quite large, but all of which serve essentially the same purpose: to provide support services for marketing managers. Depending on the size of the company, the distinction between the two areas may be either blurred on non-existent. Typical groups include training and development, advertising and promotion, market analysis, customer call center, e-Business, and commercialization and strategic planning.

Fully integrated Big Biotech companies have their own sales and marketing infrastructure with essentially the same job classifications. The main difference from their Big Pharma cousins is that biotech sales reps are specialty reps, who market products to specific and highly defined patients groups. On an experiential level, the big difference is that that very focus prevents the overreaching to the mass market that is now plaguing the marketers of broadly acting agents.

The good thing about the sales and marketing function in the biopharmaceutical industry is that once you get hired in a particular work area, it is possible, and even encouraged, to gain experience in other areas.

Field sales

This is the entry-level job in the sales function. The main purpose of the field sales force is to promote the company's products to customers—typically solo- or small-practice groups of physicians—within an assigned territory. "Reps" are carefully trained and equipped with extensive product information. They typically know their products inside out and work hard to understand the medical science on which those products are based. Within field sales are two areas—territory sales, and specialty sales.

Pharmaceutical sales representative and territory sales representative are entry-level sales positions. The next rung is medical specialist or hospital specialist. Specialty sales representatives are experienced reps, often with several years of direct sales experience. This job exists in both Big Biotech and Big Pharma companies.

The responsibilities of a pharmaceutical sales rep are well defined across the industry and fall into three distinct areas of activity. Selling is the main responsibility and requires reps to sell the company's products within the assigned territory, make

Visit Vault at **www.vault.com** for insider company profiles, expert advice, career message boards, expert resume reviews, the Vault Job Board and more.

V∧ULT CAREER LIBRARY

361

product presentations, arrange educational meetings for physicians and co-promote products (when the company has made co-marketing deals with another company). Administrative responsibilities require reps to manage the selling process (i.e., prioritize customers, take notes on call outcomes, prepare reports to the district manager), attend company meetings, manage time effectively by working out optimal sales call schedule, work out territory logistics with team members, maintain expense logs, arrange catering for lunchtime seminars with medical specialists, organize promotional materials and drug samples, and maintain the company car. Professional development responsibilities require reps to learn features, benefits and basic medical science of assigned products; learn about competing products and their advantages/disadvantages relative to own product; attend professional development training sessions; complete required online training programs; and master selling process and continually refine selling skills.

Marketing management

Marketing management is the core work of the marketing function and is where strategy is formulated and implemented. Many companies organize marketing management according to therapeutic areas (i.e., oncology drugs, cardiovascular drugs, anti-hypertensives, etc.). Until recent years, marketing had a single upward path to senior positions. With large companies merging into mega-companies (e.g., Pfizer acquired both Warner-Lambert and Pharmacia to become the largest company in the industry), some firms have opted to organize therapeutic areas and their associated products into separate business units, so that marketing management decisions get made with fewer layers of oversight and closer contact with customer physicians and targeted patient groups.

The main job title in marketing management, product manager, is consistent throughout the industry. From there, titles like product director, group product manager, and vice president of marketing represent higher level marketing management jobs. None of these are entry-level positions at the BS level, although MBAs with previous marketing experience can work in product management groups as assistant or associate product managers.

A product manager's responsibilities fall into two main categories. Product management responsibilities require the product manager to develop and manage the short-term product strategy and marketing plans for assigned products, oversee development of business plans, specify the positioning of a product among its competitors, monitor those competitor products, acquire both a quantitative and intuitive feel for customer needs, and act as an in-house champion for a product or brand. From an administrative perspective, a product manager must develop budgets, maintain records of expenses, and manage and develop entry-level support staff.

In companies organized as business units, product managers effectively become mini-CEOs and are involved in virtually every aspect of getting a product to market. Most product managers also have substantial communication and negotiation skills, as they are required to interact with professionals from every part of the organization.

Life on the Job: Pharma Sales Rep

The sales rep profiled here promotes general therapeutic products and has been on the job long enough to have earned at least one promotion. Note the nursing degree and how, combined with communication skills, it translates into an attractive base salary. Given the continual daily personal contact, the admission of an element of loneliness in this job is noteworthy.

Name of position	Pharmaceutical Executive Sales Representative
Function	Sales
Education level	Hospital Diploma RN; BS, Communications
Company type and size	Large, public, international pharmaceuticals company
Typical number of hours per week	45-50 hours
Salary range	$60K–$120K base; bonus: based on meeting and exceeding market share goals (from $5K per quarter); bonuses are uncapped.
Perks	Stock options, tied to bonus structure—top 10% will be rewarded with extra stock; each year the top 25% of sales reps are part of the Winner's Circle, get special prizes and vacations; company car and associated expenses (insurance and mileage)

Responsibilities

I am responsible for maintaining and growing the market share of my products. I'm given a list of target physicians in my territory and am expected to see 8—10 physicians per day. Through data provided by the marketing department, I know exactly what an MD is prescribing before going in to see him. I do both pre—and post-call planning. I am also expected to do business analysis—i.e., to maintain lists of market growth forms to figure out where our growth is and where our growth potential is.

I work in a team—there are two other reps on the same level I'm in. Three geographies work for the same district sales manager—that's a total of 9 reps and 1 or 2 specialty reps. I have to coordinate with teammates to determine the tactics for approaching an MD. Our team works out a routing schedule, with three-week rotations. So, for any given week, I know exactly where to go. I schedule lunches in the week where I'm going to be in that town.

I am also expected to go to two pharmacies per day—to see what they have back-ordered and what continuing education they have. I usually do a pharmacy call in the morning, since the pharmacist is not likely to be busy during that timeframe. That knocks one call out of the way. It also kind of gets your mouth in gear.

I also do a lot of continuing education, much of which happens over lunch. We usually have 2 or 3 lunches per week. We provide lunch for the entire staff, since they receive the education. Finally, we have special projects—such as arranging dinner meetings with physicians, nurses and other healthcare professionals to provide forums where specialists can talk with each other.

A typical day

7:45 a.m.	Leave home; drive to first call; do pre-call planning
8:45 a.m.-12:00 p.m.	Pharmacy visit Physician office visits
12:00 p.m.-2:00 pm	Offices closed; lunch with staff and/or physicians; great chance to talk to them; catch up on computer work; file reports. Call in specialist to—an office to talk about important issues (e.g., latest post-launch data on adverse effects or ongoing clinical results for drugs in development)
2:00 p.m.-5:00 p.m.	Pharmacy visit Physician office visits
5:00 p.m.-6:30 p.m.	Evening event set up; usually one per month. This involves making sure the meeting room is ready (i.e., slide projector, easel for note pad, writing implements, refreshments, etc.)

Visit Vault at **www.vault.com** for insider company profiles, expert advice, career message boards, expert resume reviews, the Vault Job Board and more.

VAULT CAREER LIBRARY

363

| 6:30 p.m.-9:00 p.m. | Host evening event. This involves introducing the speaker(s), moderating the meeting, and making a presentation of how my company's product fits into the disease state that the physician experts are discussing. |
| 9:00 p.m. | Follow up on the computer at home to complete post-call planning (e.g., write up notes, document questions and responses, identify outstanding issues and queries, special needs, etc.) |

Uppers and downers

Uppers	Downers
It's not a 9-to-5 job. It's an independent lifestyle. We all carry the same products and the same compensation, so that makes teamwork and collaboration very easy. We're very well taken care of. We stay in nice places and the bonus structure adds incentives to our work.	It can be lonely. You don't have an office to go to. It's pretty much you driving around all day. You don't have that office camaraderie except when we have big meetings, and that can be kind of weird. The people at the physician offices can become your family. Sometimes I bring Christmas party food and share it at a doctor's office. There are some physicians with whom you develop great rapport. Getting organized enough can be hard for some people. Some companies have networked computers that can keep track of when you are making your calls, so if you don't get started till late, that could become a problem. Access is difficult; a lot of physicians don't have a lot of time. Five minutes a piece and 15 reps a day can add an extra hour to the physician's day!

Success criteria

The most important success criteria are being flexible and being able to get along with people. Don't get crushed when they say no. See it as an opportunity to work on the problem—to let the situation evolve. So good people skills is a crucial asset.

You also have to have an ability to grasp medical knowledge—to be able to talk to a doctor. If he switches gears and talks about an area outside the product's field, you have to be able to converse with him.

Being a nurse, I've learned to figure out what a physician really needs, instead of what he says he needs. You have to be perceptive, to learn to read people. I can sense when a very nice physician is tense or not in a position to talk to me. It's not about my agenda, but theirs. Then I just say, "This doesn't seem like a good time to talk. I'll be back another day and we can talk then." They're usually very appreciative and positively disposed to talk to me the next time I call on them.

Advice for jobseekers

Get sales experience, especially in consumer products. Develop an understanding of the industry and its foremost issues to show the interviewer that you understand the challenges you will be facing. Also research the job and practice your responses to anticipated questions out loud. That will help you understand where you need to become more polished.

Pharmaceuticals/Biotech Employer Directory

Bristol Myers Squibb

345 Park Avenue
New York, NY 10154-0037
Recruiting Contact Phone: 212-546-4000
www.bms.com/career

Bristol-Myers Squibb
Hope, Triumph and the Miracle of Medicine™

Undergraduate-level students may pursue internship, co-op and permanent job opportunities in many business divisions and functions across BMS and its family of health care companies.

Genentech

1 DNA Way
South San Francisco, CA 94080-4990
Recruiting Contact Phone: (650) 225-1000
www.gene.com/gene/careers/index.jsp

Genentech
IN BUSINESS FOR LIFE

Genentech is a leading biotechnology company that discovers, develops, manufactures and commercializes biotherapeutics for significant unmet medical needs. We commit ourselves to high standards of integrity in contributing to the best interests of patients, the medical profession, our employees and our communities, and to seeking significant returns to our stockholders, based on the continual pursuit of scientific and operational excellence. From the beginning, we have selected the best and brightest people to join us, creating a stimulating culture of openness, integrity and creativity. At Genentech we emphasize working hard, collaborating and sharing rewards.

Johnson & Johnson

501 George Street
New Brunswick, NJ 08901
www.jnj.com/careers

Johnson & Johnson
Family of Companies

At the Johnson & Johnson Family of Companies you can experience a small-company environment combined with big-company impact. From our innovation in consumer health care to our life-saving pharmaceuticals and medical devices, our commitment helps people live healthier lives. Johnson & Johnson hires interns, co-ops, and full time graduates in disciplines such as Business, Accounting, Marketing, Human Resources, Operations, Engineering, Finance, and Information Management. Go to jnj.com/careers for more information and to apply.

Undergraduate schools Johnson & Johnson recruits from:
Cornell University; University of Notre Dame; Drexel; Hampton; Howard; UC Berkeley; Stanford; FAMU; U Puerto Rico, Mayaguez; Rutgers University; Penn State University; Morehouse

Abbott

100 Abbott Park Road
Abbott Park, IL 60064
Phone: (847) 937-6100
Fax: (847) 937-1511
www.abbott.com

Advanced Cell Technology, Inc.

1201 Harbor Bay Parkway,
Suite 120
Alameda, CA 94502
Phone: (510) 748-4900
Fax: (510) 748-4950
www.advancedcell.com

Allergan, Inc.

2525 Dupont Drive
Irvine, CA 92612
Phone: (714) 246-4500
Fax: (714) 246-4971
www.allergan.com

Visit Vault at **www.vault.com** for insider company profiles, expert advice, career message boards, expert resume reviews, the Vault Job Board and more.

VAULT CAREER LIBRARY   365

Pharmaceuticals/Biotech Employer Directory, cont.

ALZA Corporation
1900 Charleston Road
Mountain View, CA 94039
Phone: (650) 654-5000
Fax: (650) 564-7070
www.alza.com

Amgen, Inc.
One Amgen Center Drive
Thousand Oaks, CA 91320-1799
Phone: (805) 447-1000
Fax: (805) 447-1010
www.amgen.com

Applera Corporation
301 Merritt 7
Norwalk, CT 06851
Phone: (203) 840-2000
Fax: (203) 840-2312
www.applera.com

AstraZeneca PLC
15 Stanhope Gate
London W1Y 1LN
United Kingdom
Phone: +44-20-7304-5000
Fax: +44-20-7304-5183
www.astrazeneca.com

Bayer AG
100 Bayer Road
Pittsburgh, PA 15205
Phone: (412) 777-2000
Fax: (412) 777-2034
www.bayer.com

Becton, Dickinson and Company
One Becton Drive
Franklin Lakes, NJ 07147-1880
Phone: (201) 847-6800
www.bd.com

Bristol-Myers Squibb Company
345 Park Avenue
New York, NY 10154
Phone: (212) 546-4000
www.bms.com

Chiron Corporation
4560 Horton Street
Emeryville, CA 94608
Phone: (510) 655-8730
Fax: (510) 655-9910
www.chiron.com

Eli Lilly and Company
Lilly Corporate Center
Indianapolis, IN 46285
Phone: (317) 276-2000
Fax: (317) 277-6579
www.lilly.com

Forest Laboratories
909 3rd Avenue
New York, NY 10022
Phone: (212) 421-7850
Fax: (212) 750-9152
www.frx.com

Genentech, Inc.
1 DNA Way
South San Francisco, CA 94080
Phone: (650) 225-1000
Fax: (650) 225-6000
www.gene.com

Genzyme Corporation
5 Kendall Street
Cambridge, MA 02142
Phone: (617) 252-7570
Fax: (617) 252-7600
www.genzyme.com

GlaxoSmithKline
980 Great West Road, Brentford
London, TW8 9GS
United Kingdom
Phone: +44-20-8047-5000
Fax: +44-20-8047-7807
www.gsk.com

ImClone Systems Incorporated
180 Varick Street
New York, NY 10014
Phone: (212) 645-1405
Fax: (212) 645-2054
www.imclone.com

ImmunoGen, Inc.
128 Sidney Street
Cambridge, MA 02139
Phone: (617) 995-2500
Fax: (617) 995-2510
www.immunogen.com

Incyte Corporation
Experimental Station
Route 141 & Henry Clay Road
Building E336
Wilmington, DE 19880
Phone: (302) 498-6700
Fax: (302) 425-2750
www.incyte.com

Invitrogen Corporation
1600 Faraday Avenue
P.O. Box 6482
Carlsbad, CA 92008
Phone: (760) 603-7200
Fax: (760) 602-6500
www.invitrogen.com

Johnson & Johnson Inc.
1 Johnson & Johnson Plaza
New Brunswick, NJ 08933
Phone: (732) 524-0400
Fax: (732) 524-3300
www.jnj.com

McKesson Corporation
One Port Street
San Francisco, CA 94104
Phone: (415) 983-8300
Fax: (415) 983-7160
www.mckesson.com

Merck & Co., Inc.
One Merck Drive
Whitehouse Station, NJ 08889
Phone: (908) 423-1000
www.merck.com

Monsanto Company
800 N. Lindbergh Boulevard
St. Louis, MO 63137
Phone: (314) 694-1000
Fax: (314) 694-8394
www.monsanto.com

Pharmaceuticals/Biotech Employer Directory, cont.

Novartis AG
Lichtstrasse 35
CH-4056 Basel
Switzerland
Phone: +41-61-324-1111
Fax: +41-61-324-8001
www.novartis.com

Pfizer Inc.
235 E. 42nd Street
New York, NY 10017
Phone: (212) 573-2323
Fax: (212) 573-7851
www.pfizer.com

Roche Group
Grenzacherstrasse 124
CH-4070 Basel
Switzerland
Phone: +41-61-688-1111
Fax: +41-61-691-9391
www.roche.com

Sanofi-Aventis
174 Avenue de France
Paris 75013
France
Phone: +33-1-53-77-40-00
Fax: +33-1-53-77-42-96
www.sanofi-aventis.com

Schering-Plough Corporation
2000 Galloping Hill Road
Kenilworth, NJ 07033
Phone: (908) 298-4000
Fax: (908) 298-7653
www.sch-plough.com

Wyeth Pharmaceuticals
5 Giralda Farms
Madison, NJ 07940
Phone: (973) 660-5000
Fax: (973) 660-7026
www.wyeth.com

ZLB Behring L.L.C.
1020 First Avenue
P.O. Box 61501
King of Prussia, PA 19406
Phone: (610) 878-4000
Fax: (610) 878-4009
www.zlbbehring.com

Visit Vault at **www.vault.com** for insider company profiles, expert advice, career message boards, expert resume reviews, the Vault Job Board and more.

V∧ULT CAREER LIBRARY   **367**

Public Relations

What is PR?

It's hard to give an all-encompassing definition of public relations because it is practiced in so many different ways for different people and organizations. PR includes publicity, press agentry, book publicity, propaganda (for the government), corporate communications, crisis management, and advertising.

Like advertising, the concept of "public relations" existed long before the 20th century. Socrates is said to have remarked that "the way to a good reputation is to endeavor to be what you desire to appear." In Ecclesiastes, the Bible says, "Have regard for your name, since it will remain for you longer than a great store of gold." And Greenland was given its name because the Danish government wanted to encourage settlement there—even though "Iceland" may have been more appropriate. But the business as we know it today was born at the end of World War I. In a nutshell, PR is chiefly concerned with image management, and it is intended to help individuals, corporations, governments, and other organizations communicate effectively with the public.

The term "public" can suggest many different groups. For a corporation, it can mean employees, shareholders, environmental groups, or the government. For an individual, it could mean voters, fans, or an entire community. PR professionals deal with perception, representation, and effective communication. For example, they help employers communicate with employees, customers to understand the companies that serve them, and citizens to understand the politicians who serve their communities. At the same time, PR agents analyze trends—they study existing social attitudes and advise their clients about how they can win the support of the "publics" they answer to. In some cases, the PR agent tries to shape the attitudes of the general population so that they will respond in a positive way. At its best, PR presents a true image of reality to the public, and facilitates an effective, honest dialogue. But at the core of it all, their job is to present their clients to the public in a favorable light, which is why people tend to associate PR with "spin."

Public Relations History

A little background

Though publicity and press agentry (essentially getting clients' names into newspapers) were common in the 19th century, PR as we know it is generally considered to be a 20th century phenomenon. It was born during a period of increasing hostility toward big business. Early in the century, investigative reporters—disparagingly referred to as muckrakers—began exposing the rampant corruption of corporate America. Among the most popular of these exposes were Ida Tarbell's History of the Standard Oil Company and Upton Sinclair's *The Jungle*. The latter sparked the creation of the Federal Food and Drugs Act in 1906. In response to the scrutiny, corporations began taking steps to improve their reputations. Several railroad companies retained ex-journalists and ex-press agents to handle publicity issues. The Publicity Bureau, founded in 1900, was retained by railroad companies and other businesses who feared they were next in line for legislation. Soon thereafter, a few other publicity agencies popped up, and several organizations, including the United States Marine Corps and the University of Pennsylvania, set up their own publicity offices.

During World War I, the government began using PR extensively. In 1917, President Wilson endorsed the creation of the Committee on Public Information. Led by George Creel, the CPI was staffed by several budding architects of the PR industry, including Edward Bernays and Carl Byoir. There they learned, according to the Museum of Public Relations, that "words could be used as weapons." To gain public support for the war effort, encourage enlistment, and sell Liberty Bonds, the CPI organized public rallies, reached out to non-English speaking men eligible for the draft, and created newsreel announcements to urge people to contribute to the war effort.

Visit Vault at **www.vault.com** for insider company profiles, expert advice, career message boards, expert resume reviews, the Vault Job Board and more.

VAULT CAREER LIBRARY 369

The "Father of Spin"

Many of today's major PR firms were founded in the period directly following the war, and the basic groundwork of the industry was laid by the founders of those firms. The business as we know it was largely the brainchild of Edward Bernays, the fabled "Father of Spin." The nephew of Sigmund Freud, Bernays is said to have inherited the famed psychoanalyst's knack for understanding human behavior. He also possessed a trait critical to the PR business—the ability to anticipate changes in public opinion. Early in his career, he worked as a press agent for the theatre. As a member of the CPI, he helped sell the war as an effort to "Make the World Safe for Democracy." In 1919, Bernays set up shop in New York, calling himself a "public relations counselor," and handled communications and marketing-related "persuasion projects" for clients including the U.S. War Department and the American Tobacco Company. For the former, he convinced businesses to hire returning war veterans. For the latter, he created a campaign to convince women that smoking helped them to stay slim. He claimed smoking also disinfected the mouth, and went on to paint cigarettes as figurative "torches of freedom" for women, encouraging them to contest the taboo against female smoking in public by marching down Fifth Avenue on Easter Day in 1929, cigarettes in hand.

Bernays published the first book on the PR profession, *Crystallizing Public Opinion*, in 1922. He felt that the average man is an intellectually limited, conformist creature, so it was up to the intellectual elite to mold public opinion. He felt that the so-called "intelligent few" were essentially social scientists who could guide the masses and influence history by applying the theories of mass psychology to corporate and political agendas. Not surprisingly, Bernays was approached for counsel by both Adolf Hitler and Spain's Francisco Franco (he turned both down). An Austrian-born Jew, Bernays reportedly lamented the fact that Joseph Goebbels, the notorious Nazi, kept a copy of *Crystallizing Public Opinion* on his desk.

Bernays pioneered the practice of promoting corporate agendas through social causes. In his own words, he helped his clients "create events and circumstances from which favorable publicity would stem." To that end, he developed "public service" agendas for unnamed corporate sponsors. After WWI, for example, he was called upon to help an ailing hair net company. Bernays urged labor commissioners to require women who worked with machinery to wear hair nets for their safety and waitresses to wear them in the interests of hygiene. He never named the hair net company, but sales improved. To help sell one client's bacon, he published a survey of 5,000 doctors who agreed that Americans should eat big breakfasts. He later orchestrated "Light's Golden Jubilee," a global media event in celebration of the invention of the light bulb, which was ghost-sponsored by General Electric.

Further growth

After WWI and throughout the Depression, the PR industry continued to grow. The National Association of Public Relations Counsel was founded in 1936, and the American Council on Public Relations formed in 1939. In 1948, the NAPC and ACPR were merged to form the Public Relations Society of America, which still exists today. Just as it did during WWI, PR grew considerably during WWII. The federal government created the Office of War Information in 1942 and used PR to develop support and distribute information. The division was later renamed the United States Information Agency and continues to disseminate news across the globe.

In the 1940s and '50s, Bernays continued to help political leaders use mass persuasion to their advantage. During this period he wrote the famous "Engineering of Consent" in which he explained, among other things, the particular usefulness of visual symbols to influence the masses. And while universities and journalism schools had been offering PR courses since 1920 (the first to offer a PR curriculum was the University of Illinois), Boston University created the first school wholly dedicated to public relations in 1947.

Few people outside the industry have every heard of Bernays, largely because he was a staunch believer in the hidden yet omnipresent PR professional. For him, the PR counselor is ever the strategist, never the voice. This attitude underlies another of Bernays' innovations—the front organization. For example, in the late 1940s and early 1950s, a newly elected government in Guatemala threatened to take over some of the plantations owned by the United Fruit Company and divide them among the peasants. When Bernays was called in, he set up the Middle America Information Bureau, which was financed by—you guessed it—United Fruit. The Bureau disseminated information to American newspapers about communist influences in Guatemala, and soon the Guatemalan government was overthrown in a CIA-backed rebellion. If you think that such tactics are a thing of the past, think again. In the early 1990s, several PR firms became embroiled in ethics controversies for taking on questionable accounts. For example, Hill and Knowlton drummed up support for the war against Iraq by creating a group called "Citizens for a Free Kuwait." What became clear later was that the $11 million account was more than 99 percent funded by the exiled Kuwaiti Government. Another classic example is Burson-Marsteller's work to develop a National Smokers Alliance, funded by members of the tobacco industry.

Entertainment PR

Henry Rogers, known as the master of entertainment PR, entered the industry by launching his own publicity firm in 1936. Rogers is credited with setting many ethical and creative standards for the PR profession, and is often credited for bringing respect to the industry. In 1939, he helped make the then-unknown Rita Hayworth a household name by convincing a magazine editor to do a story on her. In 1945, Rogers launched the first full-scale Oscar publicity blitz, which helped Joan Crawford win the award for Best Actress. That campaign set a standard followed by studios and actors to this day. Within five years, Rogers became one of the most successful independent PR agents in Hollywood. In 1950, he teamed up with Warren Cowan to create Rogers and Cowan, the largest entertainment PR agency in the world. Now a division of Shandwick, R&C later expanded to serve corporate clients as well as motion picture, television, and recording stars.

Creating an industry

From the 1950s on, PR has built upon the foundation laid by Bernays, Rogers, and a few other PR notables. Daniel Edelman founded his eponymous Chicago-based firm in the 1950s, as did Harold Burson and Bill Marsteller (today their firm is one of the largest in the business). By the late 1980s, there were more than 2,000 PR agencies in the U.S. alone, and many more around the world. All of the major U.S. agencies have foreign outposts, most of which are staffed and run by local residents. Today, the strategy aspect of PR has become one of its most important components, and the agency end of the business has begun to edge in on the territory once reserved for consulting firms.

PR has essentially created a distinction between reality and what is presented by the media. Most people don't realize that many of the stories presented in newspapers, magazines, and on TV are essentially planted by PR people. Reporters don't just go out every day and look for the news—they find much of their information in press releases prepared by PR professionals. PR agents spend a lot of time brainstorming story ideas that relate to their clients and then call up journalists to pitch them. And usually, when journalists review products, it's because publicity agents send them samples and hope to get a story or a mention.

Ironically enough, the image-making industry has a negative reputation of its own. Even though many PR professionals are ex-journalists, press releases are considered the stepchildren of journalism. This may change, however, as more journalism and communications graduates choose to pass on paltry newspaper and magazine salaries in favor of more varied, better-paid gigs in PR. Additionally, PR offers greater management potential, the chance to learn business skills, and the opportunity to apply those skills to other industries.

While PR professionals uphold the fact that their major objective is to merge the client's interest with the public interest, it's important to remember that in the end, the clients are writing the checks. Even Bernays, by the end of his life, believed that the PR business had taken a turn for the worse. And PR professionals constantly cite the need to uphold ethical standards within the industry. Still PR gaffes from none other than the leading figures in the industry have caused the industry to continue to suffer from image problems. In 1996, Rich Edelman, heir to Edelman Worldwide and now its president and CEO,

Visit Vault at www.vault.com for insider company profiles, expert advice, career message boards, expert resume reviews, the Vault Job Board and more.

VAULT CAREER LIBRARY 371

said, "In this era of exploding media technologies, there is no truth except the truth you create yourself." When Esquire used that quote in an exposé of the industry that December, many PR professionals spoke out in defense of their business, noting that while spin is an essential part of PR, the term indicates "putting one's best foot forward," not manipulation. In the end, they claim that they simply want to enable an honest dialogue between their clients and the public.

Outlook

The PR industry has doubled in size over the past 15 years, and in 1999, the Bureau of Labor Statistics identified PR as one of the three fastest growing industries in the U.S. Within the PR industry, high tech has become the fastest growing specialty. Along with that growth, PR professionals expect to see a lot of changes in the business over the coming years. Because PR is too often associated with "hucksters" and "spin," many think the term PR will be phased out by agencies and some corporations. Terms such as "corporate communications" and "reputation management" (Shandwick's preferred term) will likely grow popular. PR agents also plan to improve the perception of the industry by collaborating to create a set of rules and a code of ethics to abide by. The PR Society of America has been pushing such a code for several years. There has also been talk of establishing an official education requirement for the industry.

The 1990s have been an unparalleled time for corporate mergers and acquisitions, making it a prime time for PR professionals, who have proven indispensable to the integration process. Because communications issues are so integral to a company's performance, the need for PR extends far beyond a product launch or a crisis. It is believed that the industry's reputation will improve as more executives invite PR agents to help create their management strategies, facilitate internal and external communications, and keep investors informed.

Breaking Down Public Relations

Agencies: The most common route into the public relations field is to join a public relations firm. Firms pitch their communication services to clients ranging from corporations to nonprofit organizations to government agencies. These services include organizing press events, writing press releases, launching new products, publishing, providing "damage control" for corporate missteps or miscommunication, as well as a variety of other strategic support.

Corporate Communications: Also referred to as the "client side" in the public relations world. There are two primary corporate communications roles, media relations and investor relations. Media relations focuses on relationships with media outlets like newspapers and television stations. Investor relations focuses on those shareholders with a financial stake or interest in the company, like stockholders, financial analysts and potential investors. Some senior executives in this field develop and maintain the overall corporate communications strategy.

Publicists: A public relations function in which the communications needs of a single individual, such as an author or other celebrity, is served. Referred to as press secretaries in politics. Publicists manage all relations with the media, promote their client's activities (or downplay them in some cases) and manage their public schedule.

Publicist

Any publicity is good publicity

Publicists are the vanguard for high-profile clients and the cheerleaders for obscure companies. Though publicity and press agentry (essentially getting clients' names into newspapers) were common in the 19th century, PR as we know it is generally considered to be a 20th century phenomenon. It was born out of a period when people were becoming increasingly hostile towards the violations of big business. Early in the century, investigative reporters—disparagingly referred to as muckrakers—began exposing the rampant corruption of corporate America. Among the most popular of these exposes were

Ida Tarbell's History of the Standard Oil Company and Upton Sinclair's The Jungle. The latter sparked the creation of the Federal Food and Drugs Act in 1906. In response to the scrutiny, corporations began taking steps to improve their reputations. Several railroad companies retained ex-journalists and ex-press agents to handle publicity issues. The Publicity Bureau, founded in 1900, was retained by railroad companies and other businesses who feared they were next in line for legislation. Soon thereafter, a few other publicity agencies popped up, and several organizations, including the United States Marine Corps and the University of Pennsylvania, set up their own publicity offices.

Publicists understand the way the media are perceived by the public and target certain demographic groups to get their clients' image across. They must also be chummy with journalists to ensure that the media will be receptive to their pitches. Radio and television special reports and magazine feature articles can often be traced back to a public relations firm or an independent publicist. PR specialists also plan events and programs such as speaking engagements, and often write speeches for politicians and business executives.

Hobnobbing with celebrities is one of the draws of the PR industry, but most entry-level publicists soon find out that before they can be exposed to such perks, they have to wade through grunt work and long hours. Though the pay is not high compared to other industries, the fast pace and interesting work are stimulating. Publicists are courted by the press and by their clients, and the pros enjoy a degree of celebrity themselves.

Different type of publicity employers

Work in a PR firm is one of the most popular ways to get into the business. Most major firms have departments that serve different industries, and many small to mid-size firms specialize in a few related businesses. Agencies can specialize in functions such as consumer relations, corporate communications, brand marketing, business to business relations, crisis management, event marketing, media relations, public affairs, product placement, or reputation management. Agencies also specialize in industries, such as financial services, health care, high tech and the Internet, and sports. PR agencies tend to pay pretty well—more than book publishing and nonprofits—and tend to invest the most in employee development. In addition, agency life offers the promise of structured learning and a clearly defined career path.

If you know you're interested in a specific company, or hope to move from PR to another area of a business, working for an in-house corporate communications, investor relations, or publicity department can be an exciting and fulfilling job. Though PR by definition is a behind-the-scenes job, you get a different kind of satisfaction working inside the company you are promoting. Working in publicity for a publishing house is a perfect job for people who love books and reading. Book publicists schedule book tours, work to get authors' books reviewed, and think up ways to get authors and their work featured in as many media outlets as possible.

Visit Vault at **www.vault.com** for insider company profiles, expert advice, career message boards, expert resume reviews, the Vault Job Board and more.

VAULT CAREER LIBRARY   373

Public Relations Employer Directory

Brodeur

855 Boylston Street

Boston, MA 02116

Phone: (617) 587-2800

Fax: (617) 587-2828

www.brodeur.com

Burson-Marsteller

230 Park Avenue South

New York, NY 10003

Phone: (212) 614-4000

Fax: (212) 598-6914

www.bm.com

Daymon Worldwide

700 Fairfield Avenue

Stamford, CT 06902

Phone: (203) 352-7500

www.daymon.com

Edelman Public Relations

200 East Randolph Drive

63rd Floor

Chicago, IL 60601

Phone: (312) 240-3000

Fax: (312) 240-2900

www.edelman.com

GolinHarris

111 E. Wacker Drive

Suite 1000

Chicago, IL 60601-3704

Phone: (312) 729-4000

Fax: (312) 729-4010

www.golinharris.com

Hill & Knowlton, Inc.

909 Third Avenue

New York, NY 10022

Phone: (212) 885-0300

Fax: (212) 885-0570

www.hillandknowlton.com

Hill Holiday

200 Clarendon Street

Boston, MA 02116

Phone: (617) 437-1600

Fax: (617) 573-3400

www.hhcc.com

Ketcham, Inc.

1285 6th Avenue

New York, NY 10019

Phone: (646) 935-3900

Fax: (646) 935-4499

www.ketchum.com

Manning Selvage & Lee

1675 Broadway, 9th Floor

New York, NY 10019

Phone: (212) 468-4200

Fax: (212) 469-4175

www.mslpr.com

Porter Novelli

450 Lexington Avenue

New York, NY 10017

Phone: (212) 601-8000

Fax: (212) 601-8101

www.porternovelli.com

Ruder Finn, Inc.

301 East 57th Street

New York, NY 10022

Phone: (212) 593-6423

Fax: (212) 593-6428

www.ruderfinn.com

Waggener Edstrom, Inc.

225 108th Avenue, NE, Suite 700

Bellevue, WA 98004

Phone: (425) 638-7000

Fax: (425) 638-7001

www.waggeneredstrom.com

Weber Shandwick Worldwide

640 Fifth Avenue

New York, NY 10019

Phone: (212) 445-8000

Fax: (212) 445-8001

www.webershandwick.com

Publishing

The Book Publishing Industry

By most standards book publishing is a modestly sized industry. According to the U.S. Department of Labor's U.S. Industrial Outlook, the publishing business generates over $25 billion in annual revenue, which, compared to the income of a single company like Microsoft ($32 billion in 2003) doesn't seem like much. In fact, many people would probably hesitate to call book publishing an "industry" at all since the product is "intellectual property" and publishers generally lack manufacturing operations.

Whatever you call it though, there are over 85,000 employees at book publishing companies in the U.S. busily writing, editing, designing, marketing, and selling an extremely diverse array of products for both business and consumer markets. The content of these publications runs the gamut from romance novels to children's books, tenth-grade math textbooks to bibles, and timeless literary fiction to cookbooks. In all, over two billion books are sold in the United States every year (Communications Industry Forecast, 2002) 60,000 of which are wholly new titles.

The companies that drive the publishing industry are themselves a disparate bunch, comprised of multinational media conglomerates and smaller independent presses.

Publishing operations are an eclectic mix of multinational conglomerates, private firms, associations, and educational institutions. Below is a list of the industry's largest book publishing employers in the U.S.

As you can see, ownership is heavily international, with European, Australian, and Canadian firms controlling the majority of the well-known American publishing companies.

Trade Books	Size (Revs/Growth)	Employees	Parent Co. (HQ)
Random House	$2.1 Billion (+18.3%)	6,100	Bertelsmann (Germany)
The Penguin Group	$1.4 Billion (+13.5%)	4,362	Pearson (UK)
HarperCollins Publishers	$1.1 Billion (+10.5%)	3,000	News Corp. (Australia)
Simon & Schuster	$649 Million (+8.8%)	1,518	Viacom (US)
Time Warner Books	Not available	Not available	Time Warner (US)
FSG/St. Martin's/Macmillan	$2.4 Billion (+6.8%)*	12,600	Holtzbrinck (Germany)
Educational/Professional			
Thomson Corporation	$7.8 Billion (+7.2%)	43,000	(Canada)
Reed Elsevier	$6.6 Billion (+17.6%)	34,600	(UK)
McGraw-Hill	$4.8 Billion (+3.1%)	16,500	(US)
Pearson Education	$4.4 Billion (+17.6%)	20,035	Pearson (UK)
Wolters Kluwer	$3.4 Billion (-1.5%)	19,766	(Netherlands)
Houghton Mifflin	$1 Billion (+0%)	4,400	(US)
John Wiley & Sons	$734 Million (+19.6%)	3,100	(US)
Children's			
Scholastic	$1.9 Billion (-2.3%)	3,000	(US)

*Sources: Hoover's Inc.; corporate web sites   * Includes newspaper and other non-book publishing holdings*

Visit Vault at **www.vault.com** for insider company profiles, expert advice, career message boards, expert resume reviews, the Vault Job Board and more.

VAULT CAREER LIBRARY   375

As you can see, the largest U.S. publishing operations are often units of even larger multinational media conglomerates. Each of these firms has many divisions, and within each of these divisions, there are a number of imprints (sometimes called 'lines' or 'lists'), which are the publicly used "brand" names for groups of books in a given market, format, and/or genre.

No matter what types of books they produce, however, you'll see the same types of publishing professionals at all of these organizations—editors, marketers, salespeople, and production specialists—performing very similar tasks.

Operating units/imprints

The operating units or divisions of book publishing companies are typically organized around their "imprints"—the brand names given to particular product lines. Often imprints specialize in certain genres or areas of interest and have names that reflect their focus. Other times the imprints are the names of companies that were acquired and have a publishing reputation that the acquiring company wishes to keep alive.

Here are some examples of the nation's largest trade book publishers and the imprints within them.

Trade Book Publishers	Imprints
Random House	Bantam, Doubleday, Dell; Pantheon; Knopf; Ballantine; Fodor's
The Penguin Group	Putnam; Viking; Dutton; Puffin; Dorling Kindersley; Rough Guides
HarperCollins Publishers	HarperCollins; Avon; Perennial; ReganBooks; Quill; Zondervan
Simon & Schuster	Pocket Books; The Free Press; Scribner
Time Warner Books	Little, Brown; Warner Books

Departments at a Book Publisher

Within each imprint or operating unit is a departmental organization structured along these lines:

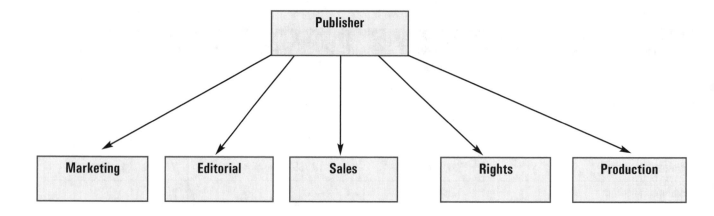

While this structure may seem fairly flat, with equally important departments reporting to a single publisher, the sales and editorial groups make the crucial business recommendations to the publisher and are responsible for delivering the most important things the company needs: quality manuscripts and sales revenue. The head of book publishing units are traditionally drawn from the editorial department, given the group's emphasis on creating compelling editorial products, although the ever-increasing emphasis on sales has meant that more top executives now come from that department.

The publisher decides which titles will be published and, of these, which titles will be pushed the hardest by the sales and marketing folks. This pecking order will be determine where the lion's share of budgeted marketing and production monies will go.

Product teams

Each title usually has a team comprised of an editor, copyeditor, proofreader, and a production staffer. Each member will handle many titles at any given time and team members will be mixed and matched throughout the operating unit. Often freelancers assist the members of the team with editing, indexing, layout, and/or graphic design.

The product teams report to their respective senior managers (developmental editors, production managers) and these senior managers work with the sales and marketing managers on things like cover art, cover copy, catalog copy, etc. The product team gets the opportunity to review and comment on everything related to the book in their particular domain (e.g., the copy editor is free to nitpick about the grammar of the marketing copy on the cover) but the senior editor responsible for the title generally gets the final say.

A Day in the Life: Book Editorial Assistant

Name: Susan Hutner

Title: Editorial Assistant

Company: The Princeton Review

Age: 22

Education

BA from Hiram College. Major in English with a minor in creative writing. I worked on the college newspaper as a contributing writer, copy editor, and photography editor and on the *Hiram Review* (a poetry journal) as one of the editors responsible for selecting the poems to be included. I also had an internship with Kent State University Press, and later worked for them as a freelance copyeditor.

Professional history

After I graduated college, I wanted to do something exciting, interesting, and vastly different from anything I'd done before. Unfortunately, the circus wouldn't have me, so I decided to look for jobs in New York City. Although I loved working at a university press, I thought that working for a commercial press would give me experience in working in a faster-paced environment. I also wanted to work on more titles and different types of books so I could gain the kind of experience that would open up more professional opportunities for me. An alumna of my college who works for The Princeton Review sent me a description of a job opening there, and I applied. I've been working for The Princeton Review for two months now.

Visit Vault at **www.vault.com** for insider company profiles, expert advice, career message boards, expert resume reviews, the Vault Job Board and more.

VAULT CAREER LIBRARY 377

Job description

I act as a copy editor, proofreader, and, occasionally, a content editor for the K-12 division, which produces educational and test preparation titles for children and high school kids. I assist the content and production editors by entering in changes made by editors, copy editing, proofreading bluelines, editing online content, and otherwise assisting the editorial staff.

One of my first projects here was editing a book designed to teach test preparation skills to third-graders in Florida who will be taking the FCAT test. This involved making sure the language was very simple and understandable, which is actually pretty hard to do. (Try explaining to an eight-year-old how to answer multiple choice questions and you'll see what I mean.) Other titles are designed for high school kids, and those are easier to edit to grade level.

Typical day

I get in around 9:00 a.m. and spend the first part of my day doing administrative types of things like photocopying, processing invoices, making travel plans for other members of the editorial team, and following up on technical support issues for the department. After this administrative work, I get to work on copy editing and proofreading tasks until lunchtime. Among the projects I'm working on now is a new title where I am taking online content and repurposing it for print.

I take an hour for lunch, which is great because we're located in SoHo and it's a very exciting neighborhood. After lunch I go back to editorial tasks and typically attend one or more meetings. Sometimes I sit in for people who can't make the meetings and I take notes on their behalf. If the meeting is related to titles on which I am working, administrative issues for which I have some responsibility, or about general production schedules, I actively participate. In either case, these meetings are a great opportunity for me to learn about new books and to better understand how the publishing operation works. I generally get to leave at 6:00 p.m., but many of the senior editors stay until 7:00 or later.

Favorite part of job

Any chance I get to work on improving a manuscript or an online product, whether it's proof reading, copy editing, content editing, or even making sure content is consistently formatted, is great. All the seemingly minor changes I make contribute to the overall accuracy and quality of the product, which is very satisfying. The best projects are ones where I get to do some significant copy editing or content editing.

Least favorite part of job

Preparing invoices and photocopying is not much fun. I understand that I'm just starting my career, though, and I've got to pay my dues with this kind of administrative work.

Advice

Intern, intern, intern. My internship with the Kent State University Press opened so many doors for me, both personally and professionally. In addition to learning editorial skills, I also learned about how a professional office works. I had great mentors there, and I'm still very close to many of them. Because I had two years of background in publishing, it was also much easier for me to find a job once I graduated. My work there was proof that I had the skills an employer needed to do the job well. My transition from college to professional life also went much smoother because I knew what sort of work I would be doing and was comfortable in an office.

A Day in the Life: Book Publicity

Name: Amy Ehrenreich

Title: Senior Publicist

Company: Random House Children's Books (New York, NY)

Age: 27

Education

B.A. in journalism; University of Florida. While at college I interned for a regional student-oriented entertainment publication. As an intern, I wrote a monthly food column and worked on public relations for the college swimsuit calendar. The calendar hosted an annual fashion show in South Beach, and I was responsible for pitching the event to the media, coordinating travel arrangements, and assisting during photo shoots. The internship was an invaluable experience that improved my writing skills and taught me how to multi-task and liaise with the media.

Professional history

As a self-proclaimed "book nerd" my dream occupation was in the book publishing industry and since publishing opportunities were in New York City, that's where I went. However, since I've always been an outgoing "people person" I wasn't sure that the lifestyle of writing and editing positions would be the right fit for me, so I looked for a promotional position. My first job was as an assistant to the marketing director at Promotions, Inc., an events-oriented firm that did both web and traditional promotions. I helped marketing managers run consumer outreach campaigns and my big project was the "Shot of a Lifetime" sweepstakes (where the winner of a half-court basketball shot would win a million dollars) to take place on NBC's Today Show. That promotion generated tons of free media and its success meant that I was assigned to more PR-oriented projects. After a year and a half of this type of work, I realized I loved working with the media, but I still wanted to work in the book publishing industry.

A friend led me to Golden Books, where I was hired as an assistant marketing manager assigned to grow their in-store event marketing programs. I wrote and produced several different "event kits" for Golden that gave bookstores costumes (e.g., The Poky Little Puppy), event ideas, and promo materials so they could attract large groups of children and parents to their stores. I also managed Golden's outside PR agency, and ultimately decided it would be best to handle our PR from in-house. By the time Golden Books was purchased by Random House, I was promoted to marketing manager and was ready to move into more of a PR role. In my new position, I was responsible for publicity on licensed properties and trade titles (new, author-driven books), which was very new and challenging, considering the many well-known authors published by Random House.

Job description

The main goal of my job is to generate an "advance buzz" in the trade and with consumers. I create demand and build momentum for our books to assure there will be a strong reader interest in our titles. Judging the return on investment in terms of revenue is difficult for publicity, so we judge most of our successes on the quality of impact and the amount of impressions achieved. The "pie in the sky" goals are getting media with big impressions, like *The Today Show* or *TV Guide*.

Specifically, my responsibilities are to create and implement publicity strategies for our children's titles and product lines. I am assigned books several months ahead of their pub date and I create a publicity campaign for each one. These involve proposing a budget and laying out a schedule of actions and events to promote the title. Among the many components of each campaign are: sending out galleys and books; setting up author tours; creating promotional materials (stationary, custom press kits, flyers, etc.); and setting up a promotional mailing schedule.

Visit Vault at **www.vault.com** for insider company profiles, expert advice, career message boards, expert resume reviews, the Vault Job Board and more.

VAULT CAREER LIBRARY

379

All of these tasks require intense logistical planning. For instance, planning an author tour involves working with the author's schedule, arranging appearances, determining the number of appearances per day, making transportation and lodging arrangements, and setting up face-to-face interviews. Knowing the media is equally important so leaving enough "lead time" and tailoring pitches to media outlets is imperative for a successful pitch. Magazines, for example, are "long-lead" media, needing galleys four to five months in advance to adhere to their press schedules. Short-lead media (local and regional TV, radio, and newspapers) can be pitched anywhere from two to four weeks beforehand.

Describe your day today

Usually I'm in the office by 8:45 a.m. and out around 7:30 p.m. The first thing I do each day is to write up a list of my top four or five goals for the day. This allows me to focus on the important tasks one at a time and still allows time for meetings and putting out the fires that pop up every day (like tracking down a missing review copy release or setting up a last-minute car service for a stranded author). Throughout the day, I'm in constant motion working on my many campaigns. This can be very challenging, but it's always rewarding, and, fortunately, I have the help of our department's two publicity assistants, one of which works very closely with me. Occasionally I travel with my touring authors.

Favorite part of job

Without a doubt my favorite part of my job is working closely with our authors. Some really amazing and incredibly intelligent people write and illustrate these books, and it's truly an honor to know them, and often astounding that they depend on me to a certain degree to ensure their books' success. Every day I am inspired by them.

Least favorite part of job

The relentless pace of a publicist's job can be challenging. It is difficult to even walk away from your desk, and especially my phone, when so many things need to be accomplished in a day. Often, just going to a meeting can throw me off schedule when things pile up so quickly. But it definitely keeps you on your toes!

Advice

Five things. 1) Be creative, assertive, and be prepared. This is not a job for the meek. Outgoing people and "out-of-the-box" thinkers make the best publicists. Try not to take rejection personally if an editor or producer is not interested in your book. Remember that the reviewers and editors need you as much as you need them. 2) Create realistic goals and hit them. 3) Keep your authors happy. 4) Make contacts and network. 5). Read!!

Publishing Employer Directory

Bantam Doubleday Dell
(part of Bertelsmann AG)
1540 Broadway
New York, NY 10036
Phone: (212) 354-6500

Condé Nast Publications Inc.
4 Times Square, 17th Fl.
New York, NY 10036
Phone: (212) 286-2860
Fax: (212) 286-5960
www.condenast.com

Harcourt Brace
15 E. 26th Street
New York, NY 10010
Phone: (212) 614-7850

HarperCollins Publishers, Inc.
10 E. 53rd St.
New York, NY 10022
Phone: (212) 207-7000
Fax: (212) 207-7145
www.harpercollins.com

Hearst Magazines
959 8th Ave.
New York, NY 10019
Phone: (212) 649-2000
Fax: (212) 765-3528
www.hearstcorp.com

Houghton Mifflin
Houghton Mifflin Company
222 Berkeley St.
Boston, MA 02116-3764
Phone: (617) 351-5000
Fax: (617) 351-1105
www.hmco.com

John Wiley & Sons, Inc.
111 River St.
Hoboken, NJ 07030
Phone: (201) 748-6000
Fax: (201) 748-6008
www.wiley.com

The McGraw-Hill Companies, Inc.
1221 Avenue of the Americas
New York, NY 10020
Phone: (212) 512-2000
Fax: (212) 512-3840
www.mcgraw-hill.com

Pearson Education, Inc.
1 Lake St.
Upper Saddle River, NJ 07458
Phone: (201) 236-7000
Fax: (201) 236-3290
www.pearsoned.com

The Penguin Group
80 Strand
London
WC2R ORL, United Kingdom
Phone: +44-2070103396
Fax: +44-2070106642
www.penguin.com

Random House, Inc.
1745 Broadway
New York, NY 10019
Phone: (212) 782-9000
Fax: (212) 302-7985
www.randomhouse.com

Scholastic Corporation
557 Broadway
New York, NY 10012
Phone: (212) 343-6100
Fax: (212) 343-6934
www.scholastic.com

Simon & Schuster, Inc.
1230 Avenue of the Americas
New York, NY 10020
Phone: (212)-698-7000
Fax: (212) 698-7099
www.simonsays.com

The Thomson Corporation
Toronto-Dominion Bank Tower,
66 Wellington Street West
Toronto, Ontario M5K 1A1, Canada
Phone: (416) 360-8700
Fax: (416) 360-8812
www.thomson.com

Time, Inc.
1271 Avenue of the Americas
New York, NY 10020-1393
Phone: (212) 522-1212
Fax: (212) 522-0602

Time Warner Books
1271 Avenue of the Americas
New York, NY 10020-1393
Phone: (212) 522-7200
Fax: (212) 522-7989
www.twbookmark.com

W.W. Norton & Company
500 Fifth Ave.
New York, NY 10110
Phone: (212) 354-5500
Fax: (212) 869-0865
www.wwnorton.com

Visit Vault at **www.vault.com** for insider company profiles, expert advice, career message boards, expert resume reviews, the Vault Job Board and more.

VAULT CAREER LIBRARY   381

Real Estate

History of the Real Estate Industry in the United States

Real estate is tangible. It's a piece of land and any building or structures on it, as well as the air above and the ground below. Everyone comes into direct contact with real estate. The places we live, work, go to school, vacation, shop and exercise, are all assets to be bought, sold and rented. And it's always been an important element of the economy.

Real estate has always been big business in the United States. Shortly after the signing of the Constitution, the federal government began transferring one billion acres of land to private owners through land sales and land grants. In the 1830s, for example, the government sold 20 million acres at roughly $1.25 per acre. This sounds like a bargain to us today, but at the time the vast majority of citizens couldn't afford that price. Consequently, a grassroots group called the Free Soil Movement formed and lobbied the government for an alternate method of distributing land.

The Homestead Act of 1862 was Congress' answer to the appeal. Settlers who did not already own what was considered a "judicious" amount of land were given title to 160 acres for each adult in the family. There was no cash exchange. Instead, the understanding was that the settlers would live on and improve the land for a period of at least five years. This program was very successful and similar federal land distribution programs followed until the later part of the nineteenth century. In total, the U.S. government distributed more than 300 million acres of public property to private landowners through the Homestead Act, creating the basis for the real estate market.

For the first time in the history of the young country, there was a system in place by which one landowner could transfer property rights to another through sale, lease or trade. This led to a tremendous amount of speculation. Some investors accumulated a tremendous amount of wealth, while others lost everything.

At the end of the 19th century, America was transitioning from an agricultural society to a manufacturing economy. Citizens flocked to urban areas to work at the burgeoning factories. For example, as the Midwest's industrial center, Chicago reached a population of one million people more rapidly than any other city in history. Settled in the 1830s, the city grew from less than 1,000 inhabitants to become the fifth largest city in the world by 1900.

The values of urban properties skyrocketed. By 1920, 50 percent of America's population lived in cities. This urban density created opportunities for real estate development as housing, office buildings, industrial facilities, hotels and retail centers were constructed to meet the demands of city dwellers.

Skyrocketing property values and associated costs began pushing people and businesses outside the city, just as advances in transportation made living outside the city easier. Suburbs, communities just outside urban centers, began to spread. Developers made these planned communities attractive by building along the transportation routes so people could easily commute to their jobs in the cities.

Technological advances influenced the building boom of the 1920s. Communities were wired for electricity, new machines such as elevators helped meet additional demand for space and allowed the construction of ever-taller buildings. Planned communities began taking shape in the suburbs, while skyscrapers changed the way the cities looked. One hundred buildings higher than 25 stories were constructed in this decade, most of them in New York City, with Chicago a distant second.

The Great Depression crippled most industries—including real estate. Values dipped below debt levels, causing a collapse. The federal government put the domestic financial markets through a major overhaul and was shrewd enough to include real estate financing as part of the New Deal programs. The Federal Housing Administration (FHA) was created in 1930 to provide mortgage insurance, lowering the risk on real estate loans and making lending more palatable for savings and loans and banks. The government also created the Federal Home Loan Bank System (FHLB) to supervise and regulate local banks. In 1938, the Federal National Mortgage Association (FNMA or Fannie Mae) was created to provide a secondary mortgage market as well as to lure investment capital in the mortgage market, and continues to play a very important role in supplying

Visit Vault at www.vault.com for insider company profiles, expert advice, career message boards, expert resume reviews, the Vault Job Board and more.

VAULT CAREER LIBRARY   383

capital to the mortgage market today. These New Deal programs ultimately made the real estate finance market more sophisticated and secure.

America and the real estate industry slowly climbed out of the Depression only to fall headlong into the Second World War. Development was put on hold during the war, but once the GIs returned from overseas, another era of prosperity began. A tremendous amount of demand for housing emerged virtually overnight. By 1946, new housing construction quadrupled to over 500,000 homes. In the postwar period, a white picket fence and peaceful green lawn proved very appealing. Two-thirds of the 15 million homes built in the 1950s were in the suburbs.

The decade was also a period of expansion for the highways, which provided access to more areas by car and truck. This enabled all types of real estate (e.g., hotels, industrial and retail centers) to be located further outside the city. Hotel chains like Holiday Inn started popping up along roadways across the country. The suburban shopping mall also became popular in this era.

As the suburbs grew, the cities slumped. By 1960, many urban centers hadn't seen new office building development in 30 years. The decay of America's urban areas didn't go unnoticed. Community activism and political pressure led to the creation of a cabinet position in 1965 focused on improving urban housing—what today is known as the Department of Housing and Urban Development (HUD). The central business districts of America's urban centers saw a number of new buildings (both commercial and retail) constructed during the last three decades of the twentieth century, spurred by growth in the service industry, increased access to financing and municipal incentives.

Today, the real estate industry is considered one of the most dynamic and healthy sectors in the American economy—people may divest their stocks, but they always need a place to live, work and shop. (To read more about the history of real estate, read *Real Estate Development* by Miles, Berns and Weiss.)

Industry Trends

As of 2006, the real estate business employed over nine million people, and opportunities abound for candidates to earn staggering income levels. Those who work in this sector often enjoy greater flexibility in job responsibilities than in other industries, though there can be drawbacks, in the form of low paying entry-level positions, competitive co-workers and long hours when starting out. Furthermore, once you're established, relocation can be detrimental to your career, as this industry is often geography-specific.

The real estate sector is largely dependent on the economy; small shifts can impact trends significantly. For example, the technology industry boom certainly helped the real estate industry in the 1990s. There was more demand for space—both commercial and residential—then ever before, and asset values skyrocketed. Unsurprisingly, the subsequent tech bust had a dramatic effect on some parts of the sector, as commercial firms that focused on office and retail development projects found the market glutted with available space.

The residential real estate market is also affected by economic swings, as unemployment and interest rates impact both consumer confidence and buying power. Although the U.S. economy was mired in recession for the first several years of the 21st century, the residential real estate market was one of the few bright spots. For example, in 2002, home sales shot up 8 percent and housing starts grew by 7 percent. The trend continued through 2005, when the real estate market was responsible for over $2 trillion worth of national economic activity.

There were many reasons for this residential housing boom. The aging U.S. population and the influx of immigrants increased the demand for homes. The rockiness of the stock market made investing in real estate look very appealing, and the Federal Reserve played a big part as well. Lower mortgage rates and minimal inflation meant that in 2003, a 30-year home mortgage could be had at a miniscule 5 percent interest rate. The drop in mortgage rates meant that homeowners could refinance, freeing up more cash for them—and in the process making real estate look like an even more attractive investment.

The wealth wasn't spread equally, however. During the real estate boom that began after the end of the 1991 recession and reached its peak between 2002 and 2005, homes and apartments in the Boston to Washington corridor and California doubled, tripled and quadrupled in value—while in other parts of the country, even in fast-growing areas such as Las Vegas, gains were more modest. This was due in part to the simple fact that there was more available land on which to build houses and apartments. Profits aside, though, the residential real estate market's remarkable gains provoked fears among some economists and homeowners that the market bubble was about to burst. The prices of homes, especially on the coasts, outpaced the means of many prospective first-time buyers, and housing market worries fueled stock drops in late 2005.

Economists' fears were confirmed in 2006, when the so-called "housing bubble" finally burst. According to *The Wall Street Journal*, increases in mortgage rates coupled with a sluggish economy produced the first decreases in real estate values in years. In fact, average residential values fell for the first time since 1995, and are expected to continue to do so. Urban markets fell along with suburban ones; *Forbes* reported that 17 out of 26 metropolitan markets that made significant gains in the boom years (examples include San Diego, Providence and Boston) have all experienced losses. And even with falling prices, first and second home sales have decreased.

Of course, home sales are still making money, though the numbers are lower. Thomas Stevens, president of the National Association of Realtors (NAR), reported appreciation in values of less than 1 percent in September 2006. On the plus side, however, while some parts of the country continue to see home prices rising, the end of the bubble may indicate the beginning of a more equitable (and affordable) housing market.

And there is still plenty of business after the burst. For one thing, the August 2006 Pending Homes Index, a measure of pending residential sales, indicated that the market was stabilizing—that is, that while a further decline in prices is possible, these are holding steady for now; good news for buyers and sellers alike. Investing in real estate can still be lucrative, too: real estate fund values have been on the rise for the past five years, and outperformed the rest of the market in the third quarter of 2006. While this is partially due to the fact that the value of real estate funds, or REITs, is reliant on commercial rather than residential properties, it is nevertheless good news for the market as a whole. It's safe to say that, while real estate is subject to ups and down just like any other industry, it remains a fairly steady—not to mention lucrative—business.

Residential Real Estate Brokers

Residential real estate agents help buyers and sellers in the process of selling or renting residential property. Some agents work with buyers, helping them find places to live and negotiating with sellers. Other agents work with the sellers. Agents rarely represent both buyers and sellers since this is perceived as a conflict of interest. For property rentals, almost all agents represent property owners. There are close to 500,000 real estate brokers and agents in the United States.

Agents are usually independent sales professionals who contract their services to sponsoring real estate brokers in exchange for a commission-sharing agreement. The commission on a home sale varies by market but is roughly five to six percent of the sale price. This commission is split four ways among the seller's agent, buyer's agent and the sponsoring brokers with whom each agent is associated. Many agents work solely on commission and don't get much in the way of benefits. Agents are expected to cover most of the overhead necessary to perform their jobs.

In order to sell real estate services, you must be a licensed professional in the state where you do business. To become a realtor, all states require that you pass a written exam focused on real estate law and transactions and be affiliated with a broker. Most states require you to be at least 18 years old and a high school graduate, and to have completed a minimum number of classroom hours. Some states waive the classroom requirements for active attorneys or offer correspondence course credit options in lieu of the classroom hour requirement. The license fee depends on the state, but expect to pay around $100 for the exam and $400 for the classes.

Visit Vault at **www.vault.com** for insider company profiles, expert advice, career message boards, expert resume reviews, the Vault Job Board and more.

VAULT CAREER LIBRARY **385**

Although there are different organizations through which you can receive your classroom instruction, the state government issues and oversees licenses. If you visit the National Association of Realtor's web site at www.realtor.org, you can find information about residential real estate as well as licensing requirements for each state and locations of authorized real estate classes.

This industry attracts all types of personalities. There's a potpourri of career switchers, from lawyers to housewives, who end up in residential real estate. If you like being your own boss and interacting with people, being a realtor can be very rewarding.

Tenant Representation

A tenant representation agent, commonly known as a "tenant rep," represents companies and other corporate clients looking to lease or buy either a portion of a property or an entire real estate asset. A large part of this job involves business development. Since tenant reps are often responsible for building their own book of business, prospecting for new clients is a big part of the job. Like residential agents, tenant reps are left to their own devices to find prospects. Although there's some direction by the broker and senior tenant reps in the office, for the most part you're cold-calling tenants or companies. First, you need to give the person on the other end of the phone a compelling reason to meet with you, then you must pitch the business. It's a tough sell.

Tenant representation is very competitive, even cutthroat. You're not only competing against outside reps but those inside your office. In fact, some tenant rep brokers think the competition inside is worse than outside the shops. Often there are disputes about who is entitled to chase what business. Ultimately, the senior brokers tend to win. Deal protocol is important to consider when you're selecting brokers because often there are disputes are common among tenant reps.

When the time comes for one of his or her clients to buy, sell or lease, the tenant rep finds a list of choices in the market, then handles the accompanying negotiations. Tenant reps usually work in teams to spread the work. Often the team is composed of one senior and one junior broker. The junior broker will make the cold calls and set up meetings with prospective clients. At the meetings the senior broker will take the lead and try to win the business. Once the process begins, the junior broker will do the legwork for market alternatives and examine options with the senior broker. All possible alternatives are presented to the client for review. The senior broker generally handles the lease or sale negotiations. This mutually beneficial system gives the senior broker a "cold caller" and provides a training platform for the junior broker. Junior brokers should expect to work at least 50 to 60 hours per week; senior brokers' hours fluctuate based on deal flow.

Once junior brokers have surpassed certain earning requirements, they're promoted to senior brokers. They still make cold calls to get leads, though not nearly as often as junior brokers. The company relies on its senior brokers to win business and handle transactions from start to finish. Sometimes senior brokers help create and execute management policy and even have equity at smaller firms.

Property Management

Real estate owners commonly employ professional property managers—either directly or through third-party management firms. Property managers are charged with the day-to-day management of real estate assets. They ensure that tenants are satisfied, the building is in good condition, rent is paid and that rents reflect market conditions. Property management provides a general introduction to real estate. As a property manager you'll learn how to efficiently operate a real estate asset in this capacity. Property managers deal with issues relating to leasing, construction, tenant relations and market analysis.

A good manager can save an owner a great deal of money by operating the asset efficiently and keeping the tenants happy. The property manager plays a crucial role in expense control; the owner relies on him to manage any and all operating expenses at the building. For instance, if there is construction work at the building, the property manager supervises the project, keeps close tabs on the progress and makes sure it doesn't go over budget. Property management also requires good interpersonal and analytical skills because tenants sometimes can be difficult and expect things to be resolved immediately. While leasing agents do much of the lease negotiations, property managers are involved in the process as well. A salesperson's license is therefore required for the position.

Visit Vault at **www.vault.com** for insider company profiles, expert advice, career message boards, expert resume reviews, the Vault Job Board and more.

VAULT CAREER LIBRARY   **387**

Employer Directory

Plum Creek Timber Company

99 Third Ave, Suite 4300
Seattle, WA 98104-4096

Recruiting Contact:
Phone: 206-467-3600
E-mail: careers@plumcreek.com
www.plumcreek.com

Job Search Website:
www.jobsearch.org/seeker/jobsearch/keyword
Search by the following keyword and location
parameters: Keyword: Plum Creek, Location: National

Plum Creek is the United States' largest private landowner with over 8 million acres of land and growing. An S&P 500 company, Plum Creek has revenues over $1.5 billion, offices in 18 states, and various positions in forestry, real estate, land management, manufacturing, accounting, human resources, and legal.

We have a collaborative, team-centric, execution oriented culture focused on delivery and strive for a good balance between career and personal life, and between cutting edge and proven technology. Plum Creek's substantial growth has created many unique career opportunities. You'll be able to build a rewarding and successful career, while enjoying the low-key atmosphere that makes life in our tight-knit communities a happy and warm place to live and visit.

Plum Creek wants to attract and keep the best people-the team who drives our success. That is why we offer superior performers opportunities for compensation that is in the top 25% for our marketplace. Benefits packages consists of a comprehensive range of benefits including Health care, Health and Dependent Daycare Funds, Life and Disability protection, Saving and Retirements benefits, Paid Vacation, Relocation, and more.

The Real Estate segment reported revenues of $292 million in 2005. The company focuses on capturing higher per-acre prices for its timberlands, increasing its sales of recreation and higher and better use timberlands. The real estate group manages acquisitions, dispositions, conservation, and development opportunities for all of Plum Creek's assets.

AMB Property Corporation

Pier 1, Bay 1
San Francisco, CA 94111
Phone: (415) 394-9000
Fax: (415) 394-9001
www.amb.com

Apartment Investment and Management Company

4582 S. Ulster Street Pkwy.
Ste. 1100
Denver, CO 80237
Phone: (303) 757-8101
Fax: (303) 759-3226
www.aimco.com

Archstone-Smith

9200 E. Panorama Circle, Ste. 400
Englewood, CO 80112
Phone: (303) 708-5959
Fax: (303) 708-5999
www.archstonesmith.com

AvalonBay Communities, Inc.

2900 Eisenhower Ave., Ste. 300
Alexandria, VA 22314
Phone: (703) 329-6300
Fax: (703) 329-1459
www.avalonbay.com

Beazer Homes

1000 Abernathy Rd.
Ste. 1200
Atlanta, GA 30328
Phone: (770) 829-3700
Fax: (770) 481-2808
www.beazer.com

Boston Capital Corporation

1 Boston Place
Boston, MA 02108-4406
Phone: (617) 624-8900
Fax: (617) 624-8999
www.bostoncapital.com

Real Estate Employer Directory

Boston Properties, Inc.
111 Huntington Avenue
Boston, MA 02199-7610
Phone: (617) 236-3300
Fax: (617) 536-5087
www.bostonproperties.com

Brookfield Properties
200 Vesey Street, 11th Floor
Three World Financial Center
New York, NY 10281-1021
Phone: (212) 417-7000
Fax: (212) 417-7196
www.brookfieldproperties.com

CarrAmerica
1850 K St. NW
Washington, DC 20006
Phone: (202) 729-1700
Fax: (202) 729-1150
www.carramerica.com

Catellus Development Corporation
201 Mission St., 2nd Fl.
San Francisco, CA 94105
Phone: (415) 974-4500
Fax: (415) 974-4550
www.catellus.com

CB Richard Ellis Group, Inc.
100 North Sepulveda Boulevard
Suite 1050
El Segundo, CA 90245
Phone: (310) 606-4700
Fax: (310) 606-4701
www.cbre.com

CBL & Associates Properties
2030 Hamilton Place Blvd.
Ste. 500
Chattanooga, TN 37421-6000
Phone: (423) 855-0001
Fax: (423) 490-8390
www.cblproperties.com

Centex Corporation
2728 North Harwood Street
Dallas, TX 75201-1516
Phone: (214) 981-5000
Fax: (214) 981-6859
www.centex.com

Century 21 Real Estate LLC
1 Campus Drive
Parsippany, NJ 07054
Phone: (877) 221-2765
Fax: (973) 496-7564
www.century21.com

CNL Hotels & Resorts, Inc.
450 S. Orange Avenue
Orlando, FL 32801-3336
Phone: (407) 650-1000
Fax: (407) 650-1085
www.cnlhotels.com

Crescent Real Estate Equities Company
777 Main St., Ste. 2100
Fort Worth, TX 76102-5325
Phone: (817) 321-2100
Fax: (817) 321-2000
www.cei-crescent.com

Day & Zimmermann Group
1818 Market Street, Fl. 22
Philadelphia, PA 19103-3672
Phone: (215) 299-8000
Fax: (215) 299-8030
www.dayzim.com

Developers Diversified Realty
3300 Enterprise Parkway
Beachwood, OH 44122
Phone: (216) 755-5500
Fax: (216) 755-1500
www.ddrc.com

Duke Realty Corporation
600 E. 96th Street, Ste. 100
Indianapolis, IN 46240
Phone: (317) 808-6000
Fax: (317) 808-6794
www.dukerealty.com

Equity Office Properties Trust
2 N. Riverside Plaza, Ste. 2100
Chicago, IL 60606
Phone: (312) 466-3300
Fax: (312) 454-0332
www.equityoffice.com

Equity Residential
2 N. Riverside Plaza, Ste. 450
Chicago, IL 60606
Phone: (312) 474-1300
Fax: (312) 454-8703
www.equityresidential.com

FelCor Lodging Trust Incorporated
545 E. John Carpenter Fwy.
Ste. 1300
Irving, TX 75062
Phone: (972) 444-4900
Fax: (972) 444-4949
www.felcor.com

Forest City Enterprises, Inc.
50 Public Sq., Ste. 1100
Cleveland, OH 44113-2203
Phone: (216) 621-6060
Fax: (216) 263-4808
www.forestcity.net

General Growth Properties, Inc.
110 N. Wacker Drive
Chicago, IL 60606
Phone: (312) 960-5000
Fax: (312) 960-5475
www.generalgrowth.com

Heitman LLC
191 N. Wacker Drive, Suite 2500
Chicago, IL 60606
Phone: (312) 855-5700
www.heitman.com

Hilton Hotels Corporation
9336 Civic Center Drive
Beverly Hills, CA 90210
Phone: (310) 278-4321
Fax: (310) 205-7678
www.hiltonworldwide.com

Visit Vault at **www.vault.com** for insider company profiles, expert advice, career message boards, expert resume reviews, the Vault Job Board and more.

VAULT CAREER LIBRARY   389

Real Estate Employer Directory, cont.

Hines Interests L.P.
Williams Tower
2800 Post Oak Blvd.
Houston, TX 77056-6118
Phone: (713) 621-8000
Fax: (713) 966-2053
www.hines.com

Hospitality Properties Trust
400 Centre Steet
Newton, MA 02458
Phone: (617) 964-8389
Fax: (617) 969-5730
www.hptreit.com

Host Marriott Corporation
6903 Rockledge Dr., Ste. 1500
Bethesda, MD 20817
Phone: (240) 744-1000
Fax: (240) 744-5125
www.hostmarriott.com

Hovnanian Enterprises, Inc.
10 Hwy. 35
Red Bank, NJ 07701
Phone: (732) 747-7800
Fax: (732) 747-7159
www.khov.com

HRPT Properties Trust
400 Centre Street
Newton, MA 02458-2076
Phone: (617) 332-3990
Fax: (617) 332-2261
www.hrpreit.com

Jones Lang LaSalle
200 E. Randolph Dr.
Chicago, IL 60601
Phone: 312-782-5800
Fax: 312-782-4339
www.joneslanglasalle.com

KB Home
10990 Wilshire Blvd., 7th Fl.
Los Angeles, CA 90024
Phone: (310) 231-4000
Fax: (310) 231-4222
www.kbhome.com

Kimco Realty Corporation
3333 New Hyde Park Rd.
New Hyde Park, NY 11042-0020
Phone: (516) 869-9000
Fax: (516) 869-9001
www.kimcorealty.com

Lend Lease Corporation Limited
Level 46, Tower Bldg.
Australia Square
Sydney, 2000, Australia
Phone: +61-2-9236-6111
Fax: +61-2-9252-2192
www.lendlease.com.au

McCormick Group, The
1525 Wilson Boulevard, Suite 500
Arlington, VA 22209
Phone: (703) 841-1700
Fax: (703) 524-2689
www.mccormickgroup.com

MeriStar Hospitality Corporation
4501 N. Fairfax Dr., Ste. 500
Arlington, VA 22203
Phone: (703) 812-7200
Fax: (703) 812-7255
www.meristar.com

MetroList Services, Inc.
1164 West National Drive
Suite 60
Sacramento, CA 95834
Phone: (916) 922-2234
www.metrolistmls.com

The Mills Corporation
1300 Wilson Blvd., Ste. 400
Arlington, VA 22209
Phone: (703) 526-5000
Fax: (703) 526-5111
www.millscorp.com

Parkway Properties, Inc.
1 Jackson Place, 188 E. Capitol St.
Ste. 1000
Jackson, MS 39201-2195
Phone: (601) 948-4091
Fax: (601) 949-4077
www.pky.com

Plum Creek Timber Company, Inc.
999 Third Ave., Ste. 4300
Seattle, WA 98104-4096
Phone: (206) 467-3600
Fax: (206) 467-3795
www.plumcreek.com

ProLogis
14100 E. 35th Place
Aurora, CO 80011
Phone: (303) 375-9292
Fax: (303) 375-8581
www.prologis.com

Public Storage, Inc.
701 Western Avenue
Glendale, CA 91201-2349
Phone: (818) 244-8080
Fax: (818) 553-2376
www.publicstorage.com

Rayonier Inc.
50 North Laura Street
Jacksonville, FL 32202
Phone: (904) 357-9100
Fax: (904) 357-9101
www.rayonier.com

RE/MAX International, Inc.
8390 E. Crescent Parkway.
Ste. 500/600
Greenwood Village, CO 80111
Phone: (303) 770-5531
Fax: (303) 796-3599
www.remax.com

RREEF America L.L.C.
101 California St., 26th Fl.
San Francisco, CA 94111
Phone: (415) 781-3300
Fax: (415) 391-9015
www.dbrealestate.com/rreef

Real Estate Employer Directory, cont.

Tishman Speyer Properties

520 Madison Avenue
New York, NY 10022
Phone: (212) 715-0300
Fax: (212) 319-1745
www.tishmanspeyer.com

Trammell Crow Residential

2859 Paces Ferry Road, Ste. 1100
Atlanta, GA 30339
Phone: (770) 801-1600
Fax: (770) 801-5395
www.tcresidential.com

Trizec Properties, Inc.

10 S. Riverside Plaza, Suite 1100
Chicago, IL 60606
Phone: (312) 798-6000
www.trz.com

URS Corporation

600 Montgomery Street, 26th Floor
San Francisco, CA 94111
Phone: (415) 774-2700
Fax: (415) 398-1905
www.urscorp.com

USG Corporation

125 S. Franklin Street
Chicago, IL 60606-4678
Phone: (312) 606-4000
Fax: (312) 606-4093
www.usg.com

Vornado Realty Trust

888 7th Avenue
New York, NY 10019
Phone: (212) 894-7000
Fax: (212) 894-7070
www.vno.com

Walton Street Capital L.L.C.

900 North Michigan Avenue
Suite 1900
Chicago, IL 60611
Phone: (312) 915-2800
Fax: (312) 915-2881
www.waltonst.com

Visit Vault at **www.vault.com** for insider company profiles, expert advice, career message boards, expert resume reviews, the Vault Job Board and more.

V\ULT CAREER LIBRARY 391

Retail

Retail Industry Overview

A shop on every corner

Unless you happen to be living in a tree, chances are good that you've had at least one interaction with the retail industry today. From the corner drugstore to the online bookstore, retail—the business of selling things made by others—is a constant presence in American life. The U.S. boasts more than 1.4 million retail establishments, which, according to the National Retail Federation (NRF), racked up sales of $4.4 trillion in 2005 alone. The sector is expected to be strong through 2006, though high gas prices and rising interest rates are taking a big bite out of consumer spending power—a situation that often results in depressed sales.

Rolling back the competition

Industry analysts are seeing growth in two sectors of retail: high-end luxury stores, which cater to wealthy consumers, and discounters such as Wal-Mart and Target, who cater to every demographic. The leading luxury stores are, by definition, too small or specialized to merit individual mention here—but not so for the discounters, a segment emphatically led by Wal-Mart, the world's largest retailer (also the world's largest company), with a revenue of $315 billion in its 2006 fiscal year. Wal-Mart's competition includes Target, with $52 billion in 2006 sales, and Kmart, back in the black after a yearlong sojourn in bankruptcy court. Home Depot and Lowe's, known in the industry as "category killers" because they put all neighboring hardware stores out of business, are also among the U.S.'s top retailers, building on a trend in do-it-yourself home-improvement projects. Wholesale shopping has also become attractive to families, which can save money by buying everything in bulk, from diapers to Dom Perignon. Costco, the leading U.S. wholesaler (with major competition from Wal-Mart's Sam's Club), reported a revenue of $52 billion in 2006. One way in which these two growth sectors, luxury and discount, interact, is consumers shopping at discounters to save money that they then funnel into luxury goods in personal interest areas, such as clothing, cars, jewelry and high-end sporting goods.

To market!

In retail, marketing makes all the difference. Despite Wal-Mart's dominance, "multi-brand" retailers, like department stores and discounters, which sell a range of other companies' brands, have a tougher battle when it comes to establishing a national brand identity of their own, according to analysis by consulting firm McKinsey & Co. But multi-brand chains are catching on to the concept of aggressive self-promotion. McKinsey notes that Target has been an innovator in marketing for the sector. According to the consulting firm, Target's distinctive "bullseye" logo, featured in early campaigns with no products on display, "places the brand and the promise of the store ahead of its merchandise"—a trend expected to grow ever more common in the sector.

Businesses are coming up with new ways to differentiate themselves and drum up sales. The concept of "experience" retailing—or giving shoppers a full range of in-store services—has been adopted by companies like Apple, which offers advice counters, seminars and group discussions on the latest computing gear, transforming stores into social spaces. Another trend in retail is "lifestyle retailing"—combining household items and wardrobe together for target markets like "elegant country" (think Eddie Bauer) and "urban hipster" (think Urban Outfitters) to appeal to a shopper's total sensibility. As the logic goes, if customers like a store's style, they will be drawn to the variety of items it sells.

Increasingly, the idea of the shopping mall is also in decline, as a decreasing number of customers are drawn to traditional department stores and generic mazes of mall space. Instead, the growing trend is to create "lifestyle centers," 130 of which have materialized around the U.S. since 2005. Lifestyle centers mimic a vibrant city street, combining outdoor space with

Visit Vault at **www.vault.com** for insider company profiles, expert advice, career message boards, expert resume reviews, the Vault Job Board and more.

VAULT CAREER LIBRARY 393

parking, shops and restaurants, creating a (some say) "neighborhood" feel to reinforce a sense of community. "Pop-up retail"—literally, shops that "pop up" in a location for a limited amount of time and then disappear—is also gaining popularity for its tendency to create buzz, lend a "fresh" feel and add an element of exclusivity.

It's a tech, tech, tech world

Technology has revolutionized retail in many ways. While online retail hasn't taken as big a bite as some Internet boosters used to predict out of traditional stores, this is mostly because it's the rare store—traditional or otherwise—that has no online presence, complete with electronic shopping cart. In addition, studies indicate that while consumers are visiting the Internet to compare prices and research products, many still like to see the merchandise in person before buying. Despite this, Forrester Research anticipates that online purchases of goods will grow from $172 billion in 2005 to $329 billion by 2010. Consumers are expanding their horizons in terms of the types of products they're willing to shop for and purchase online, and retailers are happy to offer more variety. Amazon.com, the archetypal online retailer, has expanded from books and music (which still make up a majority of its sales) to apparel, tools, gourmet foods, home furnishings and health and beauty products, to name just few.

Technology is also adding to the brick-and-mortar store experience. Two new innovations, customer relationship management (CRM) software and radio frequency identification (RFID) tags, will (maybe) make shopping more pleasant for consumers and (likely) more profitable for retailers. CRM software allows the retailer to use data about purchasing patterns to tailor suggestions of other products and services that might be of interest to the consumer. RFID, meanwhile, allows retailers to track and control products via a tiny microchip placed onto an item or its packaging. With the microchip, everyone from the producer to the stock clerk to the cashier can gather data about a product as it makes its way through the supply chain. Retailers are particularly enthusiastic about this tech because it gives detailed information about the movement of goods from the manufacturer to the consumer; they will also cut down on theft. RFID tags are still a bit too expensive (10 to 15 cents per unit) to be attached to individual products, but the price is expected to drop as manufacturers compete.

Over there, over there

Facing mature markets in their home countries, large retailers are increasingly intrigued by the expanding middle classes and swiftly growing economies abroad. Best Buy, for example, bought into China's fourth-largest appliance and electronic goods chain in 2006, while retail behemoths Carrefour and Wal-Mart are expanding there as well, giving local retail chains a run for their money. India is the growing market of the moment, though strict local regulations prohibit extensive foreign investment in its retail sector, 97 percent of which is dominated by small, independent stores. International expansion can lead to problems, however. Wal-Mart, like the stereotypical bumbling American tourist, has committed its fair share of mistakes. In Germany, the company's "Supercenter" model failed miserably, due in part to the retail giant's unwillingness (or inability) to adjust to the fact that most Germans make many small shopping trips to the butcher, fruit and vegetable vendor, and baker for daily essentials, rather than getting their weekly shopping done in one fell swoop, as is standard for suburban Americans. Other examples of Wal-Mart screw-ups include trying to sell golf clubs in Brazil, where the game is largely unknown, and ice skates in Mexico … which failure is pretty self explanatory.

Joining the retail army

Retail employees represent the single largest workforce in the country. According to the Bureau of Labor Statistics (BLS), about 11.6 percent of American employees, or some 15 million in 2005, work in retail. Most of these people are employed as retail salespersons in department or clothing stores. Furthermore, the BLS projects that employment in the sector will grow by 11 percent by 2014, a similar rate of growth as that of all other industries. Because turnover is relatively high, the sector offers an abundance of job opportunities for people of all ages and educational levels, making it the leading creator of entry-level jobs among all industries. Despite the increasing prevalence of online shopping, the BLS expects its effect on the retail sales force to be minimal, since the human element is critical in providing good customer service. Life in retail isn't always easy: while employees generally get discounts on merchandise, they must be courteous and patient at all times, even with demanding customers, and work nonstandard hours, particularly during the peak holiday season.

Retail Careers in Fashion

Retail covers the sale of apparel and related goods and services in small quantities directly to consumers. In the rush for fashion jobs, the retail sector has emerged as a promising contender. Sears, Roebuck and Co., for example, has created the "Retail Executive Development Training Program" to recruit promising new professionals. Considered a retail milestone by many, the program targets 60 undergraduate campuses. After an eight- to 10-month training program, "executive trainees" handle up to $3 million in profit/loss responsibility. Some trainees have as many as 30 people reporting to them. Retailers such as Sears, Neiman Marcus, Federated and Meryvn's offer candidates a nice deal—signficant management responsibility in a relatively short amount of time.

Some larger retail programs have established training programs. The Gap hires recent college graduates for its Retail Management Program. The program is based in San Francisco over a seven-month period. New hires gain experience in merchandising, planning and production. After successfully completing the program, the graduates have an opportunity to work full-time in the brand (i.e., Old Navy, Banana Republic, Gap Baby, etc.) in which they trained—and are placed based on Gap's needs, as well as each graduate's skills and interests.

Jobs

Retail clerk: Assists the consumer in the purchase of products and services.

Store manager: Manages the store operations and supervises the clerks.

Marketing: Works on store advertisements and catalogs.

Inventory planner: Sets monetary limits on the retail buyers' purchasing power based on historical and market analysis.

Asset protection: Minimizes store losses and track fraud and theft.

Logistics: Works with stores and buyers to optimize supply-chain.

Real estate: Manages stores that vary in size, location, and layout to keep stores new. Responsibilities may include construction and building services management.

The Scoop

Many people have a less-than-positive view of retailing. "I didn't spend four years in college to work in a store!" is a frequent gripe. This negative reaction belies the fact that retail is a good place to start or build a fashion career. Because jobs selling fine design can be extremely lucrative, retail is becoming more attractive to college graduates. Larger stores are often the best places to start since some offer standardized training programs. Comments an insider: "One of retail's biggest problems is that there is no standard training pattern. Many retailers wait for people to get on the-job-training elsewhere and then cannibalize their competitors." Despite the problem of unstructured training, retail has one indisputably stellar element: almost anyone is eligible. "We look for employees with bachelor's degrees," says an industry source. "School isn't very important. Major isn't very important. Many people who specialized in business, finance or liberal arts will do just fine."

Visit Vault at **www.vault.com** for insider company profiles, expert advice, career message boards, expert resume reviews, the Vault Job Board and more.

VAULT CAREER LIBRARY

395

On the corporate side of fashion, opportunities exist in retail buying, planning, merchandising and product development. College grads typically start out as trainees and work their way up, following established or somewhat meandering career paths. Talented and dedicated new hires, especially in large companies or department stores, can expect regular promotions—up to divisional management roles. There are also opportunities in store management, finance and human resources. More creative jobs in retail include catalog production (graphics and copywriting) and window and display design.

Image

While some insiders laud department stores, others attest to the value of small designer companies. "Department stores are out," declares one adamant source. "Smaller, more prestigious retailers—CK, Armani, Tommy Hilfiger—are the way to go. Department stores are stuffy and they convey a feeling of being 'average.' The people I know working on the selling floor of department stores want to get out." Underlying this comment are issues of prestige and class, two prominent—although seldom discussed—aspects of retail. Fashion, and retail in particular, is an image-conscious sector in which an attractive appearance, up-to-date style, impeccable grooming and an air of affluence are important. "High-end retail is a glamour job," says an insider. "The positions are high-profile and low-paying. The people who work in retail are often highly educated and parentally subsidized. The job becomes a lifestyle of fashionable wardrobes, cocktail parties, elite crowds and making the right friends." If you detect an edge of superficiality, insiders confirm it. "High-end retail jobs are often aimed at high-class young women," says a source. "They deal with a wealthy and prominent clientele. Some of the girls are old school—out to find a rich husband."

Employees may have to invest thousands of dollars on a wardrobe to wear to work. In fact, most high-end retailers require their employees to wear only their label. One contact at Ralph Lauren says she must have her work apparel approved by the company, a cumbersome and expensive process. "For a job that pays by the hour," explains a contact, "you may have to invest quite a bit of money." This dress can be very expensive, even though employees receive discounts and supplementary commissions.

Fortunately, selling takes on new meaning when employees are dealing with celebrities and high-powered execs with money to burn. Those who excel in retail know how to build relationships with their customers—"setting aside" new arrivals or sending cards and little gifts (paid for by the company, of course). Wealthy clients may need pampering, but the insiders say the money compensates for the labor. "We're talking about people who walk into a store and buy the same outfit in five different colors," says an insider.

Inventory Planning and Buying

While the retail industry offers professional opportunities in functions common to all other industries (accounting, information technology and human resources), it offers two major professional paths unique to the industry: inventory planning and buying.

Inventory planners are responsible for the making sure that the company's stores are stocked with the appropriate products. At first glance, this may not seem too demanding, but consider that many major retailers operate thousands of stores, and that these stores may carry different product mixes because of the customers they serve.

Then, consider that retailers stock different products for different seasons and promotions—think about all of the "Back to School" promotions and holiday products you see at a major retailer. At many retailers, the inventory planning department is also responsible for making sure that the actual "Back to School" signs and product displays are shipped to the stores.

Inventory planning roles are very quantitative and detail-oriented. Professionals in these must learn inventory tracking systems and software that their companies have developed or purchased. Planners generally work out of the company's corporate headquarters or major offices.

While planners are responsible for making sure that the stores are stocked, buyers are responsible for deciding what products the stores should sell. Faced with a surplus of companies all making the case that their products will be the next big thing, buyers must judiciously choose the products they believe will "sell through" to customers.

How do buyers decide? They stay on top of trends, talk with professionals in their industry to try to pick up on any "buzz" surrounding a particular product, evaluate the products' quality and appeal themselves. Then, combining all of this knowledge and the knowledge of who their store's customers are (and what they are willing to pay for certain types of items), the buyers make decisions on what products to stock. Unlike planners, buyers travel a great deal in order to meet with vendors.

Both buyers and planners are organized by the category of product they focus on: think "sporting goods" or "toddler toys" or "women's casual shoes." Inventory planning roles can be entry-level positions, while buying jobs generally require a few years' experience in retail (usually in a planning role).

Vault Q&A: Adrienne D'Ippolito, Associate Buyer, TJX

Adrienne D'Ippolito is a 2001 graduate of Stonehill College in Easton, Massachusetts. After graduating, she joined the TJX Companies' Corporate Merchandise Training Program and now is an Associate Buyer at TJX. TJX operates more than 2,000 retail outlets, most prominently its T.J. Maxx and Marshalls chains.

Vault: What is TJX's program like?

D'Ippolito: It's called the Corporate Merchandise Training Program and it begins with the PASE training program. It's basically a career path that takes you through planning before going into buying. You start as an analyst, then become a senior analyst, then an associate planner. After that, you either become a buyer or a planning manager, but you always start in planning.

Vault: Describe planning to me.

D'Ippolito: It's analyzing the business and shipping the goods. You're working with the stores one-on-one, and working with the distributors one-on-one. When you're a buyer, you're working more with the vendors. The buyers buy the product; the planners ship the product to the stores.

When I was in planning, I was in corporate offices in Framingham, which is where I still am. You mostly stay in the office, though you do travel to different stores in the area—just looking at what you're shipping. You're in charge of where the product goes, verifying that it's all there, and that you shipped it correctly.

As an Associate Planner you assist the Planning Manager. You're learning all about the numbers and the budgets, creating the plans that the Buyers buy to. You're also managing a small group of people with the help of your planning manager. You're essentially creating a budget and unit plans. We have 1,500 stores, and both TJ Maxx and Marshall's Buyers depend on the planning department. It's a lot of quantitative work.

Vault: What did you major in? Did you feel well-equipped for the type of work and is it what you anticipated?

D'Ippolito: I majored in marketing and economics, so I was pretty prepared. It's pretty much what I anticipated, I knew it was going to be a little bit challenging, and I was up to the challenge. They're not just going to make you a Buyer just for showing up. Twenty-five people started with me, and so far four people have become Buyers. Some have become Planning Managers.

Vault: How do you find buying?

Visit Vault at **www.vault.com** for insider company profiles, expert advice, career message boards, expert resume reviews, the Vault Job Board and more.

VAULT CAREER LIBRARY   397

D'Ippolito: When you're buying, you're traveling every week, and it's everywhere. Whether it's into the market or a distribution center, or a warehouse, Europe, California or wherever.

Vault: Do you like that?

D'Ippolito: I love it. I'm in New York every week—the majority of our vendors are in New York. We're in Europe twice a year, London and Paris, sometimes Italy—in Europe we're buying samples, in some cases we're working with vendors there. California, we're out with vendors too—sometimes you're in random places like Philadelphia, Ohio, wherever, with people who have warehouses.

Vault: You get to keep your frequent flyer miles?

D'Ippolito: Yes, I do. It's a nice perk, but you can get tired traveling every week… you definitely work for it.

Vault: So when you're traveling are you looking at catalogs or are you actually looking at the product?

D'Ippolito: Oh, I'm looking at the product. Every day I'm looking at product, and touching and feeling product.

You really have to know the trends, and shop every day or every week, and know what's out there. It's really strategic—thinking outside the box, thinking about the next thing, not focusing on the present, but looking to the future. In this sense, risk-taking is huge.

Vault: How do you know what risks to take?

D'Ippolito: You're going to have to read the market, find out what the department stores are buying. Some of it's gut feeling—you know what's going to be a hot item, from traveling all around, reading magazines, and word of mouth.

Vault: Do you get to choose what department you work in?

D'Ippolito: Not really, it's what the needs of the business are, and management knows what you're strengths and weaknesses are. I started off in Children's and then Men's and then Women's. I've been in Ladies' for two years. Where you are depends on the needs of the business.

Vault: How quickly do you move through the program?

D'Ippolito: For me, it was six months to senior analyst. It took me an additional year to become an associate planner. Then fourteen months to become a buyer. But it basically depends. It could take you five years; it could take you three years. It depends on the needs of the business and how aggressive you are.

Vault: Are there any training opportunities outside of your regular on-the-job training?

D'Ippolito: There's constant training—you get upgrades on the system, and you've got to train on that. And as you head up into the management positions, starting with the senior analyst and associate planner positions, you take leadership classes—things like how to handle difficult situations when you're managing people, how to give constructive criticism.

You also have a constant mentor, a "buyer buddy." It's an official program where you have an experienced buyer that helps you with any challenging issues. As an analyst in planning, you have a buyer buddy to help you get acclimated to the company. Every other month you have lunch with them.

And every March there are reviews, which provide great structure. The reviews are very helpful, they tell you what you need to work on, and where they see you going next, and it gives you sort of a road map to get where you need to go.

Retail Employer Directory

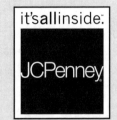

JCPenney

PO Box 10001

Dallas, TX 75301-8115

Phone: (972) 431-1000

www.JCPenney.com

Communication Subcommittee Mission Statement

Improve communications by enhancing the sensitivity level surrounding diversity & work-life impacting customer service and associate satisfaction/productivity.

Personnel Relations Subcommittee Mission Statement

To foster the upward mobility of women and minorities into all levels of management, including senior management positions, by enhancing our current recruitment programs and implementing career development plans that allow the Company to retain, train and promote qualified women and minority associates.

Work-Life Issues Subcommittee Mission Statement

Identify Work-Life Issues that affect each associate's ability to perform to full potential. Encourage a supportive work environment that allows associates to maximize their contributions towards company objectives.

Schools JCPenney recruits from

Open to all accredited colleges and universities

Albertson's, Inc.

250 Parkcenter Blvd.

Boise, ID 83726

Phone: (208) 395-6200

Fax: (208) 395-6349

www1.albertsons.com/corporate

Amazon.com

1200 12th Ave. South

Suite 1200

Seattle, WA 98144-2734

Phone: (206) 266-1000

Fax: (206) 266-1821

www.amazon.com

AutoZone, Inc.

123 S. Front Street

Memphis, TN 38103

Phone: (901) 495-6500

Fax: (901) 495-8300

www.autozone.com

Barnes & Noble, Inc.

122 Fifth Avenue

New York, NY 10011

Phone: (212) 633-3300

Fax: (212) 675-0413

www.barnesandnobleinc.com

Borders Group, Inc.

100 Phoenix Drive

Ann Arbor, MI 48108

Phone: (734) 477-1100

Fax: (734) 477-1965

www.bordersgroupinc.com

Circuit City Stores, Inc.

9950 Mayland Dr.

Richmond, VA 23233

Phone: 804-527-4000

Fax: 804-527-4164

www.circuitcity.com

Costco Wholesale Corporation

999 Lake Drive

Issaquah, WA 98027

Phone: (425) 313-8100

Fax: (425) 313-8103

www.costco.com

CVS Corporation

One CVS Drive

Woonsocket, RI 02895

Phone: (401) 765-1500

Fax: (401) 766-2917

www.cvs.com

Dillard's, Inc.

1600 Cantrell Road

Little Rock, AR 72201

Phone: (501) 376-5200

Fax: (501) 399-7831

www.dillards.com

Dollar General Corporation

100 Mission Ridge

Goodlettsville, TN 37072

Phone: (615) 855-4000

Fax: (615) 855-5252

www.dollargeneral.com

eBay Inc.

2145 Hamilton Avenue

San Jose, CA 95125

Phone: (408) 376-7400

Fax: (408) 376-7401

www.ebay.com

Federated Department Stores, Inc.

7 W. 7th Street

Cincinnati, OH 45202

Phone: (513) 579-7000

Fax: (513) 579-7555

www.federated-fds.com

Visit Vault at **www.vault.com** for insider company profiles, expert advice, career message boards, expert resume reviews, the Vault Job Board and more.

Retail Employer Directory, cont.

Gap Inc.
Two Folsom Street
San Francisco, CA 94105
Phone: (650) 952-4400
Fax: (415) 427-2553
www.gap.com

Hallmark Cards
2501 McGee Street
Kansas City, MO 64108
Phone: (816) 274-5111
Fax: (816) 274-5061
www.hallmark.com

Home Depot, Inc., The
2455 Paces Ferry Rd., NW
Atlanta, GA 30339-4024
Phone: (770) 433-8211
Fax: (770) 384-2356
www.homedepot.com

IKEA Group, The
Box 640
SE 25 106
Helsingborg Sweden
Phone: +46-42-267-100
Fax: +46-42-132-805
www.ikea.com

J.C. Penney Corporation, Inc.
6501 Legacy Drive
Plano, TX 75024-3698
Phone: (972) 431-1000
Fax: (972) 431-1362
www.jcpenney.com

Kmart Corporation
3100 W. Big Beaver Rd.
Troy, MI 48084
Phone: (248) 463-1000
Fax: (248) 463-5636
www.kmart.com/home/index.jsp

Kohl's Corporation
N56 W17000 Ridgewood Drive
Menomonee Falls, WI 53051
Phone: (262) 703-7000
Fax: (262) 703-6143
www.kohls.com

Kroger Co., The
1014 Vine Street
Cincinnati, OH 45202
Phone: (513) 762-4000
Fax: (513) 762-1160
www.kroger.com

L.L.Bean, Inc.
Casco Street
Freeport, ME 04033
Phone: (207) 865-4761
Fax: (207) 552-6821
www.llbean.com

Lands' End Inc.
Lands' End Lane
Dodgeville, WI 53595
Phone: (608) 935-9341
Fax: (608) 935-4260
www.landsend.com

Limited Brands, Inc.
3 Limited Parkway
Columbus, OH 43216
Phone: (614) 415-7000
Fax: (614) 415-7440
www.limitedbrands.com

Lowe's Companies, Inc.
1000 Lowe's Blvd.
Mooresville, NC 28117
Phone: (704) 758-1000
Fax: (336) 658-4766
www.lowes.com

May Department Stores
611 Olive Street
St. Louis, MO 63101
Phone: (314) 342-6300
Fax: (314) 342-3064
www.mayco.com

Neiman Marcus Group, Inc.
1 Marcus Sq., 1618 Main Street
Dallas, TX 75201
Phone: (214) 741-6911
Fax: (214) 573-5320
www.neimanmarcus.com

Nordstrom Inc.
1617 Sixth Avenue
Seattle, WA 98101-1742
Phone: (206) 628-2111
Fax: (206) 628-1795
www.nordstrom.com

Technology Consulting

The State of Technology Consulting

The IT factor

After sizable industry gains in the 1990s, consulting firms—especially in the technology sector—suffered crushing blows in the stock market bust of 2000-2001 and the ensuing recession and corporate cutbacks that persisted through 2003. IT spending, viewed by many corporations as a luxury, not a necessity, was often the first item slashed from budgets. Since 2004, though, as businesses recovered from the downturn and revenues started climbing, companies unfroze their hold on IT improvements and turned to tech consultants to bolster their performance and efficiency.

While things are now heading in the right direction for IT consulting firms, they're not out of the woods yet. Lower-than-expected earnings in early 2005 sparked worries in the industry regarding the pace of technology spending. In 2004, Forrester Research predicted that IT consulting will grow at a 5 percent annual rate from 2003 through 2008, and *Management Consultant International*, a newsletter produced by Kennedy Information, forecasts that the consulting industry will experience only modest growth through 2007 due to the conservative pace of spending on IT consulting.

A nip and a tuck

The slow rebound in IT spending since 2004 has forced tech consulting firms to rethink their service offerings and innovation strategies. One way some have adapted to the market is by muscling their way into the arena of management consulting, bringing the two disciplines together under one roof. EDS was one of the pioneers of this approach, acquiring A.T. Kearney in 1995 (though A.T. Kearney completed a management buyout from EDS in January 2006), followed by the 2002 acquisition of KMPG Consulting by Atos Origin and PwC Consulting by IBM in 2003. These firms maintain that the convergence trend reflects today's business environment in which technology and business strategy are inherently linked. They claim that businesses are looking for firms that can identify client needs, execute a particular IT strategy, install the system and then stay on board to provide turnkey services that include day-to-day management of the client's computer department and/or other departments. Others contend that some clients are wary of awarding an entire project to a specific firm and prefer to use separate vendors for business strategy and IT implementation.

Shoring up revenues

Another way companies are coping with reduced tech spending is by taking advantage of offshoring opportunities. While companies have been outsourcing technical work to India for nearly two generations, the practice really took off during the recession of the early 21st century, when companies were determined to cut costs. Indeed, offshoring has become just another business strategy for profitability and growth, rendering it a necessity for maintaining a company's competitive advantage in the market. A January 2006 article in *BusinessWeek* magazine cites McKinsey Global Institute in estimating that, to date, $18.4 billion in global IT work and $11.4 billion in business process services have been shifted abroad. The latest Quarterly Index from sourcing advisory firm TPI reports that although the average value of outsourcing contracts in 2005 was 24 percent lower than those in 2004, the number of outsourcing contracts continues to rise—up 11 percent from 2004—reflecting increased competition and expansion in the marketplace. In addition, a considerable number of first-generation offshoring contracts, awarded in the last seven to 10 years, are now up for renewal. Of these, TPI notes that there were $43.8 billion in renewals in 2005, and expects to see $49 billion in 2007.

Visit Vault at **www.vault.com** for insider company profiles, expert advice, career message boards, expert resume reviews, the Vault Job Board and more.

VAULT CAREER LIBRARY   401

Dissenting opinions

Although offshoring has proven to be a viable force in generating financial returns to U.S. companies, it has also been a frequent subject of hot debate. Some industry observers are concerned with offshoring's impact on traditional consulting, saying that the prevalent outsourcing model—which groups consulting services into larger outsourcing engagements—has depressed the prices of traditional consulting services and, in a sense, commoditized the business. The main concern becomes cost-savings, as opposed to selling value that can differentiate one provider from the next. Another major concern for those opposed to offshoring is that outsourcing jobs will hold down IT job growth and salaries; Forrester Research projects that IT jobs will grow slowly, at an annual rate of 3 percent through 2008, with salaries growing only 6 percent during that period.

Those in the pro camp suggest that offshoring is a win-win game. It frees up resources that can be used to generate high value, and companies can invest their savings from offshoring into new, more productive initiatives at home. For American IT consulting outfits, the rush to open offshore facilities has emerged as a competitive necessity, reducing IT spending and improving the overall corporate bottom line. As for the loss of jobs, any turnover generated by outsourcing is viewed as part of the natural flow of economic activity. These jobs will be replaced by others that will emerge when companies invest their savings from offshoring into new ventures.

Regional palates

Until recently, India has been the primary receptacle for U.S. offshoring pursuits. The country's large talent pool boasts a heavy concentration of IT consultants and an ever-ready supply of Indian recruits waving MBAs. Billing rates for skilled IT consultants are among the lowest in the world, and competition has grown rampant within the country as the leading outsourcers—Infosys, Tata, Wipro—compete head-to-head with big-league American consulting firms like IBM and Accenture for local IT development centers employing Indian engineers. Consequently, wages for mid-level employees are on the rise, and companies are offering attractive incentive plans to boost retention. With these increased wages and geographic diversification away from India, the nation's IT outsourcers have been forced to focus on emerging markets to capture cost efficiencies and market share.

Rising costs in India have encouraged consulting firms to look elsewhere for cut-rate offshoring opportunities. Countries such as China, Malaysia, Australia and New Zealand are becoming attractive locations for cost-efficient IT development centers. In fact, Kennedy Information predicts that the Chinese consulting market will prove to be heady competition for India, growing at a compound annual rate of 32 percent from 2005 to 2008, with India lagging behind at 24 percent. Demand for consultants in China is now on the rise, though the biggest challenge to growth in the country is the difficulty of training and retaining skilled labor. There are far fewer Chinese recruits wielding MBAs than there are in India. It can take up to 10 years to train a consultant and, once trained, many talented Chinese consultants opt for more lucrative positions with Western consulting firms.

Seeking specialists

With corporate America spending money on technology again, the IT job market has sprung back to life. According to Moody's Economy.com, some 125,000 tech jobs were created in 2005, with 217,000 jobs predicted for 2006—what promises to be the industry's best year since 2000. Technology consultants comprised 34,000 of those positions, a number that's expected to grow in 2006. The job market for consultants is now candidate-driven: Recruiters are having difficulty attracting enough talent to meet their hiring targets, putting candidates in advantageous negotiating positions when faced with competing job offers. The health of the industry is also evident in the upturn in voluntary turnover, which, according to *Consultants News*, reached 25 percent in 2005.

Now more than ever, clients are demanding expertise in a particular industry or functional area, and the need for generalist consultants is in decline—a trend that has taken hold in the past few years. The small size of the talent pool for specific operational issues, such as Sarbanes-Oxley regulation and national defense, coupled with heightened demand from consulting firms has caused salaries for specialists to spike.

Practice Areas

Systems integration

This is one of the traditional jobs of tech consultants, and a growth area today as companies augment their business processes with complex IT systems. When two companies merge, or a single company wants to implement new hardware or software, they turn to consultants to make all of the technology compatible. Sometimes this is a simple matter of installing upgrades or changing settings; more often, it's a long and arduous process of writing new code to allow hardware and existing software to co-exist and operate efficiently together.

Outsourcing

Another long-time area of tech consulting expertise, business process outsourcing (BPO) is the bread and butter of many firms. Some companies find it easier and more cost-effective to pay somebody else to manage their technology for them, positioning consultants, in effect, as the client's IT department. Consultants handle everything from help desk and call center operations to server maintenance and passkey and ID tag issuance. Even governments and armies outsource nowadays; CIBER has a number of contracts with the U.S. Army Reserve's Regional Support Commands and the U.S. Marine Corps and Navy, while Computer Sciences Corporation has outsourcing deals with the UK, Germany's armed forces and Australia.

Enterprise solutions

A major impact of the Enron (2001) and Worldcom (2002) accounting scandals was the summer 2002 passage of the Sarbanes-Oxley Act. SOX mandates that companies publicly listed in the U.S. market conduct internal audits, provide more detailed financial information to investors, and store financial data for a specific period of time. Many companies initially thought they could manage the IT implications of SOX on their own, and it has taken a couple of years for huge SOX-compliance IT contracts to become commonplace. Companies have found that they need vastly improved data storage, records management and security systems to maintain confidentiality of their newly prodigious amounts of financial information, in addition to process management software systems to facilitate audit, tracking and reporting requirements.

SOX compliance is just one of the major types of consulting that is generally bundled into the "enterprise solutions" category. Supply chain consulting, for example, is an even larger piece of the pie. Supply chain consultants help client companies streamline parts and materials ordering processes and reduce manufacturing input costs. Supply chain projects can focus on inventory reduction, throughput enhancement and manufacturing cost containment. Enterprise resource planning (ERP) is an extension of supply chain management that further integrates product planning, customer service, order tracking, finance and HR processes.

Customer relationship management (CRM) systems received a lot of hype in the late 1990s, only to be hit hard by an economic downturn that meant that even the most sophisticated CRM system wasn't going to grow in sales. CRM consulting engagements involve developing organized and efficient ways for clients to manage relationships, usually through a complex software solution that facilitates storing and mining large amounts of customer data.

IT strategy

IT consulting engagements that involve a broad view of the client's business or high-level tech decisions are often simply referred to as "consulting" or "strategy" projects. These engagements often entail aligning a client's IT infrastructure with its overall business strategy. Most of the large, brand-name management consulting firms have IT strategy practices, including Booz Allen's technology strategy group and Accenture's Strategic IT Effectiveness (SITE) group, which resides within its

Visit Vault at **www.vault.com** for insider company profiles, expert advice, career message boards, expert resume reviews, the Vault Job Board and more.

VAULT CAREER LIBRARY **403**

business consulting division. These IT strategy consulting groups are often managed by industry specialists (e.g., utilities, financial services) who are deeply familiar with the specific information challenges faced by potential clients.

Many IT strategy engagements fall into the category of business process reengineering (BPR). When a company decides to purchase a new software package, or simply to improve its business processes, the result is not simply a new IT system, but usually a dramatic shift in the way employees interact. BPR assignments involve rewriting work rules and shaping communication paths, calling upon consultants' general business know-how over technical computer knowledge.

Web services

Long the domain of design and hosting companies based in Silicon Alley (New York's tech center), Web services include e-commerce implementation and other secure-transaction work, though consultancies do some page design and site hosting as part of their overall deliverables as well. This specialty is receiving a lot of attention from major technology players such as IBM, HP and Accenture. Gartner predicts that Web services spending will reach $14.3 billion in 2006.

Security

Five years after the September 11 terrorist attacks and the resulting heightened awareness of security threats to U.S. residents and businesses, information security consulting work is still a hot area. IT businesses have realized there's money to be made in designing and implementing better security and identification methods. The industry has seen progress in biometrics (the science of identifying a person via retina patterns, voice, fingerprints and other unique biological characteristics), contraband detection and secure communications.

Research and development

Some consultants spend their time in the lab developing new hardware and software. Often, this work is geared toward creating new products (such as servers and analysis software) that will help companies sell work and accomplish engagements.

A Day in the Life: IT Consultant

Kristine is a consultant at a major consulting firm with many IT consulting engagements. Her role is Team Lead of the design and developer for eight Web-based training modules. She has five analysts on her team.

4:30 a.m.: It's Monday morning. Time to wake up. There's time for a shower this Monday morning—such luxury!

5:30 a.m.: I am in a cab on the way to the airport, making a mental list of anything that could have been forgotten. I ask the cabbie to tune the radio to NPR.

6:10 a.m.: At the airport I go up to the self check-in kiosk. I take the boarding pass and head down to the security line, laptop and small carry-on in hand.

6:25 a.m.: At security, I remove my laptop from my bag and place it on the tray. I move through security quickly. No alarms beep.

6:35 a.m.: After a quick stop at Starbucks, I arrive at the gate. I say hello to three other members of my project and check out the other passengers I see every week on this Monday morning flight. I board early along with the other premier fliers—one of the perks of being a frequent traveler.

7:00 a.m.: The flight departs on time. Yay! I relish my window seat close to the front of the airplane.

8:00 a.m.: The beverage cart wakes me up. I ask for coffee and scan the *Wall Street Journal* as I drink.

9:30 a.m.: I arrive at my destination and share a ride with my fellow consultants to the project site.

10:30 a.m.: At the project site. As I crawl underneath my desk to hook my laptop to the client LAN connection, one of my team members informs me that he still hasn't received feedback from his client reviewer. That's not good news.

11:00 a.m.: After checking and responding to e-mail, I call my team member's client reviewer. The reviewer agrees to send me the team member feedback on the training material by noon tomorrow.

11:15 a.m.: I remind the team of the 1 p.m. status meeting. I've got to start it on time—I have a meeting downtown at 3:15 p.m. I start to review the content outlines for the training modules.

12:00 p.m.: I scurry, along with two teammates, to get sandwiches at a nearby eatery. Mine is turkey and cheddar.

12:20 p.m.: Back at my desk, I get a call from the project manager, who is working at a client site in another state. He tells me that clients in the training department are nervous about their job security and asks that the entire team be sensitive to how the training changes may affect the training positions in the organization.

1:00 p.m.: The team holds a status meeting. I pass on the message from the project manager. Each member discusses what has been completed and what he or she expects to complete that week. Two other team members are having difficulty obtaining feedback from their client reviewers. We all brainstorm ideas on how to obtain the feedback.

2:00 p.m.: I finish up the meeting and get directions to my meeting downtown.

2:40 p.m.: Off to the 3:15 p.m. meeting.

3:15 p.m.: I meet the head of the training department to discuss the training courses. He calls in a close associate who has opinions on how the courses should be organized. The associate wants to add several more Web-based training modules. I politely suggest that part of the additional subject matter could be covered in the modules that have been agreed to in the scope of the project. We all sketch out the course structure on a white board.

4:45 p.m.: Back at the project site. I check in with my team members via e-mail.

5:45 p.m.: I complete a draft of the course flow in PowerPoint and send it to the client and my manager for review.

7:00 p.m.: I have reviewed 50 percent of the course outlines. It's time to head back to the hotel. I stop by a local diner for a quick dinner.

8:30 p.m.: Time for a workout in the hotel gym.

9:15 p.m.: I'm ready for bed. Clothes for the next day are hanging in the closet. The alarm clock is set to 6:30 a.m.

10:30 p.m.: I go to sleep.

Visit Vault at **www.vault.com** for insider company profiles, expert advice, career message boards, expert resume reviews, the Vault Job Board and more.

VAULT CAREER LIBRARY   **405**

Technology Consulting Employer Directory

Accenture
1345 Avenue of the Americas
New York, NY 10105
Phone: (917) 452-4400
Fax: (917) 527-5387
www.accenture.com

BearingPoint
1676 International Drive
McLean, VA 22102
Phone: (703) 747-3000
Fax: (703) 747-8500
www.bearingpoint.com

Booz Allen Hamilton
8283 Greensboro Drive
McLean, VA 22102
Phone: (703) 902-5000
Fax: (703) 902-3333
www.boozallen.com

BT
4201 Lexington Avenue North
Arden Hills, MN 55126-6198
Phone: (651) 415-4401
Fax: (651) 415-4891
E-mail: info.us@btsyntegra.com
www.btconsulting.com

Capgemini
750 Seventh Avenue
Suite 1800
New York, NY 10019
Phone: (212) 314-8000
Fax: (212) 314-8001
www.us.capgemini.com

CGI Group Inc.
1130 Sherbrooke Street West
5th Floor
Montreal, Quebec H3A 2M8
Canada
Phone: (514) 841-3200
Fax: (514) 841-3299
www.cgi.com

Cisco Systems, Inc.
170 West Tasman Drive
San Jose, CA 95134
Phone: (408) 526-4000 or
(800) 553-NETS
www.cisco.com

Computer Sciences Corporation
2100 East Grand Avenue
El Segundo, CA 90245
Phone: (310) 615-0311
www.csc.com

Deloitte Consulting LLP
1633 Broadway, 35th Floor
New York, NY 10019
Phone: (212) 492-4500
Fax: (212) 492-4743
www.deloitte.com

DiamondCluster International Inc.
John Hancock Center
875 North Michigan Avenue
Suite 3000
Chicago, IL 60611
Phone: (312) 255-5000
Fax: (312) 255-6000
www.diamondcluster.com

EDS
5400 Legacy Drive
Plano, TX 75024
Phone: (972) 605-6000 or
(800) 566-9337
E-mail: info@eds.com
www.eds.com

Fujitsu Consulting
333 Thornall Street
Edison, NJ 08837
Phone: (732) 549-4100 or
(800) 882-3212
Fax: (732) 549-2375
us.fujitsu.com/consulting

Getronics NV
290 Concord Road
Billerica, MA 01821
Phone: (978) 625-5000
www.getronics.com

HP Services
3000 Hanover Street
Palo Alto, CA 94304-1185
Phone: (650) 857-1501
Fax: (650) 857-5518
www.hp.com/hps

IBM Global Services
New Orchard Road
Armonk, NY 10504
Phone: (914) 499-1900
Fax: (914) 765-7382
www-1.ibm.com/services/us/index.wss

Infosys Technologies Ltd.
6607 Kaiser Drive
Fremont, CA 94555
Phone: (510) 742-3000
Fax: (510) 742-3090
www.infosys.com

Keane
100 City Square
Boston, MA 02129
Phone: (617) 241-9200 or
(800) 73-KEANE
Fax: (617) 241-9507
www.keane.com

Lockheed Martin Corporation
6801 Rockledge Drive
Bethesda, MD 20817
Phone: (301) 897-6000
Fax: (301) 897-6000
www.lockheedmartin.com

Oracle Consulting
500 Oracle Parkway
Redwood Shores, CA 94065
Phone: (650) 506-7000
www.oracle.com/consulting/index.html

Technology Consulting Employer Directory, cont.

PA Consulting Group
123 Buckingham Palace Road
London
SW1W 9SR
Phone: +44 20 7730 9000
Fax: +44 20 7333 5050
www.paconsulting.com

Perot Systems
2300 West Plano Parkway
Plano, TX 75075
Phone: (888) 31-PEROT or
(972) 577-0000
Fax: (972) 340-6100
www.perotsystems.com

Sapient
25 First Street
Cambridge, MA 02141
Phone: (617) 621-0200
Fax: (617) 621-1300
www.sapient.com

Tata Consultancy Services
101 Park Avenue, 26th Floor
New York, NY 10178
Phone: (212) 557-8038
Fax: (212) 867-8652
www.tcs.com

Unisys
Corporate Headquarters
Unisys Way
Blue Bell, PA 19424
Phone: (215) 986-4011
www.unisys.com

Wipro Ltd.
Doddakannelli Sarjapur Road
Bangalore, Karnataka 560 035
Phone: +91 (80) 844 0011
Fax: +91 (80) 844 0256
www.wipro.com

Visit Vault at **www.vault.com** for insider company profiles, expert advice, career message boards, expert resume reviews, the Vault Job Board and more.

VAULT CAREER LIBRARY   **407**

We Connect People.

From the valued customers we connect through our innovative communications services, to the employees we connect through exciting career opportunities, Cox Communications is all about bringing people together and enhancing their lives.

Innovation. Personal growth. Professional development. Recognition. Opportunity. They're the necessary components of a successful company — and a successful career. For more than 100 years, Cox Communications has succeeded by leveraging these advantages to lead the way into new markets. To be the best, we have to do our best, and that means taking it to the **MAX: Motivated, Aware, and X-traordinary**. We invite you to join our employees in building on this competitive spirit and heritage of success as we lead the way into the Digital Age for our industry, our company and our customers.

Visit us at www.cox.com/coxcareer

COMMUNICATIONS

Your Friend in the Digital Age.

Telecommunications

Telecom Industry Overview

We're all connected

In simpler times, the word "telecommunications" might conjure an image of a telephone—and not much else. These days, though, telecom is an industry encompassing everything from local and long-distance phone service to wireless communication, Internet access, and cable and digital TV. In the U.S., total telecom spending reached more than $856 billion in 2005, and is expected to surpass the $1 trillion mark by 2009, according to the Telecommunications Industry Association (TIA). In the world at large, the TIA predicts telecom spending, estimated at $1.8 trillion in 2005, to reach $2.7 trillion by 2009.

The bell tolls for AT&T

Established in 1877 as American Bell, AT&T enjoyed the largest share of the telecom industry pie for nearly a century, thanks to the government's belief that the utility constituted a "natural" monopoly. That monopoly crumbled in 1969, when the Federal Communications Commission (FCC) allowed other companies—such as MCI, which was quick to get in the game—to play in Ma Bell's sandbox. But monopolies don't disappear overnight: to encourage competition in the long-distance market, the Department of Justice (DOJ) followed up with an antitrust suit against AT&T in 1974, resulting in the company's division into a long-distance retailer and seven regional Bell operating companies (RBOCs, or "Baby Bells"), which would compete in the local call market as independent local exchange carriers (LECs). The final breakup of AT&T took place in 1984.

The industry thrived after the breakup, exploding into hundreds of smaller competitors, lowering the cost of long-distance calling dramatically. AT&T, which held about 70 percent of the market in 1984, controlled only a third in 2005, but bounced back following its buyout by SBC to once again become the biggest kid on the playground. Still, it's these so-called "Tier 1" carriers—AT&T, Sprint Nextel and Global Crossing—that make up the bulk of the long-distance market.

Untangling the wires

As the long-distance market diversified, the local exchange market remained relatively homogenous. The Telecommunications Act of 1996 aimed to change that by deregulating entry into local markets and requiring that the Baby Bells, or incumbent local exchange carriers (ILECs), retail their network elements to smaller competitors. The incumbents were required to unbundle their networks for reasonable prices, with the goal of decentralizing the system into a "network of networks." The act also temporarily blocked an RBOC from entering the long-distance market until it could prove sufficient competition in its local territory.

Another provision of the Telecom Act, allowing RBOCs the right to sell cable television services and phone equipment, proved to be a boon for the strongest RBOCs. Thanks to those services and the entry of the Baby Bells into long distance, the Act actually had the opposite of its intended effect, allowing a few RBOCs to solidify their positions and dominate the market through mergers and acquisitions. Today, there are just three RBOCs—Verizon, AT&T and Qwest—that dominate both local phone service and the burgeoning DSL (digital subscriber line) markets. Until recently there were five such companies, but the market contracted in 2005 as SBC took over AT&T (keeping the latter's name), and in March 2006 as the new AT&T announced it would purchase BellSouth.

Visit Vault at **www.vault.com** for insider company profiles, expert advice, career message boards, expert resume reviews, the Vault Job Board and more.

VAULT CAREER LIBRARY   409

Still, sniping among the RBOCs and long-distance giants like Verizon and AT&T over network access rights continues. As late as May 2004, the FCC was engaged in a dispute between the Baby Bells and the long-distance carriers, as the latter lobbied for increased access to local calling networks.

Not just at home

The dealmaking wasn't limited to America's shores. Telecom became truly global in 1997, when 70 member countries of the World Trade Organization (WTO)—which together control 90 percent of worldwide telecom sales—agreed to open up their telecom markets to each other at the start of the following year. Nearly all telecom companies around the globe had privatized in anticipation of this expanded level of competition. The accord led to a rush of international deals, especially in the world's second-largest telecom market, Japan. In 1999, British Telecommunications and AT&T partnered to acquire a 30 percent stake in LD operator Japan Telecom, combining their Japanese ventures under JT. A few months later, Britain's Cable & Wireless bought Japan's No. 6 carrier, IDC, and in 1999, Global Crossing teamed up with Marubeni to build a brand new network, called Global Access, to service Japan.

Wall Street highs and lows

As mergers and acquisitions activity heated up, Wall Street took notice: investors poured $1.3 trillion into telecom companies in the five years following passage of the Telecom Act, according to *Forbes* magazine. But with this activity came increased scrutiny and risk. Ultimately, the industry was subject to the same meltdown that hit the rest of the tech sector beginning in late 2000. Again according to *Forbes*, the industry's market value plummeted by $1 trillion after the Dow took its dive. Mergers also fell by the wayside: in July 2000, a proposed merger between Sprint and WorldCom fell through when the Justice Department filed a lawsuit that attempted to block the deal. The prospect of a lengthy DOJ suit effectively killed the merger, and it may similarly discourage future unions.

Cooking the books

Compounding the gloom, a number of major telecoms had high-profile problems in their accounting departments. The biggest offender was WorldCom, which ran afoul of the feds in 2002. WorldCom filed for the largest bankruptcy in U.S. history in July of that year, racking up $41 billion in debt and an estimated $11 billion in fraudulent expenses—leading to a $100 billion loss to shareholders. Even as the company attempted a rebound, emerging from bankruptcy in April 2004 with a lighter debt load, a moderately healthy outlook and a less tarnished name (the company had reverted to the MCI brand), it had to contend with scores of class-action lawsuits. Former CEO Bernard J. Ebbers also faced a growing list of federal fraud and conspiracy charges. In March 2005 Ebbers was found guilty on all counts, and was sentenced to 25 years in prison. Accounting firm Citigroup, which had conspired with WorldCom, announced in May 2004 that it would pay $2.65 billion to investors for its role in the scandal. Two years later, the beleaguered company was virtually no more, having been gobbled up by Verizon in a deal worth $8.5 billion.

In addition to WorldCom, about a half-dozen other providers of telecom services began Chapter 11 bankruptcy proceedings in 2002, dumping customers and employees as they went. In 2003, Sprint reorganized into separate business and consumer units in an effort to save $1 billion.

Can you hear me now?

It is a truth universally acknowledged that every person in possession of relatively good fortune must have a cell phone, or at least want one. The fact that the $174 billion American wireless market is growing by leaps and bounds and posting double-digit gains backs this up. U.S. wireless revenue increased more than 10 percent in 2005, and the industry plans on its reaching $265 billion by 2009.

The wireless market outpaced long distance for the first time in 2003, according to TIA number crunchers (LD posted $78 billion in spending to wireless's 89), the same year that the number of wireless users was estimated to be above 1 billion worldwide. By 2005 industry analysts reckoned that some 194 million people in the U.S. had a wireless phone, and projected that 270 million people would have one in 2009.

The wireless boom heralds renewed business activity in telecom. Competition began to sizzle in late 2003, as the first phase of a federal law allowing "portability"—a.k.a., letting consumers retain their mobile phone numbers when switching carriers—took effect. One notable event was Cingular's $41 billion purchase of rival AT&T Wireless, announced in February 2004, following a fierce bidding war with Vodafone. Just to show how complicated the industry's family ties are, Cingular happens to be owned by rival Baby Bells—though these huge conglomerates can't really be called "baby" anymore—AT&T and BellSouth (which former is in process of purchasing the latter); while competitor Verizon Wireless is a joint venture between Verizon and Vodafone.

Deals kept perking right along as Sprint merged with Nextel in August 2005, when the companies were, respectively, the No. 3 and 5 wireless carriers. Though the present company is one of the largest telecoms in the world, it's still No. 3 in the U.S. by number of subscribers behind Verizon and Cingular.

Wireless—if not VoIP; see below—is the wave of the future: while landlines were once seen as a source of dependable revenue and a way to spread risk, wireless companies have recently been setting up their landline units on their own and seeing them on their way. Sprint spun off its landlines in May 2006 under the name Embarq, while Alltel, after beefing up its landlines by acquiring Valor Communications, divested the unit under the name Windstream in July 2006.

An end-run around the phone

Cell phones aren't the only way consumers are making calls these days—Voice over Internet Protocol (VoIP), offered by companies like Vonage and Skype, allows users to turn their personal computers into telephones by sending voice data over a broadband connection in the same way other data is sent online. Growth in the VoIP market has been exponential: in 2005 Internet phone subscribers in the U.S. went from a mere 1.3 million to 4.5 million, according to TeleGeography, an industry research group (they also predict that there will be 19 million VoIP users by 2010).

Bypassing questions of local and long distance networks entirely, VoIP providers allow complete number portability—a subscriber in Iowa, for instance, could have a (212) Manhattan area code. (She would be all set if only the place in Chinatown with the good kung pao chicken would deliver that far.) The technology is also advantageous in terms of cost. Thanks to the FCC, VoIP is exempt from some of the taxes and regulations with which regular phone carriers are saddled. But—of course—the major telecoms are busy on Capitol Hill, trying to level the playing field. In June 2005 the FCC ruled that VoIP companies had to contribute, just like any other phone company, to the Universal Service Fund, designed to keep costs down in rural and low-income areas. The contributions to this fund will presumably be passed on to consumers in the form of higher rates.

A job market roller coaster

The numbers are intimidating: telecom seems to thrive on sudden booms and equally rapid readjustments. By some estimates, the industry slashed 300,000 jobs during the troubled period beginning in late 2000. Companies also feel compelled to trim excess fat when they merge—the 2006 MCI-Verizon merger, for example, resulted in the elimination of some 7,000 positions. Even with increased demand for telecom services, the U.S. Department of Labor's Bureau of Labor Statistics (BLS) says that employment in the industry is expected to decline by 7 percent between 2004 and 2014.

Visit Vault at **www.vault.com** for insider company profiles, expert advice, career message boards, expert resume reviews, the Vault Job Board and more.

VAULT CAREER LIBRARY   **411**

Telecommunications Employer Directory

Alltel Corporation
1 Allied Drive
Little Rock, AR 72202
Phone: (501) 905-8000
Fax: (501) 905-5444
www.alltel.com

AT&T Incorporated
175 East Houston Street
San Antonio, TX 78205-2233
Phone: (210) 821-4105
Fax: (210) 351-2187
www.att.com

BellSouth Corporation
1155 Peachtree Street, N.E.
Atlanta, GA 30309-3610
Phone: (404) 249-2000
Fax: (404) 249-2071
www.bellsouth.com

BT Group plc
BT Centre
81 Newgate Street
London EC1A 7AJ
United Kingdom
Phone: (44-20) 7356-5000
Fax: (44-20) 7356-5520
www.btplc.com

Charter Communications Inc.
12405 Powerscourt Drive
Suite 100
St. Louis, MO 63131-3660
Phone: (314) 965-0555
Fax: (314) 965-9745
www.charter.com

Cingular Wireless
Glenridge Highlands Two
5565 Glenridge Connector
Atlanta, GA 30342
Phone: (404) 236-6000
www.cingular.com

Comcast Corporation
1500 Market Street
Philadelphia, PA 19102-2148
Phone: (215) 665-1700
Fax: (215) 981-7790
www.comcast.com

Corning Incorporated
1 Riverfront Plaza
Corning, NY 14831-0001
Phone: (607) 974-9000
Fax: (607) 974-5927
www.corning.com

Nortel
8200 Dixie Road
Suite 100
Brampton, Ontario L6T 5P6
Canada
Phone: (800) 4-NORTEL
www.nortel.com

Orange SA
50 George Street
London W1U 7DZ
United Kingdom
Phone: (44-870) 376-8888
Fax: (44-20) 7984-1601
www.orange.com

Sprint Nextel Corporation
2001 Edmund Halley Drive
Reston, VA 20191
Phone: (703) 443-4000
www.sprint.com

Verizon Business
22001 Loudoun County Parkway
Ashburn, VA 20147
Phone: (703) 996-5600
Fax: (212) 885-0570
www.verizonbusiness.com

Verizon Communications
140 West Street
New York, NY 10036
Phone: (212) 395-2121
Fax: (212) 869-3265
www.verizon.com

Vodafone Group plc
Vodafone House
The Connection
Newbury, Berkshire RG14 2FN
United Kingdom
Phone: (44-1635) 33-251
Fax: (44-1635) 45-713

Vonage Holdings Corporation
23 Main Street
Holmdel, NJ 07733
Phone: (732) 365-1328
Fax (732) 231-6783
www.vonage.com

Transportation Services

Transportation Industry Overview

Planes, trains and ... trucks and buses

The vast transportation industry carries people and products (safely and on time, of course) to destinations around the globe—no small feat. Because the economy is intimately connected to getting things from where they're made to where they're bought, the transportation sector, especially express services like UPS and FedEx Kinko's, are considered a bellwether for the economy's health on both domestic and global levels. The industry can be broken into a handful of sectors: airlines; air cargo and express delivery carriers; trucks; railroads; and buses.

Carrying the load

Unlike air travel as a whole, the air cargo business remains relatively stable, with major carriers posting profits even during 2001 and 2002. Still, a few cargo carriers, including Arrow and Atlas, were forced into bankruptcy court alongside their passenger carrier counterparts. UPS, FedEx Kinko's and DHL dominate the express delivery sector, all three operating their own modes of transportation and leasing space and services on other cargo haulers' vehicles. The Internet boom has had both a positive and negative effect on the industry: while the rise in e-mail has curtailed the shipping of smaller documents, more and more Internet shoppers, online retailers and small businesses are using express delivery companies for direct shipping services and supply chain management.

Many of the challenges the sector faces, including tighter security requirements, high fuel costs and the need to replace an aging fleet of planes, mirror those on the passenger side. Others are specific to the air cargo industry—for instance, the Air Line Pilots Association (ALPA) worries that international shippers may begin routing cargo through Canada and Mexico in response to the new security restrictions, meaning reduced activity in the domestic market. Air cargo services also have to contend with other forms of transport, like ships and trucks. Despite this, the International Air Transport Association (IATA) predicts that worldwide demand for air freight will increase by more than 6 percent from 2005 to 2009.

The world delivered (on time)

In the fiercely competitive delivery market, where the industry leaders vie for massive corporate contracts as well as business from individual consumers, marketing has become a hardball game. FedEx, for one, has strengthened its market position by diversifying, namely through its $2.4 billion buyout in January 2004 of document services provider and copy shop chain Kinko's. As of 2005, there were 1,400 FedEx Kinko's locations worldwide, and the company teamed up with Microsoft to add a "Print FedEx Kinko's" extension to its Office suite of programs, which allows a document to be remotely printed at a local FedEx Kinko's. The company, with approximately 70,000 ground vehicles and an air fleet of 671 planes, operates different express, ground and freight units. UPS, on the other hand, has only 267 planes (making it the ninth-largest airline in the world, according to the company) but 120,000 ground vehicles. Even if UPS lags in the number of cargo planes, it's still the market leader in the U.S., with 47 percent of market share and a revenue of $42 billion in 2005. (FedEx is not far behind, though, with a revenue of $29 billion and 31 percent of the market).

Globally, the German logistics and express delivery firm DHL, run by German postal entity Deutsche Post, has the highest revenue, some $57 billion in 2005. The company made aggressive steps in 2003 to solidify its position in the U.S. market, where it acquired Airborne Inc. for $1.1 billion, securing its No. 3 place domestically and further strengthening its dominance in the world market for express delivery services overall. Meanwhile, FedEx Kinko's and UPS attempted to beat back the upstart by challenging DHL on regulatory grounds, particularly citing a restriction barring foreign companies from controlling U.S. airlines. As such, DHL's airline was spun off from the company not long after its acquisition.

Visit Vault at www.vault.com for insider company profiles, expert advice, career message boards, expert resume reviews, the Vault Job Board and more.

VAULT CAREER LIBRARY   413

The companies have also grown overseas: FedEx Kinko's picked up DHL's Global Express Guaranteed operations in July 2004, while rival UPS bought direct control of a jointly run Chinese delivery company, Sinotrans Group, for $100 million in December 2004. UPS, with an eye to increasing services to Japan, also swallowed the remaining stake of joint venture (with Yamato Transport Co.) Yamato Express Co. earlier that year.

Greening "Brown"

Both UPS and FedEx have taken steps recently to "green" their ground service fleets, replacing diesel vehicles with more environmentally friendly options like compressed natural gas and electricity. FedEx is also raising the green stakes by buying a percentage of the power for its retail locations from renewable sources and increasing the amount of recycled content in its packaging. While the companies get PR points for their efforts, what's really driving the green movement is, well, the green—cash, that is. Along with attracting environmentally-sensitive consumers, hybrid electric vehicles use much less fuel than traditional cars, reducing fuel costs by as much as half.

Keep on truckin'

Express delivery services also share ties—and in some cases overlap—with the trucking sector, which in 2005 alone handled 10 billion tons, or 69 percent of the volume of freight in the U.S. Dominated by bulk truckers like Quality Distribution, JB Hunt and Yellow Roadway (which recently beefed up its business with the May 2005 purchase of supply chain management firm USF for $1.5 billion), the industry is seeing increased demand for its hauling services, with 2005 sales of $623 billion.

According to the Bureau of Labor Statistics (BLS), some 3.2 million people (2.5 million of which are self-employed) worked as truck drivers in 2004, a number that is expected to increase between 9 and 17 percent over the next several years. Drivers' responsibilities vary depending on the length of their routes and the nature of the goods they carry. Some drivers specialize in shorter routes where they also act as salespeople and solicit business while they make their deliveries, while others specialize in driving long distances and may be away from home for days or weeks at a time. Some trucking jobs require loading and unloading the truck, and so drivers must be in good physical shape and able to lift heavy objects. In order to drive trucks over a certain weight, operators must obtain a CDL license from their home state, and some states and employers require additional training, depending on what the truck is loaded with. Truck drivers must have a clean driving record and good vision and hearing; people with certain medical conditions are prohibited from driving trucks across state lines.

Long-haul truckers will be in high demand as the amount of freight moving across the country continues to grow. Statistics from economics consulting firm Global Insight suggest the number of drivers needed will rise by over half a million in the next decade. And according to a June 2005 report by the American Trucking Association, the long-haul, heavy-duty truck transportation industry is currently experiencing a national shortage of 20,000 drivers—a number that could swell to 110,000 by 2014—in what many in the industry consider the tightest driver market in over 20 years.

The trucking sector also overlaps with the railroad world, with giants like JB Hunt and Schneider International teaming up with old hands on the rails such as Union Pacific, Norfolk Southern, CSX and Burlington Northern Santa Fe. With new technologies allowing real-time cargo tracking and time-specific delivery, this sector of the transportation industry is expected to become increasingly integrated. As the economy grows, both rail and truck transport services will add jobs in order to accommodate the increased quantity of goods in circulation.

Working on the railroad

While the shipping portion of the rail sector has continued to chug along, the passenger train sector has contracted dramatically in previous decades. In fact, the railroads have been in decline since the advent of the automobile and the Federal Aid Highway Act of 1956. In the 1960s, it was dealt a heavy blow when the U.S. Postal Service turned to trucks and airplanes for its first-class shipping needs. Following 1970s legislation, Amtrak took over the majority of U.S. passenger trains under its National Railroad Passenger Corporation umbrella—though the operator still has trouble turning any sort of profit; the company, after all, cannot compete with the speed offered by air lines or low fares by bus companies. Therefore, with dwindling passenger rolls and increased operating costs, Amtrak has become increasingly subsidized—the organization had taken in $29 billion in government handouts by 2006, and was operating at a loss of over one billion dollars per year in 2004 and 2005. Amtrak isn't the only railroad running at a loss: the Long Island Railroad (LIRR), the busiest commuter rail line in the U.S., had posted annual losses of $1 million by July 2006.

It should be noted that almost no form of public transport is self-supporting. All get regular infusions of capital from both states and the federal government, either directly or, in the case of bus companies, in the form of highway maintenance. There is a great deal of carping in the government and the media about the money spent on Amtrak, but, according to the Bureau of Transportation Statistics (BTS), in 2002 (the latest year for which complete data is available) the government gave Amtrak slightly over $1 billion, while giving $7.7 billion in subsidies to maintain highways, airlines and airports.

As of 2004, the BLS reports that rail transportation workers held 112,000 jobs in the U.S. Occupations in the sector include conductors and yardmasters, engineers, brake, signal, and switch operators, and subway and streetcar operators. Engineer positions are almost always filled from within a railroad's ranks and require good vision, hearing and extensive training. Almost 80 percent of the employees in this industry are unionized. While employment in intercity trains is likely to decline, the BLS predicts demand for subway and bus operators to increase as the population in cities become increasingly dense and demand for public transport grows.

On the bus

For long-haul passenger travel, about the only thing cheaper than a bus is sticking out your thumb. Intercity buses, also known as motor coaches, provide regular service to more than 42,000 U.S. communities. According to the American Bus Association (ABA), more passengers travel by motor coach in the U.S. than on any other commercial mode of transportation. The bus sector is unique in its composition: unlike the heavily subsidized rail and airline sectors, motor coach companies are more likely to go it alone (though the industry received about $25 million in grant funding for security following September 11).

There are more than 4,000 bus companies on the roads in the U.S., many of which are small, entrepreneurial operators—90 percent run fewer than 25 buses, the ABA reports. Major operators include Trailways, which has been around for nearly 70 years and operates a group of 65 member companies, and Greyhound, founded in 1914 and acquired in 1999 by Laidlaw Inc. As insurance rates have increased tenfold in recent years, access to affordable coverage is a key challenge faced by the industry, even pricing some operators out of the market.

Visit Vault at **www.vault.com** for insider company profiles, expert advice, career message boards, expert resume reviews, the Vault Job Board and more.

VAULT CAREER LIBRARY   **415**

Transportation Services Employer Directory

Amtrak
60 Massachusetts Avenue, NE
Washington, DC 20002
Phone: (202) 906-3000
Fax: (202) 906-3306
www.amtrak.com

CNF Inc.
3240 Hillview Avenue
Palo Alto, CA 94304
Phone: (650) 494-2900
Fax: (650) 813-0160
www.cnf.com

CSX Corporation
500 Water Street, 15th Floor
Jacksonville, FL 32202
Phone: (904) 359-3200
www.csx.com

DHL Holdings (USA)
1200 South Pine Island Road
Plantation, FL 33324
Phone: (954) 888-7000
Fax: (954) 888-7310
www.dhl.com

Enterprise Rent-A-Car Company
600 Corporate Park Drive
St. Louis, MO 63105
Phone: (314) 512-5000
Fax: (314) 512-4706
www.enterprise.com

FedEx Corporation
942 S. Shady Grove Road
Memphis, TN 38120
Phone: (901) 818-7500
Fax: (901) 395-2000
www.fedex.com

The Hertz Corporation
225 Brae Blvd.
Park Ridge, NJ 07656-0713
Phone: (201) 307-2000
Fax: (201) 307-2644
www.hertz.com

Houston Airport System
16930 JFK Boulevard
Houston, TX 77032
Phone: (281) 233-1800
Fax: (281) 233-1859
www.fly2houston.com

Laidlaw International, Inc.
55 Shuman Boulevard, Suite 400
Naperville, IL 60563
Phone: (630) 848-3000
Fax: (630) 579-6438
www.laidlaw.com

Massachusetts Port Authority
One Harborside Drive, Suite 200S
East Boston, MA 02128
Phone: (617) 428-2800
www.massport.com

Norfolk Southern Corporation
3 Commercial Place
Norfolk, VA 23510-2191
Phone: (757) 629-2600
Fax: (757) 664-5069
www.nscorp.com

Port Authority of New York and New Jersey
225 Park Avenue South
New York, NY 10003
Phone: (212) 435-7000
Fax: (212) 435-6670
www.panynj.gov

Sabre Holdings Corp.
3150 Sabre Drive.
Southlake, TX 76092
Phone: (682) 605-1000
Fax: (682) 605-8267
www.sabre-holdings.com

UAL Corporation
1200 E. Algonquin Road
Elk Grove Township, IL 60007
Phone: (847) 700-4000
Fax: (847) 700-4081
www.united.com

U-HAUL INTERNATIONAL, INC.
1325 Airmotive Way, Suite 100
Reno, NV 89502
Phone: (775) 688-6300
Fax: (775) 688-6338
www.uhaul.com

Union Pacific Corporation
1400 Douglas Street
Omaha, NE 68179
Phone: (402) 544-5000
Fax: (402) 271-6408
www.up.com

United Parcel Service of America, Inc.
55 Glenlake Parkway NE
Atlanta, GA 30328
Phone: (404) 828-6000
Fax: (404) 828-6562
www.ups.com

Wabash National Corp.
1000 Sagamore Parkway South
Lafayette, IN 47905
Phone: (765) 771-5300
Fax: (765) 771-5474
www.wabashnational.com

Werner Enterprises, Inc.
14507 Frontier Road
Omaha, NE 68145
Phone: (402) 895-6640
Fax: (402) 895-6640
www.werner.com

Yellow Roadway Corporation
10990 Roe Avenue
Overland Park, KS 66211
Phone: (913) 696-6100
Fax: (913) 696-6100
www.yellowroadway.com

APPENDIX

About the Author

Vault Editors

Vault is the leading media company for career information. Our team of industry-focused editors takes a journalistic approach in covering news, employment trends and specific employers in their industries. We annually survey 10,000s of employees to bring readers the inside scoop on industries and specific employers.

Much of the material in *The College Career Bible* is excerpted from Vault titles to specific industries or career titles. Vault publishes more than 100 titles for job seekers and professionals. To see a complete list of Vault titles, go to www.vault.com.

Visit Vault at **www.vault.com** for insider company profiles, expert advice, career message boards, expert resume reviews, the Vault Job Board and more.

VAULT CAREER LIBRARY   419

GO FOR THE GOLD!

GET VAULT GOLD MEMBERSHIP AND GET ACCESS TO ALL OF VAULT'S AWARD-WINNING CAREER INFORMATION

◆ **Employee surveys for 4,000+ top employers,** with insider info on
- Firm culture
- Salaries and compensation
- Hiring process and interviews
- Business outlook

◆ Access to **1,000+ extended insider employer snapshots**

◆ **Student and alumni surveys** for 100s of top MBA programs, law schools and graduate school programs and 1000s of undergraduate programs

◆ Access to **Vault's Salary Central**, with salary information for law, finance and consulting firms

◆ Access to **complete Vault message board archives**

◆ **15% off** all Vault purchases, including Vault Guides, Employer Profiles and Vault Career Services (named the Wall Street Journal's "Top Choice" for resume makeovers)

For more information go to
www.vault.com

VAULT

> the most trusted name in career information™

VAULT CAREER GUIDES
ORGANIZED BY BOOK TYPE

VAULT
> the most trusted name in career informati

VAULT CAREER TOPIC GUIDES	PRICE	PAGES	ISBN
The College Career Bible	12.95	402	1-58131-283-0
The MBA Career Bible	12.95	284	1-58131-284-9
Vault Guide to Top Internships	14.95	550	1-58131-291-1
Vault Guide to Resumes, Cover Letters and Interviews	19.95	138	1-58131-258-x
Vault Guide to Schmoozing	19.95	312	1-58131-205-9
Vault Guide to International Careers	19.95	196	1-58131-270-9
Vault Guide to Starting Your Own Business	19.95	176	1-58131-180-x
Vault Guide to Conquering Corporate America for Women and Minorities	19.95	164	1-58131-178-8
The College Buzz Book	17.95	638	1-58131-437-x
The Business School Buzz Book	17.95	678	1-58131-436-1
The Law School Buzz Book	17.95	584	1-58131-424-8
Vault Insider Guide to Medical School Admissions	29.95	192	1-58131-451-5
Vault Guide to Finance Interviews	29.95	172	1-58131-304-7
Vault Finance Interviews Practice Guide	39.95	144	1-58131-170-2
Vault Guide to the Case Interview	29.95	232	1-58131-305-5
Vault Practice Guide to Case Interviews	29.95	144	1-58131-168-0

VAULT INDUSTRY CAREER GUIDES	PRICE	PAGES	ISBN
Vault Career Guide to Accounting	29.95	128	1-58131-328-4
Vault Career Guide to Advertising	29.95	114	1-58131-267-9
Vault Career Guide to Biotech	29.95	198	1-58131-268-7
Vault Career Guide to Book Publishing	29.95	140	1-58131-269-5
Vault Guide to Capitol Hill Careers	29.95	112	1-58131-251-2
Vault Guide to Corporate Law Careers	29.95	168	1-58131-222-9
Vault Career Guide to Consulting	29.95	184	1-58131-169-9
Vault Career Guide to the Energy Industry	29.95	176	1-58131-375-6
Vault Career Guide to the Fashion Industry	29.95	128	1-58131-201-6
Vault Guide to Flight Attendant Careers	29.95	160	1-58131-303-9
Vault Career Guide to Hedge Funds	29.95	144	1-58131-302-0
Vault Guide to Human Resources Careers	29.95	128	1-58131-369-1
Vault Career Guide to Interior Design	29.95	192	1-58131-326-8
Vault Career Guide to Investment Banking	29.95	152	1-58131-306-3
Vault Career Guide to Investment Management	29.95	128	1-58131-179-6
Vault Career Guide to Journalism and Information Media	29.95	208	1-58131-355-1
Vault Career Guide to Leveraged Finance	29.95	112	1-58131-502-3
Vault Career Guide to Marketing & Brand Management	29.95	116	1-58131-406-x
Vault Career Guide to Media & Entertainment	29.95	152	1-58131-200-8
Vault Career Guide to Pharmaceutical Sales and Marketing	29.95	196	1-58131-386-1
Vault Career Guide to Private Wealth Management	29.95	216	1-58131-448-5
Vault Career Guide to Real Estate	29.95	120	1-58131-174-5
Vault Career Guide to Sales & Trading	29.95	160	1-58131-252-0
Vault Guide to Technology Careers	29.95	128	1-58131-289-x
Vault Career Guide to Venture Capital	29.95	128	1-58131-290-3

VAULT INDUSTRY EMPLOYER GUIDES	PRICE	PAGES	ISBN
Vault Guide to the Top 40 Accounting Firms	29.95	336	1-58131-418-3
Vault Guide to the Top Advertising & PR Employers	29.95	168	1-58131-383-7
Vault Guide to the Top 50 Banking Employers	34.95	598	1-58131-421-3
Vault Guide to Top Biotech/Pharmaceuticals Employers	19.95	158	1-58131-389-6
Vault Guide to the Top 50 Consulting Firms	34.95	928	1-58131-422-1
Vault Guide to the Top Consumer Products Employers	19.95	366	1-58131-323-3
Vault Guide to the Top Energy & Oil/Gas Employers	19.95	198	1-58131-318-7
Vault Guide to the Top Financial Services Employers	29.95	484	1-58131-416-7
Vault Guide to the Top Health Care Employers	19.95	232	1-58131-338-1
Vault Guide to Hospitality/Leisure Employers	19.95	244	1-58131-353-5
Vault Guide to the Top Insurance Employers	19.95	166	1-58131-320-9
Vault Guide to the Top 100 Law Firms	39.95	768	1-58131-292-x
Vault Guide to the Top Manufacturing Employers	19.95	282	1-58131-324-1
Vault Guide to the Top Media & Entertainment Employers	19.95	360	1-58131-337-3
Vault Guide to the Top Private Equity Employers	29.95	114	1-58131-453-3
Vault Guide to the Top Retail Employers	19.95	320	1-58131-322-5
Vault Guide to the Top 25 Tech Consulting Firms	29.95	366	1-58131-417-5
Vault Guide to the Top Tech Employers	19.95	360	1-58131-339-x
Vault Guide to the Top Telecom Employers	19.95	94	1-58131-403-5